MW00826969

REFORMED
ETHICS

REFORMED
ETHICS

THE DUTIES
OF THE CHRISTIAN LIFE

HERMAN BAVINCK
EDITED BY JOHN BOLT

WITH JESSICA JOUSTRA,
NELSON D. KLOOSTERMAN,
ANTOINE THERON, DIRK VAN KEULEN

Baker Academic
a division of Baker Publishing Group
Grand Rapids, Michigan

Published by Baker Academic
a division of Baker Publishing Group
PO Box 6287, Grand Rapids, MI 49516-6287
www.bakeracademic.com

Printed in the United States of America

Library of Congress Cataloging-in-Publication Data
Names: Bavinck, Herman, 1854–1921, author. | Bolt, John, 1947– editor.
Title: Reformed ethics / Herman Bavinck ; edited by John Bolt.
Other titles: Gereformeerde ethiek. English
Description: Grand Rapids : Baker Publishing Group, 2019– | Includes bibliographical references and indexes. Contents: Volume 2. The duties of the Christian life.
Identifiers: LCCN 2018036415 | ISBN 9780801098222 (volume 2 : cloth : alk. paper)
Subjects: LCSH: Christian ethics—Reformed authors. | Reformed Church—Doctrines. | Theology, Doctrinal
Classification: LCC BJ1251 .B3613 2019 | DDC 241/.0442—dc23
LC record available at https://lccn.loc.gov/2018036415

Baker Publishing Group publications use paper produced from sustainable forestry practices and post-consumer waste whenever possible.

21 22 23 24 25 26 27   7 6 5 4 3 2 1

To Richard John Mouw
For keeping Christ and the law together

Contents

Editor's Preface

This preface will be relatively brief. Since the editor's preface to volume 1 provides details about Bavinck's *Reformed Ethics* manuscript and the story of the translation project, we will not repeat that here.[1] Our focus instead will be on the relation between the foundational content of volume 1 and Bavinck's exposition of the Decalogue in volume 2.

The heart of Bavinck's understanding of the Christian life in volume 1 is found in chapter 9 with its emphasis on union with Christ and the imitation of Christ. We must first *believe* in Christ; he is our Savior and Lord, our prophet, priest, and king. But, says Bavinck, he is more: "He is also our example and ideal. His life is the shape, the model, that our spiritual life must assume and toward which it must grow."[2] The result is an ethic rooted in divine love that followers of Jesus must emulate, an ethic of Christian identity and character. On this point Bavinck learned his theological lessons from John Calvin and Ulrich Zwingli.[3] We also observe that this is an emphasis that matches the current mood in contemporary theological ethics and Christian discipleship. Among the influential ethicists that come to mind here are John Howard Yoder, Alasdair MacIntyre, Stanley Hauerwas, Edward Vacek, Glen Stassen, and David Gushee.[4]

1. *RE*, 1:ix–xvi; see also "Introduction to Herman Bavinck's *Reformed Ethics*," in *RE*, 1:xxi–xliii.
2. *RE*, 1:317.
3. See his doctoral dissertation, *De ethiek van Ulrich Zwingli.*
4. An abbreviated list of titles includes Yoder, *Politics of Jesus*; MacIntyre, *After Virtue*; Hauerwas, *Community of Character*; Vacek, *Love, Human and Divine*; Stassen and Gushee, *Kingdom Ethics.*

As Bavinck works out the concrete content of his ethics in this volume, however, he joins the long tradition of Reformed ethicists and turns to the Decalogue and the notion of duty. That move could be disconcerting for some who have recently turned to the "kingdom ethics" of union with and imitation of Christ because that emphasis is seen as a *counter* to the role of law and duty in Christian living. In fact, many who have turned to virtue and character ethics have done so because they regard the divine command ethical traditions that have traditionally schooled Protestant and Roman Catholic Christians in their discipleship to have failed.[5] Charges of "decisionism" and "legalism" accompany these critiques; it is important, so it is said, to get beyond rules and principles about right and wrong and focus attention on nurturing *persons* of character and virtue as people who *do* what is right by living the ethic of the kingdom of God.

John Howard Yoder sets this contrast clearly, asking whether the traditional use of the Ten Commandments for ethics really needs Jesus.[6] He wonders if the natural moral law discernible by human intelligence added to the Ten Commandments would not be sufficient for most Protestants. After all, for them, "the broad outlines of moral behavior are dictated by the orders of creation—the fact that the family, the school, work, and the state are instituted by God in creation and therefore binding upon us." He concludes with this: "If there had been no Jesus, our desire or capacity to be good might be defective. But what God wills, what he asks of the person who seeks to please him, would be just the same if there had been no Jesus." Yoder raises a challenging question that must be answered by those who seek to be disciples of Jesus Christ, particularly now when Yoder's general perspective is so popular among many Christian ethicists.

Yoder's own answer is to set the ethics of Jesus and his kingdom as a contradiction to any ethics using divine command or principles: "If, however, our ethics are to be guided by Jesus, then we reject the morality of common sense or reason or the 'orders of creation' because of its content and not because of its Source alone. It is an inadequate moral guide because its standards are wrong and not because humans can understand it."[7] The alternative, to put it starkly, would seem to be as follows: Christ *or* the Law; the imitation of Christ *or* divine command; the ethics of the kingdom *or* the ethics of Sinai supplemented by natural law.

---

5. This is the burden of Stassen and Gushee's *Kingdom Ethics* as well as Roman Catholic author Joseph Selling's *Reframing Catholic Theological Ethics*.

6. Yoder, "Walking in the Resurrection," 39; the cited passages that follow are to this source. I am indebted to Jessica Joustra for this reference to Yoder. Jessica also read the first draft of this preface and offered a number of helpful suggestions.

7. Yoder, "Walking in the Resurrection," 40.

Clearly Bavinck did not buy into this bifurcation; he saw no contradiction between his decidedly christoform ethics and a commitment to notions of duty and obedience to divine command. Why? Because Bavinck recognized that duties are misconstrued if they are seen only in an impersonal, abstract, Kantian, deontological sense. The duties required of us are personal; they are duties *toward God* and bear a profoundly religious character. Furthermore, these duties are not external to us; they are not arbitrarily imposed divine commands; they accord with our created nature and are *revealed* to us. These qualifications are rooted in a trinitarian, covenantal framework and have a theological-metaphysical foundation that cannot be reduced to the historical Jesus. It is an ethic, in other words, that is understood as shaped by the imitation of Christ but not restricted to it in a narrow and literal sense.[8] Let us briefly explore each element of this frame.

TRINITARIAN

Bavinck regularly describes the essence of the Christian faith in trinitarian terms: "The essence of the Christian religion consists in the reality that the creation of the Father, ruined by sin, is restored in the death of the Son of God, and re-created by the grace of the Holy Spirit into a kingdom of God."[9] This accents the importance of the doctrine of creation and the relation of redemption to creation. For Bavinck, the grace of redemption in Christ does not destroy the original creation, nor does it create a totally new world; grace *heals* and *restores* creation. Bavinck's eschatological vision denies "a destruction of substance" and sees the renewal of all things not as "a second brand-new creation, but a re-creation of the existing world. God's honor consists precisely in the fact that he redeems and renews the same humanity, the same world, the same heaven, and the same earth that have been corrupted and polluted by sin. Just as anyone in Christ is a new creation in whom the old has passed away and everything has become new (2 Cor. 5:17), so also this world passes away in its present form as well, in order out of its womb, at God's word of power, to give birth and being to a new world."[10] It is a mistake, then, to repudiate creation order and law in the name of Jesus and the kingdom of God. In trinitarian terms, the work of the Son would then undo the work of the Father, and that simply cannot be true.

8. These two sentences can be taken as the thesis and burden of my doctoral dissertation, *A Theological Analysis of Herman Bavinck's Two Essays on the* Imitatio Christi. A summary can be found in my *Bavinck on the Christian Life*, chaps. 3–5. In what follows I am providing Bavinck's hermeneutics of the *imitatio Christi*.
9. *RD*, 1:112; 2:288; cf. Bavinck, *Sacrifice of Praise*, 71; Bavinck, *Het Christendom*, 23, 62.
10. *RD*, 4:717.

COVENANTAL

Critics of command and duty ethics often seem to miss the covenantal character of Old Testament law, overlooking the prologue to the Decalogue: "I am the LORD your God, who brought you out of the land of Egypt, out of the house of slavery" (Exod. 20:2).

But the oversight goes deeper and ignores the decidedly covenantal, legal character of God's relationship with the original parents of the human race. God's blessing to be "fruitful and multiply" and have dominion over creation (Gen. 1:28) was framed by a stipulation and curse: "You may surely eat of every tree of the garden, but of the tree of the knowledge of good and evil you shall not eat, for in the day that you eat of it you shall surely die" (Gen. 2:16–17). This language—stipulation, blessing, and curse—is legal and covenantal and gave rise within Reformed theology to the notion of a "covenant of works."[11] This doctrine has a number of important implications.

The most important is the shape it gives to our understanding of the saving work of Christ and the relation between the first and second Adam (Rom. 5; 1 Cor. 15). The disobedience of the first Adam plunged the world into darkness of sin and brought death to all, but the obedience of the second Adam achieved light and life to those who believe in him. Therefore, to deny the covenantal, legal character of God's relation to humanity in its original, created condition, even apart from sin, calls into question the need for and reality of our Savior's atoning death for sinners. As the apostle Paul observed concerning the bodily resurrection of our Lord, we would still be in our sins (1 Cor. 15:17).

The insistence that duty and law be covenantally framed is especially important for the Reformed tradition because its special temptation is legalism and moralism. For Bavinck, covenant is more than the frame for morality; it is foundational to human life; it is "the usual form in terms of which humans live and work together," including "love, friendship, marriage, as well as all social cooperation in business, industry, science, art, and so forth."[12] The same is true of religion. "In Scripture 'covenant' is the fixed form in which the relation of God to his people is depicted and presented. And even where the word does not occur, we nevertheless always see the two parties, as it were, in dialogue with each other, dealing with each other, with God calling people to conversion, reminding them of their obligations, and obligating himself to provide all that is good" (569). Without covenant, the Creator God would remain "elevated

11. Since we are summarizing Bavinck's views here, we do not need to enter into the contentious discussion about the covenant of works. Bavinck's defense of the doctrine is found especially in *RD*, 2:567–88.

12. *RD*, 2:568; parenthetical page references that follow in the text are to this work.

above humanity in his sovereign exaltedness and majesty," but "religion in the sense of fellowship" would not be possible and the relation between God and humanity would be "exhaustively described in the terms 'master' and 'servant'" (569). Therefore, "if there is truly to be religion, if there is to be fellowship between God and man, if the relation between the two is to be also (but not exclusively) that of a master to his servant, of a potter to clay, as well as that of a king to his people, of a father to his son, of a mother to her child, of an eagle to her young, of a hen to her chicks, and so forth; that is, if not just one relation but all relations and all sorts of relations of dependence, submission, obedience, friendship, love, and so forth among humans find their model and achieve their fulfillment in religion, then religion must be the character of a covenant" (569). When we speak of law and duty, we are talking about our *covenantal relation* to our Creator and Redeemer.

Remarkably, Bavinck goes on to say that covenant gives human beings *rights* before God. Although by virtue of our existence alone we cannot make any claims upon God—we have nothing by which to merit such claims— nonetheless, "the religion of Holy Scripture is such that in it human beings can nevertheless, as it were, assert certain rights before God. For they have the freedom to come to him with prayer and thanksgiving, to address him as 'Father,' to take refuge in him in all circumstances of distress and death, to desire all good things from him, even to expect salvation and eternal life from him. All this is possible solely because God in his condescending goodness gives rights to his creature" (570).

Finally, covenant bestows responsible moral agency on human beings, giving them freedom and dignity. God created men and women as "rational and moral beings," maintained them as such after the fall, and continues to treat them the same way. "He deals with them, not as irrational creatures, as plants or animals, as blocks of wood, but goes to work with them as rational, moral, self-determining beings. He wants human beings to be free and to serve him in love, freely and willingly (Ps. 100). Religion is freedom; it is love that does not permit itself to be coerced. For that reason it must by its very nature take the shape of a covenant in which God acts, not coercively, but with counsel, admonition, warning, invitation, petition, and in which humans serve God, not under duress or violence, but willingly, by their own free consent, moved by love to love in return" (570–71). The sentences that immediately follow this quotation are especially germane to our concern in this preface: "At bottom religion is a duty but also a privilege. It is not work by which we bring advantage to God, make a contribution to him, and have a right to reward. It is grace for us to be allowed to serve him. God is never indebted to us, but we are always indebted to him for the good works we do (Belgic Confession, art. 24). On his part there is always the gift; on our part there is always and alone the gratitude. For that reason, religion is conceivable only in the form of a covenant and comes to its full realization only in that form." Our dutiful response of law-full obedience is an expression of gratitude and praise for who God is and for what he has done.

THEOLOGICAL-METAPHYSICAL FOUNDATION

The preceding can be summarized with the obvious maxim that moral truth is grounded in *reality*, the created reality brought into being and maintained by the Triune God. Our human capacity for responsible moral agency is structured into our very nature as image-bearers of God and the ability to tell what is right from what is wrong. There is a correspondence between our subjective human faculties and the objective reality of moral truth that is external to us.[13] In Bavinck's words: "From the beginning creation was so arranged and human nature was immediately so created that it was amenable to and fit for the highest degree of conformity to God and for the most intimate indwelling of God" (560). The doctrine here is that of the Logos. Bavinck frequently observes that the same Logos who became flesh is the one by whom all things were created.[14] Creation and redemption are unified as fully trinitarian works: "It is the Father who—not apart from the Son but specifically through the Logos and the Spirit—produces all the forces and gifts present in nature and unregenerate humankind (John 1:4–5, 9–10; Col. 1:17; Pss. 104:30; 139:7). And this Logos and Spirit who dwell and work in all creatures and humans are the same agents who as Christ and the Spirit of Christ acquire and apply all the benefits pertaining to the covenant of grace."[15] Here we have the trinitarian metaphysics that is the foundation of Bavinck's worldview. Two things follow from this.

1. The historical Jesus must never be separated from the union of his human nature with the eternal Logos, the Second Person of the Holy Trinity. A truly christoform ethics is indissolubly linked to the moral order of creation brought into being by the Father, through the Son, and in the Spirit.

2. An ethic exclusively based on the imitation of Christ is incomplete, particularly in its application of the Sermon on the Mount to contemporary

---

13. The best access to Bavinck's epistemology is his *Beginselen der psychologie* (ET: *Foundations of Psychology*).

14. E.g., *RD*, 3:235: "The Logos, who was with God and by whom all things were made, is the One who became flesh."

15. *RD*, 3:225.

life. Such an ethic is always a negative ethic—against participation in coercive power, against swearing oaths, voluntary poverty, and so on—and provides little or no constructive guidance to life in business, science, the arts, and other enterprises. To the extent that Christians participate in the public, civic square, it is as countercultural critics.

But what about Yoder's question? Does Jesus then make no moral difference at all?

First things first. The New Testament's primary concern is "restoring our proper relationship with God. The cross of Christ, therefore, is the heart and mid-point of the Christian religion. Jesus did not come, first of all, to renew families and reform society but to save sinners and to redeem the world from the coming wrath of God."[16] Redemption does not mean a radical *nova creatio*: "The differences that are present in creation by the will of God are not set aside by the Son in redemption."[17] At the same time, nonetheless, the gospel does change things.[18] How it does so is expressed both compactly and comprehensively in the final paragraph of the address by Bavinck quoted just now:

Redemption does change matters however. From the principle of reconciliation with God, all other human relationships are given a new ordering and led back to their original state. God is the owner of every human being and their possessions; we are simply tenants, renters, and must give an account of our stewardship (Luke 16:2; Matt. 25:14ff.). Husbands and wives (Eph. 5:22; Titus 2:5; Col. 3:18), parents and children (Eph. 6:1–4; Col. 3:20–21), masters and slaves (1 Cor. 7:21–22; Eph. 6:5–9; Col. 3:22), civil authorities and subjects (Rom. 13:1–7; 1 Tim. 2:1–2; 1 Pet. 2:13–16, etc.), are all brought into proper relationship with each other. Distinctions in our social life remain but they lose their sharp edge. The New Testament is overflowing with warnings against riches (Matt. 6:19; 19:23; 1 Tim. 6:17–19, etc.), but poverty is no virtue and the natural is not unclean in itself (Mark 7:15ff.; Acts 14:17; Rom. 14:14; 1 Tim.

---

16. Bavinck, "General Biblical Principles," 443. This is an address Bavinck prepared for the Christian Social Congress held in Amsterdam, November 9–11, 1891. Full title: "According to Holy Scripture, What Are the General Principles [Provided for] a Solution to the Social Question and What Pointers toward This Solution Lie in the Concrete Application Given to These Principles for Israel by Mosaic Law."

17. Bavinck, "General Biblical Principles," 443.

18. In addition to this quotation, see Bavinck, "Christian Principles and Social Relationships." Here Bavinck insists that the worth of the gospel does not depend on its effects: "Even if Christianity had resulted in nothing more than this spiritual and holy community, even if it had not brought about any modification in earthly relationships, even if, for instance, it had done nothing for the abolition of slavery, it would still be and remain something of eternal worth. The significance of the gospel does not depend on its influence on culture, its usefulness for today; it is a treasure in itself, a pearl of great price, even if it might not be a leaven" (141). But this is a contrary-to-fact conditional; the gospel *has* transformed society and culture.

4:4). Work is commended and tied to food and wages (Matt. 10:10; 1 Tim. 5:18; Eph. 4:28; 2 Thess. 3:10). In Matthew 6:25–34, Jesus himself removes for his followers all anxious concern about this earthly life. Because the redemption in Christ renews but does not eliminate the various earthly relationships in which we find ourselves, there remains a large place for the ministry of mercy. Just like the poor (Matt. 26:11; John 12:8; Rev. 13:16), so, too, the many needy will always be with us. In the same way that Jesus the compassionate High Priest is always deeply moved by those in need, so, too, he directs his followers especially to clothe themselves with the Christlike virtue of compassion ([Matt. 5:43–47]; Luke 6:36). Having received mercy from Christ, his followers are expected in turn to show mercy to others (1 Pet. 2:10; Matt. 18:33). It is for this reason that the church has a distinct office for the ministry of mercy.[19]

Thanks to Christ's incarnation, death, and resurrection, the world *has* changed and so has our moral conduct.

The completion of this volume comes with many personal debts for which I need to say "thank you." Harry Van Dyke served as the translator for the important first draft, handling a challenging task on a difficult manuscript with skill and efficiency. Our editorial team of Jessica Joustra, Nelson Kloosterman, Antoine Theron, and Dirk van Keulen scrutinized every sentence and word in our intensive summer sessions and fully deserve their mention on the title page. Others who helped with translation challenges are mentioned in the notes at the appropriate place. Calvin Theological Seminary student Adam Ramirez helped with the critical apparatus and bibliography. The editorial team at Baker Academic has once again been unfailingly helpful and supportive. Finally, the Hekman Library at Calvin University and Calvin Theological Seminary, especially its Rare Book Room, has been indispensable to my work on volume 1 and again on volume 2. However, because of restrictions on library access during the COVID-19 pandemic, I was unable to personally make final bibliographic checks on a dozen or so items. William Katerberg, newly appointed Curator of Heritage Hall, and theological librarian Paul Fields kindly chased down these references for me at the last minute. For that work of supererogation and all the others I mentioned above, thank you so very much.

This volume is dedicated to Rich Mouw, emeritus president of Fuller Theological Seminary and a longtime professor of philosophy with special interest in ethics, faith, and public life. Mouw's scholarly and popular work on Dutch

19. Bavinck, "General Biblical Principles," 443–44.

neo-Calvinism was directed more to Abraham Kuyper than to Bavinck, but in recent years he also mentored a number of doctoral students, including a member of our editorial team, to study and write about Bavinck. For that mentoring work and for his success in popularizing the vision of Kuyperian neo-Calvinism alone, he deserves a dedication of a volume such as this. Yet it is above all for his commitment to keep the tradition of divine command ethics alive but never at the expense of union with Christ that he is selected for this honor. His book *The God Who Commands* has a section, "The Triune Commander," that mentions Bavinck's imitation-of-Christ emphasis in contrast to the triumphalist appeals to creation order and kingship found in Abraham Kuyper,[20] but more importantly the trinitarian structure of Mouw's thought is thoroughly Bavinckian; his neo-Calvinist intuition anticipated Bavinck's ethical road map as we have now come to know it. Rich, you are a dear friend, and we thank God for you.

John Bolt

---

20. Mouw, *God Who Commands*, 156, 159; the entire section covers pp. 150–75.

Abbreviations

ANF	*The Ante-Nicene Fathers*. Edited by Alexander Roberts and James Donaldson. 10 vols. New York: Christian Literature Co., 1885–96. Reprint, Grand Rapids: Eerdmans, 1950–51.
art.	article
ASV	American Standard Version
Bavinck Archives	Archive no. 346 of the Historical Documentation Centre, Free University, Amsterdam.
BDB	Brown, Francis, S. R. Driver, and Charles A. Briggs. *Hebrew and English Lexicon of the Old Testament Based on the Lexicon of William Gesenius*. London: Oxford University Press, 1907. Reprint, 1968.
ca.	*circa*, about
CEB	Common English Bible
chap(s).	chapter(s)
Christ. Encycl.¹	*Christelijke Encyclopaedie voor het Nederlands Volk*. Edited by F. W. Grosheide et al. 6 vols. Kampen: Kok, n.d. [1925?–1931].
Christ. Encycl.²	*Christelijke Encyclopedie*. Edited by F. W. Grosheide and G. P. van Itterzon. 2nd rev. ed. 6 vols. Kampen: Kok, 1956–61.
CJB	Complete Jewish Bible
CO	*Joannis Calvini Opera Quae Supersunt Omnia*. Edited by Edouard Cunitz, Johann-Wilhelm Baum, and Eduard Wilhelm Eugen Reuss. 59 vols. Braunschweig: C. A. Schwetschke, 1863.
CTJ	*Calvin Theological Journal*
d.	died
Denzinger	Denzinger, Henry. *The Sources of Catholic Dogma*. Translated by Roy J. Deferrari. Fitzwilliam, NH: Loreto, 2002.
DO	Dutch original
ed. note	editor's note
ESV	English Standard Version
ET	English translation

FC	Fathers of the Church
FO	French original
Gk.	Greek
GO	German original
GrO	Greek original
HO	Hebrew original
Institutes	John Calvin, *Institutes of the Christian Religion*
KJV	King James Version
LCL	Loeb Classical Library
lit.	literally
LO	Latin original
LXX	Septuagint
NASB	New American Standard Bible
NIV	New International Version
NKJV	New King James Version
no(s).	number(s)
NPNF¹	*A Select Library of Nicene and Post-Nicene Fathers of the Christian Church.* Edited by Philip Schaff. 1st series. 14 vols. New York: Christian Literature Co., 1887–1900. Reprint, Grand Rapids: Eerdmans, 1956.
NPNF²	*A Select Library of Nicene and Post-Nicene Fathers of the Christian Church.* Edited by Philip Schaff and Henry Wace. 2nd series. 14 vols. New York: Christian Literature Co., 1890–1900. Reprint, Grand Rapids: Eerdmans, 1952.
NRSV	New Revised Standard Version
p(p).	page(s)
par.	parallel
para(s).	paragraph(s)
PL	*Patrologiae cursus completus: Series latina.* Edited by J.-P. Migne. 221 vols. Paris: Migne, 1844–65.
PRE¹	*Realencyklopädie für protestantische Theologie und Kirche.* Edited by J. J. Herzog. 1st ed. 22 vols. Hamburg: R. Besser, 1854–68.
PRE²	*Realencyklopädie für protestantische Theologie und Kirche.* Edited by J. J. Herzog and G. L. Plitt. 2nd rev. ed. 18 vols. Leipzig: J. C. Hinrichs, 1877–88.
PRE³	*Realencyklopädie für protestantische Theologie und Kirche.* Edited by Albert Hauck. 3rd rev. ed. 24 vols. Leipzig: J. C. Hinrichs, 1896–1913.
Q&A	question and answer
RD	Bavinck, Herman. *Reformed Dogmatics.* Edited by John Bolt. Translated by John Vriend. 4 vols. Grand Rapids: Baker, 2003–8.
RE	Bavinck, Herman. *Reformed Ethics.* The present translation of "Gereformeerde Ethiek." Bavinck Archives, no. 56. Historical Documentation Centre, Free University, Amsterdam.
Schaff-Herzog	*The New Schaff-Herzog Encyclopedia of Religious Knowledge.* 13 vols. Edited by Samuel Macauley Jackson. London and New York: Funk and Wagnalls, 1906–14.
ST	Thomas Aquinas, *Summa theologiae*
TBR	*The Bavinck Review*

❋ BOOK III ❋

HUMANITY AFTER CONVERSION

13

Duties, Precepts and Counsels, Adiaphora

The notion of duty or obligation involves binding human conscience to law and is an integral dimension of ethics. Duties can be divided into absolute obligations that arise from the good itself and relative or desirable duties, a categorization that leads to distinctions between morality and legality, between the necessary and the permissible, between precepts and counsels. Beginning in the early church and throughout the Middle Ages these duties were usually considered in terms of virtue, eventually becoming the four cardinal virtues of prudence or wisdom, justice, fortitude, and temperance, along with the three theological virtues of faith, hope, and love. For Protestants, duty was primarily viewed through the lens of the third use of the law—the rule of gratitude. Notwithstanding Immanuel Kant's emphasis on duty in the categorical imperative—Thou Shalt!—modern theology gradually moved away from duty and legal obligation to a morality centered in the person of Jesus Christ.

The proper ethical question to be posed to Holy Scripture is not "What is our duty?" but "What is the relation of believers to the law?" Law is not only an Old Testament notion; Jesus came to fulfill the law, and his own conduct and teaching honor the law. Jesus does and says nothing to abolish the law. He does, however, promote a righteousness that exceeds that of the Pharisees, intensifying the commandments and giving them a spiritual depth. The apostles, including Paul, were personally devout concerning the Torah but also moved beyond Jewish ceremonial practices and insisted upon Christian liberty. The law cannot give life but also no longer condemns those who are in Christ. Freed from the external authority of the law, believers are free to live according to its content. What is itself spiritual and ethical in the law already in the Old Testament is and remains eternal. Our good works do not save us; they demonstrate the new life in us and are done according to God's commandments.

Reformed ethics, therefore, was centered on the Decalogue and in opposition to both nomism *and* antinomianism. *It therefore resists all gnostic attempts to emancipate the flesh and free us from the bonds of law and authority by appealing to the special prerogatives of genius or statecraft and politics. Both God's nature and our own created human nature bind us to the law. The reality of law obligates us.*

Just as the law is summarized in one word — love — so too can all duties be reduced to a single maxim: "So whatever you wish that others would do to you, do also to them, for this is the Law and the Prophets" (Matt. 7:12). But this one duty can be distributed among many duties resulting in many questions and debates.

The Stoic distinction between precepts for all and counsels for a small group of the wise who sought a higher morality was soon adopted by the Christian church and applied to martyrs and monks ("the religious"). Precepts were obligatory, counsels voluntary. Protestants rejected this dual morality and also repudiated the scriptural warrants used by Roman Catholic defenders of the distinction. It was acknowledged that Jesus (and Paul) did grant that for some it may be profitable, for the sake of the kingdom, not to marry, but this is not a counsel that goes beyond the law and provides greater value, rank, and reward in the kingdom of heaven. Paul's advice in 1 Corinthians 7 is a concession, not a commandment. *The same is true of Jesus's challenge to the rich young ruler to sell everything and give it to the poor. For the rich young ruler this was not a matter of choice but a command. The notion that Christianity in its perfection is unattainable for all but a few aristocratic spirits, for extraordinary moral heroes, is more pagan and Pelagian than biblical. The moral law is for everyone, but each individual believer is uniquely called in different circumstances to use his or her gifts and fulfill their vocation before God.*

There has also been a vigorous debate in the Christian church about the adiaphora, the so-called indifferent things. During the time of the Reformation much of this revolved around Christian worship: liturgies and prayers, clerical vestments, altars, images, candles, incense, the use of Latin. Some, like Spener, rejected the category of adiaphora altogether, insisting that the true Christian must be completely distinct from the world. Others went to the opposite extreme and claimed that certain things were indifferent with respect to the law altogether. Most modern theologians reject the idea of the permissible in ethics, restricting it to civic life.

Along with Thomas Aquinas, Protestants acknowledge the presence of adiaphora in the abstract but insist that concrete actions that involve intention, goal, and circumstance cease to be indifferent, are to be guided by the moral law, and therefore are commanded or forbidden. Mediating positions that leave the area of the permissible to the judgment of the individual shortchange the universality of the law and end up in destructive subjectivism. Others confuse the realm of the permissible with Christian freedom, forgetting that this freedom exists within the law. The realm of the adiaphora must not be confused with things that are physical, instinctive, or natural (such as stroking one's beard), things that are indifferent for children, and variations in people's developmental stages of faith. We must also acknowledge that consciences have been historically shaped in different ways.

Ethics, finally, is concerned with "ought" rather than "may." There are actions that are permissible because Scripture does not forbid them; and we are not obligated to do something Scripture does not command. The law both proscribes and prescribes; all proscription presupposes sin. Although many actions are neither necessary nor impermissible, if they are done, they should be done in accordance with the law.

§27. THE DOCTRINE (THEORY) OF DUTY

Historical Overview

In the Dutch and German languages the word for "duty" indicates a habit to which one has become accustomed and which gradually develops into an obligation from which one cannot withdraw.[1] Objectively, the habit becomes a law, command (cf. *ethos*)—subjectively, a duty. Duty consists in being bound in my conscience to the law. From the beginning, therefore, the doctrine of duty was incorporated in ethics.

The Stoics in particular emphasized obligatory conduct, by which they meant rational action as such, or moral action apart from the influence of emotions.[2] This became a good deed[3] when it was performed with the right disposition. But Stoic idealism had to distinguish between the (absolute) good and the desirable, the relative good. And this second class of the relative good was in turn classified as three subgroups: "those which are according to nature and therefore have a value (ἀξία), being desirable and preferable (προηγμένα) in themselves; those which are against nature, and therefore without value (ἀπαξία) and to be avoided (ἀποπροηγμένα); and finally those which have neither merit nor demerit, the ἀδιάφορα in the narrower sense."[4]

---

1. DO: *plicht*; GO: *Pflicht*; from the verbs *plegen* and *pflegen* = be in the habit of; cf. Burger, "Pflicht."

2. GO: *die vernunftgemässe Handlung als solche*; GrO: καθῆκον; Zeller, *Outlines of the History of Greek Philosophy*, 244–54 (§§71–72).

3. GrO: καθόρθωμα.

4. Zeller, *Outlines of the History of Greek Philosophy*, 249 (§71). Ed. note: In the margins Bavinck provided examples of each category: things desirable include beauty, health, life, honor, money; things reprehensible include sickness, death, poverty; whether the number of my hairs is odd or even is a matter of indifference.

As a result, the Stoics were also compelled to distinguish between absolute duties (by which humans strived for the absolute good) and relative duties (which aimed for the desirable), between "perfect duties" and "conditioned" or "intermediate duties."[5] This is the difference between the virtuous life of the wise and the good and the lower life of those who also seek the desirable, between morality and legality, between the necessary and the permissible, between precepts and counsels.[6]

The work of the Stoic Panaetius is also the basis of Cicero's *On Duties*, whose three books discuss (1) what is honorable, (2) what is expedient or to one's advantage, and (3) what to do when these two conflict.[7] In the Christian church, Ambrose followed Cicero in his *On the Duties of the Clergy*, where he adopted the four cardinal virtues, pronouncing them to be Christian virtues: wisdom as worship of God, justice as piety, fortitude as courage in God, temperance as moderation.[8] Augustine adopted them and grafted them onto the root of love. Cassiodorus (died after 560) had them as well, but added the virtue of contemplation, capacity for judgment, and remembrance.[9] To these four, Pope Gregory I added faith, hope, and love.[10] This was the basic framework throughout the Middle Ages, but occasionally a few other virtues were added. The concepts of virtue and duty were used interchangeably and overlapped.

The concept of duty was also part of Protestant ethics. While the the law was always viewed as a rule of gratitude for the regenerated, the law as such remained in force.[11] After all, the law had a threefold function or use: (1) *theological/elenctic/pedagogic*: convicting of guilt or impotence; (2) *political*: curbing and bridling sin; and (3) *normative* and *didactic*: guiding Christian conduct.[12] Because the political use really belongs to the sphere of jurisprudence, the Heidelberg Catechism deals only with the first and the third uses.

---

5. GrO: καθήκοντα τέλεια and καθήκοντα μέσα. Ed. note: Bavinck's terms come from the German text (Zeller, *Die Philosophie der Griechen*[3], 3/1:265n2). The English translation of Zeller has καθορθώματα and μέσα καθήκοντα (Zeller, *Outlines of the History of Greek Philosophy*, 249 [§71]).

6. LO: *praecepta*; *consilia*.

7. LO: *honestum*; *utile*. Ed. note: Marcus Tullius Cicero's *On Duties* (*De officiis*) is divided into three books: "I. Moral Goodness"; "II. Expediency"; "III. The Conflict between the Right and the Expedient." See *On Duties* (trans. Miller).

8. LO: *prudentia*; *iustitia*; *fortitudo*; *temperantia*; Ambrose, *On the Duties of the Clergy* (NPNF[2] 10:33–89); cf. Gass, *Geschichte der christlichen Ethik*, 1:164–74.

9. Gass, *Geschichte der christlichen Ethik*, 1:179.

10. Gass, *Geschichte der christlichen Ethik*, 1:182.

11. See Heidelberg Catechism, Lord's Day 32.

12. LO: *usus legis*; *usus theologicus*, *elencticus*, *paedagogicus*; *usus politicus*; *usus normativus*, *didacticus*. Cf. Calvin, *Institutes*, II.vii.6–12; cf. Paul Lobstein, *Die Ethik Calvins*, 51–57.

The third use of the law receives less than its full and proper due in Luther.[13] The Reformed insisted that for the believer, only the curse of the law was abolished, not the law itself.[14] Therefore, they spoke of duties for the Christian.[15] The entirety of ethics was concerned with the doctrine of virtues or duties, and no distinction was made between the two.

It was especially in the age of rationalism that duties and virtues regained some honor, but they were also significantly weakened. Kant opposed this development and conceived of law—the inner "Thou Shalt!"[16]—as unconditional demand, as the categorical imperative, and once again paid homage to the majesty of duty. In this way Kant changed the entirety of ethics into lawful fulfillment of duty and failed to consider that we are unable to do this because of the radical evil[17] within us, and that the law alone can never make us moral. De Wette, in his *Textbook of Christian Morality*, therefore posited piety or godliness as the basic duty from which all other duties flow and sought the strength for their fulfillment in redemption through Christ.[18]

Schleiermacher was the first to venture into this more deeply. In his *Sketch of a Moral System*,[19] he talks about the structure of ethics and stipulates the highest good as our moral task, consisting in the unity of reason and nature.[20] In other words, the existence of rationality in nature is the highest good. Virtue is the required moral capacity consisting in the power of reason in nature. Duty is the form of moral conduct—that is, the movement of virtue toward the highest good. Rothe joins Schleiermacher in speaking about duties: duty is the formula that virtue needs for producing the highest good.[21] In normal moral development, law and duty would not be possible—for example, with angels and the saints, who *know* and who *will* the way and the manner of producing the highest good. In humanity's sinful state, duties are necessary, yet cannot be fulfilled because of sin. But now there is redemption in Christ,

---

13. Cf. Luthardt, *Die Ethik Luthers*, 39–49.

14. LO: *maledictio legis*.

15. LO: *officia*; DO: *plichten*. Ed. note: Bavinck provides as examples William Ames, Bénédict Pictet, and Johann Franz Buddeus.

16. GO: *Du sollst*.

17. GO: *das radikale Böse*.

18. GO: *Frömmigkeit*; de Wette, *Lehrbuch der christlichen Sittenlehre*, 205–12 (§§212–23).

19. Schleiermacher, *Entwurf eines Systems der Sittenlehre* (1835); this was subsequently republished by Twesten in 1841 under a different title, *Grundriß der philosophischen Ethik* (Outline of philosophical ethics); yet another version was produced by Ludwig Jonas in 1843 under the title *Die christliche Sitte nach den Grundsätzen der evangelischen Kirche im Zusammenhange dargestellt* (The Christian ethic), originally published in *Sämmtliche Werke*, div. 1, vol. 12. ET of selections from this volume: *Selections from Friedrich Schleiermacher's "Christian Ethics."*

20. GO: *Gestaltung der Sittenlehre*; *sittliche Aufgabe*.

21. GO: *Formel*; Rothe, *Theologische Ethik*, 3:351–453 (§§798–858).

who gradually leads the abnormal moral development into the normal moral development. Duty and law are still necessary because no one is yet absolutely virtuous, absolutely redeemed. But neither are duty and law superfluous, since everyone included in redemption is still relatively capable of fulfilling them. Everyone needs law and duty, precisely in order that such a rule for their conduct can lead them more and more from an abnormal moral development to a normal one. That law can proceed only from the Redeemer, and naturally with the redeemed it increasingly ceases to be law and becomes increasingly superfluous. Rothe goes on to speak of "individual moral authority"[22] that turns *the* universal duty into *my* duty, about the permissible, and about Christ and his Spirit in the community (i.e., Christian morality as our law), about collision of duties, and the like.[23]

For Martensen, "what virtue is as fulfillment, *duty* is as demand; therefore, the whole doctrine of virtue may be treated as the doctrine of duty."[24] Duty is the relation of the law to the individual. A person will say, "This is my duty," and not "This is my law." Martensen does not elaborate on the concept of duty; later, however, he maintains the third, didactic use of the law for the believers, since the old Adam is still in them.[25] Often they must still force themselves to obey Christ. They often still have to summon the imperative of duty to help them, because they are not always inclined to perform their duty. But this use of the law becomes—and must become—more and more superfluous. The Ten Commandments must be retained in the catechism but interpreted Christianly in the spirit of the New Testament. The gospel is an *invitation*, but for the conscience it is also a *commandment of duty*.[26] Christ is not only the Giver, but also the holy, commanding Authority who says, "*Thou shalt* believe."[27] Burger appears to agree with him.[28] But others, like Vilmar, say that duty has no place in theological ethics, any more than virtue and the highest good, since they presuppose a legal obligation and a legal demand while the converted have liberty and spontaneity.[29] Nevertheless, Vilmar concedes that the word "duty" can also be used figuratively,[30] but at the risk of being misunderstood.

22. GO: *individuelle sittliche Instanz.*
23. Rothe, *Theologische Ethik*, §§805, 811, 820, 849.
24. Martensen, *Christian Ethics*, 1:344 (§113); emphasis original.
25. Martensen, *Christian Ethics*, 1:438–42 (§143).
26. GO: *Einladung; Pflichtgebot.*
27. GO: *du sollst glauben.*
28. Burger, "Pflicht," 571.
29. GO: *Rechtsobliegenheit; Rechtsforderung*; DO: *vrijheid en spontaniteit*; Vilmar, *Theologische Moral*, 2/3:107–8; cf. "Law."
30. Ed. note: The Dutch original has *oneigenlijk.*

Duty and Law in Scripture

In our view, to be sure, duty is not a biblical term; it occurs only a few times in the versified Dutch psalter—for example, in Psalm 19:6:

> So, I gather from my duty,
> a clear message, O God.
> What a beautiful prospect!
> He who trusts in you
> maintains your laws,
> for they contain great reward.[31]

Yet in itself that does not disqualify the term. Duty presupposes law. The question therefore is, What is the relation of believers to the *law*? In the Synoptic Gospels we find Jesus saying the following: Righteousness[32] is an attribute of the kingdom (Matt. 6:33), with which one must be clothed as with a wedding garment in order to enter (Matt. 22:11–14); only those who do the will of God are Jesus's family (mother and brothers; Matt. 12:50), and they alone can enter the kingdom (Matt. 7:21, 24).[33] This will of God is revealed in the law and the prophets (Matt. 5:17; 7:12; 22:40); that is Jesus's point of departure (Mark 10:19): "You know the commandments" (cf. Luke 10:26). And Jesus acknowledges and upholds the entire Mosaic law; the teachers of the law and the Pharisees sitting in the seat of Moses must be obeyed, even though they themselves do not obey Moses (Matt. 23:2–3). Jesus acknowledges sacrifice in Matthew 5:23–24: "So if you are offering your gift at the altar and there remember that your brother has something against you, leave your gift there before the altar and go. First be reconciled to your brother, and then come and offer your gift." He also recognizes fasting (Matt. 6:16–18), which even in the Old Testament was commanded only on the great Day of Atonement (Lev. 16 and 23). When he says, "Woe to you, scribes and Pharisees, hypocrites! For you tithe mint and dill and cumin, and have neglected

---

31. Ed. note: The reference to Ps. 19:6 is *not* to the biblical text but to stanza 6 in the Dutch Psalm book used in the Reformed churches; translation by Harry Van Dyke. DO:
Dus krijg ik van mijn plicht,
O God, een klaar bericht.
Wat is 't vooruitzicht schoon!
Hij, die op U vertrouwt.
Uw wetten onderhoudt,
Vindt daarin grooten loon.
32. GrO: δικαιοσύνη.
33. Holtzmann, "Zur synoptischen Frage II, III"; Klöpper, "Zur Stellung Jesu"; Kirn, "Das Gesetz in der christlichen Ethik."

the weightier matters of the law: justice and mercy and faithfulness. These you ought to have done, without neglecting the others" (Matt. 23:23), he acknowledges the former as good, although it is not the most weighty. Jesus would not allow anyone to carry a vessel through the temple (Mark 11:16), because the temple is his Father's house (Matt. 23:21; Luke 2:49), which must not be turned into a den of thieves (Mark 11:17). He keeps the regular feasts in Jerusalem, eats the Passover (Mark 14:12); he orders the lepers to offer the sacrifice of purification (Matt. 8:4; Luke 17:14), and he pays the temple tax, the two-drachma tax (Matt. 17:27). In a word, Jesus did not come "to abolish the Law or the Prophets . . . but to fulfill them" (Matt. 5:17; Luke 16:17).[34] In fact, "not an iota, not a dot, will pass from the Law until all is accomplished" (Matt. 5:18)—that is, until the end of the age, when "heaven and . . . earth pass away" (Luke 16:17). Jesus came to fulfill, not to set aside, abolish, or any such thing. "The law, however, in its Mosaic basis as well as in its prophetic development, is to continue in enduring force until the end of the world, or until each of its commandments is fulfilled, as he has come to fulfil them—then, indeed it will cease as law, but only in order that it may continue in its fulfilment."[35] Thus, Jesus is very conservative; he says no word, nor performs any deed to abolish the law.

On the other hand, Jesus nevertheless opposes the Pharisees. He rejects the "commandments of men" (Matt. 15:9; Mark 7:7),[36] demands a righteousness surpassing that of the Pharisees and teachers of the law (Matt. 5:20). Therefore, in Matthew 5 he provides an internal and spiritual explanation of the law. Furthermore, Jesus seems to have had a more lenient view of the Sabbath when he permits his disciples to journey on the Sabbath (Mark 2:23–28 par. Luke 6:1–5; Matt. 12:1–8).[37] But in this instance, Jesus is not acting in conflict with the law, with the Old Testament Scripture (but only with the Jewish prescriptions), and hence appeals to the example of David. He points to the intention of the Lawgiver, that the Sabbath is made for humanity, and he claims the right as the Son of Man to interpret the law and to teach the true fulfillment of the

---

34. GrO: καταλῦσαι; πληρῶσαι.

35. B. Weiss, *Biblical Theology of the New Testament*, 1:108 (§24). Is it then appropriate to speak of Jesus as a "legislator"? Trent thinks so (Martensen, *Christian Ethics*, 1:442–59 [§§144–46]); and so do the Arminians (de Moor, *Commentarius Perpetuus*, 2:665); Eduard König investigates how Jesus related to each commandment of the first and second tables, Sabbath, ceremonial laws, and so forth. Christ came to accomplish the law, to carry out the whole law, but he also came to fulfill and perfect it, to clarify its deepest meaning. By declaring, "*I* say to you," he changed the character of the Sabbath, neighbor-love, etc. (König, "Der Christ und das alttestamentlische Gesetz").

36. GrO: ἐντάλματα ἀνθρώπων.

37. GrO: ὁδὸν ποιεῖν.

law. He never breaks the Mosaic law (Luke 13:15; 14:4), yet states that it is lawful to heal on the Sabbath.[38] Jesus was so far from breaking the Sabbath commandment that he says, "Pray that your flight not be in winter or on a Sabbath" (Matt. 24:20), for refugees might feel bound to the rule not to travel on that day. Jesus also defends his disciples against the Pharisees' stipulation about washing hands (Mark 7:1–15; Matt. 15:1–11), against their stipuation about fasting (Mark 2:18–22), and against their permission of divorce (Mark 10:2–9). Jesus always upholds the law as divine and eternal, but he views that law spiritually, internally, and lets first things be first; he proceeds from the heart and core of the law, and summarizes law and prophets as teaching the love of God and neighbor (Mark 12:28–34; Matt. 7:12). Like the prophets, he ranks mercy above sacrifice (Matt. 9:13; 12:7; Mark 12:33) and elevates the internal above the external: "There is nothing outside a person that by going into him can defile him, but the things that come out of a person are what defile him" (Mark 7:15). Thus, Jesus acknowledges the whole law as divine and enduring, but he interprets it not as the teachers of the law but as the prophets did—that is to say, spiritually. In no way does he say that the law will cease in part, except insofar as he foretells that the temple will be destroyed (Mark 13:2) and that he, who is greater than the temple (Matt. 12:6), will always be with them (Matt. 18:20). Jesus does not want to abolish the law except only in the way that arises through the true and complete fulfilling of the law (not even in Mark 2:21–22, where he warns "not against fasting, but against an untimely and immature abandonment of the old forms").[39]

The early church in Jerusalem, therefore, kept the law, continued in the temple (Acts 2:46), went up to it (Acts 3:1–2), prayed at set times (Acts 10:9), ate nothing unclean (Acts 10:14), is called "zealous for the law" (Acts 21:20) and "devout . . . according to the law" (Acts 22:12).[40] Stephen, too, said nothing against the temple and Jewish cultic practices (Acts 7). Nonetheless, at the Council of Jerusalem (Acts 15), the gentiles were freed from the law. Measures were taken merely against damaging the mission to Israel. Nothing was said about whether it was permissible to have fellowship with gentile Christians, including meals. Some zealots opposed it, and at one time Peter gave in to them (Gal. 2). But all the other apostles thought more leniently about this.

Paul also considered the law of Moses as a revelation of God's will (Rom. 2:18; 9:4; 2 Cor. 3:3, 7); though a possession and privilege of Israel, it is the law

---

38. But what about John 5:8, 11? Ed. note: This is Bavinck's question, and he leaves it unanswered.

39. B. Weiss, *Biblical Theology of the New Testament*, 1:112.

40. GrO: ζηλωταὶ τοῦ νόμου; εὐλαβὴς κατὰ τὸν νόμον.

of God (Rom. 2:27; 7:22, 25), spiritual (Rom. 7:14), holy (Rom. 7:12).[41] And by law Paul understands the entire law, including the ritual portion, because in Romans 9:4 worship belongs to Israel's privilege.[42] The whole Old Testament is sometimes called the law (1 Cor. 14:21; Rom. 3:19).[43] However, this law does not bring righteousness (Rom. 8:3), but stimulates covetous desire (Rom. 7:7–8), arouses dormant sin (Rom. 7:8–9; 1 Cor. 15:56), provokes the wrath of God (Rom. 4:15; Gal. 3:10), pronounces curse and death (2 Cor. 3:6), and increases trespasses (Rom. 5:20; Gal. 3:19). Thus, it has come between God and us and is a guardian unto Christ (Gal. 3:24). If that is the meaning and intention of the law, then it is also transitory and temporary (Gal 3:25), and the believer is no longer under a guardian.[44] With the coming of faith in Christ the end of the law has arrived (Rom. 10:4); the law—that is, the Old Testament dispensation—is "done away" (2 Cor. 3:11).[45] "Why then the law? It was added because of transgressions, until the offspring should come to whom the promise had been made" (Gal. 3:19).[46] As long as a child is a minor,[47] they are under a guardian, like Israel (Gal. 4:2–3), and are not free (v. 3), but entangled with a yoke of slavery (Gal. 5:1), under the dispensation of the law, which is symbolized by the son of the slave woman (Gal. 4:22–31).[48] That servitude to the law, however, has ceased, and freedom from the law is introduced by Christ, who himself submitted voluntarily to the law, "to redeem those who were under the law, so that we might receive adoption as sons" (Gal. 4:5).[49]

Christ has therefore provided us liberty (Gal. 5:1), to which we are now called (Gal. 5:13), and has made us children of the Jerusalem that is above, like the sons of the free woman (Gal. 4:26–31). That freedom, objectively acquired by Christ, we receive subjectively in and through the Spirit: "Now the Lord is the Spirit, and where the Spirit of the Lord is, there is freedom" (2 Cor. 3:17). "But if you are led by the Spirit, you are not under the law" (Gal. 5:18).[50] Just as a wife is set free from her husband through his death, so the believer who has died with Christ is set free from the law, to serve another lord—namely, Christ (Rom. 7:1–3; Gal. 2:19). Nonetheless this freedom of faith does not

41. GrO: νόμῳ τοῦ θεοῦ; πνευματικός; ἅγιος.
42. GrO: καὶ ἡ λατρεία.
43. GrO: ὁ νόμος.
44. GrO: ὑπὸ παιδαγωγόν.
45. GrO: καταργούμενον; Johannes Weiss, *Die christliche Freiheit*.
46. GrO: ἄχρις οὗ ἔλθῃ τὸ σπέρμα.
47. GrO: νήπιος.
48. GrO: ζυγῷ δουλείας.
49. GrO: υἱοθεσία.
50. GrO: εἰ δὲ πνεύματι ἄγεσθε, οὐκ ἐστὲ ὑπὸ νόμον.

abolish the law but upholds it (Rom. 3:31), for the "righteous requirement of the law" (Rom. 8:4)—weakened by the flesh (Rom. 8:3)—"[is] fulfilled in [those] who walk not according to the flesh but according to the Spirit" (Rom. 8:4)[51]—in those who "are released from the law" in order to "serve in the new way of the Spirit and not in the old way of the written code" (Rom. 7:6). That Spirit "gives life" (2 Cor. 3:6).[52] That Spirit must renew our mind[53] so "that by testing [we] may discern what is the will of God, what is good and acceptable and perfect" (Rom. 12:2; Eph. 5:10; Phil. 1:10), which is called a "law of the Spirit of life" over against the "law of sin and death" (Rom. 8:2).

Although Paul now views himself "under the law of Christ"[54] (1 Cor. 9:21), as serving the Lord (Rom. 12:11; 16:18; 2 Cor. 5:9), often points to the example of Jesus and himself (Gal. 4:12; 1 Cor. 4:16, 17; 11:1; Phil. 3:17; 4:9; Eph. 5:2), appeals to Christian custom (1 Cor. 11:16; 14:33), and he himself provides ordinances (1 Cor. 7:17; 11:2, 34; 16:1; Phil. 2:12), nevertheless, the Old Testament and the law remain authoritative for him. After all, everything in the Old Testament was written down for our instruction (1 Cor. 10:11; Rom. 15:4), and Paul repeatedly appeals to the Old Testament. For example, in 1 Corinthians 14:34, Paul appeals to Genesis 3:16 for the submission of a wife to her husband. In 2 Corinthians 9:9, he appeals to Psalm 112:9 for an admonition to generosity. In 1 Corinthians 1:31 and 2 Corinthians 10:17, he appeals to Jeremiah 9:23–24 for a warning against boasting. In Galatians 5:14, he appeals to Leviticus 19:18 for the summary of the entire law in one commandment—namely, that of neighbor love. In Romans 13:8–10, many commandments of the law are enumerated and summarized in terms of love. In Ephesians 6:2, he cites the Fifth Commandment. And Paul urges the fulfilling of these commandments with an appeal to the mercy of God which has been shown (Rom. 12:1), to Christ (Rom. 15:1–3; 1 Cor. 1:10), to his readers' having been bought with a price (1 Cor. 6:20), to the Spirit whose temple they are (1 Cor. 6:19), to the living fellowship with Christ (1 Cor. 6:15–16), to their Christian calling (Eph. 4:1), to doing good works (Eph. 2:10; Col. 1:10).

Thus the law is not nullified but is completely fulfilled for the first time in Christianity.[55] Christ is the true propitiation, the true Passover Lamb (1 Cor.

---

51. GrO: τὸ δικαίωμα τοῦ νόμου.

52. GrO: τὸ δὲ πνεῦμα ζωοποιεῖ. Ed. note: Bavinck has ζωοποιεῖ (without an iota subscript under the omega); this demonstrates once again that Bavinck is using an edition of the New Testament prepared by Tischendorf, who uses ζωοποιεῖ; later editions (Nestle-Aland) use ζῳοποιεῖ.

53. GrO: ἀνακαινώσει τοῦ νοός.

54. GrO: ἔννομος Χριστοῦ.

55. Thus Augustine, *Reply to Faustus the Manichaean* XIX.19 (*NPNF¹* 4:239–52); B. Weiss, *Biblical Theology of the New Testament*, 1:380–90 (§§74–75); 2:118–28 (§106). Ed. note: In addition to the passages Bavinck cites from Weiss, one more should be listed: 2:229–34 (§126).

5:7; Eph. 5:2); we are called to offer our bodies "as a living sacrifice, holy and acceptable to God" (Rom. 12:1; 15:16). These are the true sacrifices, and the church is the true temple (1 Cor. 3:16; 2 Cor 6:16). Thus, the Old Testament ordinances are "a shadow of the things to come" (Col. 2:17), Christ's sacrifice is the true atonement offering (Eph. 5:2), baptism in communion with Christ is the true circumcision (Col. 2:11), and spiritual worship is the true worship (Rom. 12:1; Phil. 3:3).[56] Thus Paul teaches that the law

1. has ceased to be able to give life and righteousness because it is "weakened by the flesh" (Rom. 8:3);
2. has ceased to be able to condemn us (Rom. 8:1; Gal. 3:13); and
3. has ceased being the institution of teaching immature Israel until the time of Christ (Gal. 3:24).

Over against all that, believers now stand under grace; they are freed, mature sons and daughters, led by the Spirit; the wall of partition between Jews and gentiles has been broken down (Eph. 2:14).[57]

Nevertheless, Paul does teach emancipation from the external authority of the law, although he in no way teaches the abolition of its content. There are many things that point to this conclusion. Even after his conversion, Paul views the law as Israel's privilege, insists that the law is confirmed by faith, and teaches that the righteousness of the law is fulfilled by the Spirit. Paul calls the law a law of God and declares it to be holy. He also acknowledges the Old Testament to be inspired (2 Tim. 3:16) and regards all things in it as having been written for our sake. He constantly appeals to the Old Testament, including the Ten Commandments. From all of this, it becomes clear that, while Paul does teach an emancipation from the external authority of the law, he definitely does not consider believers to be liberated from its content. The moral calling of Christian believers remains the same as it was for the Old Testament people of God.[58]

The Spirit in no way reveals a different or higher content; the content is and remains identical. However, the Spirit does increase believers' personal wisdom and understanding of the purpose of their life (Col. 1:9)—for example, as children of God, to be like their Father (Eph. 5:1). The Spirit increases each person's perception of what is fitting for them as they acknowledge God and

56. GrO: σκιὰ τῶν μελλόντων; λατρείαν.
57. Cf. de Moor, *Commentarius Perpetuus*, 2:662, who bases the abolition of the law on these same three things.
58. Ritschl, *Die christliche Lehre von der Rechtfertigung und Versöhnung*, 2:283–93; Ernesti, *Die Ethik des Apostels Paulus*, 63.

his law for their own regenerated being. With renewed minds, they are able to "[test and] discern what is the will of God, what is good and acceptable and perfect" (Rom. 12:2). They are able to think about "whatever is true . . . honorable . . . just . . . pure . . . lovely . . . and commendable" (Phil. 4:8). From this it follows that Paul continued to uphold the law in a threefold manner: First, he upheld it insofar as we are—by nature, and so also by our regenerated nature—obliged to fulfill it; this is the law's natural obligation, from which we are never released.[59] Second, the law brings us "knowledge of sin" (Rom. 3:20). Third, the law is a rule of gratitude—that is, a source of knowledge for a life well-pleasing to God.[60]

But, in addition, Paul appeals to various sources of knowledge: (1) To his own moral prescriptions. In 1 Corinthians 7:12–14 and 7:40, he appeals to what he has received by the Holy Spirit in contrast to the commandments taught in Scripture or by Jesus. (2) To the revelation of God in Christ, who is our example (1 Thess. 5:18). (3) To the Holy Spirit in the church, who is the rule of our walk according to the Spirit. (4) To Christian moral practice in the churches (1 Cor. 14:34; 11:16).[61] (5) Finally, as Jesus, so Paul teaches that the law has not been abolished but fulfilled, *spiritualized*, internalized. Hence what is itself spiritual-ethical (the moral law) already in the Old Testament is and remains eternal.[62]

The Law and Christian Liberty

Such, as a rule, was the healthy view of the Christian church, definitely also of the Lutheran and Reformed churches.[63] Luther maintained the necessity of good works by virtue of God's commandment, by virtue of the Christian's unique being, and by virtue of the gratitude that is due.[64] Luthardt makes the sound comment that Protestants posited as a hallmark of good works that they be done according to God's will, in contrast to Rome's self-directed religion.[65] They were thereby dependent on the revelation of God's will—that is, on the law.

---

59. LO: *obligatio naturalis*.

60. De Moor, *Commentaris Perpetuus*, 2:663.

61. GO: *Sitte*; GrO: κατὰ πνεῦμα; Ernesti, *Die Ethik des Apostels Paulus*, 68–71.

62. Martensen, *Christian Ethics*, 1:379 (§125). Ed. note: There are many different editions of Martensen's *Christian Ethics*; some earlier editions of vol. 1 are given the title *Christian Ethics, General Part*. The entire three-volume 1888–89 edition is often catalogued as *Christian Ethics, Special Part*; vol. 1 drops "General Part" and has the title "Martensen on Christian Ethics." Properly speaking, vol. 2 is "Special Ethics" and is divided into "Individual Ethics" (2/1) and "Social Ethics" (2/2).

63. For the Lutheran church, see Luthardt, *Die Ethik Luthers*, 38–39.

64. Luthardt, *Die Ethik Luthers*, 68.

65. Luthardt, *Die Ethik Luthers*, 70.

Accordingly, Protestant ethics was immediately given the form of the Decalogue, not because Protestants regarded the division into ten commandments as the best—because it was divine and on that basis they sought to revive the commandments, as Sartorius believed—but in order to highlight God's will over against the self-directed works of Rome.[66] Thus Lutheran ethicists, such as Buddeus, spoke of duties. Reformed ethicists, such as Calvin, van Mastricht, Witsius, and Alting also spoke confidently of duties.[67] The Council of Trent, too, anathematized all who say "that the ten commandments in no way pertain to Christians."[68]

With this view, we are opposing, on the one hand, the nomists, and on the other, the antinomians. Nomism turns the gospel into a new law, regards the Old Testament relation to the law as the only true one, confuses Old and New Testament dispensations, and denies the Spirit of liberty. This error is found first of all in Pharisaism, and then in the Christian church with Ebionism, Pelagian Catholicism with its many human traditions, and Pietism with its "Do not handle, Do not taste, Do not touch" (Col. 2:21).[69] In nomism, humans always

66. E. Sartorius, *Die Lehre von der heiligen Liebe*, xix–xxii; more in Hase, *Evangelische-protestantische Dogmatik*, 146–47 (§120).

67. LO: *officia*. For the Reformed church, see Calvin, *Institutes*, II.vii; van Mastricht, *Theoretico-Practica Theologia*, I.viii.2, §48; Witsius, *Economy of the Covenants*, 2:174–87 (IV.4.xxvii–lvii); H. Alting, *Theologiae Problematica Nova*, 524–25 (X.xxiii); de Moor, *Commentarius Perpetuus*, 2:662–72; cf. Schneckenburger, *Vergleichende Darstellung*, 1:109–33.

Ed. note (repeated from *RE*, 1:8n48): To understand how we are referencing van Mastricht's *Theoretico-Practica Theologia* it is helpful to know that it is divided into two parts: "how one is made spiritually alive and, being alive, how one lives to God." The first part (eight books) is a systematic theological treatment of what we need to know about God; the second part is about living before God. This second part in turn is divided into moral theology (*Idea Theologia Moralis*; three books) and the practice of piety (*Hypotyposis Theologia Ascetica, de exercitio pietatis*; four books). Bavinck usually cites the four-volume Dutch translation of this work, *Beschouwende en praktikale godgeleerdheit*. Since this work is currently being translated into English, we are citing this work by the title *Theoretico-Practica Theologia*, then by part (with part I = *Theologia* [*Godgeleerdheid*], part II = *Idea Theologia Moralis* [*Zedelyke Godgeleerdheid*], and part III = *Hypotyposis Theologiae Asceticae, de exercitia pietatis* [*Plichtvermanende Godgeleerdheid*]), book (in lowercase Roman: i, ii, iii, etc.), chapter (1, 2, 3, 4, etc.), and paragraph (§); thus, a reference such as I.ii.2, §3. Bavinck's own references (to the Dutch edition of 1749–53) are usually given simply in terms of the Dutch *volume number* (I–IV) and the page. In those instances, we will provide Bavinck's refences in square brackets [ ] after the full reference; thus III.i.2, §4 [IV, 677].

68. LO: *decem praecepta nihil pertinere ad Christianos* (session 6, canon 19); de Moor, *Commentarius Perpetuus*, 2:672.

69. LO: *traditiones humanae*; see Martensen, *Christian Ethics*, 1:382–406 (§§126–30). Ed. note: Bavinck added an interlinear reference here to Immanuel Kant; perhaps he had in mind Martensen's reference on p. 405 to Kant's essay *Zum ewigen Frieden* ("To Everlasting Peace"), on the challenge of maintaining both moral integrity and moral liberty: "A true political philosophy, therefore, cannot advance a step without first paying homage to the principles of morals, and, although politics taken by itself is a difficult art, yet its union with morals removes it from

stand under the law as slaves, and the law always stands above them as a threat, never becoming the law of liberty. This explains why the law is never viewed and interpreted in its entirety or according to its basic principle, but always in its separate commandments and with scrupulous precision and in minute detail. On the other hand, the threat of antinomianism is found already in apostolic times among those who wanted to misuse grace in order to sin and who wanted to misuse freedom as a "cover-up for evil" (1 Pet. 2:16). After that came Manichaeism, which said that *either* the Old Testament is from the true God—and then Christians are still bound to keep all his commandments—*or* the law is not binding, and then it is from a god other than the true God.[70] The same goes for all the gnostics, who believe they have transcended the limits of finitude and are equal to the gods, and who exalt themselves, together with their ideas, above the law. Antinomianism therefore is not a violation of the law[71]—every sin is that—but it is the doctrine that justifies going against the law; antinomianism is sin itself, forming itself into an ethics, under the guise of idealism. It has reappeared many times, throughout the Middle Ages among various sects: Paulicians, Cathari, Albigensians, Amalricians, the sect of the Holy Spirit (Amalric of Bena and David of Dinant), Petrobrusians, and more.[72] Then again, in the age of the Reformation, we encounter antinomianism among the Anabaptists and with Agricola and those in the Lutheran church who taught that good works were harmful for salvation. Within the Reformed churches we find antinomianism among the English, and from there to the Dutch province of Zeeland in the Hattemists and Hebrewers.[73]

---

the difficulties of art. For this combination of them cuts in two the knots which politics alone cannot untie, whenever they come into conflict with each other" (Kant, "Eternal Peace," 118; the translation from *Zum ewigen Frieden* in the note is taken from this work rather than the English translation of Martensen's *Christian Ethics*). Kant's essay was first published in 1795.

70. Cf. Diestel, *Geschichte des Alten Testamentes*, 115.

71. GrO: ἀνομία.

72. Ed. note: The Paulicians were an Armenian Christian dualistic sect that flourished between 650 and 872, when the emperor Basil I ended their military power. The Cathari were a neo-Manichaean, dualistic sect that flourished in Western Europe in the twelfth and thirteenth centuries. The Albigensians were a Cathari group in southern France; their name came from the district of Albi (ancient Albiga). The Amalricians were a thirteenth-century pantheistic and free-love movement named after Amalric of Bena; the thought of David of Dinant was also foundational; they influenced the Brethren of the Free Spirit, an antinomian sect that flourished in the thirteenth and fourteenth centuries. Petrobrusians were followers of the popular French religious teacher Peter of Bruys, who was accused of opposing church teaching on infant baptism, encouraging iconoclasm, denying the efficacy of sacraments, and deriding good works. The preceding pastiche was cobbled together from a variety of online sources including Encyclopaedia Britannica, Catholic Encyclopedia, and Wikipedia.

73. De Moor, *Commentarius Perpetuus*, 2:665–72. Ed. note: The Hattemists were followers of Pontiaan van Hattem (1645–1706), who was accused of heresy because he overemphasized the love of God, denied his wrath, and sought union with God in a quietist fashion

Today, too, we live in an age of antinomianism, emancipation of the flesh, emancipation of women, all sorts of ways to free ourselves from the bonds of law and authority.[74] It is evident, for example, in the way that some people judge great geniuses, artists, and poets mildly as if they should be judged according to a different law and have a different morality. This is similar to the gnostic distinction "between psychical and pneumatic men—between those who are bound to every-day morality, to the conventional and tradition, the 'external,' and those who have attained the stage of perfections, where everything external is indifferent."[75] In this view,

> the true Gnostic . . . lives in an uninterrupted contemplation of the divine. And just because he is so highly exalted above the sensual, which with him is reduced to be the indifferent, he can freely addict himself to all the pleasures of the flesh: for this immersion in sensuality cannot introduce any taint into his inmost being. We combat lust by addicting ourselves to lust. It is no great thing to abstain from pleasure when one has not experienced it; but the great thing is to find oneself in the midst of pleasure and enjoyment, and not to be conquered by it.[76]

This rationalization is explained by a water metaphor: "It is only the small stagnant waters which become impure when anything dirty is cast into them. The ocean, on the other hand, can receive anything into its depths without being thereby sullied. The true Gnostic *is an ocean of spiritual power*, and cannot be sullied by anything; for the impurity is at once washed away by his exalted devotion."[77]

(van der Linde, "Hattem"). "Hebrewers" is another name for "Verschoorists," followers of Jacobus Verschoor (1648–1700), who, having been denied candidacy for ministry in the Dutch Reformed Church after several attempts in different jurisdictions, began his own conventicle meetings outside the structure of the organized churches. The sect derived its name "Hebrewers" from its criticism of the "official" Dutch *Statenvertaling* of the Bible and its practice of reading the original Hebrew and Greek in its worship services. See Grosheide, "Hebreën (Secte der)."

74. Nitzsch, "Die Gesammterscheinung des Antinomianismus."

75. Martensen, *Christian Ethics*, 1:385 (§127).

76. Martensen, *Christian Ethics*, 1:385 (§127).

77. Martensen, *Christian Ethics*, 1:385–86 (§127); emphasis original. Ed. note: Bavinck refers to a father-and-son team who exemplified this; he took this from Martensen, who provides a fuller description: "Representatives of such tenets may be instanced in Carpocrates of Alexandria (second century), and his genial son Epiphanes, who died from the effects of debauchery at the age of seventeen (Faustus and Don Juan combined), after having written a work on uprightness (περὶ δικαιοσύνης), in which he expressed the opinion that the law of nature is the highest law—that the phantasies of sin proceed from those human laws which fight against the law of nature, and the dispositions implanted in man" (*Christian Ethics*, 1:386 [§127]).

This is the way that Friedrich Schlegel (1772–1829) reasoned at the beginning of the nineteenth century: the philosopher, the poet, is the true human being; genius is the true virtue. Unlike ordinary people, who see limits and boundaries everywhere, a genius sees none. Hence, in his novel *Lucinde*, Schlegel criticized marriage and said that genius is free of all customs; such unbridled subjectivism is the consequence of Fichte's philosophy.[78] One hears this all the time: geniuses are defective in virtue, and this must be judged leniently. However, a genius is also a human being—which is the highest—and must be judged by the law that holds for humans. It was therefore wrong of Jacobi when he wrote to Fichte the famous lines:

> Nay, I am that atheist, that profane person,[79] who, in despite of the will which wills nothing (that is to say, in despite of the abstract formal precepts of morality), will lie, like the dying Desdamona; prevaricate and deceive like Pylades representing himself to be Orestes; will murder like Timoleon; break law and oath, like Epaminondas and Johann de Witt; resolve on suicide, like Otho; commit sacrilege, like David; nay, pluck ears of corn on the Sabbath, only because I am hungry, and the law was made for man, and not man for the law. I am that profane person, and scorn the philosophy which calls me profane on that account—scorn it and its highest essence; for, with the holiest certainty which I have in me, I know that it is man's right of majesty, the seal to his dignity, his divine nature, to have *privilegium aggrantiandi* (right of pardon) for such offences against the absolute, universal, irrational letter of the law.[80]

Then there are also many who hold to a diplomatic or political antinomianism,[81] as if a different moral law holds for diplomacy and for the higher life of politics. Many politicians forge a new morality for themselves; for example, act now, justify later; if you did it, deny it; divide and conquer.[82] One example is Macchiavelli (1469–1527), author of *The Prince*, who, to save his country from anarchy, is willing to let the ruler reign absolutely and employ every means—violence, trickery, poison—to repel anarchy.[83] Indeed, our whole

---

78. Ed. note: The novel may have been autobiographical: "During his time in Berlin, Schlegel also began a relationship with Dorothea Veit, daughter of Moses Mendelssohn, who had left her banker husband Simon Veit in 1798. The publication in 1799 of Schlegel's novel *Lucinde*, with its frank (though by today's standards hardly risqué) portrayal of a sexual liaison widely thought to be autobiographical became for Schlegel a major scandal" (Speight, "Friedrich Schlegel").

79. GO: *Gottlöse*.

80. Martensen, *Christian Ethics*, 1:390, 392 (§128); cf. J. Müller, *Christian Doctrine of Sin*, 1:261. Ed. note: The Jacobi quote is from Jacobi, *Werke*, 3:37–38.

81. Martensen, *Christian Ethics*, 1:393–406 (§§129–30).

82. LO: *fac et excusa*; *si fecisti, nega*; *divide et impera*. Ed. note: These maxims of war and peace are from Kant, "Eternal Peace," 110–11. Kant himself is critical of them.

83. DO: *geweld, list, vergif*.

society is permeated with antinomianism, ever since Rousseau's "let's go back to Nature" presented the law of nature as the supreme law and placed all blame on society, institutions, order, rules, and moral law.[84] And many talk this way: our nature, our passions, our drives are good; they must be given free rein; desire is good but marriage is wrong, and so on.[85]

Over against nomism and antinomianism we insist that the believer is free from the law as law of the covenant of works—all of which Adam was to observe in his own strength in order to receive eternal life—and so also free from the curse and threat of the law; and free from the law as an institution of Israel.[86] But even though all people are not "under the law," they are and remain "tied to the law" and will never become "lawless."[87] God is indeed unchangeable, and so is his law; Christ has satisfied the law in our place as the law of the covenant of works, in order to earn life for us, but not in order to release us from obedience to that law as a rule of life. We are automatically bound to that law by our human nature and by God's nature.

Now where there is a law, there is also a duty. Neither law nor duty can be deduced evolutionarily, zoologically, empirically, historically from social instincts, from the idea of respect,[88] from the sanction and authority of government or parents. Law and duty are both primal, a priori, ideas; the "ought"[89] for all those theories remains unexplained and inexplicable. According to Kant, duty is the form (law, rule) of our actions, the necessity of obeying the law out of respect for the law.[90] The laws of nature are followed automatically: they do not compel respect or honor; they are not the "reason for an act," but merely the "expression of it."[91] Nor do the psychological or logical laws compel respect; they are obeyed as means to a certain end (the logical laws for finding

84. FO: *retournons à la nature*. This view is found in positivism and utilitarianism. Schopenhauer sought to banish all law from morality—an ethics that merely describes and does not prescribe. He believed that the notion of duty derives from social instincts (Janet, *La morale*, 175).

85. Martensen, *Christian Ethics*, 1:393 (§129); so also, Fourier. Ed. note: Martensen speaks of Rousseau's famous paradox: "Why has God implanted in us desires if we have not a right to satisfy them?" He then adds, "On this reasoning is found the right to emancipate the flesh and to do away with *marriage* as something merely conventional." The result is a doctrine of "'free love' (*amour libre*) and 'the lawfulness of passion' in opposition to marriage as a pernicious human institution, an 'odious' invention." François Marie Charles Fourier (1772–1837) was a radical utopian socialist who inspired many revolutionary thinkers and inspired numerous intentional communities in the nineteenth century (Janet, *La morale*, 178).

86. See van Aalst, *Geestelijk Mengelstoffen*, 1:216–30.

87. GrO: ὑπὸ νόμον; ἔννομοι; ἄνομοι; de Moor, *Commentarius Perpetuus*, 2:670.

88. As is done by von Kirchmann (1802–84): *Die Grundbegriffe des Rechts*. Ed. note: The third chapter is titled "Feelings of Respect" (*Die Gefühle der Achtung*).

89. GO: *Sollen*.

90. Janet, *La morale*, 173–92.

91. FO: *raison de l'action*; *l'expression*; Janet, *La morale*, 194.

truth); thus they are all hypothetical imperatives. Only the moral law compels respect, wants to be obeyed absolutely and purely for its own sake. According to Kant, it is a categorical imperative, but that is only formally true. Janet says that the moral law, too, is hypothetical; *if* we do not want to lower ourselves to be like animals, then we should not steal, kill, and so forth.[92] In other words, the moral law always assumes the excellence of the human personality.[93] But this hypothesis is fixed so I cannot divest myself of it; I cannot will *not* to be a human being; my conscience forbids me. Factually, therefore, the moral law is categorical after all, because the hypothesis is categorical. According to Kant, the properties of duty are that it is absolute and universal.[94] To the question, "Why is the law obligatory? Why do I feel duty-bound, to obey it?" the only possible answer is, "Because it is so, because God so wills it." Here we encounter a foundation, a primal fact.[95] Any number of formulations attempt to ground the moral good apart from God, but they fail to bring us even one step closer. Janet says that the good is good in and of itself (apart from and independent of God), and by itself entails obligation; others say that the good as well as the obligation to do the good are determined arbitrarily by God. Pufendorf claims that God determines not the good that in itself is good, but our obligation to do the good.[96] None of this advances our understanding and is nothing but a false explanation. Janet explains nothing, merely posits something, and says, "People cannot conceive their own ideal essence unless they will it and at the same time want to realize that essence."[97] But that obligation in no way depends on our will but precedes it, and it is a priori fixed. Being bound to God's law is an established fact.

In conclusion, also for the regenerate person, we can speak of law and duty. Such people are still under obligation, since they are, though not "under the law," nevertheless "tied to the law."[98] However, duty for Christians—what we are obligated to do—is no longer

a. an obligation to do the law in order to be justified;
b. an obligation to do one's duty, or to become perfect (Rothe), out of respect for the law (Kant).

---

92. Janet, *La morale*, 199.
93. FO: *l'excellence de la personalité humaine.*
94. Janet, *La morale*, 203.
95. LO: *principium.*
96. Janet, *La morale*, 217–18.
97. FO: *l'homme ne peut concevoir sa propre essence idéale sans vouloir en même temps réaliser cette essence* (Janet, *La morale*, 217).
98. GrO: ὑπὸ νόμον; ἔννομος.

Instead, Christians are obligated to perform their duty out of gratitude and love toward God, in order, from that, to be assured of their own faith and to win over their neighbors.[99]

§28. Precepts and Counsels

Single Duty: Dual Morality

Just as the law can be summarized in one word—love (Rom. 13:10; cf. Gal. 5:14)[100]—so can duty. Thus all duties can be reduced to a single duty, to one maxim or basic rule such as Matthew 7:12 (cf. Matt. 22:37–40).[101] Or as Kant put it, act in such a way that the maxim of your action can be universal law.[102] For Fichte duty is always to act according to your best conviction, according to your conscience. Rothe believed it was to submit to the Christian moral practice prevailing in your own circle, but subject to "your Protestant calling (that is, to the extent that you have one)."[103] According to Kuenen, in your interaction with others, you are to realize the idea of humanity or to promote true humanity.[104] For Janet, "every person owes it to himself to achieve the highest degree of excellence and perfection that nature is capable of."[105] But although duty is one, it can be distributed among many duties. And there are various questions about the relation of that one duty to the many.

The distinction between *precepts* and *counsels*[106] was known already among the Stoics. The absolute good could be attained only by the wise. Thus

99. Heidelberg Catechism, Q&A 86. Ed. note: See also chap. 10 in Bavinck, *RE*, vol. 1 (§23, "Security and Sealing").

100. "Love is the fulfilling of the law"; GrO: πλήρωμα οὖν νόμου ἡ ἀγάπη.

101. GrO: Πάντα οὖν ὅσα ἐὰν θέλητε ἵνα ποιῶσιν ὑμῖν οἱ ἄνθρωποι, οὕτως καὶ ὑμεῖς ποιεῖτε αὐτοῖς.

102. Ed. note: Bavinck adds the marginal reference "Arthur Schopenhauer, *Die beiden Grund-probleme der Ethik*, 232." This refers to the second of two lectures in this volume, "On the Basis of Morality" ("Ueber das Fundament der Moral"); the first lecture was titled "On the Freedom of the Will" ("Ueber die Freiheit des menschlichen Willens"). The reference is found in §19, "Confirming the Stated Foundation of Morality" ("Bestätigunen des dargelegten Fundaments der Moral"). ET: Schopenhauer, *Two Fundamental Problems of Ethics*, 233–35; a more explicit statement of the Kantian maxim can be found on pp. 161–66.

103. GO: *deines reformatischen Berufes (Soweit du nämlich enen hast)*; Rothe, *Theologische Ethik*, 3:394 (§834); cf. Rothe's discussion of other formulas for social obligation in 4:220–21 (§1005).

104. Kuenen, "Dictaat over het Geweten," §14. Ed. note: This is not a published work; it is a reference to Bavinck's own notes made from Kuenen's lectures at Leiden. The notebook can be found in the Bavinck Archives.

105. FO: *Tout être se doit à lui-même d'atteindre au plus haut degré d'excellence et de perfection dont sa nature est susceptible* (Janet, *La morale*, 217).

106. LO: *praecepta*; *consilia*.

they distinguished between absolute duties (by which humans strived for the absolute good) and relative duties (which aimed for the desirable), between perfect duties and "intermediate duties."[107] This is the difference between the higher life of the wise—who even despised desirables like food, drink, and health—and the lower life of those who set store by these things as well as the adiaphora. Thus there was a twofold morality, law, virtue, standard.

Before long, the early church made a distinction of this sort. At first, the church was called to undergo suffering, conflict, contempt of the world, martyrdom, expecting Jesus's return. But when the churches began to spread and incorporated people who worked in trade and commerce, who had a vocation in the world—when eventually suffering, persecution, and martyrdom came to an end—then the church on the one hand became worldly and sank to a lower level of morality and, on the other hand, idealized the church of the first two centuries, in particular its martyrs, and viewed it as possessing higher virtue. Ascetic monasticism attempted to hold on to that earlier ideal;[108] but since this of course could not be mandatory for everyone, in practice the distinction arose between monks (the "religious") and common laymen, and in ethics the distinction arose between counsels and precepts.

The distinction is found already in *The Pastor of Hermas*: whoever goes beyond the commandments receives greater glory.[109] It is also found in Ambrose, Jerome, Basil the Great, Gregory Nazianzus, Bonaventure, and Thomas Aquinas.[110] According to Gass, Origen combats the ethical sense of the adiaphoron, but nonetheless distinguished between precepts and counsels.[111] "Whoever does what is owed, i.e., the precepts, is but an unprofitable servant (cf. Luke 17:10). But when something is added to the precepts one will be told: 'Well

---

107. GrO: καθήκοντα τέλεια; καθήκοντα μέσα. Ed. note: Bavinck repeats here the specifics of the distinction he made at the beginning of this chapter in §27.

108. E.g., *The Pastor of Hermas*, Montanism, and Novatianism; see Gass, *Geschichte der christlichen Ethik*, 1:67.

109. LO: *mandata*; *The Pastor of Hermas*, III.5.3: "[Keep the commandments of the Lord, and you will be approved, and inscribed amongst the number of those who observe His commands.] And if you do any good beyond what is commanded by God, you will gain for yourself more abundant glory, and will be more honoured by God than you would otherwise be" (*ANF* 2:34–35); cf. E. Schwarz, "Consilia evangelica," 346; Gass, *Geschichte der christlichen Ethik*, 1:54; Luthardt, *Die Ethik Luthers*, 74; Neander, *Vorlesungen*, 148–238.

110. Ambrose, *On the Duties of the Clergy* XI (*NPNF*[2] 10:7); Jerome, *Against Jovinianus*, Book II (*NPNF*[2] 6:387–416); Bonaventure, *Breviloquium* V.9; Aquinas, *ST* Ia IIae q. 108. art. 4; Aquinas, *Summa Contra Gentiles* III, 130–38. Ed. note: Bavinck provides no references for Basil and Gregory.

111. Gass, *Geschichte der christlichen Ethik*, 1:81.

done, good and faithful servant' (Matt. 25:21)."[112] The apostle Paul teaches us what is "beyond obligation"—that is, beyond precept.[113] We learn what Paul means by "beyond precept" in 1 Corinthians 7:25, where he writes concerning the unmarried, "I have no command [*praeceptum*, Vulgate] from the Lord, but I give my judgment [*consilium*, Vulgate] as one who by the Lord's mercy is trustworthy."[114] Augustine adopted the distinction.[115] In this way there gradually arose two—or if you will, three—different lifestyles and ideals: that of the laity, the clergy, and the monks (ascetics); hence, there arose a moral dualism.

Over time, different practices were considered to be "counsels": "the desires of the flesh and the desires of the eyes and pride of life" (1 John 2:16); being a eunuch (Matt. 19:11–12); chastity (1 Cor. 7:7–40); poverty (Matt. 19:21; 1 Cor. 9:14); and obedience (Luke 14:26–27). Later, still others were added, up to a total of twelve:[116] "If your right eye causes you to sin, tear it out and throw it away" (Matt. 5:29). "Do not resist the one who is evil. But if anyone slaps you on the right cheek, turn to him the other also" (5:39). "Give to the one who begs from you, and do not refuse the one who would borrow from you" (5:42).[117] In this way, free and voluntary virtues developed alongside duties that applied to all; desirable and commendable virtues alongside those that were commanded; the contemplative life alongside and above the practical life.[118] This principle contained numerous errors: the merits of the saints and their good works, the treasury of works of supererogation, indulgences, purgatory, etc. Nonetheless, all Catholics and also the church herself accepted the principle: "A commandment implies obligation, whereas a counsel is left to the option of the one to whom it is given."[119] In the New Testament, the counsels have been added as a law of liberty to the Old Testament law of servitude. "We must therefore understand the precepts of the *New Law* to have been given about matters that are *necessary* to gain the end of *eternal bliss*, to which end the *New Law* brings us forthwith: but that the counsels are about matters that render the gaining of this end more assured

---

112. E. Schwarz, "Consilia evangelica," 346. Ed. note: The quoted material that follows is from this source.

113. LO: *supra debitum.*

114. LO: *de virginibus praeceptum non habeo; consilium autem do.* Cf. v. 6: "Now as a concession, not a command, I say this."

115. Gass, *Geschichte der christlichen Ethik,* 1:175–76.

116. Luthardt, *Die Ethik Luthers,* 78–79.

117. Schwarz, "Consilia evangelica," 346.

118. Gass, *Geschichte der christlichen Ethik,* 1:225.

119. LO: *praeceptus importat necessitatem, consilium autem in optione ponitur ejus cui datur.* Ed. note: Bavinck took this definition from Aquinas, *ST* Ia IIae q. 108 art. 4; the quoted material that follows has also been adapted from this source.

and expeditious."[120] At Trent, the church established nothing with respect to the counsels. The *Tridentine Roman Catechism* merely comments in passing, condemning "oaths sworn through a sort of contempt, such as an oath not to observe the Evangelical counsels, such as celibacy and poverty. None, it is true, are obliged to observe these divine counsels, but by swearing not to observe them, one contemns and despises them."[121] Nonetheless, with this pronouncement Trent in fact did sanction the counsels.[122] We also find the distinction in Bellarmine, Möhler, Pruner, and Schwane.[123]

The Protestants rejected this distinction out of hand. They all taught that even the regenerate could never keep the law perfectly (a thesis that Trent condemned),[124] and that even their best works were imperfect. All talk of "works of supererogation"[125] was totally out of the question. The Lutheran church spoke of the imperfection of the regenerate.[126] From the side of the Reformed, the Roman Catholic distinction was combated by Calvin.[127] The Heidelberg Catechism confesses that "in this life even the holiest have only a small beginning of this obedience" and then, in answer to the question why the commandments should be preached, it provides this reason: "so that we may never stop striving, and never stop praying to God for the grace of the Holy Spirit, to be renewed more and more after God's image, until after this life we reach our goal: perfection."[128] According to the Belgic Confession, because we are regenerated "by the hearing of God's Word and by the work of the Holy Spirit" and made "new creatures," it is impossible for "this holy faith to be unfruitful." At the same time, it is essential to remember that our

120. LO: *praecepta; melius et expeditius.*

121. LO: *cum quis juvat, se non obtemperaturum consiliis evangelicis, cuiusmodi sunt quae ad coelibatum et paupertatem hortantur; quamvis enim nemo ex necessario sequi debeat; si quis tamen iuret, nolle se illis parere consiliis, is eo iureiurando divina consilia contemnit et violat.*

122. *Catechism of the Council of Trent*, 392. Ed. note: Bavinck's source for this claim and reference is R. Hofmann, *Symbolik oder systematische Darstellung*, 62.

123. Bellarmine, *De Controversiis*, 2:217–33 (II, 7–13); Möhler, *Symbolik*, 197–203 (§§21–22); Möhler, *Neue Untersuchungen*, §49; Pruner, *Lehrbuch der katholischen Moraltheologie²*, 71; Schwane, *De Operibus Supererogatoris.*

124. R. Hofmann, *Symbolik oder systematische Darstellung*, 62. Ed. note: Canon 18 of the Council of Trent, on justification, reads: "If anyone shall say that the commandments of God are even for a man who is justified and confirmed in grace impossible to observe, let him be anathema" (Denzinger, no. 828; cf. Trent's "Decree on Justification," chap. 11 [Denzinger, no. 804]).

125. LO: *opera supererogationis.*

126. Formula of Concord art. 6 deals with the third use of the law (Kolb and Wengert, *Book of Concord*, 587–91); Chemnitz, *Examination of the Council of Trent*, 1:639–52 (part 1, topic 10, "Concerning Good Works," question 3); Gerhard, *Loci Theologici*, 3:178–92. For Luther's discussion of counsels and precepts, see Luthardt, *Die Ethik Luthers*, 72–80.

127. *Institutes*, II.vii.56–57; IV.xiii.12; cf. Lobstein, *Die Ethik Calvins*, 54.

128. Q&A 114, 115.

good works "do not count toward our justification—for by faith in Christ we are justified, even before we do good works."[129] We give the final word here to the Canons of Dort:

> Hence daily sins of weakness arise, and blemishes cling to even the best works of saints, giving them continual cause to humble themselves before God, to flee for refuge to Christ crucified, to put the flesh to death more and more by the Spirit of supplication and by holy exercises of godliness, and to strain toward the goal of perfection, until they are freed from this body of death and reign with the Lamb of God in heaven.[130]

Dual Morality Is Indefensible

The grounds adduced by Roman Catholics for this distinction are untenable:[131]

1. Consider the following passages:

a. Isaiah 56:4–5:

> For thus says the LORD:
> "To the eunuchs who keep my Sabbaths,
>   who choose the things that please me
>   and hold fast my covenant,
> I will give in my house and within my walls
>   a monument and a name
>   better than sons and daughters;
> I will give them an everlasting name
>   that shall not be cut off."

Contrary to Bellarmine, this is not a question of voluntary celibacy, of choosing more than is required and thereby gaining a place of honor. Instead, Isaiah here comforts the proselytes, the foreigners (v. 3) who, although serving YHWH, said and could say: When Israel is restored to its land, we will not be tolerated there as members of the people of God.[132] And then Isaiah comforts the eunuchs—that is, those Israelites who without becoming unfaithful to YHWH

---

129. Belgic Confession, art. 24.
130. Canons of Dort, V.2; cf. de Moor, *Commentarius Perpetuus*, 2:647–56; Vitringa, *Korte schets*, chap. 14; among the more recent literature, see Wuttke, *Christian Ethics*, 2:107–44 (§§79–85); J. Müller, *Christian Doctrine of Sin*, 1:51–52; Martensen, *Christian Ethics*, 1:425–32 (§§138–39); Janet, *La morale*, 222–40; Thiersch, *Voorlezingen over Katholicisme en Protestantisme*, 2:157; Schwarz, "Consilia evangelica," 345; J. T. Beck, *Vorlesungen über christliche Ethik*, 2:113–43.
131. Gerhard, *Loci Theologici*, 3:183–95.
132. Cf. Delitzsch, *Biblical Commentary on the Prophecies of Isaiah*, 2:361–63 (Isa. 56:2–5).

have been "cut" against their will in foreign courts and now fear they will be judged as dry trees, unworthy to dwell among God's people in Israel. Why? Deuteronomy 23:1 says plainly, "No one whose testicles are crushed or whose male organ is cut off shall enter the assembly of the LORD." To them Isaiah now says: No, but if you keep my commandments and choose them—not surpass them, as Bellarmine has it—then I will give you "a monument and a name better than sons and daughters.

b. Wisdom of Solomon 3:13:

> For blessed is the barren woman who is undefiled,
> who has not entered into a sinful union;
> she will have fruit when God examines souls. (NRSV)

Here, there is no question at all of *counsels*; the text simply comforts the barren woman. This book is also outside the canon. Moreover, New Testament counsels cannot be confirmed from the Old Testament.

c. Matthew 5:

That Matthew 5 teaches us nothing about counsels[133] is clear from verses 18–20:

> For truly, I say to you, until heaven and earth pass away, not an iota, not a dot, will pass from the Law until all is accomplished. Therefore, whoever relaxes one of the least of these commandments and teaches others to do the same will be called least in the kingdom of heaven, but whoever does them and teaches them will be called great in the kingdom of heaven. For I tell you, unless your righteousness exceeds that of the scribes and Pharisees, you will never enter the kingdom of heaven.

To "relax"[134] one of the commandments does not mean to transgress them through one's deeds, but to make them null and void through one's teaching or theory, to pronounce them finished and abolished and no longer of any concern to us. Such persons—if they fulfill the law—will enter the kingdom but be the "least."[135] By contrast, whoever has done and taught them[136] shall

---

133. Nor does Bellarmine derive an argument from this chapter, because Christ does not give his law there over against the Old Testament moral law, but instead against the laws of the Pharisees.

134. GrO: λύσῃ.

135. GrO: ἐλάχιστος; the annotation in the Dutch Authorized Version (*Statenvertaling*) has "he will in no wise enter."

136. GrO: ποιήσῃ καὶ διδάξῃ.

be called great. For (to show that doing and teaching must go together) "unless your righteousness exceeds that of the scribes and Pharisees, you will never enter the kingdom of heaven." As appears from verse 19, there are ranks in heaven, but there is no talk here of *counsels*. Similarly, verse 22 teaches that there are differences in punishments: "But I say to you that everyone who is angry with his brother will be liable to judgment; whoever insults his brother will be liable to the council; and whoever says, 'You fool!' will be liable to the hell of fire."[137] The difficulty with these passages is that one can abstain from doing any of these things without being kept outside the kingdom. There are also sins that are not deserving of the punishment of hell. From this, Rome concludes that there are venial sins and mortal sins.[138] But that would be inferring too much. Jesus simply wants to teach that our relation to the law is normative for the relation in which God stands with us.[139]

As for Matthew 5, Manichaeans and anti-Judaizing gnostics believed that here Jesus not only improves upon the Mosaic law but in fact gives an entirely different law. Many church fathers (Chrysostom, Origen, Basil, Gregory of Nyssa), most Roman Catholics, the Socinians, the Arminians, and in modern times, more moderately, Neander, Bleek, Weiss, and others hold the view that here, Jesus is giving his own commandments in weaker or stronger contrast to—as a supplement to or improvement of—the Mosaic law. But, following Western church fathers like Augustine, Jerome, and Hilary, Protestants—and most modern exegetes—claim that Jesus was not supplementing or improving the Mosaic law, but simply explaining it correctly, over against the false, hair-splitting interpretations of the Pharisees. The latter is certainly true; for these reasons:

(i) When Jesus argues with the Pharisees, he always appeals to the law of Moses. Here, in Matthew 5:17–18, he himself says that he has only come to fulfill the law, to abolish not one jot or tittle. And he says it more than once: "And why do you break the commandment of God for the sake of your tradition? . . . So for the sake of your tradition you have made void the word of God" (Matt. 15:3, 6). "Do not think that I will accuse you to the Father. There is one who accuses you: Moses, on whom you have set your hope" (John 5:45). Jesus demands that the righteousness of his disciples exceed not that of the law of Moses but that of the Pharisees (Matt. 5:20). Jesus summarizes all the

137. GrO: εἰκῇ (= rash, *temere*, without any grounds); ἔνοχος ἔσται τῇ κρίσει; ῥακά; ἔνοχος ἔσται τῷ συνεδρίῳ; μωρέ; ἔνοχος ἔσται εἰς τὴν γέενναν τοῦ πυρός.

138. LO: *peccata venialia*; *peccata mortalia*.

139. Tholuck, *Commentary on the Sermon on the Mount*, 115–292, especially 115–91 (on Matt. 5:17–48, esp. vv. 17–22). Ed. note: Much of Bavinck's discussion of the Sermon that follows has close parallels with Tholuck's treatment.

commandments in terms of love toward God and neighbor (Matt. 22:40; cf. Rom. 13:9). "So the law is holy, and the commandment is holy and righteous and good" (Rom. 7:12).

(ii) The Old Testament law forbids also what is internal—for example, desire: "For I would not have known what it is to covet if the law had not said, 'You shall not covet'" (Rom. 7:7). The law is spiritual: "For we know that the law is spiritual, but I am of the flesh, sold under sin" (Rom. 7:14). The law enjoins love toward God and neighbor; that is precisely the essence of the law and the prophets: "So whatever you wish that others would do to you, do also to them, for this is the Law and the Prophets" (Matt. 7:12).

(iii) When it is written, "You have heard that it was said to those of old . . ." the Greek word for "of old" must be in the dative case.[140] This certainly does not refer only to contemporaries of Moses but definitely also (if not exclusively) to later generations in Israel who were taught by the rabbis. Why? Because the content (what those of old time said) contains not only the Mosaic commandments but also the later interpretations. For example, in Matthew 5:21: "You have heard that it was said to those of old, 'You shall not murder'" (Mosaic law), "'and whoever murders will be liable to judgment'" (rabbinic commentary). Likewise, verse 43: "You shall love your neighbor and hate your enemy," where the second part counters Exodus 23:4–5 and Leviticus 19:18. Similarly, in verses 27, 31, 33, and 38, where Jesus argues against the false interpretation of the law. From this it follows that Jesus's interpretation of the Mosaic law against the false explanation of the Pharisees—for example, the offending eye in verse 29; turning the other cheek in verse 39; going the extra mile in verse 41—are not *counsels* but *precepts*. The simple and conclusive reason for this is that otherwise being angry in contrast to killing (v. 22), desiring a woman in contrast to adultery (v. 28), and loving your enemy (v. 44) would belong to the *counsels*—all of which is a spiritual interpretation of the law. Bellarmine was correct in dropping this passage as a prooftext.

d. Matthew 13:8: "Other seeds fell on good soil and produced grain, some a hundredfold, some sixty, some thirty." Cyprian, Augustine, and Jerome apply these words, without any basis, to celibacy, widowhood, and marriage.

e. Matthew 19:9: Here, Jesus says that "whoever divorces his wife, except for sexual immorality, and marries another, commits adultery." Whereupon the disciples say, "If such is the case of a man with his wife, it is better not to marry" (v. 10),[141] for then a man must put up with anything from his wife,

---

140. GrO: τοῖς ἀρχαίοις. Ed. note: Bavinck may have obtained this grammatical point, and the conclusion that the reference in this verse is to the later rabbinic tradition, from Tholuck, *Commentary on the Sermon on the Mount*, 160–63.

141. GrO: οὐ συμφέρει γαμῆσαι.

other than fornication, and he can never be free of her. To which Jesus replies, "Not everyone can receive this saying, but only those to whom it is given" (v. 11)[142]—that is, whom God has given the moral aptitude for it. And then Jesus goes on in verse 12 to tell us who these people are: "For there are eunuchs who have been so from birth, and there are eunuchs who have been made eunuchs by men, and there are eunuchs who have made themselves eunuchs for the sake of the kingdom of heaven." First, some eunuchs were born that way—that is, unfit for marriage by nature, from birth. Second, some eunuchs were made eunuchs by others; but, Jesus wants to say, I do not mean those. Then there is a third kind, those who have made themselves eunuchs for the sake of the kingdom of heaven.[143] These have voluntarily remained unmarried in order to be able to serve the kingdom of God "burdened with fewer cares."[144] And Jesus adds, "Let the one who is able to receive this receive it."[145] This reception is a matter not of an intellectual but a moral grasp.[146]

Thus, Jesus teaches here that for some who are able, it can sometimes be useful not to marry, for the sake of the kingdom of heaven. But Jesus absolutely does not teach here a *counsel* that goes beyond the law and provides greater value, rank, and reward *in* the kingdom of heaven. Rather, for those who have the gift, it can sometimes be useful for the sake of the kingdom of heaven to devote more labor to it. This is precisely what was done and taught by the unmarried Paul in 1 Corinthians 7. He says:

(i) To marry is good; the virgin who marries does not sin (vv. 28–30; 38). It is better to marry than to burn (v. 9). "Because of the temptation to sexual immorality, each man should have his own wife and each woman her own husband" (v. 2). "But each has his own gift from God, one of one kind and one of another" (v. 7). "Only let each person lead the life that the Lord has assigned to him, and to which God has called him" (v. 17). "Each one should remain in the condition in which he was called" (v. 20).

(ii) Nevertheless, Paul thinks that it is good for a man not to touch a woman (v. 1), wishes that all men were as he (vv. 7–8), judges that it is good to be unmarried (v. 26), and counsels the unmarried and the widows to remain single (vv. 8, 27).[147] Paul counsels those whose "passions are strong" that marriage is preferable (v. 36), but then adds, "Whoever is firmly established in his heart, being under no necessity but having his desire under control, and

142. GrO: οὐ πάντες χωροῦσιν τὸν λόγον τοῦτον ἀλλ᾽ οἷς δέδοται.
143. GrO: οἵτινες εὐνούχισαν ἑαυτοὺς διὰ τὴν βασιλείαν τῶν οὐρανῶν.
144. From the annotations of the Dutch Authorized Version (*Statenvertaling*).
145. GrO: ὁ δυνάμενος χωρεῖν χωρείτω.
146. DO: *niet verstandelijk, maar zedelijk vatten.*
147. GrO: γυναικὸς μὴ ἅπτεσθαι; μὴ ζήτει γυναῖκα.

has determined this in his heart, to keep her as his betrothed, he will do well" (v. 37). In conclusion, "So then he who marries his betrothed does well, and he who refrains from marriage will do even better" (v. 38).[148] In addition, Paul judges that an unmarried woman is happier if she remains as she is (v. 40).[149]

(iii) Now all of this is "a concession, not a command" (v. 6).[150] (In v. 6 this clearly refers to a temporary abstinence, by mutual consent, for the sake of prayer.) Paul wishes that all people, like himself, had the gift of abstinence.[151] But that is not the case. And therefore Paul can say only this: First, he tells believers who are married to unbelievers that it is good to remain married: "To the married I give this charge (not I, but the Lord): the wife should not separate from her husband . . . and the husband should not divorce his wife" (vv. 10–11). This is a command from the Lord; that is, Christ himself has pronounced on it and forbidden divorce. However, because Christ said nothing about putting away an unbelieving wife, Paul inverts his qualification: "To the rest I say (I, not the Lord) that if any brother has a wife who is an unbeliever, and she consents to live with him, he should not divorce her. If any woman has a husband who is an unbeliever, and he consents to live with her, she should not divorce him" (vv. 12–13).

The annotation in the Dutch Authorized Version [*Statenvertaling*] gets this right when it reads the "I" (Paul) in verse 12 thus: "namely as an apostle of Christ, taught and possessed by his Spirit."[152] "Not the Lord" refers to the absence of a specific, expressed command by Christ, such as the one in verses 10 and 11.[153] Similarly, with respect to virgins (v. 25), "I have no command from the Lord [i.e., no express, objective commandment from Christ], but I give my judgment as one who by the Lord's mercy is trustworthy."[154]

From all this it follows that Matthew 19:11–12 is not a commandment for all, but is a useful permission granted to some, as the annotations in the Dutch Authorized Version [*Statenvertaling*] have it.[155] Nonetheless, Paul is

148. GrO: τηρεῖν τὴν ἑαυτοῦ παρθένον, καλῶς ποιήσει; καὶ ὁ μὴ γαμίζων κρεῖσσον ποιήσει.

149. GrO: μακαριωτέρα δέ ἐστιν ἐὰν οὕτως μείνῃ, κατὰ τὴν ἐμὴν γνώμην.

150. GrO: κατὰ συγγνώμην (= LO: *secundum intelligentiam*); κατ᾽ ἐπιταγήν.

151. GrO: θέλω.

152. DO: *Namelijk als een apostel van Christus, door Zijnen Geest onderricht en gedreven.* Ed. note: This is the exact language of note 18 in the annotation of the Dutch Authorized Version (*Statenvertaling*) on 1 Cor. 7:12.

153. DO: *namelijk door een uitgedrukt bevel, gelijk het voorgaande was* (annotation, Dutch Authorized Version [*Statenvertaling*], 1 Cor. 7:12, note 19).

154. GrO: ἐπιταγὴν κυρίου; γνώμην δὲ δίδωμι; cf. J. T. Beck, *Vorlesungen über christliche Ethik*, 2:139.

155. Ed. note: The Dutch Authorized Version (*Statenvertaling*) has three annotations for the three kinds of eunuchs in verse 12, and each one is restrictive, following the formula "That is, [only] those who . . ." (*Dat is, die . . .*): a. "Eunuchs who have been so from birth": "That is,

giving his judgment.[156] To show that this is not, however, a purely subjective opinion, a suggestion by Paul that may easily be dismissed, he adds this: "as one who by the Lord's mercy is trustworthy" (v. 25).[157] Paul is alluding here to Christ's call to him to be his apostle, to the guidance he receives from Christ to be a faithful apostle. This is also evident from verse 40, where he gives his "judgment" that a woman is happier if she stays unmarried, adding, "And I think that I too have the Spirit of God."[158] Thus, it is an opinion given to him by the Spirit of God. Yet Paul does not give this judgment as an objective command, but as an opinion,[159] just as Jesus does in Matthew 19:11–12: "Not everyone can receive this saying, but only those to whom it is given. . . . Let the one who is able to receive this receive it." In other words, since it does not apply to everyone, but only to those who have the gift of abstinence, the question whether that "opinion" holds for this or that person must be left to each person's conscience.

(iv) The reasons Paul regards not marrying as possibly better than marrying are the same as in Matthew 19:12: "for the sake of the kingdom," "in view of the present distress" (e.g., persecution; 1 Cor. 7:26), and because unmarried persons can more fully devote themselves without cares to the service of the Lord (1 Cor. 7:32). Therefore, not marrying is sometimes a good thing; Paul provides here a piece of advice. Celibacy for a specific class of people is actually *forbidden* here; lacking the gift of abstinence, one is duty bound to marry.

f. In Matthew 19:21 Jesus says to the rich young ruler, "If you would be perfect, go, sell what you possess and give to the poor, and you will have treasure in heaven; and come, follow me."[160] This is a testing or challenging answer: If your boast is true, that you have kept the law, very well; to test whether you love God and your neighbor above all, go and sell all that you have.[161] This is not a universal commandment, but only imposed by Jesus in this special case in order to test the young man. It cannot be a *counsel* because then,

---

those who by nature are unsuited for marriage." b. "Eunuchs who have been made eunuchs by men": "That is, those who are made unsuitable for marriage by human beings." c. "Eunuchs who have made themselves eunuchs for the sake of the kingdom of heaven": "That is, those who, having the gift of abstinence, freely remain unmarried in order to serve God with fewer encumbrances, and thus encourage this in themselves and in others for the sake of the kingdom of heaven (1 Cor. 7:32–35). On the other hand, for those who lack this gift, it is better to marry than to burn (1 Cor. 7:9)."

156. DO: *gevoelen*; GrO: γνώμην δὲ δίδωμι.
157. GrO: ὡς ἠλεημένος ὑπὸ κυρίου πιστὸς εἶναι.
158. GrO: δοκῶ δὲ κἀγὼ πνεῦμα θεοῦ ἔχειν.
159. GrO: γνώμην.
160. GrO: Εἰ θέλεις τέλειος εἶναι, ὕπαγε πώλησόν σου τὰ ὑπάρχοντα καὶ δὸς πτωχοῖς, καὶ ἕξεις θησαυρὸν ἐν οὐρανοῖς, καὶ δεῦρο ἀκολούθει μοι.
161. GrO: πειραστικός; DO: *beproevend*.

(i) Jesus would have approved of the young man's boast and said: It is true, you have kept the whole law; but if you want to attain to a still higher level, you should go on and follow this advice.

(ii) The young man would not have sinned when he failed to follow Christ's advice, since a "counsel" does not always have to be followed.[162]

g. In 1 Corinthians 9 Paul indicates that he had the right to take along a wife, to live from the gospel, but he did not use this right.[163] Bellarmine says that he did more than was commanded and therefore he had special glory: "But I have made no use of any of these rights, nor am I writing these things to secure any such provision. For I would rather die than have anyone deprive me of my ground for boasting" (v. 15). But Paul does not mean that by giving up a salary he is earning points with God and gaining glory for God. Because "all have sinned and fall short of the glory of God, and are justified by his grace as a gift, through the redemption that is in Christ Jesus," all boasting is "excluded" (Rom. 3:23–27). "For by grace you have been saved through faith. And this is not your own doing; it is the gift of God, not a result of works, so that no one may boast" (Eph. 2:8–9). Paul rejects all of his own righteousness: "Indeed, I count everything as loss because of the surpassing worth of knowing Christ Jesus my Lord. For his sake I have suffered the loss of all things and count them as rubbish, in order that I may gain Christ and be found in him, not having a righteousness of my own that comes from the law, but that which comes through faith in Christ, the righteousness from God that depends on faith" (Phil. 3:8–9). What Paul has in mind here is glory in the eyes of others, the churches and false apostles; all this he counts as "rubbish"[164] in order to remove in Corinth every pretext, every occasion to accuse him, every hindrance to the gospel: "I was not a burden to you" (2 Cor. 11:9; 12:13–14, 16); I did not want to abuse my authority (1 Cor. 9:18–19). His boast was having good conscience (2 Cor. 1:12; Acts 24:16; 1 Cor. 4:4).

h. Luke 14:26: "If anyone comes to me and does not hate his own father and mother and wife and children and brothers and sisters, yes, and even his own life, he cannot be my disciple." This text is not a counsel but a precept; without this precept one cannot be a disciple of Christ.

---

162. LO: *consilium*; Gerhard, *Loci Theologici*, 3:187.

163. J. Müller, *Christian Doctrine of Sin*, 1:56; Neander, *Geschichte der Pflanzung und Leitung*, 746; Neander, *Das Leben Jesu Christi*, 589–92. Ed. note: Bavinck's own note provides no specifics; it reads simply "Neander"; he took this reference directly from Müller, *Sin*, 55–56; Neander also discusses the *consilia* and *praecepta* in his *General History of the Christian Religion and Church*, 5:213–16.

164. GrO: σκύβαλα = dung, refuse, garbage.

i. Revelation 14:3–4: Bellarmine considers the reference in this text to "the 144,000 who had been redeemed from the earth . . . who have not defiled themselves with women, for they are virgins," as proof that virgins have a prerogative. But included among those 144,000 are all the saints, also the married ones, and the reference here to "virgins"[165] is used metaphorically—that is, referring to those who have not committed adultery with Babylon the prostitute but remained faithful to Christ the Bridegroom.

j. Bellarmine also appeals to biblical examples such as Acts 4:32 ("they had everything in common") and Acts 21:9 (Philip had four unmarried daughters, virgins); to the church fathers; and to reason, which distinguishes between what belongs to "being" and "well-being."[166]

2. Many other testimonies of Scripture counter the Roman Catholic distinction between *counsels* and *precepts*:

a. God demands in the law (Deut. 6:5; Matt. 22:37) that we love him with all our heart, and so on, and our neighbor as ourselves, thus totally, absolutely. So there can be no counsel that goes beyond that precept; there is nothing that is greater than the absolute or more than the perfect.

b. Even our best works always contain something that needs forgiveness (Rom. 7). The need to pray to be forgiven is laid upon us all (Matt. 6). "If we say we have no sin, we deceive ourselves, and the truth is not in us" (1 John 1:8).[167]

c. When Jesus says, "So you also, when you have done all that you were commanded, say, 'We are unworthy servants; we have only done what was our duty'" (Luke 17:10), he excludes all counsels.[168]

3. The Roman Catholic distinction is actually pagan, borrowed from the ethics of Stoicism, imported especially via Ambrose, who Christianized Cicero's treatise *On Duties* in his own *On the Duties of the Clergy*.[169] Cicero divides duties into those that are "virtuous" and those that are "useful."[170]

---

165. GrO: παρθένοι.

166. LO: *esse, bene esse*; Gerhard, *Loci Theologici*, 3:192. Ed. note: Bavinck adds in the margin: "Rome understands the law as a sum total to which more can be added, as a work to be performed—like the Pharisees."

167. See Luthardt, *Die Ethik Luthers*, 73–77.

168. GrO: οὕτως καὶ ὑμεῖς, ὅταν ποιήσητε πάντα τὰ διαταχθέντα ὑμῖν, λέγετε ὅτι Δοῦλοι ἀχρεῖοί ἐσμεν, ὃ ὠφείλομεν ποιῆσαι πεποιήκαμεν. Cf. J. Müller, *Christian Doctrine of Sin*, 1:56–58, who gives an incorrect interpretation.

169. Ambrose, *On the Duties of the Clergy* (NPNF² 10:1–89). Ed. note: This is an expansion of Bavinck's treatment of Ambrose in the opening pages of this chapter.

170. LO: *honesto et utili*. See Ambrose, *On the Duties of the Clergy* I.9 (NPNF² 10:5). Ed. note: Cicero's *On Duties* (*De officiis*) is divided into three books: I. "Moral Goodness"; II. "Expediency"; III. "The Conflict between the Right and the Expedient."

Ambrose adapted this distinction, concluding, "Every duty is either 'ordinary' or 'perfect.'"[171] Ambrose viewed the ordinary duties to mean, If you want to enter eternal life, keep the commandments; and the other duties to mean, If you want to be perfect, sell all you have, and so forth.[172] Ambrose says: The excellence of the Christian religion is that perfection,[173] which was not attainable in the pagan world, now is attainable through the power of Christ. In this way, the Stoic aristocratic ideal was transferred to clerical hierarchicalism. Rome could not avoid coming to this distinction because of the false way in which she related grace to nature and God (and his worship) to the world. With Rome, grace, both before the fall and in redemption, is a "superadded gift."[174] Nature is not entirely corrupt, but instead is a "natural ability to do well."[175] But grace completes nature and turns good deeds, which are already good, into meritorious deeds. Grace and nature, God and world, heavenly and earthly vocation, thus stand alongside each other and will never become one; the more we take from the latter, the more we give to the former, and vice versa. Christianity in its perfection is therefore not attainable for all, but only for the aristocractic spirits, for clerics and monks. The fundamental error here is deistic Pelagianism. The moral law, as law for everyone, is externalized and robbed of its spiritual meaning; good deeds are detached from disposition, and works righteousness is encouraged.

4. Nonetheless, there are things that seem to speak in favor of the distinction. It is legitimate to ask whether all believers are expected to give all their possessions to the poor, to remain unmarried, or to forgo receiving a salary. Or as Thomas says, he who gives alms to a poor man, "when he is not obligated (bound), fulfills a counsel."[176] A few Protestants have indeed admitted a distinction of this kind.[177] For example, although he does it only for academic purposes, de Wette distinguishes strict duty from perfections.[178] What also speaks in its favor is that one can commend many deeds in others yet while not imposing them on anyone else, including oneself—for example, when a

---

171. LO: *Officium autem omne, aut medium, aut perfectum esse.* See Ambrose, *On the Duties of the Clergy* I.11 (NPNF² 10:7). Ed. note: Ambrose cites Cicero, *De officiis* I.iii.8.

172. LO: *media officia; rectum officia.*

173. LO: *rectum.*

174. LO: *donum superadditum.*

175. LO: *facultas naturalis ad bene agendum.*

176. LO: *quando dare non tenetur; consilium*; Luthardt, *Die Ethik Luthers*, 78.

177. Ed. note: Bavinck gives as an example von Hirscher, *Die christliche Moral als Lehre*, 2:390–94; however, he then asks, "Is he Catholic?" The answer: "Yes he is." Johann Baptist von Hirscher (1788–1865) was a German Roman Catholic theologian who taught at the universities of Tübingen and Freiburg (Breisgau).

178. De Wette, *Christliche Sittenlehre*, 3:45–49 (§433).

rich man gives away his goods or bequeaths them to the church, the poor, the arts, and so on, or adopts a poor boy as his son. That is a sacred act, an act of heroism, which we commend in others yet impose on no one.[179]

To this we must reply:

a. The moral law is always one and the same, unchangeable, and equally binding for all people without distinction. The good (love for God and neighbor) and duty in general overlap entirely.

b. In every concrete case, however, each person's conscience has to infer from the universal moral law what is good. For example, the moral law tells me that I should do well by the poor, but if a beggar comes to my door, I should not immediately give him something but first ask whether I can give without adversely affecting my family, or whether that beggar might be a fraud, and the like. The same is true with the commandment not to kill, as well as the others. In other words, when we are interpreting the moral law and applying it to concrete cases, it is always right to involve the "moral authority of the individual."[180]

Our first thesis:[181] The law stands majestically, abstractly, uniformly, above the infinite, rich variety of life and always commands the same, but we as individuals have to know the law and ask in any concrete case what the law commands in this case, and then act accordingly. That gap, that distance between the universal law and the concrete case, is bridged by the conscience. The conscience is for morality what genius is for art.[182] That application of the moral law to a concrete case by the conscience can of course be wrong (moral education is a must!).

But here is our second thesis: the good in any concrete case (that which our conscience judges to be good in a given case on the basis of the universal moral law) and the individual duty overlap completely. That which I see as good is that which I must do; that is my duty. But this thesis must not be confused with another one which is false—namely, the good in and of itself

---

179. Janet, *La morale*, 224.

180. GO: *individuelle sittliche Instanz*; Rothe, *Theologische Ethik*, 3:365 (§805); cf. J. Müller, *Christian Doctrine of Sin*, 1:38; Stahl, *Philosophie des Rechts*², 2/1:180; Reinhard, *System der christlichen Moral*, 3:198–202 (§298). For the same opinion see Ames, *Conscience*, V.xlix.8.

181. Ed. note: This reference is an insertion based on an editorial judgment. Bavinck did not indicate his first thesis but only stated his second in the following paragraph. His second thesis builds on especially the second clause, "but we as individuals have to know the law and ask in any concrete case what the law commands in this case, and then act accordingly," which is likely his real thesis.

182. GO: "So ist das Gewissen für die Moral, was das Genie für die Kunst ist." Ed. note: This quote is taken from Rothe, *Theologische Ethik*, 3:365; Rothe took the quote from Daub, *System der theologischen Moral*, 1:72.

(what is good in general) is the duty of a particular person in a given case. What is to be compared is the good in general with the duty in general—these overlap completely; and similarly what is good for particular persons in given cases also overlaps completely the duty for particular persons in given cases.[183]

c. These two rules enable us to make the application. Giving alms to the poor; remaining unmarried; sacrificing oneself for others during a plague; establishing an orphanage, as was done by St. Vincent de Paul, August Hermann Francke, and van 't Lindenhout;[184] sacrificing oneself on the barricades in June 1848 [during the June Revolution of 1848], as was done by the archbishop of Paris; like Byron, dedicating his life to the defense of oppressed Greece; for a young woman to become a sister of mercy; or to become a teacher of the deaf, like the abbot of l'Épée[185]—all that is in itself good and praiseworthy, but not obligatory for me personally. It is not a duty for me unless it is good for me; and that must be decided by my conscience. For example, to give your possessions to the poor is good, but it would be wrong for a father of a family to do so.[186] To establish an orphanage without St. Vincent's sense of calling would be wrong. It would be wrong for a young woman to become a sister of mercy out of pride or some other sinful motive. But as soon as a person's conscience senses something like that as a calling, then it becomes a duty, not a counsel but a precept. It was Paul's duty not to accept pay in Corinth; he owed that to the gospel; it was no arbitrary act, no counsel that he could just as easily have left undone, but it was laid upon him by God in those particular circumstances. In the same circumstances, it would also be our duty.

This is consonant with Paul's advice in 1 Corinthians 7: "But each has his own gift from God, one of one kind and one of another" (v. 7). "Each one should remain in the condition in which he was called" (v. 20). "In whatever condition each was called, there let him remain with God" (v. 24). In sum: "For whatever does not proceed from faith is sin" (Rom. 14:23). Beck may not objectively accept the distinction between perfect and imperfect duties,

---

183. Janet, *La morale*, 226.

184. Ed. note: Johannes van 't Lindenhout (1836–1918) was a Dutch colporteur and evangelist who founded an orphanage in 1863 that provided for 3,085 orphans in the forty-year period 1863–1903. *Christ. Encycl.¹*, 3:684–85, s.v. "Lindenhout, Johannes van 't."

185. Ed. note: The Abbé Charles-Michel de l'Épée (1712–89) was a French philanthropist who dedicated his life to teaching the deaf; he founded the world's first free school for the deaf in the 1760s (Wikipedia, s.v. "Charles-Michel de l'Épée," https://en.wikipedia.org/wiki/Charles -Michel_de_l%27%C3%89p%C3%A9e).

186. It is worth noting that the command "to sell all" was given to a "young man" (νεανίσκος; Matt. 19:20).

but he does accept degrees of subjective obligation and subjective fulfillment of one's duty.[187]

§29. DUTIES AND THE PERMISSIBLE; ADIAPHORA[188]

Historical Overview

The argument for the ethical category of adiaphora also has its origins in Stoicism.[189] It distinguished the relative or useful good in terms of the *desirable*, such as life, health, and money; the *reprehensible*, such as sickness, death, and poverty; and the *indifferent things* that lie in between—such as an odd or even number of hairs—called "neutral things" by Cicero.[190] Furthermore, these adiaphora can vary between objective things and human acts. In a broader sense, the Stoics referred to the entire range of useful or relative goods as adiaphoron. This concept, too, was imported into Christian ethics. It was the inevitable consequence of the doctrine of the evangelical counsels of perfection.[191] For the ordinary Christian, numerous actions and things are indifferent that are not so for those who follow these counsels. Already Augustine had written, "There are certain deeds of a middle kind, which can be done with a good or evil mind, of which it is rash to form a judgment."[192] Thomas Aquinas says that there are actions that are indifferent according to their species, when "the object of an action does not include something pertaining to the order of reason; for instance, to pick up a straw from the ground, to walk in the fields, and the like."[193] Objectively, therefore, there are deeds that, viewed by themselves, in their abstract form,[194] are neutral and can become good or bad depending on the circumstances, the intention, and so forth. But in article 9[195] Aquinas says that a moral action "derives its

187. J. T. Beck, *Vorlesungen über christliche Ethik*, 2:142.

188. See review of *Het Geoorloofde: Eene zedekundige studie*, by G. Vellenga, *Theologisches Literaturblatt* 17, no. 4 (January 24, 1896): 46; Mayer, *Die Lehre von Erlaubten*, 60–70; Kirn, review of *Die Lehre von Erlaubten*; Breithaupt, "Die Mitteldinge."

189. Cf. Kübel, "Adiaphora."

190. GrO: προηγμένον; ἀποπροηγμένον; ἀδιάφορον; LO: *neutra*.

191. LO: *consilia*.

192. LO: *sunt quaedam facta media quae possunt bono vel malo animo fieri, de quibus est temerarium judicare*, in Augustine, *De sermone Domini in monte* II.18, cited in Aquinas, *ST* Ia IIae q. 18 art. 8 co. English translations of the *Summa* are from the translation by the Fathers of the English Dominican Province.

193. *ST* Ia IIae q. 18 art. 8 co.

194. LO: *sua specie*.

195. Ed. note: The passage that follows from *ST* Ia IIae q. 18 art. 9 co. has been enlarged by the editor.

goodness not only from its object, whence it takes its species; but also from the circumstances, which are its accidents, as it were." And "every individual action must needs have some circumstance that makes it good or bad, at least in respect of the intention of the end." If an action is "not directed to a due end, it is by that fact alone repugnant to reason, and has the character of evil. But if it be directed to a due end, it is in accord with reason; wherefore it has the character of good. Now it must needs be either directed or not directed to a due end. Consequently, every human action that proceeds from deliberate reason, if it be considered in the individual, must be good or bad."[196] However, a human deed can also proceed "from some act of the imagination, as when a man strokes his beard, or moves his hand or foot."[197] Such an action occurs unintentionally, automatically, through the natural movement of the muscles and, "properly speaking, is not moral or human; since this depends on the reason. Hence it will be indifferent as standing apart from the genus of moral actions."[198] All the Thomists follow Thomas's opinion—Bellarmine,[199] Suarez, Valentia, Major, and Becanus. According to the Thomists, therefore, there was really no "indifferent action" except in the abstract.[200] Concretely,[201] an action was always good or bad, unless it was an involuntary movement.

A contrary view was held by Duns Scotus, the Scotists, Alexander of Hales, Bonaventure, Vasquez, and William of Durant, who argued that acts and deeds that are indifferent in their abstract form[202] remain so in concrete expression, and that there is therefore a range of morally indifferent deeds. The Pelagianism of the Scotists is once again clearly demonstrated here. Others attempted to combine the two opinions by asserting that an act that is naturally indifferent is and remains so in its concrete expression—namely, with respect to the substance of the act.[203] But it changes in concrete expression according to the circumstantial accidents.[204] Thus, the deed does not become good or bad in itself, but only reductively, to the extent that it is directed to a principle or end.[205] The deed or act, therefore, does not become necessary a priori as a result of intrinsic goodness or evil, such that it must either happen or not

196. LO: *ex deliberata ratione.*
197. LO: *ex quadam imagination; ST* Ia IIae q. 18 art. 9 co.
198. LO: *moralis vel humanus; indifferens quasi extra genus moralium actuum existens.*
199. *De Gratia et Libero Arbitrio, Libri VI,* in *Opera Omnia,* 4.1:357.
200. LO: *actus indifferens.*
201. LO: *in individuo.*
202. LO: *in specie.*
203. LO: *materia actus.*
204. LO: *accedentes circumstantiae.*
205. *Reductive tamen bonum dici, quatenus refertur ad principium, vel sinem suum, aut virtutes illas, inde actiones moderandus diximus;* Hoornbeeck, *Theologiae Practicae*[2], 2:485.

happen. But when it happens, it must happen under a certain condition. Thus, its goodness is not antecedent but concomitant; it belongs to the act by virtue of faith, or from its direction toward its ultimate end.[206] The act does not become a necessary act as a result, but faith and direction become necessary in the agent, even when one performs deeds that are indifferent in themselves. For example, people are free to marry whomever they wish, but whomever they marry, they must marry in the Lord. This was the view of Forbes, cited in Hoornbeeck.[207]

The Council of Constance (1415) took the side of Scotus and condemned the thesis defended by Hus that there are no indifferent works, but that all acts are either good or evil since they proceed from either a good or a bad person. Trent likewise condemned as heretical the view that "nothing except faith is commanded in the Gospel" and the opinion "that other things are indifferent, neither commanded nor prohibited, but free."[208] Granted, Catharine, defending Thomas's opinion, challenged this, arguing that acts indifferent in themselves ceased to be so in concrete cases. But the synod was undeterred.[209]

The Reformation really brought no change in the doctrine of the adiaphora. Luther never explicitly expressed his opinion on the adiaphora, but his relaxed stance on exuberance, dancing, games, and food and drink (reflected in the aphorism "Whoever does not love wife, wine, and song will stay a fool throughout his life") is entirely in Luther's spirit.[210] He embraced a broad range of the permissible and was very averse to any rigorism. He was firm in accepting adiaphora in the church. Luther retained a great deal in worship and church which in his opinion was indifferent. He removed only what was *proscribed* in the Bible.[211] It was precisely because Luther, unlike the Swiss Reformers, approached matters with concessiveness and not from principle that the Adiaphora Controversy arose later. Emperor Charles V, at peace after the war with France, wanted to unite Catholics and Protestants in his lands, and so in September 1547 he convened a diet in Augsburg and had an interim drawn up that would be binding for Protestants and Catholics alike until the

---

206. LO: *ex fide, aut ex directione in finem ultimum.*

207. Cf. Hoornbeeck, *Theologia Practica*, 2:485–86.

208. LO: *opera absque fide*; see Denzinger, no. 829 (Council of Trent, session 6, canon 19).

209. See Hoornbeeck, *Theologia Practica*, 2:485.

210. GO: *Wer nicht liebt Weib, Wein und Gesang, der bliebt ein Narr sein Leben lang.* Ed. note: This aphorism is often attributed to Luther but cannot be found in his extant writings (German Wikipedia, s.v. "Wein, Weib und Gesang," https://en.wikipedia.org/wiki/Wein,_Weib _und_Gesang). Bavinck's claim that Luther "never explicitly expressed his opinion on the adiaphora" is not entirely accurate; see Luther, *Disputation concerning Justification*, 155; also see Luther, *Lectures on Galatians*, 161, 202.

211. DO: *verboden.*

conclusion of a general council.[212] He wanted to enforce this everywhere, but the Augsburg Interim met with wide resistance, especially in Northern Germany. Maurice of Saxony, not daring to introduce the Augsburg Interim in his territory, consulted with Melanchthon in order to draft another interim that would be more acceptable to Protestants. Melanchthon, no longer feeling at home in strict Lutheranism and feeling freer after Luther's death (and Luther had allowed many of those adiaphora to continue), believed that Protestantism was close to extinction unless it made concessions, so he acquiesced and, together with George Major (1502–74), Paul Eber (1511–69), Johann Bugenhagen (1485–1558), Kaspar Cruciger Sr. (1504–48), and Johann Pfeffinger (1493–1573), modified the Augsburg Interim in Leipzig on December 22, 1548.[213] The Leipzig Interim reintroduced as adiaphora (which had to be tolerated) almost all Roman Catholic ceremonies, episcopal jurisdiction, the pope as "the first among equals," confirmation, extreme unction, canonical anthems, candles, choir vestments, fasting, holy days, parts of the rite of the mass in Latin, images of the saints (though not for veneration), celebrations of Mary, Corpus Christi (though without procession), and so on. Strong opposition arose from the Lutheran theologians Matthias Flacius, Nicolaus von Amsdorf, Nicolaus Gallus, Joachim Westphal (of Hamburg), Erasmus Sarcerius, Johann Wigand, and others. (Calvin also wrote to Melanchthon about it.)[214] These theologians concede that many things in Christian worship are adiaphora. But many customs are so closely intertwined with Roman Catholic superstition that they inevitably reintroduce it. The people cannot distinguish between the use of oil and the magical power ascribed to it. Those ceremonies therefore automatically become "seats and instruments of impiety and superstition."[215] In fact, the very acceptance of the adiaphora is in and of itself sinful, because it is done out of fear and deference to the emperor. The controversy was vehement until the Peace of Augsburg (1555) put an end to it.

The theologians, however, continued to debate the matter of adiaphora. And the Formula of Concord states the following in article 10 ("Concerning Ecclesiastical Practices Which Are Called Adiaphora or Indifferent Matters"): "Certain ceremonies or ecclesiastical practices that are neither commanded

212. Ed. note: The Augsburg Interim was adopted at the Diet of Augsburg on June 30, 1548. For more on the Augsburg Interim, see Issleib, "Augsburg Interim."

213. Ed. note: The first names and dates of these Lutheran (Wittenberg) theologians have been added by the editor. Bavinck's source is likely Kurtz, *Text-Book of Church History*, 2:102, who mentions Melanchthon, Major, Eber, Bugenhagen, and Cruciger as the authors of the Leipzig Interim. For more on the Leipzig Interim, see Issleib, "Augsburg Interim," 22.

214. Cf. Hoornbeeck, *Theologia Practica*, 2:486. Ed. note: In addition to Hoornbeeck, Bavinck also derives material from Kübel, "Adiaphora."

215. LO: *sedes et instrumenta impietatum et superstitionum.*

nor forbidden in God's Word, but have been established only for good order and decorum, are in and of themselves neither worship ordained by God nor a part of such worship."[216] They are not indifferent if they are forbidden in God's Word, nor when they create the appearance that our religion does not differ much from Rome, and so on. Nor are those things indifferent which do not help preserve good order or discipline or decorum but are useless, vain. However, genuinely indifferent things, which are not part of worship and must be distinguished from it, may be accepted or abolished by the church as the need arises,[217] though with wisdom. But if the enemy's intention is to divert us from true worship, then we must resist matters that are in themselves indifferent, as Paul did in the matter of circumcision, which he permitted in Acts 16:3 but not in Galatians 2:3–5. For then it is no longer a question of the middle things as such, but of the faith they express. And the Formula of Concord appeals for all of this to the Smalcald Articles and to Luther himself. Many Roman Catholic customs, including exorcism, omitting the breaking of the bread at the Lord's Supper, and the use of wafers, altars, images, and the like, have been retained and defended by the Lutherans. The Reformed were much stricter on this point; they admitted that there were adiaphora but did not recognize *those* things as adiaphora, because superstition was tied to them.[218] Melanchthon later admitted he was wrong. Calvin had written Melanchthon that he stretched the middle and indifferent things too far:[219] Roman Catholic worship is corrupt in a thousand ways. We have abolished what cannot be tolerated. Now impious people want to restore that. No wonder that many judge Lutherans to be too lax. Some of those things that you declare "middle" conflict manifestly with God's Word. Therefore, you must not concede so much, for you weaken the Word of God and give occasion and cause for mocking the gospel.[220]

The same questions that arose in Germany also came up for discussion among the Reformed in England. The Reformation of Henry VIII and Elizabeth was halfhearted: a reformation of doctrine but not of worship; it retained bishops and episcopal succession but rejected the pope, the infallibility of councils, the veneration of saints, images, and relics. It also retained the ancient liturgies and prayers, priestly vestments, congregational responses, litanies,

---

216. LO/GrO: *Adiaphorae ceremoniae* [are], *quae verbo Dei neque mandatae, neque prohibitae sunt: sed bono consilio propter* εὐταξίαν, *et ordinem, aut ad conservandam piam disciplinam in Ecclesia usurpantur* εὐταξίαν (see Kolb and Wengert, *Book of Concord*, 515).

217. LO: *pro re nata*.

218. LO: *adjunctum superstitionis*. Cf. Hoornbeeck, *Theologia Practica*, 2:487.

219. LO: *res medias et indifferentes nimis extendis*.

220. In Hoornbeeck, *Theologia Practica*, 2:486. Ed. note: Bavinck is summarizing in his own words material from Hoornbeeck's direct quotation of Calvin's letter to Melanchthon.

and a broad liturgy in worship, although it rejected altars, images, candles, incense, the mass, and the use of Latin.[221] But opposition arose from the side of those who, under the Roman Catholic queen, Mary, had fled and stayed with Calvin, Beza, Bullinger, and Vermigli.[222] After Mary's death, many returned and associated with the Anglican Church but protested against the halfhearted-ness of the reformation, the Catholic nature of the Book of Common Prayer, the hierarchy of the episcopacy, numerous ceremonies, and especially against priestly vestments: the square cap, the tippet, and the surplice. Their defenders said these were adiaphora. Their opponents agreed that they were indifferent, in and of themselves, but not under the circumstances. Such attire was Roman and therefore tainted with superstition; in a figure dressed in that way, people still saw a Catholic priest. Beza, Bullinger, and Vermigli agreed with the latter opinion, but advised the opposition to proceed slowly.[223] There was thus con-fusion within the church: one clergyman would dress ornately, baptize at the baptismal font, cross himself, serve the Lord's Supper to kneeling recipients, and so on, while another would not. Elizabeth did not tolerate this; in 1564 she ordered uniformity on pain of being deposed from office, and Archbishop Parker supported her. He summoned the nonconforming clergy and ordered them to submit: sixty-one did, thirty-eight refused and explained their reasons in writing.[224] Many now became itinerant preachers or went into exile. Walter and Bullinger advised submission; Beza agreed with the Puritans but urged caution; the Scottish clergy were on the side of the nonconformists. In 1567 the nonconformists decided to secede. The adiaphora were much debated by Forbes, Calderwood, Ames, and Parker; and by Saravia, who opposed Beza.[225]

This controversy in Lutheran and Reformed circles took place entirely in the ecclesiastical domain and concerned adiaphora in the church. Trans-posed to the ethical domain, it sparked the Second Adiaphoristic Controversy. To counter the terrible moral corruption of the church, Philipp Spener pro-moted the sanctification of life, thus leaving behind all those things that were

---

221. Weber, *Geschichte der akatholischen Kirchen*, 2.1:376–78. Ed. note: The second volume of this work, *Ersten Theiles zweiter Band: Der constructive Theil der Reformation und die puritanische Sectenbildung*, is sometimes catalogued as volume 1.2 rather than 2.1. The reason for this may be that the title of the first volume is *Ersten Theiles erster Band*.

222. Weber, *Geschichte der akatholischen Kirchen*, 2.1:424–40.

223. Weber, *Geschichte der akatholischen Kirchen*, 2.1:427.

224. Neal, *History of the Puritans*, 1:210–17; see esp. p. 211.

225. Saravia was born in 1530 in Artois, studied in Oxford, in 1582 became professor in Leiden, and in 1587 fled to England when suspected of conspiracy. Ed. note: Hadrian à Sara-via (also known as Hadrian Saravia, Adrien Saravia, or Adrianus Saravia; 1532–1612) was a Protestant theologian and pastor who became part of the company of translators of the King James Bible (perhaps the only non-English member of the team [Wikipedia, s.v. "Hadrian à Saravia," https://en.wikipedia.org/wiki/Hadrian_%C3%A0_Saravia]).

incompatible with Christian sobriety.[226] Spener and his followers maintained that a Christian is not allowed do anything unless one can say that it would be to God's honor, could be done in the name of Jesus, and would bless one's neighbor. Adiaphora do not exist, for whatever is of faith is good, and what is not of faith is sin. There is no area in between, no middle ground. On this basis Spener condemned dancing, gambling, theater attendance, jesting, and luxury in food, drink, and attire. Nevertheless, Spener made a distinction: the true Christian has a different standard to maintain than the worldly Christian; thus, Spener did not reject dance and gambling absolutely and totally, but only in their present form. The later Pietists became even stricter than Spener and rejected everything. In 1692 the controversy flared up in earnest, and many pamphlets were published on both sides. For example, advocates of adiaphora (in opposition to the Pietists) included Valentin Ernst Löscher and Gottlieb Wernsdorf; among the opponents were Christoph Matthäus Seidel and Johann Hartmann.[227] The Pietists denied the category of middle things because they demanded a direct religious purpose for all actions; thus they did not do justice to the ethical domain, exclusively promoted the salvation of the soul, accepted the natural life only apprehensively, without freedom, and viewed the world only from its bad side.[228] By contrast, the orthodox asserted that there were indeed intermediate matters, but they were equally one-sided in their claim that these were indifferent with respect to the moral law; and they, too, tried to draw up a list of actions. Pietism became fearful, withdrawn, purely religious, with no further appreciation for moral or natural life.[229] Orthodoxism carved out a realm where one was entirely detached from God and the distinction between a Christian and an unbeliever faded away. Both sides were powerless to establish the proper relationship between the religious and the ethical, between God and the world, between Christianity and humanity, between the Christian and the human, between church and

226. Cf. Paret, "Adiaphoristischer Streit," 127.

227. Ed. note: Bavinck provides no title for Löscher, only the phrase *praecismus moralis*; no such title can be found. Bavinck likely took this specific reference from Paret, "Adiaphorischer Streit," 128: "Von gegnerischer Seite schrieb z.B. Löscher über den praecismus moralis, Wensdorf über absolutismus moralis"; Wernsdorf, *Absolutismus Moralis*; Firnhaber, *De Absolutismo Morali*; Seidel, *Christliches und erbauliches Gespräch*; Hartmann, *Tantz Teuffel*.

228. DO: *slechte zijde*; see Dorner, *History of Protestant Theology*, 2:218–19. Ed. note: In Dorner's words, "Pietistic morality takes up a chiefly negative position with respect to 'the world' and is antagonistic thereto." Also, it "makes too little distinction between 'the world' and 'the world.'"

229. E.g., art and science. Ed. note: Dorner puts it this way: "Pietism acknowledges no other kind of action to be positively moral than such as contributes to awakening and conversion, and therefore to piety. Anything that cannot be thus regarded is worthless, if not suspicious and injurious" (Dorner, *History of Protestant Theology*, 2:219).

society. The conflict endured for a long time, until the end of the eighteenth century. And the contrasting choices still exist.

The Permissible in Recent Discussions

Schleiermacher conducted a scholarly treatment of the permissible.[230] He asserts that the concept of the permissible arose in the arena of civic life and belongs exclusively there. The state cannot by its laws impose norms for all expressions of people's will and actions, nor may it do so. It is in fact a good sign if the state does not do so, and if there is a multiplicity of permitted actions. But it is different in the area of morality. For the moral law imposes norms for *all* human actions; whatever a person does in freedom is connected, narrowly or broadly, closely or distantly, more or less clearly, with the moral task imposed upon one by the moral law. Thus, nothing is *adiaphoron*, indifferent. We may make time for nothing other than the obligatory. Even the enjoyment of relaxation after work—the duration and manner of that recreation—is significant, and specific cases must be normed by what the universal moral law tells each person's moral individuality with its specific disposition, character, and circumstances. All people must learn to understand and to take to heart their duty, even in the simplest and apparently most indifferent matters.[231] Thus, on the one hand, Schleiermacher recognized natural (social, political, aesthetic) life as legitimate alongside the religious life, and on the other hand, he also demanded moral, individual nurture in that natural life.[232] Following Fichte's lead, he completely banned the concept of the permissible from the realm of ethics, as early as his *Kritik der bisherigen Sittenlehre*, but especially in the previously mentioned essay on the permissible.[233] Consequently, most of the modern ethicists followed him: Richard Rothe, Christoph von Ammon, Ludwig Baumgarten-Crusius, Julius Müller, Adolf Wuttke, Gottlieb von Harless, Christian Schmid, Hans Martensen, Heinrich Merz, and J. T. Beck.[234]

---

230. GO: *Erlaubte*; Schleiermacher, "Ueber den Begriff des Erlaubten," in *Friedrich Schleiermacher's Sämmtliche Werke*, 3/2, 418–45.

231. Paret, "Adiaphora," 125.

232. GO: *Durchbildung*; cf. Kübel, "Adiaphora," 148.

233. Schleiermacher, "Ueber den Begriff des Erlaubten"; see J. G. Fichte, *Sämmtliche Werke*, 1:133–36 (§4C); 4:155–56 (§13). Ed. note: The following texts in translation may also be helpful: Schleiermacher, *Lectures on Philosophical Ethics*; Schleiermacher, *Selections from Friedrich Schleiermacher's "Christian Ethics"*; Schleiermacher, *Introduction to Christian Ethics*.

234. Rothe, *Theologische Ethik*, 3:372–77 (§§811–12); von Ammon, *Handbuch der christlichen Sittenlehre*², 1:256–62; Baumgarten-Crusius, *Lehrbuch der christlichen Sittenlehre*, 187–91; J. Müller, *Christian Doctrine of Sin*, 1:61–62. Ed. note: Müller cites with approval the second half of a maxim from Leibniz, "Every lesser good is relatively evil" (*Omne minus bonum habet*

Friedrich Stahl takes a somewhat different tack; he asserts that here on earth, holiness and blessedness (virtue and bliss) do not interpenetrate. On earth, there is a kind of satisfaction, a happiness, that is independent of ethos and virtue, yet is not sinful, such as health, a good reputation, and so on, and Stahl calls that "the sphere of the ethically permitted."[235] He writes, "The permissible is not the result of a moral commandment, but of a moral force."[236] This sphere should gradually diminish. With a different view, Johann Wirth accepts the concept of the permissible because he judges that the essence of morality cannot be determined concretely.[237] The moral law provides only universal rules; within that range, the will is free to determine itself accordingly. The standard of many actions and, similarly, some actions themselves are neither commanded nor forbidden, but are morally indifferent. Without the concept of the permissible, friendly humor, grace, and the like would fade away. Nevertheless, Wirth does not want to make everything arbitrary, but rather ties everything to the moral individuality of the agent.[238]

The Old and New Testaments recognize no adiaphora.[239] The requirement is, You shall love the Lord your God with all your heart, and so forth, and, Be holy, for I am holy. That is absolute, comprehending our whole life, norming all our actions. Everything must be done to the glory of God, even eating and drinking (1 Cor. 10:31). Everything created by God[240] is good if received with thanksgiving (1 Tim. 4:4–5). Greeting,[241] marrying—everything must be done "in the Lord." The whole of life is placed under the perspective of the kingdom of God—that is the truth to be found in Pietism. Godliness has value for all things (1 Tim. 4:8). On the other hand, natural things are not to be viewed with fear, but everything created by God is good (1 Tim.

---

rationem mali); the full statement reads: "As a lesser evil is relatively good, so a lesser good is relatively evil" (*Uti minus malum habet rationem boni, ita minus bonum habet rationem mali*). See Leibniz, *Discourse on Metaphysics*, 5 (#III). Cf. Ames, *Conscience*, III.xviii; Wuttke, *Christian Ethics*, 2:237–51 (§§120–22); von Harless, *Christliche Ethik*, 160–61; Schmid, *Christliche Sittenlehre*, 447–55; Martensen, *Christian Ethics*, 1:415–18 (§§133–34); Merz, *Das System der christlichen Sittenlehre*, 76–77; J. T. Beck, *Vorlesungen über christliche Ethik*, 2:143–53, on adiaphora, and 2:153–72, on the permissible.

235. GO: *die Sphäre des Sittlich-Erlaubten*; Stahl, *Philosophie des Rechts*², 2.1:112–14; cf. Wuttke, *Christian Ethics*, 2:122–32 (§82); von Jhering, *Der Zweck im Recht*, 2:84–86, 184–85.

236. GO: *Das Erlaubte ist nicht Ausfluß eines sittlichen Geboten, sondern der sittlichen Macht*; Stahl, *Philosophie des Rechts*², 2.1:113.

237. Wirth, *System der speculativen Ethik*, 1:114–17. Ed. note: Johann Ulrich Wirth (1810–79) was a German theologian and philosopher (OCLC WorldCat Identities, s.v. "Johann Ulrich Wirth," https://worldcat.org/identities/viaf-62341883/).

238. Paret, "Adiaphora," 125.

239. Paret, "Adiaphora," 124–25.

240. GrO: κτίσμα.

241. DO: *groeten*.

4:4);[242] the spiritual person discerns all things (1 Cor. 2:15). Much is left to such a person's freedom. One must discern what is excellent (Phil. 1:10),[243] test all things, and hold fast to what is good (1 Thess. 5:21), always discerning what is the "good and acceptable and perfect" will of God (Rom. 12:2). Such persons must stand fast in their freedom (Gal. 5:1) and not allow themselves to be judged in relation to food, drink, or Sabbath (Col. 2:16). Although Christians must flee the world, nevertheless Christianity is a life of freedom and delight. All things are yours (1 Cor. 3:22). The earth is the Lord's (1 Cor. 10:26). To the pure all things are pure (Titus 1:15).

Thus, the Reformed, in a certain sense, both accepted and did not accept the concept of adiaphora. Calvin mentions it while teaching about offenses that he classifies among middle and indifferent matters.[244] He writes more about this in his treatise on the German Interim, where, for example, he discusses the claim that peripheral things are not indifferent as long as the central things remain pure.[245] Calvin writes against a certain "unreliable mediator" who had hindered the course of the gospel in France under the pretext of promoting the peace.[246] Further, Calvin also sets forth his disapproval of any accommodation in the letter "On Shunning the Unlawful Rites of the Ungodly" and in his writings against the Nicodemites and Pseudo-Nicodemites in France (accompanied with the responses of Melanchthon, Bucer and Vermigli, and that of Bullinger).[247] He repeats this in "Four Sermons" and in his letter

242. God gave Adam something permitted (Gen. 2:16): "You may surely eat of every tree of the garden." That was permitted to Adam, but not commanded.

243. GrO: τὰ διαφέροντα.

244. *Institutes*, III.xix.13.

245. Calvin, "Adultero-German Interim"; Calvin, "True Method of Reforming the Church," 242.

246. LO: *Responsio ad versipellem quendam mediotorem, qui pacificandi specia rectum Evangelii cursum in Gallia abrumpere molitus est* [1561], CO 9:529–60. Ed. note: This work has been translated into English: Calvin, "Calvin's *Response to a Certain Tricky Middler*" (trans. Bottomly). Calvin believed that the "tricky middler" who wrote the *De officio pii ac publicae tranquillitatis vere amantis viri in hoc religionis dissidio* (Basel, 1561) was François Baudouin, but it was actually the irenicist George Cassander. See de Greef, *Writings of John Calvin*, 195–96; de Greef translates *versipellem quendam mediotorem* as "unreliable mediator"; cf. Bottomly's "tricky middler."

247. LO: *De fugiendis illicitis sacris*; Calvin, "On Shunning the Unlawful Rites of the Ungodly." Ed. note: Calvin's writings against the Nicodemites in France were a response to the crisis of conscience among French Protestants who lived in Roman Catholic countries. "In 1543 in Geneva Calvin published a 'small treatise' (*Petit traicté*) that consisted of a longer and shorter letter" (de Greef, *Writings of John Calvin*, 120). He followed this in 1544 with a treatise, *Excuse à Messieurs les Nicodémites*, in which he held fast to his view that Protestants should be open about their faith. Both works were translated into Latin and published together in 1549 as *De vitandis superstitionibus*. Responses by Melanchthon, Bucer, and Vermigli are included in an appendix (de Greef, *Writings of John Calvin*, 122–24). The "short treatise" and

"Response to a Certain Dutchman."[248] See also the correspondence of Calvin, Beza, Bullinger, and Vermigli to Knox and other Britons. Hoornbeeck shares the same judgment about adiaphora as Thomas Aquinas: there are actions that are indifferent, and they remain so also concretely—that is, in and of themselves—but here they enter into circumstances, modes, and intentions, so that they occur as good or evil actions.[249] An act is either good (prayer) or evil (stealing) or indifferent (eating, drinking, etc.) in itself; that which is indifferent becomes good or evil through what attends it as a concrete act.[250] De Moor says something similar: Although in themselves concrete acts always remain indifferent, they become good or evil "through different ends, through various circumstances, through the intervention of the magistrate, or a directive of that kind, through use or abuse."[251]

According to Rothe, the range of what is permitted includes whatever is neither commanded nor forbidden by the moral law; not anything arbitrary or morally indifferent, but whatever cannot be clearly inferred or deduced from a legal formulation.[252] This can indeed occur, since the formulation of

Calvin's response to the Nicodemites are available in English translation: Calvin, "A Short Treatise Setting Forth What the Faithful Man Must Do"; Calvin, "Answer of John Calvin to the Nicodemite Gentlemen."

248. Calvin, "Four Sermons from John Calvin"; Calvin, "Response to a Certain Dutchman." Ed. note: A second translation of this treatise can be found in *Come Out from among Them*, 239–306.

249. Hoornbeeck, *Theologia Practica*, 1:318; cf. 2:483–88.

250. LO: *in individuo*.

251. LO: *per finem varium*; *per circumstantias diversas*; *per intercedens magistratus*; *mandatum*; *per usum vel abusum*; de Moor, *Commentarius Perpetuus*, 2:656–57.

252. Rothe, *Theologische Ethik*, 3:372–77; cf. Wendt, *Ueber das sittlich Erlaubte*; Köstlin, "Studien über das Sittengesetz"; Köstlin counters Rothe, Schleiermacher, etc., and then remarks (502):

The permissible has a realm all its own, it lies on the periphery of the ethical, has no *purpose* beyond itself, exists for its own sake, and is done because it is pleasant and not forbidden; it is for natural gratification. Everyone allows the permissible to children, playing without reflection. And so also later: the natural is entitled. Body and mind must remain healthy; they cannot always be in a state of exertion. God gave us wine, etc. for refreshment and satisfaction. All this has *positive value* in itself, and also serves to equip us for our moral task. Our natural side should not be neglected. A great deal is governed by our natural *drives*, not by our *will*. That natural side must not be suppressed. Play, enjoyment, etc. are part of the ideal for our life and should be denied only for higher interests and should be enjoyed with moderation. It is not a requirement that our personality determine the whole of our material nature (Rothe) but that we respect its rights. Eating, sleeping, traveling, theater, luxury, elegant clothing, conversation, play, dance, love, banter—all have their rights. The permissible occurs most in the child, diminishes later, becomes subordinate to moral effort.

Köstlin no longer calls all this "permitted," but "morally justified." (But also commanded?) Christian Palmer, in turn, argues against Köstlin and accepts the "merely permitted" (*bloss-Erlaubtes*; "Ueber das Gesetz und das Erlaubte"); cf. Schleiermacher, "Ueber den Begriff des

law is imperfect—for example, in regulating the life of the child who still lives without law, and where the permissible covers a broad area. It occurs also when the subject becomes morally stronger, freer with respect to the law, so that the permissible also increases, since the law cannot regulate every action. In fact, every act, since it is more or less modified by the individual agent, to that extent belongs to the permissible. All of this, however, only concerns something that is permitted with respect to the law, which cannot regulate everything; it is not something that is permitted in and of itself.[253] Such acts are not at all morally indifferent but can be determined with precision[254] through moral individuality. However, we cannot determine it for others and from others; we must determine it ourselves. The permissible in the sense of what is morally determinable only on an individual basis[255] has to be taken up in ethics, but not in the sense of the morally indifferent. The permissible in a good sense is the condition for the freedom and beauty of morality.

Kübel says that the adiaphora lie beneath the moral law and are not related to it at all.[256] In this sense they are found only in the realm of nature,[257] in purely animal acts, in minors, and in purely physical phenomena in the life of adults. This is indifferent. But the permissible is something that must be distinguished from the adiaphoron; it is what is permitted, what belongs to the ethical realm. After all, ethics is divided into two areas: (1) that of duty, of "ought," the categorical imperative, and (2) that of right, of "may," the concessive, responsible freedom of choice.[258] The latter does not coincide with the former, not even in the concrete. Since the permissible occurs mostly in my relation to nature, it often coincides with what is indifferent. But the higher a person's moral development, the more the indifferent things decrease. Thus, Kübel certainly recognizes the permissible as real, but not objectively as an entity that exists, abstracted from persons, as in the legalistic reckoning of Pietism and Roman Catholicism (e.g., dance is indifferent in and of itself, as

---

Erlaubten"; Schleiermacher, *Entwurf eines Systems der Sittenlehre*, 123–24, 135–37, 244–47; Schleiermacher, *Die christliche Sitte*[2], 48–50, 511–13, 621–24, 649–51, 694–97; Schmid, *Christliche Sittenlehre*, 447–55; Palmer, *Die Moral des Christenthums*, 206; Stahl, *Philosophie des Rechts*[3], 2.1:112–14 (ed. note: Bavinck here refers to the third edition of this work, whereas elsewhere he refers to the second edition).

253. GO: *an sich*.
254. GO: *genau bestimmbares*.
255. GO: *nur in individuelle weise sittlich bestimmbare*.
256. Kübel, "Adiaphora," 148–49.
257. GrO: φύσις.
258. GO: *Sollen*; *Darf*; GrO: ἐξουσία. Ed. note: We have added the word "responsible" here to capture Bavinck's interlinear insertion at this point of the Greek word ἐξουσία = freedom of choice, ability, capability, might, power, authority, warrant. The point here (and later, where we insert "responsibility") is to emphasize the moral agent's free choice.

if dancing could exist without dancing persons). But such actions are always the actions of an individual, as the evangelical perspective judges and says; for example, one person may dance and another may not. The moral life grows and develops; what is permissible for the one is not permitted for another. The individual conscience must therefore be trained. The permissible must be left to the individual. Thus, the permissible exists or does not exist, depending on a person's condition. It no longer exists in heaven, but it does exist here below. Many people who are still children, as it were, cannot bear the responsibility for a great many things. Thus, although from an absolute standpoint there are no adiaphora for God, that absolute standpoint is still the goal to be pursued, but not the immediate duty. There are levels of faith. The case is different for an unbeliever than for a Christian. In our judgment, Kübel ascribes far too much to the individual; he fails to do justice to universal law and confuses these two: the permissible as the realm of "may"[259] increasingly diminishes and from an absolute standpoint disappears; and an unpracticed Christian is permitted less than a strong Christian, in whose case it presumably increases. Or an unbeliever is permitted to do *more* than a Christian. But in that case the realm of the permissible falls away and becomes smaller and smaller.

Martensen argues that the permissible does not fall outside the ethical but can be determined only on an individual basis. This occurs especially in the aesthetic, "by the definition of the conception of the *Befitting* or *Seemly*."[260] And then the question "May I go to the theater?" can only be answered by the individual. However, although all things are permitted, not all things are profitable (1 Cor. 6:12). The rule is, Whatever is not of faith is sin (Rom. 14:23). Now since such adiaphora exist, the question arises whether we ought not to abstain from them at times in order not to offend others, and whether at other times we should do them in order to win over others.[261]

J. T. Beck claims that, objectively speaking, some things are adiaphora—for instance, wealth and health.[262] The question is really, Are there things with which we cannot have an ethical relationship? Yes; for example, consider the case of a child who is still morally indifferent and not yet accountable. Such childlike, underage, purely natural relationships remain with us, more or less, throughout all of life—for example, with respect to modesty and shame (a peasant can act against modesty without sinning, and patriarchs could practice polygamy as persons still morally immature). Thus, if a person does not

259. GO: *das Darf*.
260. LO: *decorum*; see Martensen, *Christian Ethics*, 1:417 (§134); the quotation from Martensen was added by the editor.
261. Martensen, *Christian Ethics*, 1:418–20 (§135).
262. J. T. Beck, *Vorlesungen über christliche Ethik*, 2:143.

yet have a moral consciousness about this or that, their relationship to it can be morally indifferent. But if one is capable of moral judgment,[263] then one must act accordingly and may not be indifferent; when one is unsure whether something is good, one must attempt to find clarity. Therefore, things indifferent are always the result of deficient moral education. A distinction must be made, then, between the absolute law and one's consciousness of it. If the former has not yet been taken up into someone's consciousness, then neither is it at that moment obligatory; it is an ideal duty, but not a real duty. Protestants held only to the ideal duty, while Roman Catholics only to the real duty (that is, not everything is a duty for every person). Protestants vindicate the universal and undervalue the individual; Roman Catholics maintain exactly the reverse: they fail to appreciate the absoluteness of the law.

According to Beck, the idea of the permissible is not the same as that of the indifferent;[264] the permissible does involve the moral (as is the case with Kübel). From the legislative Old Testament perspective, the permissible is neither commanded nor forbidden by the law. But from the Christian perspective, the permissible is specifically left undecided by the law, and is thus legitimate, and as such is also an "ought."[265] This "ought" therefore belongs to the realm of "everything is permissible for me" under the "responsibility and freedom of the Christian."[266] The permissible in the New Testament is narrower than in the Old Testament, since in Matthew 5 the law is more internalized and therefore more comprehensive, and commands that eating and drinking also be done to the glory of God. On the other hand, there is a much broader sphere of freedom for the Christian. This freedom is left to the Christian positively by the law itself, as one who is under the law of Christ (1 Cor. 9:21).[267] In Christ the Christian is absolutely bound and also absolutely free. All things are permissible (1 Cor. 6:12), but all things must be done to the glory of God (1 Cor. 10:23–31). Bound with respect to Christ, free with respect to the world. Everything that falls within earthly life is thus placed in the hands of the Christian.[268] The individual conscience must decide. But the Christian has that freedom only to the degree that Christ is immanent

---

263. GO: *Urtheilsfähig.*
264. J. T. Beck, *Vorlesungen über christliche Ethik*, 2:153–72.
265. GO: *Soll.*
266. Ed. note: Bavinck uses two Greek words here: ἐξουσία (= freedom of choice, ability, capability, might, power, authority, warrant) and ἐλευθερία (= freedom). We have chosen to translate the former term as "responsibility" to capture the duality of obligation and freedom possessed by Christian moral agents.
267. GrO: ἔννομος Χριστοῦ; see J. T. Beck, *Vorlesungen über christliche Ethik*, 2:161.
268. DO: *macht*; J. T. Beck, *Vorlesungen über christliche Ethik*, 2:165.

within a person, to the extent one has the Holy Spirit;[269] otherwise one is still under the guardian. And one may use that freedom only with an eye to the flourishing of Christian life in them and in others.

Beginning with Christian Wolff (1679–1754), a distinction has been made between broad and narrow duties, imperfect (negative) duties and perfect (positive) duties.[270] The narrow ones were, for example, pay your debts, do not steal, do not kill, and so on. The broad ones were to develop your mind, comfort the sorrowing, care for the sick, teach your children—but how one does that, whether by studying Sanskrit or geometry, remains undetermined. Staying in good health, but how to do that, is similarly undefined. This is left to the individual; the law says only, Do these things as much as possible; thus, they are broad duties. But the idea of duty is always narrow, perfect, positive; only the content, the material, is sometimes difficult to determine as soon as the duty becomes spiritual—for example, showing gratitude. The content of the duty is narrow only when it consists of something physical that can be weighed and measured. In all other cases, a great deal is left to the interpretation of the individual.

SUMMARY AND SYNTHESIS[271]

1. Adiaphora and the Permissible[272]

In summary, we can discern three basic positions regarding the area of adiaphora and what is permissible: the Roman Catholic view of Duns Scotus and the Councils of Constance and Trent; the Protestant view, as well as that of Thomas, Bellarmine, and others; and a mediating position, which can be further divided into two views.

A. INDIFFERENT OBJECTS AND ACTS EXIST IN THE CONCRETE

This was the position of Duns Scotus and the Councils of Constance and Trent. In addition to things and objects that are indifferent, indifferent acts also definitely exist, not only in the abstract but also in individual, concrete cases. These have nothing to do with the moral law, since they can just as

269. J. T. Beck, *Vorlesungen über christliche Ethik*, 2:167.

270. Janet, *La morale*, 241–65. Ed. note: "Imperfect duties" and "perfect duties" are technical terms (see Kant).

271. Ed. note: This heading and those that follow in the remainder of this chapter—including subheadings—have been supplied by the editor.

272. Ed. note: Here and in what follows Bavinck pairs the German *Erlaubte* (= permissible) with the originally Greek term "adiaphora."

well be done as left undone; they are entirely independent of the law, of duty, and therefore are not morally necessary but wholly and purely arbitrary and contingent. This is the position of Pelagianism: the entire moral law is contingent; God could just as well have ordained otherwise, less, or more than he happened to have decreed by an arbitrary act. That law consists of a few purely contingent commandments, one after another, composing an aggregate, not an organism. The law therefore does not comprehend all of life but only a few actions. The law is not absolute and does not norm a person completely. There is a large domain that the law leaves free and about which it says nothing. There is an open realm beyond and an open realm beneath the law; one can do more than the law demands, but also less. Thus, on the one hand, there are counsels beyond the law; and on the other, there are *adiaphora* beneath the law. If one fulfills the law and also fulfills the counsels, then one obtains merits, and these are works of supererogation.[273] If one fulfills the law but does not abstain from the adiaphora, then one is an unprofitable servant. Abstaining voluntarily from adiaphora is the correlate of fulfilling the counsels. This standpoint is completely mistaken. The law claims us totally and undividedly and absolutely.

B. ADIAPHORA EXIST ONLY IN THE ABSTRACT

Protestants, Thomas Aquinas, Robert Bellarmine, and others hold that adiaphora, permissible things, exist only in the abstract. In their concrete form, they are always subject to the moral law—though not in themselves, but by intention, goal, and circumstance—and thus cease to be indifferent, but are in fact commanded or forbidden.[274] In their concrete form, therefore, permissible things or indifferent things vanish altogether; the only thing remaining is the law, duty, and moral necessity. Consequently, while for many things it is not possible to determine in advance and in the abstract whether something is good or evil, nevertheless Protestants—for example, Flacius and his followers in opposition to Melanchthon, the Reformed against the Anglicans—still attempted to establish everything concretely and objectively according to the moral law, not leaving it to the individual. Against Rome, therefore, Protestants maintain the absolute validity of the moral law for all people and for all time. Rome argues that, except for what the law prescribes, the individual may choose to do more or less; it is the individual's choice. Protestantism argues that every individual is always directed in the concrete form of action by the moral law.

273. LO: *opera supererogationis*.
274. LO: *in individuo; per intentionem, finem, circumstantias*.

c. The Mediating Position in Two Forms

(i) The Permissible Is an Individual Choice

Schleiermacher, Rothe, Martensen, and others say that the permissible is definitely not arbitrary, indifferent, or contingent (they regard that as the Protestant position), but neither is it subject to the law, which, after all, cannot regulate everything. The permissible, therefore, can be morally determined only on an individual basis.[275] The more we observe an action in its concrete form, however, the more we are shaped and developed morally; and we will understand our actions all the more to be either commanded or forbidden by the moral law. The realm of the permissible is therefore always decreasing, and its sphere becomes ever narrower.

Some comments are in order here.

First, this shortchanges the universal law; too much is assigned to subjective, individual opinion; dance, play,[276] theater, and so forth should also be able to be objectively determined as being either good or bad. Thus, here the permissible rests upon a defect in the law.[277]

Second, if in its individual and concrete form an action is not indifferent yet is presented by the subjective conscience on the basis of the moral law as being good or bad, then it is no longer permitted, but is either prescribed or proscribed.[278]

In the third place, how can it then also be claimed that with continuing moral development, the realm of permissible things decreases? The permissible is what is determined and stipulated by the conscience as being good or bad. Does the decrease in the realm of the permissible mean that the conscience henceforth no longer determines anything as being good or bad? Surely that cannot be. Does it mean, then, that the discipline of ethics will increasingly be able to say objectively about permissible things that they are good or that they are bad?

In the fourth place, to define the realm of the permissible as consisting only of what "can be determined on an individual basis"[279] is completely wrong. For either we end up in a terrible subjectivism, or the definition says nothing. With the former, ethics can no longer talk about worship, images of the saints, and the like, about dance, play, theater, and the like, but everything must simply be left to the individual conscience. What is good for one

275. GO: *nur in individueller Weise sittlich Bestimmbare.*
276. DO: *spel.*
277. Wuttke, *Christian Ethics,* 2:123 (§82).
278. DO: *ge- of verboden.*
279. GO: *Erlaubte* is the *nur individuell Bestimmbare.*

is bad for another, which confuses the concept of Christian freedom. With the latter, the definition says nothing, because the individual always judges in a concrete case whether something is good or evil according to the universal moral law, subsuming that concrete case under that law and then drawing a conclusion. Now that occurs with or without grounds. If it occurs (as it should be done) with grounds, then these can be objectively explained, and we are able gradually by logical reasoning to ascertain that this is either good or bad. When asked by Puritans about his view, Calvin surely could not have said, "The permissible is 'what can be determined only on an individual basis,' so it is up to you." No, he weighed the grounds pro and con and said: It is wrong. Similarly, Matthias Flacius.

(ii) The Physical Is Indifferent; the Permissible Equals Christian Freedom

Beck, Kübel, Wuttke, and others first distinguish between things indifferent and things permitted, and then identify the indifferent with the purely physical (which lies beneath the moral law), and the permissible with Christian freedom (which lies above the moral law). One progresses from the indifferent life of the immature, through the law as guardian, to true Christian freedom.[280] Thus, here for the Christian the realm of indifferent things continues to diminish and the realm of the permissible continues to increase (although Kübel says that in heaven the realm of the permissible no longer exists), and the realm of the "ought" increasingly becomes the realm of the "may," with authority and freedom.[281]

The following should be noted.

First, that the physical is indifferent is obvious. The issue is whether in the moral realm indifferent things exist; if not, then the realm of the indifferent vanishes entirely. But then one should not say: Yes, the indifferent exists, but only in the physical, not in the moral.

Second, Beck misunderstands the objective universal law. He distinguishes between ideal duty and real duty, between the law as "the goal that is to be pursued" and as "the duty that is not yet immediate."[282] "Ability determines obligation."[283] Matthew 5 and the evangelical law go beyond the Old Testament law.[284] One must distinguish the law from a person's awareness of the law.

---

280. Wuttke, *Christian Ethics*, 1:122–32 (§82).
281. GO: *Soll*; *Darf*; GrO: ἐξουσία; ἐλευθερία.
282. GO: *anzustrebendes Ziel*; *nocht nicht unmittelbare Pficht*; J. T. Beck, *Vorlesungen über christliche Ethik*, 2:151.
283. GO: *Das können bestimmt das Sollen*; J. T. Beck, *Vorlesungen über christliche Ethik*, 2:120.
284. J. T. Beck, *Vorlesungen über christliche Ethik*, 2:121, 157.

Duty depends on development, so it is something that is developing, like the Christian life itself.[285] Although Beck does maintain the law as ideal duty, and Kübel says that it is "the goal to be pursued," their view, in fact, returns us once again to the evangelical counsels. After all, the law itself leaves open a large sphere of freedom for the Christian, and thus does not regulate everything.[286]

In the third place, their position has this inconsistency: on the one hand, for them the law is the ideal, the goal to be pursued, but then the realms of the indifferent and the permissible must continually decrease, since they are beneath the law. On the other hand, the realm of the permissible is legitimate alongside the realm of the "ought," one of freedom for the Christian, a demonstration of one's strong faith, a realm of authority.[287] Existing not alongside but above the law, the realm of the permissible is then the highest and thus continues to increase. For Beck, to be loosened from the law is then the goal, and the realm of "ought" becoming the realm of "may" is the highest aim, even though Beck attempts nevertheless to bind the realm of the "may" through Christ, the Holy Spirit within us, in terms of the flourishing of the Christian life within and outside of us.[288] But this proves precisely that freedom is the goal.

Fourth, Beck confuses the realm of the permissible with the realm of Christian freedom. This freedom is not a right, power, or permission alongside obligation (Kübel), but this freedom exists *within* the law.[289] This freedom is a calling and a duty that the law imposes, one that does not extend beyond the law but instead fulfills the law. Eating food sacrificed to idols was exactly in accordance with the law, but others, who were still bound in their conscience to a different, false law, did not yet dare to eat such food.

2. The Realm of the Adiaphora

People usually assign to this realm ecclesiastical adiaphora, clerical vestments—for example, the tricornered hat and the like—images, paintings, an altar in the sanctuary, hymns, the times and length of the worship service.[290] Furthermore, this realm includes the entire domain of natural life and of the individual life: eating, drinking, caring for one's health, dressing, sleeping. It includes domestic

---

285. J. T. Beck, *Vorlesungen über christliche Ethik*, 2:125–32.
286. J. T. Beck, *Vorlesungen über christliche Ethik*, 2:161.
287. GrO: ἐξουσία; see J. T. Beck, *Vorlesungen über christliche Ethik*, 2:160.
288. J. T. Beck, *Vorlesungen über christliche Ethik*, 2:162–63, 166–67, 168–69.
289. As Beck rightly observes: *Vorlesungen über christliche Ethik*, 2:166.
290. Ed. note: The tricornered hat was the traditional garb of ministers in the Dutch Secession Christian Reformed Church (*Christelijke Gereformeerde Kerken in Nederland*); singing hymns, in addition to the approved biblical psalms, was also debated in these churches.

life: marriage, procreation, managing the household, Bible reading and prayer
at table, kneeling for morning and evening prayers, and so on. It includes social
life: bantering, joking, visiting, playing, dancing, attending the theater, traveling,
relaxing, walking, touring in a carriage, and so forth. It includes professional
life: plying a trade, devoting oneself to art, science, politics, commerce, industry, and the like. And indeed, none of this is stipulated by the moral law: what
and how much I should eat and drink, how I should dress, whether I should
go for a walk every day, whether the preacher should wear a tricornered hat,
and so on. About these details Scripture says nothing. The realm of the adiaphora seems astonishingly wide, encompassing the whole of natural life. But
that is mere appearance. In the abstract, it is equally fine to wear a tricornered
hat or an ordinary hat, to go for walks or not. But the mistake is this: people
take those things, which have all arisen historically, out of their historical context, examine them in themselves, and then ask whether they are good or bad.
No answer can be given to that abstract question. But it can be answered in a
concrete situation. The Christian religion presupposes, and everywhere meets
with, a natural, historically shaped life that has developed under God's leading.
Christianity does not reduce everything to the same level. Christianity does not
revolt, but reforms. The moral law that comes with Christianity includes universal principles, which Christianity applies to what has historically developed.
Christianity scraps only what is in irreconcilable conflict with those principles
and animates and sanctifies the rest anew.[291] Take, for example, ecclesiastical
adiaphora. Whether a tricornered hat or a regular hat should be worn cannot
be determined in the abstract, but it can be decided in concrete circumstances,
for a given preacher, in a specific congregation.[292]

Given the time and circumstances, Melanchthon and the Anglicans erred
in declaring clerical garb and related issues to be indifferent. Furthermore,
a great deal is subsumed under the adiaphora that does not belong there—
for example, dance, play, and theater. One must first address the question of
whether these things, in the abstract, are adiaphora at all. For example, play
in general is no adiaphoron. Gambling is certainly wrong for everybody; that
should not be left to the individual conscience, as if it were infallible, but it
must logically follow from the moral law that this is wrong. Protestants were
therefore right when they said that in concrete circumstances, in a specific
historical context, there are no adiaphora. Since we are moral persons, we
stand in a moral relationship to all things, even the most elementary things.

291. Ed. note: Bavinck writes in the margin: "It is not indifferent whether I marry, what
vocation I have, and so on."
292. See also Wendt, *Ueber das sittlich Erlaubte*, 16.

By intention, goal, use or abuse, and circumstances,[293] things always become moral and acquire a moral relationship to an individual and a moral significance for an individual.

3. Adiaphora and Moral/Spiritual Development

This particular matter of the adiaphora must not be confused with things that are indifferent for children and variations in people's developmental stages of faith (as is done by Beck, Kübel, Rothe, et al.). Children are not yet in a moral relationship with many things (unlike the adult), but that is because the child still lives an instinctive[294] existence and is not yet morally developed. Nature still dominates the ethos of children.[295] It is permissible for infants to cry loudly in public, for example, at their baptism in the church. This should not be called "indifferent" (for indifference relates precisely to the moral law), because no moral law functions for an infant. The issue whether it may or may not be done, whether something is permitted or not, is not at all appropriate in this case; the concept of permission does not fit. These are actions that occur entirely outside the moral law; they are natural acts. In the same way, there are natural actions among adults, since the human person also has a vegetative existence and an instinctive existence that can never be brought entirely under the power of the will. That someone strokes his beard, wiggles one's knee, is shy, nervous, has digestion issues, congestion in the head, headaches, toothaches, problems breathing, enunciating, and so forth—one's conscience does not accuse on that account (unless one has caused the illness through, for example, intemperance). That is purely the physical substratum for the ethical personality; we should not call that "indifferent" (adiaphoron).

But neither should this issue be confused with whether things are permitted or not in the various stages[296] of faith. This leads some to infer that (a) the weak in faith and the unbeliever may still do things that conflict with the moral law, things that remain *beneath* the moral law; and (b) the strong in faith may do things that transcend the moral law, elevating themselves *above* it. In the case of (a), it would be permissible to offer sacrifices and to be circumcised even though Christ has fulfilled the ceremonial law. In the case of (b), it would be permissible to eat meat offered to idols, to go for a stroll on Sunday, and the like. Two individuals would then act in completely different ways while adhering to one and the same law. How can we accept that without joining

---

293. LO: *per intentionem, finem, usum vel abusum, circumstantias.*
294. DO: *dierlijk.*
295. GrO: φύσις; ἦθος.
296. GO: *Stufen.*

Kübel and others in accepting a "may" alongside an "ought"? This is not because there is an area where the moral law does not regulate—that there is a "may" alongside an "ought."[297] Within the law itself, the possibility of both that difference and that freedom exists. For these are then two actions that do not contradict, exclusively oppose, and exclude each other, like good and evil do. But within the law itself, both actions fulfill the demand of the law. Nevertheless, as soon as one action would conflict with the law in any respect, it would be impermissible, and by that fact alone[298] would immediately be proscribed. But now, someone who, out of faith, according to the law and for God's glory, does not go for a stroll on Sundays fulfills the law just as much as someone one who, under the same conditions, does go for a stroll. And each of the actions is not merely permitted but a duty for each of those two persons: those who believe they may not go for a stroll may not do so, and those who believe they may, may do so and must indicate this even if they abstain in order not to offend. It is not the case that the one stands beneath the law and the other above it, but both stand within the law. The point is that the same law allows differing interpretations and applications by consciences that have been historically shaped in different ways.

4. Adiaphora Is Not Individual Choice

Thus, when we are interpreting and applying the universal law, the "individual moral authority"[299] is always a factor. But this must not lead to the conclusion that the permissible can be determined only on an individual basis.[300] For every interpretation of every moral commandment will, to a greater or lesser extent, involve that authority. And therefore, all actions are to some degree permissible, or have something permissible about them, as Rothe correctly concludes.

Moreover, the phrase "determine only on an individual basis" cannot mean here leaving things subjectively (in the negative sense of the word) to each person's opinion. For as long as I or another person knows this or that individual well, I or another person can determine from the moral law what such an individual must do in a specific case. Thus, the law speaks clearly to that person, leaves no room for doubt, and causes the person to hear its "ought." To be "determined only on an individual basis" is not, and must not be, set in contrast to what is determined by the law (as Rothe and company believe).

297. GO: *Darf, Soll.*
298. LO: *eo ipso.*
299. GO: *individuelle sittliche Instanz.*
300. GO: *nur indivuell Bestimmbare.*

Rather, what is determined individually is no less determined by the law, in a clear way, for the individual concerned—though not, however, for me, since I do not know that individual or the person's conscience and therefore cannot judge. Ethics may certainly discuss the realm of the permissible and come to the conclusion that, given such and such an individual, that person ought to do this or that.

Nevertheless, not all actions appear to fall under the "ought." For example, a person might say, I *must* finish my work every day, but I *may* walk an hour every day; I *must* go to church Sunday, I *may* stay home Wednesday evenings; I may smoke, drink wine, banter, play, dance, attend the theater, afford luxury, and so forth—no one would say that those things *must* be done, unless drinking wine, say, is prescribed directly for my health. Thus, there is a "may" alongside an "ought."[301] What explains that? Is it because the law contains not only prescriptions but also proscriptions?[302] Or is it because of circumstances in which we may call the one thing permissible—for example, relaxation—but only in contrast to its opposite (work), calling work itself an "ought"? (Or is it because of a deficiency in our moral consciousness, such that although every "ought" is in fact a "may," and every "may" an "ought," yet they get separated as a result of our deficient moral development?) Certainly, the first explanation is valid because of the law itself.[303] For many actions are permissible because Scripture does not forbid them. On the other hand, many actions must be done as required by scriptural command; if the law commands something, then we must do it; if the law forbids something, then we may not do it; if the law does not command something, then we need not do it; if the law does not forbid something, then we may do it. Thus, we are under obligation only where the law supplies a positive commandment; permission only becomes an issue in the case of prohibitions. The question posed above can therefore be reduced to this: What is the relation between prescription and proscription?[304] Why does the law not only prescribe but also proscribe?[305]

Proscription presupposes sin, a society thoroughly permeated by sin, a situation that has developed historically. The Ten Commandments therefore have a negative form. Every prohibition is based in a commandment, but it nonetheless differs from a commandment. Most prohibitions can be transposed into commandments, and vice versa; for example, do not lie, speak

---

301. GO: *Darf; Soll.*
302. DO: *ge- en verboden.*
303. Ed. note: Bavinck also adds *en tweede* (and the second) in the margin.
304. DO: *gebod en verbod.*
305. DO: *gebiet; verbiet.* Bavinck's marginal note: "There is an area in between commandment and prohibition."

the truth, and so on.[306] But that does not hold in every case: every "may" cannot be converted into "ought" (as Schleiermacher and Rothe wish to do in a rigoristic manner). The permission to smoke, to stay home from church, to take a stroll on Sunday cannot become an obligation (except for additional reasons, of health or the like). Conversely, "ought" cannot be changed into "may," as Rome does with its counsels. Thus, there remains an area for "may"—namely, what is not commanded and not forbidden, an area called adiaphora, or "the permissible."[307]

H. H. Wendt, teacher of theology in Göttingen,[308] understands the permissible to consist of actions that are devoted to ourselves, to our pleasure, to our physical relaxation (like playing, walking), or our mental relaxation. We perform those actions when we withdraw from the community, from the moral spheres of family, vocation, politics, and so forth. The permissible, therefore, lies outside the moral duties that exist for us in society. But the permissible may not conflict with those moral duties and may not suspend them. The permissible decreases to the extent that our duties multiply and expand, and it increases to the extent that our capacities for fulfilling moral duties expand: a healthy person is permitted to do more than a sick person. But should not all our lives be placed in the realm of duty—that is, devoted to others—so that nothing remains in the realm of the permissible? This was the approach of the rigorists, Calvin, and others. But not all people have the same moral strength and energy. Most need relaxation and the like.

On the other hand, can the permissible not be subsumed under the duties we owe ourselves, and consequently made into a duty? No, argues Wendt, for we have no duties toward ourselves, but only toward others. Thus, a realm of the permissible remains, in addition to that of duties. However, indirectly the permissible has great moral value; it may not produce vice in us; it must be virtuous and a school of virtue, and it must form a beautiful, admirable character, like duty does. But does the latter not turn the permissible once again into a duty? Are there not also duties toward ourselves—for instance, not to kill ourselves?

Wuttke argues that the "sphere of the allowed stands in the same relation to that of the express law as *play* to earnest activity." He also puts it this way: "The sphere of the allowed in general, is the wider and positive-grown

---

306. Janet, *La morale*, 243.

307. Ed. note: What follows in the remaining paragraphs was added later. This sentence is the conclusion of Bavinck's own view; what follows is Bavinck's summary of the views of Wendt, Wuttke, and Ames.

308. GO: *Privatdozent*; Wendt, *Ueber das sittlich Erlaubte*, 9–10. Cf. Windel, *Die Grenzen des christlich Erlaubten*.

extension of that of play. Here belongs *recreation* after labor, as in contrast to the positive fulfilling of the law; recreation is *per se* morally good and its essence consists in freedom; that I select precisely this path for a promenade, or busy myself thus or thus, is neither prescribed to me by any law, nor is that which I do not select forbidden."[309] That relationship is not direct, but indirect; is commanded not positively, but negatively; is a duty commanded not for the sake of oneself but for the sake of the moral. I may relax, in order later to be able to work even more energetically. In this way, freedom remains within the law.

Ames argues that there are actions indifferent in and of themselves, but they can become good or evil by means of certain circumstances.[310] In their ordinary, pure nature, however, they are indifferent—such as eating, drinking, traveling, and strolling. Some indifferent actions are more easily combined with evil circumstances, while others with good circumstances. Many actions, such as stroking one's beard, are neither morally good nor morally evil, do not fall under that category, and occur without forethought, purely through imagination. The only thing to be observed here is decency. But any action done deliberately is either good or evil; although many actions are neither necessary nor impermissible, if they are done, they should be done in accordance with the law.

---

309. Wuttke, *Christian Ethics*, 2:128 (§82). Ed. note: Extended direct quotations from Wuttke were added by the editor to clarify Bavinck's condensed summary.
310. Ames, *Conscience*, III.xviii.

14

Collision and Classification
of Duties

Because they divided their moral duties and virtues by ascribing them to various gods, pagans frequently experienced a collision of simultaneous duties. Pagan myths are replete with stories of such collisions, and their thinkers, particularly the Stoics, wrote extensively about duties. They were the first casuists.

Christian ethics also wrestled with this; Jesus himself took up questions of conflict, such as paying taxes to Caesar and healing on the Sabbath. The institutions of penance and the confessional greatly multiplied these questions in the church. Penitential books were produced to help confessors by classifying sins and their penalties. After auricular confession became canon law in 1215, extensive books of casuistry were produced, eventually leading to the Jesuit theory and practice of probabilism, in which an act was permissible so long as it was probably justifiable. In effect this meant that one could sin against God's law and even one's own conscience based on a single authority's probable opinion. The Jesuits were opposed by Pascal and the Jansenists, and the Puritan William Ames insisted that while consciences can err, no one may violate their own conscience.

Most modern Protestant ethicists insist that an objective collision of duties is impossible because the moral law is one but that subjectively flawed human beings experience such conflict. This conflict often arises from the variety of social spheres and relationships present in our lives. Many of these ethicists are averse to casuistry, but the work of Puritans such as Ames and Perkins shows how valid it is and how useful it can be. When we are faced with what appears to be a conflict, we are called to discern a hierarchy of duties: duties toward God take precedence over all others;

weightier duties take precedence over lesser ones in the same class (honor and chastity over life); duties toward the soul of one person take precedence over all material interests, including those of the community; broader duties take precedence over narrower ones (family over myself, country over family). And, when in doubt, abstain.

If we proceed from the Decalogue, we face the question of how to divide the Ten Commandments. The key question concerns the first and second commandments; are they two or one? Roman Catholics and Lutherans have three commandments in the first table and seven in the second table; others have five and five, assigning the commandment to honor father and mother to the first table; the Reformed division is four and six. This leads to the division between duties toward God and duties toward our neighbor, to the distinction between religion and morality.

Many modern ethicists reject the distinction between religion and morality. Some say that we have no duties toward God, because all duty is reciprocal and presupposes rights. If we have duties toward God, then he also has duties toward us. But this is wrong; God has no obligations to us; he is not bound to us but only to himself, to his holy nature. Our duty toward God is not reciprocal; our duties are not to benefit him; they are expressions of obedience and gratitude. Others (e.g., Immanuel Kant) say that there are no duties toward God because God cannot be known. The good must be done for its own sake and not because we know what God wills. But God is knowable; when we love the good, we love God, who is the Good One. Then, there are those who dismiss the notion of duties toward God because what are called "duties toward God" coincide with our duties toward our neighbor. Religion is morality. This too is wrong. It is true that religion involves morality; all our life is a service of God. Even stronger, our religion must be moral by answering to the moral law. But the distinction between them must remain; religion must bear a moral character, and morality must bear a religious character for both to be what they should be.

On the question of duties toward ourselves, it needs to be noted that this duty is not mentioned in the law of God. As sinners we are prone to self-centeredness and hardly need a command. In addition, duties toward ourselves are implicit in duties toward our neighbor. What we may not do to our neighbor as God's image-bearer, we may not do to ourselves. Finally, duties of faith, conversion, sanctification, and so on are prescribed through Scripture. We also have duties toward those who have died, toward angels, and to creation. We come therefore to the following classification of duties:

I. *Duties in body and spirit toward God*

II. *Duties toward ourselves*

III. *Duties toward our neighbor*

    A. *General duties*

    B. *Special duties (family, vocation, society, church, state)*

Attempts to reduce all three duties to one, whether by the category of social morality (Fichte) or by the dignity of our nature, our own self (Kant), ignore the only single source and object of duties—namely, God himself. All our duties finally come to this: Our duties toward ourselves and our neighbor stand firm in the relation we have to God in Christ. Neither we nor our neighbor (not to mention all of creation) exist in our own strength, by and for ourselves. Our love for all creatures must be a love for God.

§30. COLLISION OF DUTIES[1]

A *Survey of the Problem*

The expression "collision of duties"[2] is used for those cases where people are confronted simultaneously with two or more duties that are mutually exclusive, where to fulfill one duty means to omit another one. Such cases occurred very frequently among the pagans. According to Ebrard,[3] this can be accounted for by the fact that they divided the Good over a number of virtues and ascribed each of these to a different god: valor to Ares, chastity to Artemis, wisdom to Athena Pallas, and so forth. The virtues were not well known, nor was evil. Instead of struggles between good and evil, conflicts arose between certain duties and virtues. This conflict is especially evident in the case of Orestes, who has to avenge his father Agamemnon, slain by his mother Clytemnestra, who carries on an adulterous relationship with Aegisthus; but in so doing Orestes violates the piety he owes his mother. That is why Orestes is prosecuted by the Furies and is finally acquitted in the tribunal on the Areopagus only by the voice of the wisest of goddesses, Athena Pallas.[4]

A similar case is that of Philoctetes: Troy cannot be saved if Philoctetes (who has fallen ill and been left behind by Odysseus on the island of Lemnos) does not voluntarily return to Troy with his Herculean weapon. But Philoctetes refuses and, as Odysseus advises, has to be persuaded by deception to do his duty. Antigone wants to perform her duty toward her brother, Polyneices, by burying him, but she must also obey Creon, who has forbidden it.[5] The

1. DO: *collisie van plichten.*
2. LO: *collisio officiorum* (from *con laedo* = to injure each other; to strike each other).
3. Ebrard, *Das Verhältnis Shakspear's zum Christenthum,* 5.
4. Ed. note: The story is told by Homer (*Odyssey* I.35–43) and Pindar; Sophocles and Euripedes treat the same myth differently in their *Electra* dramas (Wikipedia, s.v. "Orestes," https://en.wikipedia.org/wiki/Orestes; Wikipedia, s.v. "Clytemnestra," https://en.wikipedia .org/wiki/Clytemnestra).
5. Ed. note: According to Greek mythology, Philoctetes was a prince, "famed as an archer, and a participant in the Trojan War." Though Philoctetes was the subject of "four different plays

conflict between a person's duties and the wishes of the gods is a recurring theme in Greek tragedy. But standing above it all is inexorable, mysterious fate: when morality has no way out, fate simply creates an escape by force.

After expounding "the way in which specific duties are derived under the several divisions of the right," Cicero observes that "between those very actions which are morally right, a conflict and comparison may frequently arise, as to which of two moral actions is morally better."[6] Furthermore, "since moral rectitude springs from four sources (one of which is prudence; the second, social instinct; the third, courage; the fourth temperance), it is often necessary in deciding a question of duty that these virtues be weighed against one another."[7] Then, according to Cicero, "those duties are closer to nature which depend upon the social instinct than those which depend upon knowledge."[8] In *On Duties* III.23 Cicero poses many cases, such as the following: When two shipwrecked men grab hold of one plank, but this plank can support only one man, is one then duty bound to surrender the plank to the other man and perish himself?[9] Cicero says that the one must surrender to the other—that is, to the man whose continued living is more important, either for his own sake or in the interest of the state. Must a son report to the magistrate that his father pillages temples? No. That he is committing treason against the government? Yes, in the end he must. Is it the duty of one who sells a slave or gold or anything else to point out any defects in what is being sold? Must one always keep his promises? For example, when Agamemnon promised Diana that he would sacrifice the most beautiful one born in his kingdom that year, did he have to sacrifice his daughter Iphigenia?[10] No;

---

of ancient Greece, each written by one of the three major Greek tragedians," only Sophocles's *Philoctetes at Troy* has survived. He is "also mentioned in Homer's *Iliad*, Book 2" (Wikipedia, s.v. "Philoctetes," https://en.wikipedia.org/wiki/Philoctetes).

6. LO: *contentio et comparatio*; *honesta*; *honestius*; Cicero, *On Duties* (*De officiis*) I.43 (LCL 30:154–55).

7. LO: *omnis honestas manet a partibus quatuour*; *cognitionis, communitatis, magnanimitatis, moderationis*; *deligendo officio*; Cicero, *On Duties* (*De officiis*) I.43 (LCL 30:154–57).

8. LO: *officia quae ex communitate*; *quae ex cognitione*; Cicero, *On Duties* (*De officiis*) I.43 (LCL 30:156–57). Ed. note: We have conformed the Latin to Cicero's own text. In addition, in the same paragraph, Cicero adds, "If wisdom is the most important of the virtues, as it certainly is, it necessarily follows that that duty which is connected with the social obligation is the most important duty." He then goes on to say that "service is better than theoretical knowledge, for the study and knowledge of the universe would somehow be lame and defective, were no practical results to follow." Therefore, "the safe-guarding of human interests" not only is "essential to human society" but also should, "therefore, be ranked above speculative knowledge."

9. Cicero, *On Duties* (*De officiis*) III.23 (LCL 30:364–65). Ed. note: The examples that follow are taken from this same source (III.23–25 [LCL 30:364–73]).

10. Ed. note: This story is told in Aeschylus's *Agamemnon* and in Euripedes's *Iphigenia at Aulis* (Wikipedia, s.v. "Iphigenia," https://en.wikipedia.org/wiki/Iphigenia).

"He ought to have broken his vow rather than commit so horrible a crime."
Cicero's conclusion: "Promises are, therefore, sometimes not to be kept; and
trusts [deposits] are not always to be restored" or returned.[11] For example, a
man who lent you his sword when he was of sound mind should not have it
returned to him after he has gone insane: "It would be criminal to restore it
to him; it would be your duty not to do so." Thus, circumstances can turn the
honorable thing into something dishonorable. The Stoics in particular made
the conflict of duties a topic for ethics; they were the first casuists. According
to Cicero, Panaetius wrote three books about duties (which Cicero followed
in his *On Duties*) and had wanted to deal in the third book with the collision
between what was apparently expedient and duty. Likewise, Panaetius's pupils
Poseidon and Hecate, as well as, earlier, Diogenes of Seleucia and Antipater
of Tarsus, often discussed such cases.[12]

These questions were taken up also in Christian ethics. Jesus himself resolves cases of conflict: "Is it lawful to pay taxes to Caesar, or not?" (Matt.
22:17–22). "Is it lawful to heal on the Sabbath?" (Luke 14:3–6). Similarly, in
1 Corinthians 7:8–11 Paul says that "it is good" not to marry and that a wife
should "not separate from her husband." In particular, the institutions of
penance and the confessional greatly multiplied these questions in ecclesiastical practice. Since penance was also part of confession, the father confessor
had to know the nature and degree of guilt of every sin and determine the
punishment accordingly. This gave rise to penitential canons and penitential
books in which all possible kinds of sins were classified along with their
corresponding penalties.[13] When auricular confession became canon law in
1215, the penitential books were no longer adequate, and books of casuistry
were produced. The most famous were the *Summa de casibus conscientiae*
of Bartholomew of Pisa/San Concordio (1338), Astesanus of Asti (1482),
Angelo Carletti di Chivasso (1486), Trovomala de Salis (1489), and Pacifico
da Novara (1574).[14] These dealt with all sorts of impossible and possible

11. LO: *promissa non facidenda (sunt) nonnunquam; neque semper deposita reddenda*;
Cicero, *On Duties (De officiis)* III.25 (LCL 30:370–71).

12. Zeller, *Die Philosophie der Griechen*³, 3/1:274n1.

13. LO: *libri poenitentiales*; cf. Mejer, "Bußbücher, Bußordnungen, Beichtbücher"; Schwarz,
"Kasuistik."

14. Ed. note: The bibliographic items that follow in this note and whose full information is
given in the bibliography are specific editions available online, whose dates may not match the
date of original publication. Bartholomew of Pisa (ca. 1260–1346) is more frequently listed
as Bartholomew of San Concordia, after his native place. See Bartholomew of Concordia,
Summa de casibus conscientiae; Astesanus, *Summa de casibus conscientiae*; Angelus de Clavasio
Carletti di Chivasso, *Summa de angelica*; Pacifico da Novara, *Summa confessionis intitulata
pacifica conscientia*; Baptista Trovamala, *Summa Roselle de casibus conscientiae* (1495); this
is an expanded and revised version of an earlier work first printed in 1484 as *Summa casuum*

questions about what to do in particular cases. Often, the answer was *nihil docet* ("to teach nothing"), hence viewed as indifferent. It often led as well to all kinds of subtle answers and advice that invoked the pronouncements of teachers but sowed confusion in consciences.

Beginning in the seventeenth century, the moralists among the Jesuits, especially the followers of Gabriel Vasquez (1549–1604), deduced from this the doctrine of probabilism.[15] Probabilism taught that an opinion, proven by the pronouncement of a respected and experienced doctor as a probable opinion, may be chosen instead of another that by itself was more probable and certain.[16] So it is with Antonio Escobar y Mendoza (1589–1669), who wrote three major works of moral theology.[17] Casuistry was opposed by Pascal in his *Provincial Letters* (1656); it was also opposed by the Sorbonne (1658, 1665) and Pope Innocent IX (1679).[18] The Jesuit Society declared in 1687 that it was not mandatory to teach probabilism, but that members of the order were allowed to challenge it. As a result, some challenged it, others altered it, and so on. In the eighteenth century, Jesuit casuistry distinguished three types of probabilism:[19]

(1) the *aequiprobabilism* of Liguori: when two moral opinions are equal, either may be followed;[20]

---

conscientiae (available online: see Baptista de Salis, *Summa casuum conscientiae*). Bavinck's source for these items is Schwarz, "Kasuistik," 555.

15. See Zöckler, "Probabilismus." Ed. note: Current scholarship also indicates the Spanish theologian Bartolomé de Medina (1527–81) and the Jesuit Luis Molina (1528–81) as key early proponents of probabilism. It is important to remember that probabilism was not intended to served as a general moral guide, but only with respect to difficult matters of conscience. The goal is to produce untroubled consciences.

16. LO: *doctor gravis*; *opinio probabilis*. Probabilism involves two rules: (a) any probable opinion [*opinio probabilis*], though contrary to God's law, exonerates one before God; and (b) of two probable opinions [*opiniones probabiles*], one may choose the least probable and least certain (Janet, *La morale*, 371).

17. Antonio Escobar y Mendoza, *Summula Casuum Conscientiae* (1626), *Liber Theologiae Moralis* (1644), and *Universae Theologiae Moralis, Receptiores absque lite Sententiae Problematicae Disquisitiones* (1652–63). Ed. note: Mendoza's *Summula Casuum Conscientiae* is not listed in WorldCat but is included in O'Neill, "Antonio Escobar y Mendoza."

18. Ed. note: Bavinck is referring to protests by the Sorbonne that led Pope Alexander VIII to condemn probabilism in decrees on September 24, 1665, and March 18, 1666 (see Denzinger, nos. 1101–45); cf. a decree of Pope Innocent IX, March 4, 1679, that condemned sixty-five probabilist propositions (see Denzinger, nos. 1151–1216).

19. Ed. note: Bavinck takes the threefold distinction that follows directly from Zöckler, "Probabilismus," 236; he also provides the following note: "Cf. Wuttke, *Handbuch*³, 1:165 (§38)" (ET: *Christian Ethics*, 1:255–73); see also Janet, *La morale*, 370–90. Janet has a similar but not identical division (*La morale*, 382).

20. Ed. note: To understand *aequiprobabilism* it is helpful to introduce another term, *probabiliorism*, "which held that it is not lawful to act on the less safe opinion unless it is more

(2) the *probabilism* of Bossuet: when one opinion is more probable than the other, then it is the safe choice that must be followed;

(3) *tutiorism*, which was found more among the Jansenists: one was to follow not the more probable, but the safer opinion.

Janet agrees with the Jesuits in (1) and with the Jansenists in (2); for (1) says no more than "obey your conscience."[21] We naturally obey only a law that we know and that appears probable to us; we cannot obey another law. The Jansenists want to judge rigorously according to the objective moral law only; the Jesuits according to the law that is subjectively known: the one who errs in good faith does not sin. However, Janet sides with the Jansenists in (2): the most probable must be chosen over the less probable. Probabilism was even worse when a single doctor of repute could make an opinion probable so that one could sin on someone else's authority (even if one believed it was not right).[22]

Ames says that conscience can err by judging as unlawful what is lawful, and vice versa.[23] Even an erring conscience is binding, since it commands under the form of God's will (thus formally it cannot err)[24] even though its content may err. Whoever dishonors someone whom he believes is the king does dishonor the king. Whoever despises her conscience despises God himself. Whoever acts against his conscience commits a sin, even if his action is good qua substance. If our conscience errs without our will or guilt, we go free when we follow it. Conscience, deeming the unlawful lawful, is binding but does not obligate (i.e., it binds one not to do the contrary but does not obligate one to do what it deems lawful). Such a conscience must be laid aside. A conscience that deems

---

probable than the safe opinion." This view served as a counter to the moral laxity nurtured by probabilism, and the two views were in contention among the Jesuits of the seventeenth century. Aequiprobabilism was an alternative in the controversy between probabilists and probabiliorists and held that it is "lawful to follow the less safe opinion if it has equal or nearly equal probability with the safe opinion" (Wikipedia, s.v. "Catholic probabilism," https://en.wikipedia.org/wiki /Catholic_probabilism). Alphonsus Liguori (1696–1787), founder of the Redemptorist order, was the main proponent of this position in his nine-volume work *Theologia Moralis*, published between 1748 and 1785. Two volumes of an English translation have been published: Liguori, *Moral Theology*. There is also a nineteenth-century synopsis prepared by "a former popish priest," Samuel B. Smith: *A Synopsis of the Moral Theology of the Church of Rome, Taken from the Works of St. Ligori, and Translated from the Latin into English*. This is a highly anti-Catholic polemical version, reflected in the name of the publisher: Office of the Downfall of Babylon. Liguori's understanding of probabilism is considered in chap. 11 of this synopsis, pp. 169–85.

21. Janet, *La morale*, 338. Ed. note: For Bavinck's extended discussion of conscience see *RE*, 1:165–214 (chap. 5).

22. On tutiorism, see Janet, *La morale*, 385–88.

23. Ames, *Conscience*, I.v.

24. Cf. Janet, *La morale*, 335–38.

unlawful what is lawful mandates that one abstain (Rom. 14:23). A conscience that considers it a duty to do that which is permissible is a conscience that obligates. But then the case may arise that we are forced by an erring conscience to sin—for example, to avenge a father's murder on one's mother or on someone else[25]—either in a material sense (by obeying it) or in a formal sense (by not obeying it). Ames says this is not a foregone necessity, because the erring conscience must be laid aside, and this conclusion is a consequence of our sin, not of God's law.[26] There is no general rule for deciding which is better: to obey an erring conscience or not to obey it.[27] Whoever doubts their conscience may in many cases follow the more probable opinion, but one may not act against one's own opinion on someone else's authority.[28] Nobody can simultaneously hold two probable opinions about the same question such that one might do either freely. In doubtful cases, one should make the safest choice—namely, the one that, in every case, is not a sin.[29] But one is allowed to act against an uneasy or hypersensitive conscience, for example, about taking communion.[30] Furthermore Ames says that after the fall the conscience is not a sufficient ground for action; if the conscience errs it must be instructed; if it is unsure we must abstain.[31] But what if the conscience condemns both doing and not doing something? That cannot happen.[32] When opinions contradict each other, one may not submit to someone else's authority but must arrive at one's own opinion. If one remains unsure, one must make the safest choice—that is, the choice in which there is no danger of sinning.[33] But what if a choice must be made, as in the case of Orestes? God's commandments cannot conflict; neglecting a lesser commandment for a greater one is really not a neglect: the greater commandment pushes the other aside. Choosing the lesser of two evils does not relate to the evil of sin, but to punishment. The conscience cannot answer the question which of two sins must be done, because the question itself goes against the conscience.

25. Ed. note: We have carefully and literally rendered Bavinck's interlinear and cryptic clause in Dutch: "*bijvoorbeeld moord van vader wreken aan moeder of [een] ander.*" We assume that the unstated presumption here is that the mother (or someone else) is the murderer.

26. Ames, *Conscience*, I.iv.13.

27. Ames, *Conscience*, I.iv.13.

28. Ames, *Conscience*, I.v.3, 4.

29. Ames, *Conscience*, I.v.5.

30. Ames, *Conscience*, I.vi.3: "If there be any man that is so molested through the consideration of his unworthiness, that he dare scarce be so bold as to come to the Lord's Table, though he find in himself true Faith and Repentance; he may and ought notwithstanding this scruple come to the Lord's Supper."

31. Ames, *Conscience*, III.xvii.20, 21.

32. Ames, *Conscience*, III.xvii.22.

33. Ames, *Conscience*, III.xvii.26.

This subject has been treated often in modern times. Reinhard says that in themselves, objectively, duties cannot collide.[34] When they conflict, that is because of us, our ignorance or our reluctance. Either our understanding does not correctly perceive our duty, or our heart is reluctant to perform the duty. In such cases we need to seek information. He posits the following rules:

1. When rights and competencies clash, what is the most useful for the common good must be done.
2. When rights (for example, pleasure) and duties clash, the latter take precedence.
3. When duties clash, one should take care, as Jesus did in Matthew 22:15–22 and Luke 20:1–8, to avoid the conflict, to prevent it. But once the conflict has occurred, the weightiest duty must be done, and preferably the duty from which one profits least.

Reinhard also quotes Kant, who also denies the possibility of conflicting moral duties,[35] and Fichte,[36] and more authors, including works on casuistry and theological responses. Schleiermacher also denies that conflict is possible; interests and relationships can clash, but not duty, which is always singular.[37] Similarly Daub, Marheineke, Baumgartner-Crusius, and Rothe:[38] the concept of duty precludes any conflict of duties, since every duty is immediate and real and, in any given moment, can be only singular. A conflict of duties does not exist, but a conflict of moral interests can exist—that is to say, partly of moral goals, partly of moral tasks.[39] This can occur when the subject is confused about whether personal and collective tasks, moral and religious tasks, are at odds. But that is not a conflict of personal and social duties, of moral and religious duties. On the contrary, duty is precisely the formula born of that uncertainty by means of the individual's prior deliberation, which then resolves the conflict. Thus, the duty arises out of the conflict. Now it is possible that two duties appear to be at odds, but never two concrete duties

34. Reinhard, *System der christlichen Moral*, 1:173–78 (§200).
35. Kant, *Einleitung in die Metaphysik der Sitten*, xxiii–xxiv (ET: Kant, *On the Metaphysics of Morals and Ethics*, 72–74). Ed. note: Bavinck's source is Reinhard, *System der christlichen Moral*, 2:173, note *a*.
36. J. G. Fichte, *Science of Ethics*, 315–28; Bavinck's source is Reinhard, *System der christlichen Moral*, 2:178, note *m*.
37. See Schleiermacher, *Grundlinien einer Kritik der bisherigen Sittenlehre*, 141–46.
38. Daub, *System der theologischen Moral*, 247–48; Marheineke, *Theologische Vorlesungen*, 1:292–93, 297–304; Baumgarten-Crusius, *Lehrbuch der christlichen Sittenlehre*, 191–94; Rothe, *Theologische Ethik*, 3:411–22 (§848).
39. Rothe, *Theologische Ethik*, 3:412 (§848).

for me. For me, there is always but one duty, the individual authority,[40] and discretionary wisdom infers my particular duty from the objective law, from the conflict. This is not easy, but it can and must be done, and it becomes easier as we mature morally.

According to Martensen, "Duties cannot come into collision when the matter is considered in a purely objective and ideal light. In a normal development the collision of duty will never come."[41] But because "the moral development of the world is not normal, but is only to be rendered so by redemption, it cannot be otherwise than that collisions should occur among the Moments of moral life."[42] For example, duties arising from love of family can clash with those arising from love of country.[43] "In the ordinary course of life, the collision of duties has most frequently its cause in a previous neglect, or because life has not been teleologically planned."[44] In that case, "the collision becomes then the doom of the individual, the punishment of his faulty relation to the law in time bygone"[45]—for example, when an individual makes "an indiscreet promise" that if kept would be sin but if broken might injure others. In that case, the sin is its own punishment.[46] The established rules to resolve the issue are of no practical help. Only our own personal moral development can help us. The more we live in communion with Christ and grow in freedom and the less we groan under former guilt, the easier it will be. Jesus experienced no moral conflict. All such cases are treated in casuistry, which ought not to be a separate discipline.[47]

E. Schwarz claims that objectively speaking, moral conflicts do not exist because duty is always only singular and therefore exists only in and for the subject. Since the very task of the subject is to try to resolve the conflict, it cannot be an objective conflict. To the extent that a person is holy, such resolution becomes easier. For the perfect person there is no collision of duties; moral conflict results from moral imperfection. It did not exist for Jesus, not even in Gethsemane. Abstract rules, an objective ordering of duties, provide no help.[48]

For J. T. Beck the concrete individual duty and freedom cannot be determined objectively but must be determined autonomously by individual con-

40. GO: *individuelle Instanz.*
41. Martensen, *Christian Ethics*, 1:430 (§139).
42. Martensen, *Christian Ethics*, 1:429 (§139).
43. Martensen, *Christian Ethics*, 1:430 (§139).
44. Martensen, *Christian Ethics*, 1:430 (§139).
45. Martensen, *Christian Ethics*, 1:431 (§139).
46. Martensen, *Christian Ethics*, 1:431 (§139).
47. Martensen, *Christian Ethics*, 1:431–34 (§§139–40).
48. Schwarz, "Collision der Pflichten"; Schwarz, "Kollision der Pflichten."

science (Rom. 14:12; Gal. 6:4);[49] errors are then unavoidable, but gradually one will improve. We should, therefore, not turn to casuistry, but instead pursue an ascetic theology[50] that demonstrates the way an individual can acquire such moral competence. Collision of duties presupposes that genuine duties genuinely collide—not just in appearance, not just duty and inclination, not just obligatory duty. Some deny them and say: they only appear that way. Others try to resolve them by means of rules; but that does not work, for the general is much too abstract, and the examples people cite from reality always occur differently nuanced. The New Testament does not know any conflict of duties. But suppose there were a conflict: then a person fulfilling one duty would not act wrongly toward the other duty (that they neglected) by not doing it, precisely because they could not act otherwise. Beck gives the example of someone who owes money and after getting some spends it on the poor out of compassion, making his creditor wait.[51] (But then he is doing wrong toward the creditor.) Thus, the good would not have been omitted, but only what is better. There is no question of guilt. The entire concept of moral conflict is rooted in a fixation on a rigid view of the law and an external concept of duty.[52] From an ethical point of view, an action that by itself is unlawful can be a personal moral act, and vice versa.[53] The New Testament does not know any collision of duties, but it does mention collision between duty and inclination (Luke 14:2–6; Matt. 14:6–9) or dereliction of duty (Matt. 22:17, 21). But although there is no collision as such, a conflict can arise owing to the diversity of the objects toward which we are to fulfill our duties.[54] Such a conflict is resolved by means of a proper coordination and subordination of those objects: the heavenly above the earthly, soul above body, necessity above honor, God's commandments above human laws, and so on. Furthermore, prayer, training, and the like are necessary.[55]

Adolf Wuttke writes that there is only a conflict of duties in paganism, not in Judaism or Christianity. Cicero's example of two men and one plank after a shipwreck is useless and vain; that cannot happen. Collision is mere appearance; it rests on lack of faith in God's guidance. During a difficult delivery the mother must be saved, the child sacrificed—this is a rule of necessity, not

49. J. T. Beck, *Vorlesungen über christliche Ethik*, 2:173–84.

50. Ed. note: Ascetic theology deals with the duties that attend growth in a believer's spiritual life and "directs us to the means by which piety is exercised, especially prayer, fasting, vigil, and so forth" (Bavinck, *RE*, 1:13; cf. *RE*, 1:462–92).

51. J. T. Beck, *Vorlesungen über christliche Ethik*, 2:180.

52. GO: *der Befangenheit an einem starren Gezetsbegriff und äußeren Pflichbegriff.*

53. J. T. Beck, *Vorlesungen über christliche Ethik*, 2:181.

54. J. T. Beck, *Vorlesungen über christliche Ethik*, 2:182.

55. J. T. Beck, *Vorlesungen über christliche Ethik*, 2:182–83.

a collision of duties—rules do not help. Only one action is ever obligatory, the other action is wrong, although it may be difficult to discern one's duty.[56]

Paul Janet passes on a few rules, contained in a footnote, toward a solution from Wolff.[57] Casuistry, though sometimes handled all too subtly, has its rightful place. Kant adopted it; J. Simon said that morality can do without all casuistry, since conscience must decide.[58] But casuistry prepares the conscience. Janet posits two rules:[59]

(a) In case of conflict, higher duties, "by reason of the importance of their object,"[60] take precedence. When one's life is threatened, is it permissible to lie or to deny one's faith in order to save one's life?[61] Janet says that life, being less than the truth, must be surrendered, and defends that against materialist and other objections.[62] Another case is, either deny the faith or lose one's virginity (*Théodore*, a play by Corneille).[63] Think of Lucretia, who was not condemned by Augustine and was yet deceived.[64]

56. Wuttke, *Handbuch der christlichen Sittenlehre*[3], 2:176–78 (§211). Ed. note: The English translation of Wuttke concludes with §152 and does not include §211, "Widerstreit der Pflichten." Wuttke also discusses Cicero's preoccupation with a "collision of duties" in *Christian Ethics*, 1:150 (§27). With respect to the question "Which of several morally good actions which cannot be reconciled with each other is to be chosen as the better?," Wuttke concludes, "Cicero answers very unsatisfactorily and unphilosophically, on the mere ground of the social comfortableness resulting therefrom (*De off.*, I, 43*sqq.*)." Collision of duties is also discussed and rejected in *Christian Ethics*, 2:136 (§84); 2:293 (§139). The index to the English translation includes a reference to 2:280 (§134) under "Cicero—collision of duties," but that is an error.

57. Janet, *La morale*, 307. Ed. note: Janet takes the following rules from Wolff, *Philosophia practica universalis*, §§210–11: "If a precept of law collides with a prohibition, the prohibition wins; if a precept of law together with a prohibition collides with a permission, the permission must yield" (*Si lex proecetiva et prohibitiva colliduntur, prohibitiva vincit; si lex proecetiva et prohibitiva cum permisiva colliduntur, permissiva cedit, etc.*).

58. Janet, *La morale*, 308. Ed. note: The reference is to Jules Simon (1814–96), the French philosopher and statesman; Janet's reference is to Simon's work *Le devoir*, first published in 1853. Janet provides no bibliographic information other than speaking of Simon as "un eminent moraliste."

59. Janet, *La morale*, 310–11.

60. FO: *en raison de l'importance de leur objet*.

61. Janet, *La morale*, 311–19.

62. Janet, *La morale*, 313.

63. Ed. note: Pierre Corneille (1606–84) was a French writer best known for his tragedies. *Théodore* was a comedy and Corneille's first failure (*Encyclopaedia Britannica*, s.v. "Pierre Corneille: French Poet and Dramatist," by Robert J. Nelson, last updated September 27, 2020, https://www.britannica.com/biography/Pierre-Corneille).

64. Janet, *La morale*, 315. Ed. note: In *City of God* I.16–20, Augustine deals with the violation of Christian virgins in captivity and uses the example of Lucretia's rape by King Tarquin's son Sextus Tarquinius to conclude that Lucretia was not an adulteress; he does, however, call her a murderer for committing suicide. He also says that anyone with "any human feeling" would forgive the deed.

Another case: to preach truth by dishonest means, or to remain silent.[65] Vivisection is a similar case.[66]

(b) The wider the group to whom a duty is owed, the higher priority it has: family above individual, state above family.[67] But this is not true without restrictions; otherwise it would be useful if one died for the entire nation (socialism). Think about this: I have to sacrifice *my* interest to that of my family, but not someone else's interest to *my* family. So, the rule is not that the individual ranks lower than the family, but that my interest ranks lower than *my* family, and so for each person.

Must I then, like Brutus and Torquatus,[68] kill my son for the state? Janet says no and yes.[69] When my country wages an unjust war, must I refuse to fight for my country and even fight *against* my country, like Moreau?[70] Furthermore, a higher good can take precedence above a wider circle, and then what? Here

65. Janet, *La morale*, 316.

66. Janet, *La morale*, 317. Ed. note: Vivisection is surgery performed on living organisms for experimental purposes. The term is usually used in a pejorative sense by opponents of all experimentation using live animals. Here is Janet's conclusion: "But, if we consider the interests of humanity, related here to the interests of science, the question takes on another face, and the right of vivisection is no more than a special case of the more general right granted to us by nature of serving animals for our utility, and sparing them all unnecessary suffering." (*Mai, si nous considérons les intérêts de l'humanité, liés ici aux intérêts de la science, la question prend un autre face, et le droit de vivisection n'est plus qu'un cas particulier du droit plus général que nous a concede la nature de nous servir des animaux pout notre utilite, et leur epargnant tout souffrance inutile.*)

67. Janet, *La morale*, 311, 319–24; Janet cites with approval the following from Fénelon: "I owe more to humanity than to my family, to my family more than to my friends, to my friends more than to myself." (*Je dois plus à l'humanité qu'à ma famille, à ma famille qu'à mes amis, à mes amis qu'à moi-même.*)

68. Ed. note: Lucius Junius Brutus (d. 509 BC) was the founder of the Roman Republic. When his sons conspired to overthrow the republic and restore the monarchy, Brutus ordered their deaths. The event is commemorated in a painting by Jacques-Louis David, *The Lictors Bring to Brutus the Bodies of His Sons* (1789; Louvre). Titus Manlius Imperiosus Torquatus (d. 340 BC) was a three-time consul and dictator of the Roman Republic who as general killed his own son for disobeying his orders in battle. The execution is captured in a painting by Dutch Baroque painter Ferdinand Bol (1661–64; Rijksmuseum) (Wikipedia, s.v. "Lucius Junius Brutus," https://en.wikipedia.org/wiki/Lucius_Junius_Brutus; Wikipedia, s.v. "The Lictors Bring to Brutus the Bodies of His Sons," https://en.wikipedia.org/wiki/The_Lictors_Bring_to_Brutus_the_Bodies_of_His_Sons; Wikipedia, s.v. "Titus Manlius Imperiosus Torquatus," https://en.wikipedia.org/wiki/Titus_Manlius_Imperiosus_Torquatus).

69. Janet, *La morale*, 322.

70. Janet, *La morale*, 323. Ed. note: Jean Victor Marie Moreau (1763–1813) was a French general who helped bring Napolean Bonaparte to power but later opposed him, was banished to the United States, and then returned to Europe and advised Swedish and Russian leaders how to defeat France (Wikipedia, s.v. "Jean Victor Marie Moreau," https://en.wikipedia.org/wiki/Jean_Victor_Marie_Moreau).

there is a new, third rule: if the order of goods conflicts with the order of duties, the former has priority over the latter; my *honor* may not be sacrificed to the *pleasure* of my family.[71]

Isaak Dorner denies that a collision of duties as such can exist; the moral law "cannot stand in opposition to itself; for we must ascribe to it perfect oneness in and with itself. Hence there can be no objective conflict of duties."[72] This unity of the law "is secured by the very fact that when I will to do a single thing, I can include in my volition the sum-total of morality, by undertaking what I have to do in the manner prescribed by wisdom."[73] Dorner does add, "On the other hand, *subjective* conflicts of duties are indeed not to be denied. Here belongs the celebrated case of the plank which two shipwrecked persons grasp, while it is able to bear only one."[74] Dorner concludes, "We still insist, after all, that *there can be no such objectively necessary conflict of duties as could not be solved by wisdom.*"[75]

Frank is of the view that harmony was disrupted by sin, that disharmony entered into the morally good, into our goals, and that therefore objective moral conflicts exist.[76] These include conflict between duties toward ourselves and toward our neighbor and God, and conflict between duties toward ourselves and toward the kingdom of God. Such conflict is not merely caused by lack of moral knowledge, but is real; in principle, however, its resolution is found in Christ.[77] At times Frank then covertly recommends a white lie—for example, to a madman who wants to hunt down and kill someone and who may be sent down the wrong path.[78]

So then, is there a conflict of duties?

1. Do Duties Collide?

Most ethicists today deny that conflict of duties is possible: Fichte, Schleiermacher, Rothe, Beck, Dorner, Wuttke, Schwartz, and others say this, because two genuine duties cannot objectively clash; concretely there are never two duties but always just one, and that one duty must be done. Nevertheless, all are compelled to assume that duties can conflict subjectively—that is, for

---

71. FO: *l'ordre des biens*; *l'ordre des devoirs*.
72. Dorner, *System of Christian Ethics*, 213 (§22).
73. Dorner, *System of Christian Ethics*, 216 (§22).
74. Dorner, *System of Christian Ethics*, 220 (§22).
75. Dorner, *System of Christian Ethics*, 220 (§22).
76. Frank, *System der christlichen Sittlichkeit*, 1:393, 406–23 (§22); cf. Schulze, *Über den Widerstreit der Pflichten*.
77. Frank, *System der christlichen Sittlichkeit*, 1:404–5, 412–14, 416–17.
78. Frank, *System der christlichen Sittlichkeit*, 1:419–21.

and in the subject. This occurs in cases where the subject feels confronted by two duties, both of which demand to be fulfilled, and the subject now tries to discover which duty should be done. Rothe says: No, only moral interests and tasks can be in conflict, but duty is singular, for it is precisely from the conflict that the subject infers what must be done. But this is playing with words; there is, after all, a conflict between moral interests and tasks. Everyone more or less admits that conflicts exist. Rothe agrees with this. According to Wuttke, there is always only one action that is obligatory, but it is sometimes difficult to select it from different cases. Dorner acknowledges subjective conflict of moral duties and so on. If the conflict as such cannot objectively exist, its cause naturally must lie with the subject. And that of course is where one looks for the cause. Reinhard says that the cause lies in the understanding, which does not properly perceive the duty, or else in the heart, which is disinclined to do it. Martensen, though accepting collision, looks for its cause also in our abnormal development, in neglect, unfaithfulness, rashness. According to Wuttke, it stems from lack of faith in God's guidance. And Beck says that the whole concept of conflict of moral duties is based on fixation on a rigid view of the law and an external concept of duty. All say that for Jesus, the Perfect One, there is no collision; Holy Scripture gives no examples of it.

Now it is undoubtedly true that the law is singular, whole, an organism, and that God's commandments by their nature never converge in such a way that a need exists to violate a commandment through sin.[79] Intrinsically, in the abstract, all commandments together form a single harmonious whole; love governs all. But the law of God comprises many commandments, specifically two tables: commandments with respect to God and commandments having to do with our neighbor. Concerning the latter there is a great variety of relationships, such as father or mother, son, brother, daughter; domestic servant toward a family; citizen toward the state; professional toward society; and so forth. In a word, we live in a great variety of spheres, and every sphere comes with its own duties. There are duties toward God, to ourselves—our soul and our body, our honor and reputation—and toward our neighbor, family, parents, brothers, country, society, to art, science, and the like. Why would it not be possible that the duties of one sphere clash with those of another? Why could there not be cases in which we are bidden to do this by the duties of one sphere and to do that by those of another? Such cases may well have been possible in the state of original perfection, and even for Jesus. Precisely because we live in various spheres, standing in various relationships to various objects, God's commandments may therefore occasionally conflict,

---

79. Thus Ames, *Conscience*, III.xvii.26.

objectively and genuinely. That is not at all in conflict with the inner unity and harmony of God's law (this remains untouched), but instead is precisely the maintaining of God's law in the various spheres of life, evidence that the law of God controls the whole of our life always and everywhere.

With the older moralists, and our contemporaries such as Martensen, Frank, and others, we accept as possible an objective conflict among God's commandments. However, in contrast to Martensen and Frank, we do not seek the cause of the objective collision in abnormal development, in the disruption of harmony within the morally good that is a consequence of sin. Yet everyone is correct in seeking the cause of collision in sin: if there were no sin, humans in such cases would know instantly and instinctively, and through holy discernment, what they had to do, and they would promptly do it. The case is not at all inconceivable that for Jesus, for example, the duty to honor his parents came into conflict with that of obeying his heavenly Father. We almost have such cases in the wedding at Cana ("Woman, what does this have to do with me?" [John 2:4]) and in the twelve-year-old Jesus in the temple, letting his parents search for him anxiously while staying behind in the house of his Father (Luke 2:41–50). Did he not sacrifice the duty of preserving his life to that of surrendering it as a ransom for many? Yet for all that, these do not seem to be conflicts of moral duties, because Jesus knew at once what he had to do, which duty he had to follow as the highest one, and that is why he exhibits a perfectly harmonious life. He had no moments of not knowing, of doubting, of wavering, of being unsure or unwilling! He was always clearly mindful of his work, his conduct, his word, and he followed it without any uncertainty. With us it is altogether different. When we are confronted by two commandments, two spheres with their distinctive duties opposing each other, we often do not know what to do: we waver, we are unsure, we are forced to investigate, deliberate, and evaluate what to do. There is time for the conflict to become clearly and objectively present in our consciousness, to make itself felt, to become an objective reality for us, as it were.

However, in no way does this mean that the singular law of God is laying upon us, in two of its commandments, differing, mutually exclusive duties that would force us in every case to violate one duty or commandment, and thereby compel us to sin. That is impossible; this would conflict with the unity and holiness of the law and of God himself. No, if two commandments come to us, and one of them, the lesser one, is neglected in order to uphold the greater one, then the lesser yields to the greater, and then the lesser commandment ceases for that time to oblige us to follow it. At that time, it is not our duty to fulfill the lesser command, but rather it is our duty, while doing the greater, not to heed the lesser. This is precisely a proof for the unity and harmony of the law; the lower commandment itself yields to the higher one. Jesus says this himself in Matthew 12:5 (NRSV): "Or have you not read in the law that on the sabbath the priests in the temple *break* the sabbath and *yet* are guiltless?"[80] (so says Ames correctly).[81] Indeed it is true what Rothe and others say, that in each concrete case my individual duty is but one and cannot be two. It is then our duty to obey the greater commandment and to leave aside the lesser. But when two objective commandments and duties oppose each other, the very thing that matters is to know what my specific duty is and what the greater commandment is.

Let us return for a moment to further describe the conflict of duties. It must not be confused with the conflict between duties and inclinations. A conflict may arise between these two, but not an actual clash. Inclination and desire must yield unconditionally to duty. Thus, there was a conflict between duty and inclination with Jesus in Gethsemane: Not my will but thine be done (Matt. 26:39). This is true time and again: we would like to go for a walk, sleep, play, relax, but we may not, because we must work. The moment duty calls, desire and inclination must be silenced. Nor must the conflict of duties be confused with the many assumed and imaginary collisions; a stingy person, for example, tries to convince both self and others that the duty to provide for self and family, or the duty to be frugal, does not permit the practice of charitable duties. This is not a collision of duties but merely a veiled struggle, in refined dress, between *inclination* and duty. That is how a physician defends unchastity with an appeal to health. It is also, for example, how the lawyer defended Jeanne Lorette,[82] appealing to her upbringing, physical constitution, childhood abuse, and lifestyle. Every violation of duty tries to cover itself with another duty. Finally, the conflict of duties must not be confused with the conflict that is born of "obligatory" duties. We sometimes, through our own fault, through neglect, through negligence, face a collision of duties

80. Ed. note: Emphasis added by Bavinck.

81. Ames, *Conscience*, III.xvii.27.

82. Ed. note: Jeanne Marie Lorette was the twenty-one-year-old mistress of Japanese envoy Thikayoshi Sakurada, whom she murdered in a hotel in Rotterdam on March 15, 1885. Her trial was a media sensation, and though Lorette was found guilty, she received only a light, three-year prison sentence because of mitigating circumstances; her attorney convinced the court that there was no premeditation in the crime. The trial and its aftermath were widely covered in the Dutch press. See the following accounts in the *Haagsche Courant*: van den Bergh, "Akte van Beschuldiging in zake Jeanne Marie Lorette"; "Zaak Lorette"; "Laatste berichten"; all are available from the Delpher database of the Royal Library of the Netherlands at www.delpher .nl; for an analysis of the "media hype" surrounding the event, see van Gils, "'Mishandelde vrouw of misdadigster.'" Note that the date of the trial is a helpful marker for dating Bavinck's manuscript.

that could have been avoided and that is unnecessary.[83] Because I neglected to do something in the past, I can later be faced with having to fulfill two duties, or because I made a rash promise to someone in the past, I can today face a situation where I either have to break my word or else cause someone harm. In that case there is indeed a conflict, but due to my own fault.[84] By conflict of duties we mean only those cases in which two real commandments or duties *really* clash, and the subject needs to know which of the two must be followed—that is, which concretely is one's particular duty—so that by fulfilling it one is also guiltless with respect to the other duty.

2. Examples of Conflicting Duties

There are a few examples that have been discussed by almost every ethicist, among others the case of the shipwreck when two people grab hold of a plank that can carry only one person. What is one to do: to drown or let the other person drown? Cicero[85] says that the plank should be surrendered to the one whose life means more to family or state; others say, to the wiser person. Fichte and also Daub say, Do nothing[86]—but then both drown. Rothe says that it depends on everyone's personal character; persons with a heroic nature will sacrifice themselves; the person with a more cautious nature will hold on to the plank without necessarily pushing the other off. But that person would certainly be a scoundrel if he calculated who was the better, the more useful, the wiser of the two, and then perhaps concluded that it was he himself. But before giving this solution (which is not a solution, because it says only what could happen, not what should happen), Rothe observes that the case rests on an impossible assumption, for if the plank cannot really carry two people, it will not carry them during the time they need to deliberate calmly what the duty is and what is to be done.[87] Similarly, Wuttke notes that if the plank carries them for as long as they need to think it over, then it will also carry them longer; if it does not carry them that long, then making a moral decision will be impossible.[88] Dorner, like Rothe, points to the different (heroic or cautious) personalities.[89] In my opinion, this cannot be determined in the abstract; in reality, the examples always occur (says Beck correctly; see above)

83. Rothe, *Theologische Ethik*, 3:416, Observation 1 (§848).
84. Martensen, *Christian Ethics*, 1:431 (§139).
85. Cicero, *On Duties* (*De officiis*) III.23 (LCL 30:364–65).
86. Ed. note: Bavinck takes the summaries of Fichte and Daub (as well as the reference to Cicero) from Rothe, *Theologische Ethik*, 3:419.
87. Rothe, *Theologische Ethik*, 3:419–20 (§848).
88. Wuttke, *Handbuch der christlichen Sittenlehre*[3], 2:177 (§211).
89. Dorner, *System of Christian Ethics*, 220 (§22).

in concrete, nuanced form, and the nuance will be decisive. For example, suppose those two are a father and a son, a mother and a child; then undoubtedly the father or mother will surrender the plank to the child and try in some other way to save themselves, and if that is impossible, will perish but not deliberately drown. The one who relinquishes the plank is not committing suicide but is sacrificing himself for the other. The father and mother will then be doing the right thing. Imagine a situation in which father or mother placed the child in a bassinet that floats while they themselves remained on the ship and perished, giving the child the best chance of survival. If they are two friends, then the nobler one will let go of the plank, and the other, with a different disposition, will hold on to the plank and remain blameless. Here again, the conflict is not an absolute one of either saving oneself or saving the other (in other words, letting either oneself or the other drown), but, rather, of letting the other or oneself have the best chance of surviving. The person who relinquishes the plank is not necessarily committing suicide but is forfeiting any chance of surviving. But the person may yet be rescued while the other with the plank may perish. God can always bring deliverance; there is no question here of suicide.

Another example is a defenseless man who, fleeing from a raging enemy who is pursuing him sword in hand, takes refuge in a house. A third party sees this and is asked by the pursuer whether the fugitive has fled into that house. If the third party answers, "Yes," that answer signs the fugitive's death warrant; if the third party says, "No," it will be a lie. (See below for more examples of lies of necessity!) For Rothe, it depends who the third party is.[90] If, for instance, that person is a soldier, then they will either tell the truth or say nothing but at the same time resist the pursuer and defend the fugitive, if need be, at the risk of their own life. Someone else will justly deceive the pursuer, since the pursuer has absolutely no right to demand the truth and is to be considered an enemy against whom one may employ a ruse. Thus, a little girl would act quite differently than the soldier yet remain blameless. However, Fichte, Daub, and Marheineke said that under no condition is one allowed to lie, and the third party should either remain silent or else tell the truth, if need be at the risk of their life.[91] Wuttke seems to agree with Rothe.[92] Lying is forbidden, but employing a ruse is something different, and if that is not possible, one must either remain silent and step back or else tell the truth but then also do everything possible to save the fugitive by calling for help or other means.

90. Rothe, *Theologische Ethik*, 3:418, Observation 3 (§848).
91. Ed. note: Bavinck takes over the characterization of Fichte, Daub, and Marheineke from Rothe, *Theologische Ethik*, 3:418.
92. Wuttke, *Handbuch der christlichen Sittenlehre*[3], 2:361–62 (§269).

A third example involves what a physician should do when, during a difficult delivery, both the life of the child and the life of the mother cannot be
saved. Should the physician sacrifice the life of the mother for the sake of her
child, or vice versa? It may be a case where the mother's pelvis is too narrow
and the baby's head cannot pass. If this is noticed in time, the physician will
resort to a caesarean section. However, if it is too late for that, mother and
child will both die unless either the child or the mother is killed! Should the
physician sacrifice the life of the mother for the sake of the child, or vice versa?
Physicians say (as does Augustine, it seems)[93] that, if necessary, the child must
be sacrificed in order to save the mother, and they also act accordingly. It has
been objected that the child still has a full life ahead, but the mother has lived
for a significant time already, and therefore the mother should be sacrificed.
But the counterargument has been that an already developed, independent
person has a higher right to life than a child who is just entering life. Moreover, the mother has a family, a husband, other children, and so on. Wuttke
agrees with this.[94] But here too there is no either/or. (The physician should
certainly be intent first of all and above all on saving the mother, but in such
a way that he never actively kills the child—which is forbidden—but tries to
save it too. If the child dies it does not die as a result of a deliberate act but
indirectly, through no fault of the physician, against the physician's will and
intent. Thus, is there a genuine conflict here?)

Apart from these stereotypical examples, the question is, Can the conflict
of duties be categorized under certain rubrics and classes? Most certainly, and
those groups correspond to the classification of duties (see §31).

Group I: Duties toward God that can come into conflict with those toward
people. This group includes duties toward oneself—for example, conflicts involving our life: whether, on the one hand, to deny the truth of God, to curse
God, to worship images, to honor ceremonies, and so on, or, on the other, to
lose one's life, to suffer a martyr's death. Or conflicts involving our honor:
to deny God or be shamefully dishonored, as many women were threatened
during religious persecution. In his tragedy, Corneille has presented this case

---

93. Augustine, *Enchiridion on Faith, Hope, and Love* 86 (*NPNF¹* 3:265). Ed. note: Bavinck's
cautious statement that Augustine *seems* to approve sacrificing the child's life for the mother's
seems to go beyond what Augustine is arguing. In the passage cited, Augustine addresses
the question "When does a human being begin to live in the womb?" He then comments,
"To deny, for example, that those fetuses ever lived at all which are cut away limb by limb
and cast out of the wombs of pregnant women, lest the mothers die also if the fetuses were
left there dead, would seem much too rash." At best, this is a concession when the fetus
is no longer viable. However, in the sentences following that does not seem to be the case
Bavinck has in mind.

94. Wuttke, *Handbuch der christlichen Sittenlehre*³, 2:177 (§211).

in connection with the virgin Theodora.[95] Or duties toward God in conflict with duties toward our parents: think of Perpetua, who had to either deny her faith or oppose her aged father. Or involving duties toward one's wife, husband, children, and so forth, whom one reduces to poverty by remaining true to one's faith, or perhaps delivers over to death or rape or slavery; compare the mother with her seven sons in 2 Maccabees 7. How often has it not been said to martyrs, Deny your faith, otherwise your father, mother, child, and family will be killed or banished? Or duties toward God in conflict with duties toward the government, ruler, emperor, country: the Christians of the first centuries in the army had to refuse to venerate the image of the emperor, taking an oath to do so or else facing death. Or duties toward God in conflict with duties toward society, state, art, science, humanity, and the like.

Group II: A clash of duties among the various duties of the second table of the law. These can be divided into several kinds:

(a) Within the duties toward ourselves, when duties toward our soul clash with those toward our body. Here one can mention Lucretia, wife of Lucius Tarquinius Collatinus, who killed herself with a dagger when she was raped by Sextus Tarquinius and faced the choice of living dishonored or ending her life.[96] One can also mention duties regarding our understanding, when they clash with those regarding our feelings: to tell the truth in a court of law or to lose our honor in the world; duties toward our honor and good name conflicting with those toward our life, and the like.

(b) Duties toward our higher interests—our soul, honor, good name, conscience, conviction—in conflict with those toward our neighbor, family, country, state, society, profession, art, and science. For example, convinced that his country's war is unjust, should a soldier join in fighting or not? If the tsar of Russia has been persuaded that Poland has been treated unjustly, should he then give back its freedom against the interests of his own people?

(c) Duties toward our lower interests, health, rest, and money, in conflict with duties toward neighbor, family, country, and so forth. To harm our health or to impoverish our family would be an example; so would practicing dishonesty or letting our children die of hunger.

(d) Duties toward our family in conflict with those toward our country. For example, should a child report a parent who is conspiring against

95. Ed. note: See n. 63 above.
96. Cf. Janet, *La morale*, 315.

the country? Or accuse them when they have stolen or murdered? Or
duties toward our family in conflict with duties toward the church. For
example, in the case of a minister who no longer agrees with the church's
confessions, should the minister injure his or her name, family, and so
on or neglect duties toward the church and dishonestly remain in the
church? Or duties toward one's family in conflict with duties toward
oneself—for example, when one is called upon simultaneously as the
only daughter to nurse her ailing father and as the wife to nurse her
ailing husband.

3. Resolving Collision of Duties

Earlier ethicists always provided rules. Wolff still supplied some; for example, "If a precept of law collides with a prohibition, the prohibition wins; if
a precept of law together with a prohibition collides with a permission, the
permission must yield."[97] Reinhard supplies these three rules:[98]

(a) When rights and competencies are at odds, then what in the given circumstances is most useful for the community must be done. This pertains to
cases involving legitimate pleasures and relaxation and to the question
of whether one should marry.

(b) When rights conflict with certain duties, then duties must take precedence. For example, the duty not to destroy a family takes precedence
over the equal right to collect a debt.

(c) When duties conflict with each other, then one must investigate whether
one can evade the conflict or fulfill both. If that is not possible, then the
weightier[99] duty should be done. And if that is not clear, then one acts
most safely by choosing that from which one benefits the least.

But more recent ethicists have an aversion to those rules and regard them
as useless; such cases, they argue, must be resolved by individuals themselves.
Everyone will find that easier the further they have advanced in morality; this

---

97. LO: *Si lex praeceptiva et prohibitiva colliduntur, prohibitiva vincit. Si lex praeceptiva
et prohibitiva cum permissiva colliduntur, permissiva cedit.* See Wolff, *Philosophia Practica
Universalis,* §§210–11; cited by Janet, *La morale,* 307n. Ed. note: Bavinck simply copied Janet's abbreviation of Wolff's maxims; originally the first one (§210) read: *Si lex praeceptiva et
prohibitiva inter se colliduntur, prohibitiva vincit praeceptiva*; the second one (§211): *Si lex
praeceptiva vel prohibitive atque permissiva inter se colliduntur, permissiva cedit praeceptiva
ac prohibitiva.* In neither case, however, was the meaning altered.

98. Reinhard, *System der christlichen Moral,* 2:175.

99. GO: *wichtigere.*

is the view of Rothe, Martensen, Schwarz, Beck, Wuttke, Dorner, and others. Therefore, in addition, they all have a strong aversion to casuistry, which should not be a separate discipline (Martensen) and should be replaced by ascetics (Beck). Casuistry, practiced mostly by theologians, was discredited by most philosophical ethicists and is today also discredited by theologians themselves. It is accused of many bad things; and casuistry has indeed often lapsed into subtle, abstract, academic investigations wholly foreign to ordinary life. As a result, people's moral sense, instead of being awakened, was blunted and dulled; casuistry left too little room for a person's moral initiative and consciousness. Casuistry went on to deal all too subtly and meticulously with all kinds of indelicate cases which any other person would be ashamed to even mention, with the argument that a father confessor must be familiar with the cases in order to be prepared to determine the punishment—as though he would not be able, in an actual case, to determine the degree of immorality himself.[100]

However, one should read Perkins, Alsted, Ames, and others to learn the validity and utility of casuistry. Casuistry seeks only to assess concrete cases objectively according to the law of God and inform people. Casuistry does not wish to deaden the moral individuality and moral character, to rob believers of the right to evaluate, but only to inform, to aid the conscience in evaluating. After all, one faces countless difficult cases in life. Never to discuss these at all will not do. Every ethicist discusses them, whether briefly or at length. Modern ethicists, when they say they must leave these cases to the individual person, are also supplying a rule. In fact, if one rejects casuistry, one is rejecting any practical ethics at all. At that point, one should not talk about suicide, dueling, killing in self-defense, divorce, capital punishment, compulsory school attendance, the right to revolt, and so on, each of which is a case of conscience.[101] In fact, the conscience, which then has to decide everything, will then likewise be engaged in casuistry—that is, it will weigh the pros and cons according to God's standards, and then make a decision.[102] Why should those subjective deliberations of conscience not be allowed to be explained objectively in ethics, so that a person's conscience can be informed and protected against wrong thinking?[103] Whether casuistry is treated separately or as part of ethics, or as part of the pastoral disciplines, is a secondary

---

100. Janet, *La morale*, 307–8.
101. LO: *casus conscientiae*.
102. Cf. Sundby, *Blaise Pascal*, 37; Brunetière, "Une apologie de la casuistique." Ed. note: This is a review of Raymond Thamin, *Un problème dans l'antiquité: Étude sur la casuistique stoïcienne*.
103. Janet, *La morale*, 309.

matter. The question is whether casuistry has a right to exist. Where would the boundary be if all casuistry were left to the individual? There is an objective law of God that governs our whole life; it is the rule for life. It is quite wrong to join Beck in explaning the entire concept of conflict of duties from a rigid concept of law, daring to say that "an action which by itself is unlawful [can be] a personal morally correct action."[104]

Let us now try our hand at formulating a few rules.

A. DUTIES OF DIFFERENT CLASSES[105]

Duties toward God take precedence over duties toward ourselves and the neighbor, family, country, government, and so forth: "We must obey God rather than men" (Acts 5:29).[106] The commandments of the first table come before those of the second table: "Whoever loves father or mother more than me is not worthy of me" (Matt. 10:37; see also v. 38). Faith may not be denied; idols may not be worshiped (Daniel and his friends); God's name may not be dishonored, even if it costs us our honor, our life, our parents; and so on. But here, there seem to be exceptions. For example, in 2 Kings 5, Naaman testifies in verse 15, "Behold, I know that there is no God in all the earth but in Israel" (a true, good, monotheistic confession), and requests permission to be allowed to take home an amount of soil, "for from now on your servant will not offer burnt offering or sacrifice to any god but the LORD" (v. 17). Except to this he adds, "In this matter may the LORD pardon your servant: when my master goes into the house of Rimmon to worship there, leaning on my arm, and I bow myself in the house of Rimmon, the LORD pardon your servant in this matter" (v. 18). And all that Elisha said to him was "Go in peace" (v. 19). Here it seems that God's commandment (You shalt not serve any other gods; do not participate in any ceremony for pagan gods) is sacrificed to Naaman's abandoning his post and being incorporated into Israel. This has been variously interpreted. Some have said that Naaman was allowed to do this because he would be bowing only to support the king; everybody knew (since he built his own altar and made offerings to YHWH on it) that his bowing was not kneeling before Rimmon, so he would be doing it for an honest purpose. But the circumstances are nevertheless suspicious, since Naaman himself does not judge it to be altogether right but asks in advance to be forgiven. Others have therefore said that under certain circumstances it is permissible to participate

---

104. GO: *eine an und für sich ungesetzliche Handlung eine personlich moralisch.*

105. Ed. note: This subheading and those that follow have been added by the editor.

106. GrO: πειθαρχεῖν δεῖ θεῷ μᾶλλον ἤ ἀνθρώποις; see de Moor, *Commentarius Perpetuus*, 2:675.

in the ceremonies of a false religion. Especially Roman Catholics have said this, trying to defend missionaries who allow people converted from paganism to keep their pagan customs. And Protestants said that this was permissible in the case of a king's servant—for example, Elector John of Saxony, who had to carry the sword of Emperor Charles V when the king attended mass.[107]

Others translated Naaman's request in the past tense. In this case it would read, "LORD, forgive your servant in this matter, that when my master went into the house of Rimmon and leaned on my hand, I too bowed down etc."— thus escaping the difficulty.[108] Bähr in Lange's commentary series, *Bibelwerk*, writes that this is a special case that can no longer occur in the New Testament. Naaman was allowed to act this way; otherwise he would have had to leave his post, his country, and go to Israel, where at that very time there was so much falling away from God. Moreover, what really mattered was that Naaman would be worshiping and proclaiming the true God in a foreign land. Keil says that since Naaman took home an amount of soil, "he was still a slave to the polytheistic superstition that no god could be worshiped in a proper and acceptable manner except in his own land, or upon an altar built of the earth of his own land."[109] Thus, Keil disapproves of it. Elisha's answer, "Go in peace," is also judged variously. It can refer either to the first request only (for an amount of soil), or to the second (about bowing down). Elisha is either approving and granting the request or condemning and forbidding the action or leaving the matter undecided and merely saying farewell. The true and simple interpretation seems to be this: Naaman's intention is to worship YHWH alone, and he no longer wants to sacrifice to other gods, but only to YHWH. That is why he takes home some of Israel's soil, either because he thinks this will be more pleasing to God since Israel's land is holy (Dan. 11:16, 41; Ps. 37:9, 29; Prov. 2:21–22), or in order to proclaim his union with Israel in worshiping YHWH and to be always reminded to worship YHWH. There is no question, therefore, that Naaman wants to hold on to pagan religion and

107. Bähr, *Die Bücher der Könige*, 291; this is vol. 7 of a commentary series, Theologisch-homiletisches Bibelwerk, edited by J. P. Lange. Ed. note: The English translation of Bähr's commentary does not include the reference to Elector John of Saxony. See Bähr, *Books of the Kings*, 2:63–64. This is vol. 6 in the Old Testament series Critical, Doctrinal, and Homiletical Commentary on the Bible, edited by Johann Peter Lange and Philip Schaff.

108. See especially Bochartus and Dr. Lightfoot. Ed. note: Samuel Bochart (1599–1667) was an influential French Protestant biblical scholar. Bavinck lists no specific source. The second reference is probably to Rev. John Lightfoot, rabbinical scholar and Master of Catherine Hall, Cambridge (1602–75), although there is no mention of a sermon or essay on Naaman or 2 King 5 in the tables of contents of his thirteen-volume *The Whole Works of the Rev. John Lightfoot, D.D.*

109. Keil and Delitzsch, *Biblical Commentary on the Old Testament*, 6:320 (2 Kings 5:17–18).

idolatry (contra Keil). But Naaman is in a quandary: he is a servant to the king, who leans on him when bowing before Rimmon. Naaman is afraid that if he bows along with him, he too may appear to be bowing before Rimmon as well, and that is not his intention; he wants to serve only YHWH. And to that, Elisha (who does not leave the question undecided but gives a definite answer) is responding: Because you do not intend to kneel before idols, and because you will never enter a temple by yourself, and because erecting an altar for yourself clearly shows that you worship YHWH alone and not the idols, and because your kneeling is therefore only a civil duty toward the king, and finally, because anyone, if they want to, can know that it is only a civic duty and that you are not bowing before Rimmon—therefore go in peace. This is also the view of Werenfels.[110] Therefore, there is no question here of violating or sacrificing a duty toward God in favor of a duty toward oneself. In my view, neither did John of Saxony sin when he carried the sword of Emperor Charles V to the mass. One may help another person in fulfilling their religious duties even if they are idolatrous—for example, by not preventing Roman Catholics from attending their church. Or, if my next-door neighbor is a Roman Catholic who cannot walk and would love to go to church, surely I may give him a ride to church in my car.[111]

Another example is the disciples plucking heads of grain on the Sabbath (Matt. 12:1–8; Mark 2:23–28; and Luke 6:1–5).[112] This could appear to be unlawful according to Exodus 16:22–26 (forbidding gathering manna on the Sabbath), but it really wasn't, although the Jews considered it unlawful. Thus, there is no question here of violating a duty toward God. But Jesus appeals to David, who, when he was hungry, entered the house of God at Nob (which was likewise forbidden—namely, in the holy place, where the showbread was located, and in the holy of holies) and took some of the showbread, which was also forbidden. Here, therefore, the duty toward one's life abrogates the duty toward the Sabbath—that is, toward God and his

110. Werenfels, "Dissertatio de Naamane."

111. Ed. note: This last sentence is a marginal note in Bavinck's manuscript, and he wrote "carriage" instead of "car." He also added this parenthetical and obscure comment: "Keller had a path constructed on the Jannerand."

112. Ὁδὸν ποιεῖν in Mark can also mean "go away" (weg gaan), not "make a way" or "clear a path" (banen); see H. Meyer, Critical and Exegetical Handbook to the Gospels of Mark and Luke, 1:33 (on Mark 2:23). Ed. note: Bavinck appears to have misread Meyer here: "The only correct explanation is: they began to make a way (to open a path) by plucking the ears of corn. . . . We must rather conceive of the field-path on which they are walking—perhaps at a place where it leads through a field of corn which it intersects—as overgrown with ears, so that they must of necessity, in order to continue their journey, make a path, which they do by plucking the ears of corn that stand in their way." Unlike Matthew and Luke, Mark makes no mention of the disciples eating.

worship. Jesus also says that the priests in the temple (according to the Jews' position that they adopted on this matter, and which logically follows from it) desecrate the Sabbath and yet are blameless. Now from the case of Jesus's disciples and David one can deduce this rule: although duties toward God come before those toward people, still the moral commandments (toward ourselves, our honor, our life) take precedence over those ceremonies commanded by God. Thus, duties pertaining to the Sabbath are made to yield to the necessities arising from hunger and life, but not of course made to yield to our inclinations or desires or laziness. The First, Second, and Third Commandments can never be displaced by anything else (e.g., nothing can ever oblige us not to worship God), but the Fourth Commandment, entailing something ceremonial, may be supplanted by moral duties of the second table, such as healing the sick. Difficulties can occur here, such as whether a soldier must participate in drills on Sunday. Must a domestic servant do the shopping on Sunday?

B. DUTIES WITHIN THE SAME CLASS

When two duties of the same class conflict with each other (for example, duties to myself or to my family), the weightiest duties take precedence. There are degrees among the virtues, among moral goods. These can be arranged in ascending order. One must rather surrender life than speak falsehood or break a promise. Desdemona did not act well when she lied while dying.[113] The soul takes precedence over the body; honor and chastity and all moral goods take precedence over life. Nevertheless, Lucretia did not act well by committing suicide after having been raped.[114] She should not have consented to her own death, even though she was pressed to do so. In this connection, one could also mention vivisection. Which takes precedence, the duty of science or that of compassion? Is not the intentional causing of suffering, also of animals, impermissible? Surely compassion must triumph over curiosity and inquisitiveness. Nevertheless, this issue can be stated differently: Does not the interest of humanity take precedence over that of animals, and are not the animals given to us for our use? Surely every needless infliction of pain, designed merely to satisfy inquisitiveness, is nonetheless to be rejected. Indeed, this rule must still be expanded.

113. Ed. note: This reference is to Shakespeare's play *Othello*; after accusing Desdemona falsely of adultery and refusing to believe her denial, Othello smothers his wife; as she is dying, her response to the question "O, who hath done this deed?" is to lie: "Nobody; I myself. Farewell. Commend me to my kind lord: O, farewell" (act 5, scene 2).
114. Ed. note: See n. 64 above.

C. Duties of the Soul above All

The interests of the soul of one person take precedence over the material interests not only of myself but also of family, country, and humanity. I may and must be prepared to lay down even my life, money, property, and name for the sake of my country, family, and so on, but I may not commit an immoral act, lie, kill, commit unchastity, and so forth on behalf of country, family, or the like. The value of virtue surpasses that of the world. The soul possesses nothing even when it gains the entire world. It is also something completely different if my country would sacrifice me on its behalf, or if the government would put a person to death so that the entire nation is not lost, as socialism desires.

D. Broader Duties over Narrower

If equal interests of myself, family, country, and humanity conflict, then those belonging to the broadest sphere take precedence over those of the narrower sphere. Those of the family take precedence over those pertaining to myself; those of country take precedence over those of family. Thus, a son is obligated to oppose his father who is conspiring against his country, and, if necessary, to turn him in. Did not justice require Brutus and Torquatus to condemn their sons on behalf of the country?[115] Janet said that nowadays we avoid such heroic actions, which always conflict somewhat with love of parents.

E. When in Doubt, Abstain

Finally, if we are uncertain and in doubt about which of two duties must be performed, then we should do nothing,[116] for everything not arising from faith is sin. Or if we must perform either of two duties, then we should perform the more probable—that is, the one that commends itself as most probable, not to the learned experts but to our own conscience.[117] It is preferable, at that point, that we choose the safest route, the one that at any rate is not a sin, and the one in connection with which we have no interest, and that we suffer disadvantage rather than seek personal advantage.[118] But we may never choose the lesser of two evils, for our conscience can never obligate us to do what it judges to be evil.

115. Ed. note: See n. 68 above.
116. LO: *in dubiis abstine.*
117. LO: *doctor gravis.*
118. Ames, *Conscience,* III.xvii. q. 12.

§31. CLASSIFICATION OF DUTIES

Ancient and Modern Classifications

The Stoics already divided duties into perfect duties and intermediate (ordinary, conditioned) duties.[119] In the Middle Ages the whole of ethics was dealt with in dogmatic theology, under the doctrine of virtue, on the basis of the four cardinal virtues (wisdom, justice, fortitude, temperance) and the three theological virtues (faith, hope, love). Since the Reformation, Lutheran and Reformed theologians have usually treated duties on the basis of the Decalogue. The Decalogue, with its first and second tables, at once suggested a classification of duties toward God and toward one's neighbor. While Lambert Daneau deals with ethics in general (free will, the form of actions, etc.) in book I of his *Ethices Christianae*, in book II he discusses all ten commandments in sequence, and in book III he enumerates virtues and vices[120] in connection with the second table. Calvin adheres strictly to the Decalogue and so classifies duties into those toward God and those toward the neighbor.[121] Polanus in his *Syntagma* likewise first discusses good works in relation to God and then good works in relation to one's neighbor, among which he therefore first deals with love toward self.[122] Ames in books III–IV of his book *Conscience* deals with duties toward God (obedience, humility, diligence, patience, temperance, drunkenness; worship, faith, heresy, confession, fate, the Lord's Supper, singing, praying, fasting, etc.); in book V he discusses duties toward one's neighbor (e.g., justice), also using the Ten Commandments.

Gradually, however, as the number of duties that had to be discussed increased, further classification became necessary. Thus, a third part was added to the twofold division—namely, duties to ourselves. This threefold classification is ancient and found already in Cyprian.[123] Not only was this series of duties toward oneself added, but the duties toward the neighbor were further subdivided as well, and some—for example, those toward state

119. Καθήκοντα τέλεια and καθήκοντα μέσα; cf. chap. 13, n. 5.

120. LO: *virtutes* and *vitia*.

121. Lobstein, *Die Ethik Calvins*, 47–50.

122. Polanus von Polansdorf, *Syntagma Theologiae Christianae*, 595–605 (IX.viii–x).

123. Ed. note: Bavinck provides the following reference: Cyprian, *Three Books of Testimonies against the Jews* 3:28; his source: Wuttke, *Handbuch der christlichen Sittenlehre*³, 1:471. Bavinck correctly takes over the Cyprian reference from Wuttke, but this chapter in Cyprian is about forgiveness of sins and especially the "sin against the Holy Ghost"; there is no mention of the threefold division of duties. The three elements can be found in Cyprian's treatise on the Lord's Prayer, though they are not specifically named as such ("Treatise IV"; *ANF* 5:447–57). It is also worth noting that the Cyprian reference is not found in the text of Wuttke's *Handbuch* but in one of the extensive annotations (#45; from 1:118 [§31]) added by Ludwig Schulze, editor of the third edition. These notes are absent from the English translation.

and government—were treated separately. Pictet,[124] for example, first considers general duties in book II (self-knowledge, knowledge of God, reading
of Scripture), then in books III–IV he examines the virtues in relation to
God (honor, fear, idolatry, superstition, diligence, prayer, oath, vow, Sabbath,
etc.). In books V–VI, Pictet discusses virtues relating to one's neighbor (love,
concord, peace, justice, usury, etc.). In book VII we find virtues relating to
oneself (self-denial, humility, modesty, temperance, hospitality, drunkenness,
prostitution, adultery, fortitude, work, watchfulness); then in book VIII relating to passions; book IX relating to state and occupation, husband and wife,
master and servant, teachers, soldiers, and merchants, and so on. Similarly,
Buddeus. In the second volume of his *Institutes*, he has the following chapters: 1: On Actions; 2: On Divine Laws; 3.1: On Duties toward God; 3.2: On
the Worship of God (love, vow, oath, etc.); 3.3: On Duties toward Ourselves;
4–5: On Duties toward Others (love, oath, usury, etc.); 6: On Duties toward
Spouses, Children, and Superiors; 7: On Duties toward Government; 8: On
Duties toward Ministers of the Word.[125] Thus, the sequence of the Ten Commandments was abandoned.

This division became authoritative especially in the previous century, thanks
to Christian Wolff. He classified duties into (1) duties of man toward himself,
and more specifically, toward his understanding, toward his will, toward his
body, and the duty in regard to our outward condition (that is, our social
position);[126] (2) duties toward God, and more specifically, love to God, fear and
reverence, trust, prayer and thankfulness, and outward wordship;[127] (3) duties
toward other people, and more specifically, toward friends and enemies, duties in regard to property, and duties in speech and in contracts.[128] Christian
August Crusius (d. 1776) regards all duties as contained in and subordinated
to the duties toward God.[129] Stapfer also classifies duties as being toward God,
to ourselves, and to our neighbors.[130] Mosheim classifies them into general
duties (and these again toward God, ourselves, and other people) and special

124. Pictet, *De christelyke zedekunst*.
125. LO: *de actionibus*; *de legibus divinis*; *de officiis erga deum*; *de cultu Dei*; *erga se ipsos*;
erga alios; Buddeus, *Institutiones Theologia Moralis*.
126. GO: *die gesellschaftliche Lage*.
127. LO: *cultus*.
128. Wuttke, *Christian Ethics*, 1:297 (§40).
129. Wuttke, *Christian Ethics*, 1:299–300 (§40).
130. Ed. note: Bavinck's own note ("Stapfer, IV, 421 v.") is not clear. The reference is to
Johann Friedrich Stapfer (1708–75), who wrote a six-volume *Sittenlehre* (1757–66) that was
translated into Dutch by Johannes Willem Haar, *De zeden-leer*. In the Dutch edition, duties
toward God begin at 4:402 and continue through 5:290; duties toward ourselves, 5:291–588;
duties toward our neighbor, 6:1–258.

duties (toward the various associations and estates in which we live).[131] Many other authors do the same. Still others, however, objected to that classification, particularly concerning duties toward God, since God neither benefits nor gains anything from our serving him. Reinhard approves of this division but for his purpose deems another one better—namely, duties with a view to our cognitive capacity, to our capacities of feeling and desiring, hence duties of Christian wisdom, of the Christian mind and of the Christian life and conduct—the latter in a very comprehensive sense.[132]

Kant was the first to distinguish sharply between the legality and the morality of our actions. The former consists in the agreement of the action (of its content, substance) with the law, the latter also in the agreement of the motive of the action (the form) with the law. The former is legal theory; the latter is ethics. Thus, the former gives legal or coercive or perfect duties, which are clear and can be enforced, while ethics deals with virtuous, loving, voluntary, or imperfect duties. Duties in ethics are distinguished by Kant as those toward ourselves, which are either instinctive[133] or moral (the latter also including the duty to practice religion and to consider the voice of conscience, to be divine),[134] and as duties toward others, which are duties of either love or respect. Ethics does not deal with duties toward God; they fall under duties toward ourselves and belong in the study of religion.[135] J. G. Fichte classified duties into two kinds—conditional or mediated duties and unconditional or immediate duties—and each of these further as general or special duties.

Schleiermacher classifies duties as "legal duties and duties arising from love, and duties of vocation and conscience, according to general and individual contributions to society and according to general and individual appropriation."[136] Rothe rejects the classification of morality and legality, perfect and imperfect duties, and says that duty is essentially singular, but at the same time a single system of particular duties.[137] These are classified as duties to self and social duties, each of which contains the whole system of duties but viewed from different angles. Rothe also repudiates the threefold classification of duties toward God, self, and neighbor.[138] Here are his reasons:

131. Mosheim, *Kern uit de zede-leer der Heilige Schrift*, 2:88.
132. Reinhard, *System der christlichen Moral*, 2:179–82.
133. GO: *animalisch*.
134. LO: *homo noumenon*.
135. GO: *Religionslehre*; see Wuttke, *Christian Ethics*, 1:332 (§43).
136. GO: *Rechts—und Liebespflichten und in Berufs—und Gewissenspflichten nach den Gegensätzen des universellen und individuellen Gemeinschaftsbildens und des universellen un individullen Aneignens*; Ueberweg, *Grundriss der Geschichte der Philosophie*, 3/1:76.
137. Rothe, *Theologische Ethik*, 3:428–47 (§§856–57).
138. Rothe, *Theologische Ethik*, 3:447–48 (§857).

(a) It is threefold,[139] whereas the moral goal or end[140] is only twofold: indi-
    vidual and general/universal. Separate duties toward God do not exist,
    for God as goal or end is nothing other than the moral goal itself. Every
    obligatory act is at the same time essentially religious, but the ethical
    and the religious coincide and do not exist alongside each other. All
    duties therefore are religious duties. Nature is always the immediate
    object of our actions.

(b) Rothe objects to this classification also because it proceeds from the
    objects of duty. After all, what is a duty *toward* someone? Because some-
    one has commanded it? But then all duties would be duties toward God,
    and there would be no duties toward ourselves. Or does that refer to the
    object of our action? But in that case, duties toward God and toward
    others would coincide, and we would also need to mention duties toward
    physical nature. And those do not exist; the object of duties is always
    people. And assuming this arrangement, where must we assign the duty
    of self-defense? Surely among duties toward our neighbor. On that as-
    sumption, no list of duties can be constructed. Or does "toward" mean
    something like "in relation to," so that the manner of our actions is
    determined by their relation to the goal of self, neighbor, or God? But,
    in that case, then there are two, not three classes of duties. Duties then
    are something like liabilities.[141] But these exist only toward others, thus
    canceling the duties toward oneself.[142]

Rothe therefore does not want to understand duties toward self and society[143] as duties *toward*[144] ourselves and our neighbors; rather, he views both
kinds from the perspective of the moral purpose for the individual.[145] Nor
does the threefold division have a basis in Scripture.[146] According to Rothe,
"If one proceeds from the object one must also ask: Are there duties toward
impersonal nature?[147] But duties toward nature do not exist, though obligatory codes of action do exist that are not specified by the object but from our
own moral purpose, and are thus duties to self or society.[148] We must employ

---

139. Ed. note: Bavinck uses the term *trichotomisch*.
140. GO: *zittlicher Zweck*.
141. GO: *Verbindlichkeiten*.
142. GO: *Selbstpflichten*.
143. GO: *Selbst-* and *Socialpflichten*.
144. DO: *jegens*.
145. DO/GO: *individuelle zedelijke Zweckbeziehung*.
146. Rothe, *Theologische Ethik*, 3:447–48 (§857).
147. Rothe, *Theologische Ethik*, 3:449 (§858).
148. According to Kant and Marheineke; see Rothe, *Theologische Ethik*, 3:450 (§858).

impersonal nature as an instrument for the kingdom of God. Rothe classifies the duties to self and society[149] in turn as general and particular.

Wuttke[150] identifies the following as objects of our moral actions:

(a) God. There are indeed duties toward God—for example, prayer—just as there are sins against God. But those duties do not exist alongside other duties: duties toward God are simultaneously duties toward ourselves.[151]

(b) People themselves. People are the object of their own moral actions, according to spirit and body.[152]

(c) Other people.[153]

(d) External nature.[154]

And in this way Wuttke views moral acting in relation to God, ourselves, others, and nature.[155] And next he discusses, under the heading of moral goods, (a) Christian perfection and (b) marriage, friendship, state, and church.[156]

Dorner also discusses the manifestation of the godlike personality[157] in relation to God, self, and others. After this he discusses in a separate section the communities of marriage, family, state, art, science, and church.

Thus, Wuttke and Dorner both conceive of Christian perfection and the particular social duties from the vantage point of the goal and fruit of moral goods, of the ideal to be pursued. But in our view, surely this no longer applies to the Christians who fulfill their duties out of gratitude, does it?!

Vilmar first deals with sanctification in general,[158] and then in relation to God and people. Duties toward ourselves fall completely within those toward

---

149. GO: *Selbst-* and *Socialpflichten*.

150. Ed. note: The italicized names that follow are original to Bavinck.

151. Wuttke, *Christian Ethics*, 2:145–48 (§86).

152. Wuttke, *Christian Ethics*, 2:149–51 (§87).

153. Wuttke, *Christian Ethics*, 2:151–56 (§88).

154. Wuttke, *Christian Ethics*, 2:156–58 (§89). Ed. note: Bavinck adds a reference to Wuttke, *Handbuch der christlichen Sittenlehre*³, 2:195–99 (§204), which is not included in the English translation.

155. Wuttke, *Christian Ethics*, 2:145–58 (§§86–89). Ed. note: In his own footnote, Bavinck refers to *Handbuch*³, 1:382–420 (§§78–88; ET 2:98–156) and 2:235–364 (§§218–51), which is not included in the English translation. This reference should be corrected to read *Handbuch*³, 2:289–448 (§§236–69), or possibly *Handbuch*³, 2:318–448 (§§243–69), which is where, after brief introduction (§§243–44), Wuttke discusses the threefold moral action toward ourselves (§§245–55), toward other people (§§256–68), and toward nature (§269).

156. GO: *die Güter*; Wuttke, *Christian Ethics*, 2:274–334 (§§131–52). Ed. note: Bavinck also adds "*Handbuch*³, 2:364v" (§252ff.). This reference should be corrected to read *Handbuch*³, 2:449–663 (§§270–314).

157. GO: *gottebenbildlichen Persönlichkeit*; Dorner, *System of Christian Ethics*, 412–13 (§49).

158. Vilmar, *Theologische Moral*, 2/3:87–200 (§§43–54).

God, for I live virtuously not for myself but for God; and my duties toward God are also those toward myself.

Luthardt accepts the arrangement of duties toward God, toward ourselves, and toward our neighbor, even though they are intertwined. He first discusses those toward ourselves, then those toward God, and then those toward church, family, state, culture, and so forth.[159]

Harless discusses these duties under the title of the "manifestation"[160] of Christian virtue and begins by discussing piety, next manifesting piety in self-edification,[161] the preservation of soul, body, earthly goods, and so on, and then manifesting piety in marriage and so forth.[162]

Beck divides ethics into

(a) the elements of the Christian life: faith, rebirth/regeneration, union with Christ, baptism, and the Lord's Supper;

(b) the development, in the church through worship, of the Christian life in union with Christ, according to the law of love toward God, self-esteem,[163] and neighbor love;

(c) the manifestation thereof in self-development[164] (self-control, prayer, and vocation) into a Christian personality, in marriage, family, and state.[165]

Martensen speaks about individual life in imitation of Christ (love and freedom)[166] and communal life.[167] Thus, he has no separate duties toward God.

Systematic Classification[168]

We now proceed to consider different systems of classifying our moral obligations:

159. Luthardt, "Die christliche Ethik," in Zöckler, *Handbuch der theologischen Wissenschaften*, 3:461–566.

160. GO: *Erscheinung*.

161. GO: *Selbsterbauung*.

162. Ed. note: Bavinck provides no reference in the original; Harless's discussion of the Christian life (with Christian piety as the mother of all virtues) can be found in his *System of Christian Ethics*, 323–510 (§§37–55).

163. GO: *Selbstschätzung*.

164. GO: *Selbstbildung*.

165. Ed. note: Bavinck provides no reference in the original; see J. T. Beck, *Vorlesungen über christliche Ethik*, 2–3:13–280.

166. Martensen, *Christian Ethics*, 1:237–343 (§§71–112).

167. Martensen, *Christian Ethics*, 1:147–236 (§§43–70).

168. Ed. note: Subheading added by editor. The ten different sets of classifications that follow are original to Bavinck, including the numbering. The descriptive headings have been added by the editor for the reader's benefit.

1. Classifying by Distinguishing Cardinal and Theological Virtues

This classification combines the four cardinal virtues of justice, fortitude, temperance, and prudence,[169] borrowed from pagans such as Aristotle, the Stoics, and Cicero, with the three theological virtues—namely, faith, hope, and love. Ambrose is the first to adopt the four pagan virtues and was followed in this by Augustine and Cassiodorus (sixth century). Pope Gregory I added the three theological virtues. This classification has been conventional since Lombard.[170] Thus there were seven virtues, in opposition to seven cardinal sins. There is some value in this classification but also something open to objection.

(a) The four virtues are borrowed from the pagans and thus not taken from Scripture. To be sure, they can be reinterpreted and forged into something with a Christian meaning, so that wisdom becomes worship of God, justice becomes godliness, fortitude becomes courage in God, and so on, but then they lose their original meaning. The classification system becomes an amalgam, rather than an integrated whole, a composite of pagan and Christian ethics.

(b) Nor are those seven virtues coordinated: faith is not one virtue alongside the others, but it is the source principle of the other virtues, their origin and guide. The virtue of justice must embody the virtue of love, and when fortitude is transplanted to the Christian foundation, it is nothing else than the perseverance that presupposes hope.[171]

2. Classifying according to the Ten Commandments

The Reformers, both Lutheran and Reformed, viewed all virtues and duties through the lens of the Ten Commandments. They did this not because they considered those commandments to be the formally correct framework for treating the virtues within ethics,[172] but because over against Rome's self-willed religion they believed that what makes a work a good work is whether it is done in accordance with God's will.[173] Indeed within systematic theology,

---

169. GrO: δικαιοσύνη, ἀνδρεία, σωφροσύνη, σοφία.

170. Cf. §27 above.

171. GrO: πίστις; δικαιοσύνη; ἀγάπη; ἀνδρεία; ὑπομονή; ἐλπίς; cf. Vilmar, *Theologische Moral*, 3:111–12 (§47).

172. E. Sartorius, *Die Lehre von der heiligen Liebe*, xix–xxii. Ed. note: This is a reference to the foreword to the "First Part of the Third Division: 'Concerning the Holy Renewing and Obeying Love'" (GO: *Zur ersten Hälfte der dritten Abtheilung: "Von der heilig erneuerenden und gehorchenden Liebe"*).

173. Luthardt, *Die Ethik Luthers*, 70: "The other thing that turns a work into a good work is God's will and command. For that is 'the first thing to know, that there are no good works except those that God has given.'"

the Decalogue remains the best guide for summarizing virtues and duties, as with Calvin[174] and the Heidelberg Catechism. This is the case if one does not want to give a complete ethics but only a summary.[175] Furthermore, the Decalogue must remain the norm also for ethics. The law remains valid also for the believer; it loses only its temporary (ceremonial) and national husk; what is eternal in it endures.[176]

Rothe is therefore wrong when he asserts with the Socinians and others that the entire Old Testament law, including the Decalogue, has been set aside and that the New Testament has brought an "altogether new" law.[177] He considers this law to be "the Christian morality in the broadest sense of the word,"[178] of which Christ through the Holy Spirit in the church is the foundation, and which is normed by the appearance of Christ and the apostolic legislation in the New Testament.[179] This is, of course, utterly wrong. The Decalogue is and remains the moral law, the sum of all ethical duties and good works. Nevertheless, the Decalogue is less suitable as a guide for treating duties within a systematic discipline of ethics for the following reasons:

(a) The Decalogue may be the sum[180] of the law, yet it has been extensively explicated, interpreted, unfolded throughout the Old and New Testaments. If we based our own ethics on the Decalogue, we would run the risk of inadequately benefiting from the rich material about family, parents and children, master and servant, Christian virtues like meekness, humility, forbearance, and so on. Even so, Sartorius still based his work on the Decalogue[181] and says that every Christian moralist should do so.[182] Our systems cover wide ground, but as a result they weaken the exalted majesty and profound impact of the divine law.

(b) If we take the Decalogue as our guide, we lose the necessary breadth, and our ethics can do little else than deal incidentally, as appendages, with topics like the moral nature of humanity and the duties toward oneself, state, church, society, art, science, recreation, socializing. The

---

174. *Institutes*, II.viii.

175. Heidelberg Catechism, Lord's Days 34–44.

176. See §27 above.

177. Rothe, *Theologische Ethik*, 3:380–81 (§819).

178. GO: *Sitte*; Rothe, *Theologische Ethik*, 3:381 (§820).

179. Rothe, *Theologische Ethik*, 3:384–85 (§821).

180. LO: *summa*.

181. E. Sartorius, *Die Lehre von der heiligen Liebe*, 275–531. Ed. note: Sartorius begins his exposition of the Ten Commandments on p. 275.

182. E. Sartorius, *Die Lehre von der heiligen Liebe*, xxi.

Decalogue gives principles, especially practical ones, but it does not talk about the spheres in which we live our lives. And a variety of commandments arise in different spheres.[183] That is why the Reformed introduced a third part about duties toward oneself, and the duties toward the neighbor are also further distinguished with respect to, for example, family life.

3. CLASSIFYING BY DISTINGUISHING CONTENT AND FORM, LEGALITY AND MORALITY

There also exists a classification of moral duties that distinguishes content and form, legality and morality. This was done especially by Kant. However, that classification is quite out of place in ethics and belongs only in jurisprudence. It is not present in Scripture. A purely legal action may be outwardly in agreement with the law and thus not punishable by the state, but it is not thereby a moral act. For an action to be moral, both its form (disposition) and content (the action itself) must conform to the law. "True ethical legality is itself morality."[184] The concept of legality is therefore out of place in ethics. And even in the sphere of law a merely legal action is still insufficient, even though it is not punishable. The law should live in people's hearts, in the disposition of citizens.[185] Accordingly, Schleiermacher, Daub, Baumgarten-Crusius, J. Müller, and others have banned the concept of legality from ethics.

This division is connected in turn to that between legal duties and duties of virtue.[186] The former can be imposed upon us by the state, but not the latter. This distinction too stems from jurisprudence, in particular from natural law. Ethics knows only duties of virtue, of love, of gratitude; for love alone is the fulfillment of the law. These two kinds—legal duties and duties of virtue—are sometimes also called compulsory duties and duties of love,[187] or also perfect duties and imperfect duties,[188] or narrow duties and broad duties, terms used by many after the Stoics. Perfect duties are those

183. Thus, also Wuttke, *Christian Ethics*, 2:26–29 (§56).
184. DO: *De ware ethische legaliteit is zelve moraliteit*. Ed. note: Bavinck placed this within quotation marks, suggesting that it was a direct quote. A possible source: Hartenstein, *Die Grundbegriffe der ethischen Wissenschaften*, 334; GO: *die wahre ethische Legalität ist selbst Moralität*.
185. Rothe, *Theologische Ethik*, 3:431–35 (§856n2); Reinhard, *System der christlichen Moral*, 2:164 (§197).
186. GO: *Rechts- und Tugendpflichten*.
187. GO: *Zwangs- en Liebespflichten*.
188. DO: *volkomen en onvolkomen plichten*; Bilderdijk, *Verhandelingen*, 61–94. Ed. note: Bavinck also added the name of Leibniz with a question mark.

which everyone has to perform, which are valid for all; imperfect duties are those that the agents themselves must recognize and about which they must convince themselves that those duties are obligatory. But that cannot be, for then the distinction coincides completely with concrete and abstract duties, or Kant's "pure and applied" duties.[189] They are also called categorical and hypothetical, general and special (and individual) duties.[190] Related as well is the distinction between duties of justice and duties of benevolence in von Hirscher,[191] and that between negative (legal) and positive (love) duties in von Ammon.[192] A duty is always strictly binding, never broad,[193] imperfect, contingent, meritorious, never a counsel[194] (for that is a notion that is really implied in the Roman Catholic idea).

4. CLASSIFYING ACCORDING TO THE DIFFERENT HUMAN CAPACITIES FOR KNOWING, FEELING, AND WILLING

Reinhard regards morality as the preeminent means for ennobling and forming our own nature. Thus he considers all duties in their relation to developing our capacities[195] for perfection, and therefore divides them into duties toward our capacities for knowing, feeling, and willing, or as duties of wisdom, of feeling, and of life or conduct.[196] Vilmar prefers to arrange them into duties of sanctification toward body, soul, and spirit (just as he arranges sins),[197] but he finds insufficient basis for this in Scripture. First Thessalonians 5:23 is not as sufficiently compelling as 1 John 2:16 for the classification of sins. Rothe arranges duties into duties to self and social

189. GO: *reine; angewandte.*

190. Von Ammon, *Handbuch der christlichen Sittenlehre¹*, 1:378; cf. Rothe, *Theologische Ethik*, 3:431–35 (§856n2).

191. DO: *plichten der gerechtigheid en der goedheid.* Ed. note: Bavinck provides no reference for von Hirscher; he likely took the reference from Rothe, *Theologische Ethik*, 3:437 (§856n2); Rothe refers to "v. Hirscher, a. a. D, II., S. 390–97. 400f." See von Hirscher, *Die christliche Moral als Lehre*, 2:390–97 (§§355–61), 400f. (§§364f). A likely terminus for the second part is p. 411 (§366).

192. In von Ammon, *Handbuch der christlichen Sittenlehre¹*, 2:262–66. Ed. note: Bavinck does not supply a specific reference for von Ammon; he cites Rothe, *Theologische Ethik*, 3:431 (§856n1), where it is found; Bavinck also adds references to Reinhard, *System der christlichen Moral*, 2:165, and to Janet, *La morale*, 241–65, for a discussion about perfect or narrow duties contrasted with imperfect or broad duties (FO: *devoirs stricts et devoirs larges*; Bavinck has DO: *volkomen of enge en onvolkomen of ruime plichten*).

193. FO: *large.*

194. LO: *consilium.*

195. DO: *vermogens.*

196. DO/GO: *als plichten der wijsheid, des Sinnes, en des levens of gedrags*; Reinhard, *System der christlichen Moral*, 2:180–81.

197. Vilmar, *Theologische Moral*, 2/3:111. Ed. note: Cf. §9, *RE*, 1:100–116.

duties,[198] as does Burger, who also rejects the threefold division, though he also believes that we have duties and even rights vis-à-vis God, which are answered by reward.[199] Yet he does not want to conceive of them in the ordinary sense of duties toward ourselves and toward our neighbor[200] but as duties with a view to the moral goal of the individual and the community. That moral goal, to be sure, is singular—every morally acting agent is by that fact alone[201] acting as a member of a moral community;[202] the law always intends both the individual and the universal moral goal. Thus, every duty has a twofold moral purpose.[203] When working on their own personal development,[204] everyone must keep both moral purposes in mind, thus also the community's goal—though not at the expense of their own personal goal—but both goals, simultaneously and entirely. Thus all duties to self are simultaneously social duties and vice versa.[205] Caring for one's own spiritual well-being simultaneously overlaps with caring for the spiritual well-being of others, even though in the present, the two types of duties still occasionally diverge.[206] Each of these two types of duties therefore contains all duties, but from different angles.[207]

Now the greatest objection to this view is that self-development[208]—the sanctification of ourselves and others—is considered the highest goal, the ultimate aim. To the question "Why ought I to do this?," the answer here is, Because it will make you and others perfect, because you ought to be perfect. Thus duties are exclusively seen from the point of view of the subject, whereas the obligatory nature of every duty lies not in my perfection and salvation, but in God, in his commandment, and has as its goal, its ultimate end, God's glory.[209] Moreover, this view of duties from the standpoint of humanity leads imperceptibly and automatically to the meritorious value of our works, of our self-development:[210] I perfect myself for my own sake, and therefore I have a reward with God. In the end, this view conflicts with the *theo*logical character of morality.

198. GO: *Selbst- und Socialpflichten*; Rothe, *Theologische Ethik*, 3:431 (§856).
199. Burger, "Pflicht"; as does Rothe, *Theologische Ethik*, 3:427–28 (§855).
200. As Rothe does, *Theologische Ethik*, 3:446 (§857).
201. LO: *eo ipso*.
202. Rothe, *Theologische Ethik*, 3:398 (§839).
203. GO: *Zweckbeziehung*.
204. GO: *Ausbildung*.
205. GO: *Selbstpflichten*; *Socialpflichten*.
206. Rothe, *Theologische Ethik*, 3:403–6 (§845).
207. Rothe, *Theologische Ethik*, 3:438–48 (§857).
208. GO: *Selbstbildung*.
209. Rothe himself admits this in *Theologische Ethik*, 3:443 (§857).
210. GO: *Selbstbildung*.

5. CLASSIFYING ACCORDING TO THE OBJECT OF MORALITY

(a) The Self[211]

Some people accept only duties toward themselves.[212] In practice these are all the selfish people who live only for themselves. Actually, they do not really accept duties toward themselves, but only rights. An example in the moral realm[213] is Thomas Hobbes, according to whom good and evil only differ in the personal opinion of the subject; self-love is the highest law, and everyone has a rightful claim to everything.[214] But the monarch brings them into harmony. According to Helvétius, self-love is the basic drive of all moral conduct.[215] And self-love is based in turn on sensual desire. Rousseau writes that the supreme moral law is to take care of your own well-being as best you can and with the least possible harm to others.[216] Fundamentally this is also the view of utilitarianism, therefore of Epicurus as well as of J. Stuart Mill, although the latter says that we must strive after "the greatest happiness of the greatest number." The position of utilitarianism has no answer for this question: Why should I follow the majority and accept its judgment about what makes people happy?

(b) Others

Then there are people who accept only duties towards others. Thus, the socialists and the communists of our day prefer to talk about the duties of other people toward them but not of their duties toward other people. We also need to mention in this connection those who deduce and explain all morality (e.g., conscience) in terms of social instincts, in contrast to egoistic instincts (Darwin, Bain, Spencer, et al.). We should also think here of Auguste Comte and his adherents, as well as of Schopenhauer, who seeks the foundation of morality in compassion. This position, however, provides no possible answer to the question "Why should I follow my altruistic inclinations and live for others?"

211. Ed. note: The identifying letters under #5, a–c, are original to Bavinck, as are the numbered headings 1–10; the subheads accompanying each number were added by the editor.

212. Ed. note: In the margin Bavinck added "Epicurus, Max Stirner, *Der Einzige und sein Eigenthum*"; ET: *The Ego and Its Own*. For more on the first English edition, see the bibliography. Stirner concludes his preface: "Nothing is more to me than myself!"

213. DO: *moraalgebied*.

214. Wuttke, *Christian Ethics*, 1:304 (§41).

215. Wuttke, *Christian Ethics*, 1:314 (§41). Ed. note: Claude Adrien Helvétius (1715–71) was a French philosopher who believed that "self-interest, founded on the love of pleasure and the fear of pain, is the sole spring of judgment, action, and affection" (Wikipedia, s.v. "Claude Adrien Helvétius," https://en.wikipedia.org/wiki/Claude_Adrien_Helv%C3%A9tius). In the margin Bavinck added "Mandeville (cf. Richard Falckenberg, *Geschichte der neueren philosophie von Nikolaus von Kues bis zur gegenwart*, 151–52, 190)."

216. Wuttke, *Christian Ethics*, 1:317 (§41).

(c) God

Other people accept only duties toward God. In a certain sense this is true (see below). But many say this while ignoring the duties toward their neighbor and toward themselves. They acknowledge only the religious life and underestimate the moral life. They make everything religious, think only of the soul, not the body; only of eternity, not of time. This is true especially of Pietists and Methodists.[217]

6. BY THE DIVISION OF THE TEN COMMANDMENTS

Viewed properly, there is only one duty, that of love, which is the fulfillment of the law (Rom. 13:10). And there actually is only one object of that love—namely, God. Everything else—people, angels, nature, art, and so forth—may and must be loved only in God and for God. The sole end of all things—ourselves, our neighbor, the state, and the like—is God's glory. God is also the only one who obligates us in his law; he alone compels us in our conscience. A duty exists only because there is a God who can obligate us. For duty is an obligation not only to do things but also to will them.[218] God obligates us in such a way that we feel obligated also to *have to will* what God commands. People and animals can force us to do things. God alone can obligate us, can oblige us to will. He alone is sovereign over our conscience, the Lord also of our innermost being, the Master of and in the deepest depth of our heart. "I am the LORD your God" serves as a heading above all the commandments. And for this reason, for this reason alone, we are not only to love him but also for his sake to love our neighbor, not kill him, and so forth. We are to love our neighbors not because they are lovable, good, beautiful, and rich, but for God's sake. Actually, therefore, there is only one type of duty—or better: there is but one single duty—toward one object only—namely, God. All other duties acquire force only in and through that and under that. All duties are therefore religious duties. Thus, the nature of duty does not disclose any classification of duties; all duty is mandatory for God's sake and at God's behest; there are no broad, imperfect duties. The end goal, too, offers no basis for classification;[219] all things must be done for the glory of God.

But besides an ultimate end there is also, under God, a subordinate end (which Pietists fail to appreciate all too much). It is not an ultimate goal, yet still a relative goal, a secure stage for our conduct.[220] That is the creation, the

---

217. Ed. note: See *RE*, vol. 1, chap. 8 (§20).
218. Bilderdijk, *Verhandelingen*, 47.
219. LO: *principium dividend*.
220. DO: *rustpunt*.

world of creatures: angels, humans, nature, art, science, and so on and so forth. They may be—nay, must be—loved in God and for God, but they are nevertheless truly objects of our love.

Therefore, God himself classifies the law as two tables: love of God and love of neighbor (Matt. 22:37–40). There are differences of opinion about how to divide these two tables. The Old Testament calls the Decalogue "the Ten Words"[221] and provides a different reading in Deuteronomy 5 than in Exodus 20.[222] Jesus divides them into two tables (Matt. 22:37–40), a division with which 1 Timothy 1:5, Romans 13:8, and Galatians 5:4 are not in conflict.

Three divisions are especially common:

i. The oldest is found already in Josephus[223] and in Philo. In the Christian church it was advocated especially by Origen, then taken over by the Orthodox Church, the Reformed churches, and the Socinians. In this division the words "I am the LORD your God" serve as the heading. "Thou shalt have no other gods etc." is the First Commandment, and "Thou shalt not make any graven images" is the Second Commandment. And the commandment against coveting is a single one.

ii. The Jewish division is as follows: the words "I am the LORD your God" are not a heading but the first word or commandment. "You shalt have no other gods etc." and "You shalt not make any graven images" together make up the Second Commandment; and the commandment against coveting is also one.

iii. In the division of Augustine, Roman Catholics, and Lutherans, "I am the LORD your God" is the heading, and "You shalt have no other gods etc." and "You shalt not make any graven images" make up the First Commandment. "You shalt not covet your neighbor's house" is the Ninth Commandment, and "You shalt not covet your neighbor's wife etc." is the Tenth Commandment.

In response, we offer the following:

(a) The Jewish view that the words "I am the LORD your God" are not the heading but the First Commandment certainly cannot pass muster. All the other commandments begin with "You shall"; this one does not, so

---

221. Exod. 34:28; Deut. 4:13; 10:4: עֲשֶׂרֶת הַדְּבָרִים; οἱ δέκα λόγοι, τὰ δέκα ῥήματα (LXX).

222. Especially in the Sabbath commandment, which in Exodus is grounded in the creation but in Deuteronomy by the deliverance from Egypt.

223. Josephus, *Jewish Antiquities* III.91–92 (LCL 242:361).

it is not a commandment. It is a heading and contains the general basis of obligation why Israel should serve God.

(b) Our (Reformed) First and Second Commandments are essentially two. Not to serve other gods does not yet imply at all that the one true God could not be worshiped in the form of an image; hence it is expressly forbidden in the Second Commandment. Oehler acknowledges this.[224]

(c) The prohibition of coveting, by contrast, is essentially one, even though it speaks of the neighbor's house and then his wife, maid-servant, and so on. The repetition of "You shall not covet" in no way justifies dividing it into two commandments. Mark 10:19–22 and Romans 7:7 and 13:9 clearly regard this prohibition of coveting as one. Moreover, the various readings of this commandment in Deuteronomy 5 and Exodus 20 assume that the commandment is one.

(d) Finally, the antiquity of this division argues for the Reformed view.

As for the division of the Decalogue into two tables, there are also three views:

(a) According to the Lutheran and Roman Catholic division,[225] three commandments belong to the first table, and seven to the second table—numbers that were then related to the Trinity and the sacred number seven. For all intents and purposes, this division agrees with that of the Reformed, but according to the latter the three commandments are really four, because worshiping other gods and making images are two distinct commandments, not one, as in the former, and because the commandment against coveting is one, not two, as in the former.

(b) Others assign five commandments to the first table and five to the second table, counting the commandment to honor father and mother as the last in the first table. Many Jews, Josephus, and Philo hold to this, as well as Irenaeus.[226] They argue that parents are not neighbors, but representatives of God, of the Creator and Ruler. Duties toward parents, therefore, belong to piety and not to uprightness.[227] But that is incorrect[228] because parents being human, the relation to them is a totally different one from the (religious) relation to God; clearly, therefore, honoring one's parents is the first commandment of the second

224. Oehler, *Theology of the Old Testament*, 186 (§85): "The command in ver. 3 to worship Jehovah alone does not preclude His being worshipped by an image."

225. De Moor, *Commentarius Perpetuus*, 2:678.

226. Oehler, *Theology of the Old Testament*, 188n18 (§85); Delitzsch, "Dekalog," 536.

227. LO: *pietas; probitas.*

228. Staudinger, *Die zehn Gebote;* de Moor, *Commentarius Perpetuus*, 2:677.

table, laying the groundwork for the entire social order. The Reformed also tried to prove that this commandment belongs to the second table based on Ephesians 6:2: it is "the first commandment with a promise." For it is simply not the first commandment with a promise; after all, the Second Commandment also contains promises (albeit along with threats!).[229] Nevertheless, it is indeed the first commandment—of the second table, that is. Otherwise a "first commandment with a promise" would also assume that it was followed by more commandments with a promise, which is not the case.

(c) According to the Reformed division, there are four commandments in the first table and six in the second.[230] This is the right division. It makes a fundamental distinction between our relationship toward God and toward neighbor, between religion and morality. It is no objection to this division to say that then far more words appear in the first table than in the second; this same objection applies equally to all other divisions as well. What matters is the content, the intrinsic differences of the "words"—that is, the commandments.[231]

And in this way the divine law itself provides the ready-made division of duties toward God distinguished from those toward the neighbor. This division is reiterated in the New Testament by Jesus and Paul and maintains the following:

(a) God is the ultimate goal. All things are in God and for the sake of God—that is, religion.

(b) The independence of the creature, over against pantheism. There are duties toward God and also duties toward the neighbor. Therefore, "*toward* God" and "*toward* neighbor" mean "in relation to."[232]

7. OBJECTIONS TO THE DISTINCTION BETWEEN RELIGION AND MORALITY

However, objections have been raised against this division between religion and morality, specifically against the notion that we have duties toward God. These objections arise not only from the side of those who do not believe in God—for example, from the materialists and from those for whom there can

---

229. Oehler, *Theology of the Old Testament*, 190 (§86n3).
230. Calvin, *Institutes*, II.vii.12.
231. For literature referring to this division, see Oehler, *Theology of the Old Testament*, 184–91 (§§85–86); Wuttke, *Christian Ethics*, 1:247–55 (§37); Wuttke, *Handbuch der christliche Sittenlehre*[3], 2:160; Suicerus, *Thesaurus Ecclesiasticus*, s.v. Δεκάλογος.
232. Rothe, *Theologische Ethik*, 3:441 (§857).

be no question of duties toward God. They arise also from the side of those who still accept a God. We can distinguish three different sets of reasons for the rejection of the idea that we have duties toward God.[233]

(a) *There are no duties toward God because all duty is reciprocal; all duty presupposes rights as well.*

If we have duties toward God, then he also has duties toward us; then not only does he have rights over and with respect to us, but we too have rights over him and with respect to him. This is Kant's position. And this can then be expanded further:[234] duties presuppose that we provide advantage to someone, make someone happier—which cannot be done with respect to God. This view presupposes that our works have merit and deserve reward, and so introduces the Pelagian and Roman Catholic view of good works as being meritorious. To be sure, among people, duties and rights are correlative: every duty toward my neighbor presupposes a right on their part, and every duty of my neighbor toward me presupposes a right on my part. Right in general is "a moral power"[235] (no matter how strong I am, I am morally powerless to kill a child in the cradle), just as duty is "a moral necessity";[236] or, right is "the possibility that is found with someone to do something or not to do it."[237] Human right is not, as Spinoza, Hobbes, and Proudon believe, originally the right of the strongest, of physical force. Nor is human right grounded in and arising from human need, as Bilderdijk and the socialists contend, for where is the beginning and end of human need?[238] In actual fact, basing a right on human need is again to say that whoever is the strongest has the greatest right.[239] Nor is human right grounded in human freedom (Kant, Fichte), because why people *ought to be free*, why their person is inviolable, is exactly what needs

---

233. Ed. note: We follow Bavinck in listing the three sets of reasons as "a–c"; the editor separated the headings from the paragraphs that follow and reworded the opening sentence in each set.

234. See Mosheim, *Kern uit de zede-leer der Heilige Schrift*, 2:89–90.

235. FO: *un pouvoir moral.*

236. FO: *une nécessité morale*; Janet, *La morale*, 266.

237. GO: *die bei Jemand vorkommende Möglichket, etwas zu thun oder zu lassen*; Reinhard, *System der christlichen Moral*, 2:165; Rothe, *Theologische Ethik*, 3:427 (§855).

238. DO: *maar waar is begin en einde van 's mensen behoeften.* Ed. note: The reference to Bilderdijk is to his *Verhandelingen*, 41–94, where Bilderdijk attempts to ground morality in the basic, created needs of human nature rather than in reason or understanding. The question that concludes the sentence is Bavinck's and is addressed to Bilderdijk's starting point. Bavinck discusses this at greater length in his *Bilderdijk als denker en dichter*, 130–35, where he summarizes Bilderdijk's position thus (135): "Rights and duties, therefore, are both grounded in human nature, in human needs" (*Rechten en plichten zijn dus beide in de natuur des menschen, in hare behoeften, gegrond*).

239. Janet, *La morale*, 271–72.

explaining.[240] According to Janet himself, human right is grounded in the "the dignity of the human nature,"[241] in its intrinsic worth, and consists in the responsibility for the dignity of that nature, which one possesses, after all, in the right to perfect oneself.[242] The dignity of human nature, however, is a false foundation for morality; it nourishes pride, cannot be defined, and can only be assumed a priori. How is one to combine it with humility, meekness, contrition, esteeming others better than oneself, and the like?

Now many say that we have rights also with respect to God, and that God has (not just rights but) duties also with respect to us.[243] Otherwise, they say, God becomes capricious, a despot and a tyrant, an absolute power, as with Hobbes. Some Reformed theologians, such as Moïse Amyraut and William Twisse, thought in terms of such an absolute power.[244] But there is no absolute capriciousness in God. His justice is his holy nature itself, and it is never separated from his love and his goodness.[245] Nevertheless, it is impermissible to say that God has duties with respect to us, because

(i)   what God does, he does spontaneously (Janet),[246] as a matter of course, according to his own holy nature, and not because a law above him constrains and commands him; and

(ii) a duty toward someone assumes that that someone is coordinate with us, of the same rank, that we are bound to that person, dependent upon that person, and thus assumes that we do something *for their sake*. And that is not the case with God. He does all things not for our sake—he is not bound or obligated by us—but only and purely for his own sake. He loves us for his own sake, not for our sake.

Therefore, God has no duties with respect to us. And for that reason, it simply is not permitted to say that we have rights with respect to God. God is not bound to us but only to himself, to his own holy nature. Rights on our part would suppose that God can or ought to act otherwise than he does. Rights secure us against possible invasion and attack. We are not permitted to say: God *may* not act otherwise than he does. Rather: he *can* and *will* not

240. Janet, *La morale*, 273.
241. FO: *dignité de la nature humaine*.
242. Janet, *La morale*, 278.
243. For example, Rothe, *Theologische Ethik*, 3:427–28 (§855); Janet, *La morale*, 289.
244. See *RD*, 2:234–35. Ed. note: Moïse Amyraut (1596–1664) was a French Huguenot Reformed theologian who studied and taught at the Academy of Saumur in Western France; William Twisse (ca. 1577–1646) was an English Calvinist who served the Westminster Assembly.
245. De Moor, *Commentarius Perpetuus*, 1:682–94.
246. Janet, *La morale*, 290.

act otherwise. And this fact—that God acts as the Supreme Wisdom, Love, and Righteousness—this secures us against everything. We have no rights, we need no rights, with respect to God. Neither we ourselves, nor our rights, nor our dignity, sustain and secure us with respect to possible encroachment and attack, but God himself. God alone grants us life, upholds us, and treats us as rational human beings, not because we are rational but because if he were to deal with us other than as rational beings he would deny *himself*, entertain a different idea about us than he actually has. But even though God has no duties toward us and we no rights with respect to him, nevertheless we do have duties toward God.

Duties and rights do not overlap. They certainly do not overlap among people. I am obligated to treat a poor person well, but does that person have a right to my benevolence? I have a duty to forgive my brother seventy times seven, but does he have any right or claim to that forgiveness? Has he not rather forfeited that? A son torments his mother and causes her to be consumed with grief, but does he have a right (also a moral right) to her forgiveness? No, rights and duties do not coincide. They do coincide in the "covenant of works," in civic relationships, and in labor relations.[247] But they do not overlap in the undergirding ethical realm, nor in the realm of grace and forgiveness. The moralists of today overlap rights and duties because they either deduce duties from rights (Kant, Fichte) or deduce rights from duties (Adolphe Franck).[248] So many rights, so many duties, and vice versa; nothing for nothing! Wages for work! Contracts keep people together, bind them to each other! For then, love, grace, and forgiveness do not exist! Eye for an eye, and so forth . . . but the Sermon on the Mount disappears! I can have more duties than rights, since my duties are not imposed upon me and my rights are not given to me by other people (if they were, yes, then indeed they would overlap), but both flow to me from God. And now I am duty bound (not for the sake of my brother but for the sake of God) to forgive him seventy times seven, even though he has not the least right to it. Now I am to love my enemies, not because they are so loveable, nor because they possess the "dignity of human nature."[249] I am to love my enemies not because I find so much to like in them, but because God wills it; not because they have a right to my love, but because God obligates me to love them. Thus, among people, there are duties without rights. How much more toward God? We have duties with respect to God because we owe him everything before conversion and far more after conversion; in other words, both in nature and in grace.

247. DO: *loonsystemen.*
248. Janet, *La morale,* 276. Ed. note: This is a reference to Franck, *Morale pour tous.*
249. FO: *dignité de la nature humaine.*

There are, therefore, only duties of gratitude. We have no obligation, therefore, to give God anything, to benefit him, to make him happier! We have duties also toward the dead, even though we cannot benefit them in any way.[250] And although God is not indifferent to our conduct, to our love, to our obedience, yet he is not served as though he needed anything (Acts 17:25). "Can a man be profitable to God?" (Job 22:2). Our sins do him no harm; our virtues do him no good. So, therefore, we have no duties by which we would gain merit with him. There is reward, but not according to the intrinsic value of our works, but only according to the gracious agreement[251] between work and reward that he wished to make.

(b) There are no duties toward God because God cannot be known.

If God cannot be known, then he cannot be the object of our moral conduct, and his will is an inadequate foundation for our actions, because the good must be done for its own sake. This was also the view of Kant, who did accept a religious duty[252]—namely, the recognition of all our duties as the moral equivalent[253] of divine commandments. But that was a duty not toward God but toward humanity itself. "To be religious is the duty human beings have to themselves."[254] If God cannot be known, then there are no duties toward him; this much is certain. For then we still do not know how and what we have to be and do with respect to him. But God is knowable.[255] Furthermore, God himself can very well be the object of our actions, though not the object of our own "formative"[256] actions, which produce the object or alter it. God can be the indirect object of our actions, whereby we act in relation to him. Thus "toward"[257] here means "in relation to," so that the manner of our action is determined by the relation in which we are placed with respect to God.[258] Finally, to do something for the sake of God is certainly a principle—in fact, the only true principle—of moral conduct. This is so because "for the sake of God" does not mean "out of fear of punishment" or "from fear of his justice." That would be in conflict with God's law. Rather, it means "out of love for him and his law." And love is simply fulfilling the law, not a perfunctory respect, as Kant wants. For only when I love *the* good—or, better, the

---

250. Janet, *La morale*, 291.
251. DO: *verdrag.*
252. GO: *Religionspflicht.*
253. Ed. note: Bavinck inserted the Latin *instar* (= figure, image) in parentheses here.
254. GO: *Religion zu haben ist Pflicht des Menschen gegen sich selbst* (cited in Rothe, *Theologische Ethik*, 3:440 [§857]).
255. See *RD*, 2:53–94 (chap. 2, "The Knowledge of God").
256. GO: *bildend.*
257. DO: *jegens.*
258. Rothe, *Theologische Ethik*, 3:441, 445 (§857).

Good *One*, for his sake—do I love God, and in him love the things of creation,
Only then do I love the Absolute Good One for his own sake, and only then
do I love everything else to the extent that it shares in that goodness of God.
Then indeed do I love the things of creation only because they are good, not
because they provide benefits.

(c) There are no duties to God because our duties to God coincide with our duties toward our neighbor.

The third view concedes that since all duties are commanded by God, and
in that sense are duties toward him, properly speaking, there are no duties
toward God, because there are no separate duties toward God alongside those
toward ourselves and our neighbor. All duties are religious duties, but they
are not separate and distinct ones. In practice, religious duties coincide with
duties to self and social duties.[259] In part, Wuttke agrees with this; he accepts
the idea of religious duties but adds that "in every duty toward God, I fulfill
also directly at the same time a duty toward myself: I cannot possibly love
and honor without exalting myself into communion with Him; whatever man
does to the honor of God is at the same time a self-transfiguration; he cannot
praise God as his Father without confirming himself as the child of God." In
addition, "the fulfilling of our moral duties toward God implies consequently
in itself, really and directly at the same time also, the fulfilling of our duties
toward those who are beloved of God." In sum, duties toward God do not
"constitute a special group entirely distinct from the others."[260] Even though
this latter claim is true, the duties toward God and toward oneself and our
neighbor are, on that account, absolutely not equal and identical. Even if it
were true, for example, that praying, thanking and praising God, the whole
of worship, would at the same time be a duty toward myself and others, of
benefit to myself and others, for spiritual nourishment and development and
so on, then that is still not what makes religion a duty. In that case religious
duty is more the result than the cause and the goal of my worship.

Religion is not a duty to self (Kant) or a social duty.[261] That would not be
religion but its very opposite. My relation to myself and others is specifically
a different one than my relation to God; although in practice they may be
inseparable, they are nevertheless distinguishable. Is it not for the sake of
God that I must often deny father, mother, all people, all creatures—yea,
my very self, soul and body? Then duty toward God surely does not coincide
with duty toward one's self and others, does it? The intention to glorify

259. GO: *Selbst- und Socialpflichten*; thus Rothe, *Theologische Ethik*, 3:442 (§857).
260. Wuttke, *Christian Ethics*, 2:148 (§86).
261. GO: *Selbstpflicht*; *Socialpflicht*.

God may coincide with that of promoting my salvation, yet these are not one and the same. In any case, Rothe is wrong when he sees morality as the content, the substance (truth), of religion and when he considers religion to be no more than the requirement for the perfection (not the existence) of morality.[262] This view in fact is rooted in pantheism, in the identification of God and the world, with the consequence that the church is allowed to dissolve into the state, into morality. Religion is then no longer its own sphere, but merely the further definition, alteration, perfection of morality.[263] Scripture, however, makes a clear distinction between the two, places love for God and love for neighbor alongside each other in relative independence, although the former is the source of the latter. Religion is something different from morality.

But here another question arises: How then can religion[264] be a topic for discussion in ethics? The subject of ethics, after all, is morality, not religion. And yet the duties toward God—that is, religion—are held before us by God himself in his moral law, and thus are part and parcel of morality. Was I therefore incorrect when, in my work on the theology of Daniel Chantepie de la Saussaye, I said that morality is always related to my neighbors and never to God?[265] To be sure, this is unclear and incomplete. Rather, this is the case: dogmatic theology is not a system of religion, but of the knowledge of God.[266] Ethics is the description of the service of God (not of religion).[267] Religion is *also* but not exclusively a service of God:[268] all of life, in all aspects,[269] including mind, will, and feeling, must always and everywhere be a service of God.[270] That is what ethics describes. Ethics therefore also describes how and when religion is a true, pure service of God. Religion therefore must also be moral—that is, it must answer to the moral law.[271] Thus, the discipline of ethics also describes religion and all religious phenomena; it provides norma-

262. DO/GO: *volkomenheid*; *Dasein*; see Rothe, *Theologische Ethik*, 1:463–82 (§§117–26); cf. *RE*, 1:62–75, under the heading "Religion and Morality."

263. Cf. Janet, *La morale*, 293.

264. Ed. note: Here and in the next two instances our use of the word "religion" is a translation of the Dutch word *godsdienst*.

265. Bavinck, *De Theologie van Prof. Dr. Daniel Chantepie de la Saussaye*, 88–89: "Zedelijk heeft altijd betrekking op onze medemenschen, op de idee van mensch, nooit op God."

266. Ed. note: Bavinck now begins to use the word "religion" (*religie*), here in tandem with *godsdienst*.

267. Ed. note: This sentence (and the next) involves a wordplay in Dutch: *Ethiek is beschrijving van de dienst Gods (niet Godsdienst).*

268. DO: *Godsdienst, religie is nu óók maar niet alleen een dienst Gods.*

269. DO: *zijden.*

270. DO: *een dienst Gods.*

271. DO: *zedelijk, zedenwet.*

tive direction for how they can truly be a work pleasing[272] to God, a service to him.[273] Therefore, religion[274] should actually be treated not so much in dogmatics as in ethics.[275] But for that reason, the distinction between religion and morality remains, as we showed earlier in §7.[276] But religion must bear a moral character, and morality must bear a religious character, in order for both to be what they should be.

8. ADDITIONAL DUTIES TOWARD SELF?

Another objection to a twofold division of duties—toward God and toward neighbor (which everyone acknowledges except the egoists)—is the question about duties toward oneself. These were mentioned separately as long ago as Cyprian and were discussed in the Reformed churches (except for Polanus, who approved of "works of love toward oneself,"[277] appealing to Tertullian and Augustine). In the third part of his *Theoretico-Practica Theologia* (*Ascetics*), van Mastricht discusses the "practice of piety with respect to himself,"[278] but in the second part (*Moral Theology*) he speaks only of (a) obedience in general (II.i), (b) obedience in relation to God, or religion (II.ii), and (c) obedience with respect to our neighbor (II.iii).[279] Pictet also discusses them, as does Lampe, who examines the duties that flow from love of self.[280] Buurt also includes a section on self-love in his work on practical theology,[281] as does de Moor.[282] Calvin does not reject the duties of self-love but merely thinks it is unnecessary to mention them.[283]

Martensen acknowledges self-love as interest in one's personal salvation and in communion with God as self-affirmation.[284] Under the heading

272. DO: *welbehaglijk*.
273. DO: *een dienst Gods*.
274. DO: *religie*.
275. See the Reformed writers—for example, van Mastricht, *Theoretico-Practica Theologia*; à Brakel, *Christian's Reasonable Service*, part II.
276. Ed. note: See *RE*, 1:49–75.
277. LO: *charitas erga se ipsum*; Polanus von Polansdorf, *Syntagma Theologiae Christianae*, 651 (X.iii).x
278. LO: *de praxis pietatis versus semetipsum*; DO: *van de Oeffeninge der Godzaligheit omtrent sich zelven*; van Mastricht, *Theoretico-Practica Theologia*, III.iv [IV, 776]. Ed. note: For details on annotations of van Mastricht, see chap. 13, n. 67.
279. Ed. note: These are the subtitles given to the three books of part II.
280. For Pictet, see above, n. 124; Lampe, *Schets der dadelyke Godt-geleertheid*, 387–447 (book II, chap. 7).
281. Buurt, *Vervolg der Daadelyke godgeleerdheid*, 195–203 (§§617–22).
282. De Moor, *Commentarius Perpetuus*, 2:676.
283. *Institutes*, II.viii.54.
284. GO: *Selbstbehauptung*; Martensen, *Christian Ethics*, 2/1:149, 157 (§67), 202 (§89), 282–337 (§§122–43).

"Christian Self-Love,"[285] he discusses "self-love in truth and righteousness, compassion with ourselves, the earthly and the heavenly calling, social life and solitude, working and enjoying, temptation and assault—suffering."[286] Janet claims that after Kant and Fichte, duties toward ourselves gained a greater importance.[287]

Kant said that one owed to others what one owed to oneself—namely, respect, resulting in a heroic (read: proud!) morality that is Stoic and not Christian. There are duties toward ourselves, our human nature, even if we were entirely alone on an island. Wuttke argues that people are themselves the object of their moral actions; one must develop oneself into a good person, sanctify oneself in body and spirit.[288] Rothe denies self-love but does accept duties toward oneself.[289] Rudolph von Jhering argues that the idea of duties toward oneself is a contradiction in terms.[290] Wendt[291] says that duties toward oneself is an impossible concept; after all, duties are always based on a relationship of interaction[292] with others, and a duty is always a reciprocal act.[293]

The notion of reciprocity is a completely wrong way[294] to look at duties; a duty is not always a reciprocal act, a wage in exchange for work, but can be imposed on us by God as a duty to ourselves. A person has value; one soul, including our own, is worth more than the whole world. People are ends in themselves,[295] not just a means for others. They are to work out their salvation with fear and trembling, and they must sanctify themselves in body and soul; they have a calling[296] also toward themselves. This does not occur, however, in the sense of Stoic or Kantian haughtiness, as though people were autonomous, their own lawgiver and lord, but in the sense that they are among the most glorious creatures by the grace of God. To despise oneself would be to rob God and his gift of honor. Thus, there are duties toward oneself. As to whether there exists a duty of self-love, see §§36–42 below. Why are these duties not mentioned in the law of God?[297]

285. GO: *Selbstliefde*.

286. Martensen, *Christian Ethics*, 2/1:282–337 (§§122–43). Ed. note: These topics are taken directly from the headings in the English translation.

287. Janet, *La morale*, 294–96.

288. Wuttke, *Christian Ethics*, 2:149 (§87); cf. 236–51 (§§119–22); on self-love see 1:175; 2:165.

289. Rothe, *Theologische Ethik*, 3:405–6 (§845n1).

290. LO: *contradictio in adjecto*; von Jhering, *Der Zweck im Recht*, 2:228.

291. Wendt, *Ueber das Sittlich Erlaubte*, 27–28.

292. GO: *Wechselverhältnis*.

293. GO: *Gegenleistung*.

294. DO: *een geheel onjuiste voorstelling*.

295. GO: *Selbstzweck*.

296. DO: *roeping*.

297. Calvin, *Institutes*, II.viii.54; de Moor, *Commentarius Perpetuus*, 2:676.

(a) Because, as a result of sin, people are already quite selfish and do not need to be stimulated to practice self-love.

(b) Because the duties toward ourselves are implicit in duties toward our neighbor; for example, "you shall not kill" also forbids suicide. Our neighbor is the standard for ourselves, since our neighbor is a human being, as we are. And what we may not do to our neighbor as God's image-bearer, we may not do to ourselves.

(c) Because these duties of faith, conversion, sanctification, and so on are prescribed throughout Scripture.

9. Duties toward Saints and Angels; Animals and Plants?

In addition to these duties discussed above, there are also duties toward those who have died—toward saints, martyrs, relatives, national heroes, and the like—but these fall under duties toward the neighbor. Additionally, there are duties toward angels, who must not be worshiped or venerated, yet must be esteemed.[298] Though there are only a few of these duties, they may be discussed from time to time. But are there any duties toward impersonal creatures like plants and animals?[299] Martensen says there are and speaks even of love for nature, as do Janet and Wuttke.[300] Jhering, however, says no.[301] Rothe mocks the idea and says that we have no duties toward animals since they have no rights.[302] However, there are obligatory actions that we owe, neither to animals nor plants, but to ourselves. Yet even if animals had no rights with respect to us, we still may owe them duties.[303] All that is required is that there be a measure of sympathy between them and us, that we are sensitive to their suffering. Moreover, those animals were given to us by God for our use, for our instruction; they groan with us and for us (Rom. 8). All of nature must be an instrument and an organ for the human spirit; it must not be misused, for example, for sorcery. Summarizing all the above, we come to the following classification:[304]

---

298. DO: *niet aangebeden of vereerd, maar toch geacht*; Janet, *La morale*, 288.

299. Schopenhauer, *Two Fundamental Problems of Ethics*, 172–73, 239–45.

300. Martensen, *Christian Ethics*, 2/1:276–82 (§§120–21); Janet, *La morale*, 283; Wuttke, *Christian Ethics*, 2:146 (§86).

301. Von Jhering, *Der Zweck im Recht*, 2:139–44.

302. Rothe, *Theologische Ethik*, 3:449–52 (§858).

303. Janet, *La morale*, 283.

304. Ed. note: In the margins Bavinck referred back to §9, where he provided a classification of sins; see *RE*, 1:106–16. By providing his summary in a list, Bavinck sketches the outline of the remaining material in his *Reformed Ethics*. In the manuscript, IV is not a separate item but subsumed under III. Only the first item in the list of "special duties" in IV (marriage and family) was completed, and it will be published in the third volume of *Reformed Ethics*.

I. Duties in body and spirit toward God, including those toward the angels (§§32–35).

II. Duties toward ourselves—that is, toward our spirit (mind, will, feeling) and toward our body (here we can also consider duties toward nature and animals) (§§36–42).

III. Duties toward the neighbor. Here, further classification is required into general (§§43–49) and special duties.

IV. The special duties teach us how we are to perform the general duties in specific spheres, such as the family and the household, one's occupation, culture, society, state, church. In all this, the final goal of all our moral actions must be the kingdom of God (§§50–58).

10. THREE DUTIES OR ONLY ONE?

Finally, we need to ask one more question: Cannot these three types of duties be reduced to one?[305] For example, concerning the moral duty we have toward nature: Cannot the duties toward animals be reduced to those toward ourselves—that is, to individual morality? Specifically, people may not be cruel and therefore may not torture animals. Further, cannot individual morality be reduced to social morality, since we must honor in ourselves what we are to honor in others? And, finally, cannot individual and social morality be reduced to religious morality, since in all things we are to love God for his sake?

Reducing all duties, also those toward God and ourselves, to social morality was done by Fichte, who viewed all duties as being owed to humanity, of which I am a member.[306] All Darwinians and socialists do the same. The view that really flows forth from pantheism and socialism is one in which the individual has no value, no immortality; only the genus known as the true humanity has value, eternal and immortal humanity, considered as the "God-man."

Reducing *all* duties to those toward ourselves, toward the dignity of our nature, was done by Kant, who even called religion a duty to self.[307] Thus, he actually looked upon God and mankind as a means for the autonomous "I." And false mysticism and false devotion lapsed into this view as well. Likewise, all individualists and egoists, all fanatics about human autonomy, and all rationalists regard a person as an isolated atom and sever all bonds. This view makes us love God and all people for our own sake.[308]

305. Janet, *La morale*, 297.
306. Janet, *La morale*, 300.
307. GO: *Selbstpflicht*.
308. Similarly, in part, Janet, *La morale*, 303–6.

All duties can even be reduced to our duties toward God, since he alone can and does obligate us in our conscience; since he alone comprehends everything, is above everything and yet in everything; since above each and every commandment are the words "I am the LORD your God, and therefore you shall love your father and mother etc." Thus, we should really and correctly say: We have duties toward God (and this is possible because he is transcendent and I stand in direct relation to him solely through the Mediator Christ, apart from any other creatures). We have duties toward God also in relation to ourselves. And we have duties toward God in relation to our neighbor. And these last two exist because God and creation do not stand alongside each other in a dualistic or deistic fashion, but because all things exist in him and he alone is in all things. No deism, therefore, but no pantheism either! And no mysticism or pietism that acknowledges duties only toward God and undervalues the natural and the creational, that joins Pascal in regarding marriage as a deicide[309] and all natural love and respect as diminishing our love for God. Then people must flee from the world and all that is in it.

---

309. FO: *un déicide*; Janet, *La morale*, 299.

OUR DUTIES TOWARD GOD

15

No Other Gods; No Images

The straightforward meaning of the First Commandment is that no other gods are to be kept as gods either instead of or next to YHWH and honored as such. The commandment thus prohibits idolatry and polytheism, heretical views of God such as Arianism, and self-justifying philosophical constructs of God by intellectuals, as well as the practical idolatry of which all are guilty who put their trust in something other than God.

The commandment also forbids superstitious attribution of power to words, things, or customs to deflect evil or obtain something good which they possess neither by nature nor according to God's word. This includes thoughts of and belief in superhuman, supernatural powers and forces, ghosts, witches, omens, and the like. People either act in accordance with such beliefs or suffer under and from fear arising from these beliefs. Superstition is always pagan, either a remnant from a pagan past or a feature of a revived new paganism. Such superstition can be objective— imaginary and false ideas about God and the supernatural world—or subjective. In the latter case human beings claim to have in their possession and at their disposal spiritual powers that can control or employ God, fate, or other spiritual entities. This is called sorcery and also magic, and Scripture warns extensively against it. The confrontation between God and Pharaoh shows the power and the limits of sorcerers. King Saul's encounter with the medium of Endor showed that the practice of sorcery and divination had not entirely been eradicated in Israel. We also read about sorcerers in Babylon (Daniel), and in the book of Acts we find several accounts of such practices. The Christian church acknowledges the reality of evil powers and human cooperation with such powers to do extraordinary things. But Holy Scripture strongly condemns all this magic and fortune-telling in many passages in both the Old and New Testaments.

Although Roman Catholic teaching distinguishes the adoration and worship that is due only to God from the invocation and veneration due to saints and angels, Protestants insist that the practice of Roman Catholics does not adequately avoid breaking the First Commandment. Angels and saints are entitled to conventional honor, but the popular piety of Roman Catholics involving pleading for all sorts of good, for mercy and healing, and the like, does look like religious adoration and risks discounting the position of Christ as Mediator.

Positively, the First Commandment prescribes faith and hope in and love for the Triune God: Father, Son, and Holy Spirit. Faith involves knowledge and trust. Faith-knowledge is both intellectual and moral; the child of God desires to know who God is and how he is to be served. To know God truly is to trust him, to rely on him for everything, to rest in the One who is completely faithful. Hope is that virtue by which we unquestionably and surely anticipate God's future blessings, especially the future completion of our salvation. The object of hope is God's promises and their fulfillment and leads to patient endurance and confession. Love follows faith and is its echo; in faith we receive, in love we give to God and to our neighbor.

The First Commandment deals with the true God; the Second Commandment deals with the true religion. It teaches us how we must worship God, according to his will and command. In accord with God's spiritual being, such worship must be spiritual and not symbolic, using images. Aversion to images and to the visual arts arose among Jews after the return from exile and captivity and may have been transferred to individual Christians in response to the idolatrous art of the pagans. The early Christian church did not share this opposition, and Christian art can be found in places like the catacombs. However, paintings were not tolerated in churches until the fourth and fifth centuries, when they were introduced as "books for the laity." Veneration of relics arose during the same time, leading to iconoclastic controversies, especially in the Eastern Church. Iconoclastic initiatives can also be found in the Western Church, but the Roman Catholic Church approved the placement and veneration of images and relics in churches at the Council of Trent. The veneration of such objects is justified as a veneration of the persons they represent and as a necessary teaching aid for the laity. It is noteworthy that the medieval church opposed laity reading Scripture on their own and strictly controlled all translations of the Bible into the vernacular.

There are good reasons for prohibiting images of the Triune God. First, it is impossible because God absolutely cannot be depicted. It is also insulting to God because all images are depictions of creatures, physical bodies: temporal, corruptible, works of sinful human beings. Images "exchange the glory of the immortal God

for images resembling mortal man and birds and animals and creeping things"
(Rom. 1:23). Idols are also destructive; they tempt people to superstition and vain
imaginations that corrupt human souls and bodies.

The commandment does not rule out depictions of spiritual beings such as
angels nor the use of symbolic or emblematic imagery (such as an eye within
a triangle) that points to God or one of his attributes. What about portraits of
Christ? Portraying Christ onstage should be ruled out because it is impossible
to portray the whole living Christ. Paintings or sculptures only portray a single
aspect of Christ's being and are a different matter. Of course, Holy Scripture
does speak about God in an anthropomorphic manner; it cannot do otherwise.
We must, however, distinguish between thinking about God and imagining
God. A conception of God is permissible, but not a material representation or
imaginative construct, since representation always requires sensory, perceptible,
physical forms, while thinking abstracts from all those forms and retains only
the pure thoughts.

Arguments used by Roman Catholics to defend the veneration of images and relics
depend on the key distinction between religious worship (latreia) and veneration
(douleia). These distinctions do not pass the test of careful biblical exegesis. The
Heidelberg Catechism provides a beautiful response to the Roman Catholic claim that
images are necessary as "books for the laity": "God wants the Christian community
instructed by the living preaching of his Word—not by idols that cannot even talk."
Faith arises not from contemplating images, but from hearing the preaching of the
Word (Rom. 10:17). Similarly, relics should definitely not be religiously venerated
because they are not means of redemption; relic veneration is a form of pagan fetishism
and amulet worship.

At the heart of the Second Commandment is the question "Who decides how
God is to be worshiped?" It forbids all self-willed worship. God alone has the right
to determine how he wants to be served; he must be worshiped and served in the
way he himself has commanded—that is, only according to his Word. Still, the
human soul yearns to see God and is inclined to make idols. God tells us that we
will not find an image of him in any creature, because that would dishonor him.
But he also tells us that Adam, that human beings bear his image, and above
all that his Son is the image of the invisible God. Whoever sees him sees the
Father. Beholding the Son and venerating him, we are changed into his likeness.
God wants, as it were, to multiply images of himself, to see nothing but images,
likenesses, portraits of himself. The new humanity in Christ, from all sides and
everyone in their own way, reflects and mirrors God. God is mirrored in us; we are
mirrored in God. God makes images of himself in us. But not we of God. God
photographs himself.

§32. THE FIRST COMMANDMENT

You shall have no other gods before me. (Exod. 20:3)[1]

The Hebrew text literally says "there will not be for you other gods before my face."[2] Abraham Kuyper put it this way: "This commandment implies: Let God be God; do not assault him in his being, but live only for him, under him, and through him."[3] Jacob Alting and Nicolaus Gürtler translate this as "except before my face"—that is, my *Shekinah*, my Son, whereby the Son is included under the prohibition of Deuteronomy 5:7 along with the Holy Spirit.[4] "Before my face" is nothing more than "in my presence" (cf. Ps. 27:8; Exod. 33:20).[5] Others translate the Hebrew preposition עַל as "except" (my face, that is, me); however, the translation "before"[6] is preferable, corresponding to the LXX πλὴν ἐμοῦ of Exodus and the πρὸ προσώπου μου of Deuteronomy (cf. Gen. 11:28; Num. 3:4). This is to say, "You will not have them anywhere, not in your heart either, hidden from people." God is pointing here, therefore,

---

1. HO: לֹא יִהְיֶה־לְךָ אֱלֹהִים אֲחֵרִים עַל־פָּנָי.

2. HO: עַל־פָּנָי.

3. Kuyper, *E Voto Dordraceno*, 3:507 (Lord's Day 34b/1); originally published in *De Heraut*, no. 741 (March 6, 1892).

4. J. Alting, *Opera Omnia Theologica*, 1:269–72 ("Commentary on Deuteronomy 5:7"); Gürtler, *Institutiones Theologicae*, 520 (chap. XXII, §109), 596 (chap. XXIV, §130). Ed. note: Bavinck's highly condensed statement follows the logic of Gürtler's argument and is worth expanding here. Gürtler (chap. XXII, §109) indicates that in his explanation of the commandment against false gods, J. Alting collates "before my face" in Deut. 5:7 with Isa. 63:9: "the Angel of the presence [face]" who is the Messiah (*juxta vel praeter faciem meum*, i.e., *praeter Messiam qui facies Dei solet appellari*). Therefore, because the Son/Messiah is referenced as the face of God or Shekinah (J. Alting, *Opera Omnia Theologica*, 1:271), the deity of Christ is honored in the Decalogue. Looking at Deut. 5:6, also through Alting's eyes, Gürtler says that "face/presence" indicates God as "your God" and therefore implies proclamation of the Messiah. Finally, Gürtler adds John 5:23—"Whoever does not honor the Son does not honor the Father who sent him"—and meditates on the fact that the prologue to the commandments references God speaking in the first person, whereas the remainder of the text, the commandments themselves, references God in the third person. Alting reads Deut. 5 covenantally, which lets him add the Angel of the Covenant and the "face/presence" of God to the Mosaic Sinai experience. This leads to the conclusion that in Deut. 5:6 there is the warning not to renounce or dishonor the Son as included in the "face/presence." If one renounces the Son as "the face of God" (first-person address), one will renounce/dishonor the Father who sent him, as referenced in the third person in the rest of the chapter. In other words, the "me" in Deut. 5:7 includes the Son, before whom Israel can have no other gods. Gürtler's references to "third person" are, of course, grammatical and not trinitarian, but Bavinck does pick up Gürtler's point (chap. XXIV, §131) that the Holy Spirit is also included in the commandment's prohibition against "other gods." I am indebted to Richard Muller for help in sorting this out.

5. De Moor, *Commentarius Perpetuus*, 2:694.

6. LO: *coram*.

to his omnipresence.[7] "Other gods" may mean "others" and also "strange ones" (Ps. 81:9; Isa. 42:8).[8] But since YHWH alone is Israel's God, "others" signifies practically and concretely the same as "foreign." It certainly does not imply that such "other gods" exist in reality, but only that many things, creatures, are revered by the nations as "gods." The commandment reads, thus, that no other gods are to be kept as gods, either *instead of* or *next to* YHWH, and honored as such, for YHWH will not give his honor and name to anyone else (Isa. 42:8).[9]

As a historical aside, while Reformed theologians traditionally explain our duties toward God through the lens of the Decalogue, this was not the case in the earliest years of the Christian church and during the Middle Ages.[10] Many more recent writers also do not connect our duties toward God explicitly to the Ten Commandments.[11]

The First Commandment prohibits the following:

1. Idolatry

Idolatry is often called "polytheism" today.[12] Today the oldest form of religion is considered to be either fetishism, animism, sabaeism (the cult of the heavenly lights, or astrology), or henotheism.[13] It was French scholar Charles de Brosses (1709–77) who sought to explain Greek polytheism in

---

7. DO: *overaltegenwordigheid.*

8. LXX: θεοὶ ἕτεροι; HO: אֲחֵרִים; LO: *alieni*; GrO: ἀλλότριοι.

9. For further explanation of this and the following commandments, in addition to *Commentaries* on the Heidelberg Catechism, see Calvin, *Institutes*, II.viii; Calvin, *Commentaries on the Four Last Books of Moses*, 1:417–2:189; Daneau, *Ethices Christianae*, vol. 2; Vermigli, *Loci Communes*, loci 3–14; Musculus, *Loci Communes*, 51–165; Zanchi, *Operum Theologicorum*, 4:211–871 (chaps. xi–xxviii); Hoornbeeck, *Theologia Practica*, 1:201–84; Gerhard, *Loci Theologici*, 3:1–108; Voetius, *Selectarum Disputationum Theologicarum*, 4:763–824; de Moor, *Commentarius Perpetuus*, 2:690–91; Owen, *Theologumena Pantopada*, 155–286 (III.i–iv).

Ed. note: Bavinck's references in this note to Daneau, Vermigli, Musculus, Zanchi, Hoornbeeck, Gerhard, and Voetius are likely taken from de Moor, *Commentarius Perpetuus*, 2:690–91. It is noteworthy that Bavinck chooses different texts from Calvin than de Moor and does not include de Moor's references to André Rivet and John Forbes of Corse.

10. See Diestel, *Geschichte des Alten Testamentes*, 214, 219, 225; Kuyper, *E Voto Dordraceno*, 3:477 (Lord's Day 34a/4); originally published in *De Heraut*, no. 727 (February 7, 1892).

11. See especially E. Sartorius, *Die Lehre von der heiligen Liebe*, 275–531; Hodge, *Systematic Theology*, 3:277–465; Wuttke, *Handbuch der christlichen Sittenlehre*[3], 2:235–69 (§§236–44) (ed. note: the English translation of Wuttke [*Christian Ethics*] only goes as far as §152); Dorner, *System of Christian Ethics*, 413–44 (§§50–55); Vilmar, *Theologische Moral*, 2/3:112–44 (§§48–51); J. T. Beck, *Vorlesungen über christliche Ethik*, 2:67–183 (§12).

12. Zöckler, "Polytheismus."

13. Ed. note: What follows is an expansion of a compact parenthesis in Bavinck's manuscript; for what follows cf. *RD*, 1:314–20.

part through fetishism (magical powers of objects).[14] Others, notably Auguste Comte (1798–1857) and Sir John Lubbock (1834–1913), saw fetishism as one of the stages[15] of religion, along with atheism, totemism, shamanism, and idolatry. Such "stage" theories were also advocated by Georg Wilhelm Friedrich Hegel (1770–1831), Theodor Waitz (1821–64), and Friedrich von Hellwald (1842–92).[16] But fetish artifacts made into amulets are found with all peoples—also with Roman Catholics, for instance—and are a corruption and degeneration of a higher God-concept.[17] Edward B. Tylor and C. P. Tiele regard animism as a cult of the soul, while Herbert Spencer, Otto Caspari, and Julius Lippert look to ancestor worship as an explanation.[18] Max Müller and Otto Zöckler consider henotheism as the oldest form of religion.[19] A consideration of the most ancient peoples by the history of religions points back to a relative monotheism or henotheism. This, in turn, assumes a pure first monotheism[20] in paradise and later, which itself was contaminated in all sorts of ways and became partly pantheistic, partly polytheistic, and linked with elements of star worship, nature worship, and worship of humanity.[21]

According to Holy Scripture, monotheism comes first, and even after the fall the knowledge of the true God remains pure for a relatively long time. Melchizedek (Gen. 14:18) and, later, Job still serve the true God. The pagan

14. Ed. note: See Morris and Leonard, *Returns of Fetishism*; this volume contains a new translation by Daniel H. Leonard of Charles de Brosses's classic 1760 text *On the Worship of Fetish Gods* (FO: *Du culte des dieux fétiches*).

15. GO: *Stufenrij*. Ed. note: See John Lubbock, *The Origin of Civilization and the Primitive Condition of Man*.

16. Ed. note: The German psychologist and anthropologist Theodor Waitz wrote the six-volume *Die Anthropologie der Naturvölker* (The anthropology of peoples who live close to nature). The first volume of *Die Anthropologie der Naturvölker* was translated into English by J. Frederick Collingwood as *Introduction to Anthropology*. For von Hellwald, see *Kulturgeschichte in ihrer natürlichen Entwicklung bis zur Gegenwart*.

17. F. M. Zahn, "Ist Fetischismus eine ursprüngliche Form der Religion?," 223. Ed. note: The next issue of *Allgemeine Missions-Zeitschrift* (vol. 7 [1880]) had a three-part series by Otto Zöckler on the original form of religion (*Die Urgestalt der Religion*). The subtitles serve as the outline for Bavinck's own treatment in this paragraph: 1. "The Alleged Original (Primitive) Atheism" (*Der angebliche Ur-Atheismus*; 7:337–54); 2. "The Fetishism- and Animism-Hypotheses" (*Die Fetischismus und die Animismus Hypothese*; 7:437–52); 2B. "The Animism Hypothesis" (*Die Animismus Hypothese*; 7:485–93); 3. "Monotheism as the Starting Point of All Religious Development" (*Der Monotheismus als Ausganspunkt aller Religionsentwicklung*; 7:533–54).

18. Ed. note: Edward B. Tylor, *Primitive Culture*; C. P. Tiele, *Elements of the Science of Religion*; Herbert Spencer, *System of Synthetic Philosophy*; Otto Caspari, *Die Urgeschichte des Menschheit*; Julius Lippert, *Die Religionen der europäischer Kulturvolker in ihrem geschichtlichen Ursprungs*.

19. Zöckler, "Polytheismus"; Augustine, *City of God* XVI.6.

20. GO/DO: *Urmonotheisme*.

21. Ed. note: Bavinck uses three technical terms here and speaks of "astrolatrische, fysiolatrische of antropolatrische elementen."

nations and with them the various languages and religions originated in Genesis 11 when the tower of Babel was built.[22] After that time idolatrous elements appear gradually in the various families and tribes. Laban's family already has *teraphim* (Gen. 31:19; 35:2). Abram also has to leave his family because of idolatry (Josh. 24:2). And this idolatry flows from the loss of the true knowledge of God and the turn to the creature (Acts 14:16; 17:29; Rom. 1:22–23). This turn is "thus from Unity to multiple forms of polytheism."[23] Yet in this diversity the false unity of the demonic appears again.[24] And 1 Corinthians 10:19–20 ascribes idolatry to demonic influences.[25]

What, then, is the essence of idolatry?[26] The Heidelberg Catechism provides this answer: "Idolatry is having or inventing something in which one trusts in place of or alongside of the only true God, who has revealed himself in the Word."[27] And that is the view of Holy Scripture on idolatry. The pagan gods do not exist, they are "nothings,"[28] impotent (Isa. 41:29; 42:17; 46:1–7), made by humans from dust (Pss. 115:4–8; 135:15–18; Isa. 41–44), dead (Ps. 106:28). And insofar as they have reality they definitely are demons[29] (Deut. 32:17; cf. 10:17; Pss. 96; 106:28; 1 Cor. 10:20; Rev. 9:20). They are worthless, "vain things" (Acts 14:15), not true gods (Acts 19:26; Gal. 4:8), only "so-called gods" (1 Cor. 8:5) that have "no real existence" (1 Cor. 8:4).[30] Holy Scripture considers serving such gods certainly as abandoning the true God (Judg. 2:12, 13; 10:6), as giving to others the honor due him (Isa. 42:8). In Israel this is specifically considered to be fornication and adultery (Jer. 3:9; Hosea 4:12 and passim) because Israel was YHWH's wife (Ezek. 16:8), and YHWH loved her with the love of one who is committed to a marriage (Jer. 2:2). Therefore God also demanded the death penalty for idolatry (Deut. 17:5), and the New Testament denies the kingdom of heaven to idolaters (1 Cor. 6:10; Rev. 9:20; 21:8).[31] According to Holy Scripture, therefore, idolatry is a

22. Thus Origen, Augustine (*City of God* XVI.6), Schelling, Kurtz, Delitzsch, Fabri, Auberten; see Zöckler, "Polytheismus," 108.

23. E. Sartorius, *Die Lehre von der heiligen Liebe*, 133.

24. E. Sartorius, *Die Lehre von der heiligen Liebe*, 136.

25. "What do I imply then? That food offered to idols is anything, or that an idol is anything? No, I imply that what pagans sacrifice they offer to demons and not to God. I do not want you to be participants with demons."

26. DO: *wezen*.

27. Q&A 95.

28. HO: אֱלִילִים.

29. HO: שֵׁדִים.

30. GrO: ματαίων; οὐκ εἰσὶν θεοί; μὴ οὖσιν θεοῖς; εἰσὶν λεγόμενοι θεοί; οὐδὲν εἴδωλον ἐν κόσμῳ.

31. Ed. note: Bavinck took these Scripture passages from Zöckler, "Polytheismus"; he also added this marginal note: "Is it good to call upon Minerva, the Muses, etc. (Ps. 16:4), to name days after them (names the Brownists wanted to change)? (de Moor, *Commentarius*

matter of not serving God, of denying and dishonoring him (Gal. 4:8; Eph. 2:12). The one necessarily excludes the other. Here there is only exclusion, opposition, choosing, not sharing.

Contemporary viewpoints are diametrically opposed to this idea. Opposition between God and all others is erased and displaced by mere distinctions between lower and higher forms of religion. All religions are viewed as worshiping the same God, the same Unknown Primal Force, but with different representations and obligations. This one religious life comes to expression in a variety of ever-more-pure forms. Such a view of religion is pantheistic[32] for the following reasons:

(a) Objectively it confuses God and the world. Because it identifies God with the world, it becomes impossible to forsake God and embrace the creature; God and the world are not distinct but are one and the same.

(b) It confuses the kinds of life in human beings. All religious life in all people is of the same sort. Opposition between spiritual and natural life does not exist. All human beings have the same set of feelings and emotional life; this indwelling of God differs in people only in degree of animation and strength.

(c) It confuses and erases the contrast between good and evil, truth and untruth in religions (and in the moral life), and thus considers deeply depraved paganism as morally equivalent to biblical faith and only behind in degree of development. This is a completely different portrait than given in Holy Scripture (Pss. 2:2; 9:17; 59:8; Matt. 6:7, 32; Eph. 2:11; 1 Thess. 4:5).[33]

But there is a more refined form of idolatry.[34] Willem Bilderdijk captures this nicely in two poems.[35] The first, "Philosophic Virtue," has as its epigraph (in Greek) this call from the apostle Peter in Acts 2:40: "Save yourselves from

---

Perpetuus, 2:703; Voetius also disapproves of this; see *Selectarum Disputationum Theologicarum*, 2:607–11)."

32. Ed. note: What Bavinck (and Kuyper) often described as "pantheism" is, in many instances, better labeled "panentheism." See Cooper, *Panentheism*. Bavinck's point about idolatry is verified by Cooper's volume, as its subtitle makes clear: *The Other God of the Philosophers; From Plato to the Present.*

33. Wuttke, *Handbuch der christlichen Sittenlehre*[3], 2:49. Ed. note: Not included in the English translation.

34. DO: *afgoderij in fijnere vorm.*

35. Ed. note: The description of "refined idolatry" that follows has been constructed by the editor from the two poems Bavinck cites, "Philosophic Virtue" ("Filozoofische Deugd") and "God, Revealed in His Word" ("God, geopenbaard in zijn woord"), in Bilderdijk, *De dichtwerken*, 5:470–71, 362.

this crooked generation."[36] Bilderdijk gives thanks that the worship of "coarser gods" has come to an end, but says that a "more refined" idolatry still plagues Christendom.[37] This is a "philosopher's god," a product of our own imagination. We create our own virtue and believe that our own rational morality will save us. Bilderdijk specifies this more clearly in another poem, "God, Revealed in His Word," where he describes this god of the new morality as a god "who is so good that he retreats from his justice," a god in whom we find no "wrath and curse," who "overlooks the sin in our hearts" and does not condemn us when we follow the inclinations of our sinful hearts.[38] Bilderdijk calls on his reader to "curse the pagan fantasy / that spooks our brains; / set aside that proud self-deception / smoked by intellectuals" and instead to worship "the God of Abraham, the God who took on sinful flesh and came to earth for us."

This refined idolatry can take on a more theoretical or a more practical form.[39] The first kind may be characterized by depicting God in thought and imagination as a human being, but especially in our day by Cartesian skepticism and indifferent disparagement of the true and pure knowledge of God and of religious truth.[40] In this case all truth is considered to be the private opinion of some, with no more validity than any other view or insight. The modern slogan is "As a man is, so is his God."[41] And such is modern polytheism, tolerant toward all gods and idols of one's own invention and making but intolerant only toward the true God. This modern polytheism absorbs all those gods into one pantheon except the One who said, "You shall have no other gods before me."[42]

The depraved heart desires to create its own God; that is the source of pantheism. Everyone today seems to think that truth and reflection are entirely outside the moral arena and considers the most flagrant aberration of idolatry

36. GrO: Σώθητε ἀπὸ τῆς γενεᾶς τῆς σκολιᾶς ταύτης.

37. DO: *grover beeldendienst*; *een fijner soort*.

38. Bilderdijk, "God, geopenbaard in zijn word," 326. Ed. note: The opening lines of this poem are

Verheerlijk God! maar niet den God	Glorify God! but not the God
Dien ge in uw binnenst schept;	You create in your deepest inner part;
Den God wien ge in uw brein gekneed,	The God you fashioned in your brain,
In 't hart gebeiteld hebt.	Chiseled in your heart. (translated by John Bolt)

39. Stapfer, *De zeden-leer*, 2:160 (IX.xciv). Ed. note: The Dutch translation is not available online in digital format; cf. the German original, *Sittenlehre*, 2:214.

40. Cf. E. Sartorius, *Die Lehre von der heiligen Liebe*, 290–91.

41. DO: *Zoals een mens is, is zijn God.*

42. Consider here also the cult of genius (da Costa), the exaltation of humanity by Auguste Comte, and statues. Ed. note: Bavinck may have had in mind da Costa's poem "Vijf en twintig jaren"; cf. da Costa, "Het Genie." Bavinck returns to the topic of "genius" below when he discusses the idolatry of erecting statues and Auguste Comte's religion of humanity.

to be morally indifferent.[43] Words such as "pagan" or "heretic" are discredited today and are mitigated or avoided. All gods of the philosophers—pantheism, deism, hylozoism,[44] and the like—are therefore "other gods." They are idols, not merely other ideas of God but other self-created gods although void of reality. For our part, we believe that the God we know is the only living God and that our understanding of God is true. Basically then, we must conclude that Jews, Muslims,[45] modernists, and many philosophers—in fact, all who obscure one or more of God's attributes or persons and thus fail to give God the glory for all his attributes together—worship "other gods."

Heresy[46] also belongs to idolatry in part, although heresy is also possible in anthropology, soteriology, and so forth. The Greek terms point to an act of arbitrarily choosing something on one's own without bowing before the Word.[47] Heresy is a deviation from the fundamentals originating from willful, subjective arbitrariness and a refusal to submit oneself to the Word. Scripture sternly condemns this (2 Pet. 2:1; Titus 3:10; 1 John 4:3; 2 John 7), and such condemnation always accompanies the dogmas established by the church in the first centuries. Among those heresies are tritheism, Ebionism (Arianism, Monarchianism), Docetism, Monophysitism, Nestorianism, and Pelagianism.[48]

However, in addition, there is also the practical idolatry of which all are guilty who put their trust in something other than God and deprive God of his honor. An idol is whatever leads us away from the living God. Paul speaks about those whose belly is their God (Phil. 3:19) and who are lovers of pleasure more than God (2 Tim. 3:4). Elsewhere we read of the proud who say, "My power and the might of my hand have gotten me this wealth" (Deut. 8:17), forgetting that it is God "who gives you power to get wealth, that he may confirm his covenant that he swore to your fathers" (v. 18). Similarly those who say, "By the strength of my hand I have done it, / and by my wisdom, for I have understanding" (Isa. 10:13). To such, God responds, "Shall the axe boast over him who hews with it, / or the saw magnify itself against him who wields it? / As if a rod should wield him who lifts it, / or as if a staff should lift him who is not wood!" (v. 15). Wisdom suggests a better way: "Trust in the LORD with all your heart, / and

---

43. E. Sartorius, *Die Lehre von der heiligen Liebe*, 3/1:123.

44. Ed. note: Hylozoism (from Greek *hylē*, "matter," + *zōē*, "life") is "any system that views all matter as alive, either in itself or by participation in the operation of a world soul or some similar principle" (*Encyclopaedia Britannica*, s.v. "Hylozoism," accessed May 26, 2017, https://www.britannica.com/topic/hylozoism).

45. Ursinus, *Commentary on the Heidelberg Catechism*, 509 (Q&A 94).

46. DO: *ketterij*.

47. GrO: αἵρεσις, ἀπὸ τοῦ αἱρεῖσθαί τι ἴδιον. Ed. note: Bavinck takes over this definition from Kahnis, "Häresie," 522.

48. Kahnis, "Häresie," 521–26.

do not lean on your own understanding" (Prov. 3:5). In the words of Jeremiah: "Let not the wise man boast in his wisdom, let not the mighty man boast in his might, let not the rich man boast in his riches, but let him who boasts boast in this, that he understands and knows me, that I am the Lord who practices steadfast love, justice, and righteousness in the earth. For in these things I delight, declares the Lord" (Jer. 9:23–24). That is also how Scripture speaks of misers, who put their hope in the uncertainty of riches rather than in the living God (1 Tim. 6:17), who say to fine gold, My trust is in you (Job 31:24; cf. Ps. 52:7; Prov. 11:28), who are thus idolaters (Eph. 5:5) and whose greed is idolatry (Col. 3:5). And furthermore, all are guilty who expect their salvation from remedies and creatures instead of from God, who is the fountain of all good, or who expect it from medicines, from their own labors (Ps. 127:1), their own reputation, name, honor, strength, influence, wisdom, goodness, righteousness, or anything that is found in creatures. In short, all are guilty who put their trust in what we humans can do and who depend on flesh for their strength (Jer. 17:5). Over against this Psalm 118:8 notes that "it is better to take refuge in the Lord / than to trust in man."[49] The sum of it is this: "But I am the Lord your God. . . ; / you know no God but me, / and besides me there is no savior" (Hosea 13:4). "All idolatry is sin, and, at the same time, all sin is idolatry."[50]

2. Superstition[51]

The Latin term *superstitio* derives, according to some, from *supersto* = to remain standing, to stand fear-struck by the divine. According to Nitzsch it is derived from *supersistere* = superfluous faith, just as in Rome foreign religions were called superstitions, but this derivation is grammatically not valid.[52] Grimm takes it from *superstes* = to stay with ideas already rejected by many long ago; according to others *superstites* were the old and superstitious people who outlived their generation. Cicero derives it from people who pray day and night that their children may be *superstites*.[53] The Greek term

---

49. Ed. note: Cf. Ps. 146:3: "Put not your trust in princes, / in a son of man, in whom there is no salvation. When his breath departs, he returns to the earth; / on that very day his plans perish."

50. DO: *Alle afgoderij is zonde, en alle zonde is eigenlijk afgoderij.* Ed. note: We placed this sentence in quotation marks even though Bavinck does not because it is taken directly from E. Sartorius, *Die Lehre von der heiligen Liebe*, 293: "Es ist nicht nur alle Abgötterei Sünde, sondern auch alle Sünde Abgötterei."

51. DO: *bijgeloof*; German: *Aberglaube* = *super* in *superstitio*. Ed. note: Later Bavinck will speak of "super-faith" (*overgeloof*).

52. R. Hofmann, "Aberglaube," 1:63. Ed. note: Hofmann provides no source for Nitzsch.

53. Cicero, *On the Nature of the Gods* (*De natura deorum*) II.28 (LCL 268:192–93). Ed. note: This reference, as well as the earlier unspecified one to Grimm, was taken from R. Hofmann, "Aberglaube," 1:63.

δεισιδαιμονία can be used for proper fear of the gods but is mostly used for a wrong fear (Acts 17:22; 25:19). In the past superstition was at times also taken to mean all false faith more broadly, but still always as a false religious phenomenon. In the previous century, it was seen mostly as mental derangement, and the concept was limited to the so-called physic superstition. And the essence of superstition was sought in it being a faith without intellectual inquiry and judgment. Kant described it as the preconceived notion to see nature as if it were not subject to the rules that are basic to the law governing the thinking itself, or elsewhere as the letting go of the laws of the mind and surrendering to pure authority, to pure facts.[54] Reinhard also considers superstition in religion as the mistake of not observing the laws of reason in our knowledge and adoration of God and instead being guided by imaginary experiences and the promptings of the imagination (polytheistic anthropomorphism and false religion).[55] Physical superstition takes place when people ascribe determining influence to natural causes and act in accordance with these beliefs.[56] The criterion here is thus something foolish and unreasonable that flows from the imagination.

In the Reformed tradition superstition is usually described as attributing power to words, things, or customs to deflect evil or obtain something good which they possess neither by nature nor according to God's Word.[57] Furthermore, if some activity is manifested, then it must be explained as from the devil or from other causes. This definition does not differ significantly from the one given by Tholuck, Ammon, or Hofmann. Tholuck defines superstition as "a mistaken theoretical or practical relation to divine causality."[58] Ammon defines it as "mistaken judgment about the causal relationship of things based on a mystical view of the unseen world."[59] And Hofmann speaks of "erroneous beliefs about the contradiction between reason and revelation that ignore the laws of nature for a causal nexus between supernatural powers and sensory

---

54. Ed. note: This statement is taken from Kant's *Critique of Judgment* (division 1, §40), where Kant summarizes his "Maxims of Common Human Understanding." The first maxim ("to think for oneself") is "the maxim of a Reason never *passive*. The tendency to such passivity, and therefore to heteronomy of the Reason, is called *prejudice*; and the greatest prejudice of all is to represent nature as not subject to the rules that the Understanding places at its basis by means of its own essential law, i.e., is *superstition*. Deliverance from superstition is called *enlightenment*" (Kant, *Kant's Critique of Judgement*, 171).

55. Reinhard, *System der christlichen Moral*, 1:414–41 (§§107–9).

56. See R. Hofmann, "Aberglaube," 63.

57. Ursinus, *Schat-boek*, 2:247–61; de Moor, *Commentarius Perpetuus*, 2:707.

58. GO: *ein verkehrtes theoretisches oder praktisches Verhalten zur göttlichen Kausalität*; Tholuck, "Aberglaube," 44.

59. GO: *ein verkehrtes Urtheil über den Kausalzusammenhang der Dinge nach einer mystischen Ansicht der unsichtbaren Welt*; cited by Tholuck, "Aberglaube," 44.

effects, and vice versa."[60] With superstition we are always in religious territory; there is also superstition in arts and science, but then this has been transferred from the religious arena. It is, namely, always faith in supernatural powers and workings (here to be distinguished from that which is unscientific), and, therefore, someone who is very scientific and knows the nature of things well and is well acquainted with what is perceptible to the senses may nevertheless be very superstitious and have all sorts of strange ideas about the supernatural (Roman Catholics). Superstition thus encompasses

a. ideas and thoughts of superhuman, supernatural powers, forces, and workings, and faith in fairies, elves, ghosts, witches, and so on;
b. acting in keeping with that belief, using all sorts of miraculous means;
c. suffering under and from that belief, fearing omens, ghosts, witches, and so forth.

Superstitions are always the remnants, the leftovers of a past religion that are retained in the new one, and thus among Christians the remnants of pagan religion.[61] This is partially true; superstition is always pagan. But it may be that the superstitions are not remnants from the past but arise once again from paganism and pagan principles and find their way into Christianity as in Roman Catholicism.[62] Superstition, for that matter, is related to unbelief; they are two sides of a coin. Where true faith recedes, both superstition and unbelief arise. Indeed, pure, unadulterated unbelief is a denial of all that is divine, supernatural,[63] but whoever applauds such unbelief posits by that very fact the divinity of the creature, of nature as existing in and by itself as something divine. This is precisely the essence of superstition. Today, instead of the conscious, living God, materialism gives us the dark, subconscious, secret forces of nature; the conscious Spirit of God makes room for the dark, incomprehensible, wild, roaming forces of nature; light makes room for darkness, and the Word for the unconscious; a clear understanding of divine wisdom makes way for the dark will and drives of nature.[64]

We may, therefore, make a distinction between objective and subjective superstition.[65]

60. GO: *irriger Glaube von einem der Vernunft und Offenbarung widersprechenden, die Naturgesetze ignorirenden Causalnexus übersinnlicher Kräfte und sinnlicher Wirkungen, und umgekehrt*; R. Hofmann, "Aberglaube," 64.

61. Vilmar, *Theologische Moral*, 1:324.

62. Wuttke, *Handbuch der christlichen Sittenlehre³*, 2:49 (§167).

63. Wuttke, *Handbuch der christlichen Sittenlehre³*, 2:48–53 (§167).

64. DO: *donkere wil en natuurdrang* (Schopenhauer and von Hartmann).

65. Ed. note: Bavinck has likely taken over this distinction from R. Hofmann, "Aberglaube," 66.

a. Objectively, superstition consists of incorrect, false ideas about God and the supernatural world. In that respect all non-Christian and false-Christian religion is superstition. One imagines God and the spiritual world to be different from what they truly are according to the Word of God. When one denies them totally or in part, it is called unbelief. When one adds other forces, beings, and so on, then it is "super-faith," superstition.[66] But in either case, one imagines realities as different from what they really are. Whoever abandons the only revelation by which these realities can be known is then delivered to subjective opinion and fantasy. Such people have no firm footing and vacillate between unbelief and superstition.[67] With every change of religious ideas, the most hardened unbeliever turns into a person filled with superstition! But, that said, "super-faith" is called superstition.[68] Then the spiritual, supernatural world is populated with all sorts of fantastic beings that exist only in the imagination, with a hidden, secret, blind fate that stands above God and all sorts of beings that are more or less connected to nature standing next to God: witches, fairies, goblins, leprechauns, dwarfs, nixies, werewolves, ghosts, elves, fairies, nymphs, will-o'-the-wisps, and devils (insofar as their depictions go beyond those found in Holy Scripture).[69]

b. Subjectively, superstition is the human idea that human beings are in possession of and have at their disposal means by which they are able to control or employ (engage for their own purposes) the Godhead, fate, or those imaginary spirits, or get something out of them.[70] In a narrow sense

66. Ed. note: Bavinck plays here on two Dutch words: *ongeloof* (= unbelief) and *bijgeloof* (= superstition). He also uses another preposition, *over* (= over; super), in parallel with *bij* (= near, with).

67. Jean Paul said, "I would rather live in the thickest foul air of superstition than under the air pump of unbelief; in the former breathing is difficult, in the latter one suffocates" (*Ich möchte lieber in der dicksten Schwadenluft des Aberglaubens als under der Luftpumpe des Unglaubens leben; dort atmet man schwer, hier erstickt man* [cited by Freybe, "Die deutsche Volksoberglaube," 183]). Ed. note: Jean Paul (1763–1825) (born Johann Paul Friedrich Richter) was a German Romantic writer, whose most famous novel was the four-volume *Titan*, published between 1800 and 1803 (Wikipedia, s.v. "Jean Paul," https://en.wikipedia.org/wiki/Jean_Paul; "*Titan* [Jean Paul novel]," https://en.wikipedia.org/wiki/Titan_(Jean_Paul_novel).

68. DO: *over-geloof*; *bijgeloof*.

69. As happened in the Middle Ages; see Wuttke, *Der deutsche Volksaberglaube*; van Heijningen, *De geestenwereld*. Ed. note: Bavinck provided no specific pages for the preceding references; undoubtedly he had the entire volumes in mind. He concludes the note in his manuscript with a reference to "Studiën en Bijdragen historische Theologie II." The full title of the journal is *Studiën en bijdragen op 't gebied der historische theologie*, and vol. 2 (1895) contains the following articles relevant to Bavinck's point: Wybrands, "De Dialogus Miraculorum"; Moll, "Bijdrage tot de kennis"; Verwijs, "Bijdrage tot de kennis."

70. Ed. note: Bavinck's source is R. Hofmann, "Aberglaube," 63; cf. Gillespie, "Superstition."

this is called *sorcery*.[71] This phenomenon is also called by the strange word *magia*, which the Latins borrowed from the Greeks, who in turn took it from the Persians. Among the Persians *magus/magi* referred to priests and wise men who were familiar with astrology, dream interpretation, and miraculous medical workings. In Hebrew, sorcerers are called מְכַשְּׁפִים (from כשׁף = to speak softly, mumble incantations).[72] The word is also found in Exodus 7:11 where it is linked with another term, חַרְטֹם (cf. Exod. 7:22), which refers to eminent writers—namely, of hieroglyphics.[73] In a broader sense, it is already sorcery when one prescribes means other than those given by God to obtain some good such as salvation from him. "For rebellion is as the sin of divination, / and presumption is as iniquity and idolatry" (1 Sam. 15:23). Examples include Roman Catholic works-righteousness, use of formulas and rosaries, water from Lourdes, the Shroud of Turin, the image of Saint Januarius,[74] relics, pilgrimages, exorcisms, consecrations, and the like. Examples from the pagan world include human sacrifices, cultic prostitution, emasculation, ascetic means—in other words, all efforts to ward off or obtain something by unauthorized ways.[75] People also try to acquire power over fate or obtain information about it. It is thought that this is associated with or dependent on specific times, days; Sunday is a lucky day, Friday is unlucky, and thus we get April 1, Walpurgis Night,[76] Sylvester,[77] New Year's Day, Easter morning, and others. These times then become the object of specific inquiry, which then turns into fortune-telling.

71. DO: *toverij*; probably from *touwen, zouwan* = to make, with the associated notion of artful; Gothic: *tanjan* = to make, to do, to complete (*tooien; voltooien*); Italian: *fattuchiero*, also pointing to *facere* = to do; cf. Lange, "Zauberei," 391.

72. Ed. note: Here Bavinck gives this citation: "Dan. 2:43, cf. Jer. 39:13." He took over these references from Lange, "Zauberei," 391, but this is clearly incorrect. The word מְכַשְּׁפִים (= conjurer, necromancer) is found in Dan. 2:2. The ESV and NRSV here translate the word as "enchanters."

73. Ed. note: According to BDB, חַרְטֹם = "engraver, writer only in a derivative sense of one possessed of occult knowledge, *diviner, astrologer, magician*." Most contemporary translations render the term as "sorcerer" in Exod. 7:11.

74. Ed. note: Saint Januarius was a third-century (d. 305) bishop and martyr; he is "the patron saint of Naples [Italy], where the faithful gather three times a year in Naples Cathedral to witness the liquefaction of what is claimed to be a sample of his blood kept in a sealed glass ampoule" (Wikipedia, s.v. "Januarius," https://en.wikipedia.org/wiki/Januarius).

75. DO: *ongeordende*; cf. R. Hofmann, "Aberglaube," 66.

76. Ed. note: Walpurgis Night (DO: *Walpurgisnacht*) is the eve of April 30 and receives its name from the feast day of Saint Walpurga (ca. 710–777/779), an Anglo-Saxon missionary to the Franks. She was canonized on May 1, ca. 870, by Pope Adrian II. The eve is also called "Witches Night" (*Hexennacht* in German; *heksennacht* in Dutch), a gathering of the witches on the Brocken, the highest peak in the Harz mountains. Bonfires are burned to ward off this gathering (Wikipedia, s.v. "Walpurgis Night," https://en.wikipedia.org/wiki/Walpurgis_Night; Wikipedia, s.v. "Saint Walpurga," https://en.wikipedia.org/wiki/Saint_Walpurga).

77. Ed. note: Sylvester refers to New Year's Eve.

Fate is also thought of as being tied to specific natural phenomena and fortuitous events:[78] comets, stars and astrology, Northern Lights, a howling dog on the property, a raven by the window, a falling mirror, the clock stopping, the call of a cuckoo, tables lifting, and so on. Fate is also linked to secret forces and beings: witches, fairies, werewolves, nixies, and vampires—the object of investigation by the secret arts. And then people also try to subdue this spirit world of elves and fairies for their own purposes through incantations (Exod. 8:7), such as the Roman Catholic practice of using the sign of the cross to ward off evil spirits or attacking them by uttering certain formulas, such as the name of the Trinity or Jesus, as the Jewish exorcists do in Acts 19:13. Holy Scripture teaches us the following about sorcery: sorcerers are mentioned first in Egypt (Gen. 41:8). Then, in the confrontation between God and Pharaoh, Egypt's sorcerers imitate Aaron's miracle by throwing down their staffs, which, like Aaron's staff, also become snakes (Exod. 7:10–12); they also change water into blood (7:22) and make frogs appear in the land of Egypt (8:7). But that is as far as they are able to go; they cannot turn dust into gnats and say, "This is the finger of God" (8:18–19). It has been suggested that Exodus 8:7, as well as the other verses, ought to be translated differently—namely, "and they [the sorcerers] did the same [they imitated Moses and Aaron] with their incantations *so that* they might make frogs come up on the land of Egypt." In other words, they tried it but were unsuccessful. Others—for example, Justin Martyr, Tertullian, Ambrose, and Jerome[79]—see these acts of the sorcerers as sleight of hand, sorcery, and cheating; for instance, a snake was hidden in a hollow staff, or their staffs were dried-up snakes, they secretly mixed the water with blood, had frogs under their garments. But most consider these acts objective miracles, possible by way of a covenant with or help from the devil. This distinguishes them from real, actual miracles, which only God can do, but they were nonetheless amazing, wondrous things that go beyond our powers and consist in a freer command over the forces and laws of nature. Scripture acknowledges demonic miracles (Deut. 13:1–2; Matt. 24:24; 2 Thess. 2:9; Rev. 13:13–15). And it was not deception, but certainly a battle between God and the powers and gods of Egypt (Exod. 12:12; Num. 33:4).[80]

Next, we meet the medium of Endor (1 Sam. 28), who had a spirit of divination.[81] There are essentially three views of this event:

78. DO: *toevallige gebeurtenissen.*
79. Staringh, *Bybels Zakelyk-Woordenboek*, 8/1: 299. Ed. note: In addition to the page number, Bavinck specifies the article: Paulus, "Tooveraars (De Egyptische)."
80. Köhler, *Lehrbuch der Biblischen Geschichte Alten Testamentes*, I/i:185–87; J. von Hofmann, *Der Schriftbeweis*, 348–55.
81. Vitringa, *Doctrina Christianae Religionis*, 2:123; Bardenhewer, *Patrology*, 297.

(a) The view of the church fathers, the Reformers, and Protestants. These do not assume an actual appearance of Samuel to Saul but only an illusionary one, a diabolical ghost in the image of Samuel. The words Samuel speaks are therefore not true divine revelation either, but a mixture of truth and lies.

(b) The rationalistic perspective of Reginald Scot and Balthasar Bekker.[82] The entire event is regarded as a ruse by the woman, having nothing to do with the devil; the woman was an impostor, and the one telling the story also considers it to be a case of deception.

(c) A more recent interpretation considers this as an actual appearance by Samuel, not really called up by the woman as if she had power over the dead but sent to her by God against the will and expectation of the woman, even though she was an impostor. The purpose was for God to make known his judgment to Saul through Samuel and the woman.[83]

Seeing Samuel, the woman is frightened (v. 12).[84]

We further read about sorcerers in Babylon (Dan. 1:20), where they are mentioned along with astrologers, enchanters, Chaldeans, and fortune-tellers (4:7; 5:11). And in the New Testament we read about Elymas the magician on the island of Salamis (Acts 13:8), Simon in Samaria (Acts 8:9), a servant girl in Philippi who had a spirit by which she predicted the future (Acts 16:16) and who made pious speeches even though she had an evil spirit. And in Acts 19:13 we read of some who drove out evil spirits, invoking the name of Jesus over those who were demon-possessed, just as we read of viper-charmers (Ps. 58:5–6; Prov. 10:11; Jer. 8:17).

82. Bekker, *De betoverde weereld*, 3:vi. Ed. note: Bavinck takes the reference to Reginald Scot and Balthasar Bekker (Keil's spelling: Becker) directly from Keil and Delitzsch, *Biblical Commentary on the Books of Samuel*, 266. Reginald Scot (ca. 1538–99) was the author of *The Discoverie of Witchcraft* (1584), a treatise against the belief in witches. There is an English translation of Bekker's work: *The World Bewitch'd, or, An Examination of the Common Opinions concerning Spirits*.

83. Voetius disputes this, observing that if God had wanted to reveal his will, he certainly would have done it through prophets, by a dream, or by other means (Luke 4:35); see Voetius, *Selectarum Disputationum Theologicarum*, 2:1114.

84. According to Keil and Delitzsch, *Biblical Commentary on the Books of Samuel*, 262: "These words imply most unquestionably that the woman saw an apparition which she did not anticipate, and therefore that she was not really able to conjure up departed spirits or persons who had died, but that she either merely pretended to do so, or if her witchcraft was not mere trickery and delusion, but had a certain demoniacal background, that the appearance of Samuel differed essentially from everything she had experienced and effected before, and therefore filled her with alarm and horror." Köhler, *Lehrbuch der Biblischen Geschichte Alten Testamentes*, II/i:232–34.

On the basis of all these references in Scripture to demonic workings, the Christian church also assumed generally that sorcery, however often mixed with deception, nevertheless was able to do extraordinary things sometimes through a covenant with the devil.[85] But Holy Scripture strongly condemns all this magic and fortune-telling:

Exodus 22:18: "You shall not permit a sorceress to live."

Leviticus 19:26: "You shall not interpret omens or tell fortunes."

Leviticus 19:31: "Do not turn to mediums or necromancers; do not seek them out, and so make yourselves unclean by them: I am the LORD your God."

Leviticus 20:27: "A man or a woman who is a medium or a necromancer shall surely be put to death. They shall be stoned with stones; their blood shall be upon them."

Deuteronomy 18:10–12: "There shall not be found among you anyone who burns his son or his daughter as an offering, anyone who practices divination or tells fortunes or interprets omens, or a sorcerer or a charmer or a medium or a necromancer or one who inquires of the dead, for whoever does these things is an abomination to the LORD. And because of these abominations the LORD your God is driving them out before you."

Notwithstanding these strong prohibitions, and although Balaam's blessing of Israel included the statement "For there is no enchantment against Jacob, / no divination against Israel; / now it shall be said of Jacob and Israel, / 'What has God wrought!'" (Num. 23:23), sorcery was nevertheless practiced in Israel. Saul had attempted to eradicate it but was still able to find a medium when he wanted one (1 Sam. 28:9–19). Therefore, the prophets continue to mention it (Isa. 47:9, 12; Jer. 27:9; 29:8; Mic. 3:7; 5:12; Nah. 3:4; Mal. 3:5). The New Testament condemns sorcery as well. Paul includes sorcery[86] among the works of the flesh along with idolatry (Gal. 5:20; cf. Rev. 9:21). Christians are commanded, "Take no part in the unfruitful works of darkness, but instead expose them" (Eph. 5:11; cf. Acts 8:9–13; 13:6–12; 19:13–20). The apostle John tells us that "the reason the Son of God appeared was to destroy the works of the devil" (1 John 3:8). The destiny of sorcerers, along with "the cowardly,

---

85. This was also the view of the Reformed: see de Moor, *Commentarius Perpetuus*, 2:706–8; Voetius, *Selectarum Disputationum Theologicarum*, 3:529–632; Heidegger, *Corpus Theologiae Christianae*, 1:292–97 (locus VIII, §§66–76); Ursinus, *Schat-boek*, 2:247, 260; Ursinus, *Commentary on the Heidelberg Catechism*, 509.

86. GrO: φαρμακεία.

the faithless, the detestable, murderers, the sexually immoral, . . . idolaters, and all liars," is "the lake that burns with fire and sulfur, which is the second death" (Rev. 21:8; cf. 22:15). The return of Christ, the apostle Paul tells us, is accompanied by a revelation of "the lawless one," whose coming is "the activity of Satan" and will be demonstrated "with all power and false signs and wonders" (2 Thess. 2:9; cf. Rev. 13:13–14; 16:14; 19:20). Sorcery, therefore, shall become mighty in the hands of the devil. According to Scripture, sorcery and divination are the Satanic, pagan imitations and caricatures of divine miracles and prophecy.[87]

3. The Invocation of Saints and Angels

In the apostolic epistles all believers are called saints. In the second and third centuries this became gradually a name of honor for those who through their faith, walk, or martyrdom were examples. Such "saints," "God-lovers," "blessed ones,"[88] were remembered after their death in their own communities and far beyond, especially on the "anniversary of their death."[89] The burial sites of these saints were considered holy and visited on the anniversaries of their deaths, their bones were esteemed more than gold, and at the commemorations of their life and death Holy Communion was celebrated on site. Besides these personal days, an All Saints' Day began to be observed in the Eastern Church in the fourth century.[90] This also came to the West in the seventh century, and here November 1 was set apart. At first a proper distinction was made between adoration of God and rendering honor to the saints.[91] But as a result of the increasing observance of rules and precepts, because of the value attached to ascetism, celibacy, monasticism, and belief in miracles performed by such saints, these saints soon were seen as intercessors,[92] as powerful protectors, as intercessors and mediators who through Christ hear our prayers and are able to help us, not only spiritually (forgiveness of sins) but also physically (e.g., in illnesses).[93] Temples and chapels were built on their graves; the ill were brought there; all kinds of precious objects (garments, gold, etc.) were hung there as votive offerings; their relics were carried around; patron saints

---

87. Wuttke, *Handbuch der christlichen Sittenlehre*[3], 2:52 (§167); Pictet, *De christelyke zedekunst*, III:vii.

88. GrO: ἅγιοι, θεοφιλέστατοι, μακάριοι. Ed. note: Bavinck's source here is likely von Grüneisen, "Heilige, deren Anrufung und Verehrung," 709.

89. GrO: γενέθλια τῶν μαρτύρων.

90. GrO: κυριακὴ πάντων τῶν ἁγίων καὶ μαρτύρων—ἑορτὴ τῶν ἁγίων. Ed. note: Bavinck's source is von Grüneisen, "Heilige, deren Anrufung und Verehrung," 709.

91. E.g., Eusebius, *Ecclesiastical History* IV.15.

92. DO: *voorbidders*.

93. LO: *patroni, intercessores, mediators*.

were chosen; ships, houses, temples, cities, church bells were placed under the protection of certain saints.[94]

Some theologians did oppose excesses and abuse,[95] but in the East, this adoration of the saints was officially adopted by the Second Council of Nicaea in 787, after John of Damascus had defended the practice. In the West theological scholarship tried to defend the adoration of saints. Just as Augustine and Jerome had done, the council distinguished *adoration*, which belongs to God alone, from *invocation*, which is appropriate to the saints.[96] According to Perrone, *invocation* is due to saints as those who share God's grace, thus *in this respect* and *analogically*, just as all of us participate in God's *being* although God alone is and remains Being itself.[97]

Thomas says that honor is due to other superiors, also among people who are still living.[98] In answer to the objection "It would seem that we ought to pray to God alone,"[99] Thomas responds:[100]

> Prayer is offered to a person in two ways: first, as to be fulfilled by him, secondly as to be obtained through him. In the first way we offer to God alone, since God alone gives, according to Psalm 83:12, "The Lord will give grace and glory." But in the second way we pray to saints, whether angels or men, not that God may through them know our petitions, but that our prayers may be effective through their prayers and merits.[101]

It is of course true, he adds, that "the dead, if we consider their natural condition, do not know what takes place in this world, especially the interior movements of the heart."[102] "Nevertheless, according to Gregory (*Moral.* xii, 21), whatever it is fitting the blessed should know about what happens to us, even as regards the interior movements of the heart, is made known

94. E.g., Rome under Peter and Paul, Spain under James, Greece under Andreas, painters under Luke, seafarers under Phocas, theologians under John the Evangelist and Augustine, jurists under Ivo. Ed. note: Bavinck's source is von Grüneisen, "Heilige, deren Anrufung und Verehrung," 709–10.

95. Namely, Augustine, Chrysostom, and especially Vigilantius in Barcelona in the fifth century.

96. GrO/LO: λατρεία/*adoratio*; δουλεία προσκύνησις/*invocatio*; Augustine, *De Trinitate* I.6.1.

97. DO: *de Zijnde*; GrO: δουλεία; σχετικῶς and ἀναλόγως; Perrone, *Praelectiones Theologicae* (1856), 1:1153–235; Pruner, *Lehrbuch der katholischen Moraltheologie*[1], 262–63.

98. Aquinas, *ST* IIa IIae q. 103 arts. 1–4; cf. IIa IIae q. 83 art. 4 arg. 1.

99. LO: *Videtur quod solus Deus debeat orari*; *ST* IIa IIae q. 103 art. 4 arg. 1.

100. Ed. note: In what follows we are providing the full quotations from Thomas in the main text where Bavinck uses partial quotes and places some of his material in footnotes.

101. *ST* IIa IIae q. 103 art. 4 co.

102. LO: *quod mortui ea quae in hoc mundo aguntur, considerata eorum naturali conditione, non cognoscunt, et praecipue interiores motus cordis*; *ST* IIa IIae q. 83 art. 4 ad 2.

to them in the Word: and it is most becoming to their exalted position that they should know the petitions we make to them by word or thought; and consequently the petitions which we raise to them are known to them through Divine manifestation."[103]

When the number of saints increased, they were hierarchically classified.[104] At the top is Mary, the mother of God, the Queen of heaven, at first honored because she is the mother of Christ, and shortly thereafter also as *perpetual virgin* (Epiphanius, Jerome). She was glorified in the apocryphal gospels and highly honored especially since the fifth century, when the term "Mother of God" or "God-bearer" was used against Nestorius.[105] Mary was placed at the head of all saints, temples and statues were dedicated to her, and miracles ascribed to her. She was depicted in art in certain ways that led to veneration and service by knights in the Middle Ages, especially by Germans, as "Our Lady" and as "the deified."[106] Mary was celebrated as possessor and dispenser of all grace, especially in the orders, among which the Franciscans (Duns Scotus and others) taught her immaculate conception.[107] In its decree on original sin, the Council of Trent declared "that it is not its intention to include in this decree, where original sin is treated of, the blessed and immaculate

103. LO: *Sed beatis, ut Gregorius dicit, in XII Moral., in verbo manifestatur illud quod decet eos cognoscere de eis quae circa nos aguntur, etiam quantum ad interiores motus cordis. Maxime autem eorum excellentiam decet ut cognoscant petitiones ad eos factas vel voce vel corde. Et ideo petitiones quas ad eos dirigimus, Deo manifestante, cognoscunt; ST* IIa IIae q. 83 art. 4 ad 2.

Ed. note: Bavinck calls attention here to a note (#1) affixed to this answer to the second objection in IIa IIae q. 83 art. 4: "This is the more probable, but even if it is not for us to know that saints hear our particular prayers, nevertheless it is not in vain that they should be directed to them, because it is sufficient for us to pray to them generally for needed supplications" (*Id probabilius est, sed etiamsi nobis non constaret sanctos cognoscere preces nostras in particulari, non tamen frustra ad illos eas dirigeremus, quia sufficeret nobis eos generaliter orare, pro supplicantium indigentia*). The note is found in the thirteenth edition of *S. Thomae Aquinatis Summa Theologica*, vol. 4, *Secunda secundae, I–XCI*, 568. The note gives the following references: "ita de Walemburch et August, apud Natal. Alexand. Saecul. V. dissert 23, quaest 11, proposit. 1; Hugo Victor lib. Ii, de suam p. 16, c. 11, Bellarm. Lib. 1 de beatitudino c. 20, Estius, m in 4, dist 45, §20, Sylvius, et alii." The reference to "Gregory, *Moral*. XII, 21" is to Gregory the Great's *The Book of the Morals: An Exposition on the Book of Blessed Job*. It can be found in *PL* vols. 75–76; ET: *Moral Reflections on the Book of Job* (trans. Kerns). Book 12 is found in vol. 3.

104. For what follows, see S. Steitz, "Maria, die Mutter des Herrn"; Hodge, *Systematic Theology*, 3:281–90.

105. GrO: θεοτόκος. Ed. note: At the Third Ecumenical Council, the Council of Ephesus, AD 431.

106. FO: *Notre Dame*; LO: *deificata*. Ed. note: This unusual juxtaposition of German knights and veneration of Mary as "Notre Dame" (in the French language) is Bavinck's own creation; the reference to German knights comes from S. Steitz, "Maria, die Mütter des Herrn," 317–18.

107. Ed. note: Hodge elaborates on the disagreement between the Franciscans and the Dominicans on the immaculate conception of Mary, concluding that "this question was undecided at the time of the meeting of the Council of Trent" (Hodge, *Systematic Theology*, 3:289).

Virgin Mary mother of God."[108] Pope Pius IX promulgated the dogma of the immaculate conception on December 8, 1854, in the bull *Ineffabilis Deus*.[109] Like Christ, Mary was immaculately conceived, was resurrected, ascended into heaven, and became a participant in the Godhead through Jesus in the same way that Jesus became a participant in humanity through her. She is thus the personification and representation of the Roman Catholic Church itself, as Thomas says: "It was fitting that Christ should be born of an espoused virgin; first, for His own sake; secondly, for His Mother's sake; thirdly, for our sake."[110] The fourth reason Thomas gives is that "because by this the universal Church is typified, which is a virgin and yet is espoused to one Man, Christ, as Augustine says (*De Sanct. Virg.* xii)."[111] Indeed, the Roman Catholic Church is the womb from which Christ is born daily with his life and sacrifice, the *mediatrix* and most blessed of all, born immaculately, maiden and mother at the same time, possessor and distributor of all grace, and so on.[112]

Concerning the veneration of saints, at the twenty-fifth session of the council (Dec. 3–4, 1563), in the decree *Invocation, Veneration, and Relics of Saints, and on Sacred Images*, Trent commanded "all bishops and others who hold the office of teaching and its administration," that "they above all diligently instruct the faithful on the intercession and invocation of the saints, the veneration of relics, and the legitimate use of images, teaching them that the saints, who reign together with Christ, offer up their prayers to God for men; and that it is good and useful to invoke them suppliantly and, in order to obtain favors from God through His Son Jesus Christ our Lord, who alone is our Redeemer and Savior, to have recourse to their prayers, assistance, and support."[113] The *Roman Catechism* teaches the same. The

---

108. Session IV, June 17, 1546 (Denzinger, no. 789.6). Ed. note: The same decree, however, did refer back with favor to Pope Sixtus IV's constitution "Cum praeexcelsa" (Feb. 28, 1476), which did affirm Mary's immaculate conception (Denzinger, no. 734). Another Pope Sixtus constitution, "Grave nimis" (Sept. 4, 1483), "reproved and condemned" preachers who taught that those who affirm the immaculate conception "sin grievously" (Denzinger, no. 734).

109. Ed. note: Denzinger, no. 1641.

110. *ST* IIIa q. 29 art. 1 co.

111. LO: *quia per hoc significatur universa Ecclesia, quae, cum virgo sit, desponsata tamen est uni viro Christo, ut Augustinus dicit, in libro de sancta virginitate; ST* IIIa q. 29 art. 1 co. Ed. note: Thomas refers to Augustine, *Of Holy Virginity* 12 (*NPNF¹* 3:42).

112. Marginal note: "Thus, also Chantepie de la Saussaye." Ed. note: Bavinck provides only the last name, giving no indication whether he is referring to the "ethical" theologian Daniel Chantepie de la Saussaye (1818–74) or to his son Pierre Daniël Chantepie de la Saussaye (1848–1920), the well-known phenomenologist of religion.

113. Denzinger, no. 984. Ed. note: Bavinck's source is von Grüneisen, "Heilige, deren Anrufung und Verehrung," 712.

saints are able to help since they reign with Christ; their intercession is effective because of their merit and Christ's merit; their invocation was not commanded, but it was said to be good and useful.[114] More recent Roman Catholic theologians appeal to Numbers 22:31; Joshua 5:15; 2 Kings 1:13; 4:37; and Revelation 5:8; 8:3–4; 20:4.[115] Protestant objections appeal to such passages as the following:

- "It is the LORD your God you shall fear. Him you shall serve and by his name you shall swear" (Deut. 6:13).
- "I am the LORD; that is my name; / my glory I give to no other, / nor my praise to carved idols" (Isa. 42:8).
- "You shall worship the Lord your God / and him only shall you serve" (Matt. 4:10).
- "To the King of the ages, immortal, invisible, the only God, be honor and glory forever and ever. Amen" (1 Tim. 1:17).
- "Then I fell down at his feet to worship him, but he said to me, 'You must not do that! I am a fellow servant with you and your brothers who hold to the testimony of Jesus. Worship God'" (Rev. 19:10).[116]

But it is not only Roman Catholics who transgress the First Commandment with their veneration of the saints, worship of relics, and pilgrimages. So do the Arians, who deny Jesus's divinity and yet worship him. Similarly, the Socinians and many modernists today, who, for instance, still use the baptismal formula, pray in Jesus's name, and so on.[117] The same is true of Albrecht Ritschl, who denies Jesus's divinity but nevertheless ascribes divine properties to him because he reveals God by living "a life of mastery over the world," which then "makes possible the community in which each Christian is to attain the similar destiny of the life eternal."[118] To this should be added

114. *Catechism of the Council of Trent*, III, ii (First Commandment). Ed. note: Bavinck took his own reference to "the Roman Catechism (III, ii qu. 4 [xix.10])" from Hodge, *Systematic Theology*, 3:283.

115. Ed. note: In a note Bavinck refers to Möhler, *Symbolik*, §45 (ET: *Symbolism*); and Perrone, *Praelectiones Theologicae* (1856), 1:1153–235. Bavinck's source for the reference to Möhler is von Grüneisen, "Heilige, deren Anrufung und Verehrung," 713. The references from the book of Revelation are from the same source, p. 712. Bavinck correctly reproduces von Grüneisen's reference to Möhler, but §45 is about ordination, not about prayer to saints. The latter topic is covered in pp. 352–57 (§52).

116. Ed. note: Bavinck includes a reference to Col. 2:18, which does not seem to fit the topic.

117. De Moor, *Commentarius Perpetuus*, 2:701.

118. Ritschl, *Christian Doctrine of Justification and Reconciliation*, 388; cf. Haug, *Darstellung und Beurteilung*, 45–60.

idolizing human beings, the worship of genius, the cult of the intellect, of art, of conquerors like Napoleon, which manifests itself in erecting statues, in the commemoration of birth and death anniversaries, in excusing the mistakes and deficiencies of the genius. Huet noted that irresponsibility is the essence of this glorification of genius, comparing it, as Victor Hugo does in his poem about genius, to Mazeppa tied to his horse and being dragged along; genius seldom makes the rider happy or better or braver.[119] Auguste Comte (1798–1867) spoke of this adoration of genius as decidedly religious. He wanted to reform society and establish a positive religion whose object was humanity in its totality—past, present, and future—a Supreme Great Being made up of all individuals, including even animals (faithful dogs).[120] Comte organized a distinct religion with prayer (a communion of humanity in its noblest representatives), nine sacraments, and a priesthood of spiritual power with Comte himself as the high priest.[121] Its organizing principle was the public veneration of religion, and its three pillars were *altruism, order,* and *progress.*[122] This Comtism is "Catholicism (in form) minus Christianity."[123] Practical adoration of people is found, for instance, with fathers or mothers who rave about and make an idol of their child, with the medieval knights

119. Huet, "Molière en de Moliéristen," 6. Ed. note: Bavinck notes Huet's reference to Victor Hugo's "Mazeppa" poem, translated into Dutch by Jacob Ten Kate. Hugo wrote the poem for his 1829 collection *Les Orientales,* inspired by the Greek War of Independence (1821–31). It was written in May 1828 and is the thirty-fourth poem of *Les Orientales.* Hugo acknowledged his own debt to Lord Byron's narrative poem *Mazeppa,* written in 1819. The story is based on a popular legend of a Ukrainian nobleman, Ivan Mazeppa (1639–1709), who has a love affair with a married Polish countess. When the affair is discovered, Mazeppa is tied naked to a wild horse and the horse is set loose (Wikipedia, s.v. "*Mazeppa* (poem)," https://en.wikipedia.org/wiki /Mazeppa_(poem); "Greek War of Independence," https://en.wikipedia.org/wiki/Greek_War _of_Independence; "*Les Orientales,*" https://en.wikipedia.org/wiki/Les_Orientales). Bavinck also adds this sentence: "Compare also the battle it caused this year in Berlin (1886)"; this seemingly casual comment with no clear referent is nonetheless an important clue for dating Bavinck's manuscript.

120. FO: *Grand-Être.*

121. FO: *le Pouvoir Spirituel; Grand-Prêtre.* Ed. note: One of these sacraments imitated infant baptism: *la presentation,* a presentation of a child to the priest, who then dedicates the child to the service of humanity.

122. Ed. note: Bavinck's own observations have been filled in by the editor from Wikipedia, s.v. "Religion of Humanity," https://en.wikipedia.org/wiki/Religion_of_Humanity. For a contemporary treatment of the subject see Davies, *Humanism,* 25–33; Wernick, *Auguste Comte and the Religion of Humanity.* Bavinck adds that "Comte's successor in Paris was Laffitte" and that "a small congregation of Comtists exists in London under Bridges, later Harrison (see my Excerpts)."

123. DO: *katholicisme (vormen) zonder het Christendom.* Ed. note: This quote is attributed to Thomas Huxley; Bavinck indicates no source, but it can be found in Huxley, *On the Physical Basis of Life,* 19: "In fact, M. Comte's philosophy might be compendiously described as Catholicism *minus* Christianity."

who adored woman, with gallant gentlemen who worship women, and with pious people who idolize "the ancient writers."[124]

Now it is certainly our duty to love our neighbor, to be modest toward all people (Phil. 4:5), to honor the king and all who have been put in places of authority (Rom. 13), to acknowledge fully every gift from God in people (artists, scholars, geniuses, godly people, martyrs, apostles, saints); it is also our duty to imitate the saints (1 Cor. 4:16; 11:1; Heb. 6:12; 13:7),[125] cherish them, and think honorably of them.[126] It is also our duty to esteem the angels (Gen. 18). In Numbers 22:31 and Joshua 5:15 we read about the Angel of the Covenant.[127] Angels and saints are therefore also entitled to conventional honor (Eph. 3:10). If this were all that is intended with the words "veneration" and "invocation," we could appreciate and approve it.[128] But what is meant by it is a religious adoration. Even though this is intended to be in a lesser measure than to God, this is not the way Roman Catholic folk necessarily experience it.[129] Religious adoration is worship, pleading for all sorts of good, forgiveness, mercy, healing, and so on.[130] In the 150 Psalms of the *Psalterium Mariae magnum*, the names of God are changed into Mary: see her epithets there.[131] Although it is said that those angels and saints grant all this through Christ, still the position of Christ as Mediator is thereby actually negated and denied.[132]

For, after all, consider the following:

(a) This does not apply to angels, who do not participate in Christ's work as mediator. In addition, the works of the saints that are accomplished in

---

124. DO: *oude schrijvers*; see Kuyper, *E Voto Dordraceno*, 1:270–77 (Lord's Day, 11/4); originally published in *De Heraut*, no. 508 (September 8, 1887). Ed. note: "Ancient writers" refers to such men of the Further Reformation as, among others, Wilhelm à Brakel, Alexander Comrie, Johannes Hoornbeeck, Herman Witsius, and Gisbert Voetius.

125. Ed. note: Bavinck added an interlinear reference to passages cited earlier as "proof-texts" used by Roman Catholics: 2 Kings 1:13; 4:37; the texts given were added by the editor.

126. Augsburg Confession, art. 21, "Concerning the Cult of the Saints," in Kolb and Wengert, *Book of Concord*, 59; Second Helvetic Confession, chap. 5, in Dennison, *Reformed Confessions of the 16th and 17th Centuries*, 2:816–18. Ed. note: Bavinck's source for these references is Grüneisen, "Heilige, deren Anrufung und Verehrung," 712.

127. DO: *Engel des Verbonds*.

128. GrO/LO: δουλεία/*invocatio*. Ed. note: We have used the double expression "appreciate and approve" to translate *te billijken*.

129. DO: *die het volk toch niet voelt*.

130. DO: *aanbidding, smeking om allerlei heil, vergeving, barmhartigheid, genezing*.

131. S. Steitz, "Maria, die Mutter des Herrn," 318–20. Ed. note: *The Psalter of the Blessed Virgin Mary* (usually attributed to St. Bonaventure) can be seen online at https://www.ewtn.com/catholicism/library/psalter-of-the-bvm-12537; the opening line of Ps. 1 reads: "Blessed is the man, O Virgin Mary, who loves thy name; thy grace will comfort his soul."

132. DO: *ontkeend en geloochend*.

them through Christ are not merits but fruits and proof rather than parts of or additions to the redemption graciously provided in Christ.

(b) To consider the good works of the saints (however accomplished in them) as additions to Christ's work that actually earn forgiveness and other benefits for others denies what Christ has perfectly fulfilled with his one sacrifice (Heb. 10:14). Rome's position is, in fact, this: just as a stone thrown into the water makes a circle and this in turn creates others and so on, so Christ is the center and starts the impact that now flows from him to others, who are prompted by him, in ever wider and diminishing circles. Protestants, by contrast, teach the scriptural truth that all must be joined to Christ individually and personally, and in that way share in Christ and his merits. The Roman notion of "implicit faith" suggests a series of "aeons/ aions" emanating from Christ, a number of mediators between Christ and my soul, no immediate connection with God, but with and through others.[133] In Rome's case this leads toward deification of humans and the church as *mediatrix*, with God at an unattainable distance, to be approached only by a few privileged persons. For the common people of God, therefore, Christ and his work recede entirely to a nebulous, dark, transcendent, deistic background, and the saints hold an ever-more-prominent place. It *is* a worship of human beings.

Now Scripture clearly forbids such worship of saints and angels in the following commandment given to us: "It is the LORD your God you shall fear. Him you shall serve and by his name you shall swear. You shall not go after other gods, the gods of the peoples who are around you" (Deut. 6:13–14; cf. Matt. 4:10). Glory and honor are to be given to God alone: "To the King of the ages, immortal, invisible, the only God, be honor and glory forever and ever. Amen" (1 Tim. 1:17). Furthermore, the saints do not know us: "For you are our Father, / though Abraham does not know us, / and Israel does not acknowledge us; / you, O LORD, are our Father, / our Redeemer from of old is your name" (Isa. 63:16).[134]

Roman Catholics, therefore, are also unable to explain how the saints know our prayers: Either God must impart the prayers to the saints—and then prayer to them is superfluous—or the saints themselves are omniscient, and then

---

133. LO: *fides implicita*. Ed. note: Bavinck also uses a Dutch transliteration for the Greek term for "emanations": *aeonen*, from the Greek αἰών = age. Bavinck thus links the Roman Catholic notion of implicit faith to Neo-Platonist and gnostic cosmology. The link is a (debatable) comparison between the gnostic notion of aeonic emanations and angels in the Christian tradition. The primary source for this comparison is the twin writings of Pseudo-Dionysius, *The Celestial Hierarchies* and *The Ecclesiastical Hierarchies*.

134. Ed. note: Bavinck adds a marginal note here: "*ST*, Suppl. IIIae. q. 72 art. 1: 'Whether the saints have knowledge of our prayers.'"

God is superfluous.[135] Some say that angels descend to earth and, returning to heaven, share these prayers with the saints. Others claim that the saints, like the angels, are equipped with marvelous speed and therefore everywhere present.[136] There are also those who say that the saints are able to see everything they need to know, whether in God or in Christ. Some say that God reveals our prayers to the saints in much the same way that he revealed things to the prophets.[137] Still others believe that it is not necessary at all that the saints know everything; it is sufficient for them to know that we are very needy in everything.[138] This surely proves that Scripture is silent about it and that the whole notion is pure fantasy. Furthermore, the saints (and angels) themselves resisted such prayers and adoration (Acts 10:25–26; 14:15; Rev. 19:10). And Rome, like the pagans, invokes those who are by nature no gods (Gal. 4:8).

*What is **commanded** in this commandment?*

The relationship in which we are to stand to God according to this commandment is frequently discussed in Holy Scripture. First, the true, living God whom we must serve is not only Father, but the Triune God. If not triune, then he is not the complete, true God. This commandment may not be explained in a unitarian way. Whoever does not honor the Son and Spirit does not honor the Father either (1 John 2:23).[139] Thus, the relationship we have with God is expressed by knowing, believing, trusting, relying, hoping, expecting, loving, fearing, honoring, being submissive, confessing, and so forth.[140] These are not tautological terms but a series of subtle distinctions and nuances of that one great relationship that we must have with God. We may reduce them to three: *faith, hope,* and *love.* But in whatever way Scripture expresses this relationship, God desires to have us *always entirely* and *everywhere* (Matt. 22:37), with all our soul, mind, and strength.[141] Sharing is not possible here. God demands us absolutely, without any condition or exception, under all circumstances, always and everywhere. There never is an excuse for not serving God. God *gives* himself entirely; he *demands* our all.[142]

---

135. Warneck, "Blicke in die römische Missionspraxis," 20. Ed. note: In an opening footnote (p. 3), Warneck refers to his *Protestantische Beleuchtung der römischen Angriffe auf die evangelische Heidenmission.*

136. LO: *quodammodo ubique.*

137. Hodge, *Systematic Theology*, 3:283.

138. *S. Thomae Aquinatis Summa Theologica*, vol. 4, *Secunda secundae, I–XCI*, 568n1; see n. 101 above.

139. E. Sartorius, *Die Lehre von der heiligen Liebe*, 302–5.

140. DO: *kennen, geloven, vertrouwen, zich verlaten, hopen, verwachten, liefhebben, vrezen, eren, lijdzaam zijn, belijden.*

141. DO: *altijd geheel; overal.*

142. DO: *geeft; eist.*

The tie to God is total. This is already true because of creation, when God gave us this commandment. And it is even more true thanks to re-creation; now we must glorify God out of gratitude with body and soul that belong to God (1 Cor. 6:20) and are God's creation (Eph. 2:10).

But does the commandment then also already demand the singular Christian virtues of faith, hope, and love toward God? This is a difficult question: If one says Yes, law and gospel seem to be confused, for the law does not make any mention of faith in the peculiar Christian sense, for then the law is inserted and sought in the gospel. If one says No, then one may decide to join the Socinians in making Christ a new Legislator,[143] who has not only fulfilled the law but added to it, completed it, deepened it, and added new commandments to it and introduced new virtues. The answer to this should be that the law certainly had no knowledge of Christ at all, knew nothing of saving faith, and so forth, but as soon as the gospel comes through proclamation—Believe in Jesus and be saved—then that believing comes to us as a demand and obligation on the basis of the law. The law requires us to believe and do whatever God may command and demand later; the law considers the command to believe as part of it, as it were, and makes it binding and mandatory for all of us. For it is a command from the God who is also the author of the law. God gives us three commands: to have faith in him, to hope in him, and to love him.[144]

A. FAITH IN GOD

Our relationship to God is called faith in God to the degree that it is the virtue by which we accept God's existence (Heb. 11:6, 11), accept as true—good, holy, and so on—whatever he says in his Word (Holy Scripture) and whatever he does (1 John 1:10; 5:10).[145] By faith we are also assured of his grace shown us in Christ; we are confident (Rom. 4:16–18; 10:10): "The righteous shall live by faith" (Hab. 2:4; Rom. 1:17; Gal. 3:11; Heb. 10:38).[146] Faith is a matter of the heart: "For with the heart one believes and is justified" (Rom. 10:10); it is a "knowing with understanding" and a "trusting with the will."[147] In other words, it is an act of the whole person, a willing and voluntary assent.[148] Faith is the one act that God always and everywhere requires of us (John

---

143. LO: *novus legislator*.

144. Ed. note: Clearly, Bavinck, like Augustine in his *Enchiridion*, structures the life of obedient Christian piety by the apostle Paul's conclusion of his great tribute to love in 1 Cor. 13.

145. Wuttke, *Handbuch der christlichen Sittenlehre*³, 2:240–41 (§237).

146. GrO: πληροφορία = full assurance, certainty; ὑπόστασις = confidence, conviction, steadfastness; πεποίθησις = trust, confidence.

147. LO: *notitia in intellectu; fiducia in voluntate*.

148. Wuttke, *Christian Ethics*, 2:217 (§113).

6:29; Acts 16:31), with the exclusion of all works of the law (Acts 13:38–39; Rom. 3:28). It is moral in character; it agrees with the moral law. In a word, it is a virtue, a virtue not only of the mind but also of heart and will, and a good, appropriate, thoroughly human attitude.[149] And, specifically, it is that virtue by which we accept God, Christ, his words, his deeds, and his gifts. It is a receiving, accepting act on our part, it is a mouth that takes food, a hand that receives the gift. Such is the attitude God requires of us, since we have nothing of ourselves and must give from what has been given to us. He is precisely the one who gives, who shares himself, who is Love, from whom all good, spiritual, and natural gifts flow.

Faith therefore has two elements: *knowledge* and *trust*.[150] There is a historical knowledge of God that precedes faith, but the knowledge of which we are speaking here follows faith.[151] This knowledge is eternal life (Jer. 31:3, 33–34; John 17:3) and is part of the image of God (Col. 3:10). This knowledge also is a virtue, often praised in Holy Scripture (Isa. 11:2, 9) and recommended (Col. 1:10; 2 Pet. 1:5; 3:18). It is fruit from God the Father (John 6:45), God the Son (Matt. 11:27), and God the Holy Spirit (1 Cor. 2:11–12). Its sources are nature (Pss. 8; 19; Dan. 2:47; 6:26–27; Rom. 1:19–20) and Scripture (Jer. 8:9).[152]

This knowledge of God also must have a moral character; it must be nurtured not for the sake of vain curiosity, human cleverness, or sophisticated casuistry, but in humility (1 Cor. 8:1), from a pure desire to know God, to honor him, and out of faith. The knowing itself is not a moral but an intellectual act, but it must be exercised in total agreement with the moral law. There is also a wrong kind of knowing (1 John 2:4; 4:8), a knowing without holiness, without love, a "Lord-Lord" declaration (Matt. 7:22, 23). And thus, all efforts to increase such knowledge, whether from nature, by searching Scripture, or in some other way, must meet the requirements of the moral law.

Second, faith involves *trust*: Trust is that virtue, generated in us by the Holy Spirit, by which we rest in God and rely on him in everything and always and forever.[153] Scripture uses these words for it. In Hebrew we have בָּטַח = to trust, be secure; אָמֵן = to trust, to believe in; חָסָה = to seek refuge. In

---

149. J. T. Beck, *Vorlesungen über christliche Ethik*, 1:195.

150. DO: *kennen; vertrouwen*. Ed. note: This is a transitional summary sentence added by the editor and picking up the opening sentence of this and the following paragraphs.

151. Wuttke, *Handbuch der christlichen Sittenlehre³*, 2:245 (§138). Ed. note: Bavinck captures this distinction in the Dutch by using two different words: "historical knowledge" translates *historisch weten*, and Bavinck uses *kennen* for the knowing that follows faith. *Weten* usually connotes factual information only, while *kennen* connotes a deeper, more intimate, and personal acquaintance.

152. Ed. note: Bavinck has taken over these passages from Polanus von Polansdorf, *Syntagma Theologiae Christianae*, 593 (IX.vii).

153. Polanus von Polansdorf, *Syntagma Theologiae Christianae*, 594 (IX.vii).

Greek, πείθομαι = to be convinced, certain.[154] That trust is the fruit of the Holy Spirit; it is born from faith in God (Eph. 3:12), comes from knowing God (Ps. 28:6–7).[155] The grounds for this conviction are that God is the One who is absolutely faithful (Ps. 33:4; 1 Cor. 1:9) and trustworthy and cannot deny himself (2 Tim. 2:13). Without his will, not a hair can fall from our head (Matt. 10:30). With and in Christ he will "graciously give us all things" (Rom. 8:32); he gives us "all these things" because he is our heavenly Father, who knows what we need (Matt. 6:25–34). As the One who promises to be with us (Gen. 26:24), he will not leave or forsake us (Ps. 94:14; Heb. 13:5), but will rescue us from all troubles:

> But the eyes of the LORD are on those who fear him,
>   on those whose hope is in his unfailing love,
> to deliver them from death
>   and keep them alive in famine.
>
> We wait in hope for the LORD;
>   he is our help and our shield.
> In him our hearts rejoice,
>   for we trust in his holy name.
> May your unfailing love be with us, LORD,
>   even as we put our hope in you. (Ps. 33:18–22 NIV)

Finally, because God is faithful, "he will not let you be tempted beyond what you can bear. But when you are tempted, he will also provide a way out so that you can endure it" (1 Cor. 10:13).

All of Scripture is full of promises, stays and supports for our trust, to instill trust in us, for God knows how mistrusting we are. Abraham is an example of this strong faith in God (Gen. 15), as is Jesus when he sleeps in the midst of the storm (Matt. 8:24).[156] This trust is a moral relationship as well, an act of the greatest devotion; all mistrust, all reliance on creatures, even on princes (Ps. 146:3), on the strength of flesh (Jer. 17:5), on temporal things and goods, and all worrying (Matt. 6:25–34; Luke 12:26–34) are therefore condemned. Similarly, all indifference,[157] every instance of "little faith"[158] (Matt.

---

154. Ed. note: Though Bavinck goes on to cite a specific passage from Vilmar's *Theologische Moral* (see n. 156 below), he does not include the key word Vilmar discusses—namely, παρρησία.

155. Ed. note: Bavinck has Ps. 20:7, which does speak of trust but less explicitly as arising from faith.

156. Wuttke, *Handbuch der christlichen Sittenlehre*[3], 2:242; Vilmar, *Theologische Moral*, 2/3:117–20 (§48).

157. DO: *zorgeloosheid*.

158. DO: *klein geloof*.

8:26; 14:31; Mark 16:14; Luke 8:13; 24:25; James 1:6), is also condemned because God cares for us (Phil. 4:6; 1 Pet. 5:7). In this regard, Holy Scripture is terribly radical: it removes everything that is unsteady and unstable in earth and heaven, every foundation and all possible support for trust that might be placed in creatures; instead it replaces all that with an eternal foundation, unshakable and solid—namely, God himself, Christ, his Word.

B. HOPE IN GOD[159]

Hope is that virtue by which we unquestionably and surely anticipate God's future blessings, especially the future completion of our salvation: "Therefore, preparing your minds for action, and being sober-minded, set your hope fully on the grace that will be brought to you at the revelation of Jesus Christ" (1 Pet. 1:13). The Old Testament Psalter is filled with the language of hope:

> Wait for the LORD;
>> be strong, and let your heart take courage;
>> wait for the LORD! (Ps. 27:14)

> I waited patiently for the LORD;
>> he inclined to me and heard my cry.
> He drew me up from the pit of destruction,
>> out of the miry bog,
> and set my feet upon a rock,
>> making my steps secure. (Ps. 40:1–2)

> I will wait for your name, for it is good,
>> in the presence of the godly. (Ps. 52:9b)

> I wait for the LORD, my soul waits,
>> and in his word I hope;
> my soul waits for the LORD
>> more than watchmen for the morning,
>> more than watchmen for the morning.

> O Israel, hope in the LORD!
>> For with the LORD there is steadfast love,
>> and with him is plentiful redemption.
> And he will redeem Israel
>> from all his iniquities. (Ps. 130:5–8)

---

159. Polanus von Polansdorf, *Syntagma Theologiae Christianae*, 598 (IX.ix); Zöckler, *Theologia naturalis*, 160, 183.

Holy Scripture calls this (in Hebrew) קוה = hope; also יחל = expectation; שמר = wait upon, attend to, watch. This hope is commended and produces wonderful fruit:

> They who wait for the LORD shall renew their strength;
>> they shall mount up with wings like eagles;
> they shall run and not be weary;
>> they shall walk and not faint. (Isa. 40:31)

Such hope rests on God's faithful promises, on God, who is our hope: "For you, O Lord, are my hope, / my trust, O LORD, from my youth" (Ps. 71:5). Our sure and secure hope for deliverance comes from no one else:

> For God alone my soul waits in silence;
>> from him comes my salvation.
> He alone is my rock and my salvation,
>> my fortress; I shall not be greatly shaken. (Ps. 62:1–2; cf. vv. 5–6)

"But for me it is good to be near God; / I have made the Lord GOD my refuge, / that I may tell of all your works" (Ps. 73:28). New Testament believers follow the apostle Paul when he speaks of the "mystery, which is Christ in you, the hope of glory" (Col. 1:27), and of "Christ Jesus our hope" (1 Tim. 1:1).

The *object* of hope is God's promises and their fulfillment whatever their content. They may be promises of grace in this life (Rom. 4:18; Hab. 2:3) or of glory in the life to come; and then it is a hope of eternal life (Titus 3:7). It is also called "the hope of salvation" (1 Thess. 5:8) and a "living hope" (1 Pet. 1:3). This is the hope in which Jacob lived and died (Gen. 49:18; Job 19:26; Ps. 17:15) and Paul stands (Rom. 5:2). And this hope will never "put us to shame, because God's love has been poured into our hearts through the Holy Spirit who has been given to us" (Rom. 5:5). It fully excludes all despair and doubt (Gen. 4:13; 1 Thess. 4:13), all uncertainty and worry, all hope in people and their promises.

Patient endurance is therefore firmly implied in this hope; in particular, *perseverance* is a fruit of hope.[160] It consists of bearing any crosses imposed on us with perseverance. This does not mean *passivity*, which actually is to do too much, but a hidden strength involving the highest energy of the soul. This requires utilizing the soul's deepest capacities and is much more than mere quiet

---

160. DO: *lijdzaamheid*; *standvastigheid*; Polanus von Polansdorf, *Syntagma Theologiae Christianae*, 606 (IX.xiii); Kuyper, "Lijdzaamheid I–II." Ed. note: We have chosen to translate *lijdzaamheid* with the two words "patient endurance" to distinguish the idea of spiritual patience (in trials and tribulation) from ordinary daily and routine patience (such as waiting in a line), for which the Dutch word *geduld* is more appropriate.

submission or resignation, the calm, patient apathy of the Stoics, or Islamic acquiescence to fate. It is the fruit of oppression, does not bend under pressure but creates rejoicing "in our sufferings, knowing that suffering produces endurance" (Rom. 5:3).[161] This creates a positive spiral of perseverance: having endured once, we are able to be patient in new adversity, and each experience of patient endurance makes us increasingly conscious of our strength. This patience, which presupposes this oppression from unbelievers, the world, and Satan, was the virtue of Job (James 5:11), and especially of Christ (2 Thess. 3:5). To be patient is to stand firm, to remain standing, and without doubt to anticipate the fulfillment of salvation, in spite of the many inward and outward attacks. Without this no child of God will enter the kingdom of heaven.

And from this flows the obligation always to *confess* God, Christ, and the truth.[162] "Whoever acknowledges me before others, I will also acknowledge before my Father in heaven" (Matt. 10:32 NIV; cf. Luke 12:8). Christ himself is "the high priest of our confession" (Heb. 3:1), "the faithful witness" (Rev. 1:5), "who in his testimony before Pontius Pilate made the good confession" (1 Tim. 6:13).[163] And so we also must confess God with the mouth (Rom. 10:9) and with deeds, so that Christ may confess our name before his Father (Rev. 3:5).[164] Christ gave himself for us, was not ashamed of us, became like us, assumed our person, and became our kin. Therefore, we are not ashamed of him. We must hold firmly to that confession (Heb. 4:14), if need be at the cost of our lives, which we should be willing to lose for Jesus's sake (Matt. 16:24–25). The martyrs are witnesses; "it is not the suffering that creates a martyr but the cause."[165] And to be allowed to suffer and die is an honor, a blessing (Phil. 1:29), not even granted angels.[166]

c. Love for God[167]

Love follows faith; it is the echo of faith. In faith we receive, in love we give: "To be known is to be loved."[168] "You shall love the Lord your God

---

161. GrO: εἰδότες ὅτι ἡ θλῖψις ὑπομονὴν κατεργάζεται.

162. DO: *belijden*. Ed. note: Note the etymological relation between "patient endurance" (*lijdzaamheid*) and "to confess" (*belijden*).

163. GrO: ὁ μάρτυς ὁ πιστός; τοῦ μαρτυρήσαντος ἐπὶ Ποντίου Πιλάτου τὴν καλὴν ὁμολογίαν.

164. Cf. Pictet, *De christelyke zedekunst*, 336–41 (IV.xv: "Concerning the Confession of Christ's Name" [*Van de Belijdenis van Christus Naam*]).

165. LO: *causa, non passio facit martyrium.*

166. Pictet, *De christelyke zedekunst*, 341–51 (IV.xvi: "Concerning Martyrdom" [*Van de Martelaardschap*]).

167. DO: *Liefde tot God*; Polanus von Polansdorf, *Syntagma Theologiae Christianae*, 599–604 (IX.x); Pictet, *De christelyke zedekunst*, 320–29 (IV.xii: "Concerning Love to God" [*Van de Liefde tot God*]); Vilmar, *Theologische Moral*, 2/3:113.

168. DO: *Bekend maakt bemind*. Ed. note: This is a popular Dutch proverb and is the name of a Dutch refugee organization's project to encourage Dutch citizens to become acquainted

with all your heart and with all your soul and with all your mind. This is the great and first commandment" (Matt. 22:37–38; cf. Deut. 6:5). Love for God is our highest duty; it is the virtue by which we love God as the highest and only Good. According to Cicero, the various Latin words for love—*dilectio (electio)*, *amor*, *caritas*—are not identical. *Caritas* is the greatest; it unites us with the object of our love. Our love for God is based on him being the only, true Good and therefore alone truly worthy of our love—this is the highest form of pure love, "disinterested love."[169] This disinterested love was advocated by the Spanish mystic Miguel de Molinos (1628–96), Francis de Sales (1567–1622), Jane Francis de Chantal (1572–1641), Jeanne-Marie Bouvier de la Motte-Guyon (1648–1717), and François Fénelon (1651–1715), the archbishop of Cambrai, France.

All of these were *quietists* who conceived human love for God to mean that every wish, longing, and will in us had to be silenced and absolutely quieted;[170] nothing may be said except "Your will be done." They neither want nor desire anything; they rest, only wait. "'To desire our soul's salvation,' says Francis de Salescus von Sales, 'is doubtless good, but it is better to desire nothing at all. But one thing ought we to seek: the glory of God.'"[171] Even the desire for salvation is set aside. "'Often have I said to the Lord,' says Madame Chantal, 'that if it should please Him to assign me my place in hell, I should be content with my lot, if it could serve to his glory.'" Everything becomes a matter of holy indifference; the soul is being transformed, "a dissolving, a melting and absorption into God; and in this absorption is holy rest." The will, the "I," has died, like a suckling child at its mother's breast. This rests on a pantheistic view that destroys human independence and individuality, causing us to be totally passive and to sink into God. "Your will be done" may be the conclusion of the prayer, but it is not the entire prayer; we certainly may pray for our bread, for salvation (the Lord's Prayer), for forgiveness. Madame Guyon said that she could no longer pray for forgiveness because she loved God completely.[172]

---

with refugees in their midst. See the website for VluchtelingenWerk Nederland at https://www .vluchtelingenwerk.nl/wat-wij-doen/onze-projecten/project-bekend-maakt-bemind.

169. FO: *amour desinteressé*; cf. Walther, "Das Wesen der Liebe zu Gott"; Bilderdijk, *De dichtwerken*, 5:277, 325. Ed. note: Bavinck has in mind two Bilderdijk poems: "Zielzucht," Universiteit van Amsterdam, September 14, 1996, http://cf.hum.uva.nl/dsp/ljc/bilderdijk/Diversen /zielzuch.html; "Liefde tot God," Universiteit van Amsterdam, August 9, 1997, http://cf.hum .uva.nl/dsp/ljc/bilderdijk/Navonkeling1/liefgod.html.

170. DO/LO: *absoluut quietivum*.

171. Martensen, *Christian Ethics*, 1:327 (§108). Ed. note: The three quotations that immediately follow are from the same source.

172. Cf. Wuttke, *Christian Ethics*, 1:276 (§39).

Now it is indeed true that we can and must love God (Ps. 73:25) because of his perfections, since he is God, the highest good (though some question whether this is possible),[173] but this is not antithetical to our salvation. Thus, we may love God also for his blessings (1 John 4:19); we love him for many reasons: "I love the LORD, because he has heard / my voice and my pleas for mercy" (Ps. 116:1). We love him precisely because he has given *himself* to us. With the quietists, the object of love itself becomes indifferent, is no longer the true God, the greatest Good, love, but mere Being. In Scripture, the love for God is quite often commended because of those blessings: ". . . but showing steadfast love to thousands of those who love me and keep my command-ments" (Exod. 20:6). "Love the LORD, all you his saints! / The LORD preserves the faithful / but abundantly repays the one who acts in pride" (Ps. 31:23). "Delight yourself in the LORD, / and he will give you the desires of your heart" (Ps. 37:4). All kinds of blessings are immediately linked to that love for God: "And we know that for those who love God all things work together for good, for those who are called according to his purpose" (Rom. 8:28; cf. Deut. 30:6, 19, 20; Heb. 11:26; James 2:5). Therefore, our love for God should not be for the reward; God must and can be loved for himself alone, and everything else in and because of him. The love for God is an affect, not a contract.[174] According to Voetius, "Good works may well be done in consideration of a reward."[175] He himself is our reward. "God is loved, not without reward, and must be loved even without consideration of reward."[176] It may come to a point that a believer says, "Do with me what you will, as long as it advances your honor."[177] This love for God is also love for Christ, for Christ in both natures, in all his offices and states. "If anyone has no love for the Lord, let him be accursed" (1 Cor. 16:22; cf. 1 John 2:22–23).

Human beings are the subjects of this love; this love may well be a fruit of the Holy Spirit, but not the Holy Spirit himself, as Lombard said, for which he was condemned by the Sorbonne.[178] And indeed, the whole person must love with strength and mind (Matt. 22:37). This love includes *fear* and *piety*.[179] This is prominent, especially in the Old Testament: "Let all the earth fear the

---

173. Pictet, *De christelyke zedekunst*, 321.

174. Polanus von Polansdorf, *Syntagma Theologiae Christianae*, 601E (IX.x).

175. LO: *bona opera; intuitu mercedis*; Voetius, *Selectarum Disputationum Theologicarum*, 2:728.

176. LO: *Non sine praemio diligitur Deus, etsi absque praemii intuit diligendus sit*; Polanus von Polansdorf, *Syntagma Theologiae Christianae*, 601E (IX.x).

177. Pictet, *De christelyke zedekunst*, 325.

178. Lombard, *Sentences Book 1*, dist. 17, chap. 2.

179. DO: *vreze, Godsvrucht*; Polanus von Polansdorf, *Syntagma Theologiae Christianae*, 605 (X.xi).

LORD; / let all the inhabitants of the world stand in awe of him!" (Ps. 33:8; cf. Isa. 66:2). But it is also found in the New Testament: "Bondservants, obey in everything those who are your earthly masters, not by way of eye-service, as people-pleasers, but with sincerity of heart, fearing the Lord" (Col. 3:22). "Honor everyone. Love the brotherhood. Fear God. Honor the emperor" (1 Pet. 2:17; cf. Rev. 11:18; 14:7; 15:4; 19:5). At the same time: "There is no fear in love, but perfect love casts out fear. For fear has to do with punishment, and whoever fears has not been perfected in love" (1 John 4:18). Nevertheless, there is still a certain amount of fear in the love for God. This is not a slavish fear, but childlike, a respect for his Highness and Majesty, a fear against doing something that displeases him and arouses his anger. This fear is a holy acceptance of God's Word, God's attributes, his promises and threats. This fear element in love maintains its purity and holiness, including the distance between Creator and creature. In addition, this love comprises devotion and *humility*.[180] Such are the people with whom God dwells and looks on with favor (Isa. 57:15; 66:2), those to whom he grants grace (Prov. 3:24; James 4:6), for before him we are as nothing (Isa. 40:15–24).

§33. THE SECOND COMMANDMENT

> You shall not make for yourself a carved image, or any likeness of anything that is in heaven above, or that is in the earth beneath, or that is in the water under the earth. You shall not bow down to them or serve them, for I the LORD your God am a jealous God, visiting the iniquity of the fathers on the children to the third and the fourth generation of those who hate me, but showing steadfast love to thousands of those who love me and keep my commandments. (Exod. 20:4–6)

Images in Scripture and Church History

The First Commandment deals with the true God; the Second Commandment deals with the true religion. It teaches us how we must worship God, according to his will and command—that is, not symbolically but spiritually, which expresses God's spiritual being. This commandment was definitely needed for Israel. Ancient indigenous superstitious practices of worshiping God[181] continued to exist for a long time among the Israelites, or new pagan worship practices entered and were assimilated into the worship of YHWH. Thus, from the beginning Israelites had *teraphim* (human-shaped figures; cf. 1 Sam. 19:13–17) as household gods, employed to receive oracles (see Hosea

---

180. Polanus von Polansdorf, *Syntagma Theologiae Christianae*, 606 (X.xii).
181. DO: *inheemse bijgelovige diensten*.

3:4; Zech. 10:2). They were brought to Canaan by Rachel (Gen. 31:19–42) and they are found there repeatedly, until the time of Josiah (Judg. 17:5; 18:27; 2 Kings 23:24). This worship of *teraphim* had nothing to do with the worship of YHWH but remained in Israel, just as superstition can still be found among us. Furthermore, Israel had been in Egypt for a long time and had become acquainted with the worship of animals; this had a long-lasting effect. Among others, we recall the golden calf of Aaron (Exod. 32); Gideon's ephod (Judg. 8:22–28); Micah the Ephraimite and his shrine of household gods (Judg. 17); the capture of Micah's idol by the tribe of Dan and their subsequent idolatry (Judg. 18:27–31); Jeroboam's formal introduction of the golden calves at Dan for the ten tribes, maintained until the deportation and beyond (1 Kings 12:25–33; 2 Kings 17:28); and the worship of Moses's bronze serpent (2 Kings 18:4).

In Judah this worship of YHWH via images was not adopted (except in Beersheba, Amos 5:5; 8:14).[182] Nonetheless, it was far more pagan idolatry that gained entrance here by means of commerce with the Phoenicians, the ancient Canaanites, and so on. They worshiped Moloch, Chemosh, Baal, Astarte, and other gods, especially during and after the time of Solomon. This image worship and idolatry came to an end only after the captivity and after an aversion to the visual arts arose.[183]

That aversion may well have transferred to individuals in the Christian church and have been strengthened by the idolatrous art of the pagans. However, the church itself thought differently about this. One finds many drawings on the walls of the catacombs in Rome and Naples, already from the second century, maybe even from the closing decades of the first century. Paintings were not tolerated in the church, however. The church fathers in those days rejected the same arguments coming from the pagans that Roman Catholics use today to defend the veneration of images. At that time pagans were also saying that they were worshiping not the images but those whom the images represented. However, church fathers like Lactantius replied, "You fear them doubtless on this account, because you think that they are in heaven; for if they are gods, the case cannot be otherwise. Why, then, do you not raise your eyes to heaven, and, invoking their names, offer sacrifices in the open air? Why do you look to walls, and wood, and stone, rather than to the place where you believe them to be?"[184] The Synod of Elvira in 306 specified in canon 36: "It has seemed good that images should not be in churches so that what is

---

182. Ed. note: The distinction Bavinck is making in this paragraph utilizes two different Dutch words: *beeldendienst* = worship/veneration of images, and *afgoderij* = idolatry.

183. Rüetschi, "Bilder bei den Hebräern."

184. Lactantius, *Divine Institutes* II.2 (*ANF* 7:41–43).

venerated and worshiped not be painted on the walls."[185] However, this strict, actually Reformed (Protestant) sentiment was not adopted beyond Spain.[186] In addition, we see from the catacombs that the paintings and drawings in the early days of the church were all symbolic in an allegorical or typological sense. This was related to the preference for a mystical-allegorical explanation of Scripture and to the practice of maintaining the secrecy of key aspects of worship for the unbaptized (the so-called Discipline of the Secret).[187]

Thus, early on, people had used the sign of the cross and the symbol of a fish.[188] Other important images included the lamb, dove, deer, eagle, rooster, peacock (symbol of the resurrection), horse, hare, ship, anchor, lily, balance-scale, vine, shepherd, sower, and the like. Historical events were also understood allegorically, such as Noah in the ark and Israel crossing the Red Sea. Images (drawings) of Christ in the catacombs date back to the first half of the second century; Jesus is portrayed as a beardless young man with a friendly soft facial expression. A few church fathers—Clement of Alexandria, Tertullian—in accordance with Isaiah 53:2–3, portrayed Christ as unhandsome, lacking any beauty.[189] In later years, with Psalm 45:2 and John 1:14 in mind,[190] he is portrayed as very handsome. Emperor Alexander Severus (222–35) placed a bust of Christ in his household shrine[191] alongside busts of Abraham, Orpheus, and Apollonius of Tyana.[192] The second-century Alexandrian followers of Carpocrates venerated images of Christ and the Greek philosophers in their temples.[193]

However, in the fourth and fifth centuries a reversal occurred. New, uncultivated multitudes of people entered the church, and the proposal was made to use

185. LO: *placuit picturas in ecclesia non esse debere, ne quod colitur et adoratur in parietibus depingatur.* Ed. note: Bavinck's source is Kurtz, *Church History*, 1:215 (§38/3).

186. DO: *gereformeerde*; see Kurtz, *Church History*, 1:215–16 (§38/3). Ed. note: It is worth noting that Denzinger includes canons 9, 27, 33, 38, and 77 of this council as part of official Roman Catholic teaching, but not canon 36 (Denzinger, no. 52a–e). This is clear evidence that canon 36 was not accepted beyond the immediate boundaries of the Spanish church.

187. LO: *disciplina arcani*; see Kurtz, *Church History*, 1:216 (§38/3).

188. Taking the letters of the Greek word for fish, ἰχθύς, as a summary of the Christian credo: "Jesus Christ, Son of God, Savior," from Ἰησοῦς Χριστός Θεοῦ Υἱός Σωτήρ.

189. DO: *onschoon*.

190. Psalm 45:2: "You are the most handsome of the sons of men; / grace is poured upon your lips; / therefore God has blessed you forever"; John 1:14: "And the Word became flesh and dwelt among us, and we have seen his glory, glory as of the only Son from the Father, full of grace and truth."

191. LO: *lararium*.

192. Ed. note: Apollonius of Tyana (ca. AD 15–ca. 100) was a Greek Neo-Pythagorean philosopher who was compared with his contemporary Jesus by fourth-century Christians (Wikipedia, s.v. "Apollonius of Tyana," https://en.wikipedia.org/wiki/Apollonius_of_Tyana).

193. Kurtz, *Church History*, 1:115 (§27/8). Ed. note: The Carpocratians were a gnostic sect; we know of them from Irenaeus, *Against Heresies* I.25.

the images as books for the laity. Some people—Augustine, the Nestorians—did warn against this.[194] According to Kurtz, the age of Cyril of Jerusalem (313–86) became the period of transition. Already in the fifth century "authentic miraculous pictures of Christ, the Apostles and the God-mother ('images not made by hands') made their appearance, and with them began image worship properly so called, with lighting of candles, kissing, burning incense, bowing of the knee, prostrations ('honorific worship').[195] Soon all churches and church books, all palaces and cottages, were filled with pictures of Christ and the saints painted or drawn by the monks. Miracle after miracle was wrought beside, upon, or through them."[196] Kurtz observes that the West "did not keep pace with the East. Augustine complains of image worship and advises to seek Christ in the bible [sic] rather than in images." Pope Gregory the Great "wishes that in churches images should be made to serve 'solely to instruct the minds of the ignorant.'"[197] He concludes, "The Nestorians who were strongly opposed to images, expressly declared that the hated Cyril was the originator of *Iconolatry*."[198]

The worship of relics arose during the same time. According to Kurtz, "The veneration for relics (λείψανα) proceeded from a pious feeling in human nature and is closely associated with that higher reverence which the church paid to its martyrs. It began with public assemblies at the graves of martyrs, memorial celebrations and services in connection with the translations of their bones held in the churches. Soon no church, no altar (Rev. vi.9), could be built without relics."[199] Miracles, healings, resurrections of dead people, and so on were attributed to relics. According to legend, Empress Helena, mother of Constantine, "found in AD 326 the Cross of Christ along with the crosses of the two thieves." The cross of Christ "was distinguished from the others by a miracle of healing or of raising from the dead." The devout empress "left one half of the cross to the church of the Holy Sepulchre and sent the rest with the nails to her son, who inlaid the wood in his statues and some of the nails in his diadem, while of the rest he made a bit for his horse." Pious pilgrims were allowed to carry with them "small splinters of the wood kept in Jerusalem, so that soon bits of the cross were spread and received veneration throughout all the world."[200]

194. Ed. note: Some of the material that follows, taken from Kurtz, *Church History*, 1:364–65 (§57/4, 5) and 1:403–6 (§66), has been added by the editor for accuracy and clarity. Bavinck's own text shows definite reliance on Kurtz.
195. GrO: εἰκόνες ἀχειροποίητοι; προσκύνησις τιμητική.
196. Kurtz, *Church History*, 1:364 (§57/4; cf. §38/3).
197. LO: *ad instruendas solummodo mentes nescientium*; Kurtz, *Church History*, 1:364 (§57/4).
198. Kurtz, *Church History*, 1:364 (§57/4).
199. Kurtz, *Church History*, 1:364 (§57/5).
200. Kurtz, *Church History*, 1:365 (§57/5).

In the East, Byzantine emperors Leo III the Isaurian (717–41); his son and successor, Constantine V (741–51); Constantine's son and successor, Leo IV (775–80); Leo V, the Armenian (813–20); and Theophilus (829–42) all opposed the images.[201] However, images were supported among the people and the monks and favored by John of Damascus and Irene—consort of Leo IV—who "used the freedom which the minority of her son Constantine VI afforded her for the introduction of image worship."[202] Although Emperor Theophilus "made it the business of his life to root out entirely every trace of image worship," his desire was thwarted by another woman, his wife, Theodora, "who after his death conducted the government as regent" and had image worship "formally reintroduced by a Synod at Constantinople in AD 842. Since then all opposition to it has ceased in the Greek church, and the day of the Synodal decision, 19th February, was appointed a standing festival of orthodoxy."[203] The Western church also supported the practice.

The Iconoclastic Controversy in the Eastern church was addressed by a number of key synods or councils. The Second Council of Nicaea (Seventh Ecumenical Council; AD 787) provided the following "Definition of the Sacred Images and Tradition":

> (I. Definition) . . . We, continuing in the regal path, and following the divinely inspired teaching of our Holy Fathers, and the tradition of the catholic church, for we know that this is of the Holy Spirit who certainly dwells in it, define in all certitude and diligence that as the figure of the honored and life-giving Cross, so the venerable and holy images, the ones from tinted materials and from marble as those from other materials, must be suitably placed in the holy churches of God, both on sacred vessels and vestments, and on the walls and on the altars, both at home and on the streets, namely such images of our Lord Jesus Christ, God and Savior, and of undefiled our Lady, or holy Mother of God, and of all the honorable angels, and, at the same time, of all the saints and of holy men.[204]

Those who look at them will be incited to remember them, "to kiss and to render honorable adoration to them, not however to grant true *latria* [worship] according to our faith, which is proper to divine nature alone." A saying of Basil is given as a rationale for this—"For the honor of the image passes to the original"—along with this application: "and he who shows reverence to the image, shows reverence to the substance of Him depicted in

---

201. Kurtz, *Church History*, 1:403–6 (§66). Ed. note: The dates following each emperor refer to the years of his reign.

202. Kurtz, *Church History*, 1:405 (§66/3).

203. Kurtz, *Church History*, 1:406 (§66/4). Ed. note: See n. 207 below.

204. Denzinger, no. 302.

it."[205] A local synod in Constantinople, convoked in 843 by Empress Theodora and Patriarch Methodius, followed suit and pronounced anathemas on persistent dissenters, who "in fact deny our salvation," because they have "cut themselves off from the common body of Christ."[206] The defeat of iconoclasm and the restoration of icons is celebrated as the Feast of Orthodoxy on the first Sunday of Lent in the liturgical calendar of the Eastern Orthodox Church and the Byzantine Rite Eastern Catholic Churches.[207]

In the West, images were permitted in the churches, but Charlemagne (742–814) and his son, Louis the Pious (778–840), vigorously protested their worship (790–825).[208] In response to the decisions of the Seventh Ecumenical Council (Nicaea, 787), Charlemagne issued his own refutation, the *Libri Carolini*.[209] In concert with the Anglo-Saxon church, Charlemagne (with Alcuin) convened a synod that "met at Frankfort in AD 794 and confirmed the positions of the Caroline books."[210] At a later gathering, "a national synod at Paris in AD 825 condemned image worship sharply, in opposition to Hadrian I, and affirmed the positions of the Caroline books."[211] In the West, apart from the Frankish kingdom, worship of saints and especially relics was zealous.[212] Shortly "after the Parisian council of AD 825," Agobard of Lyons wrote a fierce polemic against the "superstitions of those who worship holy pictures and images."[213] Agobard went "much further than the Caroline books, for not only does he regard it as advisable, on account of the inevitable misuse on the part of the

205. GrO: ἐπὶ τὸ πρωτότυπον διαβαίνει; ὑπόστασις; Denzinger, no. 302.

206. Ed. note: The quoted phrases are taken from *The Synodicon of Orthodoxy*, which was approved and used by the Constantinople Synod of 843. See Mystagogy Resource Center, February 21, 2010, http://www.johnsanidopoulos.com/2010/02/synodicon-of-orthodoxy.html.

207. Ed. note: See n. 203 above. We have corrected Bavinck's manuscript here; Bavinck gave February 19 as the date of this feast, which he took from Kurtz, *Church History*, 1:406 (§66/4). The correct day for the decision by the Synod of Constantinople is February 19, 842, which was also the first day in Lent that year, but the Feast of Orthodoxy commemorating the defeat of iconoclasm has subsequently been held on the first Sunday of Lent, whatever date it falls on (Wikisource, s.v. "Catholic Encyclopedia (1913)/Feast of Orthodoxy," https://en.wikisource .org/w/index.php?title=Catholic_Encyclopedia_(1913)/Feast_of_Orthodoxy&oldid=4654413).

208. Kurtz, *Church History*, 1:549–50 (§92). Ed. note: What follows is enhanced by the editor using material from Kurtz, the same source Bavinck used.

209. Kurtz, *Church History*, 1:549 (§92/1). Ed. note: The full title is "The Work of King Charles against the Synod" [*Opus Caroli regis contra synodum*] and consists of 120 objections against sacred images in four books. The work was not used at the time "and remained all but unknown until they were first printed in 1549." John Calvin cites it in the later editions of his *Institutes* (I.xi.14) (Wikipedia, s.v. "Libri Carolini," https://en.wikipedia.org/wiki/Libri_Carolini).

210. Kurtz, *Church History*, 1:549 (§92/1).

211. Kurtz, *Church History*, 1:549 (§92/1).

212. Kurtz, *Church History*, 1:519 (§88/4).

213. LO: *Contra superstitionem eorum, qui picturis et imaginibus sanctorum adorationis obsequiem deferendum putant*; Kurtz, *Church History*, 1:550 (§92/2).

people, to banish images entirely, but with image worship he also rejects all adoration of saints, relics, and angels."[214] He insisted that believers "should put [their] trust in the omnipotent God alone, and worship and reverence only the one Mediator, Christ."[215] Claudius of Turin exceeded even Agobard. Appointed to the bishopric of Turin "with the express injunction that he should contend against image worship in his Italian diocese," he found such excesses that "he felt himself constrained reluctantly because of the condition of affairs to cast images and crosses out of the churches altogether."[216] Popular tumults ensued in consequence, and only the fear of the Frankish arms could preserve his life and protect his office.[217] Nonetheless, the opposition eventually ceased, and one hears nothing along these lines after the eleventh century.

The Council of Trent, during session 25, in its decree "Invocation, Veneration and Relics of Saints," decided that

> the images of Christ, of the Virgin Mother of God, and of all the other saints, are to be placed and retained especially in the churches, and that due honor and veneration be extended to them, not that any divinity or virtue is believed to be in them for which they are to be venerated, or that anything is to be petitioned from them, or that trust is to be placed in images . . . but because the honor which is shown them, is referred to the protypes which they represent.[218]

Trent refers here to "the second council of Nicaea, against the opponents of images."[219] In his decree "Profession of Faith Which Is Prescribed for Orientals (Maronites)," Benedict XIV also affirmed the conclusion of Nicaea II.[220] The veneration of relics was also approved by the Council of Trent.[221] The Second Nicene Council permitted images of God the Father and the Trinity in this anathema: "Believing in one God, greatly praised in Trinity, we reverence his honored images. We anathematized those who are not so minded."[222] On December 7, 1690, Pope Alexander VIII condemned

214. Kurtz, *Church History*, 1:550 (§92/2).
215. Kurtz, *Church History*, 1:550 (§92/2).
216. Kurtz, *Church History*, 1:550 (§92/2).
217. Kurtz, *Church History*, 1:550 (§92/2).
218. Denzinger, no. 986. Ed. note: AD 787.
219. Denzinger, no. 986.
220. Denzinger, no. 1466. Ed. note: AD 1743.
221. Denzinger, no. 985.
222. Denzinger, no. 306. Ed. note: We have taken this statement from the fifth edition of Denzinger which Bavinck used and which includes both the Greek original and a Latin translation. The Greek text reads: "Πιστεύοντες εἰς ἕνα Θεὸν ἐν Τριάδι ἀνυμνούμενον τὰς τιμίας αὐτοῦ εἰκόνας ἀσπαζόμεα. οἳ μὴ οὕτως ἔχοντες ἀνάθεμα ἔστωσαν . . ."; the Latin text reads: "*Credentes in unum Deum, in Trinitate collaudatum, honoribiles eis imagines saltumumus. Qui sic not habent, anathema sint . . .*" The thirteenth edition of Denzinger omits the direct reference to

the Jansenist error: "It is unlawful to place in a Christian temple an image of God the Father sitting."[223] In the Constitution "Auctorem fidei" (August 28, 1794), Pius VI condemned

> the prescription which in general and without discrimination includes the images of the incomprehensible Trinity among the images to be removed from the Church, on the ground that they furnish an occasion of error to the untutored,—because of its generality, it is rash, and contrary to the pious custom common throughout the Church, as if no images of the Most Holy Trinity exist which are commonly approved and safely permitted.[224]

The Roman Catholic Church justifies this veneration of images in two ways.

1. The veneration of images, relics, and so on, proceeds through these objects to the persons they represent and is therefore derivative; this was already established by the Councils of Nicaea II (787), Constantinople (842), and Trent.
2. Those images and other objects are a help, books for the laity. In the words of the Fourth Council of Constantinople (869–70):

> We adore the sacred image of our Lord Jesus Christ in like honor with the book of the Holy Gospel. For as through the syllables carried in it, we all attain salvation, so through the imaginal energies of the colors both all the wise and the unwise from that which is manifest enjoy usefulness; for the things which are the sermon in syllables, those things also the writing which is in colors teaches and commands.[225]

This is also what Roman Catholic theologians teach.[226] In defense of venerating relics, Perrone appeals to the following episodes in Scripture: Moses taking the bones of Joseph back to Canaan (Exod. 13:19); the revival of a corpse when it touched the bones of Elisha (2 Kings 13:21); Josiah leaving the bones of the man of God from Judah undisturbed (2 Kings 23:17–18); a woman subject to bleeding touching the hem of Jesus's garment (Matt. 9:21; cf. Luke 6:19); healing taking place when Peter's shadow passed over people (Acts 5:15);

---

honoring images of the triune God and has the following: "We admit that images should be venerated. Those of us who are not so minded we subject to anathema."

223. "Errors of the Jansenists," #25, Denzinger, no. 1315.

224. Denzinger, no. 1569.

225. Denzinger, no. 337.

226. Pruner, *Lehrbuch der katholischen Moraltheologie*[1], 263. Ed. note: Bavinck's reference was to the 2nd rev. ed. of 1883, pp. 265ff.

and healing through Paul's handkerchiefs and aprons (Acts 19:12).[227] Support for the practice is also found in the tradition, the miracles associated with the relics that could not all be invented or fraudulent, and the reasonableness of the piety associated with relics. Perrone finds proof for the use and veneration of images in the cherubim on the ark (Exod. 25:18–19), Moses making a bronze snake for healing Israelites bitten by venomous snakes (Num. 21:8; cf. John 3:14), Joshua prostrating himself before the ark of the covenant (Josh. 7:6), and David's veneration of the ark (2 Sam. 6).[228] Whereas Exodus 20:5 prohibits making images of false gods and so on, it does not forbid making them of the true God. If that were the case, all making of images would have been forbidden. In addition, the word "idol" does not mean the same thing as the word "image."[229]

Related to this is the medieval opposition to the reading of Scripture.[230] The church fathers recommended the reading of Scripture. However, with the growing disuse of Latin among the people and the rise of the hierarchical spirit, this changed. Gregory VII had already stated that God wanted the Scripture to be kept unknown in some places—where people did not understand Latin—so that people would not draw heresy from Scripture. Nonetheless, beginning in the twelfth century, reforming sects began to appeal to Scripture against the Roman Catholic Church and began translating the Holy Scriptures. Rome therefore considered Scripture a source and cause of all heresies. The Council of Toulouse in 1229 prohibited the laity from possessing the texts of the Old and New Testaments, especially their translation. The Council of Tarragona in 1234 ordered people to bring any translations of the Bible to the bishop within eight days. The Council of Oxford in 1408 ordered that no one may translate the Bible into the vernacular without the permission of the bishop or the provincial synod. In spite of this, the Bible was disseminated more and more widely in the fourteenth century. The Council of Trent declared the Vulgate edition to be the authentic version of the Bible, restricted and supervised the printing of Bibles, but did not prohibit reading of the Bible.[231] However, in the fourth rule of his "Ten Rules Regarding the Forbidden Books," appended

227. Perrone, *Praelectiones Theologicae* (1856), 1:1193–206 (*Tractatus de cultu sanctorum*, chap. 4, "De reliquiarum cultu"). Ed. note: This is the reference Bavinck cited; the same material can also be found in Perrone, *Praelectiones Theologicae* (1838), 4:380–94.

228. Perrone, *Praelectiones Theologicae* (1856), 1:1207–30 (*Tractatus de cultu sanctorum*, chap. 5, "De sacrarum imaginum usu ac veneratione"). Ed. note: Also in Perrone, *Praelectiones Theologicae* (1838), 4:394–420.

229. GrO: εἴδωλον; εἰκών; Perrone, *Praelectiones Theologicae* (1856), 1:1209. Ed. note: Also in Perrone, *Praelectiones Theologicae* (1838), 4:397.

230. Herzog, "Bibellesen der Laien."

231. Denzinger, nos. 785–86.

to Trent's *Index of Forbidden Books,* Pius IV observed that the reading of the Bible in the vernacular often caused more harm than good and therefore was to be allowed only with the permission of the bishop or officer of the inquisition. Whoever did so without such permission received no absolution unless he had first surrendered the books to the authorities.[232] The same was decreed by Clement VIII in 1598 and Gregory XV in 1622. Yet Clement IX condemned this principle in his dogmatic constitution *Unigenitus* in 1713 in the case against French Jansenist theologian Pasquier Quesnel (1634–1719). In his *Le Nouveau Testament* of 1699 Quesnel claimed that Holy Scripture is for all and is to be read by all. Clement explicitly condemned two propositions: 1. "The reading of Sacred Scripture is for all."[233] 2. "The sacred obscurity of the Word of God is no reason for the laity to dispense themselves from reading it."[234] At the same time, Clement did not entirely forbid the reading of the Bible.[235] The judgment of Roman Catholics became milder in the nineteenth century. Although Pius VII in 1816, Leo XII in 1824, Gregory XVI in 1832, Clement XVI on May 8, 1844, and Pius IX did not prohibit the reading of the Bible, they did condemn the Bible Societies. According to Rome, reading the Bible is at any rate neither commendable nor necessary; at best it may be beneficial for some.

Here as well, the difference between Rome and us lies in our views of the church. It involves whether the church may craft regulations about religion and about the manner of serving God and whether the church may add to and subtract from those regulations of Scripture. It also involves whether such ecclesiastical regulations may, can, and must bind the conscience. Rome answers affirmatively, and consequently systematizes "self-made religion,"[236] justifying this right to make ecclesiastical religious laws on the basis of passages like Acts 15:28 and 1 Corinthians 7:25, 40. On a par with this worship of images is the creating of mental images of God according to one's own inclination. Rather than being according to God's Word, these ideals and idols of God are formed according to a subject's own ideas and according

---

232. LO: *De libris prohibitis regulae decem;* see Schmets, *Des hochheiligen, ökumenischen und allgemeinen Concils von Trient,* 224.

233. Denzinger, no. 1430.

234. Denzinger, no. 1430.

235. Ed. note: A footnote in Denzinger (p. 347n2) states, "This dogmatic constitution was confirmed by the same Clement XI in the Bull 'Pastoralis Officii' (Aug. 28, 1718); by Innocent XIII in a decree published on Jan. 8, 1722; by Benedict XIII and the Roman Synod in 1725; by Benedict XIV . . . on Oct. 16, 1756; it was accepted by the Gallic clergy in assemblies in 1723, 1726, 1730, by the councils of Avignon, 1725, and Ebred, 1727, and by the whole Catholic world."

236. GrO: ἐθελοθρησκίᾳ. Ed. note: This is a reference to Col. 2:23.

to the likeness of creatures, formed as the objects of our worship. This constitutes serving God in a manner other than he wills, a manner other than in Christ—for example, by means of good works, asceticism, pagan virtues, Stoic severity, and so on. Such images, including mental images, representations, imaginations, fantasies of God, and divine matters, are prohibited![237]

Analysis

1. *Images of the Triune God are prohibited for the following reasons:*
a. It is impossible because God absolutely cannot be depicted; that is why he prohibits it in the Second Commandment:

> Therefore watch yourselves very carefully. Since you saw no form on the day that the LORD spoke to you at Horeb out of the midst of the fire, beware lest you act corruptly by making a carved image for yourselves, in the form of any figure, the likeness of male or female, the likeness of any animal that is on the earth, the likeness of any winged bird that flies in the air, the likeness of anything that creeps on the ground, the likeness of any fish that is in the water under the earth. (Deut. 4:15–18)

"God is spirit" (John 4:24), eternal (Isa. 40:18; Acts 17:29), incorruptible, and incomprehensible.[238]

b. It is insulting[239] to God. Images are always physical bodies, temporal, corruptible, vain human work (Isa. 40; 44; Ps. 115). Whether these are images of something above or below the earth, they always "[exchange] the glory of the immortal God for images resembling mortal man and birds and animals and creeping things" (Rom. 1:23).

c. It is damaging;[240] images always tempt people to superstition and wrong notions, imaginations, and representations of God. A piece of wood is an instruction of vanities (Jer. 10:8, 14; Hab. 2:18; Zech. 10:2).

However, objections can be made against these arguments.

(i) In the Second Commandment, God does not completely prohibit making images of him, for then he would be prohibiting here the making of all images, also images of creatures. We read very straightforwardly, "You shall not make for yourself a carved image, or any likeness of anything that is in heaven above, or that is in the earth beneath, or that is in the water under

---

237. E. Sartorius, *Die Lehre von der heiligen Liebe*, 3/1:145.
238. Ed. note: For Bavinck's more thorough discussion of these divine attributes, see *RD*, 2:148–255.
239. DO: *smadelijk*.
240. DO: *schadelijk*.

the earth" (Exod. 20:4; cf. Deut. 5:8). And only then does the coordinated sentence follow: "You shall not bow down to them or serve them" (Exod. 20:5; Deut. 5:9). This commandment therefore forbids only the making of any image for veneration and religious worship (Perrone). By contrast, the Heidelberg Catechism (Q&A 97) insists that "God cannot and may not be visibly portrayed in any way," also for the arts. However, it also says that while "creatures may be portrayed, . . . God forbids making or having such images if one's intention is to worship them or to serve God through them." We acknowledge that this distinction is not sufficiently grounded in the words of this Second Commandment. Nonetheless, Scripture always speaks of the high loftiness and spirituality of God: the Israelites saw no likeness of him on the mountain (Deut. 4:12). God cannot be compared with anything, and no likeness can be applied to him (Isa. 40:18–22). God's incorruptible glory cannot and ought not to be exchanged for a corruptible image (Rom. 1:23). "God is spirit" (John 4:23; cf. Lev. 19:4; 26:1), nonphysical, immaterial, not composite, and the like.

(ii) Would it then also be prohibited to make images of angels, who are also spiritual beings? May God then not be depicted in a painting by a sun with the Hebrew letters יהוה or by a triangle with an eye, as Kuyper did in his magazine *The Herald*?[241] And what about images of Christ? Are they also prohibited? Even the Lutheran Church does not consider the prohibition against images of God to be absolute. Wuttke distinguishes between a "symbol" and an "emblem."[242] As soon as the image is intended to portray and to resemble God in any sense, and is thus a symbol, it is absolutely forbidden. However, when it is only a mere symbol or emblem to point to God or one of his attributes, it not absolutely impermissible. Certainly, this is correct. However, Wuttke wrongly states that this can happen best by means of a human form. This is incorrect, since in that case we are dealing not with a mere symbol or emblem, but with a representation.[243] It is a different matter with the angels. Angels are creatures, mortal, finite. When angels are represented by a human being with wings (think of the cherubim on the ark, the angels who repeatedly appear in human forms, the angels in the sight of the prophets, as in Isa. 6), they are not made finite by being imagined and depicted in a bodily form, for they *are* finite.

Another question altogether is this matter in relation to Christ. According to Hans Martensen, "Protestant seriousness will never be able to reconcile

---

241. DO: *De Heraut.*
242. GO: *Abbild; Sinnbild;* Wuttke, *Handbuch der christlichen Sittenlehre*[3], 2:262 (§243).
243. DO: *zinnebeeld; afbeelding.*

itself to a theatrical representation of our Lord in our public worship, and least of all to its being offered to a modern audience by way of *artistic enjoyment*. In the first place, the Saviour of the world is a subject *incommensurable* with art of any kind, one utterly transcending the power and resources of art."[244]

Portraying Christ on stage, as is done, for example, in the Passion play in Oberammergau, is absolutely impermissible. No one can express or portray him, even approximately, and by an artificial "*artistic illusion*" elicit from us an impression of Christ's "perfect *holiness*."[245] It is something different whether a painter or sculptor may make any image of him. I would not dare to prohibit these, since "the painter and sculptor make no claim to show us the *whole* living present Christ, but only a single aspect of His being, and aim by their works of art only at reviving the historical *remembrance* of Christ."[246] Such efforts portray only a specific aspect, such as his meekness, or his frame of mind in a specific moment as portrayed in Scripture, such as in the garden of Gethsemane.[247]

(iii) But did God not create an image of himself in human beings and represent himself in the likeness of a creature and appear as the "Ancient of Days" to Daniel (Dan. 7:9; cf. Isa. 43:13)?[248] And Scripture always speaks anthropomorphically about God, ascribing to him hands, feet, ears, intestines, and so on.

Response: This is most certainly the case, but the image of God exists precisely not in the physical mass of our body, but in its formal perfections[249] and in the invisible soul with its attributes. Holy Scripture does speak about God in an anthropomorphic manner, but it cannot do otherwise. Nonetheless, there is a difference between *thinking* about God and *imagining* God. The former is possible; the latter is not. A *conception* of God is permissible, but not a material *representation* or *imaginative construct*, since representation always requires sensory, perceptible, physical forms.[250] By contrast, thinking

---

244. Martensen, *Christian Ethics, Special Part*, 2/2:267 (§110); emphasis in original. Ed. note: We have enhanced Bavinck's use of Martensen here to provide a fuller context for his claim of incommensurability.

245. Martensen, *Christian Ethics, Special Part*, 2/2:267 (§110); emphasis in original.

246. Martensen, *Christian Ethics, Special Part*, 2/2:267 (§110); emphasis in original. Ed. note: Martensen at this point refers to Schleiermacher, *Die christliche Sitte*, 632. He does not indicate the edition, but it is the second edition of 1884.

247. Martensen, *Christian Ethics, Special Part*, 2:267 (§110); more about this later regarding the arts and the sacred in the arts. Ed. note: Bavinck never completed this section; see *RE*, vol. 3.

248. Ed. note: Scripture references added by editor.

249. DO: *vormelijke volmaaktheden*.

250. DO: *denk-beeld; stoffelijke afbeelding; verbeelding*.

abstracts from all those forms and retains only the pure thoughts. Nevertheless, thinking is also tied to the finite and the material. We can think of nothing immaterial except in terms of material forms (Bilderdijk).[251] Our entire language for the spiritual is metaphorical.

2. *Images may be venerated, according to the Roman Catholics, under the following considerations:*

a. *Latreia*, religious worship,[252] belongs to God alone; however, *douleia*, veneration, may be given also to creatures and images.[253] This distinction is contrary to Scripture: δουλεία is always a condition of dependence, servitude, and slavery, as opposed to freedom[254] (cf. Gal. 5:1; Rom. 8:15). The meaning of the verb is "to serve," as in the following Scripture passages: "But he answered his father, 'Look, these many years I have served you, and I never disobeyed your command, yet you never gave me a young goat, that I might celebrate with my friends'" (Luke 15:29). "No one can serve two masters, for either he will hate the one and love the other, or he will be devoted to the one and despise the other. You cannot serve God and money" (Matt. 6:24). "For you were called to freedom, brothers. Only do not use your freedom as an opportunity for the flesh, but through love serve one another" (Gal. 5:13). Apart from Christ "we . . . were . . . slaves to various passions and pleasures" (Titus 3:3), "enslaved to sin" (Rom. 6:6), serving "the law of sin" (Rom. 7:25), "enslaved to those that by nature are not gods" (Gal. 4:8). But now we serve Christ (Rom. 14:18; 16:18), "the Lord Christ" (Col. 3:24), "the living and true God" (1 Thess. 1:9).

Λατρεία is service, especially religion or the worship of God.[255]

- "They will put you out of the synagogues. Indeed, the hour is coming when whoever kills you will think he is offering service to God" (John 16:2).

251. Ed. note: Cf. Bavinck, *Bilderdijk als denker en dichter*, 106; Bavinck's source is Bilderdijk, *Verhandelingen*, 153: "We cannot think about anything immaterial except through material instruments and in material images that on their own become more clear or more opaque, and by which alone (in the best case) we correlate a certain notion that something spiritual is intended, which we feel in our heart" (*Wy denken aan niets onstoffelijks, of het is door 't stoffelijke werktuig, en onder stoffelijke beelden, die zich-zelven duidelijker of duisterer by ons opdoen, en waar meê wy alleenlijk [op zijn hoogst genomen] een zeker besef paren, dat er iets geestelijks onder gemeend wordt, 't geen wy in 't hart gevoelen*).
252. DO: *religieuze aanbidding.*
253. GrO: λατρεία; δουλεία.
254. GrO: ἐλευθερία.
255. Ed. note: Bavinck plays on the Dutch words *dienst* = service and *godsdienst* = religion or worship.

- "They are Israelites, and to them belong the adoption, the glory, the covenants, the giving of the law, the worship, and the promises" (Rom. 9:4).
- "I appeal to you therefore, brothers, by the mercies of God, to present your bodies as a living sacrifice, holy and acceptable to God, which is your spiritual worship" (Rom. 12:1).
- "Now even the first covenant had regulations for worship and an earthly place of holiness. . . . These preparations having thus been made, the priests go regularly into the first section, performing their ritual duties" (Heb. 9:1, 6).

The Greek word θρησκεία is more general, referring to a demonstration of piety. In Holy Scripture (but not in common Greek) the verb λατρεύω always points to religion and worship:[256]

- "You shall worship the Lord your God / and him only shall you serve" (Matt. 4:10).
- "That we, being delivered from the hand of our enemies, / might serve him without fear" (Luke 1:74).
- "You shall worship the Lord your God, / and him only shall you serve" (Luke 4:8).
- "But this I confess to you, that according to the Way, which they call a sect, I worship the God of our fathers, believing everything laid down by the Law and written in the Prophets" (Acts 24:14).
- "For God is my witness, whom I serve with my spirit in the gospel of his Son" (Rom. 1:9).

There is only one counterexample in Scripture. Deuteronomy 28:47–48 speaks of God's judgment on his people when they do not serve him: "Because you did not serve the LORD your God with joyfulness and gladness of heart, because of the abundance of all things, therefore you shall serve your enemies whom the LORD will send against you, in hunger and thirst, in nakedness, and lacking everything." Hence, *douleia* is also used for God. There would be no objection to using the term *douleia* to indicate veneration or honor to creatures and to reserving *latreia* for the worship of God.[257] But Roman Catholics understand *douleia* to refer not merely to "civic veneration" but

256. DO: *godsdienst.*
257. Thus, Augustine, *City of God* X.1 (*NPNF*[1] 2:180–81).

also to "religious veneration," although of a lesser sort than *latreia*.[258] In between *latreia* and *douleia* we find *hyperdouleia*, the veneration that belongs to Christ according to his human nature, to Mary, and to the crucifix.[259]

b. Rome also distinguishes "image" or "likeness" from "idol."[260] But this distinction is absurd—as if *imago* (*simulacrum*) were an image of something that exists and *idolum* an image of something that does not. In fact, there is no difference in meaning between the two terms, except that *simulacrum* is Latin and *idolum* is Greek. For example, the Greek text of 1 John 5:21 has εἴδωλον, while the Latin Vulgate has *simulacrum*.[261] Furthermore, even though an idol is nothing, Paul does call them "demons" (1 Cor. 8:4; 10:20).[262] In Acts 7:41 the image of the true God is called an εἴδωλον, and the idols of the pagans are called εἰκών in Romans 1:23.[263] It is simply incorrect to say that in this commandment God is prohibiting us only from creating images of things that do not exist.

c. In addition, Rome also claims that the veneration is transmitted through the image to the prototypes that image represents, as is mentioned in the verse in the cathedral church of Saint John, in 's Hertogenbosch.[264] This veneration is "with respect to"—that is to say, it is not directed materially to the image of wood or stone but formally—namely, as it is viewed in relation to the prototype it represents, although it truly is a proper adoration of the image itself, so that it supplies the culmination of the adoration.[265]

258. LO: *cultus civilis*; *cultus religiosus*; de Moor, *Commentarius Perpetuus*, 2:511–13.

259. Ed. note: Bavinck's definition of *hyperdouleia* is more expansive than contemporary definitions, which restrict it to veneration of the Virgin Mary.

260. HO: פֶּסֶל, to hew into shape; פֶּסֶל, image of a god; GrO: εἰκών and εἴδωλον; LO: *simulacrum* (*imago*) and *idolum*. Ed. note: The second term in each pair suggests an image of something that is imaginary, a fantasy.

261. Ursinus, *Commentary on the Heidelberg Catechism*, 525–26. Ed. note: On the Second Commandment.

262. GrO: δαιμόνια.

263. De Moor, *Commentarius Perpetuus*, 2:714–30.

264. Ed. note: In the Sint-Jan Cathedral of 's-Hertogenbosch there was at one time a wooden plaque (53 cm × 24.5 cm) affixed to a crucifix on public display (now in storage). In gold letters on a black background was this inscription:

Gedenk o mensch! Dat gij hier ziet	Beware, O man! What you see on this board
Is Christus beeld maar Christus niet;	Is only an image, not Christ the Lord;
Daarom aanbid noch hout noch steen,	So, worship neither wood nor stone,
maar Christus uwen God alleen.	but Christ your God alone.

(Translated by John Bolt with invaluable assistance from Harry Van Dyke. Thanks to I. C. M. Peters, archivist of the Sint-Jan church.)

265. LO: *in esse relativo . . . quatenus repraesentat prototypon, . . . adoratio imaginis per se et proprie, ut scilicet ipsa terminet adorationem et sit ejus objectum seu materia circa quam.* Bavinck's source is Voetius, *Selectarum Disputationum Theologicarum*, 3:879–80.

This is said to be similar to the way that we honor all creatures—for example, subjects honoring their king or children honoring their parents.[266] Honor is not given to kings or parents as human beings, but in their roles as king or parent. However, Voetius provides the correct response to this: if we accept this distinction, then everything, including inanimate matter—yes, even the devil—would have to be adored, to the extent that each has a relation to God.[267] Gregory of Valencia also agreed with this.[268] Furthermore, the question is not why or how images are being worshiped, but only whether they are being worshiped. If one could defend the worship of images by claiming that they are not being venerated "in and of themselves" but only "through another,"[269] then the same reasoning would justify the idolatry of the pagans. They also do not pray to images "as such" but "through another." They could even say that they do this "to the glory of God," and, in fact, they used the same arguments against the church fathers.[270]

d. Rome also defends images as "books for the laity." The Heidelberg Catechism provides a beautiful response to this in Q&A 98: "Q. But may not images be permitted in churches in place of books for the unlearned? A. No, we should not try to be wiser than God. God wants the Christian community instructed by the living preaching of his Word—not by idols that cannot even talk." Rome removes the Bible and its preaching and supplies the images. Faith arises not from contemplating images, but from hearing the preaching of the Word (Rom. 10:17). Preaching, not the image, should portray Christ before our eyes: "O foolish Galatians! Who has bewitched you? It was before your eyes that Jesus Christ was publicly portrayed as crucified" (Gal. 3:1). The image without verbal instruction teaches nothing. Teaching by means of visual aids does not suffice here, but instead teaches false concepts and ideas. The iconoclasts should therefore not be judged too harshly. Marnix, at any rate, does not condemn them very strongly.[271]

---

266. This is also true for portraits of a friend or king, statues, etc. (de Moor, *Commentarius Perpetuus*, 2:739).

267. LO: *quod et quatenus respectum habeat ad Deum*; Voetius, *Selectarum Disputationum Theologicarum*, 3:880.

268. Ed. note: Gregory of Valencia (1550–1603) was a Spanish humanist and scholar who defended the doctrine of Luis de Molina on grace and predestination (Wikipedia, s.v. "Gregory of Valencia," https://en.wikipedia.org/wiki/Gregory_of_Valencia).

269. LO: *per se; per aliud.*

270. See also Israel's idolatry in Exod. 32:4–5 and the worship at Bethel (1 Kings 12:25–33) (de Moor, *Commentarius Perpetuus*, 2:733).

271. Ed. note: This is a reference to Philips van Marnix, St. Aldegonde (1538–98), a Dutch writer and statesman who wrote a pamphlet justifying the iconoclasts of 1566 (Dutch: *Beeldenstorm*) who destroyed Roman Catholic art in churches and public places. Their signature action was the destruction in the Church of Our Lady in Antwerp on August 20, 1566. Van Marnix's

e. There are additional arguments offered for images: they decorate churches;[272] they exist as statues on church property.

3. Veneration of relics.

For Roman Catholics, the cross is the ultimate relic.[273] In Holy Scripture the cross figuratively represents the following:

a. Christ's death on the cross and all his suffering (1 Cor. 1:18; Gal. 6:14)
b. The doctrine of the cross of the crucified Christ—that is, the gospel (Gal. 5:11; 6:12; Phil. 3:18)
c. The persecution of Christians for the sake of Christ (Matt. 10:38; 16:24; etc.)

Literally, the word "cross" indicates either the actual cross of Christ believed to have been found by the Empress Helena or signs of the cross. The sign of the cross also served as decoration or symbol for pagans.[274] Christians began to use the sign of the cross fairly early on: on the forehead as the foremost part of the body, on the heart, from which came evil thoughts, on the mouth as the organ of speech for words; in the name of the Father, the Son, and the Holy Spirit.[275]

Luther retained the use of the sign of the cross in the morning and in the evening.[276] Lutheran and Anglican churches continue to make the sign of the cross at baptisms, the Lord's Supper, and the Aaronic benediction. Reformed churches repudiated it altogether.[277]

This use of the cross must be distinguished from images of the cross.[278] These also came into use at a relatively early period and were present everywhere.

---

literary accomplishments included a metrical translation of the Psalms (1580) and the Dutch national anthem, "Wilhelmus van Nassauwe" (Wikisource, s.v. "1911 Encyclopaedia Britannica/St Aldegonde, Philips van Marnix, Heer van," https://en.wikisource.org/w/index.php?title =1911_Encyclop%C3%A6dia_Britannica/St_Aldegonde,_Philips_van_Marnix,_Heer_van &oldid=6343595).

272. According to de Moor, *Commentarius Perpetuus*, 2:740, this was also Luther's position.
273. Voetius, "De staurolatria"; Zöckler, *Das Kreuz Christi*.
274. Merz, "Kreuzerhebung."
275. Merz, "Kreuzeszeichnen," 275.
276. Ed. note: In his Small Catechism, Luther gives the following instructions for daily prayers: "In the morning, as soon as you get out of bed, you are to make the sign of the holy cross and say: 'God the Father, Son, and Holy Spirit watch over me, Amen.'" And, "In the evening, when you go to bed, you are to make the sign of the holy cross and say: 'God the Father, Son, and Holy Spirit watch over me, Amen'" (Kolb and Wengert, *Book of Concord*, 363).
277. Ed. note: Bavinck's source is likely Merz, "Kreuzeszeichnen," 275.
278. LO: *crux exemplata*.

By the fifth century the cross image had become an amulet, especially since Constantine had seen the sign of the cross in the sky.[279] From the fifth century onward, crucifixes with images of Christ on them appeared. Roman Catholics consider this cross to be holy, blessed, and the like; this cross is the "sign of the Christian soldier," incorporates the mysteries of the faith, incites the devil to hatred, increases devotion, arouses faith and trust, and is prayed to, directly or indirectly.[280] Temples, altars, monasteries, orders, fraternities, and feasts (of discovery and elevation), litanies, and masses were all dedicated to the cross. The sign of the cross was used in connection with prayer and thanksgiving, the reading and preaching of the Word, the celebration of the sacraments, ecclesiastical blessings and consecrations of persons or things, consecrations of temples, processions, burials, and so forth.[281]

The same is true for relics, whose veneration arose out of reverence for the martyrs.[282] Venerating relics began early on, became a general practice especially during the time of Constantine, and was commended by Eusebius, Gregory of Nazianz, Gregory of Nyssa, Theodoret, Basil, and John of Damascus. The Synod of Nicaea (787) decreed that no church was to be consecrated without the presence of a relic.[283] The Council of Trent made the veneration of relics a dogma.[284] Luther said it briefly and well: "Even if we had the bones of all the saints or all holy and consecrated vestments gathered together in one pile, they would not help us in the least, *for they are all dead things that cannot make anyone holy.*"[285]

The cross and relics should definitely not be religiously venerated because, whatever they are called, they are not instruments or means of redemption.[286] God rightly took Moses away (Deut. 34:6; Jude 9). We no longer know even

279. See Merz, "Kruzifix."

280. Aquinas, *ST* IIIa q. 25 art. 4 co. Ed. note: Bavinck's source is once again Voetius, *Selectarum Disputationum Theologicarum*, 3:886–88.

281. Voetius, *Selectarum Disputationum Theologicarum*, 3:886–89.

282. Hauck, "Reliquien."

283. Second Council of Nicaea (AD 787), canon 7: "Therefore we decree that in venerable churches consecrated without relics of the holy martyrs, the installation of relics should take place along with the usual prayers. And if in future any bishop is found out consecrating a church without relics, let him be deposed as someone who has flouted the ecclesiastical traditions." Ed. note: Canon 7 is not included in the thirtieth edition of Denzinger; it is available online at Papal Encyclicals Online, last updated February 20, 2020, http://www.papalencyclicals.net/Councils/ecum07.htm.

284. Council of Trent, session 25 (Denzinger, no. 985). Ed. note: Bavinck takes this from Hauck, "Reliquien," 692.

285. GO: *Es ist alles tot Ding, das niemand heilgen kann.* Ed. note: Bavinck cites only the italicized portion of this quotation from Luther's Large Catechism on the Third Commandment (Kolb and Wengert, *Book of Concord*, 399).

286. LO: *instrumenta* or *media redemptionis.*

"Christ according to the flesh" (2 Cor. 5:16). Even though miracles were performed through these things, they would still be merely bare instruments and not to be worshiped or religiously venerated.[287] Even though people came into contact with saints, or even with Jesus himself (e.g., his cross), they are not made holy and powerful, because then the hands of the soldiers who seized Jesus and the lips of Judas who kissed Jesus would become holy.[288] All worship of relics is at base nothing more than pagan fetishism and amulet worship.

4. Self-willed religion.[289]

At its most fundamental level, the difference in connection with this commandment lies in the answer to this question: Who decides how God is to be worshiped? For Rome the answer is, Scripture and the church. In actuality this means that we humans decide, a claim made also by modernists and those who reject revelation. It is true that parents, the government, rulers, all have the right to make laws, and provided that these laws are not in conflict with God's law, we must obey them for the sake of conscience. This, too, is service to God in a broad sense, but not worship in the narrow sense.[290] It is service to God because we must obey those in authority over us *for God's sake*; he has placed them over us. In this way the church also has the right to make certain stipulations concerning the time, location, and order of preaching, the election of elders, and so on, for the sake of good order. Provided these rules do not conflict with God's Word, church members are expected to obey them, and this too is service to God[291] in the broad sense.

But none of that is religion or worship in the real sense[292] because all such regulations are binding in an incidental manner—that is, because an authority so ordered, and if the order had been different we would not be obligated, nor would we be guilty before God. Worship in a real sense pertains only to those works that people must do by the command of God, even if there is no

---

287. De Moor, *Commentarius Perpetuus*, 2:738.

288. Voetius, *Selectarum Disputationum Theologicarum*, 3:896.

289. DO: *eigenwillige godsdienst*. Ed. note: The term *eigenwillig* connotes a willfulness or obstinacy.

290. Ed. note: This sentence is clearer in the original Dutch, where Bavinck plays with the words *godsdienst* (= religion, worship) and *dienst* (= service). Perhaps the best way for English readers to understand it is to recognize that the call to discipleship in the totality of our lives in all their aspects is sometimes expressed as "all of life is worship." Bavinck does not dispute this but wants us to be conscious of the distinction and not lose sight of our need for worship in the "real sense" (*eigenlijke godsdienst*).

291. DO: *dienst Gods*.

292. DO: *eigenlijke godsdienst*. Here and in the remainder of this paragraph Bavinck uses the term *godsdienst*, which we consistently translate as "worship" in the broader sense of "service to God" and not primarily in the sense of corporate or personal worship.

corresponding human commandment. Religious worship of God, worship in the real sense, consists of serving him on the basis of his command.[293] And now this question arises: Can human beings prescribe and determine this worship in its real sense? No, they cannot, because that would invalidate and destroy the very essence of true worship. This is exactly what the apostle Paul means by "self-made religion" (Col. 2:23),[294] which makes "void the word of God" by means of human traditions (Matt. 15:6; Mark 7:13; 1 Tim. 4:3; 2 Tim. 3:5). Even less does the church have the right to do this, because her only power is a ministering power:

> But Jesus called them to him and said, "You know that the rulers of the Gentiles lord it over them, and their great ones exercise authority over them. It shall not be so among you. But whoever would be great among you must be your servant, and whoever would be first among you must be your slave, even as the Son of Man came not to be served but to serve, and to give his life as a ransom for many." (Matt. 20:25–28)

> For freedom Christ has set us free; stand firm therefore, and do not submit again to a yoke of slavery. (Gal. 5:1)

> Therefore let no one pass judgment on you in questions of food and drink, or with regard to a festival or a new moon or a Sabbath. (Col. 2:16)

> So I exhort the elders among you, as a fellow elder and a witness of the sufferings of Christ, as well as a partaker in the glory that is going to be revealed: shepherd the flock of God that is among you, exercising oversight, not under compulsion, but willingly, as God would have you; not for shameful gain, but eagerly; not domineering over those in your charge, but being examples to the flock. (1 Pet. 5:1–3)

God alone has the right to determine how he wants to be served.

5. What is prescribed in this commandment?

God must be worshiped and served in the way he himself has commanded—that is, only according to his Word. Nonetheless, there lingers deep in our soul the yearning to see God (Exod. 33:18). Therefore, God says: You will find no image of me in any creature; that would dishonor me. But if you want an image, take a look at Adam, at human beings, who are created in my likeness.

---

293. DO: *Godsdienst is alleen een dienen van God om zijn bevel*; Ursinus, *Commentary on the Heidelberg Catechism*, 520.
294. GrO: ἐθελοθρησκεία.

Above all, look at the Son, the Image of the Invisible God, God's One and Only Firstborn, God's other *I*, the expression of his self-sufficiency. Whoever sees him sees the Father. As Christ is, so is God. He is the perfect likeness, the adequate Image. Let us be satisfied with that. God may be venerated with no other image than the Son. Beholding him and venerating him, we are changed into his likeness (2 Cor. 3:18). God wants, as it were, to multiply images of himself, to see nothing but images, likenesses, portraits of himself. Human beings themselves must be God's image, and not make pieces of wood or stone into God's image. The new humanity in Christ, from all sides and everyone in their own way, reflects and mirrors God. God is mirrored in us; we are mirrored in God. "When [Christ] appears, we shall be like him [and like the Father] because we shall see him as he is" (1 John 3:2). God makes images of himself in us. But not we of God. God photographs himself.

16

The Honor of God's Name

To misuse God's name is to deny his self-revelation as YHWH and as Father, Son, and Spirit. The Third Commandment prohibits cursing, swearing falsely, unnecessary swearing, blasphemy, and any misuse of God's name.

Cursing is the opposite of blessing and is ultimately reserved for God. The Bible does give examples of human cursing, including the imprecatory psalms, but these are never personal but solely on God's instruction and for the sake of God's own honor. All other cursing of our neighbors is forbidden, especially one's parents, all authorities, and those who cannot defend themselves, such as the deaf, who are unable to hear curses. All self-cursing is condemned as well as cursing God and Christ. The curse is an expression of sinful anger, hatred, and vindictiveness and appropriates God's omnipotence to serve human, sinful passions. It insults God's majesty and holiness, making it subservient to human, sinful anger. This is demonic and makes cursing itself subject to God's curse.

Swearing falsely happens in several ways: idolatrous oaths (swearing by something other than God), false oaths (about matters that are untrue), and violated or broken oaths. Swearing by something other than God is idolatrous because God alone can search our hearts and know our minds. It is strictly forbidden in Scripture, although Israel used different formulas in daily life. In Jesus's day, because of reluctance to mention God's name, it became increasingly customary to swear by creatures and by God-related realities such as the temple and God's throne. Jesus pointed out the foolishness and idolatry of such swearing.

We swear falsely when we use an oath to affirm something untrue, in which case we call upon God to lie. We must also be certain that our oath does not violate God's law, for we then would call on God to contradict himself, to approve what he forbids or to punish what he approves. We also swear falsely when we break an oath, when we neglect an oath of promise, although we are permitted to break our oath when keeping it would transgress one of God's commandments, when mutual oaths (such as a betrothal) are broken by the other party, and when circumstances make it impossible to keep our vow. It is not permissible to break oaths when it disadvantages us, when it appears later that deceit was involved, or when the person to whom we have sworn the oath becomes an unbeliever or heretic. Oaths may not be broken when they have been taken with mental reservations or intentional equivocations. Protestants, therefore, reject the Jesuit practices of casuistry that sought to evade or conceal full truth.

It is also a sin to swear unnecessarily. There are numerous examples in the Old Testament and still among Christians today, especially in public life. Even when God's name is not explicitly called on, strong expressions such as "cross my heart and hope to die" and frequently used conversation fillers and garbled swear words such as "O my God!" and "O Jesus!" violate reverence for and the sacredness of God's Name. It diminishes God's exalted majesty to call upon his omniscience, omnipotence, and righteousness at the drop of a hat, also for the most insignificant matters.

Blasphemy is even worse than cursing God and reveals an even greater anger and demonic hardening. It was punishable by death in Israel. To blaspheme God is to say something about him that comes from the heart and directly contradicts and violates his nature and properties. It is to attribute to God the exact opposite of his true nature, to judge him as unjust, cruel, or the like; to mock his assumed holiness and love; and to represent oneself as much holier, wiser, and more just. Blasphemy is an outburst of hatred against God and his rule; it is to declare that we do not sin against God but God sins against us.

Other misuses of God's name include thoughtless prayer, indifference or irreverence in worship, using the Bible for amusement or entertainment (plays), misusing God's truth for personal advantage or to excuse sloth, despising God's gifts in nature and in people, and misusing the lot. Casting lots must be reserved for serious and important matters about which people have reached an impasse.

The Third Commandment prescribes the proper use of God's name. This includes prayer, the proper invocation and confession of God's name, and the like. Above all, the commandment deals with oaths.

Oaths are found among all peoples and in all religions. Their origin is to be sought in the ineradicable sense of responsibility to and absolute dependence on a Higher Power. To take an oath is, therefore, a religious act. Thomas Aquinas provides a solid definition of an oath, distinguishes various kinds of oaths, spells out the parameters and conditions for swearing oaths, and indicates who may swear and who is excluded from swearing an oath.

Within the Christian tradition, opposition to oaths comes from Pelagians, Anabaptists, and Socinians, among others. Christ and the apostle James are taken to have forbidden all oaths. Philosophers have also objected to oaths, and it is especially in the modern era that oaths are repudiated in the name of a secular state. In response, we need to regard Jesus's words about oaths as addressing false and evasive swearing, not as a blanket prohibition. From the rest of Scripture, we must conclude that swearing oaths is permissible. Different words and gestures are used in swearing oaths but do not affect the substance.

The oath presupposes sin, the lie, and human untrustworthiness. The essence of the oath consists of an appeal to God as true, omniscient, and omnipotent, the One who knows us and who punishes evil. It is a religious act that expresses our obligation to God. What happens when this religious dimension — "So help me God" — is removed, as many European countries did in the nineteenth century? The oath is then destroyed; a simple, moral, civil oath without calling on God is an absurdity. Remove God, and the state has no safeguard against human untruthfulness; honor and conscience become products of humans themselves. Apart from God there is no longer a foundation for truth, justice, or goodness. The oath is the cement of the state, of justice; it is the cornerstone of the edifice of the state.

Objections to oaths go beyond the religious ones derived from Matthew 5. Some claim that oaths are superstitious attempts to summon God to intervene based on fear of his wrath. But oaths do not summon God unto, but invoke a God who is already present as the all-knowing, as witness. Oaths acknowledge a person's complete dependence upon and trust in God, in his justice and goodness. Then there are those who say that there is no God or that he does not hear or know us or that we know nothing about him. Some argue that swearing oaths is insulting and distrustful of others, a destroyer of human self-esteem. The contrary is the truth: oaths honor human beings as capable of truthfulness, of being open in their speaking before God and their fellow human beings. Oaths assume the reality of the fall into sin at the same time they raise up our humanity; we have not sunk as far as Satan, who lies straight to God's face. Demons are incapable of swearing oaths.

The modern state and its pretention to be "godless" presents a difficult problem. If the oath is an article of natural rather than revealed theology, the state that promises total freedom of conscience and also tries to bind its citizens to God in oaths comes into conflict with itself. There seems to be no solution to this quandary; the godless state is practically unworkable and eventually destroys itself.

The church has a solemn obligation to imprint the sacred importance of the oath on the hearts of a people. Oaths need to be limited to only the most important cases — that is, to witnesses in court and in the oath of office. Care must be taken to preserve the solemnity of an oath ceremony. Perjury must be severely punished.

§34. THE THIRD COMMANDMENT

You shall not take the name of the LORD your God in vain, for the LORD will
not hold him guiltless who takes his name in vain. (Exod. 20:7)

The First Commandment deals with the true God, the Second with the true religion, the Third with private religion, and the Fourth with the public (communal)
exercise of that true religion. You shall not take or use[1] the name of the Lord (for
instance, in song) for idle, empty,[2] futile, trivial purposes, nor for any swearing or
lies, untruth, curses, fortune-telling, witchcraft, and the like. Although God does
not reveal himself through images and does not want to be served through them,
he has revealed himself in his Name (Exod. 3:14–15; 6:2–3).[3] The name of God
is God's revelation in a variety of relationships toward humanity; in that name
God reveals himself; and then, on the basis of this, we refer to him in accordance
with this revelation.[4] God's name is thus the sum total of his revelations. In his
name he has made himself known to us, disclosed himself. The unknown God
(Acts 17:23) is also the Unnamed, the Nameless, the Unknowable One.[5] God's
name is not an anonym (deism), not a pseudonym (polytheism); deism always
speaks of "a Supreme Being," "the most High Being," or "Heaven," as many
hymns demonstrate.[6] But God has real names, and YHWH is his proper name.
Still, we are not to think of the name YHWH alone, but of all God's names: El,
Elohim, and others, including his full name of Father, Son, and Spirit.[7]

What the Third Commandment Prohibits

The Third Commandment forbids cursing, swearing falsely, unnecessary
swearing, blasphemy, and any misuse of God's name.

1. CURSING

The Third Commandment prohibits cursing, which is the opposite of blessing. It is to pray that God will send us or our neighbor something evil, either

---

1. HO: נָשָׂא.
2. HO: לַשָּׁוְא.
3. See Keil and Delitzsch, *Biblical Commentary on the Old Testament*, 2:118 (Exod. 20:7).
4. See *RD*, 1:40–43.
5. Spencer, *First Principles of a New System of Philosophy*. Ed. note: The title of part I is
"The Unknowable."
6. DO: *Opperwezen, hoogste Wezen, de Hemel*. Ed. note: Bavinck here echoes E. Sartorius,
Die Lehre von der heiligen Liebe, 309. With his reference to hymns, Bavinck likely had in mind
the hymnbook used in the national Dutch Reformed Church, *Evangelische gezangen om nevens
het boek der psalmen bij den openbaren godsdienst in de Nederlandsche Hervormde gemeenten
gebruikt te worden* (1806).
7. E. Sartorius, *Die Lehre von der heiligen Liebe*, 309–10.

temporarily or eternally. Not all cursing is wrong. God himself curses humans (Gen. 3:16–19) and the earth and all it contains (Gen. 3:17), sends the Flood as a curse (Gen. 5:29; 8:21), and will curse those who curse Abraham (Gen. 12:3). God curses transgressors of his law (Deut. 28:15–68), Israel and its blessings (Mal. 2:2), everyone who does not remain in the book of the law (Deut. 28:58–60; Gal. 3:13), and whoever rejects Christ (1 Cor. 16:22). The curse proceeds from God (Zech. 5:3–4), and his curse strikes home (Deut. 28:15–68). With him, cursing is not just wishing evil but sending evil; his word is his command, a power that causes what is spoken to unfailingly become reality. Of course, no creature has such power. But God can nevertheless instruct people to curse in his name: Moses (Deut. 11:26) and the Levites (Deut. 27) hold up before Israel curse and blessing. People also can speak a curse in the certainty that God will confirm it: Noah curses Canaan (Gen. 9:25); Isaac blesses Jacob by cursing those who curse him (Gen. 27:29); Jacob curses the wrath of his sons Simeon and Levi (Gen. 49:7); Joshua curses the one who rebuilds Jericho (Josh. 6:26); and Peter curses Simon the Magician (Acts 8:18–21). We must also understand the imprecatory psalms in this way (Pss. 69:23–29; 109:6–20). Both psalms are quoted in the New Testament (Acts 1:16, 20; Rom. 11:9). We do not have an utterance here of personal anger or hatred or revenge, but of zeal for the honor of God. They are prophecies about the future fate of the ungodly, partly to be understood conditionally when conversion does not occur: "If a man does not repent, God will whet his sword; / he has bent and readied his bow" (Ps. 7:12).[8]

But otherwise, cursing is prohibited. It may not be done out of personal vindictiveness or vain actions, as King Saul did: "And the men of Israel had been hard pressed that day, so Saul had laid an oath on the people, saying, 'Cursed be the man who eats food until it is evening and I am avenged on my enemies.' So none of the people had tasted food" (1 Sam. 14:24). Cursing can be evidence of godlessness, as in Shimei's curse of David (2 Sam. 16:5; cf. Ps. 10:7). Cursing one's parents is especially forbidden, and the penalty is death (Exod. 21:17; Lev. 20:9; Prov. 20:20; 30:11). Also, specifically prohibited are cursing the authorities (Exod. 22:28; Eccles. 10:20; cf. Acts 23:5) and cursing deaf people, who are unable to hear curses and therefore cannot defend themselves (Lev. 19:14). We are forbidden to curse our neighbors, who are made in God's image (James 3:9); instead, we must bless even our enemies and pray

---

8. De Moor, *Commentarius Perpetuus*, 2:758; Witsius, *Miscellaneorum Sacrorum*, 1:213–20. Stapfer, *Institutiones Theologiae Polemicae*, 2:951–52 (X, §109) and 1016 (X, §203). Ed. note: Bavinck likely took this reference from de Moor and cited it in a Nederduits translation of Stapfer's *Institutiones* by Antonius de Stoppelaar, *Onderwys in de gantsche wederleggende Godsgeleertheit*; Delitzsch, "Psalmen," 291.

for their good (Matt. 5:44; Rom. 12:14). Cursing ourselves is also prohibited, and therefore Job's self-curse (Job 3:1), Jeremiah's curse (Jer. 20:14–16), the oath taken by men who wanted to kill Paul (Acts 23:12), and the one taken by Peter when he denied Jesus (Matt. 26:72–74) are all to be strongly condemned. Finally, we are never to curse God (Lev. 24:15) and Christ (1 Cor. 12:3). An undeserved curse is ineffective: "Like a sparrow in its flitting, like a swallow in its flying, / a curse that is causeless does not alight" (Prov. 26:2). God may return such curses upon the one who curses (Gen. 12:3) or change the curse into a blessing (Deut. 23:5; Balaam).

Nonetheless, it is no mere pagan superstition to attach power to curses—for instance, of parents regarding their child. History supplies remarkable proofs of this; and so have poets, writers of tragedies, and novelists. Cursing is the opposite of praying or blessing; it wishes calamities and death to happen. The curse is an expression of sinful anger, hatred, and vindictiveness and appropriates God's omnipotence to serve human, sinful passions. It is thus an insult to God's majesty and holiness and makes it subservient to human, sinful anger.[9] Instead of persons offering their wills to serve God, the curse uses God's holy will for the service of our sinful will. Cursing is not praying that God's righteousness may be revealed and shown, but demanding, requiring, charging God to punish our enemy. Cursing then is something demonic, its contents a destructive hatred.[10] Therefore, cursing is itself subject to God's curse. This brings us to the Third Commandment's second prohibition: improper oaths.

2. SWEARING FALSELY

Swearing falsely happens in several ways: idolatrous oaths (swearing by something other than God), false oaths (about matters that are untrue), and violated or broken oaths.

a. Idolatrous oaths. When someone swears by something other than God, we are not speaking of a false oath but of an idolatrous oath. One may swear only by the true, living God, who sees us and hears and knows us. In a dispute between two Israelites, it is to the LORD that oaths must be sworn: "If a man gives to his neighbor a donkey or an ox or a sheep or any beast to keep safe, and it dies or is injured or is driven away, without anyone seeing it, an oath by the LORD shall be between them both to see whether or not he has put his hand to his neighbor's property. The owner shall accept the oath, and he shall not make restitution" (Exod. 22:10–11). "Pay attention to all that I have said to you, and make no mention of the names of other gods, nor let it be heard

---

9. E. Sartorius, *Die Lehre von der heiligen Liebe*, 328.
10. Wuttke, *Handbuch der christlichen Sittenlehre*[3], 2:63 (§169).

on your lips" (Exod. 23:13). "It is the LORD your God you shall fear. Him you shall serve and by his name you shall swear" (Deut. 6:13; cf. 10:20). When the day of the Lord comes, other nations will swear by the God of Israel: "In that day there will be five cities in the land of Egypt that speak the language of Canaan and swear allegiance to the LORD of hosts" (Isa. 19:18). On that day, God will turn cursing of a rebellious people into blessing:

> You shall leave your name to my chosen for a curse,
>   and the Lord GOD will put you to death,
>   but his servants he will call by another name,
> so that he who blesses himself in the land
>   shall bless himself by the God of truth,
> and he who takes an oath in the land
>   shall swear by the God of truth;
> because the former troubles are forgotten
>   and are hidden from my eyes. (Isa. 65:15–16)

Old Testament prohibitions against idolatrous swearing are found at key moments in Israel's history. In his final charge to Israel's leaders, Joshua admonishes them to not "make mention of the names of their gods or swear by them or serve them or bow down to them, but you shall cling to the LORD your God just as you have done to this day" (Josh. 23:7–8). It is a sign of apostasy to swear by other gods:

> How can I pardon you?
>   Your children have forsaken me
>   and have sworn by those who are no gods.
> When I fed them to the full,
>   they committed adultery
>   and trooped to the houses of whores. (Jer. 5:7)

In its apostasy, Israel swore by Baal (Jer. 12:16), by the "Guilt of Samaria," by the god of Dan, and by the "Way of Beersheba" (Amos 8:14); they swear "to the LORD / and yet swear by Milcom" (Zeph. 1:5).[11] And in Matthew

---

11. Ed. note: The playful use of language as a rebuke to Israel's idolatry is neatly captured by Calvin in his commentary on Zeph. 1:5:

> As to the term מלכם, *melkom*, it may be properly rendered, *their king*; for מלך *melek*, as it is well known, means a king; but it is here put in construction, מלכם, *melkom*, their king; *they swear by their own king*. The Prophet, I doubt not, alludes to the word מולך, *molok*, which is derived from the verb, to reign: for though that word was commonly used by all as a proper name, it is yet certain that that false god was so called, as though he was a king: and the Prophet increases the indignity by saying—*They swear by*

5:34–37 Jesus says, "Do not take an oath at all, either by heaven, for it is the throne of God, or by the earth, for it is his footstool, or by Jerusalem, for it is the city of the great King. And do not take an oath by your head, for you cannot make one hair white or black. Let what you say be simply 'Yes' or 'No'; anything more than this comes from evil." James 5:12 teaches the same: "But above all, my brothers, do not swear, either by heaven or by earth or by any other oath, but let your 'yes' be yes and your 'no' be no, so that you may not fall under condemnation." We are to swear by God alone, since he searches our hearts and examines our minds (Jer. 17:10; 1 Kings 8:39; Heb. 4:13).[12]

With the Israelites, however, it was customary to swear in everyday life with different formulas, such as "by the life of Pharaoh" (Gen. 42:16) and "as your soul lives" (1 Sam. 1:26; 17:55; 20:3; 25:26). In such instances, those who swear declare the life of the person invoked as something precious to them.[13] But these formulas do not mention the name of God and are not really oaths, but strong, popular confirmations.[14] Roman Catholics cannot appeal to this for their oaths.

The more that the Israelites avoided mentioning the name of God in later times, the more it became customary to swear by creatures (Matt. 5:34–37; 23:16–22). Roman Catholics also consider swearing by saints permissible for the same reason they regard praying to them permissible. Now such an oath in the name of idols, saints, the temple, the altar, Jerusalem, and so on should be honored (even though later one might discern the error and idolatry in it), for the one who is swearing considers these things as God or as divine. Jesus pointed this out in Matthew 23:16–20 when he reminded the Pharisees that "whoever swears by the temple swears by it and by him who dwells in it. And whoever swears by heaven swears by the throne of God and by him who sits upon it" (Matt. 23:21–22). Jesus calls those who teach these things "blind fools" and points out that "whoever swears by the altar swears by it

---

Malkom. He might have simply said, "They swear by Moloch"; but he says, *They swear by Malkom;* that is, "They forget that I am their king, and transfer my sovereignty to a dead and empty image." God then does here, by an implied contrast, exaggerate the sin of the Jews, as they sought another king for themselves, when they knew that under his protection they always enjoyed a sure and real safety. (John Calvin, *Commentaries on the Twelve Minor Prophets,* 4:200)

12. Cf. Heidelberg Catechism, Q&A 102: "Q. May we also swear by saints or other creatures? A. No. A legitimate oath means calling upon God as the only one who knows my heart to witness to my truthfulness and to punish me if I swear falsely. No creature is worthy of such honor."

13. Similar confirmation formulas are found in Gen. 31:52; 42:37; 43:9; 44:9; Josh. 2:14.

14. Rüetschi, "Eid bei den Hebräern," 118; Ursinus, *Commentary on the Heidelberg Catechism,* 551.

and by everything on it" (v. 20). Subsequent insight into the idolatrous nature of such an oath shows that, in fact, we are still bound by it to the true God.

b. False oaths. We also swear falsely when we use an oath to affirm something untrue[15] and God's name is associated with a falsehood or lie: "You shall not swear by my name falsely, and so profane the name of your God: I am the LORD" (Lev. 19:12). This is what the Third Commandment teaches. Nonetheless, perjury is frequently mentioned in the Old Testament (Pss. 10:7; 24:4; 59:12; Prov. 6:19; 14:5; Jer. 5:2; Hosea 4:2; Zech. 5:3–4; 8:17; Mal. 3:5). There were no civil penalties for perjury except that the Lord would not hold perjurers guiltless. That is why a sin offering is prescribed for swearing rashly or falsely (Lev. 5:4–6). Only oaths about matters that are true are permitted; otherwise one is calling upon God to lie. We must be also certain that a matter is true, or else we are swearing with a guilty conscience, scorning God. We must also be certain that a matter is permissible according to God's law, for what God forbids us to say or do he also forbids us to promise or to swear to do. Otherwise, we would be calling on God to contradict himself, to approve what he forbids or to punish what he approves. We must also limit our swearing to matters that are possible for us because to swear to what we are incapable of doing is to swear to a lie.[16] Oaths must be limited to those matters that are necessary, that are worthy of confirmation by oath, that serve to honor God and benefit our neighbor.

c. Violated oaths. In the third place, we swear falsely when we break an oath, when we neglect an oath of promise.[17] However, sworn oaths may be broken in three circumstances:

(i) Breaking an oath is permitted when the oath involves transgressing one of God's commandments, when it leads to sin. It would have been better for Herod to have broken his oath to the daughter of Herodias (Matt. 14:7–12). David's oath to destroy Nabal's house was wrong and was properly broken when Abigail appealed to him (1 Sam. 25:22–24, 32–34).[18]

(ii) Breaking an oath is also permitted when one party to a mutual oath breaks it. Then the other party is also freed from their oath. Examples include someone breaking their promise to a betrothed.

(iii) We may break a vow when external circumstances beyond our control make it impossible to keep it. Thus, the godly promise to obey God completely and sincerely and yet fail repeatedly.[19]

---

15. LO: *juramentum affirmans*. Ed. note: Bavinck took this term from de Moor, *Commentarius Perpetuus*, 2:759.

16. Ursinus, *Commentary on the Heidelberg Catechism*, 551.

17. LO: *jusjurandum promissorium*.

18. De Moor, *Commentarius Perpetuus*, 2:761.

19. De Moor, *Commentarius Perpetuus*, 2:762.

But aside from these instances, the oath that was promised with God in view must be kept. It is not to be broken in the following circumstances:

(i) When an oath disadvantages us, when it appears that fulfilling the vow would be disadvantageous to us. Among the characteristics of the righteous person is one "who swears to his own hurt and does not change" (Ps. 15:4; cf. Lev. 5:4–6). Such an oath appears to be binding even when force may have been used to extract it. For example, a prisoner might be forced by murderers to swear that he will send them money once he is released.[20]

(ii) When it appears later that deceit was involved. The Israelites had to spare the Gibeonites (Josh. 9:15–20) and were not allowed to kill them (cf. 2 Sam. 21).[21]

(iii) When the person to whom we have sworn the oath later becomes a heretic, becomes an unbeliever, or is excommunicated. This is not the view of Roman Catholics, who believe that upon excommunication an oath need not be kept to the person excommunicated. King Sigismund of Hungary promised safe conduct to Czech reformer John Hus (1369–1415)[22] so that Hus could appear at the Council of Constance (1414–18). Nonetheless, after examination, the synod pronounced, "This holy synod of Constance, seeing that God's church has nothing more that it can do, relinquishes John Hus to the judgment of the secular authority and decrees that he is to be relinquished to the secular court."[23] Hus was then burned at the stake.[24]

In this Roman Catholic view, subordinates can be absolved from their oath to authorities or sovereigns who become heretical, and so forth.[25] Some Roman Catholics, like Becanus,[26] try to conceal this and limit their church's position to an oath that was forced, broken already by the other party, or made to do something illegal. But Abraham and Isaac also made covenants with

---

20. De Moor, *Commentarius Perpetuus*, 2:763.

21. De Moor, *Commentarius Perpetuus*, 2:763.

22. And to Jerome of Prague.

23. Ed. note: At session 15, July 6, 1415; see "Council of Constance 1414–18," Papal Encyclicals Online, last updated February 20, 2020, http://www.papalencyclicals.net/councils/ecum16.htm.

24. Ed. note: On December 17, 1999, Pope John Paul II addressed an international symposium on John Hus, called him "a memorable figure" and a man of "moral courage," adding, "I feel the need to express deep regret for the cruel death inflicted on John Hus, and for the consequent wound of conflict and division which was thus imposed on the minds and hearts of the Bohemian people" ("Address of the Holy Father to an International Symposium on John Hus," December 17, 1999, Vatican website, https://w2.vatican.va/content/john-paul-ii/en/speeches/1999/december/documents/hf_jp-ii_spe_17121999_jan-hus.html).

25. Turretin, *Institutes of Elenctic Theology*, 3:129 (XVIII.14.xvi); de Moor, *Commentarius Perpetuus*, 2:764.

26. Ed. note: Martinus Becanus, SJ (1563–1624), was a Dutch-born priest, theologian, and polemicist.

unbelievers (Gen. 21:24; 26:31), the spies did the same with Rahab (Josh. 2:14), and so did Israel with the Gibeonites (Josh. 9:15, 18). Zedekiah's defection from Nebuchadnezzar, to whom Zedekiah had made an oath, is condemned (2 Chron. 36:13; Ezek. 17:16–20). Furthermore, a marriage with an unbeliever may not be dissolved (1 Cor. 7:12–18). Prompted by Pope Eugene IV, King Władysław of Poland/Hungary broke his covenant with the Turks but was defeated and killed in battle.[27]

(iv) Oaths may not be broken when they have been taken with mental reservations or intentional equivocations.[28] Regarding equivocation, Turretin says "the question concerns a limitation supposed only and secretly understood by the speaker, amounting to a verbal or real equivocation. The verbal is when the words used themselves are of ambiguous sense and are received in that sense by the swearer (which he desires to conceal from the hearers that they may be accepted by them in a different sense)." Turretin provides an example: "As if anyone being asked, 'Is Peter at home?' should reply, 'He is not' (i.e., 'he is not eating')."[29] Words can also have "one simple sense, but by a tacit restriction or interpretation (which he keeps to himself) they are changed into another." Here Turretin points to the example of Francis of Assisi, "who being asked in what direction a certain murderer who had passed by him had gone, thrusting his hands into his sleeves, answered he did not pass in this direction, meaning that he had not passed through his sleeves."[30] "In this manner," Turretin adds, "many of the Jesuits hold that a priest being asked whether he is a priest (if he should be asked by one not a judge or has a reasonable cause for dissembling the truth), can answer that he is not a priest, provided he means that he is not a priest of Baal or that he is not a priest as to tell this to another." In former days, the Basilians and the Priscillians contended that in times of religious

---

27. Hoornbeeck, *Theologia Practica* (1666), 2:337. Ed. note: This is a reference to Władysław III of Poland (1424–44; also reigned over Hungary and Croatia from 1440). He died at the Battle of Varna (present-day Bulgaria), November 10, 1444, when the Ottoman Army defeated the Hungarian-Polish and Wallachian armies (Wikipedia, s.v. "Władysław III of Poland," https://en.wikipedia.org/wiki/W%C5%82adys%C5%82aw_III_of_Poland; Wikipedia, s.v. "Battle of Varna," https://en.wikipedia.org/wiki/Battle_of_Varna). Eugene IV was pope from 1431 to 1447.

28. LO: *mentales reservations; aequivocationes quaesitae*; DO: *gezochte dubbelzinnigheden*. Ed. note: Bavinck takes the three examples that follow directly from Turretin, *Institutes of Elenctic Theology*, 2:71 (XI.12.ii), and Turretin obtained them from de Moor, *Commentarius Perpetuus*, 2:764. Bavinck's brief summary of Turretin has been amplified by the editor.

29. LO: *An Petrus esset domi. Responderet, non est, id est, non comedit.* Ed. note: Quote amplified from Turretin; Bavinck has only "*non est (est ook = edit)*." In Latin, the word *est* can mean "he is" or "he is eating."

30. LO: *manus in manicas inmittens, respondit, non transisse illâe, intelligens, non transisse per illas manicas.* Ed. note: Also amplified from Turretin.

persecution it was permissible to disown the faith.[31] Especially Jesuit moralists such as Tomás Sanchez (1550–1610), Filliucius (d. 1622), Fernando Catro Palao (1581–1633), and Antonio Escobar y Mendoza (1589–1669) granted the legitimacy of such reservations and equivocations.[32] If someone asks to borrow something from you, then it is permissible to say: I do not have it (namely to loan to you) although I do have it. Every crime that has an excuse I may deny before the judge—namely, as a crime. All these reservations and untruths are permitted "for just cause"—namely, "when it is necessary or useful for the benefit of the body, honor, or family matters."[33] An oath is binding only when it is meant seriously, not as a joke, or the like. In addition to Jesuit moralists, others also approved these reservations and equivocations, including Doctor Navarrus (Martín de Azpilcueta, 1491–1586); Matthew of Bassi (1495–1552), founder of the Capuchins; the Dominican Domingo Bañez (1528–1604); Vincentius Candidus; Antonius Goffar; Andr. Victoral; Martín de Funes Lafiguera (1588–1653), bishop of Albarracin, Spain; and others.[34] This view was challenged, however, by other Roman Catholics.[35] Pope Innocent IX also condemned such a position in 1679.[36] To justify equivocation, Jesuits

31. Ed. note: The Basilians and the Priscillians were gnostic sects of the second and fourth centuries AD, respectively.

32. Similarly, Francisco de Toledo (1532–96), Francisco Suarez (1548–1617), Manoel de Sa (1530–96), Juan Azor (1535–1603), Gregory of Valencia (1550–1603), and Martin Becan (1563–1624). See Zöckler, "Reservatio mentalis"; Turretin, *Institutes of Elenctic Theology*, 2:71–72 (XI.12.iv–v); Wuttke, *Christian Ethics*, 1:255–57, 266–72 (§38). Ed. note: The names in this footnote are taken from Voetius, *Selectarum Disputationum Theologicarum*, 4:646.

33. LO: *ex justa causa; quando id necessario est vel utile salutem corporis honoris aut rerum familiarum*. Ed. note: Bavinck's source for this quote is Wuttke, *Christian Ethics*, 1:267 (§38); Wuttke cites as his source Diana, *Resolutiones morales*, II, tr. 15, 25ff., III, tr. 6, 30. Ed. note: Antonino Diana (ca. 1586–1663) was an Italian Roman Catholic casuist. His major work, *Resolutiones Marales* (1634), is available in many editions, but only parts of it have been translated into English, according to WorldCat. See Slater, "Antonino Diana."

34. Voetius, *Selectarum Disputationum Theologicarum*, 4:647. Ed. note: While none of the names in this list are very familiar, Bavinck's reference to Andr. Victoral is untraceable, and Vincentius Candidus, along with Antonius Goffar, can only be identified on WorldCat through their publications. Candidus is the author of a two-volume penitential *Disquisitiones morales* (Leiden: Prost, 1638); Goffar (with Martino Bonacina) is the author of *Operum de morali theologia, omnibusque conscientiae nodis, compendium* (Leiden: Landry, 1639).

35. Voetius, *Selectarum Disputationum Theologicarum*, 4:647. Ed. note: Voetius refers to Barnesius, Sylvius, and Malderus. Francis Sylvius (1581–1649) was a Flemish Roman Catholic theologian; Johannes Malderus (1563–1633) was bishop of Antwerp, 1626–28. The reference to Barnesius is unclear.

36. Zöckler, "*Reservatio mentalis*," 706. Ed. note: The papal decree of March 4, 1679, condemned, among others, the following two propositions: (#26) "If anyone swears, either alone or in the presence of others, whether questioned or of his own will, whether for sake of recreation or for some other purpose, that he did not do something, which in fact he did, understanding within himself something else which he did not do, or another way than that by

appeal to necessity, to mortal danger, to incompetent judges (for instance, heretical ones), and to careful and permissible concealment.[37]

Protestants have rejected these lies completely. Included among the Reformed who did this are Isaac Casaubon (1559–1614), Robert Abbot (1560–1617), André Rivet on the Decalogue, William Ames in his book on *Conscience*, and others.[38] Sometimes Jesuits reproach Reformed Christians that we occasionally engage in similar evasions. For instance, in 1566 Theodore Beza endorsed a confession that said that the body of Christ was "truly and actually present"[39] in the Lord's Supper. And Remonstrants, in the work *Nullitates*, assert that the Reformed are insincere because all of them signed the confession of Dort, while there is no unanimity on the subject of predestination.[40]

Now it is certainly permissible to refrain from speaking the whole truth or to be unwilling to speak at times, or to fail to utter obvious and self-evident conditions that the listener might assume (Isa. 38:1; Jon. 3:4; 1 Cor. 6:9–10). But there is a great difference between hiding something and speaking or suggesting an untruth. "It is not lying to hide the truth in silence, but to bring forth falsehood when speaking."[41] However, those Jesuit rules are nothing but lies. They create false assumptions, depend on hypocrisy and insincerity, play with God and humanity, and are hidden lies, condemned by Scripture (Jer. 9:8). According to Scripture, an oath is final (Heb. 6:16). Also, when Abraham called Sarah his sister, he was speaking the truth, yet he acted wrongly (Gen. 20), since he intentionally wanted to hide that she was his wife.

---

which he did it, or some other added truth, in fact does not lie and is no perjurer." (#27) "A just reason for using these ambiguous words exists, as often as it is necessary or useful to guard the well-being of the body, honor, property, or for any other act of virtue, so that the concealing of the truth is then regarded as expedient and zealous" (Denzinger, nos. 1175, 1176).

37. De Moor, *Commentarius Perpetuus*, 2:676.

38. Rivet, "De aequivocationibus Jesuiticis." Ed. note: Isaac Casaubon (1559–1614) was a Huguenot classical scholar and philologist and professor of Greek in Geneva, 1582–96; Robert Abbot (1560–1617) was the Regius Professor of Divinity, Oxford, 1612–15; André Rivet (1572–1651) was professor of theology in Leiden, 1620–46. Bavinck's source for these names is Voetius, *Selectarum Disputationum Theologicarum*, 4:648. Bavinck also adds the name of an unidentified "Douglas."

39. LO: *vere ac realiter.*

40. Voetius, *Selectarum Disputationum Theologicarum*, 4:648–49. Ed. note: *Nullitates* is the Latin name Voetius gave to an anonymous Dutch work usually called *Nulliteyten* and attributed to the Remonstrant Bernardus Dwinglo (see bibliography for full title). The specific reference is to pp. 71–72, which raises the question why supralapsarian Gomarus was willing to sign an infralapsarian document such as the Canons of Dort. Thanks to Donald Sinnema for help with this reference.

41. LO: *Non est mendacium cum silendo absconditur verum, sed loquenda promitur falsum*; de Moor, *Commentarius Perpetuus*, 2:768.

3. UNNECESSARY SWEARING

This brings us to the third prohibition in this commandment: swearing when it is not necessary. We see this also among the Israelites. Time and again we encounter expressions such as the following: "God is witness between you and me" (Gen. 31:50); "God . . . judge between us" (Gen. 31:53); "as the LORD lives" (Judg. 8:19); "May the LORD do so to me and more also if anything but death parts me from you" (Ruth 1:17; 1 Sam. 14:44). These and similar oaths were all too common with Israel, mostly in daily life, while they were seldom used in the courts.[42] Jesus therefore limited this practice (Matt. 5 and 23; James 5:12). Today, among us, this unnecessary swearing occurs especially in public life. Oaths are required for all occasions involving the law. But many people, even Christians, fall prey to it in daily life. This may not involve calling upon God's name, but certainly it involves using strong expressions: "Cross my heart and hope to die" or "on my life" or the like. One finds this among Jews. This often turns into nothing but exclamations, fillers—shortened, corrupted, and garbled swear words, so that at every occasion people "carelessly, lightly, and without reverence say: 'Oh Lord! oh God, oh Jesus!'—doing so out of custom, when astonished, in pain, upon sneezing, in toasting someone, in countermanding poor people, in sorrow, in foolish joking, to stir up laughter, or whatever the case may be."[43] All of this violates reverence for and the sacredness of God's name. It diminishes God's exalted majesty to call upon his omniscience, omnipotence, and righteousness at the drop of a hat, also for the most insignificant matters.[44]

4. BLASPHEMY

A fourth violation of the Third Commandment is blasphemy. Blaspheming God is even worse than cursing God and reveals an even greater anger and demonic hardening. Among Israel this carried the death penalty by stoning (Lev. 24:15–16). Notice that someone who curses God "shall bear his sin" (v. 15), but "whoever blasphemes the name of the LORD shall surely be put to death" (v. 16). That sentence is executed against foreigners as well (vv. 10–16; cf. Exod. 5:2; 14:23–30; 1 Kings 20:23; 2 Kings 18:19–40; 19:10–18; Dan. 3:15). Whoever blasphemes God indirectly shows contempt for him (Num. 16:30;

---

42. See the next section, "What the Third Commandment Requires," #3, "Customs and Formulas Used When Swearing an Oath" (pp. 203–5).

43. À Brakel, *Christian's Reasonable Service*, 3:122. Ed. note: We have provided the full passage from à Brakel that Bavinck abbreviated; Bavinck also added the term "My heavens!" (*mijn hemel*).

44. Ursinus, *Schat-boek*, 2:300.

Deut. 31:20), forsakes him (Isa. 1:4).[45] In the New Testament to blaspheme is to appropriate what belongs only to God (John 10:33). When Jesus at his trial before the Sanhedrin ascribed divine attributes to himself, he was declared to be a blasphemer (Matt. 26:65). The crowds blasphemed Jesus when he hung on the cross (Matt. 27:39; Mark 15:29). The Jews in Corinth blasphemed when Paul preached (Acts 18:6; 26:11). Paul was once a blasphemer (1 Tim. 1:13).

Blaspheming God takes place when one says something about God that directly contradicts and violates his nature and properties (Rom. 2:24). It issues from the heart (Mark 7:20–23). The early Christian church called those who renounced the Christian faith in times of persecution blasphemers. Blasphemy carried heavy penalties in the Middle Ages, and formerly also in the Netherlands.[46] And Holy Scripture calls blaspheming against the Holy Spirit unforgivable (Matt. 12:32; Mark 3:28–29; Luke 12:10; Heb. 6:4–8; 10:26; 1 John 5:16–17), because the Father and the Son do not live within us, but the Holy Spirit does live within us and works in our conscience. To blaspheme against the Holy Spirit is to directly oppose the activities of God, whom one acknowledges and must acknowledge as divine. Blasphemy is an outburst of hatred against God and his world dominion because they conflict with the sinful human reality; it is demonic madness. Humans then declare that they are not beings who sin against God, but that God sins against them; they posit their worldview as higher than and superior to God's, whose view is deemed to be unjust and unreasonable. This sin is committed in thought as well as words.[47] Blasphemy is thus not a mere denial of God's existence, properties, and providence, but instead attributing to him the opposite: to deem God to be unjust, cruel, or the like, to mock his assumed holiness and love, and to represent oneself as much holier, wiser, and just.

5. ANY MISUSE OF GOD'S NAME

Finally, we consider all misuse of God's name—that is, of all his revelations, works, words, and deeds. This takes place in various forms:

a. Thoughtless use of God's name in prayer, letting one's thoughts wander during the reading or proclamation of God's Word or during prayer. This too is sin, however inadvertently and unconsciously it happens; it is evidence of irreverence, of absentmindedness, and the like.

---

45. Ed. note: The Scripture references in this sentence and the preceding one are taken from de Moor, *Commentarius Perpetuus*, 2:755; some of the texts are puzzling in this context.

46. De Moor, *Commentarius Perpetuus*, 2:756; cf. C. Beck, "Gotteslästerung."

47. Wuttke, *Handbuch der christlichen Sittenlehre*[3], 2:49–50 (§167).

b. Misusing God's Word—for instance, by quoting a biblical event apart
from its original meaning only to create laughter. For example, when
an elderly man in the company of friends is asked if he wants old or
new wine and replies, "One does not put new wine in old wineskins."
Similarly, when a host at the beginning of a meal says, "Search all things
and keep what is good." Or to say to someone who is at a loss, "Are
you alone a stranger in Jerusalem?" Sometimes this can be innocent
and humorous, but we should be very careful here and especially not
transfer holy matters and words (that is, those dealing with sacred
things) to a mundane level. There is a difference also in the words of
Scripture.

A different misuse of Scripture is to turn it into plays for popular
amusement. Formerly the Dutch rhetoric societies[48] did this; today
the Oberammergau Passion Play does it. It is also done at dramatic
performances in church youth groups, where even tragedies involving
Jesus are enacted.[49] Further, we misuse Holy Scripture when we use
it to ascertain the future—for instance, to assume in a crisis that the
first text that catches our eye is a sign from God telling us what to
do.[50] This includes putting one's finger on a place in Scripture with
closed eyes and considering that text to be a sign. Van Velzen and
Gerdes indicated their rejection of this practice in a 1744 judgment of
the theological faculty at Groningen.[51] Such a use of Holy Scripture
use is to be rejected because the Bible is not given for such purposes
but rather for examination; the texts that catch the eye are then taken
entirely out of context and their meaning is distorted. This is to tempt
God, because we are expecting that God will give us counsel by way
of a miracle apart from our judgment and investigation (Ps. 78:15).
God nowhere commands or approves this kind of guessing; it rests on

---

48. DO: *Rederijkers*. Ed. note: The *Rederijkerskamer* (chamber of rhetoric) was a "medieval Dutch dramatic society" introduced into the Netherlands (from France) in the fifteenth
century (*Encyclopaedia Britannica*, s.v. "Rederijkerskamer," https://www.britannica.com/art
/rederijkerskamer).

49. Also in Klopstock, *Der Messias*; Ursinus, *Schat-boek*, 2:301.

50. Ursinus, *Schat-boek*, 2:301; de Moor, *Commentarius Perpetuus*, 2:751.

51. LO: *Judicium Facultatis Theologiae Groninganae*; de Moor, *Commentarius Perpetuus*,
2:751. Ed. note: Gerdes is Daniel Gerdes (1698–1765), a professor of theology at Groningen;
van Velzen is most likely Cornelius van Velzen (1696–1752), also a professor of theology at
Groningen. The *judicium facultatis* was probably a judgment passed by the Groningen faculty
at the request of a synod or classis that appealed to the university against some person who was
recommending the practice. My thanks to Richard Muller for help in identifying the persons
and the reference to the Groningen faculty. He also introduced to me the term "bibliomancy"
to describe this practice.

superstition. Augustine also rejected it.[52] Antony Driessen defended the practice, but Ursinus rejected it. Other misuses of Scripture are reminiscent of witchcraft, using amulets, and exorcism. This happens when one, for instance, like the Jews, binds texts or parts of Scripture around one's neck or hangs it on one's chest or on the wall, to abjure sickness or obtain other benefits.[53]

c. We can also sin against this commandment by misusing the truth of God. For example, one can misuse the doctrine of predestination, of election, of human inability and the need for grace, as an excuse for false resignation, sloth, sin, carelessness. From another side, one can misuse religion to justify having a good life and becoming a freeloader among the godly, praying beautifully to impress people, preaching to please people, attending church to be seen or to see someone (either sex looking to find or attract others). God's truth is also misused when people poke fun of ministers and elders, the sermon, or the sacraments.[54]

d. We also dishonor God's name when we misuse or despise God's gifts in nature and in people (including unbelievers), repudiate art, or denounce the life of the mind.[55] Similarly, when people grumble about "lousy, miserable" weather, complain about their lot in life, and, like the pessimists, speak of the world as the worst possible place. Others berate God's dominion over the world and mock his judgments.[56]

e. Misusing the lot is another way in which we can sin against this commandment. Using or misusing the lot is a religious act. The lot is a means to ascertain God's will in a specific matter, when people are perplexed or puzzled about what to do (Prov. 16:33). The lot may be used, but in Scripture it was always used for very serious matters: "The lot puts an end to quarrels / and decides between powerful contenders" (Prov. 18:18). Canaan was divided among the tribes by lot (Num. 26:54; 33:54) as were the Levitical cities (Josh. 21). After the exile, the privilege of living in Jerusalem was decided by lot (Neh. 11:1). Other occasions when the lot was used include division of the spoils (Joel 3:3; Nah. 3:10) and of

---

52. "As to those who read futurity by taking at random a text from the pages of the Gospels, although it is better that they should do this than go to consult spirits of divination, nevertheless it is, in my opinion, a censurable practice to try to turn to secular affairs and the vanity of this life those divine oracles which were intended to teach us concerning the higher life" (Augustine, "Letter 55 to Januarius," §37 [NPNF¹ 1:315]; de Moor, *Commentarius Perpetuus*, 2:752).

53. Ursinus, *Schat-boek*, 2:301.

54. Ursinus, *Schat-boek*, 2:301.

55. DO: *wetenschap*; Daneau, *Ethices Christianae*, 146.

56. Daneau, *Ethices Christianae*, 152.

clothes (Matt. 27:35; John 19:23–24), the ascension of a king (1 Sam. 10:19–21), selecting another apostle (Acts 1:26), dividing the days of ministry among the twenty-four priestly orders (Luke 1:9), and deciding difficult judicial cases (Josh. 7:14–15; 1 Sam. 14:42). In the law, using the lot was prescribed only for choosing between two goats on the Day of Atonement.[57] The lot may therefore not be used in games of chance. It may only be used when people have reached an impasse in a serious and important matter.[58]

What do we expect from the lot? A chance outcome that is somehow regulated by God? Yes, but then it cannot be used for games of chance. It is a religious act that is inappropriate for games. Often the lot causes the loser to be irritated. The public lotteries are therefore to be totally condemned—among other reasons, because they exert an immoral influence, they discourage frugality, they feed hopes of getting rich, and they make the state benefit financially from society's sins.[59] Having lotteries in Christian establishments[60] is therefore also not recommended.[61]

What the Third Commandment Requires

The Third Commandment prescribes the proper use of God's name. This includes prayer, the proper invocation and confession of God's name, and the like.[62] Above all, the commandment deals with *oaths*. Because of its profound significance, we will discuss the oath more extensively.[63]

57. Leyrer, "Los bei den Hebräern."
58. De Moor, *Commentarius Perpetuus*, 2:753–54; à Brakel, *Christian's Reasonable Service*, 3:123.
59. À Brakel, *Christian's Reasonable Service*, 3:126–27.
60. DO: *bazars*.
61. Cf. Wittewrongel, *Oeconomia Christiana*, 2:1067–83; Vermigli, *Loci Communes*[10], 249–51; Wuttke, *Handbuch der christlichen Sittenlehre*[3], 2:119 (§190), 550 (n. 27).
62. E. Sartorius, *Die Lehre von der heiligen Liebe*, 3/1:155.
63. Rietschel, "Das Verbot des Eides," 394–95. According to Socinus, Grotius, Episcopius, Bengel, Ficker, and Paulsen, Jesus only proscribed promissory oaths and not declaratory oaths. Furthermore, the oath is permitted in Holy Scripture (Deut. 6:13; 10:20; Isa. 45:23; 65:16; Jer. 12:16; 23:7–8; Heb. 6:16), even commanded (Exod. 22:10–13). Jesus himself swears an oath (Matt. 26:63–66), and an oath is implied in his uses of "amen." Paul repeatedly uses an oath (Rom. 1:9; 9:1; 1 Cor. 15:31; 2 Cor. 1:23; 11:31; Gal. 1:20; Phil. 1:8; 1 Tim. 6:13; 2 Tim. 4:1); in each of these instances Paul's affirmation is more than an ordinary "yes." Rietschel believes that not *all* oaths are forbidden, not even those with the Christian fellowship, but only *promissory* oaths, where the outcome is not in our hands. There are numerous promissory oaths in the Old Testament, but almost all the oaths in the New Testament are declaratory.

1. HISTORY

Oaths are found among all peoples and in all religions. Their origin, therefore, is not to be seen in a specific positive enactment but in the ineradicable sense of responsibility to and absolute dependence on a Higher Power. We need only think of the oaths sworn at the river Styx by the gods of Homer. For the Romans to swear by someone was the same as making that person into a god.[64] Cicero calls the oath a religious affirmation.[65] Philo considers it best and most dignified for a person not to swear an oath.[66] The Essenes rejected oaths completely, except for the one used at the initiation into their fellowship. For the most part, the church fathers considered making oaths permissible. Justin Martyr considered it dubious, and Irenaeus repudiated it.[67] Clement of Alexandria, Origen, Basil, and Gregory of Nazianz consider oaths unnecessary although not completely improper. The strongest opposition to oaths comes from John Chrysostom. He considers oaths to have been given by God to the Jews so that they would not swear by idols. Augustine does not deem swearing oaths to be sin but considers it proper only in cases of dire necessity.[68]

Thomas Aquinas concludes the following in his discussion of oaths.[69]

> Article 1: Thomas defines oaths in his response: "I answer that, As the Apostle says (Hebrews 6:16), oaths are taken for the purpose of confirmation."[70] However, while "speculative propositions receive confirmation from reason . . . particular contingent facts regarding man cannot be confirmed by a necessary reason" and therefore need "to be confirmed by witnesses." But "a human witness does not suffice to confirm such matters for two reasons. First, on account of man's lack of truth, for many give way to lying. . . . Secondly, on account of this lack of knowledge, since he can know neither the future, nor secret thoughts, nor distant things: and yet men speak about such things, and our everyday life requires that we should have some certitude about them."[71] Therefore we "need to have recourse

---

64. Horace, *Epistles* II.1.16 (LCL 185:396–97).

65. LO: *affirmatio religionis*; Cicero, *On Duties (De officiis)* III.29 (LCL 30:380–81); cf. van Leeuwen, *De eed en de moderne staat*.

66. Van Leeuwen, *De eed en de moderne staat*, 35.

67. Van Leeuwen, *De eed en de moderne staat*, 43.

68. Van Leeuwen, *De eed en de moderne staat*, 44.

69. Aquinas, *ST* IIa IIae q. 89 art. 1.

70. LO: *iuramentum ad confirmationem ordinatur* (Aquinas, *ST* IIa IIae q. 89 art. 1 co.).

71. LO: *Sed humanum testimonium non est sufficiens ad huius modi confirmandum, propter duo. Primo quidem, propter defectum veritatis humanae, quia plurimi in mendacium labuntur. . . . Secundo, propter defectum cognitionis, quia homines non possunt cognoscere*

to a Divine witness, for neither can God lie, nor is anything hidden from Him. Now to call God to witness is named 'jurare' [to swear] because it is established as though it were a principle of law [*jure*] that what a man asserts under the invocation of God as His witness should be accepted as true."[72] When God is called to witness our assertions of "present or past events," this oath is called a "declaratory oath"; when God "is called to witness in confirmation of something future," it is called a "promissory oath."[73]

Thomas goes on to nuance the legitimacy of swearing oaths in subsequent articles.

Article 2: While an oath "is in itself lawful and commendable," Thomas adds that "an oath becomes a source of evil to him that makes evil use of it, that is who employs it without necessity and due caution."[74] In other words, an oath is permitted but only in case of necessity.

Article 3: Good use of an oath requires two conditions: "First, that one swear, not for frivolous, but for urgent reasons, and with discretion; and this requires judgment or discretion on the part of the person who swears."[75] The second criterion is "that it be neither false, nor unlawful, and this requires both truth, so that one employ an oath in order to confirm what is true, and justice, so that one confirm what is lawful."[76]

Article 4: Since an oath shows reverence to God, which "belongs to religion or latria . . . it is evident that an oath is an act of religion or latria"

---

neque futura, neque cordium occulta, vel etiam absentia; de quibus tamen homines loquuntur, et expedit rebus humanis ut certitudo aliqua de his habeatur (Aquinas, *ST* IIa IIae q. 89 art. 1 co.).

72. LO: *Et ideo necessarium fuit recurrere ad divinum testimonium, quia Deus neque mentiri potest, neque eum aliquid latet. Assumere autem Deum in testem dicitur iurare, quia quasi pro iure introductum est ut quod sub invocatione divini testimonii dicitur pro vero habeatur* (Aquinas, *ST* IIa IIae q. 89 art. 1 co.).

73. LO: *ad asserendum praesentian vel praeterita = juramentum assertorium; juramentum assertorium = juramentum promissorium* (Aquinas, *ST* IIa IIae q. 89 art. 1 co.).

74. LO: *iuramentum secundum se est licitum et honestum; Sed iuramentum cedit in malum alicui ex eo quod male utitur eo, idest sine necessitate et cautela debita* (Aquinas, *ST* IIa IIae q. 89 art. 2 co.).

75. LO: *ex necessaria causa et discrete iuret . . . requiritur iudicium, scilicet discretionis ex parte iurantis. . .* (Aquinas, *ST* IIa IIae q. 89 art. 3 co.).

76. LO: *Secundo, quantum ad id quod per iuramentum confirmatur, ut scilicet neque sit falsum, neque sit aliquid illicitum. Et quantum ad hoc, requiritur veritas, per quam aliquis iuramento confirmat quod verum est; et iustitia, per quam confirmat quod licitum est* (Aquinas, *ST* IIa IIae q. 89 art. 3 co.).

(Heb. 6:16), in which God is acknowledged for "His unfailing truth and universal knowledge."[77]

Article 5: Because swearing an oath "is required merely as a remedy for an infirmity or a defect, [it is] not reckoned among those things that are desirable for their own sake, but among those that are necessary." Therefore, oaths "are used unduly whenever they are used outside the bounds of necessity."[78]

Article 6: An oath that is a "simple contestation" is to call "God as witness," and such oaths are "chiefly referred to God Whose testimony is invoked; and secondarily an appeal by oath is made to certain creatures considered, not in themselves, but as reflecting the Divine truth."[79]

Article 7: The oath is obligatory and may thus not be sworn except in certain cases. "Whoever swears to do something is bound to do what he can for the fulfilment of truth; provided always that the other two accompanying conditions be present, namely, judgment and justice."[80]

Article 8: Vows are even more binding than oaths. "A vow binds one to God while an oath sometimes binds one to man. Now one is more bound to God than to man. Therefore, a vow is more binding than an oath."[81]

Article 9: Both vows and oaths may receive dispensation by the pope, as in the case of promissory oaths under changed conditions—"to wit, in certain emergencies, it may be unlawful or hurtful and consequently undue matter for an oath."[82]

Article 10. Some are prohibited from swearing oaths: "Children before the age of puberty are debarred from taking oaths." "Perjurers are also

77. LO: *utpote cuius veritas est indefectibilis et cognitio universalis* (Aquinas, *ST* IIa IIae q. 89 art. 4 co.).

78. LO: *non quaeritur nisi ad subveniendum alicui defectui, non numeratur inter ea quae sunt per se appetenda, sed inter ea quae sunt necessaria . . . quibus indebite utitur quicumque eis utitur ultra terminos necessitatis* (Aquinas, *ST* IIa IIae q. 89 art. 5 co.).

79. LO: *per simplicem contestationem, inquantum scilicet Dei testimonium invocatur. . . . principaliter refertur ad ipsum Deum, cuius testimonium invocatur, secundario autem assumuntur ad iuramentum aliquae creaturae non secundum se, sed inquantum in eis divina veritas manifestatur* (Aquinas, *ST* IIa IIae q. 89 art. 6 co.).

80. LO: *quicumque iurat aliquid se facturum, obligatur ad id faciendum, ad hoc quod veritas impleatur, si tamen alii duo comites adsint, scilicet iudicium et iustitia* (Aquinas, *ST* IIa IIae q. 89 art. 7 co.).

81. LO: *per votum obligatur aliquis Deo, per iuramentum obligatur interdum homini. Magis autem obligatur homo Deo quam homini. Ergo maior est obligatio voti quam iuramenti* (Aquinas, *ST* IIa IIae q. 89 art. 8 s.c.).

82. LO: *quod variari potest, ita scilicet quod in aliquo eventu potest esse illicitum vel nocivum, et per consequens non esse debita materia iuramenti* (Aquinas, *ST* IIa IIae q. 89 art. 9 co.).

debarred from taking an oath, because it is presumed from their antecedents that they will not treat an oath with the reverence due to it."
"It becomes not persons of great dignity to swear." "Priests should not
swear for trifling reasons," but "it is lawful from them to swear if there
be need for it, or if great good may result therefrom."[83]

Canon law determines the age for swearing an oath at fourteen years and
determines the criteria for people who are drunk, insane, or perjurers.[84]

However, Pelagius and his followers rejected and disapproved of oaths.[85]
Perhaps the Waldensians did as well, although this is not certain.[86] They did
oppose all levity in oath swearing, which was quite common in their day.[87] In
addition, we must count the Benedictines, the Catharies, and the Anabaptists and Mennonites among those who opposed oaths.[88] The last-mentioned
considered oaths as well as polygamy permissible in Old Testament times
but wanted to abolish them now in the New Testament era. In their case, it
was part of the false doctrine of the perfect kingdom of God on earth, in
which there is no longer any room for oaths, warfare, and so forth.[89] The
Socinians contend that the new in the New Testament is Christ forbidding
frivolous oaths in ordinary cases as well as the promissory oath, but that it is
now permitted to swear by Christ (as the new second God).[90] Other groups
that reject swearing oaths include the Moravian Brethren, the Quakers, the
Kornthalers, the Raskolniken in Russia, the East Prussian Philipponen, and
many other sects in America.[91]

---

83. LO: *a iuramento excluduntur et pueri ante annos pubertatis . . . et iterum periuri, qui
ad iuramentum non admittuntur, quia ex retroactis praesumitur quod debitam reverentiam
iuramento non exhibebunt. . . . Et ideo personis magnae dignitatis non convenit iurare . . .
quod sacerdotes ex levi causa iurare non debent. Tamen pro aliqua necessitate, vel magna
utilitate, licitum est eis iurare, et praecipue pro spiritualibus negotiis* (Aquinas, *ST* IIa IIae
q. 89 art. 10 co.).

84. Cf. Richter, *Lehrbuch des katholischen und evangelischen Kirchenrechts*, 996–1004 (§261).

85. De Moor, *Commentarius Perpetuus*, 2:779; cf. Vossius, *Historiae de Controversiis quas
Pelagius*, 512.

86. Vossius, *Historiae de Controversiis quas Pelagius*, 513.

87. De Moor, *Commentarius Perpetuus*, 2:780; cf. Hoornbeeck, *Theologiae Practicae²*,
2:365–66. Ed. note: Bavinck's own manuscript cites this from the first edition (1666), pp. 335–36.

88. Van Leeuwen, *De eed en de moderne staat*, 45.

89. De Moor, *Commentarius Perpetuus*, 2:780.

90. LO: *iuramentum promissorium*; de Moor, *Commentarius Perpetuus*, 2:775–78.

91. Van Leeuwen, *De eed en de moderne staat*, 46. Ed. note: "Kornthalers" refers to the
religious community established by royal decree on September 8, 1818, in the village of Kornthal,
Germany, near Stuttgart. Kornthal was the center of Württemburg Pietism, which retained its
individuality and was known for its "nonpolemic and popular character and the greater learning
of its theological representatives." Led by Johann Michael Hahn (1758–1819), the community
had as its ideal "an apostolic life and the realization of the Sermon on the Mount." They were

Various exegetes and moralists also consider Christ and the apostle James to have forbidden the oath. Wuttke, for example, believes that Christ forbade the oath absolutely.[92] He regards Christ's oath before the high priest and that of Paul to have been merely a strong affirmation, similar to Jesus's "Truly, truly, I say to you." Wuttke incorrectly sees the essential characteristic of oaths to be pledging our eternal salvation; hence the self-imprecation "May I be damned if I . . ."[93] Nevertheless, Christians may not refuse oaths required by civil authorities, provided the oath does not involve a self-imprecation. For this oath is indeed forbidden by Christ but is in itself still not sinful because it was permitted in the Old Testament. But Wuttke believes that it would be better if the state did not base its stance on this Old Testament position. Oaths are unnecessary for Christians, fail to deter scoundrels, and are unfair to atheists.[94] Köstlin believes that Christ absolutely condemns oaths but does assume (contra Wuttke) that Christ and Paul did swear an oath.[95] He solves this discrepancy by claiming that Christ forbids swearing in Matthew 5 from the point of view of the subject, thus private oaths; but if a government authority imposes an oath, one may and must not refuse. Palmer and Schmid also repudiate oaths.[96] Rothe does defend its use but wants to abolish all promissory oaths, because of abuse. He also wonders, like Köstlin, whether oaths should not be abolished altogether in our atheistic state. Christianity should make the oath increasingly dispensable. Only the civil authorities may require oaths, never a private person; in private life, oaths should be used only sparingly.[97] Hartlieb gives several reasons for abolishing the oath in our secular society.[98] Because faith in God and religion are increasingly disappearing, the sanctity of the oath cannot be maintained; God's name is dishonored; because the oath no longer provides what it should, perjury increases alarmingly; the godly keep their word

---

"readily relieved from the obligation to military service or to take an oath" (C. Kolb, "Kornthal"). Bavinck also included two other groups, both taken from van Leeuwen: The Roskolniken [Roskolnikovians?] in Russia and the Philipponen in East Prussia. Van Leeuwen points to Bayer, *Betrachtungen über den Eid*, 128–29 (§§73–74), for more information about these two groups, indicating that the former was found among the Cossacks near the Don River and in Asia, but we have been unable to obtain further information on them.

92. Wuttke, *Handbuch der christlichen Sittenlehre*[3], 2:263–70 (§244).
93. Wuttke, *Handbuch der christlichen Sittenlehre*[3], 2:264 (§244).
94. Wuttke, *Handbuch der christlichen Sittenlehre*[3], 2:269 (§244).
95. Köstlin, "Eid," 121–22.
96. Ed. note: Bavinck provides no references, but both names are found in Köstlin, "Eid," 4:122; the references are to Palmer, *Evangelische Pastoraltheologie*, 288–98; Schmid, *Christliche Sittenlehre*, 738–43.
97. Rothe, *Theologische Ethik*, 4:375–83 (§1067); cf. Köstlin, "Eid," 124.
98. Hartlieb, *Der Eid und der moderne Staat*, 62–72.

regardless, and the ungodly do not shy away from perjury; truthfulness is dependent on fear of punishment that exists even without an oath. Finally, such oaths should be abolished because they are not specifically Christian and obligatory.[99]

But there are also objections to oaths from a philosophical point of view. Hobbes contended that outside of the civil state there is no place for oaths, that the oath is not a natural service, and that the oath adds nothing to the obligation.[100] Spinoza proposed that oaths be used "for the well-being of the fatherland and freedom, and by the highest Council of State."[101] But especially Kant[102] opposed it: he viewed the oath to be a religious act, but precisely for that reason he viewed it as superstitious, as if unless one invoked divine punishment one would not tell the truth, and as if one would not receive God's punishment when making only a promise. In addition, civil authorities cannot know beforehand that someone has a religion (which the oath presupposes), nor can it require belief in the existence of God and faith in him. On the other hand, Kant deems the oath to be indispensable in society. Many now remove the religious dimension from the oath, making and changing it into a mere moral and civil act. In the Dutch Constitution of 1798 the word "oath" was removed and replaced with the word "declaration": "I promise as a patriotic citizen, I so declare."[103] Such a civic oath had already come into fashion in Switzerland.[104] In France, since 1790, people simply say "I swear" without invoking God's name.[105] In Spain, the oath was abolished in 1869 but reintroduced in 1874.[106] Almost everywhere there are movements against oaths. In the Netherlands witness the discussion in the Second Chamber of the Dutch Parliament (October 7, 1881).[107]

99. Herman, "Eid, Schwur, schwören," 161–62; Hartlieb, *Der Eid und der moderne Staat*, 45.

100. LO: *extra statum Civitatis Juramento non esse locum, hinc Juramentum non esse Cultum naturalem, item Obligationi a Juramento nihil addit*; de Moor, *Commentarius Perpetuus*, 2:780. Ed. note: Bavinck does not indicate where Hobbes discusses oaths; see *Leviathan*, chap. 14: "It appears also, that the oath adds nothing to the obligation. For a covenant, if lawful, binds in the sight of God, without the oath, as much as with it; if unlawful, bindeth not at all, though it be confirmed with an oath" (*Leviathan*, 93).

101. DO: "bij het welzijn des vaderlands en der vrijheid, en bij den hoogsten Staatsraad" (van Leeuwen, *De eed en de moderne Staat*, 9).

102. Ed. note: Bavinck's comments on Kant that follow are taken from van Leeuwen, *De eed en de moderne staat*, 9–15.

103. DO: *verklaring; ik beloof op mijne Burgertrouw. Dit verklaar ik*; van Leeuwen, *De eed en de moderne staat*, 13.

104. Van Leeuwen, *De eed en de moderne staat*, 16.

105. FO: *je jure*; van Leeuwen, *De eed en de moderne staat*, 9–15.

106. Hartlieb, *Der Eid und der modern Staat*, 69.

107. Ed. note: Bavinck refers to a parliamentary discussion in the Second Chamber of the States-General, "the interpellation of Mr. Heydenrijk concerning the question of the oath." In

The following fought for the right to "affirm" rather than swear an oath: in England, Charles Bradlaugh (1833–91); in Breslau, Germany, Theodor Hofferichter (1815–89); in Denmark, the Jew Carl Edward Cohen Brandes (1847–1931).[108]

2. The Teaching of Scripture

The Hebrew word for "to swear" is נִשְׁבַּע, "to seven oneself." Seven is a sacred number, perhaps because of the seven days of creation, or because God's number is three and the number of the world is four.[109] The Greek term is ὅρκος (from εἴργω, arceo), "enclosure," "restriction"—that is, that which has been enclosed or restricted by God. The Latin term jurare comes from jus (right, law), which comes from jungere (to join). The Dutch word eed (oath) comes from een (one), or, more likely, from Eedh (the sun), or it comes from the stem ît (to bind). The notion of swearing[110] may possibly be related to a German word, either Schwester or Schwerdt, or it may come from svaran (truth-speaking). This is related to the English word "answer"[111] and the French word serment, which comes from sacramentum.[112] The Dutch word meineed (perjury) comes from the ancient substantive mein (Latin nequiti, worthless, bad; scelus, crime, evil deed, impious action; improbitas, badness, depravity).[113]

---

this debate the following question was posed: "Is it true or not that Mr. Hartog Heys, in one matter, concerning the law of succession, removed the promissory oath [belofte]?" Handelingen Tweede Kamer 1881–1882 07 Oktober 1881; available online at https://repository.overheid.nl/frbr/sgd/18811882/0000400152/1/pdf/SGD_18811882_0000107.pdf.

108. Ed. note: All three men refused to swear oaths in legal contexts, creating a public controversy. Bavinck provides the following sources: for Bradlaugh, see van Houten, "Charles Bradlaugh"; for Hofferichter and Brandes, see Kerkelijke Courant: Weekblad voor de Nederlandsche Hervormde Kerk, #41 (October 10, 1902). We have not been able to confirm this reference to Hofferichter and Brandes; Bavinck appears to have taken his information from Dutch church newspapers reporting on the parliamentary debates about oaths in the Dutch Senate (First Chamber). For more on Bradlaugh, see Courtney, Freethinkers of the Nineteenth Century, 97–137.

109. Van Leeuwen, De eed en de moderne staat, 24–25.

110. DO: zweren; GO: schwören, Schwur? Van Leeuwen, De eed en de moderne staat, 28.

111. Ed. note: According to the Oxford English Dictionary, "answer" comes from the Old English word andswaru and the Old Norse word andsvar, both of which contain the idea of "opposite, against" + "swear." The word "swear" is tied to Old Norse words sverja, svar, svara, which mean "to answer" (OED, s.vv. "Answer," "Swear").

112. Van Leeuwen, De eed en de moderne staat, 29. Ed. note: Van Leeuwen adds that "sacramentum in classical usage is simply another name for jusjurandum, and the oath required of soldiers was called [sacramentum]; this is the reason that the Roman soldier class was referred to by the expression sacramenta, while the soldiers themselves were called the sacrata militia" (p. 30).

113. Van Leeuwen, De eed en de moderne staat, 30.

We now turn to the exegesis of key passages.[114]

Matthew 5:33–37

> Again you have heard that it was said to those of old, "You shall not swear falsely, but shall perform to the Lord what you have sworn." But I say to you, Do not take an oath at all,[115] either by heaven, for it is the throne of God, or by the earth, for it is his footstool, or by Jerusalem, for it is the city of the great King. And do not take an oath by your head, for you cannot make one hair white or black. Let what you say be simply "Yes" or "No"[116]; anything more than this comes from evil.

The thought here is simply this: Jesus is not speaking here about swearing, but about swearing falsely.[117] For the ancients (not the Mosaic law) said: You may not swear falsely; if you have sworn by the Lord, you must keep the oath. But if you have sworn by the temple, the altar, or the like, then your oath is not binding (Matt. 23:16–22). This restricted the binding character of oaths to only those that were sworn "by the Lord." To all this Jesus says, No! *I* say to you, Do not swear at all.[118] That is to say, whenever you are inclined to swear by heaven or earth (as an evasion), don't! Instead, let your speech (not your testimony before a judge) simply be yes or no.[119] According to Abraham Kuyper, Jesus's prohibition applies only to the church.[120] If Jesus had wanted to forbid all swearing in general, he would have had to add "nor by God" to the words "not by the temple, not by the altar, etc." This was precisely the point. The Sermon on the Mount contains no commandments for the administration of justice and civil law, but only moral commandments pertaining to social interaction. This exegesis is strengthened by Matthew 23:20, where Jesus only forbids swearing by the temple, and the like (the lighthearted swearing in everyday life with appeal to all sorts of creatures). Jesus does say that such an oath is certainly binding. However,

---

114. Ed. note: The material that follows is based on van Leeuwen, *De eed en de moderne staat*, 46–60.

115. GrO: μὴ ὀμόσαι ὅλως.

116. GrO: ἔστω δὲ ὁ λόγος ὑμῶν ναὶ ναί, οὖ οὖ.

117. GrO: ἐπιορκεῖν.

118. DO/GO: *ganselijk; überhaupt.*

119. Cf. de Moor, *Commentarius Perpetuus*, 2:782–83.

120. "The commandment of Jesus not to swear does not in any way relate to the civil oath. That commandment was given to the narrow circle of his disciples and therefore holds for the church, where the oath should never be admitted. But it does not hold for civil society in relation to the state. Jesus himself swore an oath before Caiaphas" (Kuyper, *Our Program*, 81 [§67]); cf. Kuyper, *E Voto Dordraceno*, 3:617 (Lord's Day 37, chap. 1).

he does not at all forbid the oath, but on the contrary he assumes swearing oaths is permissible.

James 5:12

> But above all, my brothers, do not swear, either by heaven or by earth or by any other oath, but let your "yes" be yes and your "no" be no, so that you may not fall under condemnation.

This passage relies on Jesus when it also forbids swearing by heaven, earth, "or anything else." In view here is thus the lighthearted swearing the Jews were wont to do, and James's answer is the same as that of Jesus: Let your Yes be Yes, your No be No. In other words, if you say Yes it must be Yes. This exegesis agrees with the whole of Scripture.

The oath is commanded and considered permissible (Exod. 22:11; Deut. 6:13; 10:20). All the saints swear oaths: Abraham (Gen. 14:22; 21:23–24), Isaac (Gen. 26:31), Jacob (Gen. 31:53), Joseph (Gen. 47:31), Moses (Josh. 14:9), David (1 Sam. 20:3), Solomon (1 Kings 2:23), and Elisha (2 Kings 2:2). True, it is said of believers that they are to swear by the name of the Lord (Isa. 19:18; 45:23; 65:16). God himself swears oaths (Pss. 95:11; 110:4; Gen. 22:16; Heb. 6:13–18); so does Christ (Matt. 26:63–64), and so do the angels (Rev. 10:5–6). The apostle Paul testifies by Christ (Rom. 9:1), before God (Gal. 1:20), and calls upon God as a witness (1 Thess. 2:5; 2 Cor. 1:23). Repudiating the oath comes from a Pelagian perspective that overestimates the perfect state of Christians on earth and prematurely anticipates the future kingdom of God. Oaths are used in Scripture on many occasions, very frequently by godly people in everyday life, perhaps all too frequently; they were also used by Paul. An oath in private life is therefore not forbidden, although Jesus restricted it (Matt. 5:34–37). Public swearing of oaths (before a judge) is seldom mentioned in the Mosaic law: it is mentioned in property disputes (Exod. 22:11), in cases of perjury and restitution (Lev. 6:5), and when marital infidelity is suspected (Num. 5:19–28). Also recall the self-maledictory oath in cases of disputes between neighbors (1 Kings 8:31).

Witnesses are not commanded to swear oaths, but this may be assumed in Leviticus 5:1 and Proverbs 29:24. With respect to vows, see Numbers 30 and Deuteronomy 23:21–23. It appears, therefore, that the civil authority had the right to demand an oath.

3. CUSTOMS AND FORMULAS USED WHEN SWEARING AN OATH

The Israelites lifted their right hand to heaven (Gen. 14:22; Deut. 32:40; Dan. 12:7; Rev. 10:5) or put their hand on the thigh of the person to whom the oath was sworn (Gen. 24:2, 8; 47:29). In the latter, the thigh was considered as a symbol of offspring, as the seat of physical life. We already mentioned the formulas used in oaths earlier, the most common one being "as truly as the Lord lives." But execration or self-imprecation was frequently included as well: "And Saul said, 'God do so to me and more also; you shall surely die, Jonathan'" (1 Sam. 14:44; cf. 2 Sam. 19:13). Oaths also could incorporate judgments on, or judgments of, certain persons (Ps. 102:8; Isa. 65:15) or incorporate specific punishments (Num. 5:21, 27; Jer. 29:22; Zech. 8:13). In court it was customary for the judge to speak the oath and for the defendant to only say amen or yes (Num. 5:22, 27; Deut. 27:15–16; Matt. 26:63–66).

Gestures were also used with oaths. The Romans touched the altar of the god they swore by or held a rock in their hand.[121] The Frisians swore with a lock of hair in their left hand and put two fingers of their right hand on top of it. The Franks held stalks of straw in their hand.[122] Names of the gods—Freyr, Odin, Thor, Donnar (from which the term *donnerwetter*, thunderstorm)—were included in oaths.[123] The expression "so help me God" is a Christianized outgrowth of this.[124] A Constantinian formula of 325 reads, "As the highest divinity may be propitious to me and provide me safety, so I desire a most prosperous and thriving commonwealth."[125] The oath of Louis the German and Charles the Bald begins with "By the love of God."[126] After the Peace of Passau of 1552,[127] an identical oath was drawn up for Catholics and Protestants that ended with "So truly help me God and his holy Gospel." In America the judge says, "Do you swear . . . so truly help you God," and people assent by kissing the Gospel or by raising their hand.[128] Muslims swear with their right hand on the Qur'an and the left on their forehead, and then with bowed head on the Qur'an.[129] In France the person swearing merely says, "I swear."[130] In Belgium since 1869: "I so swear, so truly help me God."

121. Van Leeuwen, *De eed en de moderne staat*, 35.
122. Van Leeuwen, *De eed en de moderne staat*, 35.
123. Van Leeuwen, *De eed en de moderne staat*, 36.
124. GO: *so mir Gott helfe.*
125. LO: *Ita mihi summa divinitas propitia sit et me incolumen praestat, ut cupio, felicissima et florente res publica.* Ed. note: This is a post-Nicene oath from an edict of Constantine preserved in the Theodosian law code. Thanks to Richard Muller for help with this text.
126. Old German: *in Kottes minna.*
127. Ed. note: The Peace of Passau came in August 1552 when, "weary of three decades of religious civil war, [Holy Roman Emperor Charles V] guaranteed Lutheran religious freedom" (Wikipedia, s.v. "Peace of Passau," https://en.wikipedia.org/wiki/Peace_of_Passau).
128. Ed. note: Bavinck's source here is van Leeuwen, *De eed en de moderne staat*, 37.
129. Van Leeuwen, *De eed en de moderne staat*, 37–38.
130. FO: *je jure.*

In the Netherlands oath swearers raise two fingers (in Denmark, Austria, and Saxony, they raise three), a custom already in use among Germans and Frisians. In our country by raising two fingers (in Denmark, Austria, Saxony, three), already in use by the Germans and Frisians. Three fingers are used to signify the three basic requirements of oaths (Jer. 4:2): the person who swears must have true understanding and exercise good judgment in swearing, and the matter concerning which a person swears must be righteous.[131] This raising of the fingers is fairly unimportant today, but the formula is not. Should that formula be narrowly confessional, distinctly Christian, or so general that even Jews and Muslims could swear by it? In the Middle Ages the words "and his holy Gospel" or "and the relics of the saints" were added. The Reformation did not lay down any rules until after the Treaty of Passau. However, this formula was not introduced everywhere nor supplemented in keeping with the confession of the person swearing. The year 1848 brought about change in Germany, but confessional supplements were permitted.[132] In the Netherlands, the phrase was only "So truly help me God Almighty."

4. The Essence of the Oath

Like war, the oath presupposes sin, the lie, and human untrustworthiness. Betrayal on the one hand and suspicion on the other are father and mother of the oath.[133] The essence of the oath consists of an appeal to God as true, omniscient, and omnipotent, the One who knows us and who punishes evil.[134] The oath is everywhere and always considered to be a religious act, a matter not of our obligation to speak the truth, but of our obligation toward God.[135] Whoever removes the religious element from the oath destroys it. In Italy, as in France, on June 24, 1882, the formula became "I swear by my honor and conscience." In Spain it became optional on April 8, 1883, to swear "before God" or "by my honor." The religious oath has also been abandoned in Belgium and Switzerland. The atheists in Germany did not get their wish; there the formula adopted reads, "I swear by the Almighty and All-knowing

131. LO: *veritas in mente, judicium in jurante, justitia in objecto*; Scheurl, "Oath." Ed. note: Scheurl claims that this definition of a genuine oath comes from a decretal of Pope Innocent III (pope from 1198 to 1216).

132. Hartlieb, *Der Eid und der moderne Staat*, 17.

133. Hartlieb, *Der Eid und der moderne Staat*, 4.

134. See Heidelberg Catechism, Q&A 102: "Q. May we also swear by saints or other creatures? A. No. A legitimate oath means calling upon God as the only one who knows my heart to witness to my truthfulness and to punish me if I swear falsely. No creature is worthy of such honor."

135. Köstlin, "Eid," 120–21.

God, so help me God." Confessional believers, however, do not consider it sufficiently Christian.[136]

The question now is, Is a merely moral oath possible?[137] Is it then still an oath, an oath upon one's honor, conscience, or reason, for the well-being of the fatherland? The answer is, No, a simple, moral, civil oath without calling on God is an absurdity. After all, the essence of an oath consists of calling upon God as omniscient and almighty.[138] There are good reasons for this:

    a. The state and its system of justice need a safeguard that people will speak the truth. Thus, an oath presupposes human untruthfulness, which is a fact that cannot be denied. The question now becomes, Where do we find such a safeguard? Can it be found in human honor, conscience, or reason? But it is precisely for the person, for one's honor, and so on that a safeguard must be sought. Therefore, the safeguard cannot lie *within* the person, for the person; it cannot be found within one person for another person, because all people are deceitful (Rom. 3:4) and stand before the law as equals. Therefore, it is also true that this safeguard is not to be found in the state, in society, or in any creature. The safeguard can be found only in the one who is perfectly truthful, righteous, holy, and omniscient—namely, God.

    b. Reason, honor, and conscience derive their absolute character from God. Take God away, and their absolute character is lost. They fully depend on God. Without God, they become products of nurture, education, society—that is, products of humans themselves.

    c. The character of the oath consists precisely in this, that people bind themselves to One upon whom they are absolutely dependent and to whom they are absolutely accountable. But that cannot be said of any other human person, of society, or of the state. We are dependent upon and accountable to God alone.

136. Ed. note: At this point Bavinck refers to a debate in the Dutch Second Chamber between a Mr. Kist who desired a simple civil oath and a Mr. Modderman who opposed this. This debate took place on October 6–7, 1881. See n. 107 above.

137. Hartlieb, *Der Eid und der moderne Staat*, 9; van Leeuwen, *De eed en de moderne staat*, 9, 18, 73.

138. "Both in a court of law, therefore, and in establishing a relationship between a government and a subject, there is always and invariably at the basis of the relationship between the two persons a relationship of the two parties with the living God. That is why it is good and right and just that both parties also solemnly acknowledge this relationship with the living God as the basis of their action, and that they not bind themselves to each other but to him who knows the hearts" (Kuyper, *Our Program*, 80 [§66]).

d. The state, our fatherland, society, honor, conscience, and reason are not able to strengthen people against temptations. People surrender all of that for a pittance. Selfishness prevails almost always against those powers. It is true, the oath does not provide an absolute guarantee either. But those who lie even in the presence of God are completely without honor, unreliable, perjurers. If there is one safeguard, it is still the appeal to God.

e. Apart from God there is no longer truth, justice, or goodness.[139] At that point, good and evil, justice and injustice, falsehood and truth are human products with no power above humanity itself. The oath is the cement of the state, of justice; it is the cornerstone of the edifice of the state.

Whenever we call upon God in this way, we are not staking our salvation on this appeal; God's final judgment of us is not involved.[140] It is thus wrong to swear, "May God damn me if I do not speak the truth, if I do not faithfully serve in office, etc." The oath is not a self-malediction. When we say, "So help me God Almighty," we are simply calling for help in speaking the truth. But at the same time, when we swear an oath we do surrender ourselves—in case of perjury—to the judgment of God. It is an appeal to God to help, but in case of perjury, to punish. We surrender to God's justice, which certainly will punish the sin, even though the earthly judge may not discover and punish it.[141] The Heidelberg Catechism reminds us of this in its definition: "A legitimate oath means calling upon God as the only one who knows my heart to witness to my truthfulness *and to punish me if I swear falsely*."[142] But the nature and degree of that punishment may not be incorporated into the oath itself. Only God may determine it. The expression "May God do this unto me" is therefore not fully acceptable. Paul's anathema in Romans 9:1 is a unique case.

5. Objections to Oaths[143]

First, there are religious ones, derived from Matthew 5. These can be found among the church fathers, the Anabaptists, and many others. But today many more irreligious objections can be heard.

---

139. Van Leeuwen, *De eed en de moderne staat*, 76.
140. This point is emphasized by Wuttke, Palmer, and Hartlieb: Wuttke, *Handbuch der christlichen Sittenlehre³*, 2:264; Palmer, *Die Moral des Christenthums*, 450; Hartlieb, *Der Eid und der moderne Staat*, 47.
141. Van Leeuwen, *De eed en de moderne staat*, 65.
142. Q&A 102; emphasis added.
143. Hartlieb, *Der Eid und der moderne Staat*, 44ff.; van Leeuwen, *De eed en de moderne staat*, 41–80. Ed. note: These pages are a chapter: "Critique of the Oath" (*de Eedskritiek*). Bavinck

a. The oath is based on superstition, on the fear of God's wrath, on his sudden intervention. And that is incorrect. God does not let himself be summoned as a witness at someone's whim. He does not intervene miraculously. How do we answer this? Oaths do not *summon* God *unto* but *invoke* God *as* witness. After all, he is already an all-knowing and almighty witness, even without the summons. But people who swear appeal to that very reality, place themselves in the presence of God, want to speak for him, with him, in him and surrender to his justice. Those who swear are not thereby calling for an immediate, miraculous punishment—although this may also be possible—but are acknowledging themselves to be worthy of punishment if they should lie. In swearing an oath we acknowledge that God knows us through and through and will not hold the person guiltless who misuses his name. Calling for divine judgments is improper; it is to ask for an immediate divine decision, to try to force God to answer, and is based on impatience. But the oath is something entirely different; without any superstition it assumes simply that God is just and will punish in his time.

b. Atheists, deists, pantheists, pessimists, abstentionists, and the like argue that there is no God or that God neither knows nor hears us or that we know nothing about him. From their point of view the oath is absurd. Only a theist can swear an oath.

c. Human self-esteem opposes the oath. Oaths are insulting, distrustful; they assume that I will lie and consider my simple Yes insufficient. But I am an honest person; I want to be taken at my word. The answer to this objection is that, on the one hand, the oath is precisely proof of trust; it honors the person, it is sacred. The oath shows that one knows about God, that one believes in his truthfulness, and that one, *in fellowship with God*, however untruthful in oneself, can nevertheless speak the truth. But, on the other hand, the oath assumes falsity, sin, and lying and is a personal humiliation. And the law must assume this, because it is proven to be true time and again. Before the law, every person is equal. To take one person at their word, and not another, is impossible. If someone says, "I am an honest person, I do not wish to be distrusted," then the law cannot demand even a promise, for that would already assume distrust. Thus, the law would have to proceed on the assumption that everybody speaks the truth as a matter of course and will be faithful. What nonsense! The law rightly demands an oath upon assuming an office; it sometimes demands safeguards, such as sums of money as a security bond. Would all of this then not be

___

left room in his manuscript at this point for inserting additional pages, though this was never done; likely he intended to add material from this chapter.

permitted?[144] This objection is based on miserable pride, on self-deception, on a Pelagian denial of sin and lying.

d. The oath is contradictory when, on the one hand, it *trusts* and, on the other hand, it *distrusts*. It considers that I am capable of lying and yet fit to perform as sacred an act as taking an oath.[145] Some contradiction! This is true, but the oath acknowledges precisely that point: we humans in the presence of and before the face of God will still shrink from being untrue or untrustworthy. In our bond with God we are trustworthy; if we then still lie, we are lost. Demons do not swear oaths and cannot. They lie to God's face. The oath both assumes the deep fall of humanity and, on the other hand, also raises up humanity; the oath does not view humanity as having sunk as deeply as Satan, who lies straight to God's face. This is where we have a glorious contradiction.

6. Oaths and the Modern State

The modern state began in 1740 when Frederick the Great assumed his reign; he wanted to let everyone be saved in their own way[146] and began to separate state and church. The state proclaims total freedom of conscience, and state institutions lose all confessional character. This is like America (although oaths, prayer, Sunday observance, and prayer days continue). The defining characteristic of the modern state is sought in the conviction that it is not a creation ordinance instituted by God but arose purely from human nature and grew just like a plant.[147] The state is then not created by a social contract, but nonetheless, as with Rousseau, by human beings themselves. In this case, the state is not created by an act of free will but of necessity, from human nature itself. In this way, people attain a godless state,[148] as the highest manifestation and expression of the unity of the nation. Thus, the state is itself an ethical organism, a personality, the personified unity of a nation. In this state, it is said, there is no room for oaths.

In response, we must acknowledge this to be true *if* this is a true understanding of the state. However, we judge this idea of the state to be false. It is true that various branches of state functions arose gradually, while the entity that we call the state has grown gradually to full size and has constituted itself gradually. But the question is, From where does the state derive its power and

---

144. Van Leeuwen, *De eed en de moderne staat*, 72.
145. Van Leeuwen, *De eed en de moderne staat*, 77.
146. GO/FO: *nach seiner Façon*.
147. Van Leeuwen, *De eed en de moderne staat*, 99.
148. FO: *état athée*. Ed. note: It is noteworthy that Bavinck repeatedly uses the word *volk* in this paragraph.

the right to issue laws, to punish, to levy taxes, and so on? To this question there is no other answer possible than that these come from human beings. In that case, however, the state itself has no authority and right; instead, society or the people rule. Or do all these functions of the state come from God (Rom. 13)? If the latter is true, then the state cannot be godless,[149] for it then murders itself, attacks its own might and right. If, however, it derives its authority from God, then it is also accountable to God, dependent on him, bound to him, and thus not godless.[150]

Another question then follows: To what extent must the state be bound to God? As much as can be known from natural theology, or also from revealed theology?[151] If the latter, do we then accept a Calvinist or a Lutheran view of revelation? We do not have to deal with this difficult question here. For if we say with Kuyper that the state is bound to God to the extent that he can be known from natural theology, then oaths are lawful.[152] For the oath, which is present among all peoples, is an article of natural theology. But then the state comes into conflict with itself. On the one hand it promises total freedom of conscience,[153] and on the other hand, it is itself committed to God. In such circumstances, does the state really want to bind its citizens to God, as the oath indicates? This places atheists and materialists, among others, in a real quandary.

How do we solve this problem? To force atheists and similar people to swear an oath would violate their freedom of conscience, would lead to hypocrisy, and would rob the oath of its sacred character. It would be better for the state to bar atheists from taking an oath.[154] Various solutions have been suggested.

a. Let's abolish oaths altogether; they are not worth anything, and they are going to be broken anyway. Atheists want to abolish oaths, along with many Christians who favor the sanctity of the oath.[155] The modern state, they say, is no longer worthy of such a sacred matter. The nations have become godless; the sanctity of God's name demands abolition. This situation incurs God's wrath.

---

149. FO: *athée*.

150. FO: *non-athée*.

151. LO: *theologia naturalis*; [*theologia*] *revelata*.

152. "Government is directly rooted in the natural life and as such has no other than a natural knowledge of God. . . . Now it is on the basis of this purely natural knowledge of God that the state comes to honor God in its public actions; to invoke God's holy name in state documents; to respect the oath; to dedicate a day of rest to him; to proclaim national days of prayer during disasters; to practice justice even with the sword; and to allow free course to the gospel" (Kuyper, *Our Program*, 60–61 [§51]).

153. See art. 164 of the Dutch Constitution.

154. Hartlieb, *Der Eid und der moderne Staat*, 49ff.

155. Thus Adolf Wuttke, Christian Friedrich Schmid, Christian Palmer, Richard Rothe (in part), and Hartlieb. See Hartlieb, *Der Eid und der moderne Staat*, 62ff.

There is much here that is true. But we do need to take the following into account.

(i) Jurists are almost unanimous in their agreement that the state cannot do without this safeguard.[156] Oaths may be misused, but they still contain a blessing. What would happen if oaths were abolished! Perhaps—nay, certainly—something worse. The oath does not deter scoundrels, but it certainly restrains many ordinary people and those in between.[157] However, this is not the greatest objection.

(ii) All the ethicists mentioned above[158] teach that the oath should at least be permitted, but not be compulsory. It *may* be used, but does not *have* to be used.[159] Indeed, in the light of Matthew 5, it is better to have no oaths at all than to require one. But that is incorrect. There are occasions when an oath is mandatory to preserve God's honor or a neighbor's welfare, cases that especially the state must specify. God has not merely permitted the oath, but commanded it (like monogamy and baptism). The state may not dispense with this safeguard. The mistake of these ethicists is especially that they accept the godless state and sever it from God. The question is not whether we can do without the oath, whether it is misused very often, or whether it could just as well be replaced with a promise. These are utilitarian reasons. The main question is this: May the state sever itself from God? That is, may it surrender the oath, which, as is claimed, is grounded in natural theology? And to that, the answer is no.

b. Others say, Let's make oaths optional. Let those who want to swear an oath do so. Those who want to promise should be permitted to promise. Atheists will be content with a promise. This was Gladstone's proposal when the atheist Charles Bradlaugh was elected to Parliament in 1880 and refused to swear an oath, preferring instead to make an affirmation.[160] However, Gladstone's proposal was defeated by a majority of three votes, and Bradlaugh was not permitted to take his seat in the parliament.[161] There is, however, a serious objection to making oaths optional.

156. Van Leeuwen, *De eed en de moderne staat*, 114.
157. DO: *natuurlijke mensen, de middelsoort.*
158. Wuttke, Schmid, Palmer, Rothe, and Hartlieb.
159. E.g., Hartlieb, *Der Eid und der moderne Staat*, 47, 69.
160. Hartlieb, *Der Eid und der moderne Staat*, 52.
161. Ed. note: Bradlaugh's attempt to affirm as an atheist even "led to his temporary imprisonment, fines for voting in the Commons illegally, and a number of by-elections at which Bradlaugh re-gained his seat on every occasion. He was finally allowed to take an oath in 1886." He also

Making oaths optional is identical to abolishing oaths. For if the oath is no longer required, no one will still use it. This is especially true for Christians, who do not swear unnecessarily. One could argue that making oaths optional applies only to atheists. But this would be unfair toward believers! Unbelievers would then be taken at their word and thus rewarded for their honesty, but believers would be required to swear oaths. This degrades the faith. This happens in America, notably, in the oaths of witnesses.

c. Let atheists be excused from swearing an oath if they are members of an atheist society.[162] They would be excused just as the Anabaptists are. Once again, there are serious questions here:

(i)   May the state recognize an atheist society as a church? Such recognition would have to occur in advance.

(ii) Atheists would thereby be put on an equal footing with Quakers and Anabaptists. What the latter refuse to do out of religious, conscientious convictions, the former would do from unbelief and mocking God. This is too great an honor.

(iii) This proposal would force atheists to establish a church fellowship, a denomination.[163]

d. Let's declare atheists unfit to take an oath and never permit them to take one![164] Van Leeuwen does not want the state to inquire into someone's faith, but when someone declares, "I am an atheist," he believes that person should not be admitted as a witness or allowed to fill a public office.[165] This would have significant consequences:

(i)   All public offices would be closed to atheists, and they would be excused from witnessing in court. This happened to Theodor Hofferichter in Breslau.[166] Atheists would become martyrs.

(ii) Many atheists would dissemble and nevertheless take the oath for the sake of the office.

---

proposed a bill that would permit members of both houses in the British Parliament to affirm, and saw it become law in 1888 (Wikipedia, s.v. "Charles Bradlaugh," https://en.wikipedia.org /wiki/Charles_Bradlaugh).

162. Thus Windthorst; see Hartlieb, *Der Eid und der moderne Staat*, 52.

163. DO: *kerkgenootschap*.

164. Thus Malblanc, von Scheurl; this is true in Canada (Hartlieb, *Der Eid und der moderne Staat*, 53ff.; van Leeuwen, *De eed en de moderne staat*, 120).

165. Van Leeuwen, *De eed en de moderne staat*, 123–24.

166. See n. 108 above.

(iii) What happens to the person who becomes an atheist while serving in office?[167]

e. Let atheists affirm rather than swear an oath. Kuyper required four things of atheists before they could be excused from swearing an oath:[168]

(i) Proof that one is not a member of a church fellowship or denomination. Someone who is a member of a church is being hypocritical, dishonest, and unreliable in a written statement that appeals to atheism as a reason for refusing to swear an oath.

(ii) An attestation from three God-fearing persons that the person who wants to affirm is an honest, truth-loving person.

(iii) A declaration that if one should come to faith in God, then one's promise is as binding as an oath.

(iv) The atheist must be prepared to have a respectable person declare that he harbors no suspicion about the loyalty to truth on the part of this atheist in connection with the case under consideration. This would be required, however, only if the state judged it necessary.

What is good about these criteria is that they treat the atheist as an exception. Otherwise, these four requirements remain somewhat impractical and elaborate.

Any solution to this question is difficult, since the modern state is trapped in an antinomy; it promises religious freedom and freedom of conscience, *and* it must be and remain bound to God. Having separated all official power from religion, the modern state has become a godless state. Consequently, it must move toward abolishing the oath. This godless state is practically unworkable, and it leads to the suicide and self-destruction of the state.[169]

7. A Few Remaining Stipulations

The situation with oaths is alarming; perjury abounds. The oath does not live in the consciousness of the nation. The church has a solemn duty to imprint the importance of the oath on the hearts of the people. To keep the oath sacred now requires the following:

---

167. Hartlieb, *Der Eid und der moderne Staat*, 54.
168. Kuyper, *Ons Program*, 228. Ed. note: The English translation (*Our Program*, 82 [§68]) is less detailed than the original.
169. Hartlieb, *Der Eid und der moderne Staat*, 55.

a. That the state limit the use of oaths and require them only in the most important cases—that is, in the oath of witnesses and in the oath of office.[170] This could be done, for instance, by not requiring witnesses to be sworn in at every hearing, nor even at every case, but once for all occasions; also by having the oath follow rather than precede a hearing, and not requiring it in case of suspicion of perjury.

b. That the taking of an oath happen in a solemn fashion, after preparation by a clergyman.[171] Kuyper also wants to grant the state the right to first inquire whether a person believes in God.[172] Others propose that clergymen occasionally be given the right to administer the oath.[173]

c. That perjury be punished severely.[174] The perjurer mocks (not a person) but the truth, God himself, the fear of God, his holiness, justice, omniscience. At the same time, perjury is increasing steadily and alarmingly. Public opinion no longer stigmatizes the perjurer.

---

170. Hartlieb, *Der Eid und der moderne Staat*, 26ff. Ed. note: Bavinck does not specific the pages here and in nn. 173–74.

171. Hartlieb, *Der Eid und der moderne Staat*, 33; Kuyper, *Ons Program*, 228, 1128.

172. Kuyper, *Ons Program*, 228.

173. Hartlieb, *Der Eid und der moderne Staat*, 39ff.

174. Hartlieb, *Der Eid und der moderne Staat*, 55ff.

17

The Sabbath

The Fourth Commandment is about communal worship and is rooted in the creation account of God resting (Exod. 20). Other nations had rhythms of work and rest, but none of them prefigured the Jewish Sabbath, which was instituted at Mount Sinai. Because of sin, the Sabbath was also tied to salvation, to Israel's deliverance from Egypt (Deut. 5). The Sabbath was now a sign between YHWH and Israel forever, the proof and hallmark of the covenant between God and his people, a sacramental foretaste of eternal rest. Israelites had to hallow themselves on the Sabbath, separating themselves from the world and devoting themselves to God. All work was forbidden on the Sabbath, and transgression was punishable by death.

We do not know the extent of Israel's adherence to this commandment; the prophets frequently specified Sabbath sins. After the exile, the meticulous view of Sabbath observance arose and was linked to the rise of synagogue worship. Jewish life was governed by a detailed set of rules (the Talmud) covering all aspects of life from lighting fires for cooking to traveling. Jesus did not abolish the Sabbath but subordinated it to love of God and love of neighbor, which is the content of the moral law. Jesus proclaimed himself "Lord of the Sabbath."

The first Christians initially observed Jewish customs, including the Sabbath, but soon the day of Christ's resurrection became the preeminent day of Christian worship. The apostle Paul judged all days equal and insisted on Christian liberty with respect to days, though the New Testament provides evidence that Paul observed Sunday. For gentile Christians, especially, toward the end of the first century, the Jewish Sabbath was replaced by the Christian Sunday. This was not urged on the basis of the Decalogue but in view of Jesus's resurrection, and its observance was not rigorous until the time of Constantine. However, since Charlemagne (eighth century), Sunday observance has been based on the Fourth Commandment, and civil authorities were asked to support the church in this. Notwithstanding, Roman Catholic Sunday practices are quite lax—only attendance at mass is required. The Orthodox Church since the eighth century inherited a stricter view of Sunday.

Among Protestants only the Reformed advocated a more or less rigorous view of Sunday observance. For Lutherans, the outward abstaining from work is a ceremonial matter of the Old Testament that was abolished by Christ. Nonetheless, such observance is good so that laborers can rest and be refreshed and so that all people have time and opportunity to attend worship services to hear God's Word and praise him. Sunday is the appropriate day because it is the day of Christ's resurrection. In Lutheran countries Sunday observance is not very strict.

Calvin gives three purposes for the Sabbath that continue to have validity for Christians: spiritual rest from our labors and resting in God, a set time for worship (hearing the Word), and rest for servants. Calvin's Geneva practiced strict observance of Sunday rest. The debate about Sunday that surfaced in the Low Countries in the sixteenth and seventeenth centuries involved distinguishing ceremonial and moral elements in the Fourth Commandment, the extent to which proper observance required abstaining from work (which activities and by whom), and the role of the civil authorities in mandating Sunday rest for all citizens. A big question, theologically: Did the Sabbath originate in creation, or was it instituted at Sinai? Johannes Cocceius argued that the Fourth Commandment was entirely ceremonial, and he influenced some. The same controversy that raged in the Netherlands also erupted in Scotland and England in the seventeenth century, with similar polarization between stricter and more lenient views. The strict party won the day, as the Westminster Assembly and the Westminster standards are strongly Sabbatarian. This also spread to the United States of America.

A crusade against Sunday observance has grown since the eighteenth century as the unbelief highlighted in the French Revolution spread through Europe and industrialization helped turn Sunday into another ordinary day for commerce and entertainment. This gave rise to campaigns in many nations by associations (such as the Lord's Day Alliance) that promoted Sunday observance. There is only one sufficient ground for Christians to observe Sunday: the authority of God.

Ancient Israel also had feasts in addition to the Sabbath, feasts divinely instituted for memorializing God's deeds of deliverance—notably, Passover, the Day of Atonement, and some established after the exile, especially Purim and the Feast of the Dedication of the Temple, or the Feast of Lights.

The first Christians moved from coming together daily to gatherings on Sunday and eventually to Wednesday and Friday gatherings as well. Soon, additional feast days were added: *Pascha* (initially focused on Christ's death, but eventually the feast of his resurrection), *Pentecost*, *Epiphany*, and *Christmas*. In addition to these principal feasts, a number of secondary feasts were added, including countless days for saints and martyrs.

The Reformation churches abolished many of the Roman Catholic feast days but kept the great feasts—Christmas, Easter, Pentecost—and a few others. Lutherans retained some additional feasts as concessions to popular piety and for the sake of discipline and order. Calvin neither opposed nor really favored church feasts, and his spiritual followers in the Low Countries (and in Great Britain) had significant debates about them in the sixteenth and seventeenth centuries. Often the churches' views conflicted with popular piety and the civil magistrates. Over time, church assemblies repeatedly addressed the issue, and the changing orders reflected the uncertainty of church leaders, who wanted to abolish or at least significantly reduce church "holy days" except for those that fell on Sundays and Christmas. Among the Reformed in the Netherlands too, retention of feasts beyond the three great feasts was a concession to popular practice and custom. The result is that by the late nineteenth century church order canons contradicted each other; not all of them are of equal importance and binding character, and Christian liberty must be acknowledged in this matter.

Designated days for penitence, fasting, and prayer took place in Israel and in the New Testament church and have been called for in church history during critical times. The Roman Catholic Church and the Orthodox Church continue the practice of fasting in connection with the high feasts of the church year. After the Reformation general days of penance and prayer were appointed by Christian rulers during times of grave calamities, a practice approved by several Dutch Reformed church orders, including that of the great Synod of Dort.

Concerning Sunday observance, we conclude that the Sabbath was instituted at creation, that resting from work is an essential part of God's will for human beings, and that the Fourth Commandment includes both ceremonial and moral elements. The moral and permanent elements in this commandment that are abiding are public worship of God at set times, consecrating such times by resting from work and attending communal worship, and providing rest for servants and animals. An argument for observing one day in seven is not absolute but leans toward an affirmative answer. Similarly, Sunday as the day of worship cannot be said to be definitely instituted in the New Testament, but there are good reasons for this designation. It should be observed by resting from ordinary work and work that brings profit and supplies our livelihood. Works of necessity and mercy are permitted, and all forms of legalism should be avoided. Positively, we are to consecrate ourselves, dedicate ourselves to God, assemble with God's people for worship, listen to God's Word, use the sacraments, sing, gather, and present alms.

§35. THE FOURTH COMMANDMENT

> Remember the Sabbath day, to keep it holy. Six days you shall labor, and do all
> your work, but the seventh day is a Sabbath to the LORD your God. On it you
> shall not do any work, you, or your son, or your daughter, your male servant,
> or your female servant, or your livestock, or the sojourner who is within your
> gates. For in six days the LORD made heaven and earth, the sea, and all that is
> in them, and rested on the seventh day. Therefore the LORD blessed the Sabbath
> day and made it holy. (Exod. 20:8–11)

This commandment describes the proper way of engaging in communal
public worship.[1]

Scriptural Teaching

Genesis 2:2–3 teaches that God rested on the seventh day from all his work
(cf. Exod. 20:8) and—so we read in Exodus 31:17—was "refreshed."[2] Not that
God was tired, for Isaiah 40:28 teaches the opposite; not as though he now
entered an absolute *rest* or *unemployment*,[3] for John 5:17 teaches otherwise.
What this rest indicates is this:

(1) the work of creation was finished and was good, and no new species or
substances needed to be created; and

(2) God rested from his works, looked down with pleasure upon them, and
rejoiced in them (Ps. 104:31).

This resting on and hallowing of the seventh day is part of, and an essential
element in, the completion of the work of creation. For it says in Genesis 2:2,
"And on the seventh day God finished[4] his work that he had done, and he
rested on the seventh day from all his work that he had done." The completion

---

1. See Riedel, "Der Sabbath." Ed. note: What follows is not a direct quote from Riedel but
Bavinck's own summary:

> We read that the Sabbath was not instituted in Genesis 1. The Babylonians and other
> pagan nations did not have a Sabbath (as Fr. Delitzsch, *Bibel und Babel*, claims), but they
> did have a seven-day week. The Sabbath is specifically Israelite, tentatively instituted in
> Exodus 16, and later in the Law. The early Christians celebrated the Sabbath along with
> the Jews, but before long they observed the first day of the week in addition. The Sunday
> therefore did not come in the place of the Sabbath. Thus, the Fourth Commandment no
> longer applies. We did not acquire the seven-day week from Israel but from the Germanic
> tribes, who already had it, as appears from the pagan names of the days.

2. HO: וַיִּנָּפַשׁ.
3. LO: *otium* = being free from activities, doing nothing.
4. HO: וַיְכַל.

of creation consisted in this resting and blessing.[5] Next, "God blessed the seventh day and made it holy" (Gen. 2:3).[6] He set it apart from the other days as a day unto his service, for the service of the Holy One. This parallels 1 Kings 9:3, where the temple is "consecrated" or "hallowed" by God,[7] as well as 1 Corinthians 10:16, where the communion cup is "blessed."

It is clear, therefore, that the Sabbath was instituted already in connection with the creation, although no special commandment is added for humanity to observe that day.[8] Two additional factors provide additional weight to this conclusion:

(1) Exodus 20:11 and Exodus 31:17 base the Sabbath commandment on God's rest on and his hallowing of the seventh day in connection with the creation.

(2) Even before its institution at Sinai, the Sabbath is present among other nations.[9] The Egyptians and the Greeks had a ten-day week; the Romans before Christ an eight-day week. Schrader considers the seven-day week to be an ancient Babylonian institution that the Hebrews brought with them from their stay in southern Babylonia, in Ur of the Chaldees.[10] Already among the Babylonians the seventh day was called *šabbattuv* (though it may not have been observed religiously), and the seven days of the week were named after the planets, as appears from the syllabaries. Among the Aramaic Mandaeans and Sabians in the Mesopotamian city of Harran, these planetary gods were also known as gods of the weekdays.

Thus in this resting and hallowing we do not have a prolepsis of the Jewish Sabbath instituted later.[11] Granted, Genesis 2 does not mention that God spoke about an evening of the seventh day, but one may not deduce from

5. Cf. Keil and Delitzsch, *Biblical Commentary on the Old Testament*, 1:40; de Moor, *Commentarius Perpetuus*, 2:264.

6. HO: קדש ; ברך .

7. The fact that the Hebrew verb קדש appears in one place as a *piel* and in the other as a *hiphil* makes no difference.

8. Oehler and von Orelli, "Sabbath."

9. Tiele, *Outlines of the History of Religion*, 84; Schrader, *Die Keilinschriften*, 18–23; cf. also von Orelli, who corrects Oehler in Oehler and von Orelli, "Sabbath," 157–58; F. Bohn, *Der Sabbat im Alten Testament*; also the large volume of literature in the Babel-Bible controversy: J. Meinhold, *Sabbat und Woche im Alten Testament*.

10. Schrader, *Die Keilinschriften*, 18–23; Schrader, "Die babylonische Ursprung."

11. Thus Gomarus—see below, nn. 155–60; cf. also Oehler, *Theology of the Old Testament*, 328–31 (§147: "Antiquity and Origin of the Sabbath"); Keil and Delitzsch, *Biblical Commentary on the Old Testament*, 1:41.

this, with an appeal to Hebrews 4, that it would not have been an ordinary day. More important is the fact that observing the seventh day is nowhere mentioned during the time of the patriarchs; but this pervasive silence does not yet prove that it was *not* observed. (The seven-day week was probably known in Genesis 7:4, 10; 8:10, 12; 17:12; 21:4; and certainly in 29:27–28.) In fact, the word "remember" in the command "remember the Sabbath day" (Exod. 20:8) assumes that this day was already recognized as a holy day, but that it was probably no longer being observed.[12]

So then, Moses restored the Sabbath. The word *shabbat*[13] appears most often as a feminine noun and is either an abstract noun derived from *shabethet*[14]— that is, celebration, rest[15]—or a masculine *qatal* form meaning "day of rest." But in view of passages like Exodus 31:15 (the seventh day is a day of rest, the Sabbath), originally it would seem to be an abstract noun.[16] The Greek word is τὸ σάββατον, but also τὰ σάββατα; the latter, plural form with a singular meaning might have been an imitation of the Aramean form of the emphatic state (i.e., nouns with article),[17] but is probably to be explained by the analogy of the names of other sacred seasons, such as the "Feast of Rededication of the Temple"[18] (Festival of Lights, Hanukkah) and the "Feast of Unleavened Bread."[19] In addition to Genesis 2:2 and Exodus 16:5, 22–30—where it is proleptic and commands that twice as much manna has to be collected and cooked on the sixth day and none on the seventh day—the Sabbath command appears in Exodus 20:8–11 (cf. Deut. 5:12–15).[20] The Sabbath is Israel's constitution.[21]

In Exodus 20, the basis for Sabbath observance is God's day of rest after the creation; thus, human beings must follow God's example given in Genesis 2. Rest entails looking down with pleasure upon a work that is both good and completed, as the ultimate end for God and humanity alike; rest hallows the seventh day, and it completes the work of the six preceding days. But whereas Exodus 20 lays the basis for Sabbath observance in the order of creation,

---

12. HO: זָכוֹר. And Exod. 16:5, 22–30, about collecting twice as much manna on the sixth day, assumes it as well.

13. HO: שַׁבָּת.

14. HO: שַׁבֶּתֶת.

15. GO: ἀνάπαυσις.

16. LO: *abstractum*. Thanks to Michael Williams for the grammatical help.

17. Ed. note: Bavinck's manuscript has the abbreviation "*emph. stat*": the emphatic state is also called the "determined state." See König, "Emphatic State in Aramaic." Thanks to Michael Williams for the explanation and reference.

18. GO: ἐγκαίνια.

19. GO: ἄζυμα. Oehler, *Theology of the Old Testament*, 330.

20. Also in Exod. 23:12; 31:12–17; 34:21; 35:1–3; Num. 15:32–36.

21. DO: *grondwet*.

Deuteronomy adds to this another basis, derived from the re-creation:[22] "You shall remember that you were a slave in the land of Egypt, and the LORD your God brought you out from there with a mighty hand and an outstretched arm" (Deut. 5:15). Thus on account of sin, the Sabbath obtained a new meaning; working in the sweat of one's face, serving in a sinful world, slaving away in Egypt, caused human beings to yearn all the more for rest, which now became an image of deliverance from servitude. The Sabbath became a corrective against the drawbacks of heavy weekly toil that drew people away from God.[23]

The essence and significance of the Sabbath for Israel now consisted in this, that it was a sign between YHWH and Israel forever (Exod. 31:17); that is, the Sabbath was the proof, the hallmark of the covenant made between God and Israel. God wants his people to share in his divine rest; thus God's gift of the Sabbath to Israel was a gift of grace, a kind of sacrament, evidence that YHWH hallowed them, chose them to be his people (Ezek. 20:12), and would grant them eternal rest (Heb. 4). On the Sabbath, Israel rested from the troubles of life, rested in God, and devoted herself to him. Hence, Israelites had to hallow themselves—that is, separate themselves from the things of this world and devote themselves to God. This act of hallowing consisted in the following: the Sabbath was a delight, a festive day (Isa. 58:13; cf. Hosea 2:11; Ps. 92, which was a song for the Sabbath day), a day of rest for the animals (Exod. 20:10; 23:12; Deut. 5:14), a day of rest for manservants, maidservants, and strangers (Exod. 20:10; Deut. 5:14), and, of course, a day of rest for the Israelites themselves. All work was forbidden on that day: gathering and cooking manna (Exod. 16:22–23), plowing and harvesting (Exod. 34:21), lighting fires (Exod. 35:3), leaving the camp (Exod. 16:29), and gathering firewood (Num. 15:32).[24] Transgressors were put to death (Exod. 31:14–15; 35:2; according to Numbers 15:32–36, specifically by stoning). The act of hallowing the day consisted in a holy convocation (Lev. 23:3), in doubling the morning and evening sacrifice (thus two yearling lambs, two tenths of an ephah of flour, and the drink offering [Num. 28:9]), and in replenishing the showbread (Lev. 24:8). We do not know what else belonged to the observance of the Sabbath; in both the law and the prophets the positive prescriptions overshadow the negative ones.

This Sabbath did not immediately take hold, however. It appears only a few times in the historical books, as proof that it was not entirely forgotten (2 Kings 4:23; 11:5, 7, 9; cf. 2 Chron. 23:4, 8; 1 Chron. 9:32; 23:31). Solomon

---

22. DO: *herschepping.*
23. Keil, *Manual of Biblical Archaeology,* 2:1–7 (§77, "The Weekly Sabbath").
24. Keil, *Manual of Biblical Archaeology,* 2:7.

provided for it (2 Chron. 2:4) and offered sacrifices on the Sabbaths according to the commandment (8:13). So too did Hezekiah (2 Chron. 31:3). The prophets were extremely zealous about observing the Sabbath and pronounced judgment on those who defiled the Sabbath with their iniquity: "Bring no more vain offerings; / incense is an abomination to me. / New moon and Sabbath and the calling of convocations— / I cannot endure iniquity and solemn assembly" (Isa. 1:13). Nonetheless, Isaiah also pronounces a blessing on those who keep the Sabbath with integrity:

> Thus says the Lord:
> "Keep justice, and do righteousness,
> for soon my salvation will come,
>   and my righteousness be revealed.
> Blessed is the man who does this,
>   and the son of man who holds it fast,
> who keeps the Sabbath, not profaning it,
>   and keeps his hand from doing any evil." (Isa. 56:1–2)

This blessing extends beyond Israel:

> Let not the foreigner who has joined himself to the Lord say,
>   "The Lord will surely separate me from his people";
> and let not the eunuch say,
>   "Behold, I am a dry tree."
> For thus says the Lord:
> "To the eunuchs who keep my Sabbaths,
>   who choose the things that please me
>   and hold fast my covenant,
> I will give in my house and within my walls
>   a monument and a name
>   better than sons and daughters;
> I will give them an everlasting name
>   that shall not be cut off.
>
> "And the foreigners who join themselves to the Lord,
>   to minister to him, to love the name of the Lord,
>   and to be his servants,
> everyone who keeps the Sabbath and does not profane it,
>   and holds fast my covenant—
> these I will bring to my holy mountain,
>   and make them joyful in my house of prayer;
> their burnt offerings and their sacrifices
>   will be accepted on my altar;

for my house shall be called a house of prayer
for all peoples." (Isa. 56:3–7)

Jeremiah specifies Sabbath sins: "Thus says the LORD: Take care for the
sake of your lives, and do not bear a burden on the Sabbath day or bring it in
by the gates of Jerusalem. And do not carry a burden out of your houses on
the Sabbath or do any work, but keep the Sabbath day holy, as I commanded
your fathers. Yet they did not listen or incline their ear, but stiffened their neck,
that they might not hear and receive instruction" (Jer. 17:21–23). Forgetting
the Sabbath is YHWH's judgment and leads to Jeremiah's lament: "He has
laid waste his booth like a garden, / laid in ruins his meeting place; / the LORD
has made Zion forget / festival and Sabbath, / and in his fierce indignation
has spurned king and priest" (Lam. 2:6). Ezekiel sees in the Sabbaths a gift
of God and a sign between him and Israel (20:12); he exhorts the people
to hallow them (20:20); he complains about their desecration (22:26); and
he promises and prophesies that they will be hallowed in the future (44:24;
45:17; 46:1–3). Hosea announces as punishment that the Lord will put an end
to Sabbaths and feasts (Hosea 2:11). Amos laments the fact that people sell
wheat on the Sabbath (Amos 8:5). During the exile (e.g., with Ezekiel), the
Sabbath acquires increased significance; observing it is greatly emphasized.
Nehemiah impressed upon the returning Israelites that they should observe
the holy Sabbath, look upon it as a gift, as an act of God making himself
known (Neh. 9:14); he forbids buying wheat and all kinds of wares on that
day (Neh. 10:31), as well as treading wine presses, harvesting grapes, figs, and
so on, buying fish and other merchandise, and so he orders the gates of the
city to be shut on the Sabbath (Neh. 13:15–22).

After the exile, the meticulous view of the Sabbath arose.[25] Something
good had arisen after the exile: religious meetings on the Sabbath in specific
buildings built for that purpose, called synagogues. The first trace of this is
found in (probably postexilic) Psalm 74:8, where mention is made of God's
meeting places that the enemies had torched. These places were probably
older, from the time of Ezra. According to Acts 15:21, from the earliest times[26]
Moses was preached in every city and read in the synagogues on every Sabbath. Josephus ascribes the institution of the synagogue to Moses, and the
Targums date them even as far back as the patriarchs.[27] In this postexilic
era, Sabbath observance was worked out in a meticulous manner. The law

25. Schürer, *History of the Jewish People*, 2/2:52–55.
26. GrO: ἐκ γενεῶν ἀρχαίων.
27. Josephus, *Against Apion* II.17 (LCL 186:298–99); Schürer, *Lehrbuch der neutestamentlichen Zeitgeschichte*, 469.

prohibited work in general; the later Jews enumerated thirty-nine main works that were forbidden: sowing, plowing, reaping, binding into sheaves, threshing, and so forth. Each of these thirty-nine main works was specified further, and an extensive casuistry arose. For example, writing even two alphabetical letters was forbidden, but if people wrote two letters in the sand, where writing does not last, or if they wrote with their foot, mouth, or elbow, or if they wrote one letter on the wall and another on the ground so that they could not be read together, then they would be guiltless.[28] The same was true with regard to lighting a fire and carrying a burden. Part of this was also that, on the basis of Exodus 16:29, people were not allowed to travel further from their house on the Sabbath than two thousand yards (a "Sabbath's journey," Acts 1:12).

At the time of the Maccabees, going to battle on the Sabbath was deemed unlawful (1 Macc. 2:38; 2 Macc. 6:11). Mattathias therefore proposed (1 Macc. 2:41) that attacking was unlawful (2 Macc. 8:26) but fighting in self-defense was not (1 Macc. 9:43–44 involved a defensive battle), and this remained the practice.[29] Of course, enemies kept using this to their advantage. There were occasions, however, when the Jews went on the attack.[30] Further, it was forbidden, among other things, to pluck ears of grain (Matt. 12:1–2; Mark 2:23–24), to carry a bed, to heal the sick (Matt. 12:9–10; Mark 3:1–2; Luke 6:6–7; 13:10–11; 14:1–2; John 5:1–10; 9:14–15). Only imminent peril superseded the Sabbath (cf. Matt. 12:11: "Which one of you who has a sheep, if it falls into a pit on the Sabbath, will not take hold of it and lift it out?"), although the Gemara is again stricter on this point.[31] The Jewish practice,[32] though still holding the Sabbath to be a joyful day on which fasting was forbidden and three nutritious and delicious meals were to be eaten, was actually in conflict with God's commandment in the Old Testament. At that earlier time, a far more lenient practice prevailed. So, for example, the Israelites walked around Jericho for seven days, and thus also on the Sabbath day (Josh. 6). That is why Jesus repeatedly opposed the narrow-mindedness of the Jews, and here as well,

---

28. Schürer, *Lehrbuch der neutestamentlichen Zeitgeschichte*, 2/2:55.

29. Josephus, *Jewish Antiquities*, book XIV. Ed note: Bavinck specifies XIV.4.2, a reference he took from Oehler and von Orelli, "Sabbath," 162. However, this reference is an error since XIV.4 deals with Antipater scheming with King Hyrcanus II against Hyrcanus's rival, Aristobulus. References to the Sabbath don't appear until lines 63–66 (LCL 365:478–81).

30. Oehler and von Orelli, "Sabbath," 162.

31. Oehler and von Orelli, "Sabbath," 164; Schürer, *Lehrbuch der neutestamentlichen Zeitgeschichte*, 484–85. Ed. note: The Gemara (Hebrew גְּמָרָא, from the Aramaic verb *gemar* = to study) is the rabbinical analysis of and commentary on the Mishnah, the collection of Jewish oral tradition. Together, the Mishnah and Gemara form the Talmud.

32. Cf. Oort, *De laatste eeuwen van Israels volksbestaan*, 1:176.

he gave no new law but came to fulfill the Mosaic law and purify the law of the Jewish additions that had rendered it powerless. Jesus kept the Sabbath; "as was his custom,"[33] he went to the synagogue on the Sabbath (Luke 4:16); he thought that having to flee on a Sabbath was undesirable (Matt. 24:20; par. Mark 13:18 does not have the words "nor on a Sabbath").[34] Moreover, Jesus had come to *fulfill* the law (Matt. 5:17). But he resisted the Jewish additions, and for that reason he healed quite often on the Sabbath (Matt. 12:9–10; Mark 1:21–22; 3:1–2; Luke 4:31–32; 13:10–11; 14:1–2; John 5:1–13; 7:22–23); he allowed people to pluck ears of grain on the Sabbath (Matt. 12:1–2); and as the Son of Man, he called himself "Lord of the Sabbath" and declared that the Sabbath was "made for man" (Mark 2:27–28). And Jesus defends this more lenient conception of the Sabbath with various arguments: with the example of David, who was hungry (Matt. 12:3–4 par. Mark 2:25); with the priests who profaned the Sabbath in the temple and yet were blameless (Matt. 12:5); with rescuing a sheep that falls into a pit (Matt. 12:11 par. Luke 14:5); with the question "Is it lawful on the Sabbath to do good or to do harm, to save life or to kill?" (Mark 3:4); and with taking one's ox or donkey from the stall on a Sabbath and leading it away to water it (Luke 13:15). From all these examples it is clear that Jesus does not abolish the Sabbath but subordinates it to love of God and neighbor, which is the content of the moral law. And precisely as the Son of Man, who is to complete a work of love and salvation for humanity, he is Lord also of the Sabbath.

Sunday in the Early Church[35]

The Jerusalem church initially continued living according to Jewish customs. They went to the temple (Acts 2:46; cf. Luke 24:53; Acts 3:1), preached the gospel there (Acts 5:20, 25), and offered sacrifices there (Acts 21:26). They joined the synagogues, as can be deduced from Acts 9:2, 22:12, and 15:21, and from the fact that Paul always went first to the synagogue to preach the gospel.[36] As they did with the feasts (Acts 2:1–2), the early Christians in Jerusalem most

---

33. GrO: κατὰ τὸ εἰωθός.

34. GrO: μηδέ σαββάτῳ.

35. Cf. Henke, "Zur Geschichte der Lehre von der Sonntagsfeier"; Hospinian, *Festa Christianorum*; Hengstenberg, *Über den Tag des Herrn*; T. Zahn, *Geschichte des Sonntags*; L. Thomas, *Le jour du Seigneur*, deals in particular with Sunday among pagan nations and derives it from traditions dating back to paradise (see review by H. Vuillemier, in *Revue de Théologie et de Philosophie et Comte-rendu des Principales Publications Scientifiques* 26 [1893]: 360–62). Wilhelm Riedel, lecturer at the University of Greifswald, in his *Alttestamentliche Untersuchungen*, part I, has a section titled "The Three Great Jewish Feasts" ["Die drei grossen jüdischen Feste"], 52–71, and a section titled "Der Sabbath," 74–90.

36. Lechler, *Das Apostolische und das Nachapostolische Zeitalter*, 41–42.

likely joined the Jews in observing the Sabbath. But alongside these practices, there was already something new and something different. The Jerusalem church gathered in the temple not just on the Sabbath but *daily*, while breaking bread "in their homes" (Acts 2:46).[37] *Daily* the apostles preached both in the temple and in homes (5:42). And no doubt among these days, the day of the resurrection topped the list (John 20:26: "Eight days later, his disciples were inside again"). Neander claims that Sunday observance must have originated with the gentile Christians, not Jewish Christians, because people could not meet every day, and the day of the resurrection became the automatically designated day.[38] But if Sunday observance were only of gentile Christian origin, then its general spread is difficult to explain; this is not so if its spread began in Jerusalem.[39] This observance of Sunday was immediately adopted by the gentile Christians. To be sure, Paul judged that all days were equal: "One person esteems one day as better than another, while another esteems all days alike. Each one should be fully convinced in his own mind" (Rom. 14:5).[40] The Galatians observed months and times and years (4:9–10), and Paul was afraid that he had labored in vain among them. We read in Colossians 2:16, "Therefore let no one pass judgment on you in questions of food and drink, or with regard to a festival or a new moon or a Sabbath."[41]

The Reformed customarily understand these passages to refer to the Jewish feasts and the Old Testament Sabbath.[42] William Ames says that this equality of days expressed by Paul in no way precludes observing a single day, any more than not judging in food and drink precludes that bread and wine in the Supper are sacred.[43] But in addition, there is evidence that Paul himself observed Sunday and that this day was observed in the gentile Christian churches. In 1 Corinthians 16:2 Paul exhorts everyone to *personally* set something aside on the "first day of every week," and in this way gather a sum of money so that there would be "no collecting when I come."[44] Now Paul does not say that such gifts are to be brought on that first day where they hold their meetings, for he writes,

37. GrO: κατ' οἶκον.
38. Neander, *History of the Planting and Training of the Christian Church*, 159.
39. Lechler, *Das Apostolische und das Nachapostolische Zeitalter*, 50.
40. GrO: Ὃς μὲν [γὰρ] κρίνει ἡμέραν παρ' ἡμέραν, ὃς δὲ κρίνει πᾶσαν ἡμέραν· ἕκαστος ἐν τῷ ἰδίῳ νοῒ πληροφορείσθω.
41. GrO: Μὴ οὖν τις ὑμᾶς κρινέτω ἐν βρώσει καὶ ἐν πόσει ἢ ἐν μέρει ἑορτῆς ἢ νεομηνίας ἢ σαββάτων. It is also significant that mention is made repeatedly of "the first day of the week" following the Sabbath (Matt. 28:1; Mark 16:9; John 20:1, 19). From antiquity, that day has been a special day for Christians.
42. See, e.g., the annotations in the Dutch Authorized Version (*Statenvertaling*).
43. Ames, *Marrow of Theology*, 297 (II.xv, §32); de Moor, *Commentarius Perpetuus*, 2:821.
44. GrO: ὑμῶν παρ' ἑαυτῷ; κατὰ μίαν σαββάτου; ἵνα μὴ ὅταν ἔλθω τότε λογεῖαι γίνωνται.

"Each of you is to put something aside."[45] This certainly indicates a putting aside by oneself, at home;[46] yet there must be a reason why Paul mentions this first day, and then gives advice about putting money aside, not just to Corinthians but also to others, as appears from verse 1 ("as I directed the churches of Galatia"). That day must therefore have a special significance, and obviously the inference is that it was solemnly observed. That meetings were held on this day, however, does not appear from this text; for it reads "each of you."[47] This agrees completely with Acts 20:7: "On the first day of the week, when we were gathered together to break bread, Paul talked with them."[48] In Troas there was a gathering of the disciples, and the Lord's Supper was celebrated. But the text does not say that this gathering was held expressly because Paul wanted to say farewell and depart the next morning.[49] That becomes improbable, because the text adds a phrase that most English translations render as "on the first day of the week."[50] If the gathering had occurred only for Paul's sake, this addition would have been superfluous. It indicates that this day was inherently significant, even apart from Paul's departure. It appears, then, that gentile Christians observed Sunday by means of gathering together.[51] Already in Revelation 1:10 the day is referred to as "the Lord's Day."[52]

Among the gentile Christians toward the end of the first century, the Jewish Sabbath was replaced by the Christian Sunday.[53] *The Epistle of Barnabas* says: We joyfully observe the eighth day, on which Jesus arose.[54] The *Didache* says that people came together on that "Lord's Day" and broke bread;[55] Justin Martyr writes, "But Sunday is the day on which we all hold our common assembly, because it is the first day on which God, having wrought a change in the darkness and matter, made the world; and Jesus Christ our Saviour

45. GrO: ὑμῶν παρ' ἑαυτῷ τιθέτω.
46. Thus Neander, correctly: *History of the Planting and Training of the Christian Church*, 159.
47. GrO: ὑμῶν παρ' ἑαυτῷ.
48. GrO: Ἐν δὲ τῇ μιᾷ τῶν σαββάτων συνηγμένων ἡμῶν κλάσαι ἄρτον, ὁ Παῦλος διελέγετο αὐτοῖς.
49. Nowhere does it say that this Sunday observance was commanded, that it was a day of *rest*.
50. GrO: Ἐν δὲ τῇ μιᾷ τῶν σαββάτων.
51. Lechler, *Das Apostolische und das Nachapostolische Zeitalter*, 115–16.
52. GrO: ἐν τῇ κυριακῇ ἡμέρᾳ.
53. T. Zahn, *Skizzen aus dem Leben der alten Kirche*, 196–240, also speaks of Sunday in the early church ("Geschichte des Sonntags: Vornehmlich in der Alten Kirche"); cf. Lowrie, review of Zahn, *Skizzen aus dem Leben der alten Kirche*; cf. also articles by Louis Thomas, all titled "Le jour du Seigneur," in *Revue de theologie et de philosophie* between 1888 and 1892. Ed. note: The more than twenty articles in this journal were published as a two-volume work, *Le jour du Seigneur*, in 1892. See n. 35 above.
54. *Epistle of Barnabas* XV (*ANF* 1:146–47).
55. GrO: κυριακῇ ἡμέρᾳ; *Didache* XIV.1.

on the same day rose from the dead."[56] We come across similar testimonies in Ignatius of Antioch, who speaks of Christians "no longer observing the Sabbath, but living in the observance of the Lord's Day, on which also our life has sprung up again by Him and by His death."[57] Only the *Apostolic Constitutions* diverged from this and recommended observing the Sabbath as well as Sunday—perhaps to counter gnosticism, which despised the Old Testament and failed to honor the Creator.[58] On that day, since it was a day of joy, fasting and kneeling at prayer were forbidden, according to Tertullian,[59] who also combats the Sabbath.[60]

Sunday Observance in Church History

However, in antiquity Sunday observance was never urged on the basis of the Decalogue, but only in a New Testament manner, in view of Jesus's resurrection, and for its own sake, as a day of rest.[61] This is why its observance was not rigorous. After Constantine, however, stricter prohibitions appeared as early as AD 321 (modeled after the Old Testament).[62] Among the prohibited activities were court proceedings, doing business, suing for debts, and attending

56. GrO: τῇ τοῦ ἡλίου λεγομένῃ ἡμέρᾳ; Justin Martyr, *First Apology* LXVII (*ANF* 1:186); cf. Justin Martyr, *Dialogue with Trypho* X–XI, XVIII–XIX, XXIII, where he opposes the Sabbath (*ANF* 1:199–200, 203–4, 206).

57. Ignatius, *Epistle to the Magnesians* IX.1 (*ANF* 1:62). Cf. Ignatius, *Epistle to Diognetus* IV (*ANF* 1:26). In the same vein, Athanasius writes that the Sabbath was observed; Timothy of Alexandria (d. 477) writes that the Supper was distributed on that day; Cassian writes that the Scriptures were read. The Council of Laodicea prescribes it, AD 363. Both days are still observed by the Abyssinians, who were converted in the fourth century. Ed. note: Bavinck's source is Henke, "Zur Geschichte der Lehre von der Sonntagsfeier," 601.

58. Cf. Lechler, *Das Apostolische und das Nachapostolische Zeitalter*, 560–62; Zöckler, "Sonntagsfeier," 428.

59. Tertullian, *De corona* III (*ANF* 3:94): "We count fasting or kneeling in worship on the Lord's day to be unlawful."

60. Tertullian, *An Answer to the Jews* IV ("Of the Observance of the Sabbath") (*ANF* 3:155–56). Ed. note: Bavinck adds "c. haer. 4:30"; since he is speaking of Tertullian (not Irenaeus) he must be referring to Tertullian's *Against All Heresies* (*ANF* 3:649–54). Chapter 4 of this work deals with the gnostic heresies of "Valentinus, Ptolemy and Secundus, Heracleon" and says nothing about the Sabbath directly. Even when Tertullian says about Valentinus, "Of the Law and the prophets some parts he approves, some he disapproves; that is, he disapproves all in rebrobating some" (*ANF* 3:652), he reveals nothing about his own views. Only in chap. 8, where Tertullian condemns Blastus, "who would latently introduce Judaism" (*ANF* 3:654), does Tertullian seem to set gospel against law: "But who would fail to see that evangelical grace is escheated if he recalls Christ to the Law."

61. Cf. *Constitutions of the Holy Apostles* VIII.33 (*ANF* 7:495); Tertullian, *On Prayer* XXIII; Council of Laodicea (363), canon 29.

62. Marginal note by Bavinck: "The Council of Orleans (538), canon 28, prohibited field work (to ensure rest for farmers), but deemed riding, sailing, working, etc., to be lawful."

spectacles, circuses, and theater productions.[63] Emperor Theodosius the Great pronounced every transgressor guilty of sacrilege. Some synods (such as Elvira in 305, Laodicea in 363, and Carthage in 398) followed this line; a synod of Macon in 585, for example, forbade all field work and made it a punishable offense.

Since the Carolingian era, however, Sunday observance has been based on the Decalogue. Alcuin says expressly that for Christians, God has transferred Sabbath observance to the Lord's Day. In 787, Charlemagne introduced a series of prescriptions about Sunday observance with these words: "We enact according to what God has prescribed in his law."[64] Since that time, Sunday observance has been based on the Fourth Commandment.

Thomas Aquinas, for example, says that the Decalogue mentions only the Sabbath and none of the other ceremonies, because the Sabbath calls to mind the creation and the eternal Sabbath rest, but the other ceremonies call to mind only "certain particular favors that were temporal and transitory."[65] Thomas states that Sabbath and New Moon serve to remind human beings of the work of God's creation and governing of the universe, two blessings that are "bestowed in common on the whole human race."[66] In addition, he writes that the Sabbath was "a sign recalling the first creation" and that "its place is taken by the 'Lord's Day,'" which recalls the beginning of the new creature in the Resurrection of Christ."[67] Similarly, "the feast of the Passover gave place to the feast of Christ's Passion and Resurrection"; the Feast of Weeks to the Feast of Pentecost; the New Moon to "Lady Day" (the feast of Mary, "in whom first appeared the light of the sun, which is Christ through an abundance of grace");[68] the Feast of Trumpets to the feasts of the apostles; the Feast of Expiation to the feasts of Martyrs and Confessors; the Feast of Tabernacles to that of the Consecration of a Church;[69] the Feast of Assembly and Collection to the Feast of the Angels, or else the Feast of All Saints.[70]

For Thomas, the Third (which is our Fourth) Commandment describes external worship and is partly moral and partly ceremonial.[71] It is moral

---

63. Thus Jerome, on Isa. 58 and Ezek. 43 and Gal. 4:10. Augustine judged the Sabbath to be ceremonial: *Reply to Faustus the Manichaean* VI.1–2 (*NPNF*[1] 4:167).

64. LO: *statuimus secundum quod et in lege Dominus praecipit.*

65. LO: *aliqua particularia beneficia temporaliter transeuntia*; Aquinas, *ST* Ia IIae q. 100 art. 5 ad 2.

66. LO: *Haec autem duo beneficia sunt communia toti humano generi*; Aquinas, *ST* Ia IIae q. 102 art. 4 ad 10.

67. Aquinas, *ST* Ia IIae q. 103 art. 3 ad 4.

68. LO: *in qua primo apparuit illuminatio solis, id est Christi per copiam gratiae.*

69. LO: *consecratio ecclesiae.*

70. Aquinas, *ST* Ia IIae q. 103 art. 3 ad 4.

71. Aquinas, *ST* Ia IIae q. 122 art. 4.

insofar as it binds us to devote some time of our lives to the things of God; our reason itself demands "a spiritual refreshment by which our mind is refreshed in God."[72] But it is ceremonial insofar as it determines "a special time as a sign of the creation,"[73] and also insofar as it symbolizes Christ's resting in the tomb on the seventh day and it foreshadows "the restful enjoyment of God."[74] Now this commandment was placed in the Decalogue because of the moral element it contains, not because of its ceremonial element. Moreover, the Sabbath is the sign of a universal blessing—namely, the creation—and may therefore be placed in the Decalogue before any other ceremonial precepts. As to the observance and celebration of Sunday, works whereby we serve God are lawful, precisely because we are to refrain from other works of service in order to perform these. For this reason, circumcision was lawful on the Sabbath (John 7:23), priests were allowed to sacrifice in the temple and the like (Matt. 12:5), the ark was allowed to be carried, and we are allowed to teach by word or in writing. But serving sin is always unlawful. Works that are necessary "not only for ourselves but also for our neighbor,"[75] especially those that pertain to the health of the body,[76] are also lawful. Thus, one may eat, defend oneself, pluck heads of grain, or rescue an animal. Observing Sunday instead of the Sabbath is "not by virtue of a law, but by the institution of the church and the custom of Christian people."[77] That is also why it is not figurative,[78] as Sabbath observance was, and why the prohibition of work was not as strict: cooking foods and the like were lawful and were given a more lenient dispensation.

The *Roman Catechism* (*The Catechism of the Council of Trent*)[79] urges Sunday ("Lord's Day") observance and calls upon the civil authorities to support the church in this.[80] The Third Commandment (what the Reformed call the Fourth) differs from the other commandments in that, unlike the others, which are "precepts of natural law and obligatory at all times and unalterable," the Third Commandment "is not fixed and unalterable, but

72. LO: *spiritualis refectio qua mens hominis in Deo reficitur.*

73. LO: *speciale tempus in signum creationis.*

74. LO: *quietem, fruitionis Dei.*

75. LO: *non tantum sibi sed etiam proximo.*

76. LO: *quae ad salutem corporis pertinent.*

77. LO: *non ex vi praecepti legis, sed ex constitutione Ecclesiae et consuetudine populi Christiani.*

78. LO: *figuralis.*

79. Ed. note: The material that follows within quotes is taken from *Catechism of the Council of Trent*, 263–71 (III.iv: "The Third Commandment"). We will cite it as *Roman Catechism.*

80. *Roman Catechism*, 264: "Princes and magistrates are to be admonished and exhorted to lend the sanction and support of their authority to the pastors of the Church, particularly in upholding and extending the worship of God."

is susceptible of change and belongs not to the moral but the ceremonial law."[81] Worship on the Sabbath was required for the people of the Old Covenant but is "no longer obligatory after the death of Christ."[82] Nonetheless, "because the worship of God and the practice of religion, which it comprises, have the moral law as their basis . . . [namely,] the necessity of consecrating some time to the worship of the Deity," the duties of worship "doubtless form part of the moral law."[83] That is why spending a few hours "in those things that pertain to the worship of God"[84] can be found among all peoples. There is a set time for the worship of God, just as there is a set time for sleep and the like. The apostles resolved to observe the first day.[85] According to the *Roman Catechism*, "it pleased the church of God"[86] to change the Sabbath to the "Lord's Day" because "on that day light first shone on the world, so by the resurrection of our Lord on that day, by whom was thrown open to us the gate to eternal life, we were called out of darkness into light."[87] Works for the service of God and works of necessity are lawful, and attending church and listening to the sermon is a duty, as well as giving alms, visiting the sick, and comforting those who mourn.[88]

In fact, Roman Catholic Sabbath practices are quite lax. According to Pruner, prohibited is all servile work[89] (i.e., physical/manual labor for a material purpose) and legal work[90] (i.e., all public legal affairs, such as interrogating witnesses, issuing sentences, etc.)[91] and all communal activities[92] connected with disturbance of the peace (communal activities are such things as recreation, games, etc., which do not directly aim at spiritual goals, but are not simply material goals, either). But the range of the permissible is extensive, including private legal affairs (e.g., making a last will, consulting a lawyer, etc.).

Permitted are all cultural activities[93] that aim at intellectual development (e.g., study), all communal activities (e.g., games), activities that are compatible

81. *Roman Catechism*, 264.
82. *Roman Catechism*, 264.
83. *Roman Catechism*, 264–65.
84. LO: *iis quae ad Dei cultum pertinent*.
85. *Roman Catechism*, 265.
86. LO: *placuit Ecclesiae Dei*.
87. *Roman Catechism*, 267.
88. *Roman Catechism*, 268–70.
89. DO/LO: *alle opera servilia*.
90. LO: *opera forensia*. Ed. note: Bavinck's use of the Dutch qualifier *alle* is missing here because some *opera forensia* are permitted (see next sentence).
91. Pruner, *Lehrbuch der katholischen Moraltheologie*², 313. Ed. note: The details that follow are from the same source.
92. DO/LO: *alle opera communia*.
93. LO: *opera liberalia*.

with a mental focus on higher goods (traveling, shopping, etc.), and all necessary servile work or physical labor. The Roman Catholic Church nowhere states which activities belong to each of these classes, but theologians define writing a book, for example, as a cultural activity, but printing a book as servile activity. Painting by artists and stitching (in tapestry) are cultural activities, but preparing linen and painting by painters is servile work. Sculpting, since it demands too much physical labor, is not permitted. Milling grain is permitted. Moving freight or people by car or ship, annual fairs if traditional, auctions, and so on are permitted. Whether or not an activity makes a profit in no way determines whether it is lawful or unlawful. What makes an activity lawful are such components as piety toward God,[94] mercy toward the neighbor (the sick),[95] and necessity[96] (e.g., of the poor to earn some money, of mothers to do the wash, of tradesmen who have to supply something for a wedding or a funeral, the making of clothes, tools, etc., working in breweries, glass furnaces, etc.). In addition, the priest and any religious official can grant dispensation for anything. Transgressing a commandment is a mortal sin; but the sin is all the greater the more material and physical it is. All the same, if it lasts only a couple of hours, the sin is not so great. Picking flowers, for example, is entirely innocent so long as it does not completely supplant worship. But the commandment to attend the *mass* is very strict; it is mandatory for everyone older than seven. Presence at the *entire* mass is mandatory, with *one* priest, in *body* and *soul*. But again, this is accompanied by all sorts of casuistry. "Entirely"—but if necessary, one may be absent from the beginning of the mass up to and including the Gospel reading, and from the conclusion of the mass (following the consumption of the holy blood). "In body"—that is, whoever hears the mass while being more than thirty paces away, outside the church through the open door, is no longer in compliance, is no longer present in body. "In soul"—but *intentional* or *conscious* hearing is not strictly required; *implicit* or *unconscious* hearing is sufficient; involuntary distractions do not make one culpable.[97] Apart from the mass, there are no commandments to attend other and more church services on Sunday, although that would of course be very good.

The Orthodox Church since Leo III the Isaurian (685–741) and Leo VI the Philosopher (866–912) inherited a stricter view of Sunday.[98]

94. LO: *pietas erga Deum.*
95. LO: *caritas erga proximum.*
96. LO: *necessitas.*
97. LO: *intentio explicata; intentio implicata.*
98. Zöckler, "Sonntagsfeier," 430. Ed. note: Leo III the Isaurian was Byzantine emperor from 717 until 741 and founder of the Isaurian or Syrian dynasty (717–802) (Wikipedia, s.v. "Leo III

Luther said that the Old Testament law about the Sabbath and other days has ceased; for the Christian, every day is a festive day; the church observes the Sabbath and other feast days only for those who are weak, in order to proclaim to them the Word of God.[99] If we were all perfect, we would not need the Sabbath.[100] According to Luther, the Mosaic law has ended for us.[101] The true Sabbath is that we cease from our sins. And a separate Sunday is not commanded but is observed only because nature itself teaches that people must have a day of rest occasionally. Thus, Sunday or Sabbath has continued not because of Moses's commandment but because of our need for it. Otherwise, Saturday would have to be observed.[102] In other words, whoever needs no rest may also work on Sundays.[103] For Luther, this entire subject, the entire organization of religious practice, the use of altars, priestly vestments, and so on, all belong to the *adiaphora*, the things not commanded by God but open to regulation at our discretion.[104]

The *Augsburg Confession* denies that the Sabbath was replaced by Sunday "by appointment of the church," as if the church had the authority to change a commandment in the Decalogue.[105] The same article states that Sunday observance and all such ceremonies have been abolished, although the church may make such ordinances for the sake of good order, as long as they do not bind people's conscience.[106] The entire Mosaic ceremonial ministry has been abolished; the church has appointed a day merely "that the people might know when they ought to come together."[107] To that end the church chose the first day, in order that people might thereby have an example of Christian liberty and know that keeping the Sabbath or any other day is no longer necessary.

The *Lutheran Large Catechism* gives this explanation of the Third (our Fourth) Commandment: "According to its outward meaning [i.e., to abstain from all work], this commandment does not concern us Christians. It is an entirely external matter, like the other regulations of the Old Testament associated with particular customs, persons, times, and places, from all of

---

the Isaurian," https://en.wikipedia.org/wiki/Leo_III_the_Isaurian). Leo VI Sophos (the Wise or the Philosopher) was Byzantine emperor from 886 to 912 (Wikipedia, s.v. "Leo VI the Wise," https://en.wikipedia.org/wiki/Leo_VI_the_Wise).

99. Köstlin, *Theology of Luther*, 1:358.
100. Köstlin, *Theology of Luther*, 1:358.
101. Köstlin, *Theology of Luther*, 2:34–36.
102. Köstlin, *Theology of Luther*, 2:38.
103. Köstlin, *Theology of Luther*, 2:40.
104. Köstlin, *Theology of Luther*, 2:552–53.
105. LO: *institutione Ecclesiae*; Kolb and Wengert, *Book of Concord*, 94–96 (Augsburg Confession, art. 28); J. T. Müller et al., *Christian Book of Concord*, 137–38.
106. Kolb and Wengert, *Book of Concord*, 98–101; J. T. Müller, *Symbolischen Bücher*, 139.
107. LO: *ut sciret populus quando convenire deberet.*

which we are now set free through Christ."[108] We observe feast days "not for the sake of intelligent and well-informed Christians,"[109] who have no need of them, but for two reasons:

(1) For the sake of "common people—man-servants and maid-servants who have gone about their work or trade all week long"—so that they can "retire for a day to rest and be refreshed."

(2) "Second and most important, we observe them so that people will have time and opportunity on such days of rest, which otherwise would not be available, to attend worship services, that is, so they may assemble to hear and discuss God's Word and then to offer praise, song, and prayer to God."[110] Unlike with the Jews, this last purpose is not limited to fixed times, but should be performed daily. That is not possible, however, and for that reason a particular day was chosen and, for a long time now, has become customary in the Christian church. We should continue holding to that, hearing God's Word and teaching the people. Activities that cannot be postponed may be performed. Sunday observance does not consist in doing nothing, but in hearing God's Word.

The Lutheran Gerhard explains the Third Commandment as follows:[111] Morally we celebrate a specific day, ceremonially the seventh day. That day is dedicated to meetings (Lev. 23:3, 7–8, 21, 27), to explaining the Word (Lev. 10:11), and to doing works of mercy (Jesus). The apostles changed the seventh to the first day because

(1) Christ arose on that day;

(2) on that day we commemorate our deliverance, just as Israel commemorated their deliverance out of Egypt; and

(3) Christ's death abolished the Old Testament shadows, including the Sabbath (Col. 2:17).

Works that do not prevent the hallowing of this day are permitted; we have greater freedom now (Matt. 12:1; John 5:8; Luke 14:5). Works of necessity

---

108. LO: *quantum ad externum et crassum illum sensum attinet*; Kolb and Wengert, *Book of Concord*, 397 (Large Catechism, para. 82); J. T. Müller et al., *Christian Book of Concord*, 449.

109. LO: *non propter intelligentes et eruditos christianos*.

110. Kolb and Wengert, *Book of Concord*, 397 (Large Catechism, para. 83–84); J. T. Müller et al., *Christian Book of Concord*, 449–50.

111. Gerhard, *Loci Theologici*, 3:59–60.

are also permitted. In Lutheran countries, consequently, Sunday observance is not very strict.[112] In Germany, says Zöckler, there is too little rather than too much Sunday observance.[113]

A still more lenient view was held by Caspar Schwenckfeld, in *Vom christlichen Sabbath* (1532), and also by Valentin Weigel, both of whom completely spiritualized the Sabbath, declared that we were to forsake sin every day, and saw in it at most a symbol of Christ's resurrection.[114] The Socinians considered the Sabbath to have been abolished, like the ceremonies. God inserted this ceremonial law into the Decalogue only to teach Israel that even the most perfect law was still imperfect and had to be improved by Christ. Sunday observance is not a commandment of Christ but an ancient custom and is therefore permitted. Holding the same view are the Remonstrant Confession and the Remonstrant theologian Episcopius.[115] The Remonstrant *Apologia* is silent about it.[116] The Remonstrant Limborch[117] denies the institution of the Sabbath at creation and states that it is not a natural but a positive (man-made) precept, entirely ceremonial (to serve God alone—that is natural); the Sunday is observed for the sake of good order.[118]

Reformed Debates about Sabbath and Sunday[119]

Zwingli regarded the Sabbath as having been instituted at creation; the ceremonial part has been abolished by Christ, but it remains grounded in love

---

112. Tholuck, *Vorgeschichte des Rationalismus*, 2:120.

113. Zöckler, "Sonntagsfeier," 433. The church orders permit a great deal, are not strict, according to Henke, "Zur Geschichte der Lehre von der Sonntagsfeier," 601; cf. Buchrucker, "Das dritte Gebod im Unterricht," 620–23: the Sunday is not based on a divine command but on the spiritual and inner need of the congregation for a day of worship, etc.

114. Zöckler, "Sonntagsfeier," 431; Caspar Schwenckfeld (ca. 1490–1561) was a German Protestant preacher, writer, and theologian with a spiritualist bent, influenced by Thomas Müntzer and Andreas Karlstadt (Wikipedia, s.v. "Caspar Schwenckfeld," https://en.wikipedia.org/wiki/Caspar_Schwenckfeld). Valentin Weigel (1533–88) was a German theologian, philosopher, and mystical writer, a precursor of later theosophy (Wikipedia, s.v. "Valentin Weigel," https://en.wikipedia.org/wiki/Valentin_Weigel).

115. Episcopius and Remonstrantse Broederschap, *Confession or Declaration of the Ministers or Pastors*, 160–62 (chap. 12.6); Episcopius, "Disputation 36," in *Operum Theologorum, Pars altera*, 2:429–30.

116. Ed. note: This is a reference to Simon Episcopius, *Apologia Pro Confessione sive Declaratione Sententiae eorum, Qui in Foederato Belgio Vocantur Remonstrantes, super Praecipuis Articulis Religionis Christianae contra Censvram Quatuor Professorum Leidensium* (1629).

117. Van Limborch, *Theologia Christiana*, 472–75 (book 5, chap. 28, §§7–17).

118. LO/GrO: *propter/εὐταξία*.

119. According to Paul Henry, Calvin was once accused of wanting to abolish Sunday; see Henry, *Das Leben Johann Calvins*, 2:166.

toward God and neighbor, and it may be moved to another day. Work is also permitted, such as harvesting after divine worship.[120]

Calvin explains the Fourth Commandment by stating that God had three purposes with the Sabbath:

(1) So that Israel would rest and allow God to rest in them; thus they would rest spiritually. The Sabbath is an image of perpetual resting in God, which will be completed only in eternity. On the seventh day people were to meditate on that spiritual resting in God. Moreover, there is no doubt that the ceremonial part was abolished by Christ, who is truth itself (Col. 2:16–17). Superstitious observance of days was therefore disallowed.

(2) So that there would be a set time for hearing the Word and so on.

(3) So that servants could rest.[121]

According to Calvin, purposes 2 and 3 remain valid for us today. Religious meetings are prescribed for us too. All things must be done in order, so there must be one day for this. But "why do we not assemble daily . . . so as to remove distinction of days?" Calvin replies, "If only this had been given us!" But this is impossible because "of the weakness of many . . . and the rule of love does not allow more to be required."[122] So let us obey the order appointed by God. Paul is not opposed to this (Col. 2:16; Rom. 14:5; Gal. 4:10). We do not celebrate Sunday, according to Calvin, as a ceremony that represents a spiritual mystery and obscures the gospel, but as a means to keep order in the church. The Jewish day was abolished, and another day was appointed, which was necessary for the decorum, the order, and the peace of the church. The ancients substituted the first day for the seventh day, because the purpose of the Jewish Sabbath lay especially in Christ's resurrection. Calvin adds that he does not "cling to the number 'seven' so as to bind the church in subjection to it." And, he says, "I shall not condemn churches that have other solemn days for their meetings, provided there be no superstition." All he asks is that "they have regard solely to the maintenance of discipline and good order."[123] The main point is that during all our lives we should rest from our works and God should work in us; next, each one of us should repeatedly apply ourselves to the knowledge of God's works and should maintain the lawful

---

120. For Zwingli, see especially *Huldreich Zwingli's Werke*, 2/1:45–46, 106; see also *Huldrici Zuinglii Opera*, I:12–13, 34, 331; V:9, 26, 258; VI/1:120, 283, 492; VI/2:224.

121. *Institutes*, II.viii.28–34.

122. *Institutes*, II.viii.32.

123. *Institutes*, II.viii.34.

order of the church for hearing the Word and so forth; and finally, we should not oppress our subordinates. It is false to claim that the ceremonial part of this commandment was abolished but its moral part retained, for those who assert this preserve the same sanctity of that day in their hearts. In his commentary on the Fourth Commandment, Calvin explains that resting from our works, that dying spiritually with Christ, rids us of our sins.[124] Nevertheless, in Geneva Sunday was strictly observed with many meetings, and absence from them was punished.[125]

Wolfgang Musculus (1497–1563) says that the Decalogue binds us not as the law of the covenant given to Israel but to the extent that it contains natural law. In the Fourth Commandment the seventh day is now ceremonial, but natural law dictates only that we must devote some time to the worship of God.[126]

Andreas Hyperius (1511–64) says that by replacing the seventh with the first day, the apostles merely altered the commandment in circumstance, not in substance.[127] For the Fourth Commandment commands us to worship God on one of the seven days.

Peter Martyr Vermigli (1499–1562) says that the church is free to specify which day; all ceremonies have something that endures and something that changes—circumcision in relation to baptism, tithes in relation to a pastor's salary, seventh day in relation to first day, and so forth.[128]

Ursinus claims that the ceremonial part in the Fourth Commandment (i.e., the seventh day) was abolished because it was a sign between Yahweh and Israel; but the moral part is that there be some time for public worship, that God may be served, his Word known, and the church maintained.[129] Under the Old Testament the outward, ceremonial Sabbath was on the seventh day, but this changed in the New Testament. "The *new* depends upon the decision and appointment of the church, which for certain reasons has made the choice of the first day of the week, which is to be observed for the sake of

---

124. Ed. note: Bavinck cites this reference as *Commentarii in Libros Mosis in Opera Omnia* (Amsterdam, 1671), 1:485; in translation: Calvin, *Commentaries on the Four Last Books of Moses*, 2:435–36.

125. Kampschulte, *Johann Calvin*, 1:436, 457. Ed. note: In the margins Bavinck added: "Beza (on Apoc. 1:10) had a strict reading and based the Sunday on apostolic and, therefore, divine tradition. Celebrating one day in seven is commanded according to Zanchi and Bucer, according to Turretin, *Institutes of Elenctic Theology*, locus 11, Q. 14."

126. Musculus, *Loci Communes*, 174.

127. LO: *circumstantia*; *substantia*: Hyperius, *Methodi Theologiae*, 56–57.

128. Vermigli, *Loci Communes*, 270–73 (Classis Secundae, locus VII). Ed. note: Bavinck cites this reference as *Loci Communes*, 126, without providing an edition. We have given the page range of Vermigli's discussion of the Fourth Commandment in the first edition.

129. Commentary on Lord's Day 38 of the Heidelberg Catechism, Question 103, in Ursinus, *Commentary on the Heidelberg Catechism*, 557–74; cf. Second Helvetic Confession, chap. 24.

order, and not from any idea of necessity, as if this and no other were to be observed by the church."[130]

Because the Old Testament Sabbath was typical, pointing to the benefits of the Messiah, it is now set aside.[131] But the moral Sabbath (and thus also a ceremonial one in Geneva) continues to bind us—namely, that there must be a certain time to teach God's Word. But which day—Thursday or Saturday or Wednesday—is free. The apostolic church chose the first day.[132] Ursinus refutes the notion that this commandment is immutable because it was given at creation. He argues that Romans 14:5 prohibited merely the esteeming of one day above another under a mistaken notion of devotion or necessity.[133]

In the Netherlands.[134] The Convent of Wesel (1568)[135] said that "as each church sees fit, at least one day in the week shall be set aside for solemn prayer on which a public and solemn confession of guilt shall be made and a humble prayer of forgiveness for the people shall be offered, either before or after the sermon."[136] The Synod of Dort (1574) petitioned the government to forbid "buying, selling, working, drinking, taking a walk, etc., especially on Sundays while there is preaching going on," as well as the "profane and worldly shoutings that accompany buying, selling lost goods, etc., in the churches."[137] The 1618–19 Synod of Dort also addressed the question of the Lord's Day. In the *Acta* of session 14 (November 27, 1618), the Synod urged preaching from the Heidelberg Catechism on Sunday afternoons, however small the crowd (even if only the pastor's own family).[138] It also decided, in order that the common people not be distracted, to request the government

---

130. LO: *pendet ex arbitrio Ecclesiae quae elegit diem primum propter certas causas, et id est observandus ordinis causa, sed sine opinione necessitatis, quasi ab ecclesia oporteat cum observari et non alium*; Ursinus, *Commentary on the Heidelberg Catechism*, 562–63.

131. DO: *afgeschaft.*

132. Ursinus, *Commentary on the Heidelberg Catechism*, 563.

133. LO: *cum opinione cultus vel necessitatis.*

134. Ed. note: A general sourcebook for the various ecclesiastical gatherings in the Low Countries is the five-volume *Kerkelyk Plakaatboek*, prepared by Nikolaas Wiltens et al. A monograph published in 2019 provides a fresh treatment of the Sabbath controversy in the Dutch Reformed churches, making use of the most recent historical scholarship: Dieleman, *The Battle for the Sabbath in the Dutch Reformation.*

135. Ed. note: The Convent of Wesel was a clandestine gathering of leading churchmen from Dutch refugee communities in November 1568 to develop a uniform presbyterian church order; this order shaped the Dutch Reformed Church into the twentieth century. Recent historical research has questioned whether this meeting actually occurred; see Spohnholz, *Convent of Wesel.*

136. *Church Orders of the Sixteenth Century Reformed Churches*, 82 (*Acts of the Convent of Wesel [1568]*, chap. 2, art. 27).

137. *Church Orders of the Sixteenth Century Reformed Churches*, 158 (*Acts of the Provincial Synod of the Churches of Holland and Zeeland, Held in Dordrecht, June 16–28, 1574*, arts. 47 and 48).

138. LO/DO: *imo vel pro solis tantum families suis; ja slechts alleen voor hunne familiën.*

to prohibit all ordinary physical labor and especially games, drinking parties, and other desecrations of the Sabbath.[139] The *Post-Acta*[140] of the Synod (sessions 162–63) states that people are to observe Sunday, Christmas, Easter, and Pentecost (and the days immediately after Christmas, Easter, and Pentecost) and that the government will be asked to use new and stringent edicts to ban the many Sabbath desecrations that are increasing daily.[141] It also instructed a number of professors to have a "friendly conversation"[142] with the churches from Zeeland (from which the question of the necessity of the Sabbath had arisen). This conversation was to lead to a few general rules that both parties could live with until the next national synod.[143] The next session (#164), meeting in the afternoon of the same day, approved the following rules,[144] agreed upon by the professors and "the brothers from Zeeland":[145]

1. The Fourth Commandment contains a ceremonial element and a moral element.

2. The ceremonial element consisted in resting on the seventh day after creation and strict observance of the same day imposed specifically upon the Jewish people.

3. The moral element consisted in setting aside a specific, fixed day for worship,[146] a devout contemplation of which is needed both for rest and for worship.[147]

4. The Sabbath of the Jews having been abrogated, Christians must sanctify the Lord's Day solemnly.

5. This day has always been kept since the time of the apostles.

---

139. *Acta of Handelingen der Nationale Synode*, 24. Ed. note: The Latin text of the *Acta* and an English translation is underway as part of the 400th Anniversary Celebration of the Synod of Dort. A newly edited version of the Latin text has already been published: *Acta et Documenta Synodi Nationalis Dordrechtanae*, vol. 1, *Acta of the Synod of Dordt*; session 14 is on pp. 24–25.

140. Ed. note: The full Synod of Dort, including the international delegates, met in 154 sessions between November 13, 1618, and May 9, 1619. After the departure of the international delegate, the delegates continued their national synod, meeting for an additional 25 sessions (##155–89) from May 13, 1619, through May 29, 1619. The minutes of these additional sessions are known as the *Post-Acta* or *Na-Handelingen* and can be found in *Acta of Handelingen der Nationale Synode*, 934–51.

141. *Acta of Handelingen der Nationale Synode*, 938–41.

142. DO: *vriendelijke conferentie*.

143. *Acta of Handelingen der Nationale Synode*, 940–41.

144. DO: *regelen*.

145. *Acta of Handelingen der Nationale Synode*, 941. Ed. note: The rules that follow are translations of the full text; Bavinck's manuscript significantly abridges them.

146. DO: *een zekere en gezette dag den Godsdienst zij toegeëigend*.

147. DO: *en waartoe zoowel rust als tot den Godsdienst een heilige overdenking er van nodig is*.

6. This day must also be designated for worship so that, except for what is required by love and immediate necessity, people on that same day rest from all servile labor,[148] and also from all such diversions as hinder the practice of worship.[149]

In practice, the situation was woeful. Time and again resolutions and edicts were required to impose Sabbath observance.[150] That is why the churches of Zeeland brought the question of the necessity of Sabbath observance to the Synod of Dort. And the discussion did not cease at that point. Willem Teellinck wrote a tract in the interest of observing the Christian day of rest, and he defended the Synod of Dort.[151] A more lenient view came from Jacob Burs, minister on the island of Tholen, who argued that the activities of sowing, plowing, harvesting, traveling, and so forth were permissible on Sunday.[152] In 1627 Teellinck published his "Urgent Discourse," a jeremiad about the broader

148. DO: *tegenwoordige noodzakelijkheid vereischen.*

149. Thus, stricter than Calvin, but not as strict as Beza.

150. Ed. note: The summary of edicts that follows is taken from Wiltens et al., *Kerkelyk Plakaatboek*. For Zeeland (Feb. 8, 1583): loading, unloading, buying, selling, opening shop before the preaching shall be unlawful, except for seafarers, laborers, etc. (1:703–5); repeated on Jan. 24, 1673 (1:748, 855); also, on the same day: no wedding parties, wakes, or birth celebrations on Sundays, no funerals between church services, no militia drills other than early in the morning, so that no worship service will be missed (1:749). From the General States for the town and bailiwick of Den Bosch in 1680: buying, keeping shop, tavern consumptions are prohibited (1:755); similar prohibitions for the Generality Lands in 1682 (1:759); repeated in 1685 (1:772). (Ed. note: "Generality Lands" [*Generaliteitslandenen*] were territories of the United Provinces of the Netherlands directly governed by the States-General, unlike the seven provinces, which had their own States-Provincial. These territories were mostly in the South and later incorporated into the Provinces of North Brabant, Zeeland, and Groningen.) Infractions were dealt with (1685, 1:774); edicts were renewed in 1707 (1:799). For the Province of Holland in 1694: edicts against drama productions, comedy shows, rope-dancing, sidewalk retailing, hawking fruit, playing fives, ball games, drinking parties (1:791); in 1711: edicts against drama societies and the like (1:802). Cf. Wiltens et al., *Kerkelyk Plakaatboek*, 2:73 (1588), 2:134 (1598), 2:297 (1619), 2:323 (1632).

151. Teellinck, *De rust-tydt ofte tractate.* Cf. Ypeij and Dermout, *Geschiedenis der Nederlandsche Hervormde Kerk*, 3:33–36, appendix of endotes (DO: *Aanteekingeningen*) for pp. 33–36 (nn. 48–52), 15–25 (appendix starts new pagination); Vos, *Geschiedenis der Vaderlandsche Kerk*, 2:5–11; cf. 1:182; cf. Engelberts, *Willem Teellinck*, 113–32. Marginal note by Bavinck: "Godefridus Udemans (1581–1649) also advocated strict observance of the Lord's Day in 1612; see Ernst Willehelm Hengstenberg, *Ueber den Tag des Herrn*, 119."

Ed. note: Bavinck does not specify which of Udemans's writings he had in mind (nor does Hengstenberg), but it clearly was his *The Practice of Faith, Hope, and Love*, published in Dort in 1612; it includes an exposition of the Fourth Commandment that resonates with the teaching of Dort. The work is now available in English translation: Udemans, *The Practice of Faith, Hope, and Love*; the exposition of the Fourth Commandment is found on 281–308.

152. Jacob Burs, *Threnos.* Ed. note: This work, published on the island of Tholen (*Gedruckt binnen Tholen*), is very rare. WorldCat lists only the Ostfrieschische Bibliothek in Emden (Johannes à Lasco Library). Bavinck's awareness of this work is remarkable.

spiritual indifference of Dutch society, which included his own take on the Sabbath controversy of his day.[153] Teellinck found a defender in Voetius.[154] But Burs found a defender in Franciscus Gomarus for the view that the Sabbath was not instituted back in Genesis 2, where it is proleptically announced.[155] Gomarus argues that we read nothing about Sabbath observance by the patriarchs.[156] Exodus 16 does not assume knowledge of the Sabbath (and is also partially proleptic); it says: the Sabbath shall be. Blessing and hallowing the Sabbath presupposes Exodus 16.[157] The proleptic announcement in Genesis 2 expressly has Exodus 16 in view. Furthermore, gentiles were not obligated to observe the Sabbath.[158] It is not mandatory that specifically one of the seven days be observed. But there must be sufficient days for worship,[159] so not just one of a thousand days; and so on. It is likely that the first day was observed by the apostles, but it is not an institution that is binding on us.[160] It has been left up to the church, as was held by Ursinus, Aretius, Zanchius, Simler, Cuchlin, Calvin, and Thomas.[161]

In sum, there were approximately three opinions among the Reformed:

1. *The Sabbath was instituted at creation.* The moral element in the Fourth Commandment is that one of the seven days must be celebrated. The first day was established by the apostles. This was the view of Voetius, Zanchi, Beza, Hyperius, and Junius.[162]

---

153. Teellinck, *Noodwendigh vertoogh*; cf. Ridderus, *De Mensch Gods*, I:271–72, 289–90.

154. Voetius, *Lacrymae crocodilli abstersae*; cf. Voetius, *Selectarum Disputationum Theologicarum*, 3:1227–81.

155. Gomarus, "Investigatio sententiae et originis Sabbathi," in *Opera Theologica Omnia*, 2:256–76. Ed. note: In a marginal note Bavinck claims that "Henke, 'Zur Geschichte der Lehre von der Sonntagsfeier,' 645" says that "Gomarus had a strict view as did Ames, *De sabbatho* [*et die dominico*] (1658); whereas Rivet had a more lenient view." We have not been able to track down the Henke reference, but the full Ames reference is as follows: *Sententia de Origine Sabbati et die Dominico*. Bavinck provided no specific reference for André Rivet but likely had in mind his exposition of the Fourth Commandment (Exod. 20:8–11) in his *Praelectiones Pleniores in Cap. XX Exodi*, 107–23, and the appendix on the Dutch Sabbath Controversy ca. 1633, pp. 123–58.

156. Gomarus, "Investigatio sententiae et originis Sabbathi," 265.

157. Gomarus, "Investigatio sententiae et originis Sabbathi," 265–66.

158. Gomarus, "Investigatio sententiae et originis Sabbathi," 267.

159. LO: *dies sufficientes ad cultum*; Gomarus, "Investigatio sententiae et originis Sabbathi," 263–64, 269–70.

160. Gomarus, "Investigatio sententiae et originis Sabbathi," 271–72.

161. Ed. note: The names that might not be familiar to readers refer to Benedictus Aretius (1505–74), a Swiss Reformed theologian; the references to Simler and Cuchlin are ambiguous— the former could refer to Rudolf Simler (1568–1611) or Johann Wilhelm Simler (1605–72), the latter to Johannes Cuchlinus (1564–1606) or Hermannus Cuchlinus (1586–1625). All were Reformed theologians.

162. Cf. Turretin, *Institutes of Elenctic Theology*, 2:95 (XI.14.xii).

2. *The Sabbath was instituted in Exodus 16 and 20.* The moral element in the Fourth Commandment is only that God must be worshiped at specific times. The apostolic example of observing the first day is not binding. This was the view of Gomarus, Zwingli, Calvin, and Ursinus.

3. *The Sabbath was indeed instituted at creation.* The moral element of the Fourth Commandment is one of the seven days. But whether the first or another of the seven days is left up to the church. This was the view of Rivetus.

So, there were three questions regarding the Fourth Commandment:

1. Was the Sabbath instituted at creation or in Exodus 16 and 20?
2. What is the moral element in the Fourth Commandment?
3. What is the authority of the apostolic example?

Later, in the Netherlands, yet another dispute erupted about the Sabbath.[163] In 1655 Johannes Cocceius expressed his views about the Sabbath. The Sabbath, he argued, was not instituted at creation, but the blessing and hallowing of that day in Genesis 2 meant that on that day God saw that all was perfect and good and that he no longer needed to create anything more, but only had to sanctify and glorify humanity.[164] People had to consecrate themselves every day. But consecrating in the sense of resting and not working was commanded first to Israel and is something ceremonial, typifying the rest obtained by Christ. Today that Sabbath is set aside, and to observe "Sabbath" is once again to consecrate every day.[165] The dispute that arose then differed from the earlier disagreement between Gomarus and Voetius. For them it was about the origin of the Sabbath and what was ceremonial in the Fourth Commandment, but now the issue involved the Fourth

163. Ypeij and Dermout, *Geschiedenis der Nederlandsche Hervormde Kerk*, 2:472–73.
164. Cocceius, *Summa Theologiae*, 261–68 (chap. 21).
165. Cocceius, *Summa Theologiae*, 581–83 (chap. 55:6–7). In the ecclesiastical battle that ensued, Cocceius was supported by Abraham van Heyden (1597–1678) and opposed by Andreas Essenius (*Dissertatio de Perpetuâ Moralitate Decalogi* [1658]) and Johannes Hoornbeeck (*Heyliging van Godts naam, ende dag* [1659]; *Nader Bewering van des Heeren dags heyliginge* [1659]). Cocceius responded to Essenius in *Indagatio naturae Sabbati et quietis Novi Testamenti* (1658). Ed. note: Bavinck claims that Hoornbeeck would rather have seen the Sabbath question dealt with in Latin (*Nader Bewering*, 11). But this seems counterintuitive to the fact that Hoornbeeck published his polemic against Cocceius in Dutch rather than the academic Latin. Historian Jonathan Israel observes, "Voetius' ally at Leiden, Johannes Hoornbeeck (1617–66), in 1655 published a Dutch-language tract which was, in effect, an appeal to the public and the Church, against Cocceius, over the heads of the university" (Israel, *Dutch Republic*, 662, cited in Carmichael, *Continental View*, 98).

Commandment as a whole. Because Cocceius had contended that it was entirely ceremonial, this time the issue was about consecrating the day, about whether to rest and spend a specific day without doing any work. Thus, the issue now was about the Fourth Commandment *in its entirety* and about *observing* the day of rest. Therefore, in addition to those mentioned above, two more questions were raised:

4. Is the Fourth Commandment entirely ceremonial? and
5. Must the day of rest be observed by not doing any work?

Cocceius was in fact leaning toward the Socinian view. In 1659, the government prohibited the dispute among the professors.[166] In 1665 the controversy erupted once more when Utrecht professor Frans Burman (1628–79) preached about the Fourth Commandment in a Cocceian manner and was opposed by Essenius, Lodenstein, and others. The government prohibited the dispute in 1669.[167] This lenient Cocceian view of the Sabbath returns with a vengeance in Jean de Labadie (1610–74) and Anna Maria van Schurman (1607–78),[168] who also argued that the observance of a special day was not prescribed for the Christian, but that all deeds of the believer are deeds of worship; daily work does not need to be set aside on Sunday, provided the true Sabbath attitude is in the heart.[169]

In the seventeenth century, the same controversy that raged in the Netherlands was also under discussion in Scotland and England. The strict doctrine of Sabbath observance arose among the Puritans in their struggle against Roman Catholic worship practices in the Anglican Church. Voetius lists several who held this stricter view:[170] William Whitaker (1548–95),[171] Robert Rollock (1555–99),[172] William Perkins (1558–1602),[173] George Downame (ca. 1563–1634),[174] Andrew Willet (ca. 1561–1621),[175] Gilbert Primrose (ca.

---

166. Wiltens et al., *Kerkelyk Plakaatboek*, 2:377.
167. Ypeij and Dermout, *Geschiedenis der Nederlandsche Hervormde Kerk*, 3:33–35, "Appendix," 19–25 (nn. 48–51); also Koelman, *De historie van den Christelyken Sabbath*; cf. Koelman, *Het ambt en de pligten der ouderlingen en diakenen*, 269–76.
168. Ed. note: On Jean de Labadie and Anna Maria van Schuurman, see *RE*, 1:299–301.
169. Ritschl, *Geschichte des Pietismus*, 229, 253, 269; Zöckler, "Sonntagsfeier," 432.
170. Voetius, *Selectarum Disputationum Theologicarum*, 2:1239.
171. Whitaker, *Disputation on Holy Scripture*, 564–610 (question 6, chap. 12).
172. Rollock, *In epistolam Sancti Pauli Apostoli ad Colossenses*, 138–45 (on Col. 2:16–17).
173. Perkins, *Catechesis*, 687–92; Perkins, *Case of Conscience*, book 2, chap. 16.
174. Downame, *Abstract of the Duties Commanded*, on the Fourth Commandment.
175. Ed. note: Bavinck's own note reads: "*Synopsis papismi*, 426, 431?" This work, written by Willet, was first published in 1594; a ten-volume edition was published in 1852 (see bibliography). We were unable to track Bavinck's reference (note his own question mark).

1580–1642),[176] Thomas Cartwright (1534–1603),[177] William Fulke (1538–89),[178] John Weemes of Lothoquar (Scotland, ca. 1579–1636),[179] and many others.[180] But many opponents also advocated a more lenient observance.[181]

The strict party won the day at the Westminster Assembly: the Lord's Day must be kept holy as the Christian Sabbath to the end of time.[182] It consists in abstaining from all worldly employments, thoughts, and words and in public and private "exercises of divine worship" throughout the day. Similarly in the larger catechism of the Westminster Assembly, the Fourth Commandment requires that the Sabbath must be observed "throughout the entire day."[183] In 1618 James I issued a national *Declaration of Sports* (also known as the *Book of Sports*) listing the sports and recreations permitted on Sundays and holy days.[184] This declaration, which permitted certain popular recreations on Sunday, was defended by several but also condemned by many.[185]

176. Primrose, *La trompette de Sion*, 193–98.

177. Cartwright, *Confutation of the Rhemists Translation*, 370 (Rom. 14:5), 439 (1 Cor. 16:8), 479 (Gal. 4:10). Ed. note: There is one additional reference that should be added here: p. 597 (Heb. 4:4).

178. Fulke, *Confutation of the Rhemish Testament* (1834), 184–85 (Rom. 14), 231 (1 Cor. 16), 250 (Gal. 4). Ed. note: Bavinck combined the references to Cartwright and Fulke and referenced the Scripture passages to both; Fulke's work was originally published in 1582.

179. Weemes, *Christian Synagogue*, 85–92 (chap. 5, section 1).

180. It was against the testimony of these writers that an anonymous writer penned *Diatribe Angl. adversus Fr. Whitum* asserting that this was the doctrine of the Church of England. Ed. note: Bavinck also added a marginal note reference to John Forbes of Corse, *Theologia Moralis*, 75–84.

181. For example, Thomas Broad (ca. 1577–1635), Francis White (ca. 1564–1638), Christopher Dow, David Primerose (ca. 1600–ca. 1665), Gilbert Ironside the elder (1588–1671). Ed. note: Bavinck only provided authors' names; here are some of the key works: Thomas Broad, *Tractatus de Sabbatho* (1627); Francis White, *A Treatise of the Sabbath-Day* (1635); White, *An Examination and Confutation of a Lawlesse Pamphlet* (1637); Christopher Dow, *A Discourse of the Sabbath and the Lord's Day* (1636); David Primerose, *A Treatise of the Sabbath and the Lord's Day* (1636); Gilbert Ironside, *Seven Questions of the Sabbath Briefly Disputed* (1637).

182. Westminster Confession of Faith, 21.7 (ed. note: in Dennison, *Reformed Confessions of the 16th and 17th Centuries*, 4:259–60).

183. LO: *per totum diem*; Niemeyer, *Collectio Confessionum*, appendix ("Puritan Symbols"; LO: *Puritanorum libri symbolici*), 73–75, 105. Ed. note: The references are to the Westminster Larger Catechism, qq. 115–21 (also in Dennison, *Reformed Confessions of the 16th and 17th Centuries*, 4:327–29), and to the Westminster Shorter Confession, qq. 58–62 (Dennison, *Reformed Confessions of the 16th and 17th Centuries*, 4:361–62).

184. Ed. note: This declaration was issued for only Lanchashire in 1617 and extended to the nation in 1618. James's son, Charles I, reissued it in 1633. The text of the declaration is available at https://web.archive.org/web/20041204142451/http://www.wwnorton.com/nael/17century/topic_3/sports.htm; Wikipedia, s.v. "Declaration of Sports," https://en.wikipedia.org/wiki/Declaration_of_Sports).

185. It was defended by White, Dow, and others (see n. 181 above); condemned by Bownde, Bratourne, Peter Heylin, and others. Milton too, in his *Dies dominica* of 1639, taught the divine institution of the Sunday. See Milton, *Treatise on Christian Doctrine*.

The strict practice penetrated deeply into the consciousness and life of the Scottish and English people and continues to this day. Not until recent times has a softening and weakening occurred, and state legislation has given greater freedom in Sunday observance. Just as in the early church, in connection with the *Apostolic Constitutions* and the Ebionites, and just as at the time of the Reformation, in connection with a sect in Bohemia and Hungary, so too in the seventeenth century, so-called Sabbatarians became active in England. In the eighteenth century, one such sect was founded by Joanna Southcott (or Southcote; 1750–1814). Southcott passed herself off as the Bride of the Messiah and, with a view to the imminent return of Christ, pressed for the Jewish celebration of the Sabbath. Joanna believed that at the age of sixty-five she would give birth to the true Messiah, but she did not deliver, so she fraudulently substituted a child. The deception was discovered, and she died in 1814 of edema.[186] A sect of this kind arose in the seventeenth century as well; the Bampfield-Mumford Sabbatarians, founded in 1671, included John Bunyan, who favored a more lenient view, and John Milton.[187] Only recently have many in England wanted freedom from, and even abolition of, the Sunday as a strict Sabbath. A Sunday League was organized on July 2, 1875, which desired to have popular amusements—such as museums, aquariums, gardens, and so on—open to the public on Sundays; and Darwinists like Huxley, Carpenter, and Tyndall gave lectures on Sundays.[188] As in England, so in America, there is strict Sunday observance; the state still strongly upholds Sunday rest.[189]

Accordingly, since the previous century there has been a growing crusade against Sunday observance on the part of unbelievers. Rationalism could recognize Sunday at best as a day of relaxation, for going out and admiring God's goodness in nature, but it preached the churches empty and robbed the day of its holiness.[190] The French Revolution drew the consequence from this in a frightful way. In October 1793 it introduced a new calendar that was held to have begun on September 22, 1792; it lasted until December 21, 1802, and was officially rescinded on January 1, 1806. Each month had thirty days,

---

186. Reudecker, "Sabbatharier," 166–67.

187. Zöckler, "Sonntagsfeier," 431–32; see Milton, *Treatise on Christian Doctrine*, 226–30 (book I, chap. 10); 600–612 (book II, chap. 7).

188. Zöckler, "Sonntagsfeier," 433.

189. Marginal note by Bavinck: "Spener defends Sunday observance as commanded. Other Pietists like Stryk, *De jure Sabbathi* (1702), and Wagner were more lenient (Henke 649). Zinzendorf also taught a more lenient view (651). Mosheim did not consider Sunday observance commanded but grounded in nature (652)."

190. Ed. note: See *RD*, 2:432–35, where Bavinck contrasts rationalism's understanding of humanity itself as the goal of creation (*Selbstzweck*) and the biblical view that God's glory (and Sabbath) are the goal of creation.

arranged in three sets of ten each.[191] The five remaining days in the year (six during leap years) were called "complementary days"[192] or *Sansculottides* and were given over to festivals.[193] The Christian religion was set aside,[194] and the worship of Reason was introduced, soon to be replaced, in March 1794, by the Festival of the Supreme Being (restored again by the National Convention). To be sure, in 1806 Napoleon restored order and peace, legislation (Code Napoléon), higher and elementary education, religion, and so on. But unbelief remained, and so did opposition to the Sabbath. All of them—liberals, communists, and socialists—have worked day and night to remove Sunday observance from the consciousness of the people, to convert Sunday into an ordinary day on which work was not prohibited and rest was approved only for physical well-being. Modernists have emptied the churches through their preaching. Sunday laws have been abolished or are not enforced. The mail, the telegraph, railways, ferry services, restaurants, parties, meetings, theater productions, concerts, balls, and newspapers have banished Sunday observance completely from public life.

But people's eyes were gradually opened for the pit that had been dug. Oort acknowledges that the tenacity of the Jews must be ascribed especially to their Sabbath.[195] Even more strongly, Lord Macaulay said that the greatness of England is owed chiefly to the working classes who derived their strength and courage from the centuries-old custom of resting on the seventh day.[196] Consequently, a reaction has set in against the dissolution of Sunday as a day of rest. This reaction comes from two sides: Christian concern and humanitarian interests.

(1) From the side of Christians who were zealous for Sunday observance. In Germany that movement began especially after 1848, when Wichern incorporated Sunday observance in his program of domestic missions.[197] In

---

191. LO: *decadi*.

192. FO: *jours complémentaires*.

193. Ed. note: The term *sans-cullotes* (= without breeches) referred to "the common people of the lower classes in late 18th-century France" who were the driving force behind the French Revolution (Wikipedia, s.v. "Sans-culottes," https://en.wikipedia.org/wiki/Sans-culottes). The individual days were dedicated, respectively, to the celebration of talent (1), labor (2), policy (3), honors (4), convictions (5), and "Revolution Day" (6; every leap year) (Wikipedia, s.v. "Sansculottides," https://en.wikipedia.org/wiki/Sansculottides).

194. DO: *afgeschaft*.

195. Oort, *De laatste eeuwen van Israels volksbestaan*.

196. Ed. note: Bavinck cites no source for this reference to the British Whig historian Thomas Babington Macaulay (1800–1859), author of the five-volume *The History of England* (1848).

197. Zöckler, "Sonntagsfeier," 433. Ed. note: Johann Hinrich Wichern (1808–81) was a founder of the Domestic (or Home) Mission movement in Germany (German: *innere Mission*). See his *Die innere Mission der deutschen evangelischen Kirche*.

September 1849 a *Kongress für innere Mission* was established in Witten-berg, which sought to carry out this point in particular. Since then, countless meetings, treatises, and addresses have dealt with this. In 1850, appeals were made to the government, to the people, to the captains of industry, and to the large landowners. After the campaign died down in the years 1860–70, it revived after 1874, in part as a result of the *Kulturkampf*.[198] At the 1875 congress for domestic missions in Dresden, Sunday observance was a hot topic. In Germany and Switzerland several associations were formed, which joined together in an International Congress for the Observance of Sunday.[199] From Germany the movement spread to Paris, where, in 1883, a *comité* was set up. Hengstenberg[200] sided completely with the Augsburg Confession and opposed British practices, as did E. Haupt.[201]

The grounds among Christians for Sunday observance vary greatly: (a) the authority of the church; (b) the example of the apostles; (c) humanitarian and religious utility; (d) love of God and neighbor; (e) the holiness of each and every day; (f) the authority of God.

Only the last ground is sufficient.[202]

(2) From a humanitarian standpoint. Initially, the day of rest was mocked, as Juvenal and Seneca did.[203] So did many others at various times: Sunday was a lazy day, its observance was a waste of one-seventh of life (Seneca); it was the cause of poverty, idleness, laziness, and so on. But people have since

---

198. Ed. note: *Kulturkampf* (culture struggle) is the German term referring to the conflict between the Kingdom of Prussia, headed by Otto von Bismarck, and the Roman Catholic Church over control of education and church appointments. This conflict took place in the 1870s.

199. Ed. note: The association in Switzerland was headed by Alexander Lombard and in Germany by, among others, General Superintendent W. Baur. Publications included the *Bulletin Dominicae*, the *Acts* of the various congresses, and after 1877, the monthly journal *Monatschrift für innere Mission mit Einschluss der Diakonie, Diaspora-Pflege, Evangelisation und gesamten Wohlthätigkeit*, initiated by Th. Schäfer.

200. Ed. note: Bavinck is referring to Hengstenberg, *Über den Tag des Herrn*, and has in view especially Henke, "Zur Geschichte der Lehre von der Sonntagsfeier."

201. Haupt, *Der Sonntag und die Bibel*.

202. Chambers, "Substitutes for the Fourth Commandment," 480; *Acts/Proceedings of the Congress for the Observance of Sunday*.

203. Juvenal's comments are found in *Satires* XIV.96–106:

> Some who have had a father who reveres the Sabbath, worship nothing but the clouds, and the divinity of the heavens, and see no difference between eating swine's flesh, from which their father abstained, and that of man; and in time they take to circumcision. Having been wont to flout the laws of Rome, they learn and practise and revere the Jewish law, and all that Moses committed to his secret tome, forbidding to point out the way to any not worshipping the same rites, and conducting none but the circumcised to the desired fountain. For all which the father was to blame, who gave up every seventh day to idle-ness, keeping it apart from all the concerns of life. (*Juvenal and Persius*, LCL 91:270–73)

Seneca's comments are cited by Augustine, *City of God* VI.11 (*NPNF¹* 2:120–21); Reudecker, "Sabbatharier," 167.

retreated to some extent from that standpoint. The socialist Proudhon wrote *Sunday Observance in regard to Public Hygiene, Morality, Family, and Civic Life*.[204] And socialism has made it mandatory to pay attention to providing rest for the working classes. Austria enacted a law already in 1884 regulating a normal workday (eleven hours?), a day of rest, and regulating labor provided by women and children.[205] Last year (1885) these topics were debated in the German Reichstag.[206] Catholics, Conservatives, Socialists, and Liberals were all convinced of the need for improvements on this point and made proposals. Bismarck took the position of the Liberals, who were skeptical about the feasibility of the proposals which were sent to a committee that reported first about Sunday rest. Bismarck decided an inquiry was called for, which is currently taking place,[207] along with organizing meetings where employers and employees can state their views about (1) where work is being done on Sundays and holidays, (2) why work is necessary on those days, (3) what the consequences would be if that work were to be prohibited, and (4) whether such a prohibition would be workable.[208]

Holy Days

In addition to the Sabbath, ancient Israel also had feasts[209] that were arranged in terms of the number seven, that partly coincided with cosmic phenomena, and that were divinely instituted for memorializing God's deeds of deliverance:

1. *New Moon* (Num. 28:11–15), among which the first day of Tishri, the seventh month, later New Year's Day, headed the list as the "day of the trumpet blast [Feast of Trumpets]."[210]

204. Cf. Proudhon, *De l'utilité de la célébration du dimanche*. Ed. note: Bavinck cites the German translation of this French text, *Die Sonntagsfeier aus dem Gesichtspunkte des öffentlichen Gesundheitswesens* (1850). So far as we are able to determine, this work has not been translated into English.

205. Ed. note: Bavinck may have taken this from Emants, "Normale werkday," 114.

206. DO: *ten vorige jare*. Ed. note: This sentence is significant for dating the manuscript; it implies that Bavinck wrote it in 1886.

207. Ed. note: Likely in 1886.

208. Emants, "Normale werkday," 99–100. Ed. note: This article provides a fairly detailed account of the debate in the Reichstag and the specifics of laws considered and passed. Comparisons are made with other countries: Switzerland, England, Austria, North America. What is also clear is the disagreement among Christians themselves. Emants points to the fundamental difference (which Bavinck had noted above) between those who wanted to ensure a Sunday rest as obedience to God's command and those who saw it only as a benefit for human health and well-being (p. 113).

209. See Oehler and Delitzsch, "Feste der alten Hebräer."

210. Ed. note: Bavinck is citing Oehler and Delitzsch, "Feste der alten Hebräer," 428, who translate the Hebrew יוֹם תְּרוּעָה (*yom teru'ah*) as "Tag des Trompetengeschmetters." Other

2. *Passover* in Nisan (the first month, according to Exod. 12:2), to be celebrated on the eve of the fourteenth day, with the seven-day Feast of Unleavened Bread (from the fifteenth to the twenty-first of Nisan), to commemorate the sparing and saving of Israel when the Lord slew Egypt's firstborn.

3. *Feast of Weeks* or Pentecost, to be observed on the fiftieth day or seven weeks after offering the sheaf of barley to the Lord (on the second day of the Feast of Unleavened Bread—i.e., 16 Nisan), when harvesters first put the sickle to the grain (Deut. 16:9). This feast lasted one day and was called the Feast of Weeks (Exod. 34:22), the Feast of the Harvest (Exod. 23:16), and the Day of the Firstfruits (Num. 28:26).

4. *Feast of Tabernacles*, to be celebrated from 15–21 Tishri, with an eighth day as a holy convocation[211] on 22 Tishri (Lev. 23:36), as a commemoration of the blessing given by God in the harvesting of all the produce of the land, of wine, and so on, and of God's protection experienced during the exodus from Egypt.

5. *The Day of Atonement.*[212] On the tenth day of the seventh month, a "Sabbath of Sabbaths"[213] was observed in connection with the atonement of all sins and uncleanness in Israel, in the holy place.

6. *The Sabbath Year*, in which the land was supposed to rest; and the *Year of Jubilee*, the 7 × 7th year—thus, the fiftieth, the year of releasing all properties back to their original owner and of rest for the land.

Of all these feasts, only the Day of Atonement was on a par with the Sabbath; on that day as well, all work had to cease. In addition, the first and the seventh days of Unleavened Bread (Lev. 23:6–8), the first and the last days of the Feast of Tabernacles, and the New Moon were rest days or Sabbath days, but not all work was forbidden on these days, but only ordinary work,[214] so that, for example, lighting a fire or preparing food was lawful (Lev. 23:7–8, 21, 25, 35–36; cf. Num. 28:18–19). For this reason, only the Sabbath and the Day of Atonement are called "Sabbath of Sabbaths"[215] (Lev. 23:3, 32).

---

relevant Old Testament passages not mentioned by Bavinck: Lev. 23:23–25; Num. 29:1–6; 1 Sam. 20:5, 18, 24, 27; Amos 8:5.

211. HO: עֲצֶרֶת.

212. HO: יוֹם הַכִּפֻּרִים.

213. HO: שַׁבַּת שַׁבָּתוֹן. Ed. note: English translations miss the duplication "sabbath of sabbaths" but try to capture the extra dimension of the day in other ways. Thus, the term "sabbath of sabbaths" in Lev. 16:31 is rendered "sabbath of complete rest" (NRSV); "Sabbath of solemn rest" (ESV). But the KJV's "sabbath of rest" and the NIV's "day of sabbath rest" seem hardly to do justice to this extra dimension.

214. HO: מְלֶאכֶת עֲבֹדָה.

215. HO: שַׁבַּת שַׁבָּתוֹן.

After the exile, several feasts were added.[216]

1. *Days of mourning* are mentioned already in Zechariah 7:3, 5 and 8:19:

   (a) the ninth day of the fourth month, to commemorate the invasion of
       Jerusalem by the Chaldeans (2 Kings 25:3; Jer. 52:6–7);
   (b) the tenth day of the fifth month, to commemorate the destruction
       of the city and the temple (Jer. 52:12–13; cf. 2 Kings 25:8, where the
       seventh day is mentioned);
   (c) a certain unspecified day in the seventh month, to commemorate the
       murder of Gedaliah (2 Kings 25:25; Jer. 41:1–2); and
   (d) the tenth day of the tenth month, to commemorate the beginning of
       the siege of Jerusalem (2 Kings 25:21; Jer. 52:4).

2. Next, the *New Year* was moved from Nisan (Exod. 12:2) to 1 Tishri; perhaps this celebration on 1 Tishri may have been a pre-Mosaic custom,[217]
   a civil year. Sometimes in Scripture the year is reckoned to begin with
   Tishri (at the Flood, in Exod. 23:16; 34:22), likewise in determining the
   Sabbath Year (Lev. 25:4) and the Year of Jubilee (Lev. 25:9–10; Ezek.
   45:18–20 names them both).

3. Another new feast was *Purim* (lots; Esther 9:24–26), observed on two
   days, 14 and 15 Adar.

4. *A Feast of Thanksgiving* on 13 Adar, for the victory over the Syrian
   commander Nicanor in 161 BC, according to 1 Maccabees 7:49 and
   2 Maccabees 15:36–37.

5. The *Feast of the Dedication of the Temple*[218] (John 10:22), instituted
   by Judas Maccabeus in 164 BC. It lasted eight days, from 25 Chislev
   on. This was also called the Feast of Light or Lights, which took its
   name from the fact that all the houses and synagogues were illuminated,
   perhaps to commemorate the relighting of the lamps in the temple
   (1 Macc. 4:50).

6. The *Feast of the Recaptured City*, according to 1 Maccabees 13:50–52, to
   commemorate the recapture of the Acra in Jerusalem on the twenty-third

---

216. See Oehler and Delitzsch, "Feste der späteren Juden." Ed. note: In the following list,
the numbering of items 1–11 has been added by the editor for clarity and readability. They form
one contiuous paragraph in the original.

217. Ed. note: Bavinck takes the reference to "Josephus, *Antiquitates Iudaicae*, I.3.3" from
Oehler and Delitzsch, "Feste der späteren Juden," 542. Using current annotation: Josephus,
Jewish Antiquities I.80–81 (LCL 242:36–39).

218. GrO: τὰ ἐγκαίνια.

day of the second month, 141 BC. This feast does not appear to have existed very long.

7. The *Judith Feast* is mentioned only in the appendix to the book of Judith in the Vulgate. There was also the *Herod Feast*, in memory of Herod's death, which is not mentioned by Josephus.

8. The *Feast of Wood* fell on 3 Elul, on which wood was collected for the temple; Nehemiah already took steps toward that (Neh. 10:35; cf. 13:31).

9. The *Feast of Baskets* is mentioned by Philo in a newly discovered appendix to his *Septen*. It was not a standing holy day, but referred to the solemn offering of the firstfruits, as commanded in Deuteronomy 26.

10. Later, the seventeenth day of the fourth month was turned into a day of fasting, to commemorate the assault on Jerusalem by Titus; and the ninth day of the fifth month likewise, to commemorate the destruction of the temple.

11. The *Feast of the Rejoicing of the Law* was observed on 23 Tishri, when the fifty-four *parashot*[219] of the Torah were read in public.

In addition, changes were made to the biblical feasts. Among other changes, Sabbaths that were part of the feasts (except for the Day of Atonement) were replaced by two feast days, on account of the uncertainty of determining the new moon. Pentecost, New Year's Feast, and so on were celebrated for two days.[220]

Christian Feasts

At first, Christians came together daily (Acts 2:46), but eventually that was not workable. This led to gathering on Sunday. Alongside Sunday, some people continued to observe the Sabbath.[221] In the church of Rome people fasted on the Sabbath, which gave rise early on to dissension with Eastern Christians who observed the Sabbath. Innocent I commanded fasting on the Sabbath, and Gregory the Great called the prohibition of work on the Sabbath a work

219. HO: פָּרְשָׁה (= portion). Ed. note: The Hebrew term *parashah* refers to a section of a biblical book in the Masoretic Text, separated by spaces in the Torah scrolls (Wikipedia, s.v., "Parashah," https://en.wikipedia.org/wiki/Parashah).

220. Bavinck's marginal references: "Voetius, *Select. disp.*, 3:1284–85; K. A. Heinrich Kellner, *Heortologie*³."

221. Ed. note: At this point Bavinck adds a parenthetical reference to the *Apostolic Constitutions* (*Constitutiones Apostolorum*) but cites no specific passage. The obligation to worship on "the day of the resurrection of the Lord" is found in book VII, chap. 33; book V, chapters 13–20 are a "Catalogue of the Feasts of the Lord" and liberally make use of Sabbath language (*ANF* 7:387–90, 469).

of the antichrist. In this way Sabbath observance disappeared completely, and the Sabbath became a day of fasting. In addition to the Sabbath, Wednesday and Friday soon came to be observed with a *half*-fast—to commemorate the Sanhendrin's decision to kill Jesus (Matt. 26:3–4) and Christ's crucifixion. Probably for this reason, Wednesday was called "fourth day of rest," Friday the "sixth day of rest" (or "preparation"),[222] but these names are also explained differently.

But in addition to these days, *feast days* soon arose. The oldest is *Pascha* (the *Feast of Christ's Death*).[223] First Corinthians 5:7 shows that Christ was already regarded as the true paschal lamb (cf. also John 19:33 and the "Lamb"[224] of Rev. 5:6–7, and the "Lamb"[225] of 1 Pet. 1:19 [or does this refer to Isa. 53?]), although that still does not prove that the Corinthian church already celebrated Easter[226] as is claimed by some.[227] It is not certain just when the Easter feast[228] originated. But if on Wednesdays and Fridays the passion of Christ was being remembered already every week, then it was not long before it was decided to observe the week of the anniversary of the great primeval week of salvation.[229] In the second and third centuries, this Pascha[230] was exclusively a passion feast[231] (while Christ's resurrection and accompanying events were commemorated during the fifty-day Pentecost, distinct from Easter).[232] It was observed during the passion week, especially on the Friday before resurrection day, by means of a strict fast, sometimes until Sunday morning, without celebrating the Lord's Supper and with the preparation during the week prior to the passion week, from Monday onward. But since the fourth century the Pascha began

222. LO: *feria quarta*; *feria sexta*; GrO: παρασκευή.

223. Georg Eduard Steitz, "Passah, christliches." Ed. note: Although the term *Pascha* (Greek: Πάσχα) in English-language usage is ordinarily used by Eastern (Orthodox) Christians for Easter, we are retaining it in what follows, whenever Bavinck himself uses the word, to honor Bavinck's own discussion, which is primarily (but not exclusively) about our Lord's death. We will also sometimes use *Pascha* to translate the Dutch *paasfeest* (which can refer to Easter or Passover) or *Pasen* (which usually refers to Easter) and restrict our use of "Easter" to passages where the reference is clearly to our Lord's resurrection. We will provide the Dutch original for our translations when we use *Pascha* for words other than Bavinck's own use of the term.

224. GrO: ἀρνίον.

225. GrO: ἀμνός.

226. DO: *paasfeest*.

227. Ed. note: Bavinck provides as an example the single name of "Lechler." He likely had in mind Gotthard Victor Lechler (1811–88), a historian of early Christianity and author of *The Apostolic and Post-Apostolic Times*. Discussion of the early Christian participation in Jewish feasts, including the Sabbath, can be found in 1:48–67.

228. DO: *paasfeest*.

229. GO: *grosse Urwoche des Heils*; G. Steitz, "Passah, christliches," 271.

230. DO: *Pasen*.

231. GO: *Passionsfeir*.

232. DO: *Pasen*.

to include the resurrection and began to be referred to as the "crucifixion Pascha" and the "resurrection Pascha."[233] As well, the preparation days were extended from five (Monday through Friday) to forty,[234] and as such, they became a preparation for the Lord's Supper on Easter Sunday. Thereby the feast acquired a different character; in fact, the term "Pascha" was transferred in its entirety to that Sunday, and the date of the resurrection was now calculated differently—namely, on the Sunday immediately following 14 Nisan. Hence, if 14 Nisan fell on a Saturday, the resurrection feast was celebrated the very next day (Sunday; this even though there was no day in between when Jesus lay in the tomb). The term "crucifixion Pascha"[235] disappeared entirely. Pascha became the feast of the resurrection and was solemnly celebrated on the eve before the resurrection by a vigil, a torch parade, and so on, by baptism of catechumens, consecration of the baptismal water, consecration of the Paschal candle (i.e., Christ himself, whose light begins to shine into the darkness of death) as the new fire. (The German word *Ostern* comes from the Anglo-Saxon *Eostra*, Ostara, the goddess of the dawn, of the rising sun; other pagan practices are Easter bonfires and Easter eggs.) The eight days after Easter were now called "eight days of the newborn,"[236] the eight days of the neophytes who at this time continued to wear their white baptismal gowns. They take them off the following Sunday (from which we get White Sunday or Whitsunday;[237] later it was called *Quasimodogeniti*, which comes from 1 Pet. 2:2, "like newborn infants"). In the early days, festivities lasted the whole week—according to the Council of Mainz (813) only the first four days, and according to the Council of Constance (1094) only three days. Thus, as the forty days before Easter were days of sorrow, Easter with the fifty days that followed, Pentecost,[238] were days of joy.

Pentecost at first (with Tertullian) referred to all those fifty days,[239] when fasting was prohibited, prayers had to be said while standing, theater and circus were forbidden, hallelujahs had to be sung repeatedly, and the Acts of the Apostles had to be read during the worship service. But gradually (already beginning in the fourth century at the Council of Elvira, AD 305) Pentecost became the name of the fiftieth day. From early on Pentecost was highly esteemed as a grand feast. The night before Pentecost was spent in keeping vigil and fasting; baptisms were administered as well. The week after Easter was

233. GrO: πάσχα σταυρώσιμον and πάσχα ἀναστάσιμον.
234. LO: *quadragesimo*.
235. GrO: πάσχα σταυρώσιμον.
236. LO: *octo dies neophytorum*.
237. LO: *Dominica in albis*.
238. GrO: πεντηκοστή.
239. Zöckler, "Pfingsten," 567–68.

at first celebrated in its entirety but later limited—after the eighth century to four, then to three, and in the Protestant churches to two days. In the Middle Ages, the festivities were accompanied by many customs—for instance, a dove coming down from the clouds and decorating the church with green branches, perhaps in imitation of the Old Testament Feast of Weeks. In England the name for Pentecost is Whitsunday, on account of the white clothes that are worn.

The *Feast of Epiphany* is the feast of manifestation[240] (Titus 2:11; 3:4), and in the Eastern Orthodox Church until the time of Chrysostom, this feast inaugurated the cycle of Christian feasts.[241] It was linked particularly to Christ's baptism, since he was then manifested to humanity for the first time. There was as yet no separate feast of the birth of Christ (Christmas); that was celebrated together with the Feast of Epiphany on January 6 as the prelude.[242] Christ's baptism counted as the illumination[243] of Christians because by his baptism Christ had made the baptismal water into the washing of regeneration; hence this feast was also called *the lights*.[244] That is why people often had themselves baptized on this feast to be illuminated with Christ.[245] It was first celebrated in the East by the Basilideans[246] in Alexandria, and perhaps they had taken it over from Jewish Christians (Neander).[247] In the West we do not find it until the second half of the fourth century. Thus, this feast moved from the East to the West (exactly the reverse of Christmas) and could therefore change all the more easily in nature. It was also possible to view Epiphany as the manifestation of Christ to the pagans. In that case, Caesar Augustus (Luke 2) and the story of the three magi of Matthew 2:1–12 represented the pagan nations, which is why in Dutch, Epiphany is called *Driekoningen*, the Feast of the Three Kings. Or this feast could have celebrated the manifestation of Jesus's miraculous power at Cana, in which case it is *the day of the birth of the Lord's virtue*[248] and *Bethphanie*. Or it could be seen as the manifestation of Jesus's power in feeding the five thousand (*Phagiphanie*). Yet people mostly

240. GrO: ἐπιφαίνω and ἡ ἐπιφάνεια.

241. See Herzog, "Epiphanienfest," 261–63; cf. Usener, *Religionsgeschichtliche Untersuchungen*, 1:18–213 ("Christliche Epiphanie, das Alte Tauf- und Geburtsfest").

242. LO: *Praecedens*; why January 6 was chosen for Epiphany is not known; cf. Wagenmann, "Weihnachten," 689–90.

243. GrO: φωτισμός.

244. GrO: τὰ φῶτα.

245. GrO: Χριστῷ συμφωτισθῆναι.

246. Ed. note: The Basilideans were a gnostic sect founded by Basilides of Alexandria in the second century AD.

247. Ed. note: Bavinck took the reference to Neander (the German theologian and church historian Johann August Wilhelm Neander, 1789–1850) from Herzog, "Epiphanienfest," 262. Herzog provides no source for his lengthy treatment of Neander.

248. LO: *dies natalis virtutum Domini*.

thought of the three wise men from the East, and the word "epiphany" was even interpreted to refer to the appearance of the star.

Christmas[249] refers to Christusmisse—in German, *Weihnachten*, from *vih*, *weihe*, holy, referring to holy nights, originally the nights from December 25 to January 6 among Germanic peoples, in which the goddess of light combats darkness and finally wins. This is the "birthday" or "birth of Christ";[250] in Italian, *Natale*; in Spanish, *nadal*;[251] in French, *noël*. This feast was the last to appear in the Christian church, not until the fourth century. Initially all attention was paid to Christ's death and resurrection; celebrating people's birthdays also seemed to be something pagan, and the very day of Jesus's birth was also unknown. But the Feast of Epiphany led to celebrating Jesus's birthday as well. The first trace of Christmas is found in 360 under Pope Liberius (352–66). And then it spread quickly in the West, from there into the East (exactly the reverse of the Feast of Epiphany)—although not without protest—much later also in Palestine and Egypt. Why it was assigned to December 25 is uncertain. According to some (Ewald, P. Cassel),[252] this date was influenced by the Jewish Feast of Tabernacles or Feast of the Dedication of the Temple on 25 Chislev, which was December (cf. Hag. 2:18). According to others—on the basis of a tradition or a calculation from the day of the announcement of conception[253]—the choice of the date was influenced by the fact that March 25 was the beginning of spring. (But is the day of conception not rather calculated according to the day of the birth?) According to still others, December 25 was chosen because it is the shortest day, the day of the return of the sun, and Christ is the Sun of Righteousness[254] (Mal. 4:2); this day was celebrated in Rome and elsewhere as "the birthday of the invincible sun" or "the shortest day."[255] The church gave this feast a Christian stamp; hence its rapid spread; it supplanted the nature feast with the spiritual feast. From that point on, the day of the annunciation or conception was calculated

---

249. See Wagenmann, "Weihnachten," 689–90.

250. LO: *dies natalis*; *natalitia Christi*.

251. Ed. note: This is Catalan.

252. Ed. note: Bavinck provides no specific references; he likely had in mind Heinrich Ewald (1803–75), the German professor of theology and Oriental languages at the University of Göttingen and author of several books on the Old Testament and Israel. The reference to P. Cassel has in view Paulus Stephanus Cassel (1821–92), a German Jewish convert to Christianity and missionary to Jews. He is the author of a history of the Jews from the destruction of Jerusalem to 1847, *Die Geschichte des jüdischen volkes seit der Zerstörung Jerusalems*. Original title, published under preconversion name Selig Cassel: *Geschichte der Juden seit der Eroberung und Zerstörung Jerusalems und seines Heiligthums durch die Römer bis zum Jahre 1847*.

253. LO: *dies annunciationis, conceptionis*.

254. LO: *Sol justitiae*.

255. LO: *dies natalis solis invicti* or *burma = brevima (dies)*.

to be March 25, and the day of the conception and birth of John the Baptist on September 24 and June 24.

In the sixth century the *Feast of Christ's Circumcision* was introduced between Christmas and Epiphany. In addition, preparation for Christmas in *Advent*[256] is certain to have come already in the sixth century. Like the preparation for Easter, the Advent season was a season of fasting that had to be spent solemnly: no weddings were allowed, the organ had to be silent; even today in Roman Catholic churches images are veiled, altars and walls are draped with violet cloths, priests wear violet gowns—rose-colored only on the last Sunday of Advent. The length of Advent was at first forty days, six Sundays; however, it became four Sundays plus a preparatory Sunday; December 18 is the *Feast of the Expectation of the Delivery*.[257] Then follows December 24, the Christmas vigil, six o'clock at night, and then Christmas itself with three masses; the altar cloths and priests' garments are white, the church is illuminated, a manger stands in a corner, and so on. The feast is concluded on the eighth day,[258] on January 1, the *Feast of the Circumcision*, a day of penance and fasting for Christians. Especially at Christmas there are many customs whose origins are not yet clear (did they come from Christianity, Judaism, paganism?), such as the Christmas tree, lights, giving presents, and so on.

In addition to these principal feasts there gradually arose secondary feasts, such as the *Feast of the Trinity*,[259] not established for the whole church until 1334. Next came the Christ feasts: that of the Transfiguration (glorification),[260] pronounced a holy day for all of Christendom on August 6, 1456; the Feast of the Lance and the Nails of Christ, introduced into Bohemia and Germany on April 16, 1354; *Corpus Christi* on the Thursday after Trinity Sunday, introduced in 1264; the *Feast of the Discovery of the Cross*[261] on May 3 (in the East, on August 1); and the *Feast of the Elevation of the Cross*,[262] introduced on September 14, 631.

Then came the feasts of Mary: on March 25, Mary's annunciation; on February 2, Mary's purification; on August 15, Mary's assumption; on September 8, Mary's birth; on July 2, Mary's visitation; on December 8, Mary's conception.[263]

Next to appear were the feasts of the apostles and evangelists: three for John the Baptist; another for Mary Magdalene; and one each for the angels Michael

256. Alt, "Advent."
257. LO: *festum expectationis partus.*
258. LO: *octave.*
259. LO: *festum Trinitatis.*
260. LO/DO: *transfigurationis/verheerlijking.*
261. LO: *festum inventionis crucis.*
262. LO: *festum exaltationis crucis.*
263. LO: *annunciationis; purificationis; assumptionis; natalis; visitationis; conceptionis.*

and Gabriel. And then countless days for saints and martyrs: All Saints on November 1, All Souls on November 2, and so on. Here, then, we have too much of a good thing. Partially as a result of the Reformation, which abolished many holy days, and also as a result of complaints about their high number, several holy days were later canceled, at least regionally, by, among others, Urban VIII in 1642 and Benedict XIV in 1742–45, so that in several countries—Germany, Austria, and Bavaria among them—the number of holy days decreased.

The Reformation

LUTHER AND LUTHERANS

In 1517 Luther felt that all holy days might as well be abolished, including the Sabbath. The Sabbath was retained "only for the sake of the immature (imperfect) laity and the working people, in order that they may come to hear the Word of God. If we were all perfect and knew the Gospel, we might work or hold festival every day."[264] In 1520 Luther said that it would be better if there were no holy days, since they were so misused for idleness, drunkenness, gambling, and so forth. According to Köstlin, Luther did make concessions to popular piety: "If it be thought desirable to retain the festivals of the Virgin Mary and the leading saints, they might be arranged to occur upon Sundays, or they might be celebrated merely by a morning mass, and the remainder of the day be devoted to ordinary labor."[265] But what Köstlin does not say, though Bertheau does,[266] is that Luther later changed his mind: in 1528 he approved the Sunday celebration[267] of Mary's annunciation, purification, and visitation[268] and the feasts of John the Baptist, Michael, the apostles, and Mary Magdalene. Many had already been abolished, however. But Luther approved especially the Feasts of Christmas, Circumcision, Epiphany, Easter, Ascension, and Pentecost, though without the accrued legends. And others elsewhere did so as well.

The *Lutheran Church* decided to retain those rites "which can be so observed without sin,"[269] without however burdening people's consciences,[270] for

---

264. Köstlin, *Theology of Luther*, 1:358.

265. Köstlin, *Theology of Luther*, 1:380.

266. Bertheau, "Feste, kirchliche," 552.

267. Ed. note: Bavinck adds here a parenthesis taken directly from Bertheau: "(? = as feast days? Or = as feast days moved to Sunday?)"; GO: (? *Heist das die Festtage oder die auf den volgenden Sonntag verlegten Festtage?*).

268. LO: *annunciationis, purificationis,* and *visitationis.*

269. LO: *sine peccato servari possunt*; J. T. Müller et al., *Christian Book of Concord,* 113 (Augsburg Confession, art. 15).

270. J. T. Müller et al., *Christian Book of Concord,* 271–72, 707 (Apology of the Augsburg Confession, art. 8 [15], Formula of Concord, Part II, art. 10). Ed. note: Article 8 of the Apology deals with article 15 of the Augsburg Confession itself: "Of Church Rites and Ordinances." Article

the matter is entirely free,[271] and not to observe them is no sin.[272] The "holy Fathers" of the church kept certain "ceremonies and ordinances," not to earn salvation by them, but "to exercise the body, for instance, the festivals, in order that the people might know when to come together, that everything might be done orderly and decently in the churches, as a good example, and that the multitude might be kept under good parental discipline."[273] Thus we can observe the mass, Sunday, and other well-known feasts.[274] Although angels and saints pray for us, they must nonetheless not be called upon or venerated through fasting, feast days, masses, gifts, or shrines.[275] Accordingly, the Lutheran church has maintained observance of all the principal feasts. Some were abolished in the previous century:[276] the third day of the high feasts, the three days of penance, and Maundy Thursday, as well as Ascension Day (though this was later restored). On the other hand, other feast days have been added: Thanksgiving for the Harvest; since 1816 the Feast for the Dead in memory of those who had passed away during the past year; Feast of the Reformation. In addition to the three great feasts, Lutheran churches here and there also celebrate Good Friday, Ascension, Maundy Thursday, Rest Day, Epiphany, the three Mary feasts approved by Luther, and the feasts of John and of Michael—usually, however, on Sunday.

CALVIN AND REFORMED CHURCHES

In his Sixty-Seven Articles (#25), Zwingli insisted, "That time and place is under the jurisdiction of Christian people, and man with them, from which is learned that those who fix time and place deprive the Christians of their liberty."[277] There would be rest enough if the godly rested on Sunday. On other feast days it would be good to first attend church and then return to work,

---

10 of the Full Declaration of the Formula of Concord (Part II) has the same subject: "Of Church Usages." References to the Apology will be given as "art. X (y)" with the parenthetical number referring to the article in the Augsburg Confession.

271. J. T. Müller et al., *Christian Book of Concord*, 133 (Augsburg Confession, art. 28). Ed. note: The rest of this article explicitly deals with the Sabbath/Sunday question, among other things.

272. J. T. Müller et al., *Christian Book of Concord*, 273 (Apology, art. 8 [15]).

273. J. T. Müller et al., *Christian Book of Concord*, 270–71 (Apology, art. 8 [15]). Ed. note: We have expanded Bavinck's original here.

274. J. T. Müller et al., *Christian Book of Concord*, 273 (Apology, art. 8 [15]).

275. J. T. Müller et al., *Christian Book of Concord*, 371–72 (Smalcald Articles, art. 2, "Of the Invocation of Saints").

276. Bertheau, "Feste, kirchliche," 552–53.

277. LO: *tempus et locus in potestate sunt hominis*; translation from Zwingli, *Selected Works of Huldrich Zwingli*, 113; alternative translation in Dennison, *Reformed Confessions of the 16th and 17th Centuries*, 1:5; cf. Helvetic Confession, art. 24.

thus observing them only in the morning. The only feast days that could be observed commemorate the day of our Lord's birth; the day of Stephen, when all martyrs could be commemorated; the annunciation; the day of John, when church fathers and prophets could be commemorated; and the Feast of Peter and Paul, when apostles and evangelists could be commemorated. But other feasts had to be abolished, as they lead only to sin. To work after the church service is over is much better than to indulge in idleness. According to a decision of the Zurich city council in 1526, the only feasts in addition to Sunday would be Christmas, Easter, Pentecost, and All Souls, as well as the days of Stephen, Circumcision of Christ, Candlemas, Annunciation, Easter Monday, Ascension, Pentecost Monday, John the Baptist, the Virgin Mary, and Felix and Regula (patrons of Zurich). However, in 1530, all feast days related to creatures were abolished, and only the Feasts of Christ, of Easter, and of Pentecost (two days each) were retained. Later, Bullinger wrote to Calvin that here we observe only Sunday, Christmas, Circumcision, Ascension, and Pentecost (Easter?).[278]

Calvin neither opposed nor really favored church feasts. When he was banished from Geneva, along with Farel and Vinet, in April 1538, he refused to acquiesce on the question of church discipline, but was willing to accept feast days (which had already been abolished earlier by Farel and Vinet), provided that doing work after church was allowed.[279] After Calvin and his friends were banished, the feasts were restored in Geneva. Thus, he acquiesced to the wish of the people and did not abolish them after his return, but retained only a few feast days, when after 1542 shops were closed during the morning worship services but everybody was back at work in the afternoon. Only Christmas Day was celebrated in its entirety, although Calvin had told the Council (1544) that people could just as well do without it, as well as the three other feasts.[280] And when in 1551 the Council of Two Hundred, totally without Calvin's knowledge, abolished all feast days, and even moved Christmas to the following Sunday, Calvin did say that he had no part in it, although he did not at all think that it was wrong.[281]

SYNODS OF THE DUTCH REFORMED CHURCH

At the Convent of Wezel (1568), it was decided that, as each church had opportunity, at least one day each week should be set apart for solemn prayers

278. Henry, *Das Leben Johann Calvins*, 3:23.
279. Henry, *Das Leben Johann Calvins*, 1:201.
280. Henry, *Das Leben Johann Calvins*, 2:166–67.
281. Henry, *Das Leben Johann Calvins*, 3:21–23.

and for the confession of public sins, either before or after the sermon.[282] At Dort (1574), article 51[283] declared that "public evening prayers shall not be instituted in those places where it is not done. They shall be discontinued as sensitively and carefully as possible in those places where this is now the practice" (Roman Catholic vespers).[284] These were later reintroduced at Leiden, also at Rotterdam and Delft. These evening prayers were also opposed at the 1578 Synod of Dort (art. 57) and the 1581 Synod of Middelburg (art. 47).[285]

Here and there they continued to exist for a long time yet.[286] At Dort (1574), article 53 declared that "as to church holidays aside from the Sunday, it is decided that people shall be content with Sunday only. The normal material about Christ's birth shall be dealt with in the church on the Sunday before Christmas, and the people shall be exhorted not to consider Christmas as a holiday."[287] However, the people and the authorities maintained the feasts.[288] Dort (1578), article 75, states that "it would be desirable that freedom to work six days as allowed by God be maintained by the church and only Sunday be kept holy. Nevertheless, since some other festive days are observed by authority of the government, such as Christmas with the day following, the second Easter day and the second Pentecost day and in some places New Year's Day and Ascension Day, the ministers shall show diligence to have sermons in which they shall especially teach the congregation concerning the birth and resurrection of Christ, the sending of the Holy Spirit and other articles of faith and how to change the occasion to some profitable exercises."[289]

Thus, all churches should labor to cancel all feast days except for Christmas (and Easter and Pentecost, but those fell on Sundays). The Synod of The Hague (1586) already wanted to have the Lord's Supper celebrated, if possible, on

282. *Church Orders of the Sixteenth Century Reformed Churches*, 82 (*Acts of the Convent of Wesel [1568]*, chap. 2, art. 27; Hooijer, *Oude kerkordeningen*, 40). Ed. note: Bavinck cites Hooijer, *Oude kerkordeningen*, and the source of primary texts for the church assemblies he mentions below; we will add the Hooijer reference in parentheses after the De Ridder anthology of texts. Cf. Henry, *Das Leben Johann Calvins*, 2:27.

283. Ed. note: This and subsequent references to "article" are to the church orders approved at each synod.

284. *Church Orders of the Sixteenth Century Reformed Churches of the Netherlands*, 159 (*Acts of the Provincial Synod of Dordrecht [1574]*, art. 51; Hooijer, *Oude kerkordeningen*, 104).

285. *Church Orders of the Sixteenth Century Reformed Churches of the Netherlands*, 217 (*Acts of the National Synod at Dordrecht [1578]*, art. 57; Hooijer, *Oude kerkordeningen*, 153).

286. *Church Orders of the Sixteenth Century Reformed Churches of the Netherlands*, 280 (*Acts of the Provincial Synod of Middelburg [1581]*, art. 47; Hooijer, *Oude kerkordeningen*, 206).

287. *Church Orders of the Sixteenth Century Reformed Churches of the Netherlands*, 159 (*Acts of the Provincial Synod of Dordrecht [1574]*, art. 53; Hooijer, *Oude kerkordeningen*, 104).

288. Hooijer, *Oude kerkordeningen*, 93.

289. *Church Orders of the Sixteenth Century Reformed Churches of the Netherlands*, 219–20 (*Acts of the National Synod of Dordrecht [1578]*, art. 75; Hooijer, *Oude kerkordeningen*, 155).

Easter Sunday, Pentecost Sunday, and Christmas Day.[290] And Dort (1618–19), article 63, states the same thing about the Supper, and article 67 recommends that the churches observe, in addition to Sunday, also Christmas Day, Easter, and Pentecost along with the very next day, as well as the Day of Circumcision and Ascension Day.[291]

Voetius acknowledges that a church may fix specific times for gathering together, may prescribe certain days of fasting and thanksgiving, and should not immediately break communion with another church over feast days.[292] However, he denies that in addition to observing Sunday, feast days are holier than other days, for they were never instituted by God and therefore are not part of worship. Furthermore, the apostles did not observe them, and they are definitely contrary to Romans 14; Galatians 4:10; and Colossians 2:16. Christ's benefits should be commemorated each and every day; otherwise there would be distinctions of days, which lead to superstition and impose a heavy yoke. For the most part they are new and recent and of uncertain origin. Therefore, their proximate cause[293] is pagan feasts.

Voetius replied to various objections as follows: "We do not recognize the so-called holy days," as Calvin had written in a letter to John Haller, January 2, 1551.[294] The churches in Scotland recognized such holy days neither in theory nor in practice prior to 1618 (the year they were introduced);[295] the

290. *Church Orders of the Sixteenth Century Reformed Churches of the Netherlands*, 358 (*Acts of the National Synod of The Hague [1586]*, art. 56; Hooijer, *Oude kerkordeningen*, 277).

291. *Church Orders of the Sixteenth Century Reformed Churches of the Netherlands*, 555–56 (*Acts of the National Synod of Dordrecht [1618–19]*, arts. 63 and 67; Hooijer, *Oude kerkordeningen*, 456–57).

292. Voetius, *Selectarum Disputationum Theologicarum*, 3:1294–95.

293. LO: *causa procatartice*.

294. Voetius, *Selectarum Disputationum Theologicarum*, 3:1307. Calvin, *Letters of John Calvin*, 2:287–89 (#CCLXX, "Letter to John Haller"). Ed. note: John Haller (b. 1523) was pastor of the Bernese Church. Bavinck's manuscript adds: "and also to a government official [DO: *minister*] Burensis as well as to Menso Poppius in 1559." Voetius's reference (*Select. disp.*, 3:1307): 'In Epistol. Proximè frequenti ad ministrum Bureníem'; *Select. disp.*, 3:1308: 'Idem in Epistolâ as Menionem Poppim an. 1559.'" Menso Poppius was a Frisian Reformed pastor (d. ca. 1567), but the reference to "Burensis" remains unclear.

295. Ed. note: Bavinck gives "Altare Damascenus" as a source for this historical fact. It is not possible to track this down, so we are providing the full text of the fifth article approved by the General Assembly of the Kirk of Scotland, August 25–27, 1618:

As we abhor the superstitious observation of Festivall dayes by the Papists, and detest all licentions and profane abuse thereof by the common sort of professòrs; so we think, that the instimable benefits, receivit from God by our Lord Jesus Christ his Birth, Passion, Resurrection, Ascension, and Sending down of the Holy Ghost, were commendably and godly remembered at certain particular dayes and times, by the whole Kirk of the world, and may be also now: Therefor the Assembly ordains, that every Minister shall upon these dayes have the commemoration of the foresaid instimable benefits; and make choise of several and pertinent texts of Scripture, and frame their doctrine and

General Assembly abolished them again in 1640, and everything went back to the original simplicity. The Heidelberg Catechism, in Q&A 103, speaks about worship "especially on the festive days,"[296] but in order to bar all holy days, the Dutch translation reads: "especially on the Lord's Day."[297] This was the position also of Theodore Beza, Lambert Daneau, William Ames, Heinrich Alting, John Sharpe, and the Saumur theologians.[298]

Here in the Netherlands the practice of the people and the authorities has brought us, "whether we wanted it or not, from the initial simplicity of the practice to a mere deference and toleration of it; although the intention and plan remained, to change public opinion itself together with the required observation of feast days at the first opportunity."[299] The feeling was that because people are accustomed to them, they cannot easily be abolished; Dutch Reformed synods decided to hold worship services on those days to turn people away from idleness and the like.[300]

Voetius writes about feasts that are observed in the Greek Orthodox Church and the Anglican Church.[301] The latter still retained many feasts: the Feast of the Circumcision, Epiphany, Mary's Purification, Matthew, Annunciation, Mark, Philip and Jacob, Ascension, Nativity, John the Baptist, and more.[302] Lutherans like Johannes Brenz (1499–1570) and Balthasar Mentzer are somewhat more lenient and wish to keep them.[303] The Hungarian church, which

---

exhortation thereto; and rebuke all superstitious observation and licentious profanation thereof. (Maitland Club, "Acts and Proceedings: 1618, August")

296. LO: *tam praecipue diebus festis.*

297. Similarly, the Dutch Reformed Synods of Dort in 1574 and 1578.

298. Beza, "Homily 18," in *In historiam passionis et Sepulturae domin nostri J. Christi Homiliae*, 431; Daneau, *Ethices Christianae*, book II, chap. 10, pp. 171–72; Ames, *Bellarminus Enervatus*, II.vi.10, 263–66; H. Alting, *Exegesis logica et theologica*, 93 (art. 15); Sharpe, *Symphonia propetarum et apostolarum*, 155; Amyraut, Cappel, and de la Place, *Syntagma thesium theologicarum*, 3:598–613 ("Theses Theologicae de Diebus Festis"). Bavinck's source for all these references is Voetius, *Selectarum Disputationum Theologicarum*, 3:1308–11. Cf. Koelman, *Het ambt en de pligten der ouderlingen en diakenen*, 151, 165, 267. The reference to Ames was corrected; Voetius (*Selectarum Disputationum Theologicarum*, 3:1309) had: "Amesius in Bellarmino Evervato ad. Lib 3 de cultu Sanctorum," which is incomplete and incorrect.

299. LO/GrO: *a prima praxeos, simplicitate, ad συγκατάβασιν et tolerantiam illam volentes nolentes transtulit, manente tamen proposito et consilio, ipsas illas conciones et materialem dierum coactam observationem prima data occasione mutanda*; Voetius, *Selectarum Disputationum Theologicarum*, 3:1314.

300. Voetius, *Selectarum Disputationum Theologicarum*, 3:1313.

301. Voetius, *Selectarum Disputationum Theologicarum*, 3:1318.

302. LO: *purificationis Mariae, Matthiae, annunciationis, Marci Philippi et Jacobi, ascensionis, nativitatis Johannis Baptistae*; Voetius, *Selectarum Disputationum Theologicarum*, 3:1318.

303. Voetius, *Selectarum Disputationum Theologicarum*, 3:1322; the reference is to Johannes Brenz (1499–1570) and Balthasar Mentzer I (1565–1627); Voetius cites the latter's *Exegesis Augustanae Confessionis*, 451 (art. XV, "Errores Calvinianorum," #1).

adopted the Helvetic Confession, stated in its 1642 canons that she rejected the saints' days but observed Sunday and commemorated the conception, nativity, circumcision, passion, resurrection, and ascension of Christ and Pentecost.[304] The Bohemian church observed Advent, birth, death, resurrection, ascension, and Pentecost; in addition, they celebrated circumcision, epiphany, transfiguration, and eventually also days of the apostles and some martyrs.[305] The Dutch church, when it could not abolish them entirely, reduced their number. Voetius pleaded for freedom in this question[306] and does not say that these days should simply be abolished, but that churches that have done so did a good thing.[307] At present our church orders contradict each other, but not all canons should be pressed as if they were catechetical topics[308] or articles of confession.[309] The content of the canons is not uniformly important and useful; some of it is essential, while other parts are merely useful. Not all prescriptions are equally binding, such as the article on the feast days; the churches that do not observe them are no less Reformed than the churches that do.

Days of Penitence, Fasting, and Prayer[310]

In Scripture and Church History

For these purposes, Israel had the Day of Atonement (Lev. 16). In addition, during troubled times the Israelites observed separate days of penance and fasting (Judg. 20:26; 1 Sam. 7:6; 31:13; 2 Sam. 1:12; Joel 1:13–14). Kings such as Jehoshaphat proclaimed fasts (2 Chron. 20:3), and leaders such as Ezra (Ezra 8:21). At times, persons fasted privately as well (2 Sam. 12:16–23 [David]; Dan. 9:3 [Daniel]; Ezra 10:6 [Ezra]; Neh. 1:4 [Nehemiah]; Esther 4:3 [many Jews]). After the exile, the practice of fasting on specified days increased among the Jews (already in Zech. 7:5; 8:19; Sir. 34:28, 31).[311] The Pharisees fasted twice a week (Luke 18:12), and the Essenes were even stricter: they abstained from meat and wine and sometimes ate only once a day or even once every three days.

---

304. Class 3, canon 24: Voetius, *Selectarum Disputationum Theologicarum*, 3:1325. Ed. note: Voetius's source is likely Bernhard Máté and György Ráth, *Canones ecclesiastici in quinque classes distributi*, 48–49.

305. Voetius, *Selectarum Disputationum Theologicarum*, 3:1325.

306. Voetius, *Selectarum Disputationum Theologicarum*, 3:1325.

307. Voetius, *Selectarum Disputationum Theologicarum*, 3:1339.

308. LO: *capita catechetica*.

309. Voetius, *Selectarum Disputationum Theologicarum*, 3:1341.

310. Sommer, "Busstag." Cf. Kist, *Neêrland's Bededagen en Biddagsbrieven*. Ed. note: Bavinck also discusses fasting (positively) in *RE*, 1:488–90.

311. Ed. note: See pp. 249, 251 above.

We also encounter fasting in the New Testament: in the church at Antioch (Acts 13:2) and in other churches (Acts 14:23; cf. 1 Cor. 7:5; 2 Cor. 11:27). Very soon within the Christian church, days of fasting came to be observed on Wednesdays (later discontinued) and on Fridays, in preparation for Sunday, and the fast lasted till three in the afternoon. In addition to this, other times for penance arose, particularly the forty[312] days before Easter. Initially, the duration was much shorter: the forty hours of preparation for Easter were gradually extended; in the fourth century it lasted three weeks in Rome, seven weeks in Illyria, Achaia, and Alexandria.[313] Yet forty days of fasting is found already (in Jerome) with Leo I, who calls it an apostolic institution. Since fasting was forbidden on Sundays, of the six fasting weeks only thirty-six days were left, which were then supplemented with four days from the seventh week. These forty days were traced back to the forty-day fasts of Moses and Christ.[314] During the *Quadragesima* (forty-day fast) it is forbidden to consume meat, eggs, and dairy products (e.g., butter), but this is compensated for[315] with all kinds of delicacies.[316] Somewhat later than when the forty-day fast was established, a period before Christmas was instituted that acquired the character of penitence and preparation.[317]

As early as the third century we find days of penance that are tied to the change of the seasons, the so-called *Quatember days*. These were definitely formed according to the four Jewish days of mourning in the fourth, fifth, seventh, and tenth months, and according to tradition they were introduced into the Christian church by bishop Callistus (d. 223).[318] He adopted the days of fasting in the fourth, seventh, and tenth months, and after AD 440 under Leo I another day of fasting was added in the first month. In this way the year was divided into four seasons;[319] in 1095 the days were fixed by Urban II on the Wednesdays after Ash Wednesday, after Pentecost, after the Elevation

---

312. LO: *quadragesima*.

313. See Jacobson (Meyer), "Fasten."

314. See also Voetius, *Selectarum Disputationum Theologicarum*, 3:1382–83; Daillé, *De Jejuniis et Quadragesima Liber*. Carnival at first was dated from Epiphany on (January 6), later from eight days before Ash Wednesday (*dies cinerum*), on which the *Quadragesima* begins and ash is scattered upon the faithful as a sign of penitence (Voetius, *Selectarum Disputationum Theologicarum*, 3:1389–90).

315. DO: *vergoedt*.

316. Voetius, *Selectarum Disputationum Theologicarum*, 3:1385.

317. Ed. note: This is an interpretation of Bavinck's sentence: "Somewhat later than the forty day fast, there also came a period before Christmas that acquired the character of penitence and preparation" (*Iets later dan de Quadragesima kwam er ook een tijd voor Kerstmis welke het karakter can een boete- en voorbereidingstid kreeg.*)

318. Jacobson (Meyer), "Fasten," 506.

319. LO: *quattuor tempora*; hence *Quatember*.

of the Cross (September 14), and after the Feast of St. Lucy (December 13).[320] They are also known as the consecration fasts, since the very next Sunday serves to bestow the higher consecrations, also referred to as the *Fron* (= Lord) fasting, since on these days the compulsory taxes[321] were collected in civic life.

And then there still are fixed days of fasting, the Vigils,[322] the nightly preparations for the higher feasts—just as Jesus also spent a night on the mountain in prayer (Luke 6:12), and Paul and Silas sang at night in the jail (Acts 16:25). These were later abolished, already in the fourth century, and especially after the sixteenth century, but they are still mostly replaced with fasting, along with evening and morning services for the high feasts such as Christmas, Pentecost, Peter and Paul, Assumption of Mary, Matthew, and All Souls. In addition to these ordinary fast days, the Roman Catholic Church also observes extraordinary fasting days, appointed on special occasions by the bishops in their dioceses or proclaimed by the pope for the entire church. The bishops also decide what foods to abstain from.

The Orthodox Church in its various divisions has different prescriptions for fasting.[323] She has, however, maintained the ancient sentinel days[324] of Wednesday and Friday. The principal fasts are the four annual time periods:

(1) The *quadragesima* before Easter (based on Matt. 4:2)
(2) Forty days before Christmas (according to Exod. 34:28)
(3) Mary fasts, from August 1 to the Assumption of Mary on August 15
(4) Apostle fasts, from Pentecost Monday (*Trinitatis*) to June 29 (according to Acts 13:3)

In addition, the Orthodox Church has vigils and special extraordinary fasts.

Fasting in the Churches of the Reformation

On the basis of Matthew 16:6, Luther approved that people would fast several days before Easter, Pentecost, and Christmas, as well as on every Friday evening, but only if it was accepted generally and voluntarily and not made into an actual form of worship.[325] The Christian is free from all those externals,

---

320. These are still observed in the Anglican Church and were fixed as follows: *Post Luciam, cineres, post sanctum pneuma crucemque Tempora dat quatuor feria quarta* (i.e., Wednesday) *sequens*.
321. LO: *angariae*.
322. LO: *Vigiliae*. Ed. note: See Bavinck's (positive) treatment of vigils in *RE*, 1:490–91.
323. Jacobson (Meyer), "Fasten," 508.
324. LO: *dies stationum*.
325. Jacobson (Meyer), "Fasten," 508. Ed. note: Cf. Köstlin, *Theology of Luther*, 1:207–8, 358, 379, 464.

including the Sabbath.[326] Nevertheless, Luther did not underestimate the value of fasting.[327] And the Lutheran confessions speak about fasting in essentially the same way.[328] After the Reformation, what emerged in particular were the general days of penance and prayer, appointed by Christian rulers during times of grave calamities. Thus in 1633 George I of Saxony appointed a day of penance on account of the Thirty Years' War. As late as 1870, the King of Prussia appointed a day of prayer in connection with the Franco-Prussian War. Various German states still have official days of prayer—in Mecklenburg four, in Hanover three, in Saxony two. In our day, however, these are seldom observed anymore, and people would like to see them limited throughout the German Empire to two or even one.[329] Zwingli did not exactly want to abolish forty-day fasts, but he wanted to leave them a matter of liberty, since they are not prescribed in Scripture.[330] Calvin likewise deemed fasting altogether permissible, though not in and of itself, but as a support.[331] On the basis of Amos 7:13 Calvin denied that the ruler may appoint fasts. However, Daneau said that where the church is a state church, a fast day is appointed jointly by church and state after mutual consultation.[332] Voetius agreed with this because this enables the government to compel those who are not church members to rest and stop working.[333]

Days of fasting and prayer are also mentioned in the Acts of the Synods of Dort in 1574[334] and in 1578.[335] And article 66 of the 1618–19 Synod of Dort Church Order states that "in times of war, pestilence, national calamities, severe persecution of the churches, and other general difficulties, the ministers shall petition the government so that by its authority and order public fasting

326. Köstlin, *Theology of Luther*, 1:358, 379, 464; 2:30–38.
327. Köstlin, *Theology of Luther*, 1:157; 2:473.
328. See especially the Augsburg Confession, art. 26, and the Apology for the Augsburg Confession, art. 5 (8). Ed. note: See the section on Luther and the Lutherans earlier in this chapter, pp. 233–35.
329. See Sommer, "Busstag," 593–94.
330. Christoffel, *Zwingli*, 57–64.
331. LO: *adminiculum*; *Institutes*, IV.xii.14–15.
332. Ed. note: Bavinck provides as reference Daneau, *Christianae isagoges*, part IV, liber 3, chap. 32. This section, "Cur Traditiones Humanae Dicantur," is found on pp. 523–25 but contains no reference to church and state cooperation.
333. Voetius, *Politicae Ecclesiasticae* (1663), 1:993.
334. *Church Orders of the Sixteenth Century Reformed Churches of the Netherlands*, 159–60 (*Acts of the Provincial Synod of Dordrecht [1574]*, art. 54; Hooijer, *Oude kerkordeningen*, 104–5); cf. *Church Orders of the Sixteenth Century Reformed Churches of the Netherlands*, 162 (art. 81; Hooijer, *Oude kerkordeningen*, 107–8).
335. *Church Orders of the Sixteenth Century Reformed Churches of the Netherlands*, 221 (*Acts of the National Synod of Dordrecht [1578]*, art. 88; Hooijer, *Oude kerkordeningen*, 157).

and prayer days may be designated and set aside."[336] This stipulation in Dort's church order is essentially borrowed from the French National Synod of 1559,[337] which in turn had borrowed the rule from Calvin's *Institutes*.[338]

Conclusions regarding Sunday Observance

1. The Sabbath was instituted at creation (Gen. 2:2–3). Its appearance in the creation account cannot be explained from prolepsis; that would be pointless and far-fetched. Evidence for the institution:

   a. Exodus 20:11 and 31:17, where the Sabbath commandment is grounded explicitly in God's resting on and hallowing the seventh day at creation.

   b. Judging from Sabbath observance among other nations, the institution is pre-Mosaic. The fact that the Sabbath commandment states explicitly that people must keep the day does not refute this claim, since

      i. God's example, law, and command suffice; and
      ii. this is implied in the blessing and hallowing of the day (see below).

   An objection to considering Sabbath as instituted in creation is that this would obligate all nations to keep the Sabbath, whereas this is never stated in Scripture but enjoined upon the Israelites only.[339]

   Reply: Apart from the fall, humanity would certainly have observed that day. Along with the falling away from the true worship of God, the time of worship also disappeared.

2. God has set the seventh day apart from the other six days by resting. This resting on the seventh day belongs to completing the work and is an essential part of that work, of creation, for we read in Genesis 2:2: "And on the seventh day God finished[340] his work that he had done, and he rested on the seventh day from all his work that he had done." The work is completed on the seventh day in and by God's resting. That resting consisted in

---

336. *Church Orders of the Sixteenth Century Reformed Churches of the Netherlands*, 554 (*Acts of the National Synod of Dordrecht [1618–19]*, art. 66; Hooijer, *Oude kerkordeningen*, 457); see also Helvetic Confession, art. 24; Gallican Confession, art. 24; Bohemian Confession, art. 18.

337. Jacobson (Meyer), "Fasten," 509. Ed. note: A similar but lengthier article on "days of prayer and fasting" in times of "war, pestilence . . . persecution . . . and other public woes" can be found in the church order of the 1578 national Synod of Dort, art. 74 (*Church Orders of the Sixteenth Century Reformed Churches of the Netherlands*, 219; Hooijer, *Oude kerkordeningen*, 155).

338. *Institutes*, IV.xii.14–15.

339. Gomarus, "Investigatio sententiae et originis Sabbathi," in *Opera Theologica Omnia*, 2:267 (chap. 4, ##41–55).

340. HO: וַיְכַל.

a. ceasing to create in the proper sense of the word, not ceasing to work, and

b. taking delight in and rejoicing in his works.

The blessing and hallowing of the seventh day both consist and flow in this and from this. For God's delight in his creatures is a blessing for those creatures, granting them bliss and peace. By resting and by delighting in his works, God blessed and hallowed the seventh day. He blessed it by giving to the seventh day the honor and privilege for people to rest on it, to devote themselves entirely to God, and to enjoy his peace, rest, and bliss.[341] To "bless" means here to bind to that day and to promise his peace, salvation, and rest. To "hallow" means here to set apart from the other days and their activities and to positively consecrate it—that is, in connection to God himself, to participating in the pure light of divine holiness. To be sure, this is not the actual Israelite Sabbath, yet it has been given to all creatures as a continually recurring day of rest. All higher life—not vegetative life, which we also have in our stomach, kidneys, heart, and lungs, but certainly instinctive life,[342] which we have in our senses, muscles, brains, and which requires rest—needs the alternation of rest and exertion. Nature (e.g., the sun) enjoys no rest, is always moving. But God rests—that is, has completed his work, attained his goal, and carried out his plan. We do not have here the eternal Sabbath, as some people have concluded because it was not followed by an evening. Granted, the Sabbath here is the symbol of that eternal Sabbath (Heb. 4), but this Sabbath, as appears from Exodus 20:11 and 31:17, is an ordinary and actual day, on which the whole creation, especially also humanity, would be prepared for the eternal, spiritual Sabbath.

3. That the Sabbath was observed by the patriarchs cannot be proven beyond doubt, yet it is possible and not improbable, since

   a. it was observed by other nations as well;

   b. the seven-day week was well known (Gen. 7:4, 10; 8:10, 12; 17:12; 21:4; and definitely 29:27–28); and

   c. Exodus 16:5, 22–30 mentions "gather[ing] twice as much" on the sixth day, and the word *zakor*[343] in Exodus 20:8 assumes people's familiarity with (though not yet the practice of) Sabbath observance.

---

341. DO: *vrede, rust, zaligheid.*

342. DO: *dierlijk leven.* Ed. note: We have chosen to translate *dierlijk* as "instinctive" rather than the literal expression "animal-like," because "instinctive" is a more precise term to describe the sensory and physiological life human beings share with animals.

343. HO: זָכוֹר.

4. The law intervened. In Genesis 2, with Adam prior to the fall, the entire moral law, including the commandment to keep the Sabbath, was more of a privilege than a duty, more of a blessing than a command. After the giving of the Decalogue, however, it functioned in the positive form of a commandment, a law, a demand. A further difference is that the Sabbath remained a day of joy, to be sure, a feast day, a delight, a day of rest for all creatures; but still, on the Sabbath all kinds of works, identified by name, were now prohibited and transgressors were punished by death. In addition, the Sabbath is made a sign between YHWH and Israel in perpetuity, a mark of his covenant, in which God promises Israel his peace, salvation, and rest, and in which Israel binds herself to devote herself to God. The Sabbath becomes the foundation of all the other feasts (seventh day, week, month, year)—that is, of all worship of YHWH. Thus, to reject the Sabbath is to attack the entire worship of YHWH at its heart (Isaiah). Even more, the basis for the Sabbath remains God's resting (Exod. 20), but the basis is also Israel's deliverance from Egypt (Deut. 5:15)—at least, it is now urged on that basis. The basis, nature, and goal of the Sabbath are thereby altered, or at least expanded and enlarged. That is why it is stated that the Sabbath was given *to Israel* (Exod. 16:29; 31:13; Ezek. 20:12; Neh. 9:14).

5. Is the Fourth Commandment entirely ceremonial? Is it entirely moral? Or does it include elements of both?[344] These are the three basic positions:

    a. The Fourth Commandment is entirely moral—that is, still mandatory. This is the view of Judaism and, in the Christian tradition, the Ebionites, the Cerinthians, the Apollinarists, and the Sabbatarians.[345] Christian Sabbatarians appeal to Jesus and the apostles, who also observed the Sabbath. But this raises questions:

        i. The calendar is confusing and is different in different parts of the world. No one can say which is the first or the seventh day after creation. There is a grain of truth in this argument. Nevertheless, we should acknowledge the fact that we observe the first day of the week, and the Jews observe the seventh. The element of truth

344. Ed. note: Bavinck's source for what follows is Turretin, *Institutes of Elenctic Theology*, 2:77–104 (XI.13).

345. Ed. note: The Ebionites were a Jewish-Christian movement that regarded Jesus as Messiah but rejected his divinity and insisted on following Jewish law. Cerinthus (ca. 50–100 AD) was a gnostic Christian who used his own Gospel of Cerinthus, a truncated and Judaizing version of the Gospel of Matthew. The reference to Apollinarists is not clear, since Apollinarism (from Apollinaris of Laodicea [d. 390]) is a christological position that while Jesus had a truly human body, he had a divine mind instead of a human soul.

is that the seventh day can never be the absolute in every respect, or, in other words, the true religion—namely, Christianity—can never be bound to an hour or a time, no more than it is bound to a particular place, people, social rank, or the like.

ii. The moral realm is concerned with good and evil, is grounded in our nature, and is eternal and immutable.[346] The determining of a seventh day is, therefore, not in itself moral but ceremonial, for in itself a day, an hour, or a time is not and cannot be good or evil; it simply derives its holiness (not from its own nature but) from an authority that determines it. A temporal prescription therefore is always arbitrary, ceremonial, changeable.[347]

iii. The prophets often place the Sabbath and other feasts alongside each other, on a par (e.g., Isa. 1:13); together they belong to both ceremonial and positive law,[348] and therefore are transitory and mutable.

iv. The Sabbath in the Old Testament had a typological meaning: it was a sign of God's covenant with Israel (Exod. 31:13; Ezek. 20:12, 20; etc.), signifying and promising not only present but also future grace. All feast days and Sabbaths as well as the seventh day[349] were a shadow of things to come[350] (Col. 2:17). The Sabbath foreshadowed the rest of believers that was to be obtained by Christ—namely,

   (1) spiritual rest, the rest experienced by the conscience freed from the fear of divine wrath and the rest consisting in ceasing from our evil works (Matt. 11:28; Rom. 5:1; Heb. 4:3; Isa. 58:13–14), and

   (2) heavenly rest—that is, not only forsaking our sins but also resting from the labors and tribulations of earthly life (Ps. 95:11; Heb. 4:10; Rev. 14:13).

To the extent that it was typological and ceremonial, the Sabbath is now fulfilled in Christ—that is, in his passion and death, which was his rest. Jesus himself has fulfilled all righteousness, also that of this Mosaic (not the Pharisaic) Sabbath; he fully satisfied this commandment as well. The proof is his death, in which he devoted himself and gave himself over completely to God; that is, he observed the Sabbath at the cost of his life.

346. Bavinck's marginal note: "Romans 14:5: all days are equal."
347. Turretin, *Institutes of Elenctic Theology*, 2:84 (XI.13.xx).
348. LO: *juris ceremonialis et positive.*
349. Turretin, *Institutes of Elenctic Theology*, 2:84–85 (XI.13.xxi).
350. GrO: σκιὰ τῶν μελλόντων.

b. The Fourth Commandment is entirely ceremonial. This is said by Manichaeans, Anabaptists, and Socinians, as well as by Cocceius and his followers. That, too, is not possible.

    i. The Fourth Commandment is a commandment from the Decalogue, which contains not one purely ceremonial commandment. To infer from this, in agreement with the above-mentioned Sabbatarians, that the Fourth Commandment is therefore entirely moral is also incorrect. The Decalogue is mainly moral law; it gives the principles of the rule for all of life, containing also the root of all ceremonies and all civil laws.[351]

    ii. Reason already teaches that religion consists not only in silent prayer and meditation but also in worship[352] practices, in solemn public worship services, and this is always bound to some time or other—that is, it must occur at a specified time.

    iii. This commandment, just like the others, is grounded in love toward God and neighbor.

    iv. The commandment was given already before the fall, instituted at creation. From this it does not follow that it is entirely moral, for the probationary commandment was not a moral law but a positive law.[353] Nevertheless, it shows that the Sabbath commandment was not only something for Israelites, as a schoolmaster unto Christ, but that it has a deeper meaning even apart from sin and is valid for the entire human race. That universally human quality, though it be also a positive law, remains. Colossians 2:16–17 does not negate this. Food and drink are today also clean, yet in the Lord's Supper they are still consecrated for special use.[354]

6. Now if the Fourth Commandment contains something ceremonial and something moral, then what is passing and what is abiding? In any case, the elements that are ceremonial and have passed are these:

a. The stipulation of exactly the seventh day of the week, which after all was changed already in the New Testament to the first day

b. Consecrating that day in the Israelite sense—that is, strict observance from evening to evening, by abstaining from all work, lighting a fire, cooking, and walking, and by bringing sacrifices and displaying the showbread

---

351. Turretin, *Institutes of Elenctic Theology*, 2:86–88 (XI.13.xxvi–xxix).
352. LO: *cultus.*
353. Lat. *juris positivi.*
354. Turretin, *Institutes of Elenctic Theology*, 2:87–88 (XI.13.xxx).

   c. Using the Sabbath as a type and shadow of the spiritual and heavenly rest to be gained by Christ (Col. 2:16)

The moral and permanent elements in this commandment are these:

   a. Worshiping God at set times; worshiping him communally in assemblies; maintaining church services, schools, and so on[355]

   b. Consecrating such set times, negatively by abstaining from ordinary, everyday work and positively by attending church services, studying God's Word, using the sacraments, and so forth

   c. Giving rest to servants and animals[356]

A difficult question is, Does the Fourth Commandment also obligate us morally, permanently, to observe not specifically the seventh day, but surely *one* of the seven days? Of course, God could just as well have given us one in ten or twenty days to observe; but given this positive commandment, are we duty bound to observe one of the seven days? This cannot be settled with certainty, beyond doubt. But the following arguments can be advanced for an affirmative answer:

   a. The seven-day week is grounded in the work of creation. After seven days the week ends and starts over again. God himself has instituted this order. It is entirely natural and fitting that God set aside one of those seven days for worshiping him.

   b. If none of the seven days is binding, then we are without any directive. Then we can speak with Gomarus merely of a sufficient number of days[357] for worship. And who determines that number?

   c. The New Testament churches did change the day, but maintained the weekly cycle, surely not arbitrarily or accidentally.

   d. Even if one says, No, only a sufficient number of days is being commanded here, then one still retains a ceremonial element; if not one of every seven days, then one of every ten or twenty days, and so on.

7. Is the first day, Sunday, instituted by God? Roman Catholics base this on canon law and the authority of the church. Others (Junius et al.) base it on the authority of Christ, who consecrated it by his resurrection, his appearances, and his outpouring of the Holy Spirit. The latter is all true, but these do not yet establish an institution. Texts like Acts 20:7; 1 Corinthians 16:1–2; and Revelation 1:10 do show that this day was soon observed by the churches in coming together when preaching and

---

355. Heidelberg Catechism, Q&A 103.
356. Turretin, *Institutes of Elenctic Theology*, 2:90 (XI.13.xl).
357. LO: *dies sufficientes*.

sacraments would be administered. That change occurred, if not at the apostles' command, nonetheless with their approval. In any case, it was not done arbitrarily or accidentally, such that it could just as well be undone today. It must be ascribed to the leading of the Holy Spirit, for the following reasons:

a. Such a change cannot be made in a commandment of the law—in the Decalogue, no less—by anyone other than God himself, who is the Lord of the Sabbath and who alone can grant a dispensation from a commandment.

b. If the change were not good, the apostles would certainly have withheld their approval and have urged observance of the Sabbath, which, however, according to Colossians 2:16, had been set aside.

c. The Christian church, consisting of both Jews and gentiles, from the outset unanimously observed Sunday. Thus, we can say that the change occurred by divine authority,[358] by the leading of the Holy Spirit among the apostles and the churches. That we cannot find a special command for this should not surprise us. God dealt in the same way with the abolition and replacement of all the Old Testament ceremonies. A formal commandment for abolishing circumcision does not exist, either. That children must be baptized, that women must partake of the Lord's Supper, and so on are not written anywhere, either. Jewish Christians continued to practice circumcision for a long time, alongside baptism. "In whatever condition each was called, there let him remain with God" (1 Cor. 7:24; cf. vv. 17–24). Gradually, and not by power or might, the Holy Spirit guided the churches to the new and caused them to outgrow the old. The old has not been replaced or abolished by the new, but in the new the old has been fulfilled, incorporated, and elevated. Thus, circumcision is fulfilled in baptism. Every ceremony is fulfilled in Christ. Sunday is the day of resurrection. Under the Old Testament the pattern was first work, then rest—that is, worship of God. Now, we are first strengthened by the worship of God, and from there we undertake everything with vigor. Then, moving toward the Sabbath was climbing up *toward* God. Today, we move *from* God into the wide world. Then, people ascended; today, we descend. Then, earth moved toward heaven; today, heaven comes down to earth. Then, the promise; today, fulfillment. Then, expectation; today, enjoyment. Then, from outside

358. LO: *auctoritate divina.*

to inside, from the periphery to the center. Today, just the reverse. Then, shadow; now, substance.

8. How is Sunday supposed to be observed? Negatively by abstaining from ordinary (servile) works[359] and from all work that brings profit and earns something toward our livelihood. Permitted are all works that directly pertain to divine worship (Matt. 12:5; John 5:8–9), all works of mercy (Matt. 12:10; John 5:9; 9:14; Luke 13:15), and all works of necessity (Mark 2:27).

Thus, no Jewish strictness![360] Cooking food, lighting a fire, making a bed, dressing, eating, and walking are certainly permitted. Nowhere does the New Testament teach that Sunday was observed by abstaining from work. Resting as such is still only negative and has no value in itself[361] (so the Lord's Day Alliance[362] is mistaken) and is only a means for practicing the positive. Positively, rest consists in consecrating oneself, dedicating oneself to God: congregational assemblies (Lev. 23:3; Acts 20:7), reading God's Word (Heb. 10:25), using the sacraments (Acts 20:7), singing (Col. 3:16; Acts 1:14), and gathering and presenting alms (1 Cor. 16:2).[363]

---

359. LO: *opera servilia.*
360. DO: *joodse gestrengheid.*
361. Turretin, *Institutes of Elenctic Theology,* 2:97–98 (XI.14.xxiv).
362. DO: *de Vereniging vor Zondagsrust handelt.*
363. Kuyper, "Uit de pers," states, "When discussing the question of Sunday observance, be sure to read the Epistle to the Galatians and the Heidelberg Catechism. To be sure, worldliness must be avoided, the day of rest must be used for its purpose, but that can happen only slowly. Churches should not take over the task of the conscience by determining in every case what is lawful, for then new questions will always arise for which Scripture gives no definite answers."

OUR DUTIES TOWARD OURSELVES

18

General Bodily Duties to Self

We also have duties to ourselves. Although grounded in our duty to God, these are distinct from our duty to God and arise from our being made in his image. A variety of classifications of duties have been proposed, but there is substantial agreement that we can arrange them into a number of duties toward the life of the body and duties toward the life of the soul. The former can be related well to the second table of the Ten Commandments; the latter toward the human faculties of intellect, feelings, and will.

Is it appropriate to call these duties "self-love"? After all, we are commanded, "Love your neighbor as yourself." From Augustine on, this question has been much discussed by theologians. It is best not to understand our duties toward ourselves as self-love. The notion is uncomfortable, open to misunderstanding, and never commanded in Scripture. It is better to subsume all duties toward self under the single duty of self-preservation, which is not identical to the instinct for self-preservation. It is a moral obligation.

Self-preservation finds its limit in the duty of self-denial, which helps us avoid the sin of selfishness. Selfishness is an idolatrous yearning for self-preservation and fails to accomplish its goal. Scripture teaches us that true self-preservation is, in fact, the loss of self. Our outer or carnal self, dominated by the sensual world, must be put to death so that our inner self, the true essential self that is created in God's image, may come alive. As the apostle Paul says, "I have been crucified with Christ. It is no longer I who live, but Christ who lives in me" (Gal. 2:20). Christian self-denial constitutes self-preservation.

We also have duties toward our bodies. We were created as embodied souls, and our bodies are not accidental to our humanity but an essential part of it, created in *the image of God and redeemed in Christ. Christ was bodily raised from the dead, and that is also the Christian's firm hope. Christianity is opposed to both ascetic spiritualism—whether it takes the form of Platonism, Neo-Platonism, or modern rationalism—and materialistic sensuousness, which pursues the liberation of the flesh.*

Christianity insists that we take care of our bodies, beginning with our health. Due to sin, the body has become more independent of and emancipated from the spirit and has become far more dependent on and bound to nature, to material things. Thus, our bodies often seduce our spirits, tempting us though the lust of the eyes and the lust of the flesh. Our bodies are also slavishly dependent on our outward nature and subject to various disorders and sicknesses. Scripture connects sickness and pain with death and locates its source in sin. Illnesses of the body and of the soul have deep moral significance. Being sick should not be despised as a "waste of time," but neither should we pursue a cult of health with its excessive focus on bodily ailments. Illnesses are often an excellent pedagogical means in God's hands. They pluck us out of our busy earthly occupational life, force us to rest, to be quiet, to experience solitude, and to contemplate our life, especially as we face eternity.

Nevertheless, even though a sickness is sent to us by God, we may fight it and pray for healing and look for means to cure it. God himself has supplied powers and means in nature for healing, and only God-ordained means may be used; Christians should avoid incantations, charms, and the like. Magnetism or hypnotism is not the same as spiritism; it does not involve summoning spirits. Yet it is not advisable to put ourselves in the power of someone else. Miraculous healing as a charism is in principle still very possible and cannot be denied but is likely reserved for extraordinary times. Positively, we may care for our health, because life is the prerequisite for performing our duties; we have been created with the desire to live.

§36. GENERAL DUTIES (SELF-PRESERVATION)

There are duties toward self.[1] Aristotle already knew the concept of self-love:[2] truly good persons love themselves fully, but this is not selfishness, for they love in themselves what is good and promotes that good.[3] The Stoics saw the common, basic instinct of all creatures in the drive toward self-preservation or self-love, in the "possessing life to preserve itself"[4] whereby every creature strives after what agrees with its nature. The highest good or happiness is

1. On duties to self, cf. chap. 14, §31, #8.
2. GrO: φιλαυτία; Aristotle, *Nicomachean Ethics* IX.8–9.
3. Wuttke, *Christian Ethics*, 1:111–13 (§19).
4. GrO: τὸ ζῷον ἴσχειν ἐπὶ τὸ τηρεῖν ἑαυτό.

found then in living in accordance with one's nature.[5] Thus Cyprian enumerates all the duties toward self, alongside those toward God and neighbor.[6] Thomas says that one can exercise the virtue of justice also toward oneself.[7]

Calvin also accepts self-love and duties toward self but deems it unnecessary to explain them.[8] We find them also with Polanus,[9] van Mastricht,[10] Pictet,[11] Lampe,[12] de Moor,[13] Buurt,[14] and Buddeus.[15]

1. The Existence of Duties toward Self

We do have duties toward ourselves. Vilmar, among others, denies this, and says that our duties toward ourselves fall entirely within and under those toward God; for I live honorably, for example, not for myself but for God; and conversely, our duties toward God are at the same time duties toward ourselves. Yet he does speak of the duties we have to sanctify our body, soul, and spirit.[16] Wendt says that having duties toward self is an impossible concept; after all, they are always based on a mutual relationship with others; duty is always a quid pro quo.[17] But we must raise the following objections:

a. Contra Vilmar, it must be said that God's honor is certainly the ultimate objective and basic reason of our moral behavior toward ourselves, as well as of all moral behavior toward nature and the neighbor; yet I am certainly the closest direct object of my moral actions. I believe unto my salvation; I sanctify myself; and so on.

b. Contra Wendt, it is incorrect to say that duty is always a quid pro quo, a compensation for something received; duty is not always based on justice. Duties are imposed upon us by God, who commands that we work out our salvation.

5. Zeller, *Outlines of the History of Greek Philosophy*, 245–47.

6. Ed. note: On the reference to Cyprian, see n. 123 in chap. 14 above.

7. Wuttke, *Christian Ethics*, 1:211 (§34); see Aquinas, *ST* IIa IIae q. 58 arts. 2 and 4.

8. *Institutes*, II.viii.54.

9. Polanus von Polansdorf, *Syntagma Theologiae Christianae*, 651–52.

10. Van Mastricht, *Theoretico-Practica Theologia*, III.iv.1–15 [IV, 776–840]. Ed. note: See chap. 13, n. 67, above for specifics on our annotation of van Mastricht's work.

11. Pictet, *De christelyke zedekunst*, 598–693 (book VII: "Van de Pligten en Deugden eens Christens met betrekking op zichzelven").

12. Lampe, *Schets der dadelyke Godt-geleertheid*, 387–447 (book II, chap. 7: "Van de Pligten, die uit de *zelfsliefde* vloeyen").

13. De Moor, *Commentarius Perpetuus*, 2:676.

14. Buurt, *Vervolg der Dadelijke godgeleerdheid*.

15. Buddeus, *Institutiones Theologiae Moralis*, 446–47 (book 11, chap. 3, §3).

16. Vilmar, *Theologische Moral*, 2/3:110–11 (§47).

17. Wendt, *Ueber das sittlich Erlaubte*, 27–28.

That we have duties toward ourselves is clear from this:

a. Every human being,[18] every individual, is God's image (Gen. 1:26; James 3:9), has inestimable worth, has been created for eternity, has an immortal soul of more value than the whole world (Matt. 16:26; Mark 8:36; Luke 9:25), and nothing among all creatures can be exchanged[19] for one's soul. This value or worth was expressed and clearly revealed first by Jesus.[20]

Pagans did not know the worth of an individual person and always thought in terms of whole people-groups (*volk*). The pantheists, materialists, socialists, communists, and others[21] do not know this value either and therefore do not know the concept of duty toward self. The state, the unit, society is everything for them. Thus, they demand an all-powerful state; everything becomes a matter of the state; all people become citizens of the state. Over against this, the worth of the individual is maintained more prominently by Kant with his categorical imperative; so too by Schleiermacher in his *Monologen* (*Soliloquies*),[22] and especially by Vinet[23] and also by Ritschl. A person is not a tool of the state, existing merely for its sake; on the contrary, we are ends in ourselves and have our own destiny and purpose.

b. Scripture also treats persons as those who have duties toward themselves. While socialism says it is better that one person die for the people than that the whole nation perish (cf. John 11:50; 18:14), Christianity is individualistic, focusing on the individual, on conscience, on what is most individualized within the person. In election, Christianity maintains the value of the individual.[24] Christianity brings the individual into a personal relationship with God (without any mediator except Christ alone) and commands every individual to believe, to repent, to work out their own salvation (Phil. 2:12), and to sanctify themselves (1 John 3:3) in soul, spirit, and body (1 Thess. 5:23). Believers are the apple of God's eye (Deut. 32:10; Ps. 17:8; Zech. 2:8).

c. However, although the person is the object of duty toward oneself, the basis of such duty does not lie in the person. We are not subjects who

18. Marginal note by Bavinck: "It is an honor to be human. Christ became a human being."
19. GrO: ἀντάλλαγμα.
20. See Matt. 6:25–32; 10:29–30; 12:3–8, 11–13.
21. Ed. note: Bavinck adds between the lines: "and the catholics."
22. Schleiermacher, *Friedrich Schleiermachers Monologen*; ET: *Schleiermacher's Soliloquies*.
23. Cf. Cramer, *Alexandre Vinet als christelijk moralist*, 46–48.
24. Vinet, *Essais de philosophie morale*. Cf. Cramer, *Alexandre Vinet als christelijk moralist*, 48.

obligate ourselves, we are not our own lawgiver (Kant), but God obligates us in our conscience. Reason and conscience are not an independent, autonomous basis of this duty, but are dependent on God, who establishes them, although they are immanent within us.[25]

2. Classification of Duties toward Self

What are those duties toward self? Here are several examples of classifications. Pictet includes the following in the seventh book of his *Christian Ethics*:[26] self-denial (1), humility (3), modesty (sober-mindedness) (4), moderation (5 and 10), feasts (11), intoxication (13), fornication (15), adultery (16), bravery (20), work (23), watchfulness (24); thus, he does not attempt to arrange them as yet.[27]

In his list of the Christian's duty to self, van Mastricht speaks of [occupation and] leisure, [use and abuse of] sustenance/provisions, [use and abuse of]

25. J. T. Beck, *Vorlesungen über christliche Ethik*, 2:185–90.

26. Chapter numbers are provided in parentheses after the title. Ed. note: It will be readily apparent that Bavinck's list is incomplete; the significance of this incompleteness is discussed in the next note. As it stands, this list, as well as those of van Mastricht and Lampe, also mixes positive and negative duties (virtues and vices) and gives credence to Bavinck's contention at the end of the paragraph that we do not see here a clear classification.

27. DO: *zelfverloochening; nederigheid; zedigheid; matigheid; gastmalen; dronkenschap; ontucht; overspel; dapperheid; arbeid; waakzaamheid*; Pictet, *De christelyke zedekunst*, 598–693 (book VII). Ed. note: Because Bavinck only provides a partial list of Pictet's virtues and vices, his point that Pictet does not attempt to classify them does not tell the full story. Because it is incomplete, Bavinck fails to incorporate Pictet's own pattern of subordination, especially of vices to virtues.

Book VII of *De christelyke zedekunst* is titled "The Duties and Virtues of Christians with Respect to Themselves" and contains twenty-five chapters, of which Bavinck mentions only eleven. Here are the missing chapters: 2: "Cross-Bearing and Following Christ" ("Kruis van Christus opnemen en hem navolgen"); 6: "Knowledge and Ignorance" ("Kennis en onwetenheid"); 7: "Carefulness" ("Voorzigtigheid"); 8: "Wisdom" ("Wijsheid"); 9: "Foolishness" ("Dwaasheid"); 12: "Gluttony and Debauchery ("Gulzigheid en brasserij"); 14: "Chastity" ("Kuisheid"); 17: "Moderation in Sleeping, Relaxation, and Games" ("Matigheid in 't slaapen, d'Uitspanningen en de spelen"); 18: "Stout-heartedness and Steadfastness" ("Kloekmoedigheid en standvastigheid"); 19: "Magnanimity and Generosity" ("Grootmoedignheit, edelmoedigheit"); 21: "Honesty" ("Eerlijkheid"); 22: "Propriety and Decency" ("Betaamlijkheid, Gevoegsaamheid"); 23: "Work, Industriousness, Laziness" ("Arbeid, naarstigheid, luiheid"); 25: "Contentment of Spirit, of Mind" ("Vergenoeging des geests, of des gemoeds"). From this it is evident that the vices of feasting (partying; #11), gluttony and debauchery (#12), and drunkenness (#13) are the vices that come from failures to exercise the first five virtues of self-denial, cross-bearing, humility, modesty, and moderation. Also, fornication (#15) and adultery (#16) are failures with respect to the specific virtue of chastity (#14), along with the first five. Furthermore, the virtues listed in ##16–25, along with their attendant vices, are the active, even public, demonstrations of Christian discipleship. Pictet's classification is very loose and not explicitly stated, but it is not without its own order and reflects the long-standing Christian tradition's examination of the virtues.

clothing, [use and abuse of] recreation, [use and abuse of] prosperity, [use and abuse of] world, cross-bearing [and its abuse], [use and abuse of] temptations, one's [bodily] cross [and its consolation],[28] horrors, blasphemous objections, spiritual desertion, doubt, and [the duties of piety concerning] death.[29]

Lampe speaks, for instance, of carelessness, lack of self-understanding, faintheartedness, intemperance, avarice, wastefulness, desire for recognition,[30] grandiosity, pursuit of fame, carousing, laziness, slothfulness[31]—over against concern for salvation, self-examination, moderation, kindheartedness, labor (sleep), sobriety, and fasting.[32]

With Wolff we find this arrangement: he identifies the "duties of man toward himself, and more specifically, toward his understanding, toward his will, toward his body" and distinguishes these from "the duty in regard to our outward condition (that is, our social position)."[33]

Stapfer arranges duties toward ourselves into four classes:

a. General duties as basis for the rest of our duties—namely, self-knowledge (1) and self-love (2)

b. Duties that avert harm: alertness and caution (3), abstinence and moderation (4), chastity (5), patience and equanimity (6)

c. Duties toward the soul: spiritual care and preparation for death (7)

---

28. Ed. note: This repetition is not an error. Van Mastricht's first reference to the cross (*Theoretico-Practica Theologia*, III.iv.8 [IV, 809–13]) concerns "bearing the cross, and its misuse"; the second (*Theoretico-Practica Theologia*, III.iv.10 [IV, 822–25]) deals with the "bodily cross and its consolation." (See chap. 13, n. 67, for specifics on our annotation of van Mastricht's work.)

29. DO/LO: *ledigheid/otio*; *levensonderhoud/alimentorum*; *kleding/vestitus*; *uitspanning/recreationum*; *voorspoed/prosperitatis*; *wereld/mundi*; *dragen van kruis/crucis tolerantia*; *verzoekingen/tentationum*; *kruis/crucis [corporalis]*; *verschrikkingen/melancholicis terroribus*; *godslasterlijke opwerpingen/suggestionibus blasphemicis*; *geestelijke verlatingen/desertionibus spiritualibus*; *twijfel/dibitationibus*; *dood/mortem*; van Mastricht, *Theoretico-Practica Theologia*, III.iv.1–15 [IV, 776–840]. Ed. note: Bavinck's list here is also incomplete; our additions in square brackets complete van Mastricht's full chapter topics. The Dutch originals in this note are exactly as in Bavinck's manuscript; the equivalent Latin originals were added by the editor. Bavinck also lists, in order, fourteen of the fifteen topics covered by van Mastricht in book 4 of his *Sketch of Ascetic Theology*; Bavinck does not include III.iv.7 [IV, 803–08]: "The Vanity of Human Things." For good reason, Bavinck does not repeat his complaint against Pictet about failure to classify. Van Mastricht's careful and precise ordering of material can be seen in the "Methodical Arrangement of the Whole Work," in van Mastricht, *Theoretical Practical Theology*, 1:61–62.

30. DO: *staatzucht*.

31. DO: *zorgeloosheid*; *onkunde van zichzelf*; *kleinmoedigheid*; *onmatigheid*; *gierigheid*; *verkwisting*; *staatzucht*; *grootsheid*; *overdadigheid*; *naamzoeking*; *breasserij*; *gemakzucht*; *luiheid*.

32. DO: *zorg voor zaligheid*; *zelfonderzoek*; *matigheid*; *zachtmoedigheid*; *arbeid (slaap)*; *soberheid*; *vasten*; Lampe, *Schets der dadelyke Godt-geleertheid*, book II, chap. 7.

33. According to Wuttke, *Christian Ethics*, 1:296 (§40).

d. Duties toward the body: care of the body (8), improvement of all the capacities of soul and body (9), duties toward outward prosperity (10), and industriousness and redeeming the time (11)[34]

Reinhard classifies all duties into those toward mind, feelings, and will.[35] To the first he reckons the formation of the mind in general, love of truth (184–91, §203), memory training (192–96, §204), imagination (196–209, §205), investigation (218–22, §207), faith (222–37, §208), self-knowledge (237–58, §209), self-esteem (258–61, §210), knowledge of human character and of the world (261–82, §211), knowledge of religion (278–304, §§212–13), banter (305–15, §214), ideals (315–31, §215), and the relation between intellect and feelings (331–38, §216).[36]

Among duties toward feelings,[37] Reinhard discusses emotions (339–45, §217), general formation (345–47, §218), self-esteem (347–57, §219), perfection (357–62, §220), dissatisfaction with oneself (362–63, §221), conformity to God and Jesus (364–75, §222), gratitude toward God (376–82, §223), obedience (382–92, §224), trust (393–404, §225), patience (405–17, §226), religiosity (417–19, §227), being conscientious (420–24, §228), attitude toward Jesus (424–34, §229), human appreciation (435–41, §230), kindness toward people (444–47, §232), generosity (448–63, §233), ambition (464–74, §234), meekness (474–81, §235), heavenly mindedness (481–86, §236), and simplicity (487–88, §237).[38]

---

34. Stapfer, *De zeden-leer*, 5:304–5.

35. Reinhard, *System der christlichen Moral*, 2:179–80. Ed. note: Page references that follow in the text are to this work, second volume.

36. DO/GO: *waarheidsliefde/Wahrheitsliebe*; *vorming van het geheugen/Bildung des Empfindungsvermogens und das Gedachtenisses*; *verbeelding/Heerschaft über die Einbildungskraft*; *onderzoek/Untersuchungsgeist*; *geloof/Glaubenspflicht*; *zelfkennis/Selbsterkenntnis*; *zelfwaardering/Selbstschätzung*; *wereld-en mensen kennis/Welt- und Menschenkenntnis*; *godsdienstkennis/Religionserkenntnis*; *scherts/Uebung und gebrauch des Witzes*; *idealen/Umweisung der Ideale*; *verstand en gevoel/Verhältnis Vernunft [und] Gefühlsvermögen*. Ed. note: Bavinck does not include Reinhard's §206, "Culture of Fantasy" ("Cultur der Phantasie"), 310–18, as a separate category. Bavinck has only one category for "knowledge of religion" (*godsdienstkennis*), while Reinhard divides the topic into "General" (§212) and specifically Christian (§213).

37. Ed. note: Reinhard starts a whole new section here: "Christian Perfection in Feelings, or Concerning the Duties of the Christian Senses" ("Christliche Volkommenkeit im Empfinden, oder Von den Pflichten des christlichen Sinnes").

38. DO/GO: *gevoel/Gefühle und Gesinnungen*; *algemene vorming/allgemeine Erläuterung über den christlichen Sinn*; *zelfachting/Selbstachtung*; *volmaking/Gefühl für Vollendung*; *ontevredenheid met zichzelf/Unzufriedenheit mit sich selbst*; *gelijkheid met God en Jezus/dankbaarheid jegens God/Dankbarkeit gegen Gott*; *gehoorzaamheid/Gehorsam gegen Gottes Gesetze*; *vertrouwen/Vertauen auf Gott*; *geduld/Geduld im Leiden*; *religiositeit/herrschende Religiosität*; *consciëntieusteit/Gewissenhaftigkeit genzindheid jegens Jezus/Gesinnungen gegen Jesum*; *waardeeering van de mens/Werthschätzung der menschlichen Natur, welwillen jegens mensen/herrschendes Wohlwollen gege die Menschen*; *grootmoedigheit/Grossmuth*; *eerzucht/Ehrbegiert*;

Among the duties toward the will,[39] Reinhard speaks first about

a. Those toward our body (2:511–646, §§242–64): health, self-defense, moderation, emotions, fasting, chastity, gracefulness, clothing, illnesses, and death[40]

b. Those connected with striving after external happiness[41] (3:1–120, §§265–83): wealth, property, the increase and use of wealth and property, honor, dominion, sensual enjoyment, and pleasures[42]

c. Those connected with promoting of the common good[43] (3:122–296; §§284–306): toward animals, people, justice, benevolence, alms, truth, politeness, sociability; toward strangers and the dead[44]

d. Those connected with specific relationships[45] (298–676, §§307–48): marriage, parents, children, the state, the arts, and so on[46]

e. Those relating to the worship of God (678–818, §§349–58)[47]

Immanuel Kant arranges duties toward self into those arising from our animal nature and those arising from our moral nature; to the latter belong also the duties to be religious and to consider conscience as divine.[48]

---

deemoed/Demuth; hemelse zin/himmlischer Sinn; eenvoud/Gefühl für Gleichförmigkeit und Zusammenstimmung aller unserer Thätigkeiten. Ed. note: Bavinck does not include Reinhard's §231, "Works Sympathetic to the Troubles of Humanity" ("Theilnehmendes Werken auf die Ungelegenheiten des menschlichen Geschlechts"), 442–44, as a separate category.

39. Ed. note: Reinhard starts another new section here: "Christian Perfection in Actions, or, Concerning the Duties of Christian Conduct and Life" ("Christliche Volkommenkeit im Handeln, oder, Von den Pflichten des christlichen Betragens und Lebens; 2:509–3:296).

40. DO: *gezondheid; noodweer; matigheid; affecten; vasten; kuisheid; bevalligheid; kleding; krankheden; dood.* Ed. note: We are only providing Bavinck's Dutch originals here; his list is selective (only ten sections out of twenty-two), and he summarizes with one term material to which Reinhard dedicates a number of sections, each with subtle nuances.

41. DO/GO: *streven naar uitwendig geluk/Betragen beim Suchen und dem Genusse des äusserlichen Glücks.*

42. DO: *rijkdom, eigendom, vermeerdering [van rijkdom and eignedom], gebruik [van rijkdom and eignedom], eer, heerschappij, zinlijke genietingen, vergenoegens.* Ed. note: We again provide only Bavinck's Dutch originals; once again his list is selective and simplifies Reinhard's discussion.

43. GO: *Beförderung des allgemeines Besten.*

44. DO: *jegens dieren, mensen, gerechtigheid, welwillen, aalmoes, waarheid, beleefdheid, gezelligneid, jegens vreemdelingen, gestorvenen.* Ed. note: See nn. 40–42 above.

45. DO: *bepaalde verhoudingen.*

46. DO: *huwelijk, ouders, kinderen, Staat, kunsten.* Ed. note: See nn. 40–42 above; Bavinck's "and so on" covers a number of significant missing topics: divorce and remarriage (§§322–23), duties arising from class (§§329–30), friendship (§§331–32), duties of patriotism (§§334–37), war (§340), relation of church and state (§§346–48).

47. Ed. note: Bavinck does not include the specifics found in Reinhard, including prayer (§351), vows (§352), family worship (§353), feast days (§354), oaths (§355), confession and martyrdom (§356), religious zeal (§357), and prudence (§358).

48. Ed. note: Bavinck provides no references for these statements about Kant.

After a number of introductory sections on "Duties to Self" (§§859–69),[49] Rothe engages in a lengthy discussion of "Ascetics"[50] (464–526, §§870–86). The disciplined life in general makes it possible to fulfill the "particular duties toward the self" (§§887–1003).[51] He then notes that there are as many duties toward self as there are virtues,[52] and specifies self-development toward the following sixteen personal virtues: self-possession, happiness, strength of personality, self-control, health, purity, skill, independence, significance, love, professional competence, respectability, education, beauty, piety, character.[53]

Despite differences, there is nevertheless substantial agreement regarding duties toward self. We can arrange them as follows:

I. Duties toward the life of the body: making provision for one's[54]

    1. health
    2. sustenance
    3. clothing   } Sixth Commandment
    4. life

    5. chastity→Seventh Commandment

    6. honor, renown→Ninth Commandment

    7. property→Eighth Commandment

49. GO: *Selbstpflichten*; Rothe, *Theologische Ethik*, 3:454–63; page and section numbers that follow are to this volume.

50. GO: *Die Asketik*; Rothe, *Theologische Ethik*, 3:464–526 (§§870–86). Ed. note: Rothe divides this material into "Means of Moral Virtue" ("Die sittlichen Tugendmittel"; 3:464–89 [§§871–75]) and "Means of Religious Virtue" ("Die religiösen Tugendmittel"; 3:489–526 [§§876–86]).

51. GO: *bezonderen Selbstpflichten*; Rothe, *Theologische Ethik*, 4:1–219 (§§887–1003).

52. Rothe, *Theologische Ethik*, 4:1–219 (§§887–1003); cf. 3:207–23 (§§609–34). See HathiTrust Digital Library, https://babel.hathitrust.org/cgi/pt?id=hvd.hnxe9f&view=1up&seq=227.

53. GO/DO: *Eigenthumhaftigkeit* (§§888–99), *Glückseligkeit/gelukzaligheid* (§§900–905), *Kräftigkeit der Persönlichkeit/kracht* (§§906–11), *Selbstbeherrschung/zelfbeheersing* (§§912–13), *Gesundheit/gezondheid* (§§914–16), *Reinheit/reinheid* (§§917–20), *Vermöglichkeit* (§§921–26), *Selbstständigkeit/zelfstandigheid* (§§927–29), *Gewichtigkeit* (§§930–31), *Liebe/liefde* (§§932–38), *Berufstüchtigkeit* (§§939–52), *Ehrenhaftigkeit* (§§953–64), *Erbildetheit* (§§965–71), *Schönheit* (§§972–77), *Frömmigkeit* (§§978–90), *Charakter/karakter* (§§991–1003). Ed. note: We have reversed our usual DO/GO order in this note because Bavinck uses more of Rothe's original German terms than Dutch ones in this list and misses the key notion of "personality" in the third one. In Rothe, the full import of this list is clarified by the heading "The duty, to train oneself" (*Die Pflicht, sich selbst zu erziehen*) and, in each of the sixteen duties: "to the capacity for" (or "ability to"; *zu tugendhafter . . .*).

54. Ed. note: In his manuscript Bavinck designates this as §37 but then actually covers the material in §§37–41.

II. Duties toward the life of the soul[55]

    1. toward temperament, character

    2. toward intellect, memory, judgment, imagination

    3. toward feelings

    4. toward the will

3. On Self-Love

Can all these duties be reduced to the single duty of *self-love*?[56] Augustine already discussed this and found it in the commandment "You shall love your neighbor *as yourself*" (Lev. 19:18; Matt. 22:39).[57] Concerning the resurrection of the flesh, Tertullian says (about one's own flesh), "There is none, after the Lord, whom you should love so dearly; none more like a brother to you, which is even born along with yourself in God."[58] Chrysostom and Augustine say the same.[59] Calvin also accepts the duty of self-love, but adds that it is self-evident that self-love has been omitted from the law and that the person who leads the best and holiest life is the one "who lives and strives for himself as little as he can."[60] And when God commands that we are to love our neighbor as ourselves, he does not mean that he ranks self-love[61] first and love of others second, but that he wants us to transfer our natural disposition toward self to others; love does not seek its own (1 Cor. 13:5). Love toward others is not subject to love of self. "But he shows that the emotion of love, which out of natural depravity commonly resides within ourselves, must now be extended to another, that we may be ready to benefit our neighbor with

55. Ed. note: In his manuscript Bavinck designates this as §38 but then actually covers the material in §42.

56. Cf. Bavinck, *Foundations of Psychology*, 188. Ed. note: In a section on human "drives," Bavinck states his case cautiously:

> Perhaps all these drives are to be traced back to the drive for self-preservation. Every created thing is implanted with a striving to persevere in its existence. All beings value themselves, seek what is advantageous, avoid what is harmful, and strive for happiness. This self-love is the root from which all activities of the desiring faculty arise. It is the condition without which there could be no drive or desire, longing or act of will, hope or fear, joy or sorrow, love or hate.

Original: *Beginselen der psychologie*, 139. On self-love (*eigenliefde*) see Teyler's Godgeleerd Genootschap, *Verhandelingen, raakende den natuurlyken en geopenbaarden godsdienst*, 18:331.

57. Augustine, *On Christian Doctrine* I.23–26 (NPNF[1] 2:528–29). Ed. note: Bavinck's source is Polanus von Polansdorf, *Syntagma Theologiae Christianae*, 651.

58. Tertullian, *On the Resurrection of the Body* 63 (ANF 3:594), Christian Classics Ethereal Library, https://ccel.org/ccel/tertullian/resurrection_flesh/anf03.v.viii.lxiii.html.

59. Cf. Polanus von Polansdorf, *Syntagma Theologiae Christianae*, 651.

60. LO: *quam minimum fieri potest, sibi vivet ac studet*; *Institutes*, II.viii.54.

61. Gk. φιλαυτία.

no less eagerness, ardor, and care than ourselves."[62] This shows that Calvin has little use for self-love.

Polanus accepts the duty of self-love because (a) it is commanded by God (James 4:9);[63] (b) it is approved by David, the apostles, and Christ (Matt. 12:3–4, 7); (c) it is evident in Christ himself, who avoided personal dangers when his hour had not yet come; (d) we are of great value, since Christ gave himself up for us; and (e) we are temples of the Holy Spirit. Polanus places self-love over against hatred of self and inordinate self-love.[64]

The duty of self-love is discussed also by Bernard de Moor and Frederik Lampe.[65]

Wuttke states that there is an "*ante-moral* love, one that is *per se* not yet moral but which simply leads to the moral."[66] It is the same with self-love; it is involuntary and natural, also with animals. It must be formed into a moral love by subjecting it to love for God. If this is not done voluntarily, then self-love becomes immoral and sinful. Scripture recognizes self-love (1 Sam. 18:1, 3; Matt. 22:39; Luke 10:27; Rom. 13:9; Gal. 5:14; Eph. 5:28–29, 33; James 2:8). The phrase *as yourself* (in the command to love your neighbor as yourself) "is not a mere comparison of two parallel forms of love—both are at bottom but *one* love; a truly moral love of one's self as a moral personality; . . . true love of neighbor is also at the same time true self-love."[67] Thus, true love of self as a moral person is true neighbor love, and the reverse; feigned neighbor love is also feigned self-love (Matt. 5:46–47; Luke 6:32).[68] I love my neighbor not for my sake, but for God's sake, but loving my neighbor is a moral enjoyment.[69] True self-love is the model and measure of neighbor love (Matt. 7:12). Likewise, self-love is good.[70] Christians must love themselves with their whole heart. Sin really consists of loving

---

62. LO: *Sed ubi naturali pravitate solebat amoris affectus in nobis residere, ostendit aliuo jam oportere diffundi*; *Institutes* II.viii.54.

63. Ed. note: James 4:9 does not appear to address the question of self-love, either directly or indirectly. We have retained the reference here because Bavinck correctly cites Polanus, and there may be reasons he refers to this verse that are as yet unknown to us. Polanus approves of Christian self-love "because it is commanded by God, James 4:9" ("*quia est à Deo præcepta, Jacob. 4. v. 9*").

64. LO: *inordinatus amor dei*; Polanus von Polansdorf, *Syntagma Theologiae Christianae*, 651.

65. Ed. note: Bavinck provides no source references.

66. Wuttke, *Christian Ethics*, 2:163 (§92); Wuttke gives the example of "the child at its mother's breast" (164 [§93]).

67. Wuttke, *Christian Ethics*, 2:256 (§124).

68. Wuttke, *Christian Ethics*, 2:256 (§124).

69. DO: *zedelijk genot*; Wuttke, *Christian Ethics*, 2:257–59 (§125).

70. Wuttke, *Handbuch der christlichen Sittenlehre*³, 2:6 (§154).

self instead of loving God.[71] Love for God sanctifies self-love. Self-love then is loving oneself as a child of God, in fellowship with him, and thus also hating the sin within us.

Schwarz says that passages like Matthew 22:39 do not command self-love but assume it, just as they assume the duties of self-examination and self-evaluation.[72] Philosophical ethics may therefore adopt the concept of self-love as an acknowledgment, also within itself, of the idea of our humanity. Theological ethics requires the duty of self-love as a disposition to preserve spiritual life (2 Cor. 7:1), to renew it (Eph. 4:23), and in this way to be glorified (2 Cor. 3:18). Therefore, the subject here is the Christian.[73] In self-preservation, the person is the subject; self-preservation is pure feeling and leads to solipsism (2 Cor. 10:12). Every duty toward self is a duty toward the neighbor, and vice versa. Christian self-love, then, is self-esteem, self-development, and so on.

Burger also accepts the duty of self-love, distinguishing it from egoism and selfishness.[74]

Julius Müller states that self-love differs from the propensity toward self-preservation, which, of course, is not yet moral.[75] Self-love is recognized in Scripture,[76] and though the phrase is not very apt, it does indicate that persons are the object of their own moral obligation.[77] Being an object of one's own moral obligation cannot occur in one's "existing for self," in one's pure naturalness (this is only the drive toward self-preservation in the form of a reflex), but only in relation to God and the value of human being that flows from that relation, as the image of God.[78] The object of the moral duty, therefore, is the person in fellowship with God. Therefore, self-preservation and selfishness[79] must be contrasted with true Christian self-love.[80]

---

71. Wuttke, *Handbuch der christlichen Sittenlehre*³, 2:36–39 (§163).

72. Schwarz, "Selbstliebe," 22.

73. Thus, this is a specifically Christian virtue in human persons. Cf. Aquinas, *ST* IIa IIae q. 77 art. 4.

74. DO: *Eigenliefde, zelfzucht*; Burger, "Liebe," 667.

75. J. Müller, *Christian Doctrine of Sin*, 1:138–39: "As an ethical conception [self-love] must be carefully distinguished from that merely natural impulse towards self-preservation which man has in common with the lower animals" (138).

76. J. Müller, *Christian Doctrine of Sin*, 1:140.

77. J. Müller, *Christian Doctrine of Sin*, 1:140.

78. J. Müller, *Christian Doctrine of Sin*, 1:141.

79. GO: *Selbsterhaltung; Selbstsucht*.

80. J. Müller, *Christian Doctrine of Sin*, 1:141. Ed. note: Müller explains nicely that we have a threefold relation to ourselves: "First there is the natural instinct of SELF-PRESERVATION, which is not, to begin with, of a moral character, but the conception of which includes the natural desire of man for a state of satisfaction conformable with his individual nature. Upon the awakening of his moral consciousness two contrasted paths present themselves to this

Thomas Aquinas says that self-love,[81] as such, is good and is a duty (Lev. 19), but inordinate self-love is the cause and origin of all sin.[82] He says elsewhere that self-love is found in all people insofar as they love their own self-preservation (all people love themselves, their own existence).[83] Only for those who are good does this hold insofar as they love their inward self; for those who are evil, this holds insofar as they love the outward self, their sensitive and corporeal nature.[84] However, since this latter group does not know themselves well, they do not truly love themselves either; they do not seek spiritual things; their natural love is thus faulty.[85]

Isaak Dorner also acknowledges the duty of self-love.[86] Others deny that self-love exists as a proper moral category. Fichte denies it and tries to derive the duties we have toward self from the moral community.[87] He says that each person is an end for the other but that for oneself, the person is only a means and instrument of the moral law.

Rothe denies the duty of self-*love*, for love presupposes more people and assumes the other as object.[88] There is no evidence in Scripture for this. The true element in this claim is the duty to develop into a character who possesses virtue. True self-love and social love are one and the same. Duties toward the self are thus simultaneously duties toward society, and vice versa.

Sartorius also denies the duty of self-love.[89] The essence of love is self-denial,[90] presupposes a "Thou," is a surrender to the other, does not seek its own (1 Cor. 13:5), is self-denial but not loss of self (Eph. 5:28, 33). People who love their neighbor love themselves, but not vice versa. As soon as one relates love to oneself in isolation, then it is not love, but selfishness. Scripture does not command the duty of self-love, but it does command self-denial (Matt. 16:24–25). The phrase "as yourself" (Matt. 22:39) is not self-love, nor is it a model for neighbor love. It does not say "as you love yourself," but commands us to seek the object of our love not in self but in our neighbor,

---

natural impulse, the one downwards, the other upwards. It may sink down into SELFISHNESS, or it may rise into MORAL SELF-LOVE by self-denying obedience to the divine law, whose germ is love to God."

81. LO: *amor sui.*

82. LO: *inordinatus amor sui causa et initium est omnis peccati*; Aquinas, *ST* Ia IIae q. 77 art. 4 ad 1.

83. LO: *diligunt sui ipsorum conservationem*; Aquinas, *ST* IIa IIae q. 25 art. 7 ad 1.

84. LO: *naturam sensitivam et corporatem*; Aquinas, *ST* IIa IIae q. 25 art. 7 co.

85. Aquinas, *ST* IIa IIae q. 25 art. 7 co.

86. Dorner, *System of Christian Ethics*, 445–503 (§§56–68).

87. J. G. Fichte, *Sämmtliche Werke*, 4:254–71 (§§19–20).

88. Rothe, *Theologische Ethik*, 2:405–6, Observation 1 (§845).

89. E. Sartorius, *Die Lehre von der heiligen Liebe*, 64–65.

90. GO: *Entselbstigung.*

to view our neighbor as we view our own self or another self, whereby a stranger becomes a neighbor.[91]

Wendt, too, refuses to acknowledge self-love and denies even duties toward self.[92] Schenkel also speaks about self-love.[93] Hoekstra also rejects the idea of self-love.[94]

Summary Evaluation of the Idea of Self-Love

Certainly, as we have seen (above), we have duties to self.[95] But there are good reasons why these cannot be understood as self-*love*:

1. Love toward self, also according to Müller,[96] is somewhat uncomfortable and seemingly improper; it is open to misunderstanding[97] and yet indispensable. Love always presupposes an "other," since it is not "I" oriented but "you" oriented[98] (Sartorius), and consists in self-surrender and self-denial; it does not seek its own (1 Cor. 13:5). Therefore, self-love is a contradiction. Self-love destroys the essence of love. Love demands an object. God is love, because he is triune.

2. Scripture repeatedly commands love for God and the neighbor, but never love for oneself.[99] But is self-love not presupposed in Matthew 22:39, Luke 10:27, Romans 13:9, Galatians 5:14, and James 2:8—all of which are taken from Leviticus 19:18—and cannot self-love be derived from this? Self-love certainly is not present directly. Jesus does not intend to teach how we should love ourselves, but how we should love our neighbor. Now we must certainly add "you shall love"[100] to the phrase "as

91. E. Sartorius, *Die Lehre von der heiligen Liebe* (1:65n), appeals to Luther's commentary on Gal. 5:14; to Schleiermacher, *Entwurf eines Systems der Sittenlehre*; and to Augustine, *On Christian Doctrine* I.23–28 (NPNF[1] 2:528–30).

92. Wendt, *Ueber das sittlich Erlaubte*, 27.

93. Schenkel, *Die christliche dogmatik*, 2/1:16, 235–37.

94. Hoekstra, *Vrijheid in verband met zelfbewustheid*, 164. Ed. note: Hoekstra contends that the notion of self-love (DO: *eigenliefde*) or love to oneself (DO: *liefde tot zichzelven*) is a combination of two words that are mutually exclusive (DO: *waarvan het eene het andere buitensluit*).

95. GO: *Selbstpflichten*.

96. J. Müller, *Christian Doctrine of Sin*, 1:137.

97. Burger, "Liebe," 667.

98. Ed. note: Bavinck here uses the two terms used by E. Sartorius, "egoism" and "tuism" (*Die Lehre von der heiligen Liebe*, 65).

99. Marginal note by Bavinck: "Indeed, it even forbids the φιλῶν τὴν ψυχὴν αὐτοῦ (John 12:25); thus Vilmar, *Theologische Moral*, 1:288, 290." Ed. note: Bavinck takes this variation of the Greek text directly from Vilmar. See HathiTrust Digital Library, https://babel.hathitrust.org/cgi/pt?id=hvd.ah4kcd&view=1up&seq=308.

100. GrO: ἀγαπᾷς.

yourself,"[101] as Ephesians 5:28–33 also proves.[102] Nevertheless, self-love is not being proposed here as an example and standard of neighbor love. The two are not compared and equated. But neighbor love is here being urged and described in terms of what it should be like. Namely, people feed and care for their own bodies (Eph. 5:29), treat themselves well, care for themselves, instinctively and naturally. So then, neighbor love must be just as spontaneous, prompt, automatic, and natural. Love your neighbor as if your neighbor were your own self; your neighbor will be the object of your love as if your neighbor were as close to you as you yourself are. We are closest to ourselves, the saying goes, but Jesus says, No, the neighbor (the closest one)[103] is as close to you as you are to yourself.

Thus, it is also written in Matthew 7:12: "So whatever you wish that others would do to you, do also to them, for this is the Law and the Prophets." This is a very practical precept, made clear and illuminated by the human habit to choose for oneself what is good. Paul makes a similar point about marriage: "In the same way husbands should love their wives as their own bodies. He who loves his wife loves himself. For no one ever hated his own flesh, but nourishes and cherishes it, just as Christ does the church. . . . However, let each one of you love his wife as himself, and let the wife see that she respects her husband" (Eph. 5:28–29, 33). This clarifies the notion that the reverse (he who loves himself loves his wife) is not true, but it is the way Paul puts it. Why? Because the wife is his own body (just as the church is the very body of Christ, vv. 29–30) and has become one body with him (v. 31). And this is a profound mystery (v. 32). So that is to say: You must love your wife as if she were you yourself, for she is surely not a stranger to you, but she is your own self, one flesh with you, your own body. The neighbor—in this case, the wife—must be loved as one who is just as near to you as you are to yourself. That is the idea.

3. But even if, properly speaking, there is no self-love, nevertheless no one has ever hated his own body, but feeds it and cares for it (Eph. 5:29). That is true. There is an instinct for self-preservation[104] (cf. the Stoics and Spinoza: every creature seeks to maintain its own existence). Nevertheless, our duties toward ourselves cannot be reduced to self-preservation, either,

---

101. GrO: ὡς σεαυτόν.

102. J. Müller, *Christian Doctrine of Sin*, 1:140n.

103. Ed. note: Bavinck draws a contrast between *naast* (near) and the superlative *naaste* (nearest).

104. GO: *Selbsterhaltungstrieb*.

as Hobbes and Spinoza wanted. This instinct is a property of animals, of all existing beings; it is therefore natural, obvious, and necessary. It is a property of all our organs—the eye, ear, hand, finger, and so on. This instinct also does not exist in Spinoza's sense, for then suicide, attempted self-destruction, would be inexplicable—just as inexplicable as surrendering oneself to sensuality or all sorts of sin, loving death, and willfully injuring oneself (cf. Prov. 8:36). At that point the demand for self-denial would be impossible.[105] Moreover, the instinct for self-preservation is not yet moral but natural. After all, we are ourselves the object of moral action, for we may and must work out our own salvation. It is therefore difficult to find a general duty that includes the specific duties toward self. Is that the reason they are not mentioned separately in the Decalogue?

4. It may also be argued against self-love that if self-love is legitimate, then sin would appear to proceed merely from something good in itself, thus from excessive or inordinate self-love[106] (Aquinas). And does not the distinction between good and evil in this way then become entirely a matter of degree? Conversely, if there is no love for ourselves, then there appears to be no duty toward self, either (Wendt, Fichte), and then the Ten Commandments contain no duty toward self.

5. It is better to subsume all duties toward ourselves under the single duty of *self-preservation* (not the instinct for self-preservation).[107] This is not an inevitable or automatic instinct; it is moral and valid both for the soul and for the body. Save yourselves for your life's sake (Gen. 19:17; Acts 2:40). "To save"[108] is a genuine biblical notion. Beck also rejects self-love and speaks of "self-regard,"[109] but nevertheless he uses the term "self-love."[110]

4. On Self-Denial

The duty of *self-preservation* finds its limit in the duty of *self-denial*. Through sin, the duty of self-preservation has degenerated into and been twisted into

---

105. Cf. Baumann, *Handbuch der Moral*, 130.

106. LO: *nimius amor sui*; *amor sui inordinatus*. Ed. note: The first Latin phrase is from J. Müller, *Christian Doctrine of Sin*, 1:136; the second is from Aquinas, *ST* Ia IIae q. 77 art. 4 ad 1.

107. DO/GO: *zelf-behoud*; *Selbsterhaltungstrieb*.

108. HO: הוֹשִׁיעַ; GrO: σῴζω.

109. GO: *Selbstschätzung*; Gk. λογίζεσθαι ἑαυτόν = to regard oneself.

110. GO: *Selbstliebe*; J. T. Beck, *Vorlesungen über christliche Ethik*, 2:184–231 (see esp. 195).

a love of one's own life[111] (John 12:25), into a pleasing of self[112] (Rom. 15:1), into a seeking of self[113] (1 Cor. 13:5)—that is, into selfishness.[114] That does not mean always isolating oneself from others or withdrawing from society. No, the selfish person lives in the midst of the world, society, and people. Selfishness means making oneself the center of one's thoughts, desires, feelings, and actions, defining and assessing everything in terms of one's own self: "Man is the measure of all things."[115] Selfishness originated with the claim that "you will be like God" (Gen. 3:5), with withdrawing oneself from subjection to God, with isolating oneself from God. When God is no longer the center, then immediately our own ego, our own individual existence, our own right, happiness, esteem, honor, money, fame, and name become the center. And then conflict arises automatically, not only with God but also with the neighbor. Everything, including the neighbor, is then judged and treated from the perspective of the self rather than from the perspective of God and his law. Selfishness then makes us seek what is pleasing, suitable, and beneficial, and that is what we then consider to be the good. We are then always looking for self-advancement, self-glorification, and self-gratification. We seek to flatter our ego, to treat our ego well, to enliven our ego, and to provide our ego with whatever it desires and with whatever the world can give. And thus we become slaves of our own ego and of the world around us.[116] And that selfishness is *singular*, whether it manifests itself more sensually as hedonism or more spiritually as pride.[117]

This selfishness, then, is a yearning for self-preservation (Matt. 16:25; Mark 8:35; Luke 9:24; 17:33); it is a loving of one's life (John 12:25). But Scripture condemns this yearning for self-preservation and considers it a false yearning and the opposite of duty. Over against this false yearning for self-preservation, Scripture sets before us the duty of self-denial[118]—that is, the duty of true, genuine self-preservation. For God demands that we give up not something essential, something real, and something good, but only the delusion that selfishness truly provides self-preservation. That self-preservation, Scripture says, is indeed the loss of self. For Holy Scripture makes a distinction between parts of a twofold self, a twofold ego within us:

111. GrO: φιλεῖν τὴν ψυχὴν ἑαυτοῦ.
112. GrO: ἑαυτοῖς ἀρέσκειν.
113. GrO: ζητεῖ τὰ ἑαυτῆς.
114. DO: *zelfzucht.*
115. Gk. ἄνθρωπος μέτρον πάντων (Protagaras). Ed. note: For more on selfishness and egocentricity, see *RE*, 1:100–116.
116. J. T. Beck, *Vorlesungen über christliche Ethik*, 2:195–97.
117. Burger, "Selbstsucht."
118. DO: *zelfverloochening.*

a. The carnal ego[119] (Rom. 7:14) and "our outer self"[120] (2 Cor. 4:16), the untrue ego, the depraved ego, the ego dominated by the sensual world, the ego that looks to the sensual world for self-preservation, and

b. "Our inner self"[121] (2 Cor. 4:16), not identical to the regenerated person or to the new person,[122] but the true essential self within us, the person who has been "made in the likeness of God"[123] (James 3:9), "the hidden person of the heart"[124] (1 Pet. 3:4)

Concerning all of this, Scripture says and demands that we deny, kill, and hate that first ego, with its instinct for self-preservation.[125] Nevertheless, even in connection with this ego, a distinction must again be made. The outer self[126] is not, as a matter of course, identical with the old self,[127] with the carnal self.[128] Our ego, as sinful, as carnal, must not be denied, but killed, crucified, buried with Christ (Gal. 2:20; Rom. 6; Col. 3). But that same ego, not as sinful, but as mere natural, sensual, external, must be denied as soon as it conflicts with higher interests. Now, satisfying the yearning for self-preservation of the external ego by means of food, drink, marriage, and so on is in itself often not impermissible. But as soon as that yearning conflicts with the demand of Jesus, of the kingdom of heaven, the entire external ego must be denied, not given a hearing, refused, and rejected.[129] Yes, then even the inherently good love for parents and the like must be denied: father and mother must be hated (Matt. 10:37; Luke 14:26); the young man must sell his goods (Matt. 19:21); eye and ear and hand must be cut off (Matt. 5:29; 18:9–10); house and fields must be forsaken (Matt. 19:29; Mark 10:29; Luke 18:29); Abraham must sacrifice his son (Gen. 22); the dead must be left behind, and one is not to look back (Luke 9:62–63). Yes, and then one's own life, and one's own soul,[130] in this sense, must be given up (Matt. 10:39; 16:25; 26:35; Luke 22:33; John 13:36; Acts 20:24; Rom. 16:4; 2 Cor. 12:15; Phil. 2:17, 30; 2 Tim. 4:6; 1 John 3:16; Rev. 2:13; 12:11). Our entire earthly existence and life—often termed

119. GrO: ἐγὼ δὲ σάρκινος.
120. GrO: ἔξω ἄνθρωπος.
121. GrO: ἔσω ἄνθρωπος.
122. GrO: καινός ἄνθρωπος.
123. GrO: ἀνθρώπους τοὺς καθ᾽ ὁμοίωσιν θεοῦ γεγονότας.
124. GrO: ὁ κρυπτὸς τῆς καρδίας ἄνθρωπος.
125. GO: *Selbsterhaltungstrieb*.
126. GrO: ἔσω ἄνθρωπος.
127. GrO: παλαιὸς ἄνθρωπος.
128. GrO: σάρξ.
129. See Cremer, *Biblico-Theological Lexicon*, s.v. "Ἀρνέομαι" and "Ἀπαρνέομαι."
130. GrO: ψυχή.

"body"[131]—must be sacrificed to God; this is our reasonable worship (Rom. 12:1), as a spiritual sacrifice (Heb. 13:15–16; 1 Pet. 2:5). Whoever lives must live not for self but for Christ (2 Cor. 5:15); those who are married must live as though they were not (1 Cor. 7:29). And all of this should happen not on the basis of obligation, because of compulsion, so that it is experienced as a sacrifice, but willingly, joyfully, without grumbling or doubt, for the sake of Jesus (Phil. 2:14; 1 Pet. 4:9). The cross should be taken up willingly (Matt. 16:24; Luke 9:57–58). Jesus himself is the example of this self-denial; he did God's will (John 5:30; 6:38), drank the cup (John 18:11), endured the cross and scorned its shame (Heb. 12:2), made himself nothing (Phil. 2:6–7), and gave his life for the sheep (John 10:11–18).[132]

But in this self-denial our ego does not perish and is not destroyed. What perishes and is put to death is the outward person, the vain, paltry existence, the spurious ego, which is part of us and around us, the natural, sensual ego, the person as existing for this world; but our inner self, our proper self, that inner ego that we are, our true eternal being that now dwells only in that temporary form, is being preserved, kept, and strengthened precisely through and in this self-denial (Matt. 16:25; 2 Cor. 4:16). Self-denial is thus self-preservation. Giving up the outer self and the sensual life, losing one's soul (Matt. 10:39), is really gaining the authentic self: "I have been crucified with Christ. It is no longer I who live, but Christ who lives in me" (Gal. 2:20). Christ lives in me—and yet: the preservation and rescue of authentic spiritual life takes place in *me* as *I* now live in the body; in this way I find my soul.[133]

Thus, Christianity does indeed demand self-denial,[134] but that self-denial actually constitutes self-preservation.[135] Christianity does not demand self-destruction. To be nothing, to lose oneself in God, to lose one's existence, one's being, thinking, willing, and so forth, to enter a state of nirvana, is indeed the demand of pantheistic, quietistic mysticism, but it is not the demand of Christ.[136] God did not create something out of nothing so that there would be nothing. And Christ re-creates us, brings us back to true being, and

---

131. GrO: σῶμα.

132. Wuttke, *Handbuch der christlichen Sittenlehre³*, 2:251–54 (§241); J. T. Beck, *Vorlesungen über christliche Ethik*, 2:197–99.

133. Ed. note: This sentence is an interpretation of Bavinck's complex sentence: "Christus leeft in mij—en toch: wat ik in het vlees leef, behoud en redding van het waarachtige geestelijke leven, is vinden van mijn ziel." Bavinck is simply reiterating the point he made about self-denial in the opening sentence of this paragraph: "But in this self-denial our ego does not perish and is not destroyed."

134. DO: *zelfverloochening*.

135. DO: *zelfbehoud*.

136. Cf. van der Hoeven, *De godsdienst, het wezen van de mensch*.

makes us into a new creature[137] (2 Cor. 5:17), so that we may bear his image (Rom. 8:29), to the praise of God's glory (Eph. 1:12).[138] The principle of sin is only self-destruction: through sin we lie to ourselves and pervert ourselves.[139]

§37. DUTIES TOWARD BODILY LIFE

We also have duties toward our bodies. The body, after all, is not an accidental but an essential part of a human being; although of dust, it is not sinful as such. In a certain sense the body, too, is created in the image and likeness of God; it, too, is redeemed and saved through Christ. One day it will rise again and share in eternal salvation; it is a marvelous organ of our soul, a temple of the Holy Spirit. And Christ himself took on flesh and blood.

Spiritualism, which penetrated the Christian church through Platonic and Neo-Platonic influences since the fourth century and remained influential in the church during the Middle Ages, was revived by the rationalism of the eighteenth and nineteenth centuries. And the cause of sin was sought in the Pauline concept of "flesh."[140] The life of the spirit begins only at death, said Rousseau in his *The Profession of Faith of a Savoyard Vicar*.[141] Here, sin is sensuousness, something for which we are not responsible; it was created in us by God and automatically ends at death. Materialism reacted against this spiritualism by denying the spirit and identifying human nature with the body. Thus Feuerbach, for example, claimed that "human beings are what they eat."[142] Recently, many in Germany vigorously pursued the emancipation or liberation of the flesh, the setting free of sensuality.[143] This school of thought is to some extent still dominant. Care for the body is the only and supreme duty.

Christianity takes a position in between the two: it is neither one-sidedly spiritual nor one-sidedly material.[144] It commands taking care of the body, as

---

137. GrO: καινὴ κτίσις.

138. J. T. Beck, *Vorlesungen über christliche Ethik*, 2:200.

139. Cf. Wuttke, *Handbuch der christlichen Sittenlehre³*, 2:53–55 (§168); 2:74–75 (§173).

140. GrO: σάρξ.

141. FO: *Profession de foi du vicaire Savoyard*. Ed. note: This profession (or creed) is found in book IV of Roussea's *Emile*.

142. GO: *Der Mensch ist, was er ißt*. Ed. note: Bavinck provides no source; the aphorism can be found in Ludwig Feuerbach, "Das Geheimniß des Opfers, oder Der Mensch ist, was er ißt."

143. DO: *Zorg voor gezondheid*; e.g., Ludwig Börne, Heinrich Heine, Karl Gutzkow, Heinrich Laube. Ed. note: This group of German writers was known as "Young Germany" (*Junges Deutschland*), a progressive youth ideology that opposed "the dominant spirit of absolutism in politics and obscurantism in religion" and "maintained the principles of democracy, socialism, and rationalism" (Wikipedia, s.v. "Young Germany," https://en.wikipedia.org/wiki/Young_Germany).

144. Wuttke, *Christian Ethics*, 2:61–62 (§64).

the apostle Paul prays in 1 Thessalonians 5:23 that the body too (along with our spirit and soul) may "be kept blameless at the coming of our Lord Jesus Christ."

1. Care for Our Health[145]

Due to sin, the body has become more independent of and emancipated from the spirit and has become far more dependent and bound to nature, to material things. Thus, the body often seduces the spirit (Matt. 5:29: "if your right eye causes you to sin"); it is filled with lusts (Rom. 6:12–14; 7:23); and it opposes the spirit (Gal. 5:16, 19–21). The body tempts us through the lust of the eyes, the lust of the flesh, and the pride of life (1 John 2:16). It refuses to serve the spirit and is sluggish and weak (Matt. 26:41). Further, it is slavishly dependent upon our outward nature and subject to various disorders and sicknesses.

Scripture connects sickness and pain with death and locates its source in sin: "In pain you shall bring forth children" (Gen. 3:16). "If you will diligently listen to the voice of the LORD your God . . . I will put none of the diseases on you that I put on the Egyptians, for I am the LORD, your healer" (Exod. 15:26; cf. Deut. 7:15). "You shall serve the LORD your God, and he will bless your bread and your water, and I will take sickness away from among you. None shall miscarry or be barren in your land" (Exod. 23:25–26). If they do not serve God, he will send panic, wasting disease, fever, and pestilence (cf. Lev. 26:16, 25; Num. 14:12; Deut. 28:21–24, 27–28, 35, 59; 29:22; 32:24). God often sends illnesses as a punishment for sins: tumors on the Philistines who took the ark (1 Sam. 5:6, 9, 12), the pestilence because of David's census (2 Sam. 24:15), leprosy on Gehazi because of his theft (2 Kings 5:27), diseases on Jehoram because of his sin (2 Chron. 21:15, 18), and afflictions on Israel (Ps. 107:17–20; Jer. 16:4; Ezek. 7:15; 14:19). That is why Jesus personally took our sicknesses upon himself (Matt. 8:17). He healed the sick no less than he forgave sins; he saw a connection between sin and sickness. To the paralytic he says, "Your sins are forgiven" (Matt. 9:2); to another he says, "Sin no more, that nothing worse may happen to you" (John 5:14). Likewise, Paul connects sin and sickness in 1 Corinthians 11:29–30 when he states that "anyone who eats and drinks [at the Lord's Supper] without discerning the body eats and drinks judgment on himself. That is why many of you are weak and ill, and some have died." Yet God does not want us to look for the cause of every specific illness in a specific sin (John 9:2–5). He also sends afflictions purely to test us, as in the case of Job, and he gave Paul a thorn in the flesh to keep

---

145. Ed. note: Bavinck's #1 encompasses this entire section (§37); chap. 19 deals with #2 (food and drink; §38) and #3 (clothing; §39).

him from becoming conceited (2 Cor. 12:7). Sickness is sometimes for the glory of God (John 11:4).[146]

THE MORAL SIGNIFICANCE OF ILLNESS

Sicknesses have a deep moral significance that philosophers ignore entirely. The Pythagoreans had a unique theory about the origin of diseases.[147] Plato attributes bodily illnesses to three causes:

a. The nature of the basic material elements, such as an excess or deficiency or uneven distribution of elements

b. The organic constituents of the body (marrow, bone, flesh, sinew, blood)

c. Irregularities in the distribution and nature of the pneumatic elements, such as mucus and bile[148]

In addition, there are also illnesses of the soul. These stem from physical causes and are of two kinds: lunacy and ignorance.[149] As for the healing of illnesses, Plato places far more emphasis on a sound care of the body than on medicines, and he recommends an integrated treatment of the entire person in soul and body. According to the Stoics, sicknesses arise through changes in the spirit, and illnesses of the soul are affections that have become habitual in their excess.[150] Schleiermacher wrote a treatise, "On Plato's View of Medical Practice,"[151] in which he says that Plato's view is that when we are ill we should go to a physician, so that he will be able to heal us through fast-working remedies. If that is impossible, we must leave the doctor, and rather than submitting to lengthy medical treatment and time-consuming rules, we should accept our unhealthy condition and be content with the health of our sound will. Schleiermacher agrees with this because this method is easy to follow and leaves no one in doubt about what to do. He goes on to say that "when the doctor prescribes a lengthy treatment, an *active* man[152] has no time to be sick in that way and leave his affairs in the lurch."[153] Then one becomes no

---

146. See Wuttke, *Handbuch der christlichen Sittenlehre*[3], 2:140–41 (§197).

147. Zeller, *Die Philosophie der Griechen*[4], 1:417–18; Zeller does not say what this theory was.

148. GrO: πνεύματα; Plato, *Timaeus* 81e–86a. See Zeller, *Die Philosophie der Griechen*[3], 2/1:732n7.

149. Plato, *Timaeus* 86b–87b.

150. Zeller, *Die Philosophie der Griechen*[4], 3/1:205n4, 232.

151. Schleiermacher, "Ueber Platons Ansicht von der Ausübung der Heilkunst." Ed. note: Bavinck's source here and in the notes that follow is Rothe, *Theologische Ethik*, 4:37 (§916).

152. GO: *der thätige Mann*.

153. GO: *wenn der Arzt Anstalt mache zu einer langwierigen Behandlung . . . nicht zeit, auf solche Weise krank zu sein, nämlich seine Geschäfte lange im Stich lassend*; Schleiermacher, "Ueber Platons Ansicht," 277.

more than a nurse and a servant[154] of one's illness; one neglects one's affairs, prolongs one's death—the one grandiose act of dying—by numerous pauses over an extended period of uselessness in which one becomes effeminate and weak. Accordingly, Schleiermacher formulates the rule "that a medical treatment which does not restore the ability to perform what is one's own must not be accepted even by the person who has something to do."[155] Hence a doctor does not do well by keeping a person alive as long as possible when a person is so sick that they cannot perform their task. To keep the body alive is not the task of the doctor but of the cook.

Here Schleiermacher completely misjudges the moral significance of being sick; he considers it an absolute waste of time because only being active and busy in one's occupation can be moral. So, if we cannot be cured immediately by a doctor, then do not waste any time or money, and do not spend any time caring for the body. It is better to do what we are still capable of doing, or if our health condition does not improve, to choose a different occupation in which our condition hampers us less. Rothe partially agrees. He believes, of course, that medical assistance is good, but he wonders to what extent doctors may restrict their patients' occupational activity for the sake of their health, and also to what extent patients may suspend their activities to concentrate on their health. In the case of acute illnesses, this is not an issue; they are intense and last for only a short time. But the problem arises with chronic illnesses. The individual circumstances of each person must decide here.[156] But while everybody these days holds to the more lenient approach, one ought to investigate whether the stricter approach of Plato and Schleiermacher is not better. In any event, the independence of our spirit should be maintained as much as possible with respect to the life of our senses,[157] particularly as the latter weakens and approaches its end.

In this there is some truth in opposition to those many people in our time who are guilty of a cult of health. To that cult belong all of those who run to the doctor for every little ache and pain. This is especially common among the poorer classes who have a social-assistance doctor.[158] It includes those for whom nothing is more important than to fret about their own

---

154. GO: *Pfleger und Aufwärter seiner Krankheit*; Schleiermacher, "Ueber Platons Ansicht," 280; Rothe, *Theologische Ethik*, 4:37 [§916].

155. GO: *daß eine ärztliche Behandlung, welche die Fähigkeit nicht wiederherstellt, das Seinige zu verrichten, auch von dem, der etwas zu verrichten hat, nicht angenommen werden darf*; Schleiermacher, "Ueber Platons Ansicht," 278.

156. DO/GO: *Ieders individuele Instanz*; Rothe, *Theologische Ethik*, 4:36 (§916).

157. DO: *zinlijk*.

158. Ed. note: Bavinck's term here is *armendokter*—literally, "poor-doctor," a doctor for the poor.

well-being and who are constantly wondering and probing if something might be wrong with them and constantly taking remedies. This may be truer for women but is also true for men, in particular those who employ homeopathic remedies. It includes, above all, the thousands of bathers who spend their summer season at seaside resorts and mineral spas.[159] They spend weeks and months this way, without any real need for rest and relaxation, purely as a pastime, purportedly for their health—people, in other words, who do nothing but lead a vegetative life without the least moral value. Plato was right when he wished that there would be no physicians for such people in his republic. For all those people, the body—its health and well-being—is not the means but the end, a goal in itself.[160] This is completely at odds with Scripture, which subjects not only health but all of life to the kingdom of heaven (Matt. 16:25; John 12:25).

Moreover, being sick has profound ethical significance. Schleiermacher may well have said that one must not take time to be sick, but whether we want to or not, God often gives us time to be sick. He casts us down on a sickbed. It is absolutely not true that we have time given to us only to be active, to work, and to have enjoyment—as though everything else is a waste of time. Time has also been given us for suffering, for being sick, even for being bored. The last of these is given that we may learn how impoverished time and everything in the whole world are in themselves, so that we may long for something lasting and enduring. It is God who sends us that suffering and that sickness, and not the devil. The latter belief was widely held in the early church[161] and by the Roman Catholics. Luther also attributed all evil and misfortune to the devil, as do many Lutheran theologians.[162] The nineteenth-century Lutheran theologian J. C. K. von Hofmann considers the difference between someone who is demon possessed and other sick people to be merely a matter of degree.[163] In fact, the Lutheran confessions ascribe all chaos, quarrels, war, hatred, murder, and plagues to the working of Satan. This is entirely wrong. To be sure, according to Scripture there are certainly demonic sicknesses—think of

---

159. DO: *badgasten.*

160. GO: *Selbstzweck*; Dorner, *System of Christian Ethics*, 458 (§60). Ed. note: Dorner is clearly the inspiration for the entire preceding paragraph.

161. Hagenbach, *Lehrbuch der Dogmengeschichte*, 102–4 (§51). Ed. note: This section in Hagenbach has the title "The Devil and Demons" [*Teufel und Dämonen*].

162. Philippi, *Kirchliche Glaubenslehre*, 3:341.

163. GrO: δαιμονιζόμενοι. Ed. note: Johann Christian Konrad von Hofmann (1810–77) was a Lutheran professor of systematic and historical theology at Erlangen; see his *Weissagung und Erfüllung*, 2:103; J. von Hofmann, *Der Schriftbeweis*, 1:445–63; cf. Hahn, *Die Theologie des Neuen Testaments*, 372–84 (§§143–45). Bavinck's source for these references is Philippi, *Kirchliche Glaubenslehre*, 3:341.

Job, or of the demon-possessed in Jesus's time. But, when Hebrews 2:14 says that the devil has "the power of death,"[164] this means only that all who have not been set free by Christ must necessarily fall under the power of death unleashed by Satan. Moreover, it is God who has the power of death. He is the Creator also of darkness and evil—that is, of disasters (Isa. 45:7). He determines the end of our life (Job 14:5; Pss. 31:15; 39:5; 139:5; Acts 17:26). Scripture itself distinguishes clearly between natural and demonic sicknesses (Matt. 4:24; 8:16; Mark 3:15).[165]

The Pedagogical Significance of Illness

For that reason, illnesses are excellent pedagogical means in God's hand.[166] They pluck us out of our busy earthly occupational life, force us to rest, to be quiet, to experience solitude, and to contemplate our life. They make us realize the vanity of our strength, our youth, our money, our courage, our years, our life. Every illness is a harbinger of death, a warning from God: "Set your house in order, for you shall die" (Isa. 38:1). An illness exhorts us to ponder our state as we face eternity. It serves to arouse faith, to test it, to strengthen it (John 9:3–17; 11:4). Thus we ought to receive illness as God's messenger, as a prophet who proclaims to us that we should seek the things of heaven (Ps. 41; Isa. 38:1–5), as a messenger who urges us to humble ourselves, but also to have faith. It is on our sickbed that we discover that our health, too, is but a relative good. A chronic sickness can also be a thorn in our flesh (1 Cor. 11:30; 2 Cor. 12:7), and thus may have a pedagogical purpose, in order that we follow Christ with patience and humility.[167]

164. GrO: τὸ κράτος τοῦ θανάτου.

165. See Delitzsch, *System of Biblical Psychology*, 345–60.

166. Willem Teellinck wrote a tract about how one ought to conduct oneself in time of sickness and the like: *De schending van het recht*. Original title: *Wraeck-sweert, bepleytende het recht van Godts verbondt door bloedige oorloge, diere-tijdt, bleecke pestilentie*. Cf. Engelberts, *Willem Teellinck*, 45.

167. Cf. "The prayer for the sick and the distressed, Comfort for the Sick; Some Proverbs of Consolation." Ed. note: This was found in the liturgical section of the old Dutch Reformed psalter (*Het gebed voor de kranke en aangevochten mensen. De Ziekentroost. En enige troostelijke spreuken*). An English translation of two such prayers can be found in the Canadian Reformed Book of Praise: "A Prayer for the Sick and the Spiritually Distressed" (##9–10), Canadian & American Reformed Churches, accessed November 20, 2020, https://canrc.org/prayers. See also Martensen, *Christian Ethics, Special Part*, 366–70 (§154); J. T. Beck, *Vorlesungen über christliche Ethik*, 3:188–90; Pictet, *De christelyke zedekunst*, 958–65 (IX.xxvii).

In the margins Bavinck writes, "also Proosdij on Calvin." It is not possible to determine with certainty what Bavinck had in mind; he may have been thinking of C. van Proosdij's translation of and introduction to three Calvin sermons from the French: Calvin, *De Offerande van Abraham*, esp. 37, which deals with sickness. The passage concludes, "Let us, therefore, in

Healing, Spiritism, Magnetism, and Hypnotism

But even though a sickness is sent to us by God, we may fight it and pray for healing and look for means to cure it. A remedy was provided for Hezekiah (Isa. 38:21); Jesus himself heals sick people with saliva, mud, and the like. We are permitted to long for life and health—for example, when we are not yet ready to die because it would be difficult for us to be missed by our children, our spouse, our church, or our work. Thus, Paul deemed his life necessary for the sake of the believers (Phil. 1:23), even though he otherwise really wanted to die.

God himself has supplied powers and means in nature for healing. Bilderdijk thought that every illness brought its own appropriate means of healing, just as an animal instinctively looks for healing and eats grass.[168] All the same, only the God-ordained means may be used. The Christian church has always condemned healing through incantations, charms, blessings, and the like.[169] In America a peculiar school known as Christian Science has recently arisen, led by Mrs. Eddy, an idealist pantheist who teaches that sin does not exist, sickness is not real, everything is spirit.[170]

Especially nowadays, the phenomenon of animal magnetism (mesmerism, somnambulism) has become important. Among the Greeks it was the Pythia,[171] and among the Romans it was the Sybil of Cumae[172] (according to

---

agreement with this, consider ourselves warned, so that when God tests us, we bow our necks and accept his test."

On a separate piece of paper between pp. 718 and 719 of the original manuscript, Bavinck had written several notes and suggested correlations between personality types and different religious temperaments; cf. his treatment of this topic in *RE*, 1:417–22. The text reads (with English translation and editor's annotation in square brackets): "Temperamenten Mach, Die Willensfreiheit, 155 and Martensen, *Dogmatik*, p. 166." The first reference is to Mach, *Die Willensfreiheit des Menschen*, 155; the second is to Martensen, *Christian Dogmatics*, 182–83 (§95, Observations). Bavinck then took the classic four types of temperament and related them to religious types.

Cholericus is orthodox [choleric people (short-tempered/angry) are orthodox];

sanguinicus is vrijzinnig [sanguine (self-confident, optimistic) people are liberal/freethinking];

melancholicus dweeper [melancholic (sad/depressed) people are fanatics/enthusiasts/zealots];

phlegmaticus indifferentisch [phlegmatic (low-key, agreeable) people are indifferent/apathetic].

168. Cf. Bilderdijk, *Verhandelingen*, 11. See also Bilderdijk, *De ziekte der geleerden*, where pain is considered a warning, a blessing.

169. Pictet, *De christelyke zedekunst*, 959 (IX.xxvii.15).

170. See Greene, "Christian Science or Mind-Cure"; Stöcker and Schwabedissen, *Christliche Wissenschaft und Glaubensheilung*; *Was lehrt man in der Kirche Christi des Scientisten?*; H. Kuyper, "Genezing door geloofsgebed."

171. Ed. note: "The Pythia was the name of the high priestess of the Temple of Apollo at Delphi who also served as the oracle, also known as the Oracle of Delphi" (Wikipedia, s.v. "Pythia," https://en.wikipedia.org/wiki/Pythia).

172. Ed. note: "The Cumaean Sybil was the priestess presiding over the Apollonian oracle at Cumae, a Greek colony located near Naples, Italy." Virgil refers to her in *Aeneid* VI (Wikipedia, s.v. "Cumaean Sybil," https://en.wikipedia.org/wiki/Cumaean_Sibyl).

Virgil), who uttered oracles in a trance or in a sleeping state. The cures they prescribed were always familiar remedies.

Paracelsus[173] was probably the first magnetizer; he cured epilepsy, hysteria, and similar disorders. People believed that magnets could heal all kinds of sicknesses and even wounds. In the middle of the seventeenth century, for example, a remedy called "weapon salve" became popular.[174] Shortly thereafter people began to believe they could achieve the same result by massaging with bare hands. Many scientists devoted themselves to the study of magnets, until Father Maximilian Hell (1720–92), a Jesuit astronomer in Vienna, cured sicknesses by placing steel plates of a peculiar shape on the bare body. He communicated this, among others, to Franz Mesmer (1734–1815), who in 1775 announced his discovery of animal magnetism.[175] He went to Paris, set up a hospital, and healed many patients. One of his students, Amand-Marie-Jacques de Chastenet, Marquis of Puységur (1751–1825), also cured many. As a result of the French Revolution, this work fell into oblivion. But in 1813 there appeared a book by Joseph-Philippe-François Deleuze with the title *Critical History of Animal Magnetism*.[176] Abbé Faria (José Custódio de Faria; 1756–1819) believed that hypnosis worked by suggestion rather than animal magnetism, and he gradually put five thousand patients to sleep by simply using the word *sleep*. In Germany, Mesmer's student Joseph Ennemoser (1787–1854) taught that the magnetic force of a human could affect all humans, animals, plants, and organic entities. He became famous and even won the support of Fichte, Schleiermacher, Hegel, Krause, and Schopenhauer. Joining Ennemoser were Dietrich Georg von Kieser, who called "siderism"[177] a new force, and Karl

173. Ed. note: Paracelsus (1493/1494–1541) was a Swiss physician, alchemist, and astrologer whose major work, *Astronomia magna* (1571), was a "treatise on hermeticism, astrology, divination, theology, and demonology" and gave rise to "Paracelsus's later fame as a 'prophet'" (Wikipedia, s.v. "Paracelsus," https://en.wikipedia.org/wiki/Paracelsus).

174. DO: *wapenzalf*. Ed. note: "Weapon salve" is also called "powder of sympathy" and was "a form of sympathetic medicine, current in the 17th century in Europe, whereby a remedy was applied to the weapon that had caused a wound in the hope of healing the injury it had made. The salve consisted of the patient's blood and human fat, the wound itself being wrapped in wet lint. This doctrine was supported by Wilhelm Fabry, Robert Fludd, and Jan Baptist van Helmont, who attributed the cure to animal magnetism" (Wikipedia, s.v. "Powder of Sympathy," https://en.wikipedia.org/wiki/Powder_of_sympathy).

175. Ed. note: This theory held "that there was a natural energetic transference that occurred between all animated and inanimate objects" (Wikipedia, s.v. "Franz Mesmer," https://en.wikipedia.org/wiki/Franz_Mesmer).

176. Deleuze, *Histoire critique du magnétisme animal*.

177. Ed. note: Merriam-Webster defines "siderism" as "a phenomenon similar to animal magnetism formerly supposed to result from the bringing of iron or other inorganic bodies into connection with the human body" (*Merriam-Webster*, s.v. "siderism," https://www.merriam-webster.com/dictionary/siderism). With Adam von Eschenmayer and Christian Friedrich

Ludwig Freiherr von Reichenbach (1788–1869), who theorized about a "field of energy combining electricity, magnetism, and heat, emanating from all living things, which he called the Odic force" (from a Sanskrit word *od*, "to blow").[178] He wrote about this in a two-volume work, *The Sensitive Person and His Relation to Od.*[179]

Magnetism, or its later preferred term, hypnotism, should be distinguished from spiritism, which involves summoning spirits.[180] Spiritism claims such a summons is useful for proving that there is a world of spirits, that miracles are possible, that the soul is immortal, and so on. But hypnotism involves a hypnotist who is able to put a subject to sleep or into a sleep-like condition; the subject becomes unaware of the external world and because of the stiffening of the muscles, among other things, is now insensible to impressions from the outside, such as painful manipulation. Negatively this involves closing off the spirit to the outside world. But in addition, the hypnotist is sometimes able, by touching certain parts of the body, to evoke certain passions, sensations, feelings in the subject; the hypnotist can transfer their feelings onto the subject, dominate their consciousness, and guide them to the subject the hypnotist wishes to discuss. Positively this involves the absolute domination by the hypnotist of a subject, of their consciousness and will, and making them serve the hypnotist so that the subject thinks about what the hypnotist wants them to think, and so on.

In the third place, subjects, having their spirits disengaged from the outside world, withdrawn into themselves and elevated above the normal boundaries of space and time, presumably become clairvoyants who can see more than

---

Nasse, von Kieser published the twelve-volume *Archive for Animal Magnetism* (*Archiv für den thierischen Magnetismus*) (Wikipedia, s.v. "Dietrich Georg von Kieser," https://en.wikipedia .org/wiki/Dietrich_Georg_von_Kieser).

178. Ed. note: See Wikipedia, s.v. "Carl Reichenbach," https://en.wikipedia.org/wiki/Carl _Reichenbach; see also "Carl Reichenbach," in *New American Cyclopedia*.

179. Von Reichenbach, *Der sensitive Mensch.* Ed. note: Bavinck's possible source for this reference is Kirchner, *Der Spiritismus*, 11, 16n27. Several works by Reichenbach are available in English translation, including *Physico-Physiological Researches in the Dynamics of Magnetism, Electricity, Heat, Light, Crystallization, and Chemism in Their Relations to Vital Force*; and *The Od Force: Letters on a Newly Discovered Power in Nature and Its Relation to Magnetism, Electricity, Heat, and Light.* These works have been republished with slightly altered titles.

180. Ed. note: Bavinck's statement here is correct with respect to nomenclature but fails to take note of important differences between the two. Theoretically, magnetism operates from the premise that there is a universal force (animal magnetism) that influences health; hypnotism, initiated by Scotsman James Braid (1795–1860), replaced "the supernatural theory of 'animal magnetism' with a new interpretation based on 'common sense' laws of physiology and psychology" (Wikipedia, s.v. "Hypnosis," https://en.wikipedia.org/wiki/Hypnosis). In what follows, the terms "hypnosis" and "hypnotist" are our (converted) translations of Bavinck's *magnetisme* and *magnetiseur*.

others. With their consciousness, such people can even transport themselves to another place—say, America—and have a better understanding of the causes and connections of things and solve and cure much. In 1882, in London, the Society for Psychical Research (SPR) was established to investigate these and similar phenomena,[181] and many scientists support it: the philosopher Henry Sidgwick, the naturalist Alfred Russel Wallace, the chemist William Crookes, and others.[182]

A few observations at this point:

a. It is an open question whether there is such a thing as immediate transfer of thoughts,[183] whether we can influence someone else's thoughts, feelings, or will other than by way of the normal human capacities. In other words, the question is whether we can accept the reality of a suprasensual connection and correspondence of souls that transcends the body. There are still many scientists who dispute and deny this. However, the possibility cannot be denied out of hand. We know from dogmatic theology that the Holy Spirit can work directly upon our heart, will, and consciousness and can change them.[184] The devil also can operate internally and immediately on the boundaries of the sensitive and bodily faculties of the soul.[185] The devil can operate particularly upon the imagination, and hence indirectly work upon the mind and the will. Yet he probably cannot affect the latter directly and immediately; otherwise, the idea of temptation would be lost, and guilt and responsibility would be gone. It therefore seems improbable that one human being can act immediately upon another and can enlist another's consciousness and will. The art of reading someone's mind does not prove this in any way; that is done directly by closely observing the hands and facial muscles, as well as by subtly guiding the other's thoughts in a certain direction.[186]

b. But suppose that it is possible for a hypnotist to control a subject to such an extent (and the subject desires this—having surrendered to the

181. Ed. note: Bavinck adds this note: "See my excerpt from 'Telepathie und Geisterseherei in England.'" Bavinck likely has in mind a summary he prepared of an essay by William T. Preyer, "Telepathie und Geisterseherei in England." The essay was also published as a book in 1886.

182. Ed. note: Other members included physicist Oliver Lodge, philologist Frederic W. H. Myers, and psychologist William James.

183. GO: *unmittelbare Gedankenübertragung.*

184. *RD*, 4:50–53, 76; Bavinck, *Saved by Grace*, 44–49.

185. LO: *interne et immediate operari circa facultates animae sensitivas et corporeas.*

186. Think of the mentalists Stuart Cumberland (1857–1922), Washington Irving Bishop (1855–89), and John Randall Brown (1851–1926); see Preyer, *Die Erklärung des Gedankenlesens.*

hypnotist, after all): it is an altogether different question whether it is permissible.[187] Hypnotists control their sleeping subjects by means of their gaze, their demeanor, their voice, their fiery and penetrating eyes, their self-confidence and will; they overwhelm them, daze them (as a teacher does a pupil, or a master a dog). Hypnotists pour their atmosphere, their emanations, into those of the subject (think of the astonishing influence exerted by a single hug, a kiss, a handshake). Even more: the subject reads in the mind of the hypnotist, feels through the body of the hypnotist. The hypnotist thinks for the subject, and the subjects imagine the hypnotist's thinking to be their own. Hypnotists exert their will on their subjects, and subjects acknowledge the hypnotist's will as their own. Now, this is nothing less than a condition of possession, of one person being possessed by another. Those who are possessed lose their selfhood; with all the faculties of body and soul, they become an instrument of the hypnotist. Bilderdijk comments that such a form of possession may occur only in the marriage between husband and wife.

c. Finally, we ask whether the hypnotized soul is elevated above space and time and sees many things that we don't see. That is not impossible. Think of the analogous ecstasy of the prophets, whose spirits were detached by God's Spirit from their surroundings, their time, their consciousness. And many phenomena seem to show that, for example, when sleeping or when dying, when the soul is more detached from the body, it enters another world and begins to see everything in a different and deeper and better light.[188] Think, for example, of premonitions, sadness for unknown reasons that become known later, "second sight" or extrasensory perception in Scotland, and the like.[189]

d. However, especially because of what is mentioned under points (a) and (b), consulting hypnotists is not advisable. It is wrong for such subjects to put themselves in the power of someone else in that way.[190]

---

187. See Bilderdijk, "Over het Dierlijk Magnetismus." Ed. note: In what follows, Bavinck is paraphrasing Bilderdijk.

188. See Splittgerber, *Schlaf und Tod*.

189. Ed. note: Bavinck's reference to Scotland here may come from the Gaelic notion of "the two sights" (*an sa shealladh*) (Wikipedia, s.v. "Extrasensory perception," https://en.wikipedia .org/wiki/Extrasensory_perception).

190. Ed. note: Bavinck adds, "In Paris, the medium Slade acted as the prophet of *Fakirism* (M. A. Gooszen, "Verschijnselen des tijds," in *Geloof en Vrijheid* 20/6 [1886]: 551ff.)." "Fakir" or "faqir" is an Arab term (root *faqr* = poverty) and is "an Islamic term traditionally used for a Sufi Muslim whose contingency and utter dependence upon God is manifest in everything they do and every breath they take." The term has also been "applied to refer to Hindu ascetics (e.g., sadhus, gurus, swamis, and yogis)" (Wikipedia, s.v. "Fakir," https://en.wikipedia.org

MIRACULOUS HEALING

Another method of healing is that of anointing with oil or prayer and the laying on of hands.[191] Miraculous healings occur repeatedly in the Old and New Testaments. Jesus heals the sick or raises persons from the dead by a word, by saliva, by mud, sometimes preceded by prayer (John 11:41–42). He gives that power to his disciples and apostles: "Heal the sick, raise the dead, cleanse lepers, cast out demons" (Matt. 10:8). "They will lay their hands on the sick, and they will recover" (Mark 16:18). Hence, the gift of healing was found in the church (1 Cor. 12:9). The apostles healed the sick (Acts 3:6; 8:7), even by the shadow of Peter (Acts 5:15). Paul healed a man "crippled from birth" when he perceived that the man "had faith to be made well" (Acts 14:9). These signs and wonders[192] are often mentioned in the New Testament (Acts 2:43; 4:16; 5:12; 6:8; 8:6, 13; 14:3; 15:12; 19:11; Rom. 15:19; 2 Cor. 12:12; Gal. 3:5; Heb. 2:4). Then we come across Mark 6:13 ("and they cast out many demons and anointed with oil many who were sick and healed them") and James 5:14–15 ("Is anyone among you sick?")—two passages on which Rome bases the sacrament of extreme unction. However, this sacrament is a preparation for dying, whereas the anointing in those two passages is for healing. This gift of healing remained in the Christian church for a long time.[193] But Origen notes in his commentary on Proverbs 1:6 that these charismata were already diminishing.[194] Chrysostom calls the charismata an obscure area since they are now lacking. And Augustine also remarks that miracles no longer occur as gloriously as in former days.[195]

/wiki/Fakir). Bavinck explicitly links fakirism to spiritism in the context of India. The reference to "Slade" is likely to Henry Slade (1835–1905), a famous, well-traveled fraudulent medium, especially known for his "slate-writing" trick. Bavinck then continues, "Some people in Paris believe they are in communication with Buddhists. In the Hague we had the performance of Donato, editor of the *Le Magnétisme, revue générale des sciences physio-psychologiques*; he has people move their limbs, call out their name, throw off their clothes, etc." Ed. note: Donato was the pseudonym for the hypnotist Alfred-Édouard d'Hont (1840–80), known for his spectacular cabaret shows of hypnotism (French Wikipedia, s.v. "Alfred D'Hont," https://fr.wikipedia.org /wiki/Alfred_D%27Hont).

191. Cf. the missionary J. L. Zegers, *De geloofsgenezing*.

192. Gk. σημεῖα and τέρατα.

193. See Justin Martyr, *Dialogue with Trypho* II.82; Justin Martyr, *First Apology* I.45; Irenaeus, *Against Heresies* II.31.2; II.32.4; V.6.1; Eusebius, *Ecclesiastical History* V.16.7; Tertullian, *Ad Scapulam* 2 and 4; Tertullian, *Apologia* 23, 27; Tertullian, *De anima* 9; Cyprian, *Epistola* 76; Origen, *Contra Celsum* I.2.46, 67. Ed. note: Bavinck's source for these references and those that follow is Böhmer, "Geistesgaben," 738–39.

194. According to Böhmer, "Geistesgaben," 739.

195. Augustine, *City of God* XX.8; cf. Tholuck, *Vermischte Schriften*, vol. 1; Böhmer, "Geistesgaben," 738–40. Ed. note: Bavinck refers without further specification to vol. 1 of Tholuck's *Vermischte Schriften*. It is likely that he had in mind the lengthy second chapter (pp.

So they have gradually diminished and disappeared. They were no longer necessary because the wide expansion of Christianity was itself the great miracle (Augustine). The Roman Catholic Church, however, still believes that miraculous healings occur regularly; think of the Holy Robe (the seamless robe of Jesus) in Trier, the water at Lourdes, and similar phenomena. Protestants generally consider the time for miracles to be over; only a few—Grotius, Vitringa, Vossius—judged that miracles could still occur. Irvingians, Darbyists, and other sects have reintroduced healing through prayer and the laying on of hands.[196] To be sure, miraculous healing as a charisma is in principle still very possible and cannot be denied. Perhaps it still occurs. But it is certain that miracles are not a regular phenomenon, that God reserved that gift for extraordinary times, that the prayer of the righteous accomplishes much and still often saves a sick person (James 5), but prayer does not exclude means, but accompanies them. What James 5 clearly teaches is that in sickness, we must not wait passively but may apply means toward its cure. Jesus therefore commands his disciples to heal the sick, and he himself heals the sick. Paul gives Timothy some medical advice: "Use a little wine for the sake of your stomach and your frequent ailments" (1 Tim. 5:23). "Do not be anxious about your life, etc." (Matt. 6:25–34) does not prove the opposite.[197] Positively, we may care for our health, because life is the prerequisite for performing our duties; we have been created with the desire to live. We can keep our bodies healthy by strengthening our muscles and ligaments through exercise and by hygiene; physical weakness is no virtue.[198]

28–148): "Concerning the miracles of the Catholic Church and particularly concerning the relationship of these miracles and biblical miracles to the phenomena of magnetism and somnambulism" (*Ueber die Wunder der katholischen Kirche und insbesondere über das Verhältnis diser und der biblischen Wunder zu den Erscheinungen des Magnetismus und Somnambulismus*).

196. Ed. note: Bavinck added the following marginal note here: "At a congress in 1884 in New York some speakers said that sickness is from the devil. Salvation of the soul is also healing of the body. A person can be cured of sickness, if he really wants, for once he prays to God for healing, God must answer. A Christian may not be sick or die other than from old age, like Moses."

197. Cf. Wuttke, *Handbuch der christlichen Sittenlehre*[3], 2:284.

198. Reinhard, *System der christlichen Moral*, 2:515.

19

Basic Necessities of Bodily Life

The resources on which we depend for our life — light, air, drink, food, shelter, clothing — are given to us from outside; we cannot exist by ourselves and from our own resources. What we use for food, for example, is a gift from the Creator. At the same time, God appoints humans as coguardians of their lives; they have to earn their bread. This is our calling as God's image-bearers: maintain our households and share with the needy.

All religions have dietary laws and require discrimination in what people may eat. Mosaic law forbade certain kinds of meat and established laws for clean and unclean foods although we are not certain about all the reasons. Bans on eating all meat are found in some religious traditions and among some ascetic philosophers. In modern times vegetarianism has been on the rise. Scripture, however, does not forbid killing animals and eating meat; what is impermissible is inflicting cruel and unnecessary pain on animals. Although a concern for human dignity may hold us back from eating certain meats, for New Testament Christians there is no food that is inherently unclean.

The matter of drinking is a challenge for Christians, especially alcoholic beverages. On the one hand, Scripture speaks positively of wine as one of God's good gifts and blessings. At the same time, it warns strongly against excess. The effects of drinking alcohol are terrible on the human body and on life in human society, where alcohol abuse leads to many other sins and misdeeds, even crimes. Alcohol abuse destroys what is spiritual in us, the image of God. Opioid addiction is even worse. Tobacco and coffee are also addictive.

The misuse of food, or gluttony, was not foreign to Israel either, although God limited it through dietary and sacrificial regulations. History provides numerous examples of excesses in eating and drinking. Epicures, connoisseurs, and gourmands have countless exemplars from the past, people who, in the most literal sense of the word, make a god of their belly.

Asceticism, abstinence, and vegetarianism are all responses to the misuse of food and drink. The nineteenth century saw the rise of temperance movements around the globe, but especially in the United States. Asylums to treat alcoholism as a disease arose in the US in the same century and spread to other countries as well. Attempts by governments to restrict abuse of alcohol through repeated increases of excise taxes only encourage cheating and, because the trade in alcoholic beverages is incredibly lucrative for governments, provide a perverse disincentive to such efforts at restricting its use.

Holy Scripture warns against immoderate use and acknowledges the good of abstinence in the case of Nazirites, the Rechabites, and John the Baptist. We must do everything to the glory of God, and self-denial is expected of Jesus's followers, especially out of love for the neighbor. These truths have led some Christians to become teetotalers. This cannot be demanded of us. The use of alcohol is not forbidden as such in Scripture; perhaps forbidden in connection with and for the sake of some circumstances, but not in and of itself. On this matter, we have Christian freedom. To reject alcohol and its use as inherently evil is a Manichaean and gnostic dualism that Scripture opposes. Instead, Scripture commands moderation and gives us permission to rejoice and feast before God. All created gifts of God are good; the dividing line is in the person of the Christian, who is expected to live a holy life and to accept such gifts with prayerful gratitude; mealtime prayers are a long-standing Christian tradition. Our prayers acknowledge that, notwithstanding our sweaty work, our food is an unmerited gift of God, we are wholly dependent of him for all blessings, and we put all our trust and hope in him. In all things: "Nothing in excess!"

Human beings need clothing because through sin they feel uncovered, naked, and ashamed. Shame presumes that we fell yet did not become animals and arises especially with respect to defects that cannot be helped. Shame assumes that these defects are permanent and cannot be remedied and yet are grounded in our will. While other creatures are self-sufficient with regard to clothing, human beings need to borrow from plants and animals to clothe themselves.

Clothing readily moves beyond mere function to ornament, adornment, finery. Historically, among the ancient peoples and Israel, ornaments and finery in clothing (Joseph's coat of many colors) became matters of ritual (linen clothing for priests) and occasions for sin that required regulation (distinct garb for men and women, veils). The Old Testament prophets warned against the luxuries of Israel and Judah, and the New Testament warns against luxury and calls for modesty and self-control.

The Christian church has from its beginnings opposed excessive adornment and luxury. In the Netherlands, the seventeenth-century Golden Age was a period of such excess, and Reformed pastors, especially those with Puritan leanings, complained vigorously, even from the pulpit. A great controversy, up to the synodical level, erupted about long hair for men. Ministers preached repeatedly on 1 Corinthians 11:4–8; Isaiah 3:24; 23:9; and 1 Timothy 2:9. The dispute eventually died down, and, as usual, fashion won. Even pastors began to wear long hair or periwig.

Head coverings deserve special attention, especially those of the clergy. Fashion is determinative here and with respect to clothing in general. Nonetheless, because clothing expresses individuality and character, it has a very great moral significance. Clothing differs among nations, generations, families, and persons, differing from one country to another, from one place to another, from one time to another, from one situation to another. Modern fashion is more global and uniform and, in its uniformity, becomes characterless.

Why do we wear clothing? For four basic reasons: (a) To cover our nakedness. Intentional public nudity is sinful. (b) To protect us from nature's elements. While animals are protected by their fur and hair, we humans are helpless and borrow our weapons from the outside, from plants and animals, and are able to do so since we are spirits. (c) To identify us according to sex, age, and social class. Clothing also distinguishes among time and occasions: celebrations call for clothing that is different from work clothes; mourning clothes differ from party dress. Here, too, the leveling impulse of democratism leads to greater uniformity. Distinctive clothing for clergy is appropriate but not required; it is a matter of liberty, though indifference and nonchalance is not an act of piety. (d) To adorn. Clothing does adorn, and Scripture gives us permission to do so while warning against misuse, excess, and pride. The rule of moderation and modesty suggests that neither blind submission to fashion for vain ostentation nor open opposition and resistance by openly wearing unfashionable clothing is appropriate. Our bodies are properly a work of art, and our deportment and adornment should reflect the refinement of our souls. Excessive attention and time devoted to adornment as well as counterfeit beauty have been disapproved by church leaders through the ages. Worldliness does not befit the Christian.

§38. FOOD AND NOURISHMENT

2. Concern about Food and Drink[1]

A. FOOD AND WORK[2]

In the natural realm, too, we depend on what is given. We exist and live only as long as we receive.[3] The earth and the heavens are our storehouse. We receive light, air, drink, food, shelter, and clothing from outside ourselves. We cannot exist for a moment by ourselves and from our own resources, neither naturally nor spiritually; absolute isolation would spell certain death. Without our "environment" we are nothing. The environment for our physical living is the earth. God gave human beings dominion over the fish of the sea and other creatures and gave them every plant yielding seed and every tree yielding seed for their food; to the animals, on the other hand, he gave every green plant (Gen. 1:26–30). God appoints humans as coguardians of their own lives; they have to earn their bread: "If anyone is not willing to work, let him not eat" (2 Thess. 3:10). Even paradise was no land of plenty for the lazy.[4] There are creatures who are not able to contribute anything to their existence: they survive, or they grow and decline, according to their nature. But to a certain extent, we humans have power over our life, to maintain and take care of it, freely and independently.[5]

After the fall the ground is cursed for Adam's sake:

> Because you have listened to the voice of your wife
>   and have eaten of the tree
> of which I commanded you,
>   "You shall not eat of it,"

---

1. DO: *Zorg voor voedsel*. Ed. note: We see here the fundamental continuity with the second part of the previous chapter (§37); #1 was "Care for Our Health."

2. Ed. note: This heading and all others in this chapter have been added by the editor for the sake of clarity and readability. Since Bavinck inserts the subject of opium tobacco and even salt after discussing the addictive character of alcohol in section (c), and there is some repetition in his argument, it may be helpful to provide here the outline of his main sections: (a) "Food and Work"; (b) "What Food May We Eat?"; (c) "What Beverages May We Drink?"; (d) "Sins of the Belly, Including Gluttony"; (e) "Responses to Alcohol Abuse; Temperance"; (f) "What Does Holy Scripture Teach?"

3. Drummond, *Natural Law in the Spiritual World*, 256.

4. DO: *luilekkerland* = lazy-luscious-land.

5. According to Oscar Peschel, the world's peoples find food in wild-growing plants and in all kinds of animals: fish, foxes, bats, rats, snakes, hyenas, worms, and caterpillars. The Chinese eat swallow's nests. Cannibalism was practiced in ancient Mexico, among the Batta on Sumatra, among Polynesians, the Aimoré in eastern Brazil, Papuans, and Negroes along the Congo River (see Peschel, *Races of Man*, 155–66). Ed. note: The Aimoré are part of a group of people in eastern Brazil called Botocudo in Portugese. Bavinck refers to them as "Botokuden."

> cursed is the ground because of you;
>> in pain you shall eat of it all the days of your life;
> thorns and thistles it shall bring forth for you;
>> and you shall eat the plants of the field.
> By the sweat of your face
>> you shall eat bread,
> till you return to the ground,
>> for out of it you were taken;
> for you are dust,
>> and to dust you shall return. (Gen. 3:17–19)

That was a punishment but also a blessing for humanity. Intense labor keeps people from many sins; idleness is the devil's workshop. Developing over the course of time were crop farming (Cain), animal husbandry (Abel), hunting (Nimrod), the nomadic life (Jabal), the arts (Jubal: harps and pipes), and industry (Tubal-Cain, an instructor of artisans in brass and iron).[6]

None of this is sinful. It is true that Jesus instructs us, "Do not be anxious about your life, what you will eat or what you will drink"[7] (Matt. 6:25), and, furthermore, urges us, "Do not work for the food that perishes, but for the food that endures to eternal life" (John 6:27).[8] What Jesus condemns there are the anxious worriers who have no trust in God, the multitudes that seek Jesus out for the sake of bread, not for the food unto everlasting life. Our liturgical form for the solemnization of marriage says it so beautifully: "You are to labor diligently and faithfully in the *divine* calling in which God has set you, that you may maintain your household in all godliness and honesty and likewise have something to share with the needy."[9] And Scripture teaches the same about diligence: "The hand of the diligent makes rich" (Prov. 10:4). "The hand of the diligent will rule" (12:24). "The diligent man will get precious wealth" (12:27). "The soul of the diligent is richly supplied" (13:4). Paul

---

6. On food and drink, see von Jhering, *Der Zweck im Recht*, 2:424–42.

7. GrO: μὴ μεριμνᾶτε τῇ ψυχῇ ὑμῶν τί φάγητε καὶ τί πίητε.

8. GrO: ἐργάζεσθε μὴ τὴν βρῶσιν τὴν ἀπολλυμένην ἀλλὰ τὴν βρῶσιν τὴν μένουσαν εἰς ζωὴν αἰώνιον.

9. DO: *zo zult gij getrouw en naarstig in uw Goddelijk beroep arbeiden, opdat gij uw huisgezin met God en met eer moogt onderhouden en ook daarenboven iets hebt, om aan de nooddruftigen mede te delen.* Ed. note: This line is taken from the "Liturgical Form for Solemnizing Marriage in the Church of Christ" ("Formulier om den huwelijke staat voor de gemeente van Christus te bevestigen"), in use in the Dutch Reformed Church since the Synod of Dort (1618–19) (Online-bijbel.nl, http://www.online-bijbel.nl/liturgie/formulier/6/). An abbreviated version is in use in the Canadian and American Reformed Churches: "Work faithfully in your daily calling, that you may support your family and help those in need" ("Form for the Solemnization of Marriage," Canadian and American Reformed Churches, https://canrc.org/forms/form-for-the-solemnization-of-marriage).

commands believers to work with their own hands, "so that you may walk properly before outsiders and be dependent on no one" (1 Thess. 4:11–12). Similarly, "If anyone is not willing to work, let him not eat" (2 Thess. 3:10). Paul condemns people who "walk in idleness, not busy at work, but busybodies," and commands them "to do their work quietly and to earn their own living" (2 Thess. 3:11–12). Another instruction: "Let the thief no longer steal, but rather let him labor, doing honest work with his own hands, so that he may have something to share with anyone in need" (Eph. 4:28). The book of Proverbs repeatedly makes this point: "The sluggard does not plow in the autumn; / he will seek at harvest and have nothing" (20:4). "The sluggard says, 'There is a lion outside! / I shall be killed in the streets!'" (22:13). "Slumber [idleness] will clothe [a person] with rags" (23:21). "I passed by the field of a sluggard, / by the vineyard of a man lacking sense, / and behold, it was all overgrown with thorns; / the ground was covered with nettles, / and its stone wall was broken down" (24:30–31). "As a door turns on its hinges, / so does a sluggard on his bed" (26:14).

B. WHAT FOOD MAY WE EAT?

We encounter dietary laws in practically all religious traditions.[10] Herodotus reports that the Egyptians distinguished between clean and unclean foods.[11] According to Porphyry, the Egyptians had to abstain from all foods and beverages imported from abroad, because only the land of Egypt and its products were holy and consecrated.[12] But other Egyptian animals were unclean as well, such as the animals of prey devoted to Typhon, four-footed and winged "flesh-eaters."[13] Similarly, the Egyptians abstained from the hippopotamus, the mouse, swine, donkeys, and the like, classifying them in general as "quadrupeds that had solid or many-fissured hoofs."[14] The gazelle,[15] which was permitted in Deuteronomy 14:5, is unclean in Egypt, as is all meat from the cow; and meat from the bull is permitted only during sacrificial meals. All fish are unclean, of the birds especially the hawk. Also unclean were vegetables like legumes, beans, and onions.

10. Leyrer, "Speisegesetze bei den Hebräern"; more expansive than von Orelli, "Speisegesetze bei den Hebräern."

11. GrO: καθαρός, μιαρός; Herodotus, *Histories, I and II*, II.37, 47 (LCL 117:318–21, 332–35). Leyrer, "Speisegesetze bei den Hebräern," 610–13.

12. Porphyry, *Select Works of Porphyry*, 141–42 (*On Abstinence from Animal Food [De abstinentia]* IV.7).

13. GrO: σαρκοφάγα.

14. GrO: τετράποδα δὲ μώνυχα ἢ πολυσχιδῆ ἢ μὴ κεράσφορα; Porphyry, *Select Works of Porphyry*, 141 (*On Abstinence from Animal Food* IV.7).

15. GrO: ὄρυξ.

Then we consider the Avestan[16] food laws found among the Persians, who divide all of nature dualistically into an unclean realm of *Ahriman*[17] (to which belong wolves, tigers, snakes, scorpions, moles, lizards, bees, flies, worms, and others) and a clean realm of *Ohrmazd*[18] (eagles, vultures, dogs, foxes, horses, camels, and others, none of which may be eaten but are cared for).[19] Then there are Indian food laws, which forbid eating all four-footed animals whose hooves are not split and that do not chew the cud, including pigs, camels, and so on; all birds that are carnivores; most fish; and amphibians that are carnivores. In the Sabaean food laws we find similar regulations.[20] Mohammed derived his food laws partly from the Arabian pagans (with the exception of the ban on wine), partly from the Mosaic law—for instance, the ban on blood, pigs, donkeys, ravenous beasts, and animals offered to idols.[21] Food laws were also found among the Greeks and the Romans.

Accordingly, we also find dietary laws among the Jews. As to whether the eating of meat was forbidden before the fall, see below.[22] Noah was given meat for food, but not meat with the life (i.e., with blood) in it (Gen. 9:4; Deut. 12:23). For blood is the manifestation of a creature's life; it atones by means of the life. Mosaic law forbids the following:[23]

1. Certain pieces of fat on the sacrificial animal, and the firstfruits; especially

    a. the prohibition of eating blood, repeated more than once (Lev. 3:17; 7:25–27)

    b. the fat that surrounds the intestines (Lev. 7:25–35)

    c. the firstfruits of trees and fields

16. Ed. note: Bavinck uses the term *zendische* (*Zendic*; from *Zend*) which is no longer used by contemporary scholars, who use the term "Avesta/Avestan" to refer to the Ancient Iranian people and language. The *Avesta* is the primary collection of religious texts of Zoroastrianism (Wikipedia, s.v. "Avesta," https://en.wikipedia.org/wiki/Avesta).

17. Ed. note: *Ahriman* is the Middle-Persian equivalent of Angra Mainyu, "the Avestan-language name of Zoroastrianism's 'destructive spirit'" (Wikipedia, s.v. "Angra Mainyu," https://en.wikipedia.org/wiki/Ahriman).

18. Ed. note: Ohrmazd (which Bavinck spells "Ormuzd") is an alternative name for Ahura Mazda, the Avestan name for the creator and sole God of Zoroastrianism (Wikipedia, s.v. "Ahura Mazda," https://en.wikipedia.org/wiki/Ahura_Mazda).

19. Ed. note: Bavinck's source for this statement (including the term "Zendic") is Leyrer, "Speisegesetze bei den Hebräern," 611.

20. Ed. note: Bavinck's source for this statement is Leyrer, "Speisegesetze bei den Hebräern," 612; the Sabaeans were an ancient people living in the South Arabian peninsula. The Sabaean Kingdom existed between 1200 and 800 BC (Wikipedia, s.v. "Sabaeans," https://en.wikipedia.org/wiki/Sabaeans).

21. Leyrer, "Speisegesetze bei den Hebräern," 612.

22. Leyrer says yes: "Speisegesetze bei den Hebräern," 594.

23. Leyrer, "Speisegesetze bei den Hebräern," 595–606.

2. Using (though not touching) unclean animals—that is, those who have no cloven hooves and do not chew the cud; even if they chew the cud, like the camel, or have a split hoof, like the pig

3. All aquatic animals except fish; and among fish, also those that have no fins or scales, such as the eel

4. Some birds that are identified by name rather than characteristics; up to twenty-one in number, such as eagles, vultures, ravens, ostriches, and hawks

5. Small land animals (except the grasshopper), creeping animals, insects, and so on

6. The meat of slaughtered clean animals and beasts of the hunt that were not killed according to the law but died of themselves or were torn by other animals, like animals that died of suffocation, carrion, meat stored in a mortuary, and meat and wine offered to idols

The rabbis erected an entire casuistry on the basis of these laws. The basis for all these laws is uncertain. Some see the basis in national-economic goals; others in sanitary-political ends; still others in dietary-moral purposes; but all this is incorrect.[24] The Persians trace it back to a dualistic creation of the world, and this is incorrect. Nonetheless, after the fall an evil-demonic[25] principle is manifest in the animal world as well. This became evident first in the serpent. The animal world, too, is grievously involved in the consequences of the fall into sin, in the groaning of creation[26] described in Romans 8:22. The image and character of various passions and vices are mirrored in the aversion, fear, and repulsion that are aroused by creepy and scary animals. There certainly is some truth to the remark of the church fathers that some animals portray human sins and passions, so that they instill abhorrence: pigs and dogs portray filth and unchastity; beasts of prey portray wrath and violence; snakes and vermin portray evil spirits (cf. Matt. 7:6; 10:16).[27] Animals have a profound symbolism. Among the ancients, an instinctive fear, an involuntary horror of

24. Leyrer, "Speisegesetze bei den Hebräern," 611; Leyrer attributes these proposals to Michaelis but judges them contrary to the "character of Old Testament religion."

25. Ed. note: Bavinck borrows a coined Greek/German (Dutch) term: *kakodemonisch* (from Ionic Greek: κακοδαιμονία = possession by a demon; raving madness).

26. GO: συστενάζει καὶ συνωδίνει.

27. Novation, *On the Jewish Meats* (ANF 5:647); Philo, *On the Special Laws* IV.16–25 (LCL 341:65–93); *The Letter of Aristeas*, 246–313 (§§128–71); *Epistle of Barnabas* X (ANF 1:143–44); Origen, *Homilies on Leviticus 1–16*, 129–52 (*Homily 7*); Theodoret of Cyrus, *Questions on the Octateuch*, vol. 2, *On Leviticus, Numbers, Deuteronomy, Judges and Ruth*, 28–33 (question 11). Ed. note: Bavinck provided the specific references to Origen and Theodoret given here; the others were filled in by the editor. Bavinck's source is Martensen, *Christian Dogmatics*, 213 (§112).

nature,[28] functioned much more powerfully than among us, whose sense of nature has been weakened and dulled by art. With us, reflection is dominant, and through artificial culture our insight into the nature and lot of animals has been spoiled. Among the ancients there was a much closer correlation and correspondence between the ethical and the natural, the cosmic and the lawful, the psychical and the physical, all of which were not as separated as with us.[29]

Furthermore, the ban on eating meat was honored by many people for many centuries. In India those who aim at greater holiness abstain from all meat.[30] A Brahmin may consume meat and fish but with expressly mentioned exceptions.[31] The Buddha himself did not forbid fish and meat, provided they are clean in three respects: they do not look evil, are not known to be evil, and are not suspected of being evil.[32] But in the rules of Buddhist monks, ghee, butter, oil, honey, sugar, fish, meat, milk, and curds are forbidden.[33] In the course of time people in India followed the food rules of the Brahmins with increasing strictness, although they admit that the ban on meat did not arise until the Iron Age—that is, after the nirvana of the Buddha; prior to that time, the Buddha himself ate pork. In many places, Buddhists adapt to local customs; in Burma (Myanmar), Ceylon (Sri Lanka), and Bali they do eat meat. Much stricter are the Jains, who protect animals to an absurd degree.[34] The reason for food bans and animal protection lies in the rebirths that persons must go through after their death in order to enter nirvana.

Pythagoras taught the doctrine of the transmigration of souls, or regeneration;[35] whether he and the Pythagoreans abstained entirely from meat is uncertain; later authors make that claim,[36] but others report this only about the meat of male goats and bulls.[37] Empedocles also assumed that the souls of wicked people migrated into the bodies of humans, animals, and plants, and accordingly he forbade eating meat and killing animals, which he considered just as bad as killing a human being. He did not apply this consistently to

28. LO: *horror naturalis*.
29. Leyrer, "Speisegesetze bei den Hebräern," 597–98; cf. Bilderdijk, who considered vermin to have been created after the fall; "Concerning the Creation of Snakes, Worms, and Vermin" (*Over de schepping van slangen, gewormte, and ongedierte*), in *Opstellen van de Godgeelerden en zedekundigen inhoud*, 1:119–36. In another place he considered them incarnations of fallen angels: *De Dieren, Dichtstuk*.
30. Leyrer, "Speisegesetze bei den Hebräern," 611–12.
31. Kern, *Geschiedenis van het Buddhisme in Indië*, 2:59.
32. Kern, *Geschiedenis van het Buddhisme in Indië*, 1:187.
33. Kern, *Geschiedenis van het Buddhisme in Indië*, 2:58.
34. Kern, *Geschiedenis van het Buddhisme in Indië*, 2:59–61.
35. GrO: μετεμψύχωσις; παλιγγενεσία; Zeller, *Outlines of the History of Greek Philosophy*, 1:481–84.
36. E.g., Ovid, *Metamorphoses* XV.60–142 (LCL 43:300–307).
37. Zeller, *Outlines of the History of Greek Philosophy*, 1:344–46.

plants, forbidding the consumption of only a few plants.[38] The same goes for the later Neo-Pythagoreans.[39] The Essenes also ate no meat and killed no animals.[40] The Therapeutae of Egypt[41] ate only bread and drank water; they abstained from meat and wine; in fact they regarded eating and drinking as gratifying the body and therefore unclean, and they did not eat before sunset; food was not allowed to see the light of day; some members ate only once every three or six days.[42] Similarly Porphyry forbade meat because animals have reason and are related to us; eating them makes us carnal. It would be best if we could do without food, but that is impossible, and so one's diet should be as simple as possible.[43] The same was true for Iamblichus, Syrianus, and Proclus.[44]

These influences of asceticism penetrated the Christian church as well.[45] In general, people considered meat consumption to have been permissible first with Noah;[46] it did not exist in paradise. The same picture of a golden age when only plants were eaten is found also in pagan literature—Virgil, Ovid, Horace, Theocritus, Hesiod, Plutarch, and more.[47] The gnostic sect of the Encratites of Tatian,[48] the gnostics, and the Manichaeans were all under the influence of Persian ideas.

By way of the monks, the notion that the patriarchs were vegetarians became the dominant one in the church. Jews, Roman Catholics, Lutherans, Arminians, and some Reformed—Zwingli, Musculus, Junius, Piscator,

---

38. Zeller, *Outlines of the History of Greek Philosophy*, 2:174–75.

39. Zeller, *Die Philosophie der Griechen*[3], 3/2:92, 145, 147, 157.

40. Zeller, *Die Philosophie der Griechen*[3], 3/2:286n1.

41. Ed. note: The Therapeutae were a monastic order, similar to the Essenes, found among the Jews of Egypt. The primary source for information about the Therapeutae comes from the Alexandrian Jew Philo, in his treatise *On the Contemplative Life* (*De vita contemplativa*) ("Therapeutae," in *1911 Encyclopaedia Britannica*, 26:793; available online at https://en.wiki source.org/wiki/1911_Encyclop%C3%A6dia_Britannica/Therapeutae).

42. Zeller, *Die Philosophie der Griechen*[3], 3/2:304.

43. Zeller, *Die Philosophie der Griechen*[3], 3/2:721.

44. Zeller, *Die Philosophie der Griechen*[3], 3/2:771, 812, 844. See HathiTrust Digital Library, https://babel.hathitrust.org/cgi/pt?id=wu.89094323862;view=1up;seq=795. Ed. note: Iamblichus (ca. 245–ca. 325), Syrianus (d. 437), and Proclus Lycaeus (412–85) were significant Neo-Platonist philosophers; Syrianus was the teacher of Proclus (Wikipedia, s.v. "Neoplatonism," https://en .wikipedia.org/wiki/Neoplatonism).

45. Martin, "Vleeschverbruik in de Middeleeuwen."

46. Cf. Rom. 14:2: "The weak person eats only vegetables."

47. Virgil, *Eclogues* IV.21–25; V.60 (LCL 63:30–31, 38–39); Ovid, *Metamorphoses* I.89–112 (LCL 42:8–11); XV.96 (LCL 43:370–71); Horace, *Odes and Epodes*, "Epode XVI" (LCL 33:306–11); also in *Odes and Epodes of Horace*, 504–11; Theocritus, *Idylls* XXIV.84 (LCL 28:293–94).

48. Ed. note: The Encratites were an ascetic Christian sect during the second century; they forbade marriage and discouraged eating meat. Eusebius (*Ecclesiastical History* IV.28–29) attributes the founding of this heresy to Tatian the Syrian (ca. 120–ca. 180).

Lightfoot—held the same view.[49] Calvin alone broke with the notion, and consequently Heidegger, Voetius, André Rivet, Cappellus, Samuel Bochart, de Moor, Marck, and others had a more liberal view.[50]

In modern times, animal welfare and vegetarianism are the order of the day.[51] A Vegetarian Society was founded in London by James Simpson on September 30, 1847. Meat was considered to be harmful for morality and health and to be the source of many social wrongs. The group also forbade liquor and spices, though milk, butter, eggs, and cheese were permitted.[52] A similar society was established in Germany in 1869 under the direction of Eduard Baltzer (1814–87). Many people have taken up the pen to advocate for vegetarianism.[53] Opponents of this vegetarianism have also been vocal.[54] Vegetarians claim that their practice explains the longevity of the patriarchs, and they note that at the Last Supper Christ instituted only bread and wine, not meat. The poets John Milton and Percy Bysshe Shelley, the scientist Isaac Newton, and the French poet and politician Alphonse de Lamartine (1790–1869) were all vegetarians.[55]

Now it is probable that even before the fall, eating meat was quite permissible.[56] For in Genesis 9:3, eating meat is expressly permitted, and absolutely

49. Zöckler, *Die Lehre vom Urstand der Menschen*, 276.

50. DO: *vrijere opvatting.* Ed. note: While the other names in this sentence are clear, Bavinck's reference to Cappellus is not, particularly since his source for the reference to Calvin, Heidegger, and Rivet is Zöckler, *Die Lehre vom Urstand der Menschen*, 276, but his source for the other six names is unknown.

51. Cf. Schopenhauer, *Two Fundamental Problems of Ethics*, 243–45.

52. Dock, *Iets over het Vegetarianisme.*

53. Ed. note: Bavinck listed the following: Amos Bronson Alcott (1799–1888), Sylvester Graham (1794–1851), Charles Lane (1800–1870), Jean-Antoine Gleïzès (1773–1843), Eduard Baltzer (1814–87), Theodor Hahn (1824–83), Gustav Karl Johann Christian von Struve (1805–70), John Eyton Bickersteth Mayor (1825–1910), and Francis William Newman (1805–97). Bavinck also listed Gustav Henske, who remains elusive to internet searches.

54. The physiologists Rudolf Virchow (1821–1902), Carl Friedrich Wilhelm Ludwig (1816–95), and Otto Funke (1828–79). See Winkler Prins, *Geïllustreerde Encyclopaedie*, s.v. "Vegetarianisme" (14:145ff.); also see Gleïzès, *Die Enthüllung des Christenthumes.* Ed. note: Bavinck does not specify which edition of the Winkler Prins encyclopedia he is using. He would have had the second edition (published 1884–88) available to him as well as the first (published 1870–82), but there are good reasons to believe he used the first edition. For example, the second edition has a brief article on "vegetarians" (*vegetarianen*) but none on "vegetarianism." Similar omissions in the second edition lead to the conclusion that he was using the first edition. Unfortunately, while the second and third editions are available online (in the Hathi Trust Digital Library, https://catalog.hathitrust.org/Record/012314807), the first edition is not.

55. Ed. note: See Shelley, *Vindication of Natural Diet*; Shelley, *On the Vegetable System of Diet.*

56. Cf. Wuttke, *Christian Ethics*, 2:269 (§129); contrary to Leyrer, "Speisegesetze bei den Hebräern," 594.

no mention is made of an earlier ban.[57] Nor can one think of a reason why
eating meat should become permissible for the first time after the Flood. In
fact, one would sooner expect restrictions after the terrible Flood than expansion of claims on nature. To have "dominion over the fish of the sea and
over the birds of the heavens" (Gen. 1:28) makes no sense if it did not include
eating them. Immediately after the fall, Abel "brought of the firstborn of
his flock and of their fat portions" (Gen. 4:4), and God gave Adam and Eve
"garments of skins" (Gen. 3:21). Furthermore, if meat consumption were
merely a concession on God's part because of our sinfulness and because the
fruitfulness of the earth had diminished (Gen. 3:17; 5:29), then surely meat
consumption would have been forbidden at the Passover and the sacrifices.
Then Jesus would certainly have abstained from meat. However, he "came
eating and drinking" and was therefore called a "glutton and a drunkard"
(Matt. 11:19; see also Mark 2:19; John 2:2–11), and he joined in the Passover
meal (Matt. 26:17–19). Peter was shown a sheet filled with "all kinds of animals
and reptiles and birds of the air" and was commanded, "Rise, Peter, kill and
eat. . . . What God has made clean, do not call common" (Acts 10:12–13, 15).
Paul considers it a weakness not to eat meat (Rom. 14:2, 21; 1 Cor. 10:25);
if meat eating offends some people, he himself wants to abstain from and
forbids it to others (Rom. 14:21). The animals are there to be killed for food
(Deut. 12:15, 50; 2 Pet. 2:12). Schopenhauer also does not consider killing
and eating animals unlawful, since especially in the north people cannot live
without meat; however, he would have animals killed by means of chloroform.[58]

Thus, according to Scripture, killing and eating meat is not impermissible; what is impermissible is torturing and painfully killing animals (Prov.
12:10), and to that degree, animal welfare societies have a legitimate point.[59]
Sometimes there is something immoral in the killing of animals. Many cannot
wring the neck of a pigeon, cannot stand to hear a pig squeal and gurgle,[60] are
so sensitive that they cannot kill a spider or a fly. What also hurts feelings is
killing one's loyal pet: dog or cat or horse. We have a natural aversion to eating
the meat of many animals. Horse meat has come into fashion only recently.
During the 1870 siege of Paris—during the Franco-Prussian War—people ate
rats prepared with champagne and spices.[61] A good rat cost sixty cents, and
the number of rats in Paris was estimated at twenty million.

---

57. Marginal note by Bavinck: "Isaiah 11:6–9 and 65:25 speak of a messianic kingdom in
which no harm is done to any animal."
58. Schopenhauer, *Two Fundamental Problems of Ethics*, 245.
59. Schopenhauer, *Two Fundamental Problems of Ethics*, 239–45.
60. DO: *rochelen*.
61. Kepper, *De oorlog tusschen Frankrijk en Duitschland*, 2:559–60.

Just as we find in the Old Testament, "You shall not eat any flesh that is torn by beasts in the field" (Exod. 22:31; cf. Lev. 17:15; 22:8; Deut. 14:21; Ezek. 4:14), so too we read in the New Testament that carrion, blood, what was strangled and torn (in addition to sexual immorality and eating food offered to idols) were forbidden (Acts 15:20, 29; 21:25). This prohibition is no longer binding upon us; it was a temporary compromise. Paul considered the eating of meat offered to idols quite lawful.

Similarly, the prohibition against the consumption of blood comes directly from Old Testament prohibitions (Gen. 9:4; Lev. 3:17; 7:26–27; 17:10; 19:26; Deut. 12:16, 23; 1 Sam. 14:32) and reappears in the New Testament (Acts 15:20, 29; 21:25). Among the Semitic peoples, drinking blood mixed with wine was a common practice during sacrifices. However, the practice is coarse, uncivilized, and cannibalistic-like, and it exerts a wrong influence upon us; makes us harsh, savage, and cruel; and imparts to us something animalistic. That is why meat must not be eaten raw (as nomads do), but needs to be somewhat prepared. Eating steak and blood sausage is therefore quite permissible.[62]

Finally, although there is much meat and other food that we would not eat because they are revolting to us, and although some food and plants are not appropriate for human consumption, and although the best and finest of plant and animal is worthy of human consumption, and although also in this respect we must uphold human dignity—because there is some truth to Feuerbach's dictum "One is what one eats"[63]—nevertheless now in the New Testament dispensation there is no single food that is inherently unclean. The dietary laws, too, have been fulfilled by Christ. In Matthew 15:11 we read, "It is not what goes into the mouth that defiles a person, but what comes out of the mouth; this defiles a person" (similarly, Mark 7:15–19). From Acts 10:15 we learn that God has made all things clean. From Romans 14:17 we learn that the kingdom of God does not consist in food and drink, but righteousness and peace and joy in the Holy Spirit. From this, Paul concludes, "Do not, for the sake of food, destroy the work of God. Everything is indeed clean, but it is wrong for anyone to make another stumble by what he eats" (Rom. 14:20). And he also says, "To the pure, all things are pure, but to the defiled and unbelieving, nothing is pure; but both their minds and their consciences are defiled" (Titus 1:15). The apostle also declares that "food will not commend us to God" (1 Cor. 8:8) and that no one should "pass judgment on you in questions of food and drink" (Col. 2:16). God fills our hearts with food and joy (Acts 14:17). "Foods that God created [are] to be received with thanksgiving

---

62. Wuttke, *Handbuch der christlichen Sittenlehre*³, 2:285 (§249).
63. GO: *Der Mensch ist, was er ißt.*

by those who believe and know the truth. For everything created by God is good, and nothing is to be rejected if it is received with thanksgiving, for it is made holy by the word of God and prayer" (1 Tim. 4:3–5). Here full freedom rules; the kingdom of heaven does not depend on what we eat.

c. What Beverages May We Drink?[64]

Let us first consider the teachings of Holy Scripture on this matter:[65]

In addition to water, milk, and so on, the Jews especially drank wine. Terminology: Hebrew: יַיִן; Arabic: وَيْن;[66] Greek: Ϝοῖνος;[67] Latin: *vinum*, wine (perhaps from יַיִן ,יגן, to tread).[68] עָסִיס (from עסס, to trample, press, or compress) is must (new wine): unfermented, unrefined "sweet wine" (Isa. 49:26; Amos 9:13). The term חֶמֶר (from Chaldean חַמְרָה) refers to fermented, refined wine, "pure wine" (Deut. 32:14; Isa. 27:2); סֹבֶא (Isa. 1:22; Nah. 1:10) appears to have been a particularly strong, undiluted wine. מִשְׁרַת עֲנָבִים (Num. 6:3) is freshly pressed grape juice; תִּירוֹשׁ (from ירשׁ) is new wine mixed with grain (דָּגָן) and is wine that is still sweet and fermenting (Gen. 27:28); שֶׁמֶר is wine that is kept in the dregs or sediment.[69]

Along with grain, oil, and figs, wine is repeatedly mentioned in Scripture as one of the blessings and promises of God in the land of Canaan (Deut. 6:11; 8:8; 11:14). But there were also mixed wines:[70] מֶסֶךְ (Ps. 75:8); מִמְסָךְ (Prov. 23:30; Isa. 65:11); מֶזֶג (Song 7:2); יַיִן הָרֶקַח (Song 8:2). Mixed, spiced wines are also mentioned in the New Testament: "wine mixed with myrrh" (Mark 15:23); "the wine of the wrath of God, which is poured out without mixture" (Rev. 14:10 KJV).[71] The idea was to mix into the natural wine all kinds of

---

64. Ed. note: Bavinck also treated this subject in *RE*, 1:120–22 (§10).

65. Ed. note: Bavinck's source for much of what follows is Leyrer, "Wein und Weinbau"; cf. Keil, *Manual of Biblical Archaeology*, 2:112–17 (§97: "Articles of Food, or Meats and Drinks"); Winer, *Biblisches Realwoerterbuch*, 2:683–87 (the articles "Wein, natürlicher" and "Wein, künstlicher").

66. Ed. note: Bavinck took this Arabic term وَيْن (wayn[un]) from his source, Leyrer, "Wein und Weinbau," 708; to the best of our knowledge this is the only place in Bavinck's writings where we find Arabic in Bavinck's own hand. Bavinck, it is worth noting, also studied Arabic during his student years at Leiden; see his letter exchange with his friend, the renowned Arabist Chr. Snouck Hurgronje, in de Bruijn and Harinck, *Een Leidse vriendschap*. For the facsimile of Bavinck's own handwritten manuscript, see the critical edition edited by Dirk van Keulen, *Gereformeerde Ethiek*, 869.

67. Ed. note: Bavinck took this from his source, Leyrer, "Wein und Weinbau," 708: "the Greek οἶνος with Digamma Ϝοῖνος."

68. Ed. note: Bavinck took these two Hebrew terms from his source, Leyrer, "Wein und Weinbau," 708; יגן means "wine press," but the root meaning of יון is uncertain (see BDB, s.v. יון ,יגן).

69. Ed. note: Bavinck adds here the Latin term: *vinum faecatum*.

70. Ed. note: Bavinck has "artificial wines" [*kunstwijnen*].

71. GO: ἐσμυρνισμένον οἶνον; οἴνου τοῦ θυμοῦ τοῦ θεοῦ τοῦ κεκερασμένου.

herbs, myrrh, musk, rose oil, absinth, incense, pepper, and the like in order to give them a more powerful taste and a more fragrant aroma.[72] In Jesus's parable (Luke 10:34), the Samaritan binds up the man's wounds with oil and wine.[73] The Greeks and Romans always drank their wine mixed with water; that this was a custom in Israel cannot be proved: Isaiah 1:22 and Proverbs 9:2 do refer to it, but Isaiah 1:22 actually condemned the practice, probably because it adulterated the wine. It is not spoken of until the Talmud. There was also a general name for any drink that has an intoxicating effect, also for wine at the time of sacrifice (Num. 28:7): שֵׁכָר (from the verb "to fill": to drink to excess and become drunk). This term is mostly found in parallel with יַיִן—that is, "wine and strong drink" (methylated spirits; Lev. 10:9; Num. 6:3; Deut. 29:6; and more)—and refers to drinks made from grain, fruit, honey, dates, or pomegranates (Song 8:2). Wine made from barley was already known in Egypt but is not found in the Old Testament. חֹמֶץ (vinegar of wine; Num. 6:3) was mixed with a bit of oil and was a drink for laborers (Ruth 2:14).

Alcoholic Beverages

Today we have alcoholic beverages.[74] *Alcohol* is an Arabic word, the name of the intoxicating element in drinks. Formerly, in the Middle Ages, the spirits in drinks were called[75] vegetable solvent, heavenly light, heavenly soul, living spirit, star, Diana, and, in particular, vegetable mercury[76] (all ingredients that could be expelled or evaporated from a body through heat were called "mercurial"). The term "alcohol" began to appear in the sixteenth century. The word entered Spanish from the Arabic; here it denoted sulphuric acid.[77] The Arabs distilled wine and used it as a medicine, but the method of preparing it was kept a secret; however, Arthur de Villeneuve taught it in the fourteenth

---

72. In 3 Macc. 5:2, the king orders Hermon, the elephant keeper "to drug all the elephants—five hundred in number—with heaping handfuls of frankincense and much unmixed wine on the following day" (CEB).

73. GO: ἔλαιον καὶ οἶνον.

74. See Fuchs, "Der Alkoholismus und seine Bekämpfung"; published separately as Fuchs, *Der Alkoholismus und seine Bekämpfung*. Also consider Martius, *Der Kampf gegen den Alkoholmissbrauch*; Malins, *Temperance Movement*. Ed. note: Most of what follows is taken directly from Fuchs. We will cite this work by first indicating the page number in the separate volume, followed by the page number in the original journal, thus: 1 (409).

75. E.g., by Raymund Lull (ca. 1232–ca. 1315).

76. LO: *menstruum vegetabile*; *lucerna coeliac*; *anima coeliac*; *spiritus vivus*; *stella*; *mercurius vegetabilis*. Ed. note: "Menstruum" is a noun that refers to any "substance that dissolves a solid or holds it in suspension; solvent" (*Merriam-Webster*, s.v. "menstruum," https://www.merriam-webster.com/dictionary/menstruum). Bavinck's source for these terms is Fuchs, *Der Alkoholismus und seine Bekämpfung* 5 (411).

77. GO: *Schwefelantimon*.

century. Ezekiel 23:40—"You . . . painted your eyes"[78] (Hebrew *kachal*)—is translated into Spanish as "Alcoholaste tu ojos."

The sixteenth-century alchemists used alcohol in preparation for pulverizing material into finely divided substances; for example, creating "gold alcohol" as a raw material.[79] Yet the word "alcohol" was little used for spirits, not even in the seventeenth century; "to alcoholize" usually meant to pulverize; the French expression for "milk of sulphur"[80] is "flower of alcoholized sulphur."[81] Not until the eighteenth century is the term "spirits" used to refer to alcoholic beverages, thanks to the work of Herman Boerhaave (1668–1738), who used it to refer to the strongest wine spirit. The term became common especially after the introduction of antiphlogistic nomenclature in 1787, in reference to the finest extract of wine.[82] Alcohol is now present in all spirits, in wine and beer as well as in brandy. Those who oppose alcohol have opposed this and said that the wine spirit in fermented drinks differs essentially from the alcohol in distillates, that the former is a natural, the latter an artificial product, and that the former is harmful only in excess, the latter is inherently harmful. Chemistry shows, however, that all those beverages—wine, beer, brandy, gin—contain an identical ingredient—namely, alcohol.

Alcohol of this type does not occur in nature, but originates through the breakdown of certain organic compounds, of sugar, along with the action of other agents that are called yeast. Fermented yeast (i.e., natural yeast) is usually a decomposing substance containing nitrogen; all decomposing substances are in a state of fermentation—that is, they can cause matter to ferment. According to Pasteur, fermenting matter always contains microscopic organisms. Artificial yeast is made in beer breweries and gin distilleries by letting milled barley or rye malt, adding carbonic acid, natron, and sulphuric acid, and then letting things ferment.[83] Fermentation in general is the breakdown of organic material; the process varies depending on the fermenting material, the most important one being alcoholic fermentation in the making of wine,

78. HO: כְּחַלְתְּ.

79. LO: *alcool auri*. Ed. note: We have amplified Bavinck's explanation using Hiortdahl, *Fremstilling af Kemiens Historie*, 68.

80. GO: *Schwefelmilch*.

81. FO: *fleur de soulfre alcoholisée*. Ed. note: "Milk of sulphur" is "sublimed sulfur boiled with lime water, the lime being removed from the precipitate by washing with diluted hydrochloric acid; used in preparing sulfur ointment and in the treatment of various skin disorders" (Free Dictionary, s.v. "milk of sulfur," https://medical-dictionary.thefreedictionary.com/milk+of+sulfur).

82. Ed. note: "Antiphlogistic" is defined by *Merriam-Webster* simply as "anti-inflammatory" (*Merriam-Webster*, s.v. "antiphlogistic," https://www.merriam-webster.com/dictionary/antiphlogistic).

83. Winkler Prins, *Geillustreerde Encyclopaedie*[1], s.v. "Gisting" (7:575ff.).

beer, brandy, and bread. Alcohol fermentation consists in dissolving the sugar ingredients in wine spirit and oxygen (wine spirit when exposed to air changes into vinegar). Distillation is changing a liquid substance into a gas and then back into a liquid state in order to separate out one or another ingredient—for instance, methylated spirits. Materials containing sugar produce alcohol through fermentation or distillation.[84]

Alcohol is present in different beverages in various proportions, with some distilled spirits having an alcohol content as high as 70 percent (rum), while beers, for example, run from 3 to 7 percent and higher. But pure alcohol is always poisonous, because it shrivels up the intestines by absorbing the water.[85]

The effects of drinking alcohol are terrible,[86] first of all on the organism of drinkers themselves. Alcohol affects all parts of the body, eventually making a person's blood turn watery and fatty while losing its essential components. Alcohol results in additional fat storage, leading the drinker to obesity. Alcohol directly affects the digestive organs through loss of appetite and otherwise through a desire for spicy food. Alcohol has a particular effect on the nervous system; an excess of blood is sent to the brain, which causes headaches, ringing in the ears, flashes before the eyes, and so on. Deep depression alternates with manic episodes, and often this leads to migraines or bleeding on the brain and deliria. Often this results in epilepsy. Often the spinal cord is damaged, with the further consequence of shaking and trembling of the drinker and dizziness and the like. There can also be eye disease, leading to blurred vision and color blindness.

Beyond all this, we need to acknowledge the law of heredity. Aristotle and Plutarch already said, "One drunkard begets another."[87] Darwin observed that in 1406 cases of alcoholism, 980 had parents who were also alcoholics.[88]

---

84. Ed. note: Bavinck's manuscript at this point begins to introduce details about alcohol and statistics that are clearly dated. Much of this has been deleted in the English translation and summarized by the editor.

85. Ed. note: For the detailed list of percentages that Bavinck himself used, see Fuchs, *Der Alkoholismus und seine Bekämpfung*, 7–8 (413–14). Bavinck picks up Fuchs's particular warning about the highly poisonous nature of wine made from potatoes.

86. Fuchs, *Der Alkoholismus und seine Bekämpfung*, 12–35 (418–41).

87. LO: *Ebrii gignunt ebrios.*

88. Ed. note: The reference to Darwin is unspecified and requires some bibliographic source-archaeology. Bavinck takes the reference from Fuchs, *Der Alkoholismus und seine Bekämpfung*, 17–18 (423–24). Fuchs's source is a literature review in the *Allgemeine Zeitschrift für Psychiatrie und psychisch-gerichtliche Medizin* 28 (1872): 235, by Richard von Krafft-Ebing (1840–1902), of an American journal, *The Quarterly Journal of Psychological Medicine and Medical Jurisprudence* 3 (1869). In the October issue of this journal (3/4:625–47), Krafft-Ebing highlights an article by Stephen Rogers, "Hereditary Diseases of the Nervous System, Unattended by Mental Aberration." The reference to Darwin can be found on p. 630: "A hundred years ago, the great naturalist and physician and poet, Darwin, remarked, that *all* the diseases from drinking

But not only alcoholism is hereditary; so are epilepsy, intellectual disabilities, tendency towards vagrancy, onanism, thievery, various defects, frailty of body and soul (cough, croup, fever, atrophy, etc.). Fortunately, marriages between alcoholics are not very fertile—marriages involving alcoholics average 1.3 children, whereas marriages that do not involve alcoholics average 4.1 children—and many of their children die young and are unfit for military service. Mortality rates rise as a result of alcohol abuse. Sirach 31:30 said that wine slays many. The statistics about deaths from alcohol abuse are staggering, involving delirium, suicide, and mental illness.[89]

Finally, then, alcohol abuse causes many other sins and misdeeds. People calculate that three-quarters of crimes are due to alcohol abuse, which is particularly strong in Ireland. Alcohol is also often involved in divorce, moral languor and apathy, poverty, vagrancy, and destruction of character: alcohol abuse destroys what is spiritual in us, the image of God.[90]

Because of these terrible effects, many in our country want to replace distilled spirits (gin and brandy) with beer as the popular drink. In Sophocles and Aeschylus, beer is called barley wine; its invention is ascribed to King Osiris of Egypt in the twentieth century BC, or also to Gambrinus, king of Brabant, in AD 800; the latter is included among the saints of the Catholic Church. Beer was already the common drink among the Germanic tribes; it was widely popular in Germany as early as the sixth century AD. Toward the end of the fifteenth century, a strong beer was brewed in the monasteries for

---

spirituous or fermented liquors are liable to become hereditary, even to the third generation, gradually increasing, if the cause be contained till the family becomes extinct." From this it is clear that the reference is not to Charles Darwin as one might expect, but to his grandfather, Erasmus Darwin (1731–1802).

89. Ed. note: At this point, Bavinck provided data about the direct consequences of alcohol abuse. Because the information is dated, we removed it from the main body of the text but are including it in this footnote to indicate the concreteness of Bavinck's claims about alcohol. Bavinck believed that social science research was helpful and important for doing theology.

Between 1847 and 1874, 22,723 people died in England from delirium; between 1870 and 1875, 3,828 died there as a direct result of alcoholism. In America in 1872 one in 40 deaths resulted from alcohol abuse. Add to that the indirect consequences, which amount to no less than 20 percent of all deaths. Then there is suicide; of the 1,250 suicides in Prussia between 1823 and 1837, three-fifths or 750 resulted from drink. Between 1871 and 1873 there were 583 suicides in France as a result of drink. And so on.

Next, insanity. Fifteen to 20 percent of male and 7 percent of female lunatics have this condition as a result of drink, and 10 percent as a result of alcohol abuse by the parents; this number varies widely, and where brandy is consumed, it is worse than where wine or beer is the common beverage.

Bavinck's source: Fuchs, *Der Alkoholismus und seine Bekämpfung*, 7 (413).

90. Ed. note: Here and in what follows, we are not including Bavinck's nineteenth-century statistics. Once again, Bavinck's source is Fuchs, *Der Alkoholismus und seine Bekämpfung*, 12–35 (418–41).

the prior (father's beer),[91] and a weaker beer for other monastics (convent beer).[92] In the sixteenth century there were distinguished brewers' guilds, especially in the towns of Flanders. In Germany, especially in Bavaria, beer is still the popular drink. However, the nutritional value of beer has been highly exaggerated; during the brewing process, one-fourth of the starches and one-fifth of the barley proteins are lost.[93] There is no way beer can replace rye bread and meat in terms of nutritional value. Excessive consumption of beer is also injurious to one's health; it fosters thickening of the blood, obesity, sluggishness, and apathy.

Other Addictive Substances[94]

Let me add a word about opium and tobacco.[95]

Opium. Opium is the dried sap from unripe seed pods of the opium poppy (*papaver somniferum*). It is an excellent narcotic medicine and was known in antiquity. The abuse of opium, however, probably did not begin until much later (Sanskrit seems to have no word for it)—namely, among Muslims, who derived from it valor and contempt of death. From there, it came by way of Persia to India, where it was cultivated in Malwa as early as the thirteenth century.[96] China became acquainted with opium through the Arabs, but used it only as a medicine, until the second half of the seventeenth century, when smoking opium came into vogue. It is now used in the Orient among Turks, Greeks, Persians, especially Chinese, and among North Americans and Englishmen. The British East India Company undertook opium cultivation in Bengal, held a monopoly on it, and shipped ever larger amounts of it to China. In 1875, four million (Dutch) pounds[97] of opium entered China. Since 1853, opium has been grown in China as well.

91. DO: *paterbier.*
92. DO: *conventbier.*
93. Winkler Prins, *Geillustreerde Encyclopaedie¹*, s.v. "Bier" (4:18ff.).
94. Ed. note: Bavinck's comments here about opium, and later about tobacco and salt, don't quite fit in this section on what beverages are permitted, but are a continuation of his comments on addiction. The subheads were added by the editor.
95. See Winkler Prins, *Geillustreerde Encyclopaedie¹*, s.v. "Opium" (11:365ff.); cf. Kuyper, *Ons Program*, index; Perelaer, *Baboe Dalima* (a novel). Ed. note: The index for the original (1879) platform of the Dutch Calvinist *Anti-Revoluionaire Partij*, to which Bavinck refers here, has eight references to opium. The burden of Kuyper's argument weighs against the colonial exploitation of the Dutch East Indies and enrichment of the Dutch treasury through the state monopoly of opium licenses. See especially Kuyper, *Ons Program*, 344–46, 1016–19. Kuyper compares state profit from opium to profiting from prostitution and lotteries. Cf. brief references to opium in Kuyper, *Our Program*, 306, 318.
96. Ed. note: The west-central India region of Malwa remains one of the world's largest producers of legal opium (Wikipedia, s.v. "Malwa," https://en.wikipedia.org/wiki/Malwa).
97. Ed. note: There are two Dutch pounds (*pond*) in a kilogram; one Dutch *pond*, therefore, = 1.10231 pounds. Bavinck's four million *pond* = 4,409,240 pounds or 2,204.62 tons.

The effects of opioids are horrific. After one takes opium, within an hour it induces a sleep of five to six hours, with wonderful dreams; upon waking, one is indolent and miserable and craves more opium. The drug disturbs the nervous system, disrupts the action of the senses, whitens the face, stretches the neck, dulls the eyes, and twists the tongue. Bilderdijk also used far too much of it.

Tobacco. Smoking tobacco was native to America.[98] The Spanish adopted its use and introduced it to Portugal, and then it came to France, and in 1565 to Germany and Italy. The English became acquainted with tobacco in Virginia and brought it to the Netherlands. In the seventeenth century, its use spread to Sweden and Norway, Russia, Turkey, Persia, and Asia, all the way to China; today, its use has even spread as far as the islanders in the South Pacific.

At first, the use of tobacco was combated by princes, magistrates, church synods, and the like. Voetius actually considered it useful only as a medicine.[99] Johann Heinrich Alsted (1588–1638) included an article on tobacco in his seven-volume *Universal Encyclopädie*.[100] Smoking tobacco was universally considered shameful and harmful, yet the practice continued to spread, even to religious leaders and rulers (see the student song about the pipe).[101] Bilderdijk was disgusted by "that stinking vapor-blowing" and favored barley beer over noxious French wines.[102]

Bilderdijk attributed his poetic inspiration to *coffee*.[103]

98. Von Hellwald, *Kulturgeschichte in ihrer natürlichen Entwicklung*, 2:467.

99. Voetius, *Selectarum Disputationum Theologicarum*, 4:389–90.

100. Ed. note: Johann Heinrich Alsted, "Tabacologia," in his *Encyclopaedia Septem Tomis Distincta*, 7:2383–86 (§23); Bavinck's source for this reference is Schweizer, "Alsted, Joh. Heinrich," 308.

101. Ed. note: Bavinck himself smoked cigars. In his daily journal he records receiving birthday gifts of cigars from a friend (Albert Gunnink) on December 13, 1875, and from members of his Franeker congregation on December 13, 1881 (Bavinck Archives, map 16). Cf. his *De Vrouw in de hedendaagsche maatschappij*, 107–8, where he speaks of a *man's* need for relaxation with "beer and tobacco, wine and cigars." To which "student song" Bavinck is referring cannot be known with certainty. It may have been the one which begins:

> *Een student is een vent met een pijp in den kop* [A student is a fellow with a pipe in his beak]
> *En een pet or een muts scheef erop.* [With a hat or a beanie askew on his peak.]

Thanks to Nelson Kloosterman for his superb help with this translation.

102. Bilderdijk, *De dichtwerken*, 14:369–70 ("Het Tabakrooken"); cf. Kuyper, *Ons Program*, 905; Keibel, *Hoe moeten wij rooken?*

103. DO: *bezieling*. Ed. note: See Bilderdijk, *De dichtwerken*, 6:429 (his poem "De Ziekte der Geleerden"). Bavinck adds a reference here to Peschel, *Races of Man*, 166; Peschel counters the claim made by Bilderdijk and countless others that the use of stimulants enhances productive creativity and progress: "The Mosaic conception of God, the Zoroastrian dualism, Christianity and Islam, Indian legends and philosophies, have all arisen without the aid of narcotics. During the age of Chinese invention, that is to say, during the first three dynasties, tea was unknown in

Salt was unknown to many people.[104]

According to Bilderdijk, after the discovery of America, a flood of calamities inundated Europe, due to the introduction of potatoes, spices, infectious diseases, strong drinks, venereal diseases, and tobacco.[105]

D. SINS OF THE BELLY, INCLUDING GLUTTONY[106]

These sins were not foreign to Israel either. But while sexual sins are more common among some groups of people, sins of the belly are more common among others.[107] However, we immediately have two examples at the beginning of Scripture: Noah (Gen. 9:20) and Lot (Gen. 19:32–38). The Canaanites were especially guilty of idolatry, fortune-telling, sorcery (Lev. 19:31; 20:6–7; Deut. 18:10–14), and shameful lust, as with Sodom (Gen. 19; cf. Lev. 18:3–23; 20:23; Deut. 9:4; 12:31).[108]

Although Israel did not escape the sin of gluttony, God limited it through dietary laws, laws concerning the Nazirites (Num. 6), sacrificial meals from which the fat had to be removed, and the like. Nonetheless, overindulgence and drunkenness did occur in Israel. Nabal's meal was like that of a king, and he was very drunk (1 Sam. 25:36). David made Uriah drunk (2 Sam. 11:13). The brothers of Joseph got drunk with him (Gen. 43:34). Banquet preparations were not uncommon. David prepared a banquet for Abner and company (2 Sam. 3:20), Solomon for his servants (1 Kings 3:15), Absalom for his brothers and Amnon (2 Sam. 13:23), and King Jehoram for the Syrians (2 Kings 6:23); and Job and his children feasted (Job 1:4–5). At those banquets there was music and wine (Isa. 5:12). In addition, the warnings and admonitions of the prophets provide sufficient evidence that sins of excessive eating

China. Copernicus devised his system, Galileo confirmed it, and Kepler proved it by his laws, without coffee and without knowing its name."

104. Peschel, *Races of Man*, 170–71.

105. Bilderdijk, *Opstellen van godgeleerden en zedekundigen inhoud*, 2:117–18 ("Teekenen der Tijden").

106. DO: *buikzonden*. Ed. note: Though Bavinck begins this section with examples of drunkenness, notice how he shifts his attention in the second paragraph to gluttony. Bavinck's concern in this section is with excessive partying involving food and drink (Bacchanalia). We highlight the attention to gluttony in our subhead to distinguish it from the next section, which deals with alcohol abuse.

107. Vilmar, *Theologische Moral*, 1:262–63.

108. Ed. note: This comment initially may seem out of place in a chapter on food and drink, but Bavinck is focused here on *excessive* eating and drinking as one form of self-indulgent sensuality. The Dutch word we translated as "shameful lust" is *wellust*, which can also be translated as "sensuality," "lechery," "lasciviousness," or "voluptuousness," according to the Van Dale dictionary. Van Dale also places *wellust* in its definitions of *bacchant* and bacchante—i.e., "someone who yields him- or herself to drunkenness and *wellust*."

and drinking were present among the people of God in the Old Testament. Israel was a merry and zestful people; their feasts were probably not always very edifying.[109]

Initially, the Greeks and Romans were very moderate. Only at the banquets of Dionysus, which were very sensual, were men older than forty permitted to drink themselves drunk.[110] During the *Symposium*[111] there was much chatter and drinking going on. Socrates could hold his liquor so well that no one ever saw him drunk. As for Rome, excess and luxury arrived from Asia in the second century BC, when it became an empire. At that time, banquets and Bacchanalia were the order of the day. All kinds of meats, pork, fowl, and particularly mollusks such as oysters, mussels, and sea snails were favorites and were imported at exorbitant prices from every region of the Roman Empire. Apart from domestic and foreign wines from Greece, Asia Minor, Spain, and Gaul, men drank *mulsum* (wine sweetened with honey), *calidum* (warm wine and water), *hydromeli* (mead—i.e., water and honey), and fruit wines. Greeks and Romans always drank their wine mixed with water. The drinking bouts at which a *symposiarch*[112] was selected to oversee matters were filled with excess, so that Sulla, Caesar, and Augustus even enacted laws against them, though to no avail. As the cups were raised, speeches were given (see Plato's *Symposium*) and toasts made: to the health of his girl a man would drink as many cups[113] as there were letters in her name.[114] Plato

109. There is even mention in the New Testament of excesses at *agape feasts* (1 Cor. 11:17–34).

110. Von Hellwald, *Kulturgeschichte in ihrer natürlichen Entwicklung*, 1:377.

111. Ed. note: The word "symposium" comes from the Greek word συμπίνειν = to drink together. The symposium "was a part of a banquet that took place after the meal, when drinking for pleasure was accompanied by music, dancing, recitals, or conversation" (Wikipedia, s.v. "Symposium," https://en.wikipedia.org/wiki/Symposium). Cf. Garnsey, *Food and Society in Classical Antiquity*, 136.

112. GrO: συμποσίαρχος. Ed. note: Between the lines Bavinck adds a reference to Horace, "Carmen, II, 7,25," found in Horace, *Odes and Epodes of Horace* (Lytton), 186–87 ("Ode to Pompeius Varus"). Bavinck also adds some Latin equivalents: *magister* (*rex, arbiter*) *convivii* (*bibendi* = master [king, ruler] of drinking banquet).

113. Ed. note: Bavinck has *cyathi* (plural of *cyathus*, from Greek κύαθος = cup).

114. Martial, *Epigrams* I.71 (trans. Ker, LCL 94:75): "Let Laevia be drunk in six measures, and Justina in seven, in five, Lycis, Lyde in four, Ida in three. Let each of my girls be numbered by the Falernian [wine] in my cup; and since none of them comes, do you, Sleep, come to me." Ed. note: Bavinck adds, "cf. de Antiquiteiten en Athenaeus Deipnosophistae." The former is likely a reference to J. G. Schlimmer, *Handboek der Romeinsche Antiquiteiten voornamelijk uit den tijd der Romeinsche Republiek* (Groningen: Wolters, 1877). Athenaeus, *Deipnosophistae* (from Gk. Δειπνοσοφισταί, combination of δειπνο- [= dinner] and σοφιστής [= expert, one knowledgeable in a particular art], is "an early 3rd-century AD Greek work by the Greco-Egyptian author Athenaeus of Naucratis. It is a long work of literary, historical, and antiquarian references set in Rome at a series of banquets held by the protagonist Publius Livius Larensis for an assembly of grammarians, lexicographers, jurists, musicians, and hangers-on" (Wikipedia, s.v.

labeled the stages of drinking successive cups as follows: 1. Health; 2. Love; 3. Sleep; 4. Arrogance; 5. Clamor; 6. Carousing; 7. Fighting; 8. Madness.[115] According to Lecky, the Romans forbade women to drink wine.[116] Blood relatives therefore would kiss a woman to find out if she had drunk wine. Sometimes men killed their wives for their drinking. Later, by the time of Tertullian, this custom was obsolete, and for the saintly Monica a drink of wine was at one time a great temptation.[117] Even the Stoics called immoderate drinking a virtue.[118]

Germanic tribesmen were first-rate drinkers, especially of beer, which they drank from the skulls of their enemies. In the Middle Ages, particularly in the fourteenth and fifteenth centuries, gastronomy increased in popularity; we know this from the cookbooks and invoices that have survived from that time. Banquets were the order of the day: at baptisms, at funerals, at the first mass by a young priest, and at weddings. People bequeathed money to monasteries and other institutions for banquets. The last meal of a convict condemned to death consisted of finer foods than usual.[119] Every guild had its banquets, paid for from the "dues" contributed by their members; attendance was mandatory.[120] These meals did not stand out for their quality, however, or the delicacy of the dishes, but for their quantity. They lasted for three or more days; the menu included cow foot and tripe, potato stew and peas, hotchpotch, and so on, but in enormous quantities, and the leftovers were always eaten the following day or night. In the sixteenth and seventeenth centuries these meals became more luxurious; compare the seventeenth-century painting *Banquet at the Crossbowmen's Guild in Celebration of the Treaty of Münster (Schuttersmaaltijd)*, by Bartholomeus van der Helst,[121] with the much simpler, sixteenth-century (1533) *Banquet of Members of Amsterdam's Crossbow Civic Guard*

"Deipnosophistae," https://en.wikipedia.org/wiki/Deipnosophistae). It is available in English as Athenaeus of Naucratis, *Learned Banqueters*.

115. GrO/LO: ὑγιείας/*sanitatis*; ἔρωτος/*amoris*; ὕπνου/*somni*; ὕβρεως/*contumeliae;* βοῆς/*clamoris*; κωμῶν/*comessationum*; ὑποπίων/*ictuum et contusionum*; μανίας/*furoris*; Voetius, *Selectarum Disputationum Theologicarum,* 4:509.

116. Lecky, *History of European Morals,* 1:96n.

117. Augustine, *Confessions* IX.8. Ed. note: Bavinck's source for this is Lecky, *History of European Morals,* 1:96n.

118. GrO: ἀρετὴ συμποτικὴ; Fuchs, *Der Alkoholismus und seine Bekämpfung,* 31 (437).

119. DO: *galgenmaal*; ter Gouw, *De Gilden,* 59. Ed. note: Ter Gouw provides the following description (n. 1): "Prisoners who were due to be executed, the day and night before their execution, were brought into the hearing chamber, where *they were treated [onthalen] with better food than was usually provided, and with wine*" (emphasis added).

120. GO: *Schottelgelt*; ter Gouw, *De Gilden,* 60.

121. Ed. note: These paintings are at the Rijksmuseum and can be viewed at Google Arts & Culture, https://artsandculture.google.com/asset/banquet-at-the-crossbowmen-s-guild-in -celebration-of-the-treaty-of-m-nster/_QE9lAmMRgI7dA?hl=en.

(*Braspenningsmaaltijd*), by Cornelis Antonisz.[122] The meals excelled in their large number of guests, their quantity of entrées, and their long duration; incidentally, rich and poor ate virtually the same.[123] Gluttony and drunkenness were common among all classes;[124] they were especially common in the world of university students.[125] That is why laws against drunkenness were made.[126]

Nevertheless, gastronomy and luxurious appetites have not died out or decreased.[127] For many people, culinary art is still the supreme science, which has advanced at an astonishing rate. There are still many epicures, connoisseurs, and gourmands, who have their exemplars from the past, notably Heliogabulus.[128] In the most literal sense of the word, such people are making a god of their belly (Phil. 3:19).

Gastronomy (or gastrology) contains the rules of higher culinary art; gastrosophy prescribes the rules for how people must behave in order to obtain maximum enjoyment of table pleasures without losing their health or dignity.[129] The art of cooking is a noble and important skill for preventing bad food practices and keeping the body and thereby the mind in a healthy state. Cooking reflects the character of a people: practical and forceful among the English, languid among the Italians, highly refined with Louis XIV, simple and plain with the heroes of Homer. Later among the Greeks cooking was more refined, and it was discussed by Mithaecus, Actides, and Philoxenus and widely practiced especially in the time of the Roman Empire.[130] After eating,

122. Ter Gouw, *De Gilden*, 65–66. Ed. note: The painting by Antonisz. (= Antoniszoon = Anthony's son) can be found at Wikipedia, s.v. "Cornelis Anthonisz.," https://en.wikipedia .org/wiki/Cornelis_Anthonisz.#/media/File:Anthonisz,_Cornelis_-_Banquet_of_Members_ of_Amsterdam%27s_Crossbow_Civic_Guard_-_1533.jpg.

123. Von Hellwald, *Kulturgeschichte in ihrer natürlichen Entwicklung*, 2:325.

124. And laws were passed against them: Fuchs, *Der Alkoholismus und seine Bekämpfung*, 31 (437).

125. Tholuck, *Vorgeschichte des Rationalismus*, 1:270.

126. Fuchs, *Der Alkoholismus und seine Bekämpfung*, 52 (458).

127. Ed. note: Apropos to his day, Bavinck mentions the Boers of the Transvaal.

128. Ed. note: Heliogabulus, also known as Elagabulus, was the Roman emperor Marcus Aurelius Antonius Augustus (ca. 203–22), known for his debased lifestyle. In a footnote Bavinck adds the names Lucullus (118–57/56 BC) and Cleopatra (69–30 BC). Bavinck also discusses "eating sins" in *RE*, 1:119–22.

129. See von Vaerst, *Gastrosophie*, vols. 1–2.

130. Ed. note: Mithaecus (ca. fifth century BC) was a cook and the first known author of a cookbook (not extant). Only a brief recipe survives and is quoted in the *Deipnosophistae* of Athenaeus (see n. 114 above) (Wikipedia, s.v. "Mithaecus," https://en.wikipedia.org/wiki/Mi thaecus). Actides of Chios is referred to in literature about the great cooks of Greece (including Athenaeus's *Deipnosophistae* [XIV.81]) but is otherwise elusive; there is no mention of him in WorldCat. Philoxenus of Leucas was a poet who wrote the poem *The Banquet* (a "description of a splendid dinner written in dactylo-epitrites and dithyrambic language"). He is likely also the author of the *Cookery-Book*, a poem "written in dactylic hexameters and quoted by

people took emetics so they could start all over again. The Roman gourmand and lover of luxury Marcus Gavius Apicius (first century AD) took poison to kill himself when he judged his substantial income was no longer adequate to maintain his culinary lifestyle.[131]

E. RESPONSES TO ALCOHOL ABUSE; TEMPERANCE[132]

No wonder then that people sought to combat this frightful abuse! There were all sorts of restrictions in Israel. That also explains the institution of the Nazirite, which bound a person to abstain from wine and strong drink and every intoxicating drink—in fact, from anything from the vine (Num. 6:1–21). Some Nazirite vows were only for a limited period; others for an entire lifetime (Amos 2:11–12). This is apparent from the examples of Samson, Samuel, and John the Baptist. Samson's mother (Judg. 13:4) had to abstain from wine during her pregnancy. Nazirites still appear in 1 Maccabees 3:49, and, in a comment on Luke 1:24, John Lightfoot refers to three hundred Nazirites who "came together at once" during the reign of King Alexander Jannaeus (103–76 BC).[133]

It is uncertain whether Paul's vow when he shaved his head at Cenchreae (Acts 18:18) was a Nazirite vow. For Nazirites were allowed to dwell only in Israel, and if they lived elsewhere, then upon entering the Holy Land they had to remain a Nazirite for thirty days (according to the rabbinic school of Shammai) or start over again from the beginning (according to the rabbinic school of Hillel). According to the law, the Nazirite vow had to be concluded in the temple, and the head had to be shaved there. Or did Paul begin the period of his Nazirite vow when first his head was shaved? Perhaps it was not an actual Nazirite vow after all. The vow (Acts 21:23–26) is a Jewish custom also mentioned elsewhere.

Jeremiah 35 speaks of Rechabites—sons of Jonadab, son of Rechab—who observed the commandment of their father not to drink wine or build a house, sow seed, plant, or own a vineyard, and instead live their entire life in huts on the land. Jeremiah praises them and holds them up to the people of Judah as examples of obedience. Jonadab probably lived at the time of Jehu (1 Chron. 2:55; 2 Kings 10:15, 23). Rechabites were prominent men, though

---

the Athenian comic poet Plato" (*Oxford Classical Dictionary*, "Philoxenus," https://oxfordre.com/classics/view/10.1093/acrefore/9780199381135.001.0001/acrefore-9780199381135-e-5023).

131. Von Jhering, *Der Zweck im Recht*, 2:424–42.

132. Ed. note: There is overlap here with the previous section, but Bavinck here turns to remedies for the abuse of alcohol, including vows of abstinence (temperance) and prohibition. See n. 106 above.

133. Lightfoot, *Horae Hebraicae et Talmudicae*, 3:24.

of Kenite origin. Similar to these Rechabites are the nomadic Nabataeans[134] and the Wahhabist Muslims. Later than the Rechabites, we encounter the Essenes, the Therapeuts, and the Neo-Pythagoreans. In the Christian era, we encounter the ascetics, monks, nuns, and so on.

Today, we encounter the prohibitionists and the teetotalers. We find traces of them also in former centuries. In 1139, a society was founded by the archduke of Austria, later the emperor Frederick III; another society was founded in 1524 by the elector of Trier and the Palatinate; a society was founded around 1600 by Maurice of Hessen that forbade brandy but allowed some two bottles of wine for each member. But the great temperance movement commenced in the nineteenth century.[135] In 1808 in America, Dr. Benjamin Rush (1747–1813) drew attention to the damaging consequences of alcoholic spirits, and that same year, in the town of Moreau in Saratoga County, New York, forty-three men gathered together to promise total abstinence from alcoholic spirits. In 1813, a temperance society was founded in Boston. This society failed. But in 1826, the American Temperance Society was founded in Boston. This group spread widely; it worked and still works with a number of representatives and publications and is supported by all Christian temperance societies.[136] The governments of some states also supported the Temperance Society. Drinking alcoholic spirits was prohibited in the state of Maine. Here and there people occasionally overreacted. In 1874 a formal crusade of women against barkeepers included surrounding the taverns and singing and praying until the owner promised to close the tavern. In Ohio and Indiana, about 450 bars were closed and twenty thousand people became prohibitionists. Drinking alcoholic spirits was prohibited. In Kansas a law was passed forbidding all manufacture and sale of spirits, brandy, wine, ale, and beer. The law prohibited pastors from serving wine at the Lord's Supper. Before the celebration of the Lord's Supper, an Episcopalian minister, Rev. Dr. Archibald Beatty in Lawrence, Kansas, declared that "the bishop and the clergy were not going to pay attention to this law."[137] One must know

134. According to Diodorus Siculus, *Bibliotheca Historica* XIX.94; cf. Winer, *Biblisches Realwoerterbuch*, 2:129–30 ("Nabatäer").

135. Fuchs, *Der Alkoholismus und seine Bekampfung*, 50–67 (457–75). Ed. note: In what follows we are omitting most of Bavinck's outdated statistics.

136. Ed. note: Bavinck here lists the *Temperance Recorder* (with 250,000 subscribers) and the *Youth's Temperance Banner* (with 130,000 subscribers). He also mentions 300 Catholic associations with 350,000 members holding a congress in 1872 in Baltimore.

137. GO: *daß der Bischof und die Geistlichkeit diesem Geseße keine Beachtung shenken würden*; Fuchs, *Der Alkoholismus und seine Bekämpfung*, 8n3 (414). Ed. note: Fuchs introduces his comment on Dr. Beatty thus: "Naturally the church fellowships could not accept this law" (*Natürlich können die Kirchengemeinfchaften diesem Gesetze nich gehorchen*).

the terrible alcohol abuse in America to be able to assess these overreactions properly. Annually, thousands of people die, and millions of dollars are spent on alcohol.[138] Temperance societies also sprang up in many other places around the globe.[139]

In addition, there have arisen *asylums* to treat alcoholics. The first one was founded in 1854 by Dr. Turner in New York; since 1867 it has belonged to the state, and today it is called the New York State Inebriate Asylum; so too in Boston (1859), Pennsylvania (1867), and other states—about forty institutions throughout America.[140] In Germany there is one in Lintorf on the Rhine under the direction of Rev. Hirsch. These asylums often treat alcoholism as a disease. People want to replace pubs with coffee houses—an idea that began in Ireland—called coffee taverns. Here in the Netherlands as well we find a Society for Community Coffee Houses, and coffee wagons travel about to offer coffee, chocolate, tea, and milk for a small price.[141] Finally, governments attempt to restrict abuse through repeatedly increasing excise taxes. But as taxation in Sweden shows, this only encourages cheating. In Sweden, the distillation time is limited to two months every year, a measure

138. Ed. note: Bavinck takes the figures of sixty thousand people dying of alcohol abuse per year and a total of $6.7 billion annually spent on alcohol in the United States from Fuchs, *Der Alkoholismus und seine Bekämpfung*, 53n1 (459).

139. Ed. note: What follows in this note is an abridgment of Bavinck's text: Temperance societies began in Great Britain and Ireland (1829), as well as teetotaler or total abstinence societies, which soon eclipsed the temperance movement. The Irish Capuchin monk Father Theobald Mathew (1790–1856) persuaded large numbers to take the pledge: 700,000 in London; in the rest of England, 180,000; in the US, 600,000. Temperance associations were founded on the Sandwich Islands (Hawaii; 1851); in India (1832), on the Society Islands (1834), in Australia (1833), at the Cape [of Good Hope], and among the KhoiKhoi (formerly, Hottentots; 1835). In the Netherlands, temperance societies were founded in Utrecht (1835), Dragten (1842), and Amsterdam (1843), and an Abolition Society [*afschaffingsgenootschap*] in Leiden in 1842. In Germany the cause found adherents thanks to the American agent R. Baird and was promoted by pastor J. M. Boettcher, author of *Geschichte der Mäßigkeitsgesellschaften in den norddeutschen Bundesstaaten*, and the Roman Catholic curate J. M. Seling in Osnabrück. Since 1848 the greatest flowering of temperance has passed in Germany. Cf. Martius, *Handbuch der deutschen Trinker- und Trunksuchtsfrage*; see review in *Theologisches Literaturblatt* 12.

140. Fuchs, *Der Alkoholismus und seine Bekämpfung*, 61–62 (467–68). Ed. note: The New York State Inebriate Asylum in Binghamton was chartered in 1854 and admitted its first patients in 1864; it was later known as the Binghamton State Hospital and was converted to a mental hospital in 1879; its building remained in use as a mental hospital until 1993 (Wikipedia, s.v. "New York State Inebriate Asylum," https://en.wikipedia.org/wiki/New_York_State_Inebriate _Asylum). Neither Bavinck nor Fuchs identifies "Dr. Turner" more specifically. According to Recovery.org, the New York State Inebriate Asylum was "opened in 1864 under the direction of Dr. Joseph Edward Turner. It was the first medically monitored addiction treatment center in the U.S. and is considered the first alcohol rehab center" (see "Timeline: History of Addiction Treatment").

141. DO: *Maatschappij voor Volkskoffiehuizen.*

specified because of surplus. The city of Gothenburg targeted particularly the barkeeper, who was granted no benefits, was not allowed to sell on credit or barter, was required to keep his establishment well ventilated, and was required to sell food.[142]

f. What Does Holy Scripture Teach?

Opponents of alcohol adduce four grounds for their position.[143]

a. Holy Scripture warns against immoderate use, as in the cases of Noah and Lot and in biblical instruction: no drunkard will inherit the kingdom of God (1 Cor. 6:10).

b. According to Scripture, abstinence is sometimes good: for Nazirites, John the Baptist, the Rechabites, Aaron and the priests as they approach the tent of meeting (Num. 6:3–4), and kings (Prov. 31:4). Similarly, overseers in the church must not be drunkards, and deacons "not addicted to much wine" (1 Tim. 3:3, 8).

c. We must do everything to the glory of God, eat and drink in faith, with prayer and thanksgiving (1 Tim. 4:3–5)—and that is not possible with alcohol.

d. Abstinence is a requirement of Christian self-denial, which sometimes demands our life, our possessions; it is necessary for the sake of weaker believers (Rom. 15:1–2; 14:15; 1 Cor. 8:12; and esp. Rom. 14:21). And this little, negligible bit of self-denial is commanded by neighbor love, by the terrible needs and misery and circumstances of our time. Most teetotalers do permit alcohol for medicinal purposes, as did the apostle Paul (1 Tim. 5:23).

142. Ed. note: We are including Bavinck's dated statistics here in this note as evidence of his own interest in concrete, detailed Dutch statecraft matters as early as 1885. They also reveal how incredibly lucrative the trade in alcohol was and is for governments, even in such small countries as the Netherlands: "In the Netherlands the excise on liquor amounted to *fl* 9,215,000 in 1865 and *fl* 23,512,000 in 1885 (i.e., *fl* 2.61 per head in 1865 and *fl* 5.49 in 1885). In recent years the excise tax rate on liquor has been *fl* 60 per hectoliter."

Using the Historical Currency Converter (created by Rodney Edvinsson, professor in economic history, Stockholm University), an instrument based on the purchasing power of gold, we find that the US dollar was worth 1.5519 Dutch guilders in 1865; the 1885 rate was $1 US = *fl* 2.499. This translates the 1865 Dutch excise of *fl* 9,215,000 into $5,937,883 US and the 1885 excise of *fl* 23,512,000 into $9,408,563 US. See https://www.historicalstatistics.org/Currency converter.html. For comparison, in inflation-adjusted 2021 dollars, $9,408,563 in 1885 equals a staggering $250+ billion (calculations derived from the US Bureau of Labor Statistics, CPI Inflation Indicator, at https://www.in2013dollars.com). Thanks to Antoine Theron for help in finessing this footnote.

143. Mulder, *De geheel-onthouding en de Heilige Schrift*.

Here are some guidelines:[144]

a. Alcohol seems to be good for strengthening muscles and nerves; for the appetite; for combating fever, including that caused by infection and blood poisoning; for chronic melancholy; and for the kidneys, to encourage urination. But the medicinal value of alcohol has been grossly exaggerated, especially in former days, when it first came into use (among the common people particularly during and after the Thirty Years' War).[145] The physician Arnaldus de Villa Nova (1240–1311) believed that the human race had become old and weak; therefore, God gave brandy to rejuvenate it. Brandy, he said, is a fountain of life; that is why it is called water of life.[146] In the sixteenth century a German author, Theoricus, attributed still stronger effects to alcohol.[147] In the seventeenth century, however, the question arose whether it should not rather be called water of death.[148] Many physicians no longer assign such high medicinal value to alcohol, although lately cognac is once again being highly praised.[149] Then again, it is pointed out that people cannot do without strong drink. All nations have such beverages.[150] Laborers need them for refreshment—as Bismarck said on March 28, 1881—as do soldiers occasionally before entering battle after an exhausting march.[151] This is exaggerated. Opponents of alcohol rightly oppose this argument. But let's return to Scripture.

b. The use of alcohol is not forbidden as such in Scripture; perhaps forbidden in connection with and for the sake of some circumstances, but not in and of itself. Mulder also says: Holy Scripture maintains Christian freedom in this matter.[152] People reply, however, that neither does Scripture command it! Of course not; nor is it commanded either to eat, to drink, to relax, to engage in this or that sport. Scripture *assumes* the natural life. But

144. Ed. note: Bavinck begins a new series of points here that serve as his own summary.
145. Ed. note: 1618–48.
146. LO: *aqua vitae*; Fuchs, *Der Alkoholismus und seine Bekämpfung*, 46 (452).
147. Ed. note: Bavinck's source is Fuchs, *Der Alkoholismus und seine Bekämpfung*, 46 (452); Fuchs provides the following reference: A. Baer, *Der Alcoholismus*, 561; Baer provides an additional source: R. Baird, *Geschichte der Mässigkeits-Gesellschaft in den vereinigten Staaten Nord-Amerika's*. According to Baird, Theoricus was a sixteenth-century chronicler who wrote an entry in the *Chronik des holinsched*, on the wonderful healing power of brandy-wine (Baird, *Geschichte*, 4–5). Among the mentioned health benefits: "It delays old age and strengthens youth; it promotes digestion, dissipates melancholy and gladdens the heart; it enlightens the mind and enlivens the soul; it crushes kidney- and gall-stones [and much more]."
148. LO: *aqua mortis [et damnationis]*. Ed. note: Bavinck only uses the term *aqua mortis*; the full term, *aqua mortis et damnationis*, is used by Baird, *Geschichte*, 4.
149. Fuchs, *Der Alkoholismus und seine Bekämpfung*, 46–53 (452–59).
150. Fuchs, *Der Alkoholismus und seine Bekämpfung*, 36–48 (442–54).
151. Fuchs, *Der Alkoholismus und seine Bekämpfung*, 36–48 (442–54).
152. Mulder, *De geheel-onthouding en de Heilige Schrift*, 27.

in Scripture wine and strong drink had to be offered to God (Exod. 29:40; Num. 28:7). God gives "wine to gladden the heart of man" just as he gives "bread to strengthen man's heart" (Ps. 104:15). Jesus came eating and drinking (Matt. 11:19) and he was called a "glutton and a drunkard" (Luke 7:34). He changed water into wine (John 2:2–12) and used wine in the Last Supper (Matt. 26). He says that we are not defiled by anything that goes into our mouth (Matt. 15:11; Mark 7:15, 18). Paul says that the kingdom of God does not consist in food and drink (Rom. 14:17). Furthermore, everything is pure (Titus 1:15), every creature of God is good (1 Tim. 4:4), and a little wine is sometimes good (1 Tim. 5:23). We have the right to eat and drink (1 Cor. 9:4). The New Jerusalem will witness the wedding feast furnished with new wine (Matt. 26:29; Mark 14:25; Rev. 19:7, 9). The natural is good. God is the Creator of heaven and earth. We reject Manichaeism and Anabaptist dualism!

c. Opposing alcohol and its use as inherently evil proceeds from a wrong, anti-Christian, dualistic, gnostic principle. Marital unfaithfulness and immorality are just as shockingly widespread as alcohol use. Should marriage be abolished simply because so many defile it?[153] The same goes for eating, dressing, walking, traveling, relaxing, playing games, and so on. All kinds of societies and associations are being established these days to combat specific sins and evils in connection with prostitution, food and drink, unscrupulous food practices, and clothing. In France recently an association was set up to combat atheism. There is a society for the defense of immortality, a tract society, a missionary society, an organization for the protection of orphans. Everything is analyzed, dissected, individualized—instead of one central and comprehensive fight and assault on the principle from which all those evils flow! It's comparable to a guerrilla war, with the tactics of the Cossacks. In my opinion, Field Marshal Moltke's strategy is preferable: "On to Paris!"[154] Preach the gospel, restore the church, free the university, bring the gospel to bear on state and society and family, and you will automatically vanquish those evils.

d. To be sure, a vow to abstain is in and of itself lawful. We find that vow with the Nazirites, Rechabites, and others to signify devotion to God. There are circumstances in which taking that vow is a duty. For example, alcoholics can overcome their bondage to alcohol only by totally abstaining from it. But the opponents of alcohol want me to take the vow of abstinence for the

---

153. Fuchs, *Der Alkoholismus und seine Bekämpfung*, 45 (451).

154. Ed. note: Bavinck refers here to German general Helmuth von Moltke the Elder (1800–1881), commander of the Prussian forces in the Franco-Prussian War (1870–71).

sake of others, and that cannot be. I can do that for the sake of my brothers and sisters who are weak—abstain from meat and wine—but these must be brothers and sisters who would be offended and injured in their spiritual life. But since drunkards are not my brothers, nor are they offended when I drink in moderation, this argument based on brotherly love fails. Is it then commanded by neighbor love? Not at all; marriage does not need to be abolished just because someone else abuses it. One can take a vow only personally and voluntarily, not for the sake of others. Even if I abstain for the sake of others (say, for my children), that is still not a vow, but purely a measure of prudence. The temperance societies have been blessed; in some places alcohol abuse and crime have been reduced.[155] But the energy has evaporated. These societies have not brought about a radical cure. Their greatest flourishing is already gone. How then is this evil to be combated? The state has a calling; thus far it has made itself a partner in the liquor trade everywhere and has regulated the sale of liquor only to benefit the treasury, just as it has done with the opium trade.[156] It has made money from sins of the people. Instead it should reduce the public esteem for the occupation of barkeeper, it should grant the barkeepers no benefits, it should tax them heavily, and so on. In the final analysis, only genuine conversion can avail.[157]

e. Holy Scripture strongly and repeatedly forbids any and all abuse of alcohol (Gen. 9:21; 19:32). A son that is a glutton and a drunkard must be stoned (Deut. 21:20). Consider the example of Nabal (1 Sam. 25:36). Zimri kills King Elah after Elah drinks himself drunk (1 Kings 16:9–10). Prophets pronounce judgment:

> Woe to those who rise early in the morning,
>> that they may run after strong drink,
> who tarry late into the evening
>> as wine inflames them! (Isa. 5:11)

155. In Ireland, through the work of Theobalde Mathew, alcohol use and crime decreased (Fuchs, *Der Alkoholismus und seine Bekämpfung*, 57 [463]).
156. Mulder, *De geheel-onthouding en de Heilige Schrift*, preface.
157. Kuyper, *Ons Program*, 767–74, 903–4; Kuyper, *Our Program*, 232–34. Ed. note: The second reference in *Ons Program* is to an appendix in which Kuyper spells out the moral dilemmas of government excise duties for distilled alcoholic beverages. On the one hand, Kuyper acknowledges the terrible human cost of alcohol abuse. At the same time, he points to two problems with proposals to increase these duties as a means to discourage alcohol use (i.e., a "sin tax"): (a) The government has become dependent on the revenue and has a vested interest in actually *increasing* use of alcohol to increase its revenue. (b) Moral renewal is not the responsibility of the state: "Only conversion can touch the root of the sin, and the Christian church can stand nowhere but on the Word of God for healing the heart of the nation."

Isaiah points to the iniquity of Israel on the day when the "Lord GOD of hosts / called for weeping and mourning, / for baldness and wearing sackcloth," only to find "joy and gladness, / killing oxen and slaughtering sheep, / eating flesh and drinking wine." Their motto had become: "Let us eat and drink, / for tomorrow we die" (Isa. 22:12–13). God's punishment on Israel is announced by Hosea, also for their love of wine:

> I will punish them for their ways
>   and repay them for their deeds.
> They shall eat, but not be satisfied;
>   they shall play the whore, but not multiply,
> because they have forsaken the LORD
>   to cherish whoredom, wine, and new wine,
>   which take away the understanding. (Hosea 4:9–10)

Abuse of alcohol shows a lack of wisdom: "Wine is a mocker, strong drink a brawler, / and whoever is led astray by it is not wise" (Prov. 20:1). "Whoever loves pleasure will be a poor man; / he who loves wine and oil will not be rich" (Prov. 21:17). And the words of King Lemuel from his mother:

> It is not for kings, O Lemuel,
>   it is not for kings to drink wine,
>   or for rulers to take strong drink,
> lest they drink and forget what has been decreed
>   and pervert the rights of all the afflicted. (Prov. 31:4–5)

Wine and women lead intelligent men astray, / and the man who consorts with prostitutes is reckless. (Sir. 19:2 NRSV; cf. 31:28)

The intoxicating, calamitous effects of drink are often an image of divine judgment (Isa. 29:9; 51:17, 22; Jer. 25:15; 49:12; 51:7; Lam. 4:21; Ezek. 23:31–34; Hab. 2:16; Zech. 12:2; Pss. 60:3; 75:8; and similarly Rev. 14:10; 16:19; 17:4). God's wrath is a cup that he compels nations to drink.

The New Testament, accordingly, condemns serving our "appetites" (Rom. 16:18)[158] in a variety of ways: "But watch yourselves lest your hearts be weighed down with dissipation and drunkenness[159] and cares of this life, and that day come upon you suddenly like a trap" (Luke 21:34). "Let us walk properly as in the daytime, not in orgies and drunkenness,[160] not in sexual immorality

---

158. GrO: δουλεύουσιν ἀλλὰ τῇ ἑαυτῶν κοιλίᾳ; Vilmar, *Theologische Moral*, 1:263–67 (§21).
159. GrO: κραιπάλῃ καὶ μέθῃ.
160. GrO: μέθαις.

and sensuality, not in quarreling and jealousy" (Rom. 13:13; cf. 1 Cor. 5:11; Gal. 5:21). "Their end is destruction, their god is their belly,[161] and they glory in their shame, with minds set on earthly things" (Phil 3:19). Leaders must be "not given to wine"[162] (Titus 1:7; 2:3 KJV); God's people are not to drink without a care for the consequences[163] (1 Pet. 4:3) or out of habit[164] (1 Pet. 4:3).

The twin sins of gluttony, excessive eating and drinking, are combined and condemned (Rom. 13:13; Gal. 5:21; 1 Pet. 4:3) as κῶμοι and ἐγκωμία—that is, reveling in boisterous banquets with music and poetry, common in ancient times as well as in the fifteenth and sixteenth centuries, and still common today. It is wanton, riotous living[165] (1 Tim. 5:6; James 5:5; 2 Pet. 2:13), a form of sybaritism with its motto: "The flood comes after us."[166] It is to lead a soft, frolicking, sensual life of pleasure and luxury.

f. Over against all that, Holy Scripture commands *moderation.* Wine and liquor are not nutritious, nor is beer; brandy has absolutely no nutritional value, and beer not much either. These beverages are all indulgences; they do not belong to our needs in the strict sense, but to luxury, to the pleasures of life.[167] As we have seen, when used in moderate amounts they can benefit the nerves, muscles, and so on, but they are not everyday staples; they are occasional foods and drinks, items of enjoyment. That is why Scripture recommends not abstinence but moderation. Not abstinence, for God gives us permission to be merry and to enjoy life. As Paul himself testified to the crowd in Lystra, "Yet he did not leave himself without witness, for he did good by giving you rains from heaven and fruitful seasons, satisfying your hearts with *food and gladness*" (Acts 14:17).[168] Every creature of God is good (1 Tim. 4:4). Even meat offered to idols may be eaten, for the earth is the Lord's (1 Cor. 8:4–13; 10:23–32).

When we turn to the Old Testament, we find that God wanted Israel to rejoice before him at the feasts (Lev. 23:40; Deut. 12:7, 12, 18). Israelites who could not bring their tithes of grain, new wine, and olive oil and the firstborn of their herds and flocks to the place where the LORD would choose "to set

161. GrO: ὧν ὁ θεὸς ἡ κοιλία.
162. GrO: πάροινον.
163. GrO: πότοις.
164. GrO: οἰνοφλυγίαις.
165. GrO: τρυφή and σπαταλάω.
166. FO: *Après nous le deluge.* Ed. note: In this form the saying is attributed to the official mistress of Louis XV of France (1710–74), Madame de Pompadour (1721–64); in its more familiar form, *Après moi le déluge* ("After me comes the flood"), it is usually attributed to the king himself. See Laguna, "The Expression 'Après moi le déluge.'"
167. Fuchs, *Der Alkoholismus und seine Bekämpfung*, 38 (444).
168. GrO: τροφῆς καὶ εὐφροσύνης.

his name there," because the way was too long to carry it all, were instructed to turn their tithes "into money and bind up the money . . . and go to the place that the LORD your God chooses and spend the money for whatever you desire—oxen or sheep or wine or strong drink, whatever your appetite craves. And you shall eat there before the LORD your God and rejoice, you and your household" (Deut. 14:23–26; cf. 16:11; 27:7).[169] Thus, the psalmist praises the LORD who

> makes grass grow for the cattle,
>   and plants for people to cultivate—
>   bringing forth food from the earth:
> wine that gladdens human hearts,
>   oil to make their faces shine,
>   and bread that sustains their hearts. (Ps. 104:14–15 NIV; cf.
>   Judg. 9:13)

However, Scripture does advise and recommend moderation[170]—that is, prudence and sobriety. In Holy Scripture this means remaining within the bounds of life ordained by God. This soundness of mind[171] too is a gift of God: "For this reason I remind you to fan into flame the gift of God, which is in you through the laying on of my hands, for God gave us a spirit not of fear but of power and love and self-control" (2 Tim. 1:6–7). In Titus 2:12 Paul equates "self-controlled, upright, and godly lives" with renouncing "ungodliness and worldly passions."[172] The Christian must be sober, sensible, and "not overindulging in wine" (1 Tim. 3:3 NASB). This requirement pertains to church leaders (1 Tim. 3:2–3; cf. Titus 1:8), to their wives (1 Tim. 3:11), and to the elderly (Titus 2:2). First Peter 4:7–8 calls upon everyone to be self-controlled and sober-minded for the sake of their prayers. Sobriety and self-control are essential for Christians who prayerfully await the end of all things (cf. Luke 21:34). Thereby Scripture forbids all flippancy and frivolity.[173] Our body, too,

---

169. Levi prepared a great feast for Jesus (Luke 5:29); copious amounts of wine were consumed at the wedding in Cana (John 2:10); see Perkins, *Works of William Perkins*, 8:399 (*Case of Conscience*, III.iv.2). Ed. note: This annotation for Perkins's *Case of Conscience* differs from that in *RE*, vol. 1; vol. 8 in *The Works of William Perkins*, which includes Perkins's writings on conscience, was published in 2019 and not available for our use in the preparation of vol. 1. To facilitate use of other editions, we are including the book, chapter, and section reference as above.

170. DO: *matigheid*; GrO: σωφροσύνη = whoever is of pure and sound mind [*qui sanae et integrae mentis est*].

171. GrO: σωφροσύνη.

172. GrO: σωφρόνως καὶ δικαίως καὶ εὐσεβῶς ζήσωμεν; ἀσέβειαν καὶ τὰς κοσμικὰς ἐπιθυμίας.

173. DO: *lichtzinnigheid*; *frivoliteit*.

is a temple of the Holy Spirit (1 Cor. 6:19–20) and is a member of Christ's body (1 Cor. 10:14–22).

g. Scripture knows no dividing line in the gift itself; all gifts are good. But Scripture does draw a dividing line in Christians themselves. Christians must be sober and watchful and must not, through drunkenness and revelry, let themselves be robbed of the noblest thing that human beings have—namely, their consciousness. Intoxicating drink murders the soul and body alike, attacks the image of God in us, and reduces us to the level of an animal. Furthermore, when we say that "everything created by God is good," we must also remember that "nothing is to be rejected if it is received with thanksgiving, for it is made holy by the word of God and prayer" (1 Tim. 4:4–5; cf. Eph. 5:20).[174] God wants all his gifts to be enjoyed with thankful hearts. Only through grateful enjoyment is creation's goal fulfilled. Every gift is made holy (not declared holy but made holy—for food in itself is neither sacred nor profane) for those who enjoy it by "the word of God"[175] and by prayer.[176] Is Paul perhaps thinking of Jewish mealtime prayers?

h. The Mosaic law stipulates no requirement of a prayer at mealtime or any other time. But public prayers were attended by growing numbers (Isa. 1:15); shortly before the exile there were already ordained intercessors (1 Chron. 23:30; cf. Neh. 11:17). Soon after, the thrice-daily prayer makes its appearance (Daniel)—namely, at the third hour (8:00–9:00 a.m.; Acts 2:15), the sixth hour (Acts 10:9), and the ninth hour (Acts 3:1; 10:30). Among the Jews the midday and the evening meals are also accompanied by prayer. The father cuts the loaf of bread in half, covers it with both hands, and gives thanks, whereupon the others say "Amen" and then eat; next, he blesses the wine, and the others again say "Amen"; then the father recites Psalm 23, and the meal is enjoyed. At the close, there is another antiphony with "Amens."[177] Meals were begun and concluded with washing hands and saying prayers (Matt. 14:19; 15:36;

---

174. GrO: μετὰ εὐχαριστίας λαμβανόμενον, ἁγιάζεται γὰρ διὰ λόγου θεοῦ καὶ ἐντεύξεως.

175. GrO: διὰ λόγου θεοῦ. The "word of God" in this case could mean a number of things: (i) Wahl and Leo understand it as "speaking to God," as a synonym of petition or prayer. But the term "word of God" never occurs in this sense. (ii) A specific word in Scripture—e.g., Gen. 1:31 or Acts 10:15. (iii) The teaching of Christianity. (iv) The word of God occurring in a prayer of thanksgiving. (v) Prayers and intercessions to God (1 Tim. 2:1; thus, de Wette, van Oosterzee, and Meyer). Ed. note: The references are to Christian Abraham Wahl (1773–1855), Gottlob Eduard Leo (1803–81), Wilhelm Martin Leberecht de Wette (1780–1849), and J. J. van Oosterzee (1817–82). See de Wette, *Kurze Erklärung der Briefe an Titus, Timotheus, und die Hebräer*, 120 (commentary on 1 Tim. 4:5); van Oosterzee, *Two Epistles of Paul to Timothy*, on 1 Tim. 4:5; Bavinck's source is H. Meyer, *Critical and Exegetical Commentary on the New Testament*, 11:171–72 (on 1 Tim. 4:5).

176. GrO: ἐντεύξεως.

177. W. Pressel, "Gebet bei den alten und bei den heutigen Hebräern."

26:26; Luke 9:16; John 6:11).[178] Jesus himself follows this custom of prayer (Matt. 14:19; cf. Luke 9:16; John 6:11); he commanded the multitude to sit down on the grass, and he took the five loaves and the two fish and blessed them. He did the same with the seven loaves and a few fish (Matt. 15:36) and at the Passover meal (Matt. 26:26).

God's blessing on the food must be invoked, because "man does not live by bread alone, but . . . by every word that comes from the mouth of the LORD" (Deut. 8:3). Without that blessing, we will eat but not be satisfied (Lev. 26:26). God can take away our entire supply of bread and water (Isa. 3:1; cf. Ezek. 4:16).

The Christian church has adopted this custom. The *Apostolic Constitutions* provides the following mealtime prayer: "You are blessed, O Lord, who nourishes me from my youth, who gives food to all flesh. Fill our hearts with joy and gladness, that having always what is sufficient for us, we may abound to every good work, in Christ Jesus our Lord, through whom glory, honor, and power be to You forever. Amen."[179] In fact, we find this usage in Acts 27:35, where Paul gave thanks with the ship's crew and ate with them. We find it also in Tertullian.[180] Commenting on 1 Timothy 4:5, Calvin calls sitting down to eat and forgetting God "a beastly way of eating."[181] Saying grace before mealtime is thus customary in most Christian countries, whether before every meal—and even before a sandwich and cup of coffee—or, as in Scotland, only in the morning and in the evening. See also the hymns and form prayers for before and after meals in the liturgical section of old Reformed psalters. The fourth petition of the Lord's Prayer is "Give us this day our daily bread." Even though the food is already on the table and we have therefore already received it, prayer is still useful and necessary. Here are three good reasons:

    i. Prayer makes us aware that, notwithstanding all our labor in the sweat of our brow, food is still an unmerited gift of God. After all, through sin we have forfeited our right to the earth and our dominion over it. For us just to take the food without acknowledging God is therefore, to speak with Calvin, an "unclean use."[182] By prayer and thanksgiving, however, the gifts become sanctified when we acknowledge that God in Christ gives us a sacred right to them as children. Although it is true

178. HO: בְּרָכָה; GrO: εὐλογία; εὐχαριστία.
179. "Constitutions of the Holy Apostles" VII.39 (*ANF* 7:748); cited by H. Meyer, *Critical and Exegetical Commentary on the New Testament*, 11:172n1 (on 1 Tim. 4:5).
180. Tertullian, *Apologia* 39; cf. Wuttke, *Christian Ethics*, 2:188 (§102).
181. LO: *belluinum gerendi morem*.
182. LO: *impuram usurpatio*; Calvin, *Commentaries on the Epistles to Timothy, Titus, and Philemon*, 105–6, on 1 Tim. 4:5.

that we must work for our livelihood, nevertheless God has also given us the intelligence, the strength, and the health to work.

ii. Prayer makes us acknowledge that God is "the only fountain of all good,"[183] that all blessings come from him, and that all things depend on that blessing. God gives every living thing its food "in due season" (Ps. 145:15–16). As Israel is about to enter the promised land, she is told, "And you shall eat and be full, and you shall bless the LORD your God for the good land he has given you" (Deut. 8:10).

But then a warning follows:

> Take care lest you forget the LORD your God by not keeping his commandments and his rules and his statutes, which I command you today, lest, when you have eaten and are full and have built good houses and live in them, and when your herds and flocks multiply and your silver and gold is multiplied and all that you have is multiplied, then your heart be lifted up, and you forget the LORD your God, who brought you out of the land of Egypt, out of the house of slavery. (Deut. 8:11–14)

For our labor and our dishes of prepared food on the table do not benefit us without God's blessing (Deut. 8:3; Lev. 26:26; Isa. 3:1; Ezek. 4:16; Ps. 127:1–2; Luke 5:5–6). Thus it is fitting also for the rich to pray this petition, for they too need God's blessing on their bread, so that they may consume it in good health and be nourished by it, for without God's blessing the most nutritious food often does not nourish. We must pray so that, on the one hand, we do not waste God's gifts, and on the other hand, we are able to use them and not be parsimonious.

iii. Prayer leads us to withdraw our trust from all creatures and place it in God alone[184] (Matt. 6:25, 31–32; Ps. 62:10; Prov. 30:8–9)—and not attach our hearts to these transitory goods, nor to be too concerned about them. Avarice and anxiety do not suit us as Christians. "But godliness with contentment is great gain, for we brought nothing into the world, and we cannot take anything out of the world. But if we have food and clothing, with these we will be content" (1 Tim. 6:6–8).

Although Christ commands us to pray *today* for our daily bread, although he condemns all worry about life (Matt. 6:25, 33), although Agur prayed to have neither riches nor poverty (Prov. 30:8), although wealth is a great danger (Matt. 13:22; 1 Tim. 6:9), nevertheless we

183. Heidelberg Catechism, Q&A 125.
184. Heidelberg Catechism, Q&A 125.

are allowed to save up and lay aside for tomorrow (Joseph in Gen. 41:47–49; Christ in John 6:12; the apostles in Acts 11:28–29), to be stewards (Luke 16:1–12) and share with the needy (Eph. 4:28); and we may even make ample use of all those gifts. Indeed, we may hold feasts (John 2) and banquets, as God prescribed for Israel (see above), provided they do not degenerate into revelry and drunkenness. In all things the motto holds: "Nothing in excess!"[185]

The following five errors must be avoided with our mealtime prayers: doing things in haste, ostentation, excess, violence, fanaticism.[186] Dinner parties should not have too many guests (somewhere between the number of Graces and Muses!),[187] not always wealthy guests, who invite us in return, but also poor people, the disabled, crippled, blind (Luke 14:13; who does that?), and not only likeminded guests. Jesus sat down with tax collectors (Matt. 9:10) and with Pharisees (Luke 14:1). Paul includes this instruction in his guidance to the Corinthians on food: "If one of the unbelievers invites you to dinner and you are disposed to go, eat whatever is set before you without raising any question on the ground of conscience" (1 Cor. 10:27; cf. 5:10–12). So this concourse with unbelievers is not illegitimate even, for example, for pastors, but always be careful! The practice of Jesuits and monks is therefore not good; Roman Catholic dinner laws[188] and monastic diets are arbitrary.[189] Furthermore, those dinner parties should not be held during seasons of fasting, during the week of preparation for the Lord's Supper, on Saturdays and Sundays, in times of mourning. There must be love at

---

185. LO: *Ne quid nimis!*

186. LO: *praepropere; laute; nimis; ardenter; studiose*; Voetius, *Selectarum Disputationum Theologicarum*, 4:500; de Moor, *Commentarius Perpetuus*, 2:875.

187. Ed. note: Bavinck says, "somewhere between the number of Graces (3) and Muses (9)." The nine Muses in Greek mythology are Calliope (epic poetry), Clio (history), Erato (love poetry), Euterpe (music, song, and lyric poetry), Melpomene (tragedy), Polyhymnia (hymns), Terpsichore (dance), Thalia (comedy), and Urania (astronomy) (Wikipedia, s.v. "Muses," https://en.wikipedia .org/wiki/Muses). The three Graces are Aglaia (elegance, brightness, splendor), Euphrosyne (mirth and joyfulness), and Thalia (youth, beauty, and good cheer) (Greek Mythology.com, s.v. "The Graces," https://www.greekmythology.com/Other_Gods/The_Graces/the_graces.html).

188. LO: *leges cibariae.*

189. Ed. note: Bavinck provides the following as reference: "cf. Zwingli Opp I"; he likely has in mind Zwingli's April 16, 1522, sermon: "Concerning choice and liberty respecting food— Concerning offence and vexation—Whether anyone has power to forbid foods at certain times" (*Von erkiesen vnd freyheit der speisen. Von ergernüß vnd verböserung. Ob man gewalt hab die speyßen zu etlichen zeiten verbieten*), in Zwingli, *The Latin Works and the Correspondence*, 1:70–112. The sermon came in defense of Zurich printer Froschauer, who with his workers broke a Lenten fast by eating sausages, claiming that otherwise they would not have the strength to deal with a heavy backlog of work.

the dinner table (Prov. 15:17), and the meal should be spiced with witty conversations about literature, art, history, and philosophy and with music and singing—in order that the human spirit, too, might be fed and entertained. Toasts, which had infiltrated Christianity from the pagans—the Greeks and the Romans—are illegitimate according to Voetius, since they lead to intemperance and drunkenness, because they force people to drink.[190] In our day, we need far more to return to simpler customs—even if they are not puritanical—than to be convinced that partying is illegitimate. There are plenty of parties, meals, dinners, suppers, brunches, formal banquets. A person can manage with little food, as is clear from those who have fasted for long periods of time.[191]

§39. Clothing

3. Concern about Clothing[192]

Human beings need clothing because through sin they feel uncovered, naked, and ashamed. Wuttke says that even in the absence of sin clothing would have been necessary.[193] Shame can relate to different parts of the body: among some peoples only the face, or the back of the head, or the navel, breasts.[194] Shame presumes that we fell yet did not become animals. Shame arises especially with respect to defects that cannot be helped (even more than with respect to sinful deeds that were voluntarily committed)—for example, blindness, deafness, and deformity.[195] Shame does not presume free will, yet does assume (1) that the defects are permanent and cannot be remedied and (2) that they are grounded in our will.[196] Shame does not arise with respect to

---

190. Voetius, *Selectarum Disputationum Theologicarum*, 4:500; de Moor, *Commentarius Perpetuus*, 2:875.

191. Ed. note: Bavinck provides two examples from his own day that help date his manuscript: "Succi recently fasted for 30 days, and in Paris, Stephano Merlatti from Piedmont fasted for 50 days (Nov.–Dec. 1886)." "Succi" is a reference to Giovanni Succi, who fasted for thirty days in August–September 1886. There were numerous accounts of this in Dutch newspapers. See the Delpher database of the Royal Library of the Netherlands at www.delpher.nl.

192. Ed. note: This continues the numbering that began in §37 ("1. Care for Our Health") and was resumed at the beginning of §38 ("2. Concern about Food and Drink").

193. Wuttke, *Christian Ethics*, 2:245 (§121): "Clothing did not first become necessary because of sin. The Biblical account implies only, that it became necessary prematurely, and for other than its normal reason—namely, before the development of personal character had led to its invention as an adornment."

194. Peschel, *Races of Man*, 171–75.

195. Scholten, *De vrije wil*, 210–14.

196. Von Hellwald, *Kulturgeschichte in ihrer natürlichen Entwicklung*, 1:142. Ed. note: To this interlinear note Bavinck adds "and Darwin, (ibid., 142)"; the reference is to von Hellwald's

illness, headaches, and so on but does arise with respect to sexual urges and the call of nature.[197] Often there is also false shame, with respect to poverty, one's Christian faith, and other things. God respects the feeling of shame in Adam and Eve and furnishes them with "garments of skins" (Gen. 3:21). Ever since, human beings have had to borrow from plants and animals to clothe themselves, while every other creature—angel, animal, plant—is self-sufficient with regard to clothing.

A. CLOTHING IN SCRIPTURE, HISTORY, AND CULTURE

Adornment and Luxury

Under the influence of culture, human beings soon changed this garb to cover their shame into an ornament, adornment, finery. Among primitive peoples, a loincloth is often the only dress, or nothing at all.[198] Hair and beard are allowed to grow or are partially cut. Among many of those peoples the body is adorned with tattoos, a woman's breasts are repressed (in sixteenth-century Spain), and ear adornment and ostentation soon increased. Oriental people like the Assyrians and the Babylonians already had cotton and perhaps also silk; the silk robes of Assyria, the carpets of Babylon, and so on were highly sought after.[199]

Finery in clothing developed apace among the Israelites too.[200] Alongside animal hides (Gen. 3:21) came clothes of sheep's wool (Gen. 31:19; 38:12), of goat hair (Prov. 27:26), of flax (first mentioned in Exod. 9:31; cf. linen workers, 1 Chron. 4:21), of cotton and linen (שֵׁשׁ), and later, fine linen (בּוּץ, byssus, בַּד, ὀθόνη). Ornaments, too, were present already at the time of the patriarchs: golden earrings and bracelets (Gen. 24:22, 30) and silver and golden ornaments and garments (Gen. 24:53). Joseph was given a coat of many colors (Gen. 37:3, 23). On account of its purity and radiance, white linen clothing was used for festive and formal occasions, as an image of light, happiness, and holiness (Eccles. 9:8; Zech. 3:4; Luke 23:11; John 20:12; Acts 1:10; 10:30; Rev.

---

footnote 1: "Concerning this, see the interesting chapter about blushing (*Erroten*) in Darwin, *The Expression of the Emotions in Man and Animals*"; the reference is to chap. 13: "Self-Attention—Shame—Shyness—Modesty: Blushing," pp. 310–47.

197. DO: *noodzakelijke behoefte*.

198. Peschel, *Races of Man*, 171.

199. Von Hellwald, *Kulturgeschichte in ihrer natürlichen Entwicklung*, 1:249.

200. Cf. Schotel, *Bijdrage tot de geschiedenis der kerkelijke en wereldlijke kleeding*, part 2, chap. 1 ("The Clothing of the East in the Time of Jesus and His Apostles"); cf. Leyrer, "Kleider und Geschmeide." Ed. note: The Leyrer article is Bavinck's source for the detail that follows. Schotel's one-volume book consists of two parts, each with its own pagination: "Hair, Wigs, and Tricorns" (DO: *Het Hair, de Pruik, de Steek*) and "Toga, Long Coat, and Tabs/Collar" (DO: *De Toga, Mantel, en Bef*). We will cite them as 1:xx and 2:xx.

3:18; 4:4; 6:11). Variegated purple and blue vestments made of wool and linen were the garments of kings and nobles among the Midianites, Phoenicians, Canaanites, Assyrians, Babylonians, and Persians (Judg. 5:30; 2 Sam. 1:24; Esther 8:15). Silk (σηρικόν) is mentioned first in Revelation 18:12.

The Torah prohibited wearing clothing made of linen and wool together (Lev. 19:19; Deut. 22:11) and instructed priests to wear linen clothing. In Deuteronomy 22:5, men are forbidden to wear women's clothing, and vice versa. When offering sacrifices, priests had to wear linen undergarments (Exod. 28:42). Ordinary clothing included an undergarment (כֻּתֹּנֶת, χιτών, *tunica*), a kind of knee-length shirt of wool, linen, or cotton, in white, blue, or variegated, with a sash; in later times, another shirt was worn underneath that (סָדִין, σινδών, Isa. 3:23; Prov. 31:24), and an outer robe, a large, four-sided rectangular robe or cloth, roughly six yards long and three yards wide (בֶּגֶד or שִׂמְלָה, ἱμάτιον, *toga*). Additionally, women wore various kinds of robes and veils. Israelites also wore turbans of various shapes on the head, shoes, bracelets, earrings, nose rings, rings for the fingers (as signet rings), collars, and small anklets with tinkling bells (Isa. 3:16–23). Beginning in the time of Solomon, and even more after Uzziah and Ahaz, luxuries increased greatly in Israel, and the prophets repeatedly spoke out against them with the LORD's judgment: "The LORD will strike with a scab / the heads of the daughters of Zion, / . . . will lay bare their secret parts / . . . take away the finery . . ." (Isa. 3:17–18). God turns their world upside down:

> Instead of perfume there will be rottenness;
>   and instead of a belt, a rope;
>   and instead of well-set hair, baldness;
>   and instead of a rich robe, a skirt of sackcloth;
>   and branding instead of beauty. (Isa. 3:24; cf. Jer. 4:30; Lam. 4:5;
>   Ezek. 16:8–39)

God adorns his bride Israel; "foreign attire" is the mark of disloyalty (Zeph. 1:8), and clothing is the symbol of vanity and transitoriness, since it is consumed by moths (Job 13:28; 27:16–17; Jer. 50:9; 51:6, 8; Sir. 11:4; 14:17; 42:13).

The New Testament too contains repeated warnings against luxury in dress. Paul instructs Timothy, "Women should adorn themselves [this is permitted!] in respectable apparel, with modesty and self-control, not with braided hair and gold or pearls or costly attire, but with what is proper for women who profess godliness—with good works" (1 Tim. 2:9–10). Older women "are to be reverent in behavior" (Titus 2:3).[201] Peter instructs wives, "Do not let

---

201. GrO: ἐν καταστήματι ἱεροπρεπεῖς (ed. note: "as becometh holiness" [KJV]).

your adorning be external—the braiding of hair and the putting on of gold jewelry, or the clothing you wear—but let your adorning be the hidden person of the heart with the imperishable beauty of a gentle and quiet spirit, which in God's sight is very precious. For this is how the holy women who hoped in God used to adorn themselves" (1 Pet. 3:3–5). In 1 Corinthians 11, the head covering is a sign of submission (exactly the opposite of our custom, where inferiors remove their hats before a superior). The Jewish custom was to pray with the head covered; the Greek custom was to perform sacred rites with a bare head. Paul follows the latter custom, sees in it an act consonant with the place of husband and wife. Paul would have the husband uncover his head during prayer, while the wife is to cover her head (as subject to her husband, because she stands under him),[202] "because of the angels"—that is, lest she grieve the angels with her disorderliness.

Greeks and Romans at first wore only a tunic and a toga.[203] Later, these were supplemented by outer garments and undergarments. Before long, a tendency arose toward ornamentation. The first barbers arrived from Sicily in Rome in 269 BC. The Romans, who used to wear long beards and still did later when in mourning, now had their hair styled. Hadrian and other emperors let their beards grow long again, but it did not catch on. The Romans wore many rings on their fingers. The women focused on hairstyles, tied their hair in buns or wore it in curls or braids; they used a lot of pomades and hair creams, especially to dye their hair golden blonde (like the Germanic women). If the hair fell out, they wore wigs;[204] they also used false teeth, as well as earrings, chains, rings, veils, fans, parasols, cosmetic face powder, painted eyebrows, and so on.

Church Opposition to Adornment and Luxury

The church fathers campaigned vehemently against all luxury among Christians, and most of them were somewhat ascetic.[205] Initially, the clergy wore the same clothing as the laity, but gradually they developed distinctive garments, especially after the seventh and eighth centuries.[206]

---

202. With ἐξουσία (= authority) as a symbol of masculine power.

203. Schotel, *Bijdrage tot de geschiedenis der kerkelijke en wereldlijke kleeding*, 2:24–58. The ancients wore clothes made of wool; they had to bathe daily (we have our *clothes* bathed = washed by others) or else suffer many skin diseases. We wear a (linen) shirt that is washed every week.

204. LO: *capillamenta*.

205. See Tertullian, in particular *On the Apparel of Women* II (ANF 4:18–26) and *On the Veiling of Virgins* (ANF 4:27–38); Cyprian and Chrysostom (see Voetius, *Selectarum Disputationum Theologicarum*, 4:411–12); *Apostolic Constitutions* I:3 (ANF 7:392); Reinhard, *System der christlichen Moral*, 2:614; Schotel, *Bijdrage tot de geschiedenis der kerkelijke en wereldlijke kleeding*, 1:61–62; 2:58–84.

206. Schotel, *Bijdrage tot de geschiedenis der kerkelijke en wereldlijke kleeding*, 2:63, 83.

In the Middle Ages,[207] simplicity was pushed aside by the growth of commerce and industry, by the connection with Italy and Greece, and especially by the Crusades and acquaintance with the Orient. Wealth and luxury arose. In the fourteenth and fifteenth centuries, the authorities often passed laws and ordinances against luxury in clothing and meals, particularly among the lower classes. The very fabric and shape of clothing were sometimes prescribed. Stockings and shirts, as well as soap, were still unknown. In the Middle Ages and among our ancestors, clothing was picturesque and richly variegated and differed for various classes and places. Seventeenth-century paintings show the expensive clothing of men and women. Home interiors featured fancy furniture, shiny kitchen utensils, and embossed silverware.[208] People could eat and drink quite exorbitantly.[209] In the Netherlands, high society followed French fashion. In his satire *Tryntje Cornelis*, Constantijn Huygens talks about women wearing dresses with a low neckline attending the theater in The Hague.[210] In another work, *'t Voorhout*, Huygens portrays all the young women from The Hague as having fake hair and false bosoms.[211]

The Reformed pastors, especially those with Puritan leanings, complained vigorously, even from the pulpit. Clothing and cosmetics were ostentatious. The church observed all that luxury and protested. The provincial synod of North Holland did so in Amsterdam in 1640 and repeated it in Hoorn in 1641. The Synod of South Holland followed suit in Gouda, as did the Synod of Gelderland in 1643 and Utrecht in 1644.[212] The issue especially concerning long hair for men was being discussed everywhere. The fuse was lit by a sermon

207. Ed. note: At this point Bavinck adds a marginal reference to "Hermann Weiss, *Kostümkunde*, I. Oudheid, 2. Mittelalter, III. Vom 14 Jahrhundert bis zur Gegenwart." Bavinck does not specify the volume he has in mind nor the edition.

208. Huet, *Het land van Rembrand*, 2/2:195; Quack, *Studiën en schetsen*.

209. Huet, *Het land van Rembrand*, 2/2:197. Ed. note: Regarding costumes, Bavinck adds, "See J. Quicherat, *Histoire du Costume en France depuis les Temps les plus reculés jusqu'a la Fin du XVIIIᵉ Siècle* (on France); Schotel, *Bijdrage tot de geschiedenis der kerkelijke en wereldlijke kleeding*, 2:121–33 (on Germany); 2:134–46 (on England); 2:147–74 (on The Netherlands)."

210. Huygens, *Tryntje Cornelis*; cf. J. Smeth, "J. Uytenbogaert," in the journal edited by Kist and Royaards, *Nieuw Archief voor kerkelijke geschiedenis* 2 (1854): 256. Uytenbogaert pointed to a couple of women with exposed breasts in church (*J. Uytenbogardus olim Hagae foeminas quasdam nobiles, quae pecus mamaque nudabant, publice acriterque moniuit, a turpi habitu ut abstinerent, nec aliis scandalum darent*).

211. Huet, *Het land van Rembrand*, 2/2:270. Ed. note: The work Bavinck had in mind is *Batava Tempe, dat is 't Voor-hout van 's Gravenhage* (Middelburgh: Hans vander Hellen, 1622). This work is usually paired with *Kostelick mal* (Exquisitely foolish), a satirical look at the "ostentatious finery of the townspeople" (see Huygens, *Constantijn Huygens' Koselick mal*) (*Encyclopaedia Britannica*, s.v. "Constantijn Huygens," https://www.britannica.com/biography/Constantijn-Huygens).

212. Cf. Schotel, *Bijdrage tot de geschiedenis der kerkelijke en wereldlijke kleeding*, 1:10–13; Ypeij and Dermout, *Geschiedenis der Nederlandsche Hervormde Kerk*, 1:226–27.

preached in Dort by Jacob Borstius (1612–89) about long hair, in connection with 1 Corinthians 11:14.[213] A surprising dispute arose. Each person chose for or against long hair. Things calmed down somewhat in 1645 due to an intervention by Classis South Holland.

Not only in Dort but also elsewhere, ministers preached repeatedly on 1 Corinthians 11:4–8; Isaiah 3:24; 23:9; and 1 Timothy 2:9.[214] Especially in the Province of Zeeland, Godfried Udemans, the minister of the church at Zerikzee, published a tract, *Absalom's Hair* (1643).[215] However, Professor Boxhorn of Leiden opposed him in his booklet *The Little Mirror, Showing the Long Hair and Locks Worn by the Old Hollanders and Zeelanders* (1644),[216] as did Claudius Salmasius.[217] Johannes Polyander wrote a conciliatory tract, cosigned by Frederick Spanheim and Jacob Trigland.[218] Gisbert Voetius, however, condemned long hair, as did Carolus de Maets, Meinard Schotanus, and Johannes Hoornbeeck.[219] The dispute died out, and, as usual, fashion won. And the pastors fell in line: toward the close of the seventeenth and the beginning of the eighteenth centuries, pastors wore long hair or periwig and again defended this with Scripture, appealing to the Nazirites, among other scriptural warrants.[220]

213. "Does not nature itself teach you that if a man wears long hair it is a disgrace for him?"

214. 1 Cor. 11:4–8: "Every man who prays or prophesies with his head covered dishonors his head, but every wife who prays or prophesies with her head uncovered dishonors her head, since it is the same as if her head were shaven. For if a wife will not cover her head, then she should cut her hair short. But since it is disgraceful for a wife to cut off her hair or shave her head, let her cover her head. For a man ought not to cover his head, since he is the image and glory of God, but woman is the glory of man. For man was not made from woman, but woman from man."

Isa. 3:24: "Instead of perfume there will be rottenness; / and instead of a belt, a rope; / and instead of well-set hair, baldness; / and instead of a rich robe, a skirt of sackcloth; / and branding instead of beauty."

Isa. 23:9: "The LORD of hosts has purposed it, / to defile the pompous pride of all glory, / to dishonor all the honored of the earth."

1 Tim. 2:9: "Women should adorn themselves in respectable apparel, with modesty and self-control, not with braided hair and gold or pearls or costly attire."

215. Irenaeus Poimenander (a pseudonym of Godfried Udemans), *Absaloms-Hayr off Discours, Daerinne ondersocht wordt.*

216. Van Boxhorn, *Spiegeltjen Vertoonende 't cort hayr.*

217. Schotel, *Bijdrage tot de geschiedenis der kerkelijke en wereldlijke kleeding*, 1:33. Ed. note: Claudius Salmasius (Claude Saumaise [1588–1653]) was a French classical scholar and prolific author. He was a professor at Leiden from 1631 (*Encyclopaedia Britannica*, s.v. "Claudius Salmasius," https://www.britannica.com/biography/Claudius-Salmasius).

218. Schotel, *Bijdrage tot de geschiedenis der kerkelijke en wereldlijke kleeding*, 1:39–41.

219. Schotel, *Bijdrage tot de geschiedenis der kerkelijke en wereldlijke kleeding*, 1:43–50. Ed. note: Carolus de Maets (1597–1651) was a Dutch Second Reformation theologian who taught at Utrecht, 1640–51; Meinard Schotanus (1593–1644) was a professor of theology at Franeker (1626–37) and at Utrecht (1637–44).

220. Schotel, *Bijdrage tot de geschiedenis der kerkelijke en wereldlijke kleeding*, 1:57.

The use of fake hair, long locks, and shaved beards had been in vogue among effeminate Greeks and Romans. Wigs[221] came into fashion around 1620–30 among all classes, at first quite simple, then very large and long (called "in-folio" wigs). Louis XIV had forty-eight wigmakers; his era was the age of fashion par excellence. The rococo style emerged during the reign of Louis XV. All natural relationships were turned upside down; artistic skill had to be applied everywhere. Political life, social life, ethics, and aesthetics became artificial and affectatious. Hedges and palm trees were given the shape of pyramids, for example.[222] Under Louis XVI wigs were gradually replaced with coiffed hairstyles. Gentlemen attempted by means of their clothing to look like an Adonis and a Hercules at the same time. The French Revolution saw to the disappearance of the wigs. But professors in Oxford and Cambridge still wear them to this day.[223] The eighteenth century was the Age of the Periwig (up to ten layers), but the French Revolution looked upon these as symbols of the aristocracy and banned them.

Head Coverings

Let us now consider head coverings. The papal tiara received its first tier with Pope Alexander III (1169).[224] The cardinal's hood dates from the thirteenth century, and the beret[225] became common in the thirteenth century among the spiritual class in varying shapes, colors, and fabrics.[226] In the fifteenth century, tricornered or four-cornered hats were adopted for all Roman Catholic clergy, professors, and scholars (four-cornered for scholars, three-cornered for the clergy?).[227] The *skullcap* (the mother of wigs)[228] came along with the beret; the skullcap was the headdress of retired pastors in the sixteenth century,[229] and in the seventeenth was worn by doctors, professors, and literary people.[230] The hood[231] was in common use in the early church. The cape[232] emerged in

221. DO: *pruiken*; etymology unknown; formerly the word meant head hair, not fake head hair.
222. Gürlitt, *Geschichte des Barockstiles, des Rococo und des Klassicismus.*
223. Schotel, *Bijdrage tot de geschiedenis der kerkelijke en wereldlijke kleeding*, 1:89.
224. Schotel, *Bijdrage tot de geschiedenis der kerkelijke en wereldlijke kleeding*, 1:112.
225. DO: *baret* (*birretum*, from the red of *birrus* or *burrus*).
226. Schotel, *Bijdrage tot de geschiedenis der kerkelijke en wereldlijke kleeding*, 1:115.
227. Schotel, *Bijdrage tot de geschiedenis der kerkelijke en wereldlijke kleeding*, 1:119.
228. FO: *calotte*; Schotel, *Bijdrage tot de geschiedenis der kerkelijke en wereldlijke kleeding*, 1:120.
229. Schotel, *Bijdrage tot de geschiedenis der kerkelijke en wereldlijke kleeding*, 1:123.
230. DO: *letterkundigen*; Schotel, *Bijdrage tot de geschiedenis der kerkelijke en wereldlijke kleeding*, 1:124. Ed. note: Schotel adds to the list: nobility (*edellieden*), magistrates (*magistraatspersonen*), lawyers/jurists (*rechtsgeleerden*), and artists (*Kunstenaars*).
231. DO: *kap.*
232. DO: *kaproen*; Schotel, *Bijdrage tot de geschiedenis der kerkelijke en wereldlijke kleeding*, 1:131.

the thirteenth century, fell into disuse during the sixteenth century, and like the bonnet, was worn by both sexes.[233] Hats originated in France during the thirteenth century and continually changed in shape and material: with or without broad brims; with or without plumes.[234] In 1672, when the French invaded the Low Countries, they introduced the broad hat with the brim folded high at the front and low at the back, and it was worn straight or at an angle. That hat became fashionable in the Netherlands. Around 1697 the small tricornered *chapeau-bas* emerged, which was carried under the arm so as not to damage the wig. Soon here in the Netherlands, people tied to fashion wore the smallest possible style. More sophisticated citizens wore larger or smaller tricornered hats.[235] The oblong cocked hat or cap emerged near the end of the eighteenth century, and the liberty cap with the French Revolution. In the seventeenth century, ministers wore a hat, but in the eighteenth century they wore the pointed or tricornered hat and kept it even after the style changed.[236] The long coat[237] is a remnant of old local costume; the clerical band (or "tabs") came from the collar;[238] the toga was adopted by Dutch Lutherans in 1840 and by the Remonstrants in 1844 and was recommended by the Synod of the Dutch Reformed Church in 1854.[239]

Fashion is very influential in the arena of clothing. It has often been maligned, also by Kant in his anthropology, who considered fashion altogether vain and foolish. Since the time of Louis XIV, France has set the tone in this area.[240] In the late nineteenth century, women increasingly adopt the form of men's clothing, at least for the upper body: hat, collar, vest, shawl, narrow sleeves, cuff-links with buttons—a sign that women want to be men: she writes, reads, composes poetry, studies, swims, rows, rides, smokes, shoots, hunts, climbs the Alps, and so on—all proof that the nineteenth century is the century of the *man*. In the Middle Ages—specifically, the twelfth and thirteenth

---

233. Schotel, *Bijdrage tot de geschiedenis der kerkelijke en wereldlijke kleeding*, 1:135.

234. Schotel, *Bijdrage tot de geschiedenis der kerkelijke en wereldlijke kleeding*, 1:140.

235. Schotel, *Bijdrage tot de geschiedenis der kerkelijke en wereldlijke kleeding*, 1:147.

236. DO: *punthoed; steek*; on the costumes of the Protestant clergy, see Schotel, *Bijdrage tot de geschiedenis der kerkelijke en wereldlijke kleeding*, 2:206–37; Bunz, "Kleider und Insignien."

237. DO: *mantel*.

238. DO: *bef, kraag*. Ed. note: The word "collar" might suggest that the "clerical band" (*bef*) that Bavinck is referring to here is what we think of as the "Roman collar" worn by clergy. But a *bef* is different; it is "an ornamental pair of bands worn hanging onto the chest, notably as part of formal dress by certain Catholic and protestant clergy, magistrates and professors" (WordSense.eu, s.v. "bef," https://www.wordsense.eu/bef/). A *bef* is white, and the appearance is like a very neat untied bowtie. Preaching bands are still available at stores that sell clergy accessories.

239. Schotel, *Bijdrage tot de geschiedenis der kerkelijke en wereldlijke kleeding*, 2:218, 222, 235. Ed. note: See also Aalders, *De komst van de toga*, 105ff.

240. Cf. Rothe, *Theologische Ethik*, 4:152–55 (§976).

centuries—the woman dominated (love songs, knights). Notwithstanding crusades and wars, this era was lyrical, soft, sentimental, feminine, and gushing, and the clothing worn by men closely resembled that of women, and their appearance was feminine: smooth face, long locks, long skirt, feminine cloak. This reversed again in the fourteenth century, when a great variety arises in clothing and fashion. In the fifteenth century, men lead and women follow. But in France, this reverses again: men wear feminine shoes,[241] silk stockings, shoes with pompons, wigs, no beards, powder in their hair, and tailcoats. This is reversed yet again during the French Revolution.[242]

Now then, we see that clothing has a very great moral significance. Individuality and character are expressed in clothing[243] and in this way supply it with a moral significance. Thus clothing differs among nations, generations, families, and persons, differing from one country to another, from one place to another, from one time to another, from one situation to another. Such variety was pronounced especially earlier, when there was no global fashion, when every locality had its own costume, when there was as yet no single model for all. Our modern apparel is therefore in keeping with the dearth of character[244] in our age; it is characterless.[245] Uniformity is the curse of modern life (Kuyper);[246] one cut is the same for all, without exception. Taste is gone. The guideline for men's fashion seems to require highlighting the original forms of the body. But among the ladies the least elegant members are decorated the most—just think of the bustle.

B. Why Do We Wear Clothes?

Finally, we come to the purpose of our clothing. There are four basic purposes.

(1) To Cover Our Nakedness

Clothing reminds us of our sin, dishonor, shame (Gen. 3:7). Clothing, therefore, ought to humble us instead of making us proud.[247] Clothing is a

---

241. GO: *Spitzen.*

242. *Über Land und Meer: Allgemeine Illustrirte Zeitung* 29, no. 58 (1886–87); cf. von Jhering, *Der Zweck im Recht*, 2:230–41. Ed. note: Bavinck's reference to *Über Land und Meer* is general and indicates the entire issue. Likely he had in mind the drawing that is found on p. 891: "Figuren aus dem Residenzpublikum." See HathiTrust Digital Library, https://babel.hathitrust .org/cgi/pt?id=mdp.39015035332645;view=1up;seq=395.

243. Rothe, *Theologische Ethik*, 4:41, Observation 3 (§918).

244. DO: *karakterschaarste.*

245. DO: *karakterloos.*

246. Kuyper, "Uniformity." Ed. note: Here is what Kuyper says about the men's clothing of his day: "All that is called male, of whatever vocation or title, rank, or status, is clothed in the same ill-fitting, undistinguished garments" (p. 29).

247. Pictet, *De christelyke zedekunst*, 614–16.

bulwark against lust, covering the dominion of the flesh but leaving uncovered the face, which reveals the spirit, while at the same time pushing the purely sensual life into the background. Nevertheless, nakedness and immorality are not identical. Customs make a big difference. Most people groups wear at least some cloth around the waist. But among them immorality is no greater than in our fully clothed society; in fact, the opposite is more often the case. It should also be observed that color may make a big difference. Among darker-skinned people, the shame of nudity may be less obvious (blushing), overshadowed and hidden, as it were, by the color of their skin. Yet although one may not immediately assume that nakedness equals immorality, matters are different in our society. There are differences among us too. Rural peasants associate with one another much more informally than gentlemen and ladies from the city. Refinement imparts restraint, causes the spontaneous, naïve attitude of childlike innocence to retreat in the face of reflection. No one is offended by the rolled-up sleeves and bare arms of children and maids, but if ladies sported them we would think differently about it. The actions of the Adamians—a second-century Christian sect in North Africa—of worshiping without any clothing, were wrong and immoral.[248] So were the actions of Bohemian neo-Adamites in the fifteenth century and the Anabaptists in Amsterdam in 1536.[249]

The story is told of Francis of Assisi that he sometimes went naked and that when a woman once caught him at it and tried to seduce him, he sat down on a bed of glowing coals and said, "Come and lie down with me!"[250] Scholars like Joseph Vicecomes and G. J. Vossius believed that in the early church, people undressed completely in connection with baptism by immersion.[251] However, Voetius disputes this because nothing like this is noted in connection with John's baptism recorded in Scripture and because the enemies of Christians never mention this. Voetius believes that it is also wrong for our women to bare their arms and neck too much and to wear skirts that are too short. Already in the seventeenth century, it was common for women to wear low necklines and expose their bosom. The Roman Catholic casuists Sylvester, Navarrus, and Azorius say it is not a mortal sin "to show the naked female breast without

248. Epiphanius, *The Panarion of Epiphanius of Salamis, Books II and III*, 68–70 (§52).

249. On the Quakers see Buddensieg, "Quäker." Ed. note: Bavinck cites pp. 433f. and provides no terminus. He could have added to his list: the Brethren of the Free Spirit in the thirteenth century, the Taborites in Bohemia in the same century, and the Beghards in fourteenth-century Germany (Wikipedia, s.v. "Adamites," https://en.wikipedia.org/wiki/Adamites).

250. LO: *Hic mecum cuba!*; see Voetius, *Politicae Ecclestiasticae* (1663), 1:687.

251. Joseph Vicecomes (Giuseppe Visconti), *Observationes ecclesiasticae, in quo de antiquis baptismi ritibus, ac caeremoniis agitur* (1618); G. J. Vossius, *Disputatio de Baptismo* (1619). Ed. note: Bavinck's source for these two references is Voetius, *Politicae Ecclesiasticae* (1663), 1:684.

evil intent."[252] Alsted concurs, provided it is the custom of the land.[253] But Voetius, along with many others whom he cites, strongly disagrees, because "where there is smoke, there is fire."[254] Some writers appeal to Scripture and observe that also among Israel people sometimes walked about naked (e.g., Isa. 20:2–4) and barefoot (cf. Saul in 1 Sam. 19:24). But in Scripture, the word "naked" often means "without an outer cloak," like our "undressed" (cf. Isa. 58:7; Ezek. 18:7, 16; Matt. 25:36–44). Perkins also opposed baring the neck, shoulders, and breasts.[255] Indeed, today we should also disapprove of such levels of undress. Paul counsels women to "adorn themselves in respectable apparel, with modesty and self-control"[256] (1 Tim. 2:9; cf. Exod. 28:42).

(2) To Protect Us from Nature's Elements

Another purpose of clothing is to protect us from the elements of nature: cold, frost, heat, outside air (Prov. 31:21). That is why the pledged clothing of a poor man must be returned to him before sundown (Exod. 22:26–27). That is why clothes must really protect the health of the body. Professor Jäger currently recommends all-wool outfits, since they retain heat. Perkins claims that after the fall the world experienced a strange intemperance of heat and cold and that that is why God ordained clothes.[257] This purpose of clothing must be kept carefully in mind. Many clothes of children and women need to be rejected because they injure personal health. For example, consider the light and flimsy children's clothing, especially for girls, in spring or summer; and for women, consider the corsets and other tight-laced garments, as well as high heels and the like. Clothes should also vary according to the different seasons, altitudes, temperatures, and so on. Clothing is a weapon protecting us against nature. Thus, animals are protected by their fur and hair, but we humans are helpless and borrow our weapons from the outside, from plants and animals, and are able to do so since we are spirits.

(3) To Identify Us according to Sex, Age, and Social Class

Clothing distinguishes us according to our sex, our age, and our social rank.[258] That clothing is particular to our sex is taught in Deuteronomy 22:5:

---

252. LO: *foeminam nudum pectus gestare sine mala intentione*. Ed. note: Bavinck's source for this Latin quote is Voetius, *Selectarum Disputationum Theologicarum*, 4:461.

253. Voetius, *Selectarum Disputationum Theologicarum*, 4:461.

254. LO: *semper flamma fumo est proxima*; Voetius, *Selectarum Disputationum Theologicarum*, 4:460–93. Ed. note: The Latin proverb is attributed to Titus Maccius Plautus (ca. 254–184 BC).

255. Perkins, *Works of William Perkins*, 8:411–12 (*Case of Conscience*, III.iv.3).

256. GrO: ἐν καταστολῇ κοσμίῳ.

257. Perkins, *Works of William Perkins*, 8:411 (*Case of Conscience*, III.iv.3).

258. Von Jhering, *Der Zweck im Recht*, 2:232–34, 311–29.

"A woman shall not wear a man's garment, nor shall a man put on a woman's cloak." The distinction in dress between the two sexes should be preserved; for that reason, some articles of clothing for women deserve to be rejected. The same goes for the distinction in age: a girl should dress differently from a married woman, a society lady; a boy should be dressed differently than a young man or an adult male.

Clothes should also to some extent express the sentiments of our heart.[259] Oriental people do so more strongly than we: they sprinkle ashes on their head, rend their clothes, put on sackcloth, and so on. Nonetheless, fortunately fashion among us still distinguishes mourning clothes from party dress. Moreover, we have our Sunday clothes, and this is of great value and moral significance. The Sabbath is a festive day; the way we dress declares that on Sunday we are free, that we serve no human being, only God, that we get to eat what is freely given us. O, Sunday clothes do so much good! They preserve purity and cleanliness, nurture the exalted feeling of freedom and independence, awaken in the breast of the lowliest workman a festive mood and attitude, a zest for life. Moreover, it is appropriate for us to appear before God on Sunday in pure, clean clothes, in festive garments! Sunday observance is of immeasurable benefit; it makes us, at least for one day of the week, a "child of God," not just servants, laborers, or hired hands. Finally, clothing also serves to distinguish between the classes in society—between rich and poor, indeed, but also between those in authority (e.g., government leaders, judges, professors and students, different ranks within the military) and those subject to authority.

However, such variety in clothing is disappearing more and more; the uniformity of fashion and the leveling impulse of democratism prevail. Inequality is disappearing, everything flows together pantheistically. Nevertheless, distinctive clothing is based on something essential. Each class uniquely forms and develops the human person, creates a type, of which clothing is an expression and a symbol. This is also true for the class of religious leaders. In the Old Testament, God prescribed a separate, elegant clothing for priests. In the New Testament, Jesus, the apostles, the first ministers of the church, wore ordinary clothing. As we have seen, separate dress for the clergy gradually came into vogue. The Roman Catholic Church and the Orthodox Church have always developed this more extensively. They have a separate vestment for each clerical rank, for each order of monks and nuns. In Christianity, distinct clerical clothing is not mandatory; it is completely a matter of liberty (also among the Reformers). Yet this does not mean that we should disapprove of

259. Von Jhering, *Der Zweck im Recht*, 2:323–24.

such distinctive clothing. Wearing a toga, as in the national Dutch Reformed Church,[260] is desirable, to hide defects, to protect against cold and heat, to enhance dignity, and so on. However, clerical clothing should be subdued, in keeping with the clergy's estate. It is not recommended that pastors visit church members wearing wooden shoes (clogs),[261] puffing on a long pipe, or wearing a bathrobe.[262] Clothes ward off temptations and guard against aspersions and insinuations.[263] We need to recover character, taste, and form also in our clothing. Indifference or nonchalance in this area is not an act of piety. Goethe was strongly opposed to wearing spectacles.[264] Cleanliness is happiness.[265]

(4) To Adorn

Clothing also serves to adorn. God prescribed for the high priest an elegant garment. Ecclesiastes 9:8: "Let your garments be always white. Let not oil be lacking on your head." In Proverbs 31:19–22 the woman is praised who puts her hand to the spindle, who makes bed coverings, and who is clothed in fine linen and purple. According to Scripture, gold, silver, precious stones, silk, velvet, purple, and the like may be used to adorn oneself.[266] They are gifts from God, expressly given for adornment. Abraham had his servant give Rebecca a golden earring and two bracelets (Gen. 24:22). Pharaoh dressed Joseph in "garments of fine linen and put a gold chain about his neck" (Gen. 41:42). The Israelites wore golden earrings (Exod. 32:3). In Solomon's day, silver in Jerusalem was as common as stone (2 Chron. 9:27). Psalm 45:7–8 praises the robes of the Lord's anointed as "all fragrant with myrrh and aloes and cassia." Jesus speaks approvingly of Solomon's glory (Matt. 6:29). And although passages such as Isaiah 3:18–24, 1 Timothy 2:9, and 1 Peter 3:3 speak against braids, gold, pearls, and precious garments, they are speaking more against their misuse, against the excess and pride therein, than against their use. We must observe Christian modesty also in the way we dress. In Matthew 6:28 Jesus forbids worrying about clothing and has us consider the lilies of the field, more beautiful than Solomon. We are to be content with food and clothing (1 Tim. 6:8). We are to share with the poor from our abundance: "Whoever

---

260. Ed. note: *Nederlands Hervormde Kerk.*
261. DO: *klompen.*
262. Ed. note: Bavinck uses the English term "chambercloak."
263. Wuttke, *Handbuch der christlichen Sittenlehre*[3], 2:561n63.
264. Harnack, *Goethe in der Epoche seiner Vollendung*, 76.
265. Ed. note: Bavinck uses the English expression here but gives no indication of its source. The conventional expression, usually attributed to John Wesley, is "Cleanliness is next to godliness."
266. Perkins, *Works of William Perkins*, 8:405–6 (*Case of Conscience*, III.iv.3).

has two tunics is to share with him who has none, and whoever has food is to do likewise" (Luke 3:11). This must not be taken absolutely; Jesus had two coats and kept both.

The same general rule applies also to clothing: "Whatever is true, whatever is honorable, whatever is just, whatever is pure, whatever is lovely, whatever is commendable, if there is any excellence, if there is anything worthy of praise, think about these things" (Phil. 4:8). Elijah wore simple clothes (2 Kings 1:8), as did most prophets (Zech. 13:4), including John the Baptist (Matt. 3:4). The Christian may not follow after vain ostentation or silly fashion but, on the other hand, should also guard against strikingly unfashionable clothing, straight hanging hair,[267] uncleanliness, and indifference. So, we desire neither blind submission to fashion nor open opposition and resistance to what is fashionable!

Unnatural marring of the body is not good. Leviticus 19:27–28 forbids shaving the corners of head and beard and cutting and tattooing the body (cf. Lev. 21:5; Ezek. 44:20). Paul wants the church at Corinth to follow local custom (1 Cor. 11). Scripture emphasizes the clothing of the soul, the robes of righteousness (Isa. 61:10), good works (1 Tim. 2:9–10), a meek and quiet spirit (1 Pet. 3:4). Nonetheless, it is certain that spiritual purity is also expressed in external beauty and cleanliness. Only the person who with Plato deems the body a prison and despises and denigrates this life can live in a barrel like Diogenes, can find pleasure in filth.[268] Conversion among pagans results also in lifestyle changes and cultural refinement. In women especially, filthiness is something offensive, a sin.

Limits have also been placed on the adornment of the body.[269] To be sure, we are created in God's image and must develop ourselves in terms of beauty, including outward (and especially inward) beauty, and to answer to the requirement of beauty. Human beings are the showpiece of God's creation, wonderfully made (Ps. 139). The somatic organism must be and become a work of art and evoke pleasant and gratifying feelings in others, especially through deportment, gestures, and tone; no one should be unrefined.[270] Such refinement comes about through influencing and forming the soul.[271] The time for that formation of beauty is especially the years of youth and young adulthood, although every season of life—including those of husband and wife, of mother and graybeard with silver hair—has its own

---

267. DO: *sluik neerhangende.*
268. Wuttke, *Handbuch der christlichen Sittenlehre*[3], 2:288.
269. Kuyper, "In eerbaar gewaad."
270. GrO: ἄμουσος (i.e., without the muses); Rothe, *Theologische Ethik*, 4:150 (§973).
271. Rothe, *Theologische Ethik*, 4:151 (§974).

beauty.[272] And to enhance that beauty, adornment is morally legitimate, provided it fulfills the requirements developed above. But then that adornment should be chosen with taste, not for its glamor and gleam;[273] people should individualize the general fashion according to their own character, social class, and so on.

However, the adornments that are allowed should not involve deception. If the applied adornments are intended to deceive others about the design and build of our body and our form, they are not altogether morally innocent. Roman Catholics permit women to cover a defect by means of clothing and to feign a beauty they do not have. Thomas says that a married woman may adorn herself to please her husband (1 Cor. 7:34) (not to seduce him, Prov. 7:10), but an unmarried woman should not adorn herself to please a man, although then it is only a venial sin.[274] Also, it is one thing to counterfeit a beauty one does not have,[275] but quite another to hide a disfigurement arising from some cause;[276] the latter is permitted (1 Cor. 12:23). Alsted also approved of this, but other Roman Catholics, some church fathers, Voetius, and Perkins condemned it.[277] Peter Martyr Vermigli also disapproved of such adornment and deemed it legitimate only for the sake of the husband (just as when a mother sings to rock her child to sleep).[278] Vermigli also speaks of cosmetic rouge[279] and comments that many Scholastics approve of it on the basis of 1 Corinthians 7:34 and 12:23, but condemns it himself.[280] Why? Because one

272. Rothe, *Theologische Ethik*, 4:151 (§975).

273. As is alleged about the Jews (DO: *joden*).

274. Aquinas, *ST* IIa IIae q. 169 art. 2 co. Ed. note: According to Thomas, "if a married woman adorn[s] herself in order to please her husband, she can do this without sin." Thomas then distinguishes the mortal sin of unmarried women who "adorn themselves with this intention of provoking others to lust" from the sin of adorning "from frivolity or from vanity for the sake of ostentation." This sin is "not always mortal, but sometimes venial."

275. LO: *fingere pulchritudinem non habitam*.

276. LO: *occultam turpitudinem ex aliqua causa provenientem*.

277. Alsted, *Theologia Casuum*, 355–56 (XIX.2); Voetius, *Selectarum Disputationum Theologicarum*, 4:417–28, 429–61. Ed. note: Bavinck did indicate these two sections separately, although he indicated them simply as "417v." and "429v." The two sections are the fourth and fifth disputation in Voetius's discussion of the Seventh Commandment, *De excelcis Mundi, ad VII Decalogi Praeceptum, primus quae est de Choreis* ("The Highest Worldliness with Respect to the Seventh Commandment of the Decalogue, the First of Which Is Dancing"). The subject of disputation 4: *quae est de luxu et vanitate in vestibus, dominibus, et suppellectile* (concerning extravagance and vanity in apparel, dwelling place, and jewelry); that of disputation 5, *quae est de ornatu faciei et capillorum* (concerning the ornamentation of the face and hair). Perkins, *Works of William Perkins* (*Case of Conscience*, III.iv.3), 8:413.

278. Vermigli, *Loci Communes*[2], 175A.

279. LO: *fucus*. Ed. note: Bavinck defines this as *blanketsel, eigenlijk een verfkruid* (cosmetic face powder, actually a kind of cosmetic coloring).

280. LO: *focus*; Vermigli, *Loci Communes*[2], 175B–79.

should seek to please Christ, not other people; one cannot make one's hair black or white (Matt. 5:36); one may not disguise oneself.

Men are therefore also forbidden to wear women's clothing; we must all glorify God in our body.[281] Voetius says that one may wash one's face (Matt. 6:17) when it is burned by the sun, clean it and restore its original beauty; but one may not try to change the shape of the face with which one was born, for no one can make a single hair black or white. Hence the misuse of cosmetic face powder is not permitted. Removing pimples, plucking eyebrows, and teeth whitening[282] are allowed, but the use of ivory teeth, glass eyes, and so on does not seem to be approved.[283] Nose rings and earrings are likewise not allowed (does Gen. 24:22, 47 speak of nose rings?). It is permissible to use mirrors, but not in excess (Isa. 3:18–23). Voetius also forbids fake hair, but Alsted permits it.[284] Of a *capillitium alienum* (wig or hairpiece) he says, "I prefer not to feign in that way."[285] Rothe also opposes whatever serves to misrepresent the organism, although he does not condemn wigs or false teeth when they are required for health reasons.[286] Admonition on this score is not always out of place; everything can be falsified: false hair (hair buns,[287] wigs), false ears, eyes, teeth, false bosoms, false legs, feet! "The world wants to be deceived; so let it be deceived."[288] A warning is also due when women take an excessively long time to dress up! Sometimes hours and days! In order, for example, to adorn their hats, women in America needed five million birds, whereas science required only five hundred thousand.[289] Worldliness does not befit the Christian (Rom. 12:2).[290]

---

281. Vermigli cites Tertullian (*De cultu en de habitu muliebri*), Cyprian, Ambrose, Chrysostom, Jerome, and Augustine.

282. LO: *Pustulas tollere, oculorum sinus mundare, dentes albificare.*

283. LO: *non videtur affirmandum.*

284. Alsted, *Theologia Casuum*, XIX.2.

285. LO: *malim modum illum non affectari.*

286. Rothe, *Theologische Ethik*, 4:152–55 (§976).

287. FO: *chignons.*

288. Ed. note: Bavinck's text reads: "Mundis decipitur"; the full Latin phrase is *Mundus vult decipi, ergo deciipiatur.*

289. *De Standaard* (Jan. 15, 1887).

290. Cf. van Mastricht, *Theoretico-Practica Theologia*, III.iv.3 [IV, 788–91].

20

Bodily Duties to Our Souls

God gives us life, and we are accountable to him for its care and use in his service. Self-defense is therefore an obligation; we defend not only ourselves but the moral law, the moral community, and justice. This duty to preserve our own life rules out self-harm, self-mutilation, self-flagellation, and all forms of self-destruction. It also rules out all notions of redemption as release from being, whether as in the religions of India or in philosophies such as Neo-Platonism and its derivatives, including that of Schopenhauer. When Christians die to self, they die to self-centered sinfulness, not to their own existence.

Even suicide has been defended by some, including the Greek Cynics, the Stoics, John Donne, David Hume, and Montesquieu. Suicide came into vogue among the young after Goethe published his The Sorrows of Young Werther *in 1774. From the middle to the end of the nineteenth century, suicide grew at an alarming and steady rate. There seems to be something contagious about it. Suicides follow some patterns, but statistics fail to clarify motives; mental illness is a major factor. The notion of a "noble suicide" can be found among pagans, as a free and wise act, but never among Christians, who know the moral quality of this life and the future after this life. Since we belong to God and to others, suicide is a sin against God and the neighbor. We do not have free rein over ourselves but are bound by duties toward ourselves. Our lives must be dedicated to fulfilling God's will, which can never demand that we kill ourselves. That would mean that God's will destroys itself; suicide is rebellion against the moral law itself.*

Christians also may never intentionally expose themselves to mortal danger, as Satan tempted Jesus to throw himself off the temple roof. Those who appeal to the example of Samson to defend such action overlook the special command of God and inducement of the Holy Spirit; Samson's act came from faith (Heb. 11:32, 34), and his death was a type of Christ's death. Another needless exposure to harm is willfully remaining behind during a plague or refusing to flee persecution. The situation is different for pastors, who should stay behind to offer help and comfort. Killing oneself rather than accept being forced to sin was much discussed in the early church. Augustine gave the best counsel: We may not do evil to bring about good; if we were permitted to kill ourselves to avoid sin, we should kill ourselves immediately after being baptized. Whether or not someone who commits suicide can be saved is a judgment we must leave entirely to God. In conclusion, all reckless deeds, all toying with human life, done usually to tickle people's pride and ambition, are morally condemnable.

What about longing for death? There is genuinely Christian desire to depart and be with Christ, arising from the inner desire to die completely to sin and live in communion with Christ. But this should never arise from an aversion to life and a despondency with it, what has been called acedia by spiritual writers. Acedia arises from excess of pleasures, from wallowing in sensual pleasures that ends in loathing and is usually accompanied by deep melancholy or profound bitterness — occasionally by both at the same time. It leads to misanthropy, weariness of life, and despair about God and frequently ends in suicide. The young are particularly prone to this; many in the 16–20 age group have already been sated with earthly pleasures; there is nothing new for them, and they are spent with life. This state arises especially in periods of sentimentality or romanticism. Schopenhauer and Karl Robert Eduard von Hartmann organized it into a system, and poets like Goethe, Lord Byron, and Giacomo Leopardi celebrated it. In the early church a similar school of thought was manifest in a fanatic and frenetic longing for martyrdom.

The Seventh, Eighth, and Ninth Commandments also call us to attend to our bodily life. Scripture generally designates sins against the Seventh Commandment as "uncleanness," "filthiness," or "defilement." Included in the list of such sins are fornication, adultery, homosexuality, pedophilia, and incest. The New Testament terms for purity cover not only sexuality but also our speech, our eating and drinking, and our outward appearance. We are to purify our "heart" or inner person by crucifying our flesh with its sinful passions and dedicating our bodies to the Lord. Chastity pertains to our eyes, ears, hands, thoughts, inclinations, and tongue.

The Eighth Commandment comes from God's gift of the earth to humanity. God gave Adam the garden to dress it, keep it, and commanded him to subdue the earth. This is the basis (and right) to culture, to cultivation and labor that puts a human stamp on nature. From this we derive the right of possessions and property. As economic transactions moved from barter trade to consistent and common means of exchange (money), the challenges brought about by inequities intensified. While

Scripture does not condemn wealth as such, it repeatedly warns against riches, both in the Old and New Testaments.

It is not surprising that the early church considered wealth to be dangerous, living initially in a community of shared property according to the book of Acts. Over time the church elevated voluntary poverty as a higher virtue. Having wealth was a permitted necessity for Christians who lived in the world, but this was a concession; poverty was regarded as morally superior to wealth. The Reformation restored the rights of the natural. Calvin called for a golden mean between an ascetic life, restricted to absolute necessities, and the intemperance of a luxurious, indulgent lifestyle. We must subordinate our love for this world to our desire for the heavenly life, all the while being grateful to God the Creator and Giver of all good things. Both poverty and wealth come with grave dangers: poverty may lead to moral regression, dishonesty, and indifference. The embarrassments of poverty and the temptations of wealth are both perilous. Poverty can be an occasion for idleness, laziness, mendicancy, theft, and so on, but it can also be a stimulus to effort, frugality, moderation, helpfulness, meekness, and trust in God. Voluntary poverty fails to provide the virtues people expect from it, makes virtues like generosity impossible, and opens one up to pride, self-righteousness, idleness, and mendicancy. It does not put to death the seed of sin in us but supplies sin with different forms of manifestation.

As stewards we must guard against the two vices of covetousness and wastefulness. Covetousness or the love of money is a sin against God, the neighbor, oneself, and every Christian virtue. It enslaves people, drawing them away from God and leading them into all kinds of temptation, and creates unrest, anxiety, and fear. Covetousness comes in two forms: hoarding what one has (stinginess, miserliness) and pursing what one does not have (avarice, greed). Wastefulness does not only apply to money and property but also to physical and spiritual strength, to words, work, time, and energy. The evil here is not so much in the quantity wasted as in the proportion between what one spends and what one has. The poor can also be guilty of wastefulness. Frugality is good but must never become stinginess or a spur to avarice. The Eighth Commandment teaches us righteousness (faithfulness in our work, being honest, justice, and so forth) and compassion (care of the poor, gentleness, charity, clemency).

The Ninth Commandment concerns our good name and reputation. God's honor and honor from God are more important than our own honor from others. Otherwise we risk becoming more concerned for our image than for what we truly are before God. Ambition seeks fame, praise, and an immortal reputation with contemporaries and descendants, often using flattery and other means to please people. It is appropriate to defend our honor and good reputation, but not by the outmoded practice of a duel.

Our individuality yields duties toward our soul as we honor God's variety of gifts in temperament, character, intellect, emotions (feelings), and will. This diverse individuality is good but always partial; each individual person exhibits the idea of humanity from a specific angle that complements others. Humanity is the full true, human being. Classically, four temperaments have been distinguished: sanguine (optimistic, social); melancholic (pensive, withdrawn); choleric (short-tempered, irritable); and phlegmatic (relaxed, peaceful, passive, emotional). Each temperament has its strengths and shadow side; even the apostles display different temperaments, as do different nations. None of this should be understood in a deterministic manner, as evolutionists do; temperament is the soil for moral action, not its final cause. Morally responsible people are called to know themselves and to supplement their own temperament with that of others and thereby make their soul-life healthy. All persons must emancipate their personality from strict adherence to their temperament and transform what is natural to them into something ethical. Our temperament must be brought under the nurture and discipline of God's Word; we are called to develop ourselves into persons of Christian character.

Character is the hallmark of what has become of a person's innate disposition and temperament under the influence of nurture, education, experiences of social life, examples, and moral principles. Character is the individuality that our personality has imparted to ourselves and that has become second nature; it is generally "conditioned" by temperament and nature. It always bears an ethical character and is produced by the development of a person's moral life. Persons who do not seek to shape their temperaments by religious-moral principles develop ingrained sinful characters, drawn to vice, to self-acquired active sin and cherished inclination. Christ is the model for our Christian character; his alone is the perfectly harmonious character, while all others are more or less one-sided. The first feature of the Christian character is purity, followed by steadfastness, strength, energy—without inflexibility—and firmness. There are great variations of Christian character across time and among the nations and diverse Christian traditions. The modern age with its materialism, secularism, and nihilism is most unfavorable for the development of character; it is bereft of moral characters and even more so of truly Christian characters.

We are called to develop Christian character in our intellects, our emotions, and our will. The first of these requires instilling a love of truth, all truth. This requires, first, developing our capacity to pay attention and to observe. Having observed, we must remember—God's Word and law, his acts of lovingkindness and human acts of kindness, which should be inscribed in marble, while insults should be written in sand. Our imagination, which often enchants us and leads us into sin, is a gift that must be restrained and controlled by scriptural, rational considerations. It then becomes an eminently valuable capacity that shapes our ideals and helps us pursue grand goals and perform brave and heroic deeds. It must be trained to be attentive to real truth, goodness, and beauty. The intellect must be warned especially against pedantry, which is an excessive acquiescence to general concepts and rules that ignores concrete experience. The direct opposite of the pedant is the genius who sets *aside all maxims, including moral ones, to follow their own light and become a law unto themselves.*

Feelings mediate between our consciousness and our will; they arise and function independently of our will. Nevertheless, we are responsible for them; our passions are not sinful as such and do not need to be eradicated (as the Stoics believed), but they do need to be disciplined; disordered passions are sinful. It is possible to distinguish different classes of passions. According to the Stoics, passions may have good or bad things as their object, either in the present or in the future, resulting in feelings of pleasure and desire, grief, and fear. For Spinoza, the principal passion is desire, which becomes either joy or sadness; all other affections are derived from these two and are governed by and subject to knowledge. Suffering and pain disappear when we know we are one with the infinite Being, when our love of earthly things is absorbed by the mind's love toward God. Schopenhauer believed that the will and human affections cannot be changed; we can improve our intellect but not our heart. It is true that the affections cannot be controlled—let alone be purified and sanctified—by reason and intellect. Nonetheless, regenerated and led by the Holy Spirit, we must master our passions. Governed by the love of God and the example of Jesus, we are to cultivate the mind of Christ within ourselves and, with it, noble, holy dispositions.

In regeneration, our will is set free from bondage and enabled to serve God freely. It must be increasingly purified of all contamination and sanctified in the service of God. Our wills must become one with God's will. The will becomes freer to the extent that it increasingly is more determined by God's will. The notion that we become truly free when our will is autonomous, separated from God, is nothing but slavery.

§40. Our Duty to Life Itself

Life, too, is a gift of God (Acts 17:25). God is the creator of all things (Rev. 4:11), by his Spirit (Ps. 104:30). He kills and he makes alive (Deut. 32:39; 1 Sam. 2:6; 2 Kings 5:7; Neh. 9:6). Life is entrusted to us for a time, during which we are to fulfill our life's task, but we are not our own judge;[1] we do not exercise autonomous and arbitrary control over life, but are accountable to God for it. And he commands us to take care of this life as his gift. It is one of the greatest gifts, greater than food and clothing (Matt. 6:25). Nevertheless, however great a gift (as Job 2:4 puts it, "Skin for skin! All that a man has he will give for his life"), life is not the highest good.[2] Even the duty to take care of life may have to yield to other, higher duties (cf. §30 above), and

1. LO: *nostril juris.*
2. GO: *Das Leben ist der Güter höchstes nicht*; Schiller, *Die Braut von Messina*, 4:10; Schiller, *Bride of Messina.*

self-preservation may have to yield to the duty of self-sacrifice (cf. §36 above; cf. Matt. 10:39; 16:25–27; Mark 8:35; Luke 14:26, 27; John 12:25; 1 John 3:16), just as Jesus himself gave up his life (John 10:11–18; 15:13; in Paul, 2 Tim. 2:24, and many heroes of faith under the old covenant: Heb. 11:33–39). This shows that we do not have life merely to possess it, that it is not absolute, an end in itself,[3] but that we have received it in order to expend it in the service of God, our neighbor, and our own eternal interests. Sensory life is subordinate to the higher, moral life. But apart from this higher moral goal, to which sensory life must be sacrificed, care for sensory life is mandated, and neglect, dismissal, disdain, and contempt for it is a sin, and in principle is suicidal.

Self-Defense

In fact, that care is mandatory to such an extent that we are all held to the duty of self-defense.[4] This is definitely a duty[5]—not just permissible but obligatory, commanded. Self-defense does not mean that under the force of circumstances one does what is actually not good, but denotes the right and duty to pit a force of divine justice within one's own person over against the violence of an ungodly injustice. If someone attacks us with violence and without legitimacy, in order to kill us or rob us of our possessions, self-defense is a duty. Self-defense may not set out to kill the attacker; its only aim is to defend oneself and one's goods; but if that is impossible without killing the other person, then this is warranted. For I am then fighting first of all for my own life and property, to be sure, but in so doing, also for the moral community, for the moral law, for justice. And in the attacker's assault upon my life, the attacker has forfeited their own life, having brought it into conflict with justice. In that case, my self-defense is a duty, because in that momentary danger the government cannot act. But after having repelled the attack, I must report it. Reinhard says,[6] however, that if the attacker is intent only upon our possessions, we may not take their life in order to protect property, for human life is worth more than our possessions. Others have condemned self-defense because, when we take the attacker's life, we have also deprived them of the possibility of repentance, and thus of salvation, whereas by allowing ourselves and our possessions to be taken, we may yet win the attacker over and give them an opportunity to repent.[7]

---

3. GO: *Selbstzweck.*
4. De Moor, *Commentarius Perpetuus*, 2:860–62.
5. Rothe, *Theologische Ethik*, 4:9–12 (§894).
6. Reinhard, *System der christlichen Moral*, 2:524n.
7. Reinhard, *System der christlichen Moral*, 2:527n.

As for Reinhard's own view, it can be difficult at the time to determine whether the attacker is going after only our wallet or also our life. After all, they are demanding our life for the sake of the wallet. And as for the second view, who says that the attacker will repent? Or that the person attacked is always themselves a convert and ready to die? The attacker has forfeited their life, and they alone are responsible for that. Holy Scripture has no specific instance or command about self-defense, but neither does it forbid it anywhere. Reinhard appeals to Acts 23:12–22, where the conspiracy against Paul is reported to the commander by his nephew, and to Romans 13:3–4, but this is insufficient proof.

Self-Harm

Self-harm, self-mutilation, self-flagellation, and self-destruction conflict with the duty of self-preservation (cf. §36; Gen. 19:17; Acts 2:40). These are systematized in the religions of India, in Brahmanism and Buddhism. Existence itself is evil, sin, and suffering; evil originates not in a misdeed but in being as such. Redemption consists of release from being. Thus, what nature envisions with death as a natural end becomes in this tradition a moral end. One tries to retrace the steps by which all existence developed out of Brahma, back to union with Brahma, to kill one's individual existence, to annihilate within oneself one's personality, will, self-consciousness, and feeling. People are called to die not to their sin (as in Christianity) but to their existence, their thinking, willing, feeling, and acting. The means thereto are asceticism, withdrawing from life, sinking within oneself, and horrific self-harm.[8] The same is found among the Neo-Platonists:[9] redemption consists in returning from multiplicity to unity. The way to attain to the highest stage of the mystic contemplation of God is to forget oneself, to lose oneself. The more I am an independent, free, self-determining personality, the further I am removed from God. The self-conscious personality is foreign to God, who is the Completely Absolute One. Thus, our personality must not be sanctified, but suppressed. Morality consists, therefore, not in action and the like, but in extinguishing the will, deadening feelings, doing nothing, resting.

Via Pseudo-Dionysius the Areopagite and John Scotus Eriugena, this school of thought also influenced Christians. It fostered the medieval mysticism of Eckhart (ca. 1260–ca. 1328), Johannes Tauler (ca. 1300–1361), and others,[10]

8. Wuttke, *Christian Ethics*, 1:47–54 (§8).
9. Wuttke, *Christian Ethics*, 1:144 (§26).
10. Wuttke, *Christian Ethics*, 1:225–33 (§35). Ed. note: Wuttke also mentions Jan van Ruusbroec (ca. 1293–1381).

the quietism of Molinos, Madame de la Motte-Guyon, and Fénelon (d. 1715).[11] J. G. Fichte, in "his rhetorical work 'Direction for a Holy Life' (1807) [from the second period of his life], in which he already departs from his earlier views [advocating an active and acting morality], and takes a rather mystic-Pantheistic turn, . . . expressly presents as the goal of morality, complete 'self-annihilation'[12]—not, however, in the Christian sense of moral self-denial, but rather in the sense of the religion of India. The belief in our self-existence must be absolutely destroyed; by this course the ego that was, sinks away into the pure divine essence."[13] Thus, all morality is self-destruction, and belief in our independence must disappear. "So long as man yet desires to *be* any-thing himself, God comes not to him; but so soon as he annihilates himself fully, utterly and radically, then God alone remains and is all in all. In anni-hilating himself man continues in God, and in this self-annihilation consists blessedness."[14] Schopenhauer, too, locates morality in the extinguishing of individuality, in breaking with the will to live. "The will must turn away from existence, must turn to will-lessness; for existence is absolutely null, and the will a delusion, from which we must become free."[15]

Often coupled with that self-annihilation are horrible self-harm and self-injury, practiced among the people of India, monks, and the flagellants of the thirteenth to the fifteenth centuries (in imitation of Jesus, who was flogged), a practice that spread from Italy throughout all of Germany.[16] Origen castrated himself (cf. Matt. 19:12).

Such self-injury and self-destruction are forbidden in Holy Scripture. Granted, Holy Scripture does make use of self-destructive imagery in its portrayal of Christian discipleship: "If your right eye causes you to sin, tear it out and throw it away. . . . And if your right hand causes you to sin, cut it off and throw it away" (Matt. 5:29–30). "It is better for you to enter eternal life crippled or lame than with two hands or two feet to be thrown into the eternal fire" (Matt. 18:8). Jesus even talks about those "who have made themselves eunuchs for the sake of the kingdom of heaven" (Matt. 19:12). The apostle Paul says about himself, "I discipline my body and keep it under

---

11. Wuttke, *Christian Ethics*, 1:273–77 (§39).

12. GO: *Selbstvernichtung*.

13. Wuttke, *Christian Ethics*, 1:341.

14. Wuttke, *Christian Ethics*, 1:341 (§45); cf. van der Hoeven, *Over het wezen der godsdienst*, 16. Ed. note: Wuttke later observes that Fichte's son, Immanuel Herman von Fichte (1796–1879), in his "System of Ethics" returned to "a decidedly theistical stand-point, and strongly emphasizes the idea of personality, which in Hegel [and in his father!] falls into so dubious a back-ground" (Wuttke, *Christian Ethics*, 1:358).

15. Wuttke, *Christian Ethics*, 1:358 (§47).

16. See Herzog, "Geißler," and *RE*, 1:329–30 (§21).

control" (1 Cor. 9:27). But undoubtedly these are figurative expressions, which command only that the person who is in Christ, the spiritual person, must rule over their bodily lusts and sins. Self-destruction, after all, is expressly forbidden; according to Leviticus 19:27–28, shaving the corners of head and beard, cutting the flesh, or making marks in the flesh is unlawful (cf. Lev. 21:5; Deut. 14:1–2). Paul calls rigorous asceticism—"Do not handle, Do not taste, Do not touch"—a form of "self-willed religion"[17] that is of "no value in stopping the indulgence of the flesh" (Col. 2:21–23).

He warns Timothy against people who forbid marriage, demand abstinence from foods, and so forth, and says that bodily exercise[18] is of little profit (1 Tim. 4:1–8). Self-imposed injuries are but an invention of the deceitful human heart, to transfer repentance and contrition from the soul to the body, thereby to enter heaven—that is, by many good works and much suffering. They proceed from the false assumption that the body with its senses is the seat of sin, that whippings and spiked belts can kill sin. In this way they fail to extract the roots of sin and instead foster spiritual pride.[19] Wicked and unconverted people really enjoy hearing talk of hell: "Let me have it!"[20]

Suicide[21]

Suicide was defended by the Cynic philosophers. These men practiced bearing everything with equanimity. They hardened their bodies, like Diogenes, who tortured himself in summer by rolling in hot sand, in winter by walking barefoot through snow and hugging ice-cold columns. But if life for some reason became unbearable, the Cynics reserved for themselves the right to kill themselves to save their freedom. When Antisthenes became impatient during his illness, Diogenes offered him a dagger, but Antisthenes was not minded to kill himself. That Diogenes ended his own life is often told, but proof is lacking. However, Metrocles and Menedemus did kill themselves.[22] The Pythagoreans

---

17. GrO: ταπεινοφροσύνῃ καὶ ἀφειδίᾳ σώματος. These Greek terms refer to giving "a shew of wisdom in will worship, and humility, and neglecting of the body" (KJV).

18. GrO: σωματικὴ γυμνασία.

19. Cf. Wuttke, *Handbuch der christlichen Sittenlehre*[3], 2:287, 561; Lange, *Zur psychologie in der Theologie*.

20. DO: *Sla er maar op*.

21. Ed. note: Suicide statistics were available to Bavinck in D. E. Siegenbeek van Heukelom, "De zelfmoord als peilschaal van het maatschappelijk geluk," *De Gids* 63 (1899): 58–89.

22. Zeller, *Socrates and the Socratic Schools*, 271n8. Ed. note: Metrocles (active ca. 32 BC) was a Cynic philosopher whose story is told by Diogenes Laertius, *Lives of Eminent Philosophers* VI.96–98 (LCL 185:98–101); Menedemes of Eretria (345/344–261/260 BC) was a Greek philosopher whose story is told by Diogenes Laertius, *Lives of Eminent Philosophers* VI.104–9 (LCL 185:108–9).

did regard the body as a prison, but they opposed suicide because God had placed souls in the bodies, and they were therefore not allowed to set them free.[23] Life in the body was a way to purify the soul and was guided by God.[24] Plato also opposed suicide on the same grounds—namely, because we are servants of God[25] and because no more than a soldier may we abandon our post.[26] Voetius, however, claimed that Plato allowed it in some cases.[27]

By contrast, the Stoics defended suicide. They made fatalism into a dogma, and they preached submission to the universal link between cause and effect and the universal nature of reason. The highest goal is to want nothing except what inheres in the nature of things. Therein lie the tranquility and happiness of the wise and the harmony of life—that is, virtue. Nevertheless, the Stoics made one exception: if fate places the wise person in an intolerable situation, they may free themselves from it by committing suicide. In fact, suicide, which the Stoics called "departure" or "going out,"[28] was for them the best proof of the freedom of the wise from all things external.[29] Seneca praises the act of Cato the Younger,[30] who killed himself on account of the end of the republic, and regards this act as the supreme triumph of the human will.[31] He also says that death as the path of freedom must be not be despised.[32] Whoever denies the right to suicide "does not see that he is shutting off the path to freedom. The best thing which eternal law ever ordained was that it allowed to us one

23. Zeller, *Die Philosophie der Griechen*[4], 1:419.

24. Zeller, *Die Philosophie der Griechen*[4], 1:426.

25. DO: *dienstknechten Gods*. Ed. note: Zeller says that human beings are "the property of God" (*ein Eigenthum der Gottheit*; see *Die Philosophie der Griechen*[4], 2/1:929).

26. Plato, *Phaedo* 61D–89A; cf. Zeller, *Die Philosophie der Griechen*[4], 2/1:929. Ed. note: English translation in Plato, *Euthyphro, Apology, Crito, Phaedo, Phaedrus* (LCL 36:212–307).

27. Voetius, *Selectarum Disputationum Theologicarum*, 4:255–56. Ed. note: Bavinck cites Voetius's reference to Plato, *De legibus* 9, and provides a Latin version of IX.873c where Plato distinguishes between two kinds of suicide: on the one hand, when a man is either "ordered by the city's judicial decree" or "compelled by some terribly painful and inescapable bad luck that's befallen him" or has "been allotted some baffling shame that he can't live with" and, on the other hand, when "out of lack of effort and unmanly cowardice [a man] inflicts an unjust penalty upon himself." Plato implies acceptance of the former but gently discredits the latter by placing their burial in separate and unmarked tombs "in uncultivated and nameless boundary regions" (translation taken from Plato, *Laws of Plato*, trans. Pangle, 268–69).

28. GrO: ἐξαγωγή.

29. Seneca, *Ad Lucilium Epistulae Morales I*, 70–71 (XII.10).

30. On Cato, see Augustine, *City of God* I.23–24 (NPNF[1] 2:16).

31. Seneca, *Moral Essays I*, 10–13 (*De providentia* II.9–12); cf. Seneca, *Ad Lucilium Epistulae Morales II*, 82–83 ("Epistle 71 [16]").

32. Seneca, *Moral Essays I*, 44–47 (*De providentia* VI.6); cf. Seneca, *Ad Lucilium Epistulae Morales II*, 64–65 ("Epistle 70 [14]"); Seneca, *Ad Lucilium Epistulae Morales I*, 456–57 ("Epistle 65 [22]"); Seneca, *Ad Lucilium Epistulae Morales III*, 352–55 ("Epistle 117 [21–24]"); Seneca, *Ad Lucilium Epistulae Morales III*, 388–93 ("Epistle 120 [14–20]").

entrance into life, but many exits."[33] The masters of this school of thought put this doctrine into practice as well. Zeno hanged himself at an advanced age because he had broken his finger. For even less weighty reasons Cleanthes ended his life by starving himself. Antipater later followed their examples.[34] For them, suicide is not only occasionally permissible but is honored as the supreme act of moral freedom. Not that it is recommended for just anyone, yet everyone is required to kill themselves if no higher duty connects them to life and if external circumstances make life no longer desirable.[35]

According to Seneca, there is sufficient basis for suicide if one or another disruption robs us of work and peace of mind—for example, failing strength, incurable disease, the tyranny of a despot, or severe poverty.[36] Diogenes calls suicide for the sake of others lawful as well. Others enumerate five grounds given by the Stoics for suicide: for the sake of others (e.g., for one's fatherland) and in cases where one is forced to do something unlawful or is subject to poverty, lengthy illness, or mental weakness. For the Stoics, after all, life and death are adiaphora. The wise shed their life when it no longer fits them, like a garment; one escapes as from an uninhabitable house—leaves it as freely as one leaves a party. Wise people choose their manner of dying like people choose a ship for their journey: life is merely a means.[37] Countless Roman Stoics put an end to their lives. In Massilia (modern Marseilles), suicide was lawful. In Rome a person who committed suicide remained unburied, yet there were also legitimate reasons why someone would not refrain from self-injury—namely, weariness of life, shameful indebtedness, and impatience with ill-health.[38]

Among the later Cynics, Demonax defended suicide and killed himself.[39] And during the Olympic Games of AD 165, Peregrinus, half fearing death but craving fame and applause, threw himself into the flames of a funeral pyre.[40]

---

33. LO: *non videt se viam libertatis eludere. Nil melius aeterna lex fecit, quam quod unum introitum nobis ad vitam dedit, exitus multos*; Seneca, *Ad Lucilium Epistulae Morales II*, 64–65 ("Epistle 70 [14]").

34. Ed. note: Bavinck's source for the preceding is Zeller, *Die Philosophie der Griechen*[3], 3/1:306.

35. Epictetus, *Discourses, Books 1–2*, 98 (*Discourses* I.9–16).

36. Seneca, *Ad Lucilium Epistulae Morales I*, 406–9 ("Epistle 58 [33–37]"); Seneca, *Ad Lucilium Epistulae Morales II*, 56–72 ("Epistle 70"); Seneca, *Ad Lucilium Epistulae Morales III*, 106–7, 112–13 ("Epistle 98 [16, 17:9]"); Seneca, *Moral Essays I*, 292–94 (*On Anger* III.xiv.3–4).

37. Zeller, *Die Philosophie der Griechen*[3], 3/1:305–9; cf. Wuttke, *Christian Ethics*, 1:139–40 (§24).

38. LO: *justae causae, quibus adductus aliquis sibi non parcere debeat; taedium vitae, pudor aeris alieni, valetudinis impatientia.*

39. Ed. note: The little that is known about the Greek Cynic philosopher Demonax (ca. 70–ca. 170), including his suicide by self-starvation, comes from his pupil Lucian of Samosata's brief biography, in *Lucian in Eight Volumes I*, 142–73. The suicide of Demonax is in lines 65–66 (*Lucian in Eight Volumes I*, 172–73).

40. Zeller, *Die Philosophie der Griechen*[3], 3/1:772–74.

Plotinus rejects the Stoic recommendation of suicide, yet does not consider it illegitimate under all circumstances.[41] Cicero hesitates, but he leans toward regarding it as legitimate.[42]

The defense of suicide reappears in the ethics of modern philosophy, in Hume and Holbach.[43] Schopenhauer defends a negation of the will to live, but not suicide, which is actually the affirmation of the will. The one seeking suicide wills life, after all, but is discontent with its manner, with suffering. Suicide proceeds not from the will but from a rational decision.[44] In modern times, suicide is defended by John Donne (in his Βιαθανατος: *A Declaration of That Paradoxe, or Thesis, That Selfe-Homicide Is Not So Naturally Sinne, That It May Never Be Otherwise* [1644]);[45] by Hume; by Duvergier, abbot of St. Cyran (d. 1643), in his *Question Royalle* (1609);[46] by Montesquieu; and by Rousseau (?), who hesitates.[47] In Germany, suicide is defended by the Jesuit Johannes Robeck,[48] who killed himself. Suicide came into vogue especially after the publication of Goethe's *The Sorrows of Young Werther* (1774), during the period of extravagant enthusiasm for Romanticism. In his *Ethics*, Kant condemned it outright, as did Fichte in his *Ethics*.[49]

In our day suicide is spreading at an alarming rate.[50] We are being told that this is only apparent, because formerly, reports were not so accurate. But even in the period when accurate statistics were kept (especially after 1848), the suicide rate has risen steadily in every European country, except of late in the Scandinavian countries.[51]

41. Zeller, *Die Philosophie der Griechen*[3], 3/2:600–602. Cf. also von Baumhauer, *Verum philosophorum praecipue Stoicorum doctrina de morte voluntaria.*

42. Cicero, *On Ends*, 276–81 (*About the Ends of Goods and Evils* III.18); Cicero, *On Duties* I.31 (LCL 30:112–17); Cicero, *Tusculan Disputations* V (LCL 141:425–548). For a contemporary discussion on Cicero and suicide, see Harding, "The Virtue of Suicide and the Suicide of Virtue."

43. Hume, "On Suicide"; Wuttke, *Christian Ethics*, 2:312, 322 (§41); 2:551; cf. Wuttke, *Handbuch der christlichen Sittenlehre*[3], 2:551n32. Ed. note: Hume's essay was first published anonymously and then posthumously; it has appeared in a number of anthologies. It is available as a facsimile reprint in *Essays on Suicide and the Immortality of the Soul* and as "Of Suicide" through Hume Texts Online, https://davidhume.org/texts/su/.

44. Scheffer, *Arthur Schopenhauer*, 813.

45. Published in London by John Dawson, 1647.

46. Ed. note: Check bibliography for complete information.

47. Rousseau, *Julie*, book I, chaps. 20ff. Ed. note: Bavinck provides no terminus ad quem.

48. Robeck, *Exercitatio Philosophica.*

49. Cf. Rothe, *Theologische Ethik*, 4:13n3 (§895).

50. Cf. von Oettingen, *Die Moralstatistik*, 737–85.

51. "In the fifty-three years for which reliable statistics are available, in twenty-two European countries, the number of suicides has approximately tripled, from 47 per one million inhabitants in the five-year period 1821–25 to circa 120 per one million inhabitants during 1876–80. In the last five years [1876–80] the absolute number for twenty-two European countries has increased from 20,306 to 24,910, thus from 80 to 97 cases per one million inhabitants." Ed. note: The

In Europe, about one hundred suicides occur on average per one million inhabitants. To be sure, suicide statistics are difficult to obtain; many families keep it a secret, ascribing the death to other causes; many cases, such as drowning, cannot with any certainty be counted as suicide; as well, countless attempts at suicide are unsuccessful, and so are not recorded. The record of reported suicides is therefore likely to be unreliable. The remarkable thing is that while suicide seems to be an act of free will, nevertheless the number of cases is rather constant and rises each year at a steady rate. This is evidence that suicide is the result of the circumstances of the time, of prevailing despair in society, and of miserable social conditions.[52] Suicide is a contagious disease.[53]

Most suicides occur in June and July, fewer in November, December, and January; their numbers rise and fall in proportion to the hours of daylight. Buckle inferred from this that nature desires a fixed number of suicides annually, just like a fixed number of deaths. In summer the will to resist is apparently weaker than in winter. Most occur at night or in the evening; in addition, most occur on Mondays and Tuesdays among men, on Sundays among women.

Suicide is performed in a variety of ways: by hanging, drowning, shooting, or poisoning. The first method is becoming steadily more common. Proportionately, suicide occurs in the cultural centers of London, Paris, Marseilles, Lyon, Rome, Berlin, and Vienna; the highest rate is found in Saxony. It was more common among the Germanic tribes than among the Romans and the Slavs; and it occurs among Protestants (190 per one million) three times as often as among Catholics (60 per one million), since Protestantism does more to develop individuals and their freedom, and hence Protestants are more easily given to doubt, dreariness, despair. Moreover, suicides increase with culture (think of the Greeks, Romans, Chinese, and Buddhists); it is rare among uncivilized peoples. It is promoted by excessive cultural refinement,

---

content of this note was originally in the body of the manuscript. Because of the dated statistics we have placed it in a footnote and slightly altered Bavinck's text in keeping with the original source. Bavinck's source for this data, and for the statistics in the next note, is von Oettingen, *Die Moralstatistik*, 742–46.

52. Ed. note: At this point Bavinck inserted between the lines a Dutch translation of a phrase that von Oettingen placed between quotation marks: *op een myriad schuldigen komt één offer* (GO: *auf eine Myriade Schuldiger Ein Opfer kommt* [von Oettingen, *Die Moralstatistik*, 767]). Von Oettingen's point is that a rise in suicide rates reflects social problems and is not simply an individual sin. Bavinck repeats the saying in the body of the text only two paragraphs later to make the same point.

53. "In England and Wales, suicides rose from 1,275 in 1857/58 to 1,764 in 1878; in Prussia from 2,076 in 1851/52 to 4,881 in 1879; in France, from 3,639 between 1851 and 1855 to 5,147 between 1866 and 1869 and to 6,434 in 1878; the proportionally largest increase occurred in Saxony, from 231 in 1874 to 408 in 1878." Ed. note: The content of this note was also originally in the manuscript body; slight corrections have been made to conform to the original source.

hypersensitivity to suffering, competition, social misery, alcohol, immorality, industrialization, and so on. The brighter the light, the darker the shadows! In Saxony, Protestant spirituality meshes with Germanic high culture, and these factors result in the highest number of suicides. The highest numbers come from prostitutes, prisoners, servants, and soldiers.

As for the causes of suicide: "The multitudes are guilty, but only one is sacrificed."[54] The seed for suicide lies within every sinner. Thousands nurse the thought. With one, the thought produces the act. There is a divinely regulated causal connection here between the sinful deed of the individual and the sins of society. We are all guilty of the general sins of hyperculture, nervous rush, competition and rivalry, luxury, pauperism, and so on, all of which together drive some people to suicide. "Our education leads to powerlessness, and powerlessness leads to suicide."[55] We are guilty of thinking too lightly of suicide, too cheaply of life. The particular influences that lead a person to commit suicide are rooted in the organically connected society. Evidence for this is also found in the fact that more men than women kill themselves: three hundred to four hundred males for one hundred females; there is more inducement among men, more struggle, more occasion for despair. The desire for suicide rises as people grow older: ages sixty to seventy yield the largest contingent. But in recent years, large cities show an increase among those under twenty-one, among high school and university students, young men from aristocratic families, apprentices, commercial people. Proportionally, more unmarried and divorced people than married people kill themselves, and more married people who have no children than those who do. About the motives of suicide, the statistics are still very uncertain. Mental illness is the leading cause; next come regret and fear of punishment, alcohol, and so forth.[56]

Suicide can be committed directly but also indirectly. Avarice, which withholds from oneself the necessities of life; masturbation and fornication, which sin against one's own body; drunkenness, which kills one's body and mind; and in a certain sense every sin that corrupts is suicide; likewise neglect of the body, of clothing, food, shelter, and so on.

Holy Scripture definitely condemns suicide.[57] In Genesis 9:5–6 God says that a human being may not be killed, for God made every person in the

54. Ed. note: For the German original, its source, and Bavinck's Dutch translation, see n. 52 above. A more literal translation would be "A myriad of culprits brings forth one sacrifice."

55. FO: "Nôtre éducation mène à l'impuissance et l'impuissance au suicide" (von Ottingen, *Die Moralstatistik*, 769).

56. Cf. Darwin, *Descent of Man*, 1:163; cf. Lecky, *History of European Morals*, 1:223–35.

57. Suicide is praised in 2 Macc. 14:41–46, but Josephus, *Jewish War* III.8.5, condemns it (LCL 487:678–83).

image of God. In Exodus 20, the Sixth Commandment reads: "You shall not kill." As the apostle Paul says, "No one ever yet hated his own flesh, but nourishes and cherishes it, just as Christ does the church" (Eph. 5:29). The image of God in others and in ourself may not be desecrated. Holy Scripture includes examples of suicides but without approving them: Abimelech (Judg. 9:54); Samson (Judg. 16:23–30); Saul (1 Sam. 31:4); Ahithophel, who hanged himself (2 Sam. 17:23); Judas, who hanged himself (Matt. 27:5). Suicide is the clearest manifestation of the brokenness caused by sin, of the disruption of life,[58] of the inner discontent and disharmony of our existence. Moreover, Scripture teaches us to trust in God in all things (Matt. 5:36; 6:27; Rom. 14:7–8), and to honor our body (1 Cor. 6:19; 3:16–17; Acts 16:28: "Do not harm yourself"!).

Revelation 9:6 is applicable to suicide: "And in those days people will seek death and will not find it. They will long to die, but death will flee from them." Suicide is a sin not just against the body (Harless, Schmid) but also against the soul, a denial of immortality (any person who believes in immortality believes in eternal perdition and cannot kill themselves), incompatible with the thought of an eternal life.[59] Rothe says, "Certainly noble suicides can also occur, but not among us, in the Christian world."[60] And it is true: among pagans, suicide did not always arise out of despair, but was viewed as something noble, an act of freedom and wisdom. Vilmar comments correctly: pagans did not regard suicide as being all that evil, since everything was wrapped up in this earthly life; whenever that was disrupted by anything, it was no longer a "life worth living," and they discarded it.[61] This is why Cicero says, "You know the old saying, '*When once your powers are passed, why wish your life to last?*'"[62] Pagans who condemned suicide did so because it was an offense against the state.[63]

In Christianity, however, the moral quality of this life and the future after this life are clearly revealed to us; erroneous conviction[64] can no longer be the cause of suicide among us, no more than vain ambition.[65] With us, the causes are different: mental illness, melancholy, dread of shame and punishment,

---

58. GO: *Zerrütung des Lebens.*

59. Wuttke, *Handbuch der christlichen Sittenlehre*[3], 2:138–42.

60. Rothe, *Theologische Ethik*, 4:13n3 (§895).

61. GrO: βίος βιωτός; Vilmar, *Theologische Moral*, 1:340–41 (§30). Ed. note: The next two citations, from Cicero and Aristotle, are taken directly from Vilmar.

62. LO: *Vetus est enim: ubi non sis qui fueris, non esse cur velis vivere*; Cicero, *The Letters to His Friends II*, VII.iii.4 (LCL 216:18–19).

63. GrO: ἀδικεῖ τὴν πόλιν; Aristotle, *Nicomachean Ethics* V.11.

64. LO: *falsa persuasio.*

65. LO: *vana ambitio*; Voetius, *Selectarum Disputationum Theologicarum*, 4:244–61.

misery and poverty, obsessive unrequited love,[66] doubt, despair, and so on. It was Christianity that first taught us clearly that we are not "autonomous," a law unto ourselves,[67] that we cannot do what we want. We belong to God, to our neighbor (family, state, society, etc.). Suicide is therefore a sin against God and the neighbor; it is wicked and immoral. We have free rein over our property (e.g., money); the property is ours and is for us. But we do not have free rein over ourselves. For that, we are bound to duties that we cannot and may not shrug off.

According to Kant, Fichte, and Rothe, those who commit suicide grant themselves the competence to withdraw from all obligations, something that is impossible.[68] People are ends-in-themselves[69] and thus cannot treat themselves as mere means. My life must be dedicated to fulfilling God's will, and his will can never demand of me that I kill myself, for then that will would have destroyed itself. The one who commits suicide rebels against the moral law itself. Animals do not commit suicide. Neither do uncultured people. But cultured people do, corrupted by immature civilization. Suicide is cowardice in comparison with the grander task of bearing one's suffering;[70] in comparison with virtuous people. However, it is heroic in comparison with the "good-for-nothing" who endures every disgrace with indifference, satisfied merely to exist.[71]

What is condemned along with this suicide is exposing oneself deliberately and voluntarily to danger, as Jonah perhaps did when he told the crew to throw him into the sea (Jon. 1:12) (or did he do this at God's command?). Jesus was tempted by Satan to commit this sin by throwing himself down from the pinnacle of the temple (Matt. 4:5–7). To this category belongs sacrificing oneself in war, as van Speyk did in 1831 when he blew up his ship in the harbor of Antwerp lest the Belgian rebels capture it.[72]

66. DO: *dwepende en teleurgestelde liefde.*

67. LO: *nostri juris.*

68. Rothe, *Theologische Ethik*, 4:13n3 (§895).

69. GO: *Selbstzweck.*

70. Fichte, quoted in Rothe, *Theologische Ethik*, 4:13n3 (§895).

71. DO: *nietswaardige.* Ed. note: Bavinck adds the following epigram from Martial in the margin: "In narrow means 'tis easy to despise life: he acts the strong man who is wretched and can endure" (LO: *Rebus in adversis facile est contemnere mortem. Fortiter ille facit, qui miser esse potest*) (Martial, *Epigrams* XI.56 [trans. Ker, LCL 95:280–81]).

72. Ed. note: Jan Carolus Josephus van Speyk (1802–31) was a Dutch naval lieutenant who was given command of a gunboat when the Belgian War of Independence began in August 1830. On February 5, 1831, a storm blew the gunboat into the port of Antwerp, where it was stormed by Belgian troops who demanded his surrender. According to legend he shouted "I'd rather be blown up" (*Dan liever de lucht in*) and ignited the ship's gunpowder, killing himself and twenty-eight crewmen along with dozens of Belgians. Van Speyk is regarded as a naval

Acts like this have been defended with an appeal to Samson (Judg. 16:26–30). Voetius and de Moor justify this in the case of Samson by saying that Samson acted by a special command and inducement of the Holy Spirit, in faith (Heb. 11:32, 34), after first saying a prayer (v. 28), not in order to kill himself but to kill many foes, so that his death is also a type of Christ's death.[73] Augustine judged similarly:[74] Samson's strength was expressly returned to him so he could perform that deed. Deeds that cannot be condoned are those of Eleazar, who passed under the elephant on which he thought the king was mounted and stabbed it to death so that the elephant fell upon Eleazar and crushed him (1 Macc. 6:43–46), and the deed of Razis, who when cornered by the enemy fell upon his sword, preferring to die bravely rather than to fall into the enemy's hands (2 Macc. 14:37–42). Augustine rightly says, "Not all that is grand is good, since even crimes can have grandeur."[75]

To this category also belongs willfully and needlessly remaining behind during a plague. The Christian must not tempt God (Matt. 4:7), and so may not go or remain where he is not called. Tertullian was of the opinion that the Christian was not permitted to flee from persecution.[76] But others, such as Cyprian, were more sensible. Not everyone can or may flee the plague. Particularly pastors should stay behind in such a situation and offer help and comfort.[77] In 1634 Voetius wrote about this to an anonymous Remonstrant pastor.[78] Voetius says that Episcopius wanted to release pastors from the duty to remain behind. But this is wrong. That would be unbelief, without

---

hero in the Netherlands (Wikipedia, s.v. "Jan van Speyk," https://en.wikipedia.org/wiki/Jan _van_Speyk).

73. Voetius, *Selectarum Disputationum Theologicarum*, 4:256–68, 281–92; de Moor, *Commentarius Perpetuus*, 2:868–70; annotation of the *Statenvertaling* on Judg. 16:28 ("O Lord GOD, please remember me and please strengthen me only this once, O God, that I may be avenged on the Philistines for my two eyes"): "He prayed this in faith and was heard by God, who, after the Philistines had gouged out his eyes and (so they believed) made him incapable of fulfilling his calling, on this occasion, in answer to Samson's prayer, gave him extraordinary strength and conferred on him a more miraculous victory than in his life; to the glory of his holy name, the mocking of idols, and the shame of his enemies."

74. Augustine, *City of God* I.21; Augustine, *Contra Gaudentium* I.31. Ed. note: Augustine's anti-Donatist writing *Answer to Gaudentius, a Bishop of the Donatists* (*Contra Gaudentium Donistarum episcopum*, PL 43:81–83) is scheduled to appear in English translation through New City Press in its series *The Works of Saint Augustine: A Translation for the 21st Century*.

75. LO: *non enim bonum est omne quod magnum est, quoniam magna etiam sunt mala*; Augustine, *Saint Augustine Letters, Volume V, 5 (Epistle 204)*, cited by de Moor, *Commentarius Perpetuus*, 2:870.

76. See Tertullian, *De Fuga in persecutione*.

77. Cf. Voetius, *Selectarum Disputationum Theologicarum*, 4:269–70; cf. Voetius, *Politicae Ecclesiasticae* (1663), II.iii.8 (question: *An quis fugâ confessionem declinare possit, seu an persecutionem fugere luceat*).

78. See Voetius, *Selectarum Disputationum Theologicarum*, 4:270–74, 307–9.

precedent in Scripture, and ultimately not very helpful. Pastors especially ought to remain behind and care for the sick.[79] As for fleeing persecution, Voetius says that before he turned to Montanism, the early Tertullian deemed it legitimate.[80] But Athanasius,[81] Augustine,[82] and the later Beza,[83] Lavater,[84] Vermigli,[85] and Ames[86] all affirm fleeing persecution as legitimate.

Yet another question in the early church was whether one may kill oneself if forced to commit a sin.[87] During persecutions it happened that women and girls would kill themselves to escape shameful violation. Many lauded this and counted such women among the saints—for example, Eusebius,[88] Chrysostom, and Neander.[89] However, Augustine condemned it,[90] since chastity does not reside in the body but in the heart, and the heart can stay pure even when a person is violated.[91] Augustine says that suicide is never good, neither to pursue good things nor to avoid bad things.[92] He repeats this in *Epistle 60* and

---

79. Second Helvetic Confession, chap. 18; Voetius, Τα Ασκητικα *sive Exercitia Pietatis*, chap. 24.

80. Tertullian, *Of Patience* XIII ("Of Bodily Patience") (*ANF* 3:715–16); Voetius, *Politicae Ecclesiasticae* (1663), 3:101.

81. Athanasius, *Defence of His Flight* (NPNF[2] 4:255–65).

82. Augustine, *Letters 156–210*, 158–60 (*Epistle 180* [to Oceanus]).

83. Beza, "Homilia decima (Luke 24:29–35)."

84. Lavater, *Liber Nehemiae*, 35 (*Homily 20*). Ed. note: This is a commentary on Neh. 6:11. Nehemiah responds to Sanballat's death threats and the request from Shemaiah to meet secretly in the temple with the following: "Should a man like me run away?" (LO: *Nunquid mei similis fugiat*). In his commentary, Lavater concludes from the example of David, among other things, that it is permissible to flee (LO: *fugere iinterdum licet*).

85. In a letter published together with his *Loci Communes*, according to Voetius, *Politicae Ecclesiasticae* (1663), II.iv.101, and *Quatuor Libris Adornata*, 101: "*Martyr in epistola quadam, quae inter alias cum locis communibus ipsius edita.*"

86. Ames, *Conscience*, IV.iii. q. 6.

87. De Moor, *Commentarius Perpetuus*, 2:861–62.

88. Eusebius, *Church History* VIII.14.12–17 (NPNF[2] 1:337); cf. Eusebius, *Life of Constantine* I.34 (NPNF[2] 1:492).

89. Neander, *Vorlesungen*, 154, 210; Wuttke, *Handbuch der christlichen Sittenlehre*[3], 2:286–88. In his commentary on Jonah, Jerome says that "in times of persecution one must not die at one's own hand—except in the situation where chastity is endangered" (LO: *nisi forte castitas periclitetur*; commentary on Jon. 1:12; translation from Hegedus, "Jerome's Commentary on Jonah" [1991], 22). Another translation can be found in Jerome, *Commentaries on the Twelve Prophets*, vol. 1. Rothe, *Theologische Ethik*, 4:13–14 (§895n3), approves of committing suicide in order to avoid being forced to sin, since it is not possible to undergo sin in purity.

90. Augustine, *City of God* I.16–28 (NPNF[1] 2:12–19).

91. Ed. note: Between pages 796 and 797 of the manuscript there is a small paper with notes. The text reads: "Suicide statistics from Oettingen. Also Siegenbeek in *De Gids*, Jan. 1899. Dr. C. J. Wijnaandts Francken, *De zelfmoord; een sociologische studie* (The Hague: Nijhoff, 1899)." The reference to Oettingen is to von Oettingen, *Die Moralstatistik*, referred to earlier in this chapter; see above, nn. 50–55. "Siegenbeek" is a reference to D. E. Siegenbeek van Heukelom, "De zelfmoord als peilschaal van het maatschappelijk geluk." See n. 21 above.

92. LO: *nec propter bona assequenda nec propter mala vitanda.*

Epistle 204.[93] But in *City of God* I.26, he hesitates[94] to censure these examples of women who killed themselves to preserve their chastity. On the one hand, the command was immutable: You shall not kill; on the other hand, those examples were lauded by the church. It is possible that, like Samson, the women were moved by an impulse of the Spirit.[95] But Vermigli is right in saying that this comparison is invalid because the impulse of the Spirit has been established in Samson's case but not in the case of the women; hence their deed must be condemned. Suicide may also not be committed for the greater glory of God,[96] as some contend. One may not do evil to bring about good. Augustine observes correctly that if we were permitted to kill ourselves in order to avoid a sin (as those women did), then we ought to kill ourselves immediately after being baptized.[97]

Here is a difficult question: Are all those who commit suicide lost?[98] We may not answer this with a definite yes. Voetius,[99] Hoornbeeck,[100] Saldenus,[101] and Knibbe[102] counsel caution in our judgment.[103] Suicide is a great sin, of course, deserving eternal perdition, but though the sin may be terrible, the sinner may still be justified. The judgment about a person must be made on the basis of that person's entire life rather than on the basis of one act. It has not been demonstrated sufficiently that each and every sin must be followed by a distinct and explicit act of repentance[104] in order to receive forgiveness. Furthermore, we do not know what God can work at the very last moment in the heart of such a sorely tried person. In any case, formally speaking, suicide is not the sin against the Holy Spirit, and thus can be pardoned. There are in fact many cases of suicide by godly people—for example,

93. Augustine, *Letters 1–99*, 243–45 (letter to Aurelius); Augustine, *Letters 156–210*, 372–77 (letter to Dulcitius).

94. LO: *de his nihil temere audio judicare*; "Of such persons I do not presume to speak rashly" (*City of God* I.26 [NPNF¹ 2:17]). Similarly, Hoornbeeck, *Theologiae Practicae*, 243; according to Vermigli, *Loci Communes²*, 132b and 133a.

95. LO: *instinctus Spiritus.*

96. LO: *ad majorem Dei gloriam.*

97. Cf. Augustine's comments about Lucretia in *City of God* I.19 (NPNF¹ 2:13).

98. Gerhard, *Loci Theologici*, locus XVI, 24. Ed. note: It is not clear which edition of Gerhard Bavinck was using here. In the 1657 revised edition, locus XVI, 24 (3:114–16), deals with Levitical laws concerning clean and unclean. Gerhard does consider suicide (αὐτοφονία) in his discussion of the Sixth Commandment (Lutheran Fifth Commandment), in locus XV, 155 (3:64–65).

99. Voetius, *Selectarum Disputationum Theologicarum*, IV:246, 247, 268–69, 288–90.

100. Hoornbeeck, *Theologia Practica*, 1:243–44.

101. Saldenus, *Toetssteen van eens Christens oordeel*, 196–218 (chap. 15).

102. Knibbe, *De Leere der Gereformeerde Kerk*, 643 (Lord's Day 40, Q&A 105).

103. De Moor, *Commentarius Perpetuus*, 2:870.

104. LO: *poenitentia distincta et explicita.*

Samson and Pelagia and a mother with her two daughters.[105] Thus we cannot say with certainty that they are all lost. We must leave the judgment to God. This was the conclusion of Augustine,[106] Melanchthon,[107] and Luther. Friedrich Balduinus distinguishes between those who kill themselves out of "despair or malevolence" and those who commit suicide "from madness or melancholy"; the latter are not definitely lost.[108] Episcopius thought the same.[109]

To be subsumed under suicide are also various acts of recklessness—for instance, speed skating on ice, the neck-breaking stunts of acrobats on horseback and the like, the dangerous feat of, say, crossing Niagara Falls on a wire, crossing the ocean in a small boat, swimming across the English Channel, fasting for fifty days like Succi,[110] contests involving drinking the most glasses

---

105. Cf. Ambrose, *Concerning Virgins* 7 (*NPNF²* 10:386–88). Ed. note: Ambrose mentions "Saint Pelagia [who] lived formerly at Antioch, being about fifteen years old, a sister of virgins, and a virgin herself." He goes on to tell how she, her mother, and her sister, fleeing persecutors, regarded the raging river as a baptism of forgiveness, waded in, and gave up their lives. Bavinck also adds "Nicephorus 7:12," a reference to the Greek church historian Nicephorus Callistus Xanthopulus (ca. 1320), *Ecclesiastical History* VII.12 (*PL* 145:1230).

106. Augustine, *City of God* I.16, 26.

107. Ed. note: Bavinck's reference is "Melanchthon, Consol. Theol. II. p. 220." Bavinck took this directly from Hoornbeeck, *Theologiae Practicae²*, 1:244. To what is Hoornbeeck referring? It is not Melanchthon's pastoral consolation to pastors in times of persecution, *Epistola Consolatoria Theologorū in Misnia / ad Pastores in finibus Bohemiae et Lusatiae / qui persecutionem propter puram Euangelij doctrinam / jam ferunt* (Dresden: Matthes d.Ä. Stöckel, 1555). Possibly, the reference is a typographical error and the work intended is Melanchthon, *Consilia sive Iudicia Theologica, Itemque Responsiones Ad Quaestiones De rebus variis ac multiplicibus secundum seriem annorum digestae* (Neustadii: Harnisius, 1600). Pages 220–21 of the second part (*De actis tempore interim. Anno 1548*) concern *iudicium de ius, qui sibiipsis mortem consciuerunt, vel alias repentina morte obierunt* (verdict concerning those who choose their own death or otherwise experience sudden death).

108. Ed. note: The full text of Balduin reads: *Ita si quis non ex desperatione aut malo proposito, sed ex phrenesi aut melancholia laborans, sibi ipsi mortem consciuerit, nostrum non est, praecipitare iudicium, praefertim si antè piè vixerit.* (Thus, if a man chooses to kill himself, not out of despair or malevolence, but suffers from madness or melancholy, we should not judge rashly, especially if he lived piously before this.) Friedrich Balduin, *Tractatus Luculentus Posthumus*, 706.

109. Simon Episcopius, *Opera Theologica*, 66–67 (*Responsio ad quaestiones theologicas LXIV*, no. LXI). Ed. note: This treatise starts a new pagination in this volume after p. 440.

110. Ed. note: This is Bavinck's second reference to the fasting of Giovanni Succi (see chap. 19, n. 191). In that note Bavinck gave the example of Succi fasting for thirty days in August–September 1886, a feat well documented in Dutch newspapers (see the Delpher database of the Royal Library of the Netherlands at www.delpher.nl). His use of "fifty days" here does not contradict the preceding. While there are numerous accounts of Succi's thirty-day fast in various cities around the world, there are also reports of twenty-five-day, thirty-five-day, forty-day, and forty-five-day fasts. Succi was a professional faster who staged his fasts as public performances, not without controversy (he was accused of cheating during a thirty-day fast in Vienna in April 1896). His death was reported in the *Rotterdamsch*

of beer or gin, and so on. To be sure, what is risky for one person is not so for another. Gymnastic exercises can give the body a suppleness and flexibility that enable others to engage in impossible feats that are mortally dangerous. But we may never toy with life; it is too serious for that. Moreover, all the reckless feats mentioned are useful only for tickling people's pride and fostering their ambition and are without any moral value. The first bullfight held in Paris occurred on January 16, 1887.

Finally, we should mention here the kind of longing for death that is wrong and reprehensible. There is certainly a genuinely Christian desire to depart and be with Christ (2 Cor. 5:1–10; Phil. 1:23), which has sprung forth from the inner desire to die completely to sin and to live in communion with Christ. But it is wrong to harbor an aversion to life[111] and a despondency with life.[112] In the Middle Ages such a condition was called ἀκήδεια (literally: unconcern), *acedia*, and arose frequently in the monasteries.

Acedia is that condition in which everything is indifferent to us, in which our emotions arising from the ups and downs of life are completely stifled, in which we consider the greatest wisdom to be "vanity, all is vanity," in which we look down contemptuously on people's joys and sorrows. This "is a special form of hypochondria,"[113] of melancholy, and arises not only in the monasteries but also in the centers of culture (as with Solomon in the book of Ecclesiastes). It arises from excess of pleasures, from wallowing in sensual pleasures that ends in loathing. It is a condition that occurs often in the pagan world, which is a world without God, without Christ, without hope (Eph. 2:12), articulated in this aphorism: "Hope is the name for an uncertain thing."[114] Scripture affirms this: "Worldly grief produces death" (2 Cor. 7:10). The slogan of this attitude is "Let us eat and drink, for tomorrow we die" (1 Cor. 15:32b). The question it asks is that of Pilate: "What is truth?" (John 18:38). Among Israel, too, we find a Job (chap. 2) and a Jeremiah (15:10; 20:14) who curse the day they were born, and the Preacher of Ecclesiastes, who is pessimistic. However, here it is done from a different standpoint; they are in a state of transition. Hamlet is the exemplar of this pessimistic school, with his exclamation "O, that the Everlasting had not fix'd his canon 'gainst

---

Nieuwsblad of October 17, 1918. He is believed to have been the inspiration for Franz Kafka's short story "A Hunger Artist" (1924). The references to Niagara Falls and the English Channel are original to Bavinck.

111. LO: *taedium vitae*.

112. GO: *Lebensüberdruss*.

113. Martensen, *Christian Ethics, Special Part*, 2/1:378 (§159).

114. LO: *spes incertae rei nomen est*. Ed. note: It was not possible to determine the source of this saying.

self-slaughter!"[115] and with his monologue that includes the words "To die, to sleep—to sleep, perchance to dream."[116]

Acedia, born of excess, surfeit, and superabundance, is usually accompanied by deep melancholy or profound bitterness, occasionally by both at the same time. It leads to misanthropy, weariness of life, and despair about God and frequently ends in suicide. People in such a state are removed far above all that they have ever learned, received, enjoyed, observed, and experienced; all of this is not good enough for them. Particularly in our day this disease is very common; many people in the ages of sixteen to twenty have already tasted every earthly pleasure; there is nothing new for them anymore, and they are spent with life. The disease arose especially in the period of sentimentality (romanticism, "Werther fever"),[117] was dominant in the years 1820–50, and was represented by Leopardi, Byron, and others.[118] It was organized into a system by Schopenhauer and von Hartmann.[119] Byron shrouded it in the mist of poetry. Accordingly, this disease is viewed among many as world-weariness, apathy, European exhaustion, world fatigue, and as something respectable.[120] Sentimentality is coquetry with suffering,[121] a surrender to morbid feelings and moods.[122] It appears interesting, distinguished, appears to be proof of one's profound outlook on life, one's seriousness; but it is in reality a sickness, a form of hypersensitivity without moral value, a contempt of God, a complaint against his world rule,[123] able to be linked with various sins.[124] In the early church a similar school of thought was manifest in a fanatic and frenetic longing for martyrdom.

115. Shakespeare, *Hamlet*, act 1, scene 2, lines 129, 131–32.
116. Shakespeare, *Hamlet*, act 3, scene 1, lines 63–64; cf. de Laveleije, "Hamlet."
117. DO: *Wertherkoorts*. Ed. note: "Werther fever" refers to the influence Goethe's 1774 novel *The Sorrows of Young Werther* had on many young men in Europe who tried to emulate the lifestyle of the novelist's protagonist, including his suicide. For a recent essay on the phenomenon, see Belinda, "Goethe's *Werther* and Its Effects."
118. Ed. note: Giacomo Leopardi (1798–1837) was a renowned and influential Italian romantic poet; George Gordon Byron (Lord Byron [1788–1824]) was a leading romantic poet who died of disease while fighting for the Greek War of Independence from the Ottoman Empire.
119. Ed. note: While Bavinck does cite Schopenhauer specifically, he makes no specific reference to von Hartmann, even leaving his identity uncertain. He is undoubtedly referring to the German philosopher Karl Robert Eduard von Hartmann (1842–1906), author of *Philosophy of the Unconscious* (1869), a pessimistic work that builds on Hegel and Schopenhauer and influenced later thinkers such as Rudolf Steiner and Carl Jung (Wikipedia, s.v. "Karl Robert Eduard von Hartmann," https://en.wikipedia.org/wiki/Karl_Robert_Eduard_von_Hartmann).
120. GO: *Weltschmerz*; *Blasiertheit*; *Europamüdigkeit*; *Weltmüdigkeit*; Vilmar, *Theologische Moral*, 1:271–73.
121. Vilmar, *Theologische Moral*, 1:145.
122. Vilmar, *Theologische Moral*, 1:294.
123. Wuttke, *Handbuch der christlichen Sittenlehre*[3], 2:298.
124. Fabius, *De Fransche Revolutie*, 59–71.

§41. ATTENDING TO BODILY LIFE IN THE SEVENTH THROUGH NINTH COMMANDMENTS

In §§37–40 we discussed duties with respect to health, food, clothing, and life itself, all of which are directly or indirectly grounded in the Sixth Commandment. We have yet to discuss our duties with respect to chastity (Seventh Commandment), property (Eighth Commandment), and honor and reputation (Ninth Commandment). In part these duties already touch upon duties toward the life of the soul (e.g., chastity, fornication) and other topics still to come, such as duties toward neighbor, property, vocation, and so on. For this reason, at this point we will be brief!

Attending to Chastity: The Seventh Commandment

Sexuality is at the heart of natural life. The sex drive is the strongest of all drives. The genitals are the root, the flashpoint of the will.[125] Nevertheless that drive, though it is the pivot of all movement and lord of the world, is kept almost entirely hidden and secret. In Scripture, the most general designation of sins against this commandment is "uncleanness"[126] (KJV; 2 Cor. 12:21; Gal. 5:19; Col. 3:5; Eph. 5:3), "filthiness"[127] (James 1:21), and "defilement"[128] (2 Cor. 7:1). It is manifested in many forms: fornication,[129] adultery,[130] and unnatural lusts such as homosexuality,[131] pedophilia[132] (Rom. 1:27; 1 Cor. 6:9; 1 Tim. 1:10),[133] sodomy (for which Lev. 20:13 imposed the death penalty), and incest[134] (Lev. 18 and 20; Deut. 27). These sins will be discussed later.[135]

A direct sin against oneself is masturbation (Gen. 38:9), the self-disruption of the image of God, and then also "obscene talk" (Col. 3:8),[136] "filthiness" (Eph.

---

125. Schopenhauer, *The World as Will and Idea*, 3:310–15.
126. GrO: ἀκαθαρσία.
127. GrO: ῥυπαρία.
128. GrO: μολυσμός.
129. GrO: πορνεία.
130. GrO: μοιχεία.
131. GrO: ἀρσενοκοίτης.
132. DO: *pederastie*; GrO: μαλακὸς εἶναι.
133. Ed. note: At this point Bavinck takes over from Schopenhauer a comment about pederasty being especially common among ancient Greeks and Romans. See Schopenhauer, *Die Welt als Wille und Vorstellung*, 2:643–51 (appendix to chap. 44). This entire appendix was omitted in the English translation. See Schopenhauer, *The World as Will and Idea*, 3:375n7.
134. DO: *bloedschande*.
135. Vilmar, *Theologische Moral*, 1:249–61. Ed. note: This is a broad reference to Vilmar's chapter "Concerning Sins of the Flesh" (*Von den Fleischessünden*); the chapter opens with a section, "Sexual Sins" (*Geschlechtssünden*).
136. GrO: αἰσχρολογία.

5:4),[137] "corrupting talk"[138] (Eph. 4:29), unchastity in images, paintings, clothing, debauchery, and so on. By contrast, chastity is also a duty toward ourselves. For this, the New Testament uses the words ἄγνεια and ἁγνότης, which denote purity with respect not only to sexuality but to all pleasures, including eating, drinking, and clothing, as in 1 Timothy 5:22: "Keep yourself pure."[139] This is an imperative not only to "cleanse your hands,"[140] or outward appearance, but also to "purify your hearts,"[141] or the inner person (James 4:8). Pure conduct is an essential quality of Christians (1 Pet. 3:2; cf. 1 Tim. 4:12), who have crucified the flesh with its affections and lusts (Rom. 6:1–23; Gal. 5:24), and dedicated their bodies to the Lord, not to the prostitute (1 Cor. 6:13–20). Thus, the chastity of the Christian is something other than proper shame (which is good in itself) in the area of natural life, which Scripture praises as well (1 Tim. 2:9).[142] Christian purity[143] is the fruit of wisdom from above (James 3:17), since our body is a temple of the Holy Spirit (1 Cor. 6:19) and is made possible through the power of the Holy Spirit (Rom. 8:13; Gal. 5:22). We are therefore also to be on guard against filthy talk (Eph. 4:29; 5:4) and to think on what is pure (Phil. 4:8). It is not old age, but only repentance that supplies us with that chastity.[144] Chastity pertains to our eyes, ears, hands, thoughts, inclinations, and tongue. Joseph is an example of that kind of chastity, as is Job (31:1).[145]

Attending to Property: The Eighth Commandment

At creation, the world is not finished and completed.[146] But God gives the earth to humanity (Ps. 115:16).[147] He gave Adam the garden in order to

---

137. GrO: αἰσχρότης.

138. GrO: λόγος σαπρός.

139. GrO: σεαυτὸν ἁγνὸν τήρει. Ed. note: Confirming Bavinck's point here, according to Cremer, "The expression, ἐν πάσῃ ἁγνείᾳ, in 1 Tim. 5:2, may, indeed, grammatically be referred to the whole clause, and would not be unsuitable, compare with 4:12 and 5:22; but it may also be more closely conjoined with the last words, παρακάλει . . . νεωτέρας ὡς ἀδελφὰς ἐν π. ἁγν.;—ἁγνεία would then denote the chastity which shuts out whatever impurity of spirit or manner might be mixed up with the παράκλησις" (Cremer, Biblico-Theological Lexicon, s.v. "Ἁγνεία, purity").

140. GrO: καθαρίσατε χεῖρας.

141. GrO: ἁγνίσατε καρδίας.

142. Ed. note: Bavinck also provides Heb. 12:28 as a reference here, which does not seem relevant to the point he is making about proper shame.

143. GrO: ἁγνεία.

144. Ed. note: Bavinck adds "(ancient High German: chûsci, Middle High German: kiusche, from kiusan, to choose; cf. Hebrew: kosher, Latin: castus)." See Vilmar, Theologische Moral, 2/3:138–41; Burger, "Keuschheit," 661–63; Rothe, Theologische Ethik, 4:38–43 (§§917–20).

145. Cf. also Pictet, De christelyke zedekunst, 647–52 (VII.xiv).

146. Marginal note by Bavinck: "God the Father cares for us, but also for our possessions."

147. Interlinear note by Bavinck: "God is the Owner, Possessor, Sovereign, Creator! Animals have no property. Man is the image of God, lord, even though he comes from the earth."

dress and keep it (Gen. 2:15), and he commanded him to subdue the earth (Gen. 1:28). He divided the inheritance among the nations (Deut. 32:8) and determined the bounds of their habitation (Acts 17:26). On this rests the right to culture—cultivation, labor, consciously putting a human stamp on [nature][148]—and therefore to possessions and private property. The legal basis of private property is sometimes difficult to establish, and often varies. One can be the owner of something through occupation, such as land and its fish, animals, and birds; through purchase (Abraham bought the cave of Machpelah); through a gift (God gave Palestine to Israel); through inheritance; through long-term possession; and so on.[149]

There soon arose among people the contrast between rich and poor. The socialists contend that the formation of capital is a phenomenon of modern times, found sporadically in the Middle Ages through trade with Venice and the East, found more often after the Reformation, and especially after the loosening of all ties and the opening of society to competition as a result of the French Revolution. However, there has always been capital formation, though in ancient times and among primitive peoples it came in the form of material things: cattle, hunting tools, land, tents, clothing, jewelry, and so forth.[150] Nevertheless, there is some validity to the claim of the socialists:[151] in the Middle Ages people were unaware of the power of money, of capital; money was regarded as something inert that produces nothing, and so people refused to charge interest on their loans. In those days everything was bound; today everything is free. Back then everything was immobile; today everything is mobile. Back then the chief factor was labor; today it is capital. Back then agriculture, the trades, and crafts were highly regarded, and commerce was held in contempt; today almost the reverse. Back then money was nothing; today it is everything.[152] Earlier there was only barter trade: one product would be exchanged for another. Every person needed only a small portion of the products they themselves produced, but needed other people's products, and that is how barter arose.

But this barter exchange proved inadequate, for sometimes the one who wanted to trade already had enough of what was being offered in exchange. Thus, something like a means of exchange had to be found that would always

148. DO: *bewerking, arbeid, stempeling met gedachte.*
149. Marginal note by Bavinck: "Not of private property, (a) man is lord, image of God, (b) for the sake of fulfilling our moral calling, (c) right, righteousness, equity/fairness, mercy."
150. Interlinear note by Bavinck: "And then in Phoenicia, in Greece after the Persian Wars, in Rome; von Hellwald, *Kulturgeschichte in ihrer natürlichen Entwicklung*, 1:93–101."
151. Cf. Uhlhorn, *Das Christenthum und das Geld*, 7–10.
152. Uhlhorn, *Das Christenthum und das Geld*, 9.

be practical for everyone and that no one ever had in sufficient quantity. Initially that was cattle (Latin *pecus, pecunia*): in Homer the armor of Diomedes cost nine oxen, that of Glaucus one hundred. In Abyssinia, salt served as a means of exchange; in Africa, some kind of shell; in Newfoundland, dried cod; in Virginia, tobacco; and so on. But gradually, and very quickly, metal came into use as a means of exchange. The Spartans used iron, the Romans copper, unminted until Servius Tullius. People had to personally test and weigh those pieces or bars of metal. Abraham weighed out the four hundred shekels of silver (Gen. 23:16). In civilized countries, the minting of metal by the government came into use, and the weight was indicated on the edge or the surface of the coin. The oldest names of coins are thus taken from the act of weighing: *as* (Latin), *livre* (French), *pound* (English).[153] Similarly in Greek. But money, originally a means, has today become the goal of every pursuit; it has become the soul of commerce, a virtually boundless and all-dominant power.

To be sure, on the one hand wealth is indeed a good thing in Scripture; it is a privilege, a gift and blessing of God. Abraham was very rich in cattle, silver, and gold (Gen. 13:2; cf. 14:23). In the Old Testament, wealth was limited and private property was maintained by the law of Moses. The Lord makes rich and he makes poor (1 Sam. 2:7; Prov. 22:2); the blessing of the Lord makes rich (Prov. 10:22); Solomon received from God riches and honor (1 Kings 3:13; 10:23; 1 Chron. 29:12; 2 Chron. 1:12), as did Jehoshaphat (2 Chron. 18:1) and Hezekiah (2 Chron. 32:27). Riches and honor are tied to wisdom (Prov. 8:18). Jesus was with the rich in his death (Isa. 53:9). One may not curse a rich man (Eccl. 10:20). Riches are a reward for diligence (Prov. 10:4), for humility (Prov. 22:4); they are a gift of God (Eccles. 5:18; 6:2); wisdom and money are a defense (Eccles. 7:11–12). All good gifts are from above (James 1:17); parents must gather treasures for their children (2 Cor. 12:14); God richly provides us with everything to enjoy (1 Tim. 6:17b); and these are good when received with thanksgiving (1 Tim. 4:4).

But the warnings against riches are more plentiful. Proverbs 23:4: "Do not toil to acquire wealth." Proverbs 28:20: "Whoever hastens to be rich will not go unpunished." Jeremiah 9:23: "Let not the rich man boast in his riches." Trusting in riches is strongly condemned (Pss. 49:7; 52:7; Prov. 11:28); such a person will fall (Prov. 11:28) and be abandoned by wealth (Jer. 17:11). Recall Agur's prayer: "Give me neither poverty nor riches" (Prov. 30:8). This warning is stronger still in the New Testament, which has not a single word of comfort

---

153. Winkler Prins, *Geillustreerde Encyclopaedie*[1], s.v. "Geld" (7:430); Winkler Prins, *Geillustreerde Encyclopaedie*[1], s.v. "Munt" (10:724).

for the rich. Recall that Jesus himself was poor (Luke 9:58; 2 Cor. 8:9).[154] In Matthew 19:23 we are told that a rich man shall enter into the kingdom of heaven "only with difficulty"[155] (cf. Mark 10:25; Matt. 19:24 par. Luke 18:25: it is "easier for a camel to go through the eye of a needle . . .").[156] Jesus speaks woe against the rich: "for you have received your consolation" (Luke 6:24). Concerning property, Jesus himself acquired none, and he refused to arbitrate when two brothers quarreled about an inheritance. He considers that rich man to be a fool who "lays up treasure for himself and is not rich toward God" (Luke 12:21).[157] He bids the rich young ruler to give away everything (Matt. 19) and sends out his disciples without provisions (Matt. 10:9–10). He pronounces the poor blessed (Luke 6:20; Matthew adds "in spirit").

He blames the "deceitfulness of riches" when the Word bears no fruit (Matt. 13:22). He admonishes people to invite to dinner not their rich neighbors but instead the poor, the blind, and the like (Luke 14:12–13). In all kinds of ways he shows concern for the poor, preaches the gospel to them (Luke 7:22), commends them to us (Matt. 26:11; John 10:28), praises the poor widow (Mark 12:43), and warns against "lay[ing] up . . . treasures on earth" (Matt. 6:19). Paul says the same: "Those who desire to be rich fall into temptation" (1 Tim. 6:9), but having "food and clothing, with these we will be content" (1 Tim. 6:8). He commands the rich "not to be haughty, nor to set their hopes on the uncertainty of riches" (1 Tim. 6:17). The apostle James is very blunt: "But the rich should take pride in their humiliation—since they will pass away like a wild flower" (1:10 NIV). "Listen, my beloved brothers, has not God chosen those who are poor in the world to be rich in faith and heirs of the kingdom, which he has promised to those who love him?" (2:5). And immediately adds, "Are not the rich the ones who oppress you, and the ones who drag you into court?" (2:6); and then finally: "Come now, you rich, weep and howl for the miseries that are coming upon you" (5:2). Holy Scripture is not favorable toward wealth.[158] For these reasons, Jesus has been accused of being an Ebionite,[159] and Christianity of false asceticism, of depreciating the

---

154. Regarding Jesus's poverty, see Buddeus, *Institutiones Theologiae Dogmaticae*, 781–83 (book IV, chap. 2, §21).

155. GrO: δυσκόλως.

156. GrO: εὐκοπώτερον, κάμηλον διὰ τρυπήματος ῥαφίδος εἰσελθεῖν. Ed. note: Bavinck is following Tischendorf's text edition of Luke 18:25.

157. GrO: εἰς θεόν.

158. Cynics and Stoics also despised wealth (Diogenes). But Socrates said to Antisthenes, "I can see your vanity through the holes in your cloak."

159. Renan, *Renan's Life of Jesus*, 114: "Pure *ebionism* then—the doctrine that the poor (*ebionim*) alone will be saved, that the reign of the poor is at hand—was the doctrine of Jesus." Ed. note: Bavinck said that Renan claimed Jesus was an Essene and provides a general reference

natural. Add to this that the early Christian church lived in a community of shared property (Acts 2:44–45),[160] and the socialists call Jesus the first socialist (Proudhon and others).

This perspective continued to dominate throughout the early Christian centuries. Wealth was considered to be dangerous. Many who converted to Christianity surrendered their property. Later, voluntary poverty was officially elevated by the church as a higher virtue, with the claim that there can be no holiness where there is no true poverty.[161] This was a "counsel"[162] (of perfection) for monks and ascetics that was higher than the "precepts"[163] for the laity.[164] Throughout the Middle Ages the deeply held notion was dominant that the original, normal situation was that property was not private but shared.[165] Sin is the cause of "mine and thine"; the acknowledgment of private property is a concession. Poverty is morally superior to wealth; out of necessity wealth was permitted to Christians who lived in the world.

The Reformation restored the rights of the natural.[166] Luther sees something good in eating, drinking, wealth, and so on; wealth, intelligence, and beauty are gifts of God.[167] Wealth is the smallest gift, beneath beauty, health, intelligence, and so forth. "That is why our Lord God usually gives wealth to the coarse donkeys, to whom he otherwise grudges nothing."[168] Calvin says

---

to chap. 11 of Renan's book, which has the title "The Kingdom of God Conceived as the Accession to Power of the Poor." There is no mention of the Essenes in either the French original or the English translation. Bavinck also refers to Graetz, *History of the Jews*, 150, who does connect Jesus with the Essenes:

> Jesus must, from the idiosyncrasies of his nature, have been powerfully attracted by the Essenes, who led a contemplative life apart from the world and its vanities. When John the Baptist—or more correctly the Essene—invited all to come and receive baptism in the Jordan, to repent and prepare for the Kingdom of Heaven, Jesus hastened to obey the call, and was baptized by him. Although it cannot be proved that Jesus was formally admitted into the order of the Essenes, much in his life and work can only be explained by the supposition that he had adopted their fundamental principles. Like the Essenes, Jesus highly esteemed self-inflicted poverty, and despised the mammon of riches.

160. Cf. Kuyper, "De Liefde X."

161. LO: *Non potest esse sanctitas, ubi non est vera paupertas.*

162. LO: *consilium.*

163. LO: *praecepta.*

164. LO: *consilium; praecepta.* Marginal note by Bavinck: "Augustine says: stolen goods are had by those who enjoy abundance, etc."

165. The Middle Ages honored a theory that today would pass for socialism, says Dr. Heinrich von Eicken, *Geschichte und System der mittelälterlichen Weltanschauung*, 496–97; cf. van der Wijck, "Twee pleibezorgers van den godsdienst," 360; Uhlhorn, *Das Christenthum und das Geld*, 13, 23.

166. Uhlhorn, *Das Christenthum und das Geld*, 24.

167. Uhlhorn, *Das Christenthum und das Geld*, 24.

168. GO: *Darum gibt unser Herr Gott gemeinlich Reichthum den groben Eseln, denen er sonst nichts gönnet.*

that two errors must be avoided: on the one hand, allowing earthly goods only for necessities; on the other, a luxurious lifestyle.[169] The basic rule is, property must be used for the purpose for which God created it; thus, not merely for alleviating want but also for making life more pleasant. God also created flowers and gave gold, silver, and ivory their glitter and glamor. Yet excess must be avoided as well, by thanking God for his gift. Gratitude and intemperance cannot go together. Moreover, this life is subordinate to the heavenly life. We must be on guard against overestimating earthly goods. We should remember that someday we will have to give an account.

This was the judgment of almost all Reformed people. Commentaries on Heidelberg Catechism, Lord's Day 50, about the fourth petition of the Lord's Prayer, usually said: We are allowed to pray for wealth—that is, wealth taken in the sense of what is needed for one's sustenance, which is different for a king than for a subject. If God gives more than what is needed, this excess must not immediately be thrown away but must be saved, as was done by Joseph (Gen. 41:46–49), and by Jesus (John 6:12; cf. Acts 11:28–29; Prov. 30:8). The Reformation has taught us to see wealth as a good, although it was not blind to its dangers. Many pious people today are rich yet miserly. To combat that, the Anabaptists in Münster wanted communal property. And many Christian sects are more or less hostile toward wealth. Fichte (to a degree) and today's socialists want to destroy wealth, prevent the accumulation of capital, and abolish actual money.[170]

Both poverty and wealth come with grave dangers. Poverty, too, is not desirable; it often causes moral regression, dishonesty, and indifference. Agur's prayer is very wise: "Give me neither poverty not riches; feed me with the food that is needful for me" (Prov. 30:8). The embarrassments of poverty and the temptations of wealth are both perilous.[171] Nevertheless, in the abstract it is impossible to fix a level above which a person is not allowed to increase their wealth. Wealth, like poverty, is a very relative concept. Some will say that to be rich is to own more than you need, and to be poor is to have less than you need. But Croesus says: He is rich who can support an entire army for a whole year. Our liturgical marriage form says it so beautifully: "Work faithfully in your daily calling, that you may support your family and also help those in need" (cf. Eph. 4:28).[172] Reinhard says that it is even a duty to seek earthly goods, and he believes that the warnings of Scripture in passages such as

169. Calvin, *Institutes*, III.x; cf. Lobstein, *Die Ethik Calvins*, 108–10.
170. Fischer, *J. G. Fichte und seine Vorgänger*, 535.
171. Rothe, *Theologische Ethik*, 4:43–51 (§923).
172. Ed. note: The liturgical form for the solemnization of marriage used in Bavinck's church in the nineteenth century goes back to the Synod of Dort. A contemporary English translation,

Matthew 10:37–39, Mark 10:23–27, and 1 Corinthians 1:26–28[173] are valid
only for their time, when wealth was very harmful in connection with persecution, and the Jews viewed the messianic kingdom as an external kingdom;
or else, he says, the pronouncements applied only to specific people (Acts 6:2;
Matt. 19:16–26; Mark 10:17–27; Luke 18:18–27), or they must be interpreted
differently.[174] Mark 10:24–25 is about entering the kingdom of heaven, about
accepting Jesus's teaching, not about being saved. Pursuing wealth is a good
thing, because loving God and neighbor is the most vital activity for the good
of the world, which is not possible without having wealth. Nowadays, without
money you cannot accomplish very much for the kingdom of God. Moreover,
the desires for honor, wealth, and power are ineradicable desires of our heart,
desires that are not wrong in themselves; but these desires simply must be
sanctified. Money is a means for cultural refinement, for the formation of
the mind, the heart; and many believers were rich (Matt. 27:57). Helvetius,
in his work *De l'homme*, severely attacked the Christian disdain for wealth
and pointed out how harmful this attitude was.[175] But elsewhere, Reinhard
acknowledges that poverty does have a few advantages as well.[176] To be sure,
it can often be an occasion for idleness, laziness, mendicancy, theft, robbery,
sycophancy, uncleanliness, foulness, and murder.[177] The poor constitute the
greatest population of prisons. But poverty can also be a stimulus to effort,
frugality, moderation, helpfulness, humility, meekness, and trust in God. Many
a great person came from the lower classes.

What about voluntary poverty? Some take voluntary poverty as a vow,
perhaps sometimes for the sake of a noble vocation (Socrates gave instruction
free of charge), for the sake of the kingdom of heaven (Jesus; Paul, 1 Cor.

from which our translation is taken, is available from the website of the Canadian and American
Reformed Churches, https://canrc.org/forms/form-for-the-solemnization-of-marriage.

173. Ed. note: In Matt. 10:37–39 Jesus warns his disciples against loving family more than
him and the necessity of losing own's life through cross-bearing; in Mark 10:23–37 he tells them,
to their amazement, that it is more difficult for a rich man to enter the kingdom of God than
for a camel to go through the eye of a needle; in 1 Cor. 1:26–28 the apostle Paul describes the
Corinthian Christians as being uninfluential, of lowly status, and foolish by worldly standards.

174. Reinhard, *System der christlichen Moral*, 3:6–16 (§266).

175. Ed. note: Bavinck obtained this reference to Helvetius from Reinhard, *System der christlichen Moral*, 3:16n1; neither Reinhard nor Bavinck provides further bibliographic information
(see Helvetius, *De l'homme*, in the bibliography). Claude Adrien Helvétius (1715–71) was a
materialist and utilitarian; in his major work *De l'esprit* (*On Mind*), he argued that all human
faculties arise from sensation and that self-interest is the only motive for human action. *De
l'homme* was published posthumously (Wikipedia, s.v. "Claude Adrien Helvétius," https://en
.wikipedia.org/wiki/Claude_Adrien_Helv%C3%A9tius).

176. Reinhard, *System der christlichen Moral*, 4:548–68 (§442).

177. DO: *ledigheid*; *luiheid*; *bedelarij*; *diefstal*; *roverij*; *onzindelijkheid*; *kruiperij*; *gruw-
zaamheid*; *moord*.

4:12), or for the sake of one's fatherland.[178] Nonetheless, such vows are to be condemned because they fail to supply the virtues people expect from them and render impossible other virtues, like generosity, compassion, and help. Furthermore, a vow of poverty in itself is open to other dangers—pride, self-righteousness, idleness, mendicancy—and does not put to death the seed of sin within us, but at most supplies sin with a different form of manifestation.

In connection with seeking and possessing wealth, we must always remember that we are stewards, that we have brought nothing into the world and will carry nothing out (1 Tim. 6:7–8), that we should not become arrogant (1 Tim. 6:17), nor put our trust in wealth (Jer. 9:23; Pss. 49:6; 52:7). Thus, we are to guard against the two vices of covetousness and wastefulness.

Covetousness is strongly and repeatedly forbidden in Scripture:

- "If riches increase, set not your heart on them" (Ps. 62:10).
- "Incline my heart to your testimonies, and not to selfish gain!" (Ps. 119:36).
- "Whoever is greedy for unjust gain troubles his own household, but he who hates bribes will live" (Prov. 15:27).
- "Woe to those who join house to house" (Isa. 5:8).
- "Take care, and be on your guard against all covetousness" (Luke 12:15).

Ephesians 5:3, 5, and 1 Corinthians 6:10 teach that no covetous person will inherit the kingdom of God.

- "Put to death therefore what is earthly in you: . . . covetousness, which is idolatry" (Col. 3:5).
- "As for the rich in this present age, charge them not to be haughty, nor to set their hopes on the uncertainty of riches, but on God, who richly provides us with everything to enjoy" (1 Tim. 6:17).
- "Keep your life free from love of money" (Heb. 13:5).

Jesus provides the basic warning: "You cannot serve God and money" (Luke 16:13). Pagans also condemned this vice,[179] and they mocked Hermocrates,

---

178. Ed. note: Bavinck supplies the following two references: "Phocion, in Nepos 1; Epaminondas, in Nepos 4"; he took the references to Cornelius Nepos from Reinhard, *System der christlichen Moral*, 4:562, notes *p* and *q*. The reference is to Cornelius Nepos, author of *De viris illustrabus*. For ET, see Nepos, *Lives of Eminent Commanders* (2015); Nepos, *Lives of Eminent Commanders* (trans. Watson [1886]). Phocion is no. XIX (pp. 405–8); Epaminondas is no. XV (pp. 375–84). The online version of Watson's translation comes from a number of different published versions.

179. Cf. also Pictet, *De christelyke zedekunst*, 747–48.

who made himself heir to his own estate.[180] "For the love of money is a root of all kinds of evils" (1 Tim. 6:10), including stealing, robbing, hating, envying, murder, and manslaughter.[181]

This love of money[182] is a sin against God, against the neighbor, against oneself, against every Christian virtue: faith, love, compassion, generosity, and more. It leads to lies, falsehood, perjury, deceit, theft, fraud, wagering, lottery, gambling, counterfeiting, advertising techniques,[183] bankruptcy, indebtedness, betrayal, and murder; think of Judas! Covetousness enslaves people more than any other drive. The miser[184] is drawn away from God (cf. Matt. 13), falls into all kinds of temptations (1 Tim. 6:9), and lives in constant unrest, fear, and anxiety. This love of money[185] is manifested in two forms: in hoarding what one has and in pursuing what one does not have—in other words, stinginess and avarice.[186]

The other vice is wastefulness,[187] which can be practiced not only with respect to money and property but also with respect to physical and spiritual strength, to words, work, time, and energy. This evil consists not so much in the quantity wasted as in the proportion between what one spends and what one has. Thus, the poor, too, can often be guilty of wastefulness and incur more poverty.[188] "Wealth gained hastily will dwindle, but whoever gathers little by little will increase it" (Prov. 13:11). "Whoever loves pleasure will be a poor man; he who loves wine and oil will not be rich" (Prov. 21:17). Consider as well those passages where extravagance and luxury are condemned: Isaiah 5:11–12; Ezekiel 16:49; Amos 6:4–6; Luke 16:19–31. The root of wastefulness

180. Ed. note: Bavinck obtains the reference to Hermocrates from Pictet, *De christelyke zedekunst*, 748. He also adds references to Juvenal, *Satura*, 14; Molière, *The Miser* (*L'Avare*). Pictet cites the following passage from Juvenal in which the poet answers the question of "what measure of fortune is enough": "as much as thirst, cold, and hunger demand" (*Mensura tamen quae sufficiat census, siquis me consulat, edem: in quantam sitis atque fames et frigora poscunt*). Translation by G. G. Ramsay, LCL 91:286–87.

181. DO: *stelen, roven, haten, benijden, moord, doodslag*. Ed. note: This list was an interlinear note by Bavinck. Bavinck does not cite the Dutch *Statenvertaling*—which has *geldgierigheid* (avariciousness for money) for 1 Tim. 6:10—exactly here; his manuscript simply has *gierigheid*, which can be taken as avarice and as miserliness, as Bavinck indicates in the next paragraph.

182. Ed. note: To prevent confusion arising from Bavinck's distinction at the conclusion of this paragraph, we have translated *gierigheid* here in a general sense.

183. DO: *reclamemiddelen*.

184. DO: *gieraard*.

185. Ed. note: We have supplied the subject for this sentence; Bavinck uses the impersonal "zij openbaart zich."

186. DO: *gierigheid (schraperigheid)*, *hebzucht*; LO: *avaritia*; GrO: πλεονεξία, φιλαργυρία.

187. DO: *verkwisting*. Interlinear note by Bavinck: "LO: *gula, ebrietas* (gluttony, revelry), food, drink, dress, luxury, excess/superabundance, the right to luxury. God lets flowers grow and covers them with splendor."

188. Wuttke, *Handbuch der christlichen Sittenlehre*[3], 2:112.

is pleasure seeking (Prov. 23:30–35; Luke 15:13–16). Wastefulness is the work of the fool (Prov. 21:20).

Between these two vices is frugality, that genuine Dutch thriftiness that can easily, however, become stinginess, tightfistedness, parsimoniousness, avariciousness.[189] Jesus himself practiced frugality (John 6:12) and taught it (Luke 15:8–10; cf. Isa. 65:8). Two virtues in particular are being taught in this Eighth Commandment: righteousness (faithfulness in our work, being honest, just, etc.) and compassion (care of the poor), gentleness, charity, clemency.

Concern for Honor and Reputation: The Ninth Commandment[190]

Scripture is concerned about our good name and reputation: "A good name is to be chosen rather than great riches, and favor is better than silver or gold" (Prov. 22:1). "A good name is better than precious ointment, and the day of death than the day of birth" (Eccles. 7:1). And this is said about our Lord: "And Jesus increased . . . in favor with God and man" (Luke 2:52). Elders in the church are required to have a good reputation among outsiders (1 Tim. 3:7). That is also why we may defend our good name: "Answer a fool according to his folly" (Prov. 26:5). "In your hearts honor Christ the Lord as holy, always being prepared to make a defense to anyone who asks you for a reason for the hope that is in you; yet do it with gentleness and respect, having a good conscience, so that, when you are slandered, those who revile your good behavior in Christ may be put to shame" (1 Pet. 3:15–16). Paul defends himself (cf. Acts 16:28) against his slanderers (2 Cor. 11:21–30) and will not allow others to make his boast vain (1 Cor. 9:15). And Jesus appeals to the reputation of his good works (John 10:32; cf. 8:46; 18:37). Honor and a good name are great goods; honor lost—greatest loss.[191] And self-defense is not pride; modesty can go hand in hand with self-esteem, self-respect, knowing one's own worth, for Christians know their worth through and in God (1 Cor. 15:10). We are to give honor to whom honor is due (Rom. 13:7). It is wrong, however, to accept honor from people and not seek honor from God, since honor from God is higher (Pss. 3:3; 73:24; 112:9; John 5:44; 12:26, 43; Rom. 2:6–11; 5:2).

189. DO: *schrilheid*; *karigheid*; *krenterigheid*.

190. The Anabaptists disapprove of seeking public office and honorary posts; the Quakers reject all public honor and homage (Reinhard, *System der christlichen Moral*, 3:52, note). Is one permitted to strive for posthumous honor? Uhland refused any knighthood; see Kübel, "Ehre," 106. Ed. note: The reference is to Ludwig Uhland (1787–1862), the German poet, philologist, literary historian, and politician.

191. DO: *eer verloren—veel verloren*. Ed. note: This is captured by a quotation from Publilius Syrus: "He who has forfeited his honor can lose nothing more." *The Moral Sayings of Publius Syrus: A Roman Slave*, 31 (#264).

Seeking honor from people but not from God is what the Pharisees did (John 5:44); at that point, then we are more concerned about appearances than about reality, about what others think of us rather than about what we are in reality—that is, what we are to God—concerned more about the image we project upon other people's consciousness than about our true being. Then we become hypocrites, we become false; we focus on and conduct ourselves according to a false standard, according to a human standard, human customs, mores, society, and so on. By contrast, Paul's statement is relevant: "But with me it is a very small thing that I should be judged by you. . . . It is the Lord who judges me" (1 Cor. 4:3–4; cf. Matt. 5:11; Acts 5:41). If we are not vindicated today, then tomorrow—"So shall my righteousness answer for me in time to come" (Gen. 30:33 KJV)[192]—or else in the final judgment. Honor is important but is not everything.[193] Ambition strives to please people by means of pontificating, passion, flattery, and posturing.[194] Ambition seeks fame, praise, and an immortal reputation with contemporaries and descendants. It enslaves us to other people's judgment, induces us to hunger for the sensational impact.[195] Honor is an awesome power, an ethical bond between people. To lose one's good name in society results in standing entirely on the outside, all by oneself, alone (boycotted), a "broken-off leaf soon to wither away."[196] Honor is the reflex of our character in the consciousness of people. God himself seeks his honor, defends his good name, and is jealous (Exod. 14:4; 1 Sam. 2:30; Ps. 46:10; Isa. 42:8, 48:11; Ezra 8:22; John 5:23; Rom. 11:36; 16:27). And for people, honor is a gift and a blessing (Pss. 7:1–8; 49:12; 84:11; Prov. 3:16, 35; 8:18; 11:16; 21:21; 22:4; 29:23; Phil. 2:29).[197] For that reason, Paul preferred to work with his hands (Acts 18:3; 20:33–35; 1 Cor. 9:4–6; 2 Cor. 11:7; 12:13–15). God himself admonishes us to let our good works be seen by others (Matt. 5:16; Phil. 2:15; Eph. 5:8). He personally promises Abraham a great name (Gen. 12:2; cf. Josh. 6:27; 1 Sam. 18:7, 30). Paul repeatedly emphasizes the need for a good reputation (Acts 6:3; Rom. 14:18; 16:7; 2 Cor. 4:2; 5:11; 9:2, 4; 1 Tim. 5:10; Titus 1:6; 2:15; 3 John 12), also among unbelievers (Acts 16:2; 22:12; Rom. 14:16; 2 Cor. 6:3; Col. 4:5; 1 Tim. 3:7; 5:14; Titus 2:5, 8; 1 Pet. 2:12; 2 Pet. 2:2).[198]

192. LO: *Cras mihi respondebit justitia mea.*
193. Martensen, *Christian Ethics, Special Part,* 2/1:353–58 (§151).
194. DO: *prediking; toorn; vleierij; houding.*
195. DO: *knaleffect.*
196. Wuttke, *Christian Ethics,* 2:254 (§123).
197. Wuttke, *Christian Ethics,* 2:331 (§150). Ed. note: Bavinck takes this and the preceding series of Scripture references directly from Wuttke.
198. Ed. note: Bavinck refers here to "Wuttke, *Handbuch*³, 1:446f." (*Christian Ethics,* 2:313ff. [§145ff.]). Wuttke deals with honor on pp. 330–32 but the discussion is general, does not refer specifically to the apostle Paul, and uses different Scripture texts. Martensen, on the other hand,

To defend one's honor by means of the duel ("a duel is war") is reprehensible.[199] It is a remnant from the medieval custom of judgment by ordeal and was very common among the knights. It assumes that the one that loses is the guilty party. This duel must not be confused with a contest like that between David and Goliath (1 Sam. 17:8–51; cf. 2 Sam. 2:14–17) or with a similar custom among the Romans. All moralists condemn dueling—which, however, is still popular in America, and among army officers and university students in Germany. It is a senseless way of defending one's honor. After all, the duel has no relation whatever to the insults: it makes no sense that insulting someone (e.g., by calling them a fraud, traitor, fornicator, or perjurer) can be erased by shedding blood. Someone can be a mean scoundrel and still have the courage to engage in this form of combat.

The coward is certainly not always the offender. Furthermore, there is absolutely no certainty that the innocent party will not be killed. The duel is not a divine judgment. Furthermore, it constitutes reckless playing with life: in principle, it is suicide or possibly homicide, a form of revenge that does not befit the Christian (Rom. 12:18–19). Many duels are staged on the basis of all kinds of foolish and silly notions about honor, demonstrated in daredevilry and excessive eating and drinking.[200] It is the Christian's duty to be kindly disposed toward one's opponent (Matt. 5:25). Rothe condemns dueling,[201] though sometimes one may risk one's life for the sake of honor— when, for example, fighting for one's country, but not for the one's own honor that has been attacked and insulted. Living for what is moral within society is higher than personal honor, so one's life may not be sacrificed for mere personal honor. At most, a duel supposedly proves something, as when a certain person's courage has been insulted or cast into doubt, and he proves his courage precisely by daring to accept the challenge. Yet even then, the moral duty trumps courage. Dueling is also in conflict with the willingness to forgive, with love. It is based on excessive self-esteem.

---

does refer to the apostle Paul defending his office and his "personal worth," but without the series of Scripture texts. See Martensen, *Christian Ethics, Special Part*, 2/1:355.

199. LO: *duellum = bellum*; cf. Luthardt, review of *Zur Duellfrage*, 45; de Moor, *Commentarius Perpetuus*, 2:876. In 1844 a professor in the Dutch Military Academy (Van Bolhuis) challenged an officer to a duel (because the officer had criticized his rudeness) and consequently lost his life (Kemper, *Geschiedenis van Nederland*, 3:448–49). Even stronger: in February 1846, Van Dam van Isselt spoke to Minister Van Hall about the persecution of the press. Van Hall had said, "If what has been said [by Van Dam] were said outside this chamber I would declare it slander." The angry Van Dam issued a veiled challenge to the minister. But a duel was averted (Kemper, *Geschiedenis van Nederland*, 5:99–100).

200. Reinhard, *System der christlichen Moral*, 1:622–27 (§138); Wuttke, *Handbuch der christlichen Sittenlehre*³, 2:451–53 (§289).

201. Rothe, *Theologische Ethik*, 4:131–41 (§963).

Just as Wuttke, Rothe would like to see honor trials alongside regular courts, because the duel is not a crime and is not inherently dishonorable.[202] Even if one does not kill but only spills blood in a duel, Rousseau's question remains relevant: "What do you want to do with that blood, you savage? Do you want to drink it?[203] On December 13, 1886, a motion introduced by August Reichensperger to restrain duels was debated in the German Reichstag. A committee of fourteen members was appointed to investigate the matter. It remains to be discussed.[204]

§42. DUTIES TOWARD THE SOUL

Each of us has a distinctive individuality from birth, and although we are all human beings, we are as distinct from one other as leaves on a tree. That difference is not the result of sin. A multiplicity of gifts exists quite apart from sin as well, such as in the church, for example. Sin has simply caused all those gifts and capacities no longer to have their unity and center in love for God; it caused that diversity to become one-sidedness and self-centeredness: each person wants to be an Ego by and for oneself. God is unspeakably rich: a poet or painter can depict only a certain number of characters, of individualities, and then his well is dry, but God created millions of individual entities— plants, animals, humans. None is like the other. God never makes copies or portraits; rather, he creates. So, from birth we have differences in sex, in gifts of intellect, disposition, will, and also temperament.

Temperament[205]

The Latin word *temperamentum* means in the first place an instrument to moderate or to mitigate, and then it refers to the proper constitution of a thing, a constitution that has the right proportion. By temperament, we understand "the different tempers of the spirit in its bearing to the outer world, as determined by differences of bodily peculiarities."[206] It is an innate,

---

202. In France, a heated debate between General Boulanger and Prime Minister Floquet resulted in a duel between the two on July 13, 1888. The latter wounded the former so severely that he was unable to continue.

203. FO: *Qu'en veux tu faire de ce sang, bête féroce? Le veux tu boire?* Monod quotes Rousseau's question in his sermon on Exod. 20:13 (Monod, "Êtes-vous un meurtrier?," 239).

204. Ed. note: Bavinck's source for this story is "Die Duellfrage im Reichstag"; the 6/4 (1887) issue of *Schorers Familienblatt* was dedicated to the theme of duel, and fifteen additional short articles on the topic can be found on pp. 141–65.

205. Fouilée, *Tempérament et caractère*.

206. Wuttke, *Christian Ethics*, 2:71 (§68).

uneven relationship of the elements of our sensory nature and the influence of this relationship on our spirit. As such this is neither sinful nor wrong. Individuality is not defective or imperfect as such; it is not "an incorrect formation of the human being," nor a false and untrue natural organism.[207] Every individual does not embody the full idea of a humanity in its variation. But neither should that be the case; every individual exhibits the idea of humanity from a specific angle[208] and therefore complements the others. Humanity is the full, true human being: Christ and his church.[209] Each temperament has a basis that has been created by God and is imparted to us. The inclination to cling exclusively to this basis over against other temperaments becomes sinful, egoistic, and concupiscent only from our universal sinful condition.

People usually distinguish four temperaments.[210] The sanguine and melancholic lean more toward the side of the intellect; the choleric and phlegmatic more toward the side of will. They do differ from each other in terms of a certain kind of intensity (irritability, exuberance, agitation) or in terms of a certain kind of weakness (depression). The sanguine temperament consists of a disproportionate strength or stimulability of the intellect; the melancholic temperament consists of a disproportional weakness or depression of the

---

207. GO: *positiv unrichtige Formation des menschlichen Seins*; Rothe, *Theologische Ethik*, 1:496 (§132). Even more strongly in Schopenhauer: "For at bottom every individuality is really only a special error, a false step, something that had better not be; nay, something which is the real end of life to bring us back from" (*The World as Will and Idea*, 3:286). Ed. note: Schopenhauer's "solution" for human blessedness is that every person "become what he is not . . . cease to be what he is" (*The World as Will and Idea*, 3:286). Bavinck likely took the Schopenhauer quote from Rothe, *Theologische Ethik*, 1:496, note * (§132). Rothe's comment: "Which, of course, overshoots the target" (GO: *Was freilich weit, uber das Ziel hinausschietst*). After the Schopenhauer quote, Bavinck adds, "Similarly, many mystics" (*Zo ook vele mystici*).

208. DO: *van een bijzondere zijde*.

209. Ed. note: This cryptic sentence is stated more completely in *RD*, 2:577: "Not the man alone, nor the man and woman together, but only the whole of humanity is the fully developed image of God, his children, his offspring. The image of God is much too rich for it to be fully realized in a single human being, however richly gifted that human being may be. It can only be somewhat unfolded in its depth and riches in a humanity counting billions of members. Just as the traces of God (*vestigia Dei*) are spread over many, many works, in both space and time, so also the image of God can only be displayed in all its dimensions and characteristic features in a humanity whose members exist both successively one after the other and contemporaneously side by side."

210. Ed. note: Bavinck briefly alluded to these temperaments when he observed that the human "moral disposition . . . is shaped by differences of social class, environment, and personal temperament" (*RE*, 1:229). The four classic personality types hark back to the Greek physician Hippocrates and were tied to the notion of four bodily "humors": the sanguine (blood: optimistic and social), choleric (yellow bile: short-tempered or irritable), melancholic (black bile: pensive, withdrawn), and phlegmatic (phlegm and other clear body liquids: relaxed, peaceful, passive, emotional) (Greek Medicine.Net, "The Four Humors," http://www.greekmedicine.net /b_p/Four_Humors.html).

intellect. The choleric temperament is the disproportionate strength of the will, while the phlegmatic temperament is the disproportionate weakness of the will. For this reason, the sanguine and the melancholic temperaments are mutually exclusive, as are the choleric and the phlegmatic temperaments. But the sanguine and the choleric can go together, and so can the melancholic and the phlegmatic; in fact, they are usually connected in some way.

The sanguine and the phlegmatic are also mutually exclusive, as are the choleric and the melancholic. The sanguine and the melancholic tempera-ments are seated especially in the feelings,[211] which constitute the strength of the former and the weakness of the latter. The choleric and phlegmatic tem-peraments are seated especially in the drives,[212] which constitute the strength of the former and the weakness of the latter.[213]

The sanguine temperament tends toward enjoyment and naïveté,[214] is open and receptive to external impressions, more receiving than giving, more stimulable than spontaneous. Therefore, it is especially the temperament of childhood. It is the gift of God for receptivity to the things of this world, to the joy in the world; it is the basis of the *charismata* of teaching, helping, and comforting.[215] This temperament enables a person to move about in the world with ease, to enjoy the fullness and delight of life, and to have an eye for what is beautiful, grand, and noble. It induces one to live entirely in the present, for the moment, to live from one day to the next, moving easily from one thing to another.

But it also has its shadowy side: it can easily turn into concupiscence, reveling in sin, being obsequious,[216] and carnal desire. In Martensen's words: "But the same temperament opposes great hindrances to the fulfilment of duty, because it disposes to flightiness, superficiality, and so to split up life into an unconnected multiplicity, as well as, finally, to indecision and unreliability."[217] An example of this sanguine temperament is Peter, whose

211. GO: *Empfindung*.
212. GO: *Trieb*.
213. Rothe, *Theologische Ethik*, 1:493–95 (§131).
214. DO: *naïeve*.
215. GrO: διδασκαλία, ἀντίληψις [ἀντιλήμψεις], παράκλησις.
216. DO: *ogendienst*.
217. Martensen, *Christian Ethics, Special Part*, 1:9; cf. Vilmar, *Theologische Moral*, 1:249ff.; Lotze, *Mikrokosmus*, 2:352. Ed. note: We have left Bavinck's reference to Vilmar as open as he did; it is not clear whether he intended to call attention to the immediately following §20 ("Sexual Sins") or to the entire chap. 3 ("Sins of the Flesh"), which also includes §20 ("Gluttony"; GO: *Bauchsünden*) and §21 ("Sins of Sloth"; GO: *Trägheitssünde*). For more on temperament, see Daub, Schleiermacher, and others in Rothe, *Theologische Ethik*. Bavinck adds no further bibliographic information, which we are adding here. Rothe, *Theologische Ethik*, 1:493, note ** (§131); Daub, *System der theologischen Moral*, 2:144–49; Schleiermacher,

personality made him energetic and unstable, leading him even to deny Jesus. Nonetheless, "transformed by grace," Peter, "with the lightly moved temperament, formerly a pliant reed, became the rock on which the Lord has built His Church."[218]

The melancholic temperament involves being passive, long-suffering,[219] and sentimental. It is the serious temperament. With respect to external impressions, the melancholic temperament is less receptive and more active; it deepens what it absorbs. It has an ideal, but often without being properly aware of its content. Such a temperament lacks self-awareness. It always looks at life from the most serious side, tends toward sadness, inclines a person to live in the past or in the future. It is the temperament particularly of the young man, especially if love awakens in him—love of the female sex, love of the ideas he absorbs but cannot yet master, love of a lofty but not entirely clear ideal. This temperament equips a person for deeper reflection, devotion to duty, not being satisfied with sensual pleasures and with the outward appearance of things. It is a gift of God for being receptive toward the ideal, toward the divine in nature and history, the basis for the *charisma* of knowledge.

But it also has its shadow side. It easily degenerates into a tendency to live by one's mood, to nurse one's melancholy, to times of "darkness,"[220] to the sentimental. The sanguine person leaps immediately from one mood to the other; the melancholic lingers for a long time in the same mood; what the sanguine person loves about the present, the moment, the melancholic esteems as trifling. As a result, the melancholic becomes impractical, dwelling mostly in the past or the future. And then the mood can change into self-satisfied and self-absorbed aloofness, into arrogant self-congratulation, into useless and fruitless brooding.[221]

The sanguine person is one-sidedly optimistic; the melancholic person is a one-sided pessimist, who sees everything from the darkest side, despises the "hum-drum" nature of existence,[222] exalting oneself high above it. The sanguine person risks surrendering to sensual sins; the melancholic to spiritual sins, to pride, to looking down with contempt on everything, to self-exaltation. An example of this temperament is the gloomy Thomas, who is thoroughly gallant but easily doubts, who turns despondent at the drop of a hat, and says,

---

Erziehungslehre, 695–97, 700, 776–77; I. von Fichte, *Psychologie*, 1:67. Rothe adds one more reference that proved to be untraceable: "Jeffen, *Versuch einer Wissenschaftl: Begründing der Psychologie*, 301ff."

218. Martensen, *Christian Ethics, Special Part*, 1:283.
219. DO: *lijdende*.
220. DO: *tot de 'zwarte' tijd*.
221. GO: *Grübeleien*.
222. DO: *het 'proza' des levens*.

"Let us also go, that we may die with him" (John 11:16). Thomas is the one who maintains his mood of disbelief about Jesus's resurrection; he refuses to accept the testimony of the other disciples and hardens himself in his doubt. Thomas was obstinate and proud, exalted himself above, and knew better than those other credulous disciples.

The choleric temperament is oriented toward the practical; with respect to impressions from the outside, it is very open and receptive, but at the same time self-motivated, affecting and impacting the outside world. It is the hot temperament. It is more characteristic of adulthood;[223] it equips a person for action, for living energetically and seizing life, displaying courage, perseverance, initiative, and strength. It is the gift of God for being busy in the world, the basis for the *charismata* of administration, governing,[224] the performance of mighty deeds (cf. 1 Cor. 12:10).[225]

But it too has a shadow side. It tends toward thoughtless fixation on a plan once decided, to passionate zealotry, inflexibility, obstinacy, hardheadedness, single-minded pursuit of a solitary goal to the exclusion of all others. The choleric easily becomes a particularist, a fanatic, a lonely eccentric who is haughty, domineering, irritable, jealously bent to his or her own goal while condemning everything else. We meet this temperament in Paul, especially before his conversion; at that time, he was a fanatic persecutor of God's church who fancied that he was doing God a service—an inflexible, hard, merciless man. But through conversion this temperament turned into a world-conquering, world-defying heroism of faith.

The phlegmatic temperament is the contemplative, quietist temperament, less receptive to external impressions and at the same time inactive and tranquil, cold; it is the temperament of peace, tranquility, stillness, reflection, levelheadedness. It is God's gift for resting in God amid the transitoriness of the world; it is the basis of faith and wisdom;[226] it makes for harmony with the world, undisturbed by passions.

The shadow side is that the phlegmatic person becomes indifferent, insensitive, sluggish, lethargic, and plodding. The phlegmatic seeks safety in a false quietism, unconcerned about the world, putting up with everything as it comes, having a cold, hard, and unfeeling heart, indifferent also with respect to sin, never becoming angry or indignant, and subscribes to the motto "live and let live."[227] We find this temperament in John, with his contemplative-

223. DO: *mannelijke leeftijd.*
224. GrO: κυβέρνησις.
225. GrO: ἐνεργήματα δυνάμεων.
226. GrO: πίστις, σοφία.
227. DO/FO: *het laisser passer huldigt.*

mystical disposition, his profound speculation, his intimate love, peace, and rest. He enjoyed leaning on Jesus's breast. Nations can also display such temperaments. The Dutch are phlegmatic, the French sanguine, the English choleric, the Germans melancholic.[228] (This is true also about churches; are Reformed churches choleric?)[229]

Now then, temperament as such is neither a vice nor a virtue. It is premoral, as Paul says: "I was once alive apart from the law" (Rom. 7:9). Aristotle distinguished between natural and ethical virtues. The natural is very important, forming the foundation for the ethical. Some people are born good-natured, mild-tempered, or good-hearted;[230] others are quick-tempered, chastely modest, seething with passion; some are thrifty, frugal, others wasteful and thoughtless. Nevertheless, not everything should be ascribed to the natural, as is done in physical determinism and evolutionism. People place blame on the sun, moon, and stars, "as if we are villains by necessity."[231]

Temperament is the soil for the moral—influences it but is not identical with it. The special calling of the responsible person is to learn to know and to supplement their own temperament from and through that of others, and thereby make their soul-life[232] normal and healthy. All persons must master their own temperament, make their personality independent of it (emancipate it), and put their temperament especially into the service of the moral personality. What is purely natural must be transformed and changed into something ethical. Temperament must be determined by the moral will and must be made moral.[233] Thus people with a sanguine temperament must not only cultivate their natural friendliness but also combat the flightiness to which such a temperament is prone. The melancholic person must guard against "selfishness and narrowness"; the choleric against "passionateness and revenge," the phlegmatic against "indifference and indolence."[234] Temperament must also be brought under the nurture and discipline of God's

---

228. This comparison of Frenchmen and Germans is found in Matyas Vallady, *France et Allemagne*, 336 (reviewed in *Deutsche Rundschau* 55).

229. Mountain dwellers differ from those of the plains, sailors from farmers, people who live on the moors from those living in clay belts. The sons of Jacob, the tribes of Israel, each have their own individuality; see Kuyper, "Twelve Sons of Jacob."

230. Rothe, *Theologische Ethik*, 3:197n (§992), referring to Reinhard, *System der christlichen Moral*, 2:74–78.

231. Edmund, in Shakespeare, *King Lear*, act 1, scene 2, line 122.

232. DO: *zielenleven*.

233. DO: *gemoraliseerd*; Rothe, *Theologische Ethik*, 2:12 (§174).

234. Wuttke, *Christian Ethics*, 2:73.

Word. That is to say: As Christians, we must shape and develop ourselves into persons of Christian *character*.

Character[235]

Character, as the inscribed mark, hallmark, and characteristic property,[236] is what has become of a person's innate nature, disposition, aptitude, temperament, and general temper, under the influence of nurture, education, social life, examples/models, experiences, and especially moral principles.[237] Character is the individuality that our personality has imparted to us and that has become second nature; it is generally "conditioned" by temperament and nature. People cannot simply choose the character they prefer. There are just as many characters as temperaments. Character always bears an ethical character. Without the action of moral principles, no character comes into existence; a person without principles is characterless.[238] Character is the product of the development of the moral life.[239] To the degree that it is mature, a character is always marked by steadiness; it inspires trust and is predictable as to what it will do. If people do not shape their temperament, do not form their aptitude, do not guide their temperament by religious-moral principles, then their sinful tendency becomes their character trait, their second nature; then characters come into being that are short-tempered, violent, reckless, loveless, hard-hearted, and so on. The inborn sinfulness then turns into a definite vice, into a self-acquired active sin and cherished inclination.[240] Christ alone is a perfectly harmonious character; all other characters are more or less one-sided.[241] He is our example; we are to model our Christian character after him. We are to grow into adulthood and not remain children in our understanding: "Be watchful, stand firm in the faith, act like men, be strong" (1 Cor. 16:13). This calls for maturity: "Let those of us who are mature[242] think this way" (Phil. 3:15).

The features of the Christian character include, first, purity.[243] This is found where character is not self-consciously determined by outside authorities, but only by love toward God, by pure moral principles, by the law of God, by

235. GrO: χαρακτήρ; Hagemann, *Was ist Charakter*[4], 5.
236. DO: *ingekrast merk; kenteken; kenmerkende eigenschaap.*
237. Beets, *Karakter, karakterschaarschte, karaktervorming,* 7. Ed. note: This was Beets's inaugural address as professor of church history at the University of Utrecht, delivered on March 16, 1875.
238. DO: *karakterloos;* Beets, *Karakter, karakterschaarschte, karaktervorming,* 7.
239. Rothe, *Theologische Ethik,* 3:220–23 (§§629–34).
240. Wuttke, *Handbuch der christlichen Sittenlehre*[2], 2:53 (§165), 102 (§176).
241. Martensen, *Christian Ethics,* 1:252 (§67): "Only in Christ do we behold that perfectly harmonious character which affords inexhaustible fulness to our contemplation."
242. GrO: τέλειοι.
243. DO: *reinheid, zuiverheid.*

what is Christian, without any admixture of pagan, Jewish, Stoic, pantheistic, humanitarian, and materialistic principles.[244]

Additionally, Christian character includes steadfastness, strength, energy, without inflexibility—firmness, like Joseph showed toward Potiphar's wife (Gen. 39:8), like Joshua recommended in order to preserve souls in loving God (Josh. 23:6, 11), and like Proverbs 4:26–27 urges, "Ponder the path of your feet; / then all your ways will be sure. / Do not swerve to the right or to the left; / turn your foot away from evil" (cf. Prov. 24:10). Christians must be "rooted and grounded in love" (Eph. 3:17), rooted and built up in Christ (Col. 1:23; 2:7), holding their "original confidence firm to the end" (Heb. 3:14), establishing their confidence through grace (Heb. 13:9), enduring to the end (Matt. 24:13), not "tossed to and fro by the waves and carried about by every wind of doctrine" (Eph. 4:14). It is God who strengthens them (Eph. 6:10), whereas they are weak in themselves (2 Cor. 12:10). God restores, confirms, strengthens, and establishes them (1 Pet. 5:10).[245]

But the widest diversity exists among the characters of Christians as a result of aptitude, temperament, time, people, country, and confession, as well. The Christian character displays a different stamp in the first, fifteenth, and nineteenth centuries. The Christian character is different among Italians, Norwegians, and other people groups. It also varies in Roman Catholic, Lutheran, and Reformed churches. There are contemplative, energetic, practical, passive, quiet, masculine, and feminine characters.[246] Our age, however, is bereft of moral characters, and even more of truly Christian characters. This age is most unfavorable for the formation of character, due to its circumstances, its ideas, its materialistic teachings and systems, its spirit, its current system of nurture and education, nihilism, and so on.[247] There are talents, which are born in quiet tranquility, but no characters, which originate only "amid the turmoil of life."[248]

244. Martensen, *Christian Ethics*, 1:339–41 (§111).
245. Wuttke, *Handbuch der christlichen Sittenlehre*[3], 2:382.
246. Martensen, *Christian Ethics*, 1:342–43 (§112).
247. Bavinck's source is Beets, *Karakter, karakterschaarschte, karaktervorming*, 12–35, passim.
248. GO: *im Geräusch der Welt*. Ed. note: Except for the citation (from Goethe), Bavinck builds this claim indirectly from Beets, *Karakter, karakterschaarschte, karaktervorming*, 25, 40. Beets asks the question "Did not the poet speak the truth?" and then, without reference to Goethe, cites two lines:

> *Es bildet ein Talent sich in der Stille,* [Talent is nurtured in solitude;]
> *Sich ein karakter in dem Strom der Welt.* (25) [character in the stormy billows of the world.]

He adds a postscript to the published work: "Concerning the quoted lines of poetry on p. 25, I am not entirely certain whether the poet (Göthe) didn't write 'im Geräusch der Welt,' but

Intellect

We are to develop a Christian character with respect to the intellect.[249] To that end we must first of all instill a love of truth—not just saving truth but also scientific truth and truth in everyday life. This love of truth is not only of formal (logical) truth—that is, not just the freedom of our propositions from contradiction—but also the love of material, factual truth. Christianity has given us knowledge of God as the Truth (John 17:3; 14:6) and given us proper love for the truth, not for its own sake (which is ultimately for our own sake, egotistically), but made possible for the sake of God. The Word, a lamp unto our feet, the truth (John 17:17), enables us to pursue truth, to recognize it, to distinguish it from the lie (Acts 17:11; 1 Cor. 2:14–16; 1 John 4:1; 1 Thess. 5:21). Indifferentism and skepticism are therefore not permitted for the Christian—are a sickness of the soul that needs healing. And we are called to abound, to mature, to grow in knowledge (Rom. 12:4–8; 1 Cor. 12 and 13; Phil. 1:9; 4:8; 1 Thess. 5:21; Titus 3:8–9; 2 Pet. 3:18).

But the arena of the intellect contains other faculties, each of which also needs to be developed. These include the capacity to pay attention and to observe, for to observe[250] is better than the fat of rams (cf. 1 Sam. 15:22). Not paying attention is a great sin (2 Chron. 33:10; Prov. 1:24; Zech. 7:11). In every field, attentiveness, both spiritual and natural, is so difficult. We must compel our senses to observe well, and we must practice this. To see, hear, touch, and read well is such an art. Next, there is memory and the capacity of recollection: the cupbearer forgot Joseph (Gen. 40:23); Israel repeatedly forgot the covenant, forgot the Lord (Deut. 4:23; 6:12; 8:11–16; 32:18), forgot God's works and wonders (Ps. 78:7, 11), forgot their Savior (Ps. 106:21); we are forgetful hearers (James 1:25). The believer, however, is seized with a desire to remember it all—God's acts of loving-kindness (Ps. 48:9), his works (Ps. 77:12)—in order to remember his word, law, and ordinances and not forget them (Ps. 119:16, 61, 83, 176). The same is true in the natural arena: kindnesses should be inscribed in marble, but insults written in sand.

I have not had the opportunity to check this" (40). The passage is from Goethe's *Torquato Tasso*, I.2.66. Translation from "Your Dictionary" at https://quotes.yourdictionary.com/author/quote/539086. Beets had it correct in his original address and should not have second-guessed himself.

249. Reinhard, *System der christlichen Moral*, 2:182–91 (§§203–4); Pictet, *De christelyke zedekunst*, 620–23; Wuttke, *Handbuch der christlichen Sittenlehre³*, 2:289–97; Dorner, *System of Christian Ethics*, 382–400 (§§46–47). Ed. note: Bavinck adds a further general reference to "Rothe." He may have had in mind *Theologische Ethik*, 3:365–69 (§806).

250. Ed. note: The *Statenvertaling* has *opmerken* (to observe, notice). English translations include "hearken" (KJV, ASV), "heed" (NIV, NRSV), "heeding orders" (CJB), "to listen" (ESV).

Next is the faculty of imagination, a marvelous capacity that makes the abstract—indeed, the entire world—come alive, often entices one to sin, transforms the idea into an ideal, and in this way arouses the desire and will to pursue it (Matt. 5:27–30; 18:8–9; Rom. 6:12; 7:7; Gal. 5:24; James 1:14–15; 1 John 2:16). Rationalism and supranaturalism were very averse to imagination, looking to it as the wellspring of all fanaticism, theosophy, and mysticism.[251] But in our century, some reaction to this antipathy has developed once again—for example, in works such as Hildebrand's *Camera obscura* and Chateaubriand's *Génie du christianisme*, in the school of Romanticism, and the like.[252]

To be sure, it is the imagination that often conceives the desire and then gives birth to death. The imagination calls up images of lust, honor, fame, power, rule, wealth, and so on in lifelike colors. It enchants us and carries us along. Eve looked at the tree. But Joseph fled from Potiphar's wife, without indulging in deliberations and arguments.[253] A person must be the master of one's thoughts, of one's imagination; one must practice self-control, preserve one's imagination from lack of restraint. Restrained, controlled imagination is eminently valuable; without it there would be no ideal, no pursuit of anything grand, no brave and mighty deed. But that is the very reason why it needs to be mastered, to be regulated by scriptural, rational considerations. Imagination must be made attentive to real truth, goodness, and beauty, not fed with bad novels, paintings, and so forth.

Because each person has ideas, and each person has a measure of imagination as well, therefore each person also has ideals, more or less lofty, numerous, grand.[254] Christianity has acquainted us with many ideals; Christ himself is the realized ideal (John 14:9; Col. 1:15–16; Heb. 4:14–15); the kingdom of God is an ideal (John 3; 18:36–37; Rom. 14:17–18; Eph. 4:1–16); and we have the ideals of perfection, of eternal salvation, of faith, of love. Christianity is an ideal spiritual world and awakens in us a longing for the ideal, for something suprasensory, eternal, spiritual. But it is our calling to give our ideals the proper content, clarity, and direction, as well as to test them against Scripture, to bring them into coherence and harmony with one another and with other principles and thoughts. Our calling is not to exaggerate the ideal of valor, for example, at the price of compassion and humility, but instead to make all of our ideals fruitful for life and not let them be a mere game

251. Cf. Reinhard, *System der christlichen Moral*, 2:196–218 (§§205–6).

252. Ed. note: Bavinck refers to Hildebrand (pseudonym of Nicolaas Beets), *Camera obscura*; Chateaubriand, *Genius of Christianity*.

253. Martensen, *Christian Ethics, Special Part*, 1:87 (§31), 411–14 (§169).

254. Reinhard, *System der christlichen Moral*, 2:315–31 (§215).

of our fantasies and dreams. We must not allow them to dominate us while neglecting and despising real life, not allow them to seduce us into discontent with what is, and so on.

Moreover, in a word, according to 2 Corinthians 10:4–5, we are to "destroy arguments[255] and every lofty opinion raised against the knowledge of God and are to take every thought captive to obey Christ."[256] To be rejected are all futile thinking (Rom. 1:21) and foolishness (Mark 7:22); all fancied, proud, external knowledge without reality or life; worldly, carnal wisdom that would measure the divine will against earthly standards (1 Cor. 1:17–25); knowledge falsely so called (1 Tim. 6:20) and vain philosophy (Col. 2:8, 23). But true knowledge and wisdom are highly esteemed in Scripture. It is more valuable than the choicest gold (Prov. 8:10). We are to grow up (2 Pet. 3:18); indeed, we are to be mature[257] in understanding (1 Cor. 14:20).

A warning is in order especially against *pedantry*. Derived from the Italian word *pedante* (steward, butler), it is a species of the genus folly.[258] Schopenhauer writes that pedantry arises from a person's lack of confidence in their own capacity to know immediately what is correct. Therefore, a pedant always places his or her understanding under the tutelage of reason and "tries always to proceed from general concepts, rules and maxims, and to confine himself strictly to them in life, in art, and even in moral conduct."[259] Thus the pedant is a stickler for form, manner, expression, and word, which function in place of the essence of things. But those maxims will not suffice; they are inadequate for living life. The pedant is thus shown to be foolish, lifeless, stilted, and artificial.[260] Pedants know things only abstractly, not concretely—as do the doctrinaires, the theoreticians, the ivory-tower scholars.[261] Thus pedants take pride in a few, often poorly understood, abstract propositions; they order their life, their conduct, and their attitude according to these few propositions; they apply them everywhere and want to judge and fashion life according to them. Directly opposite to this is the *genius*.[262] These people set aside all maxims,

255. GrO: λογισμοὺς καθαιροῦντες.
256. GrO: αἰχμαλωτίζοντες πᾶν νόημα εἰς τὴν ὑπακοὴν τοῦ Χριστοῦ; νόημα = every product of our mental capacity.
257. GrO: τέλειοι.
258. DO: *narheid*.
259. Schopenhauer, *The World as Will and Idea*, 1:78. Ed. note: In what immediately follows, Bavinck summarizes in his own words Schopenhauer's comments on pedantry.
260. DO: *onverstandig; levenloos; stijf; gemaniëreerd*.
261. Schopenhauer, *The World as Will and Idea*, 1:79: "When we speak, especially in connection with politics, of doctrinaires, theorists, savants, and so forth, we mean pedants, that is, persons who know the things well in the abstract, but not in the concrete."
262. Regarding this, see Schopenhauer, *The World as Will and Idea*, 1:238–47, 251–53; 2:245–49; 3:138–66; J. Meyer, *Probleme der Lebensweisheit*, 85ff. ("Genie und Talent"); also

including the moral ones, are led by their own discoveries and hunches, and, mocking morality, are a law unto themselves.[263]

The Formation and Development of Feelings[264]

Feelings mediate between consciousness and will. Feelings exist and initially function independently of our will. Involuntarily, we feel something affect us, agreeably or disagreeably. Nevertheless, it is our calling to cultivate our feelings. Our feelings, our passions,[265] are unregulated, disharmonious, and tend toward wrong objects. Feelings cannot and may not be left to themselves. They carry us away either to insensitivity or to hypersensitivity, emotionalism, sentimentality. The passions[266] as such are not sinful, so they need not be eradicated (as in Stoicism), but what is wrong is their undisciplined disorder.[267]

Aristotle calls the right relation to the emotions "moderation," the wrong relation "intemperance."[268] He further distinguishes both from the self-control[269] of the passions by the will and from lack of control[270] resulting from weakness of the will. The Stoics distinguished four types of passion. All passions are generated by ideas.[271] These have as their object either good or bad things, either in the present or in the future. Thus, there are four main classes: the unwise opinion about present goods breeds *craving*; about future goods, *desire*. The unwise opinion about present goods breeds *worry*; about future goods,

the poem of Nicolaas Beets, da Costa?, etc. Ed. note: Bavinck does not provide the details of the Beets poem, and the question mark after da Costa is his. Since Meyer's *Probleme der Lebensweisheit* is not available online, we were unable to specify the pages here and in the next note beyond Bavinck's terminus a quo.

263. J. Meyer, *Probleme der Lebensweisheit*, 179–98 ("Die Geschmacks- und Geniemoral").

264. DO: *gevoel*; Reinhard, *System der christlichen Moral*, 2:339–494 (§§217–37); Pictet, *De christelyke zedekunst*, 694–727; Wuttke, *Handbuch der christlichen Sittenlehre*[3], 2:297–99 (§252).

265. Ed. note: In what follows Bavinck uses the Dutch word *affecten*, which when translated into English as "affections" could be misleading. The term, from the Latin *affectus*, can also mean "desire," "emotion," or "passion," and that is the meaning in the discussion that follows. Our translations of *affecten* reflect this variety; when we use the term "affections," the reader should associate the term with the human faculty of desiring rather than any connotation with the notion of "affectionate" in ordinary English usage.

266. GrO: παθήματα; LO: *passiones*; GO: *Leidenschaft*.

267. GrO: ἀταξία.

268. Zeller, *Die Philosophie der Griechen*[3], 2/2:659. Ed. note: Bavinck's terms are *matigheid* and *onmatigheid*; Zeller's, *Mässigkeit* and *Unmässigkeit*.

269. GrO: σωφροσύνη. Ed. note: Zeller uses the term *Selbstbeherrschung*.

270. Ed. note: Bavinck's DO: *teugelloosheid*; Zeller: *Zügellosigkeit*; both words point to dissoluteness, lawlessness.

271. DO: *voorstellingen*; GO: *Vorstellungen*; Zeller, *Die Philosophie der Griechen*[3], 3/1:230.

fear.[272] Therefore, we have four classifications: pleasure and desire, grief and fear.[273] In Virgil's words about the human condition: "Hence their fears and desires, their griefs and joys."[274] These four are then divided into many subclasses.[275] For example, to grief belong pity, jealousy, zeal, distress, and sadness.[276] To fear belong fright, hesitation, shame, anguish, and alarm.[277] To pleasure belong delight and merriment.[278] And to desire belong courage, passion, and longing.[279] And these passions are all wrong, according to the Stoics; they are disruptions of spiritual health, "objectionable impulses of the spirit, sudden and vehement; they have come so often, and so little attention has been paid to them, that they have caused a state of disease."[280]

These diseases gradually become "hardened and chronic vices."[281] Moderation (as Plato and Aristotle wanted) is therefore not enough; moderation in

272. DO: *lust, begeerte, bekommering, vrees.*

273. GrO: ἡδονή and ἐπιθυμία, λύπη and φόβος.

274. LO: *hinc metuunt, cupiuntque, dolent gaudentque.* Ed. note: Bavinck does not identify the source of this quotation. It is from Virgil, *Aeneid* VI.733 (LCL 63:556–57).

275. GrO: ἔλεος = sympathy, pity; φθόνος = ill-will, envy, jealousy; ζῆλος = zeal, emulation, rivalry; ἄχθος = burden (of sorrow), distress; ὀδύνη = pain, grief, sadness.

276. GrO: λύπη: ἔλεος, φθόνος, ζῆλος, ἄχθος, and ὀδύνη.

277. GrO: δεῖμα: ὄκνος, αἰσχύνη, ἀγωνία, and δέος.

278. GrO: ἡδονή: τέρψις and διάχυσις.

279. GrO: ἐπιθυμία: μῖσος, ὀργή, and θυμός.

280. LO: *motus animi improbabiles soluti et concitati*; Seneca, *Ad Lucilium epistulae morales* I.12 ("Epistle 75") (LCL 76:142–43). Ed. note: The second clause in this sentence was added by the editor to provide transition to the one that follows.

281. LO: *inveterate vitia et dura*; Seneca, *Ad Lucilium epistulae morales* I.12 ("Epistle 75") (LCL 76:142–43). Aquinas divides the passions as follows: The appetitive power in action generates inclination (*inclinationem, seu aptitudinem, seu connaturalitatem*), propensity (movement; *motum ad assequendum*), and habit (rest; *appetitus quietationem*). The appetitive power can be inclined to the good ("love"; *amor*) or to evil ("hatred"; *odium*); it can be pulled to the good (desire or concupiscence; *desiderii vel concupiscentiae*) or drawn to evil (aversion or dislike; *fuga vel abominatio*); when it rests in the good, it finds delight or joy (*delectationem vel gaudium*), and when it rests in evil, sorrow or sadness (*dolor vel tristitia*).

Ed. note: Bavinck freely summarized Aquinas, *ST* Ia IIae q. 23 art. 4 s.c. In addition to slight editorial alteration of the preceding, we are adding the following direct quote from the article for summary and clarification:

> On the other hand, in the irascible passions, the aptitude, or inclination to seek good, or to shun evil, is presupposed as arising from the concupiscible faculty, which regards good or evil absolutely. And in respect of good not yet obtained, we have "hope" and "despair" [spes en desperatio]. In respect of evil not yet present we have "fear" and "daring" [timor et audacia]. But in respect of good obtained there is no irascible passion: because it is no longer considered in the light of something arduous. . . . But evil already present gives rise to the passion of "anger" [irae]. Accordingly, it is clear that in the concupiscible faculty there are three couples of passions; viz. love and hatred, desire and aversion, joy and sadness. In like manner there are three groups in the irascible faculty; viz. hope and despair, fear and daring, and anger which has no contrary

vice is impossible;[282] evil, even when moderate, is still an evil.[283] Such diseases must therefore be totally suppressed.

In his *Ethics* Spinoza defines passions as those emotions of our body whereby our physical and mental energy diminishes or increases, is suppressed or reinforced.[284] The principal passion, according to him, is desire. This then becomes either joy or sadness. And from these two, Spinoza derives all other affections: love and hate, hope and fear.[285] According to Spinoza they are governed by and subject to knowledge. The passive affection ceases to be an affection as soon as it is known in its essence. At the stage of clear knowledge, there is no longer any suffering or any pain. A person knows that they are one with the infinite Being, that the affections of their body and soul are merely modifications of that Being, and that love of earthly things is merely a modification of the highest love, love toward God. The knowledge of God (of the coherence of nature) is the highest form of knowledge and is necessarily connected to the highest and most blissful of all affections, the mind's love[286] toward God.

Schopenhauer writes that the will, human affections, cannot be changed. It is possible to improve someone's head, but not their heart.[287] Only regeneration could help. Passions are indeed tremendously strong, dragging us along and enslaving us in shackles. They are like a fire that consumes everything, like wild horses on the run, like waves and billows that toss us to and fro, like bullies that torture us, like tyrants that coerce us.[288]

It is true that the affections cannot be controlled, let alone be purified and sanctified, by reason and intellect. That approach results only in expelling one

---

passion. Consequently, there are altogether eleven passions differing specifically; six in the concupiscible faculty, and five in the irascible; and under these all the passions of the soul are contained.

282. LO: *mediocritas morbi*.

283. LO: *malum, etiam mediocre, malum est*; Cicero, *Tusculan Disputations* III.10 (LCL 141:252–53). Ed. note: We have corrected Bavinck's Latin here; taking the Cicero quote directly from Zeller, *Die Philosophie der Griechen*[3], 3/1:233n3, Bavinck renders the passage as "evil, even when moderate, is great" (LO: *malum, etiam mediocre, magnum est*).

284. Van Vloten, *Baruch D'Espinoza*, 284. Ed. note: Cf. Spinoza's own definition of emotion: "By EMOTION (*affectus*) I understand the modifications of the body by which the power of action in the body is increased or diminished, aided or restrained, and at the same time the ideas of these modifications" (*Spinoza's Ethics*, 86–87 [part III, proposition 2]).

285. Ed. note: See Spinoza, *Spinoza's Ethics*, 98 (part II, proposition 18, n. 2).

286. LO: *amor intellectualis*. Ed. note: See Spinoza, *Spinoza's Ethics*, 159: "The greatest good of the mind is the knowledge of God, and the greatest virtue of the mind is to know God" (part IV, proposition 28).

287. Schopenhauer, *Two Fundamental Problems of Ethics*, 252–55.

288. Ed. note: Bavinck provided no specific references for this rich imagery, and a search of Schopenhauer's *Two Fundamental Problems of Ethics* yielded no results. Bavinck likely summarized Schopenhauer's view in his own words and imagery.

affection in order to admit another. Jesus alone had perfect self-control, never allowed himself to be carried away by his love or his anger and knew when to speak and when to remain silent. We are to imitate him in this. We must get to know our affections, learn what objects easily arouse them. We must bridle our imagination and conquer our passions.[289] We must gain mastery also over our heart. We must be governed by the love of God poured into our heart, cultivate the mind of Christ[290] within ourselves (1 Cor. 2:16; Phil. 2:5), and in this way cultivate noble, holy dispositions within ourselves.

We are called to be pure in heart (Matt. 5:8; 1 Tim. 1:5; 2 Tim. 2:22), to be led by the Spirit of God (Rom. 8:14), and to walk according to the Spirit, not the flesh (Rom. 8:4–5). Feelings must be formed and developed in such a way that they are moved and aroused in a perfectly normal way by various objects in keeping with their nature. Our feelings should be rich, variegated, tender, deep, and healthy, and they then will be exceptionally valuable. They enable us to know the value of things, to enjoy them, and to be thankful for them.[291] Their underlying orientation should be love toward God, and then they are blessed from the start (Matt. 5: blessed are the pure of heart).[292]

The Formation and Development of the Will[293]

The will, initially bound, is set free from sin in regeneration (John 8:36). To serve God voluntarily—that is true liberty.[294] Religion, after all, is the proper, original, and natural component of the will. Our will must therefore increasingly absorb this will of God. Not making oneself will-less, as the mystic says, not losing oneself, but being of one will with God—that is true virtue. Our cross consists in this: that our will and God's will, rather than coinciding, are

---

289. Pictet, *De christelyke zedekunst*, 694–700 (book VIII, chap. 1, "On the Passions in General" [*Van de Hartstogten in 't algemeen*]); Reinhard, *System der christlichen Moral*, 2:534–44 (§246, "Control of the Passions" [*Herrschaft über die Affecten*]).

290. GrO: νοῦν Χριστοῦ.

291. Wuttke, *Christian Ethics*, 2:248–50 (§122).

292. Wuttke, *Christian Ethics*, 2:283–84 (§136).

293. Wuttke, *Handbuch der christlichen Sittenlehre*[3], 2:299–301 (§253). Ed. note: Bavinck also refers to Reinhard, *System der christlichen Moral*, 2:495ff.; from this open-ended citation it is not clear whether Bavinck had in mind only the two-page §238 ("Moving to a New Investigation" [*Uebergang zur neuen Untersuchung*]), the larger introductory part of chap. 4 (§§238–40), or the entire fourth chapter, "Christian Perfection in Action, or Concerning the Duties of Christian Conduct and Life" (*Christliche Volkommenheit im Handeln, oder Von den Pflichten des christlichen Betragens und Lebens*), §§238–64, pp. 495–646. To complicate matters even more, vol. 2 covers only the first part (*erste Abtheilung*) of chap. 4; chap. 4 continues in vol. 3, part 2, §§265–83; part 3, §§284–306; part 4, §§307–48; part 5, §§349–58. Volume 4 begins a whole new section.

294. LO: *Deo servire, libertas*.

at cross-purposes. Our will must therefore be increasingly purified of every contamination of the flesh and of the spirit and must perfect holiness in the fear of God (2 Cor. 7:1). Not to have a will of one's own, to kill one's will, is not the highest virtue. Still higher and more glorious is to personally will and desire with all our might what God wills.[295] Within the Christian, there is still a large gap between willing and doing (Rom. 7:14–24), yet the believer does have the capacity to will and a sincere desire to live according to all God's commandments.[296] That will must be trained, reinforced, until the believer can say without fail, "Not my will, but yours, be done" (Luke 22:42; cf. Ps. 40:8; Matt. 6:10; John 5:30). It must become our food and drink to do the will of the Father (John 4:34), not out of coercion, but voluntarily, through love becoming one in will with God.[297] In this way all arbitrariness, all randomness will increasingly disappear from this will. The will becomes all the more free to the extent that the Christian acts more confidently, more consciously, more ethically, and allows oneself to be increasingly determined by God's will.[298] This freedom of the will is therefore altogether different from the free will of the Pelagians, and also of Fichte, who always proceeds from the "I," with everything produced from the "I," and has all of nature subjected to and controlled by the "I." He writes, "You shall be free even vis-à-vis God: free fellow citizens of his kingdom." Or Schiller: "Take the deity into your will, / and it will descend from its world throne."[299] Such a freedom, separated from God, is nothing but slavery.

---

295. Van der Hoeven, *De godsdienst, het wezen van den mensch*, 45.

296. Ed. note: Bavinck summarized in his own words the second part of the answer in Q&A 114 (Lord's Day 44) of the Heidelberg Catechism, in response to the question "But can those converted to God obey these commandments perfectly?": "No. In this life even the holiest have only a small beginning of this obedience. Nevertheless, with all seriousness of purpose, they do begin to live according to all, not only some, of God's commandments." Translation by the joint task force of the Reformed Church in America and the Christian Reformed Church in North America, website of the Christian Reformed Church in North America, https://www.crcna.org/welcome/beliefs/confessions.

297. Wuttke, *Christian Ethics*, 2:251 (§122).

298. Wuttke, *Christian Ethics*, 2:283–84 (§136); van der Hoeven, *De godsdienst, het wezen van den mensch*, 45.

299. GO: *Nimmt die Gottheit auf in euren Willen, und sie steigt von ihrem Weltenthron herab.* Cited by Reinhard, *System der christlichen Moral*, 2:348. Ed. note: The citation is from Schiller's poem "Das Ideal und das Leben"; see Schiller, *Sämtliche Werke*, 1:201–5. The translation is ours; E. P. Arnold Foster translates it as follows: "Thy Spirit and the Deity's cement, / And God half way will meet thee from His throne" (*Poems of Schiller*, 227 ["The Ideal and Life"]); another version has it thus: "And with divinity thou sharest the throne, / Let but divinity become thy will!" ("The Ideal and the Actual Life," in "Project Gutenberg's *Poems of the Third Period*, by Friedrich Schiller," EBook #6796, Project Gutenberg, https://www.gutenberg.org/files/6796/6796-h/6796-h.htm).

21

Loving Our Neighbor

Love for other human beings is not uniquely a biblical virtue but a given of natural law, and versions of it can be found in the world's religious traditions. However, these do not arrive at the fullness set forth in Holy Scripture. At best they offer notions of justice and a general love of humanity.

Scripture teaches the common origin of all human beings and a love to the neighbor. Jesus's parable of the good Samaritan reminds us that the issue is not about asking who my neighbor is but about how one becomes a neighbor—namely, through serving love. Love, therefore, defines our humanity; the true relation of one human being to another is that of love, and this love must include all people, extensively and intensively. Both excessive love of and contempt for human beings is wrong. The former can be found in parents who idolize their children, in lovers who idolize each other, in ancestor worship—the last of these among society's elites, who despise the masses.

Neighbor love is based on love toward God; the second table of the law follows the first, and both are headed by "I am the LORD your God." We must love our neighbor because he or she is a fellow human being, an image-bearer of God. Of course, we cannot actually and factually love all people. That is why Scripture never speaks of a universal love of humanity, but of neighbor love. And our neighbor is everyone, no matter who and what they are, who needs our help; and we are their neighbor without any regard to their race, nation, or religion, because they are human, because they bear God's image. This is not "natural," because it runs counter to our sinful nature; it is also not the same as the natural love between parents and children, friends, and countrymen. Real and genuine neighbor love is a gift of the Holy Spirit, a supranatural habitude.

At the same time, there are different degrees of love; some neighbors are closer to us than others. These degrees include those who have died, sinners, enemies, those in distress, brothers and sisters in Christ, angels, animals, and nature in general. There is a variety in the way societies show respect for their dead and dispose of their bodies. The religions of China emphasize veneration of ancestors, and most peoples buried their dead, although some cremated them. The biblical and Christian custom is burial. Since the nineteenth century there has been a revived interest in cremation. Economic and hygienic reasons are the primary grounds for cremation. Arguments against cremation include concerns about compulsion, challenges to the justice system's ability to investigate deaths of victims, the break with Christian custom, the lack of reverence for the dead, and conflict with the idea of resurrection. However, Scripture does not provide specific prescriptions with regard to burial—only examples, such as the tender way Jesus was buried by his disciples. For Christians, mourning and sadness are permitted, but Christians do not grieve as those who have no hope. Intercessory prayer for the deceased, a common custom in the early church, was rejected by the Reformation, although the Lutheran church does not forbid it absolutely.

Our respect for the dead, however, goes beyond respectful burial. We owe our dead gratitude for the spiritual and material goods that they acquired, bequeathed, and gave to us. We also owe them proper piety, neither criticizing them beyond measure nor whitewashing their wrongdoings, but explaining them in the context of their time. While we should not condemn or prohibit all anatomical dissection, it does conflict somewhat with Christian sensitivities and should be limited and done with reverence toward the deceased and family.

Our love should also embrace our offspring. We ought to leave behind a good, rich heritage: God's Word the greatest treasure, a pure confession even more pure, a fine remembrance, our treasures in art and scholarship, an honorable, untarnished reputation. We must guard against creating debt, both material and spiritual.

Love toward sinners is a most difficult duty, bringing two obligations into tension: hatred of sin and love for the neighbor who is a sinner. We must judge sin; we may not call what is sinful good. At the same time, we must love the sinner. This is possible when we distinguish between the human being created after the image of God and what is sinful in the neighbor. In fact, hatred of the second must be done for the sake of the former.

Love of one's enemy is rarely found among the pagans, although the Stoics did teach that every person, simply as a human being, deserves our sympathy and kindness. Love of enemy is definitely taught in the Old Testament, but most clearly in the New Testament. It is a defining mark of Jesus's teaching that is misinterpreted if it is taken as a moral obligation to forgo self-defense, be passive in legal matters, and be a pacifist in wartime. Nonetheless, we are to practice unlimited forgiveness, and nothing demonstrates our love for our enemies more than when we pray for them in all sincerity. All this is about our personal enemies; we are never to be reconciled with God's enemies. In the final judgment, "Christ will cast all his and my enemies into everlasting condemnation" (Heidelberg Catechism, Q&A 52). That is why Scripture never says that we must love Satan or the demons, even though they are creatures of God.

The virtue of compassion toward those in distress—the poor, the sick, widows, orphans, strangers, prisoners—was unknown to pagans but was a clear and important part of biblical teaching in the Old and New Testaments. Christians may not harden their heart to the poor, but also not give them preferential treatment in court out of sentimental sympathy. Justice and mercy are called for, and their aim is to heal and relieve human distress, a continuation of Christ's compassionate High Priestly office.

Jesus was the first to call his disciples "brothers," and our love for brothers and sisters in the Lord is rooted in our common union with Christ our brother. It is this union with Christ through the Holy Spirit that is the "new" in the "new commandment" he gave us (John 13:34). Outside of the human and Christian families, we are to show respect to angels and care for animals and all creatures. Animals may not be worshiped nor treated cruelly. Organizations set up specifically to protect animals from cruelty are a disgrace for a Christian society and misguided in principle: should we set up separate societies for every sin or evil?

The Sixth Commandment is about protecting and promoting our neighbor's life because the image of God in human beings has royal, priestly character, is sacrosanct, and may not be violated. This clearly forbids murder in the literal sense of killing another human being, either directly or indirectly, but it also covers the spiritual murder of hate and the killing of another person's soul by seduction or in other ways leading them into sin. It does not exclude capital punishment or war.

The Seventh Commandment is given to protect our neighbor's chastity and to promote honorable and healthy human sexuality. We were created male and female with a goal of multiplying the human race as an organic whole and not as a society of individuals. Forbidden are adultery, concubinage and polygamy, fornication, incest, and sins against nature. Also forbidden is all unchastity of the heart and whatever seductive means incline us to such unchastity. In short, what is commanded is chastity in soul and body, in word, gesture, and deed, both within and outside marriage.

Dominion over the earth belongs to the content of the image of God in humans; to subdue the earth is our human calling and forms the basis for the right of ownership. Even without the fall there could well have been private property, but now it is necessary to avoid disputes and to stimulate industry. We should be grateful for what we have received and be content, possessing as though not possessing and being good stewards. All theft is forbidden by the Eighth Commandment because we may not take from our neighbors what God gave them, their goods as well as their life. Not only theft by violence (robbery) but also theft by cunning, perverting justice with false weights and measures, adulterating merchandise, gambling, incurring debts and not repaying them, evading taxes and excises, and the like. We are commanded to promote and protect our neighbors in terms of their possessions.

The Ninth Commandment concerns our duties toward our neighbor's reputation. All lies and deceit are forbidden in our daily relations with our neighbor, in courts of law, and in all forms of communication. There are different kinds of lies, and some regard only intentional, malicious lies as sins. The Reformed acknowledged these differences but regarded all forms of lying to be sin. Scripture forbids even every idle word. This commandment also forbids all insulting, name-calling, vilifying, malicious gossip, and mocking those with disabilities. We are not to delight in such things but rebuke them. Positively, we are commanded to show concern for our neighbors' honor and reputation as precious and, in a nutshell, to love the truth, form true representations of things, and convey the truth we obtained by communicating in our language with objective purity. Be true, when you think and when you speak!

Reformed exegetes judge that the Tenth Commandment, about covetousness, applies to the entire Decalogue and not only to the second table. The commandment does not forbid all desiring, only disordered desire. Desiring is innate to our human nature; sin does not destroy our desiring capacity but directs it to impermissible objects, creates inordinate desires, and leads to satisfying our desires in ways other than those intended by God. This commandment, therefore, points out to us that our nature is corrupt and that we are culpable for our condition as well as our actual sin. This is the doctrine of original sin. Our desire needs to be redirected to God and his righteousness; only the regenerating and renewing work of God the Holy Spirit can accomplish this. The Tenth Commandment drives us to Christ!

§43. NEIGHBOR LOVE IN GENERAL

Neighbor love is a commandment of the natural law[1] (Rom. 2:14) and is not altogether unknown to pagans.

Buddhism

Buddhist morality distinguishes itself by its gentleness and resistance to all selfishness. The moral precepts for laity and spiritual leaders are five in number:

1. Do not kill, not any living creature whatsoever.

1. LO: *lex naturalis.*

2. Do not steal.

3. Do not be unchaste.

4. Do not lie.

5. Do not consume alcohol.

In addition, spiritual leaders are to abstain from

1. meals at prohibited hours;

2. worldly amusements;

3. beauty lotions, perfumes, jewelry;

4. luxurious beds;

5. accepting monetary gifts.

These are the ten good moral practices.[2] Lay people are to observe the first five, but if they also follow the other five or at least the first three of them (all together, eight), all the better. Buddhist morality is distinguished into a lower, intermediate, and higher morality. Morality, abstinence, and avoiding anything harmful for others and ourselves are more valuable than virtue or positive actions.[3] The more one resembles a dead person, the higher the level of spiritual development one has attained. Thus, the ethics of the Buddha is predominantly negative. There is no question here of actual positive love toward the neighbor. Performing good deeds is a good thing for lay people to do, but only as training toward quietism.[4] The doctrine of activism is heretical. Buddhist ethics emphasizes one's attitude or state of mind; it wants to foster goodwill, compassion, joyful sharing, and equanimity.[5] The core of its moral teaching is: "An act that you would not want done to yourself, you should not do to others." "Whatever you desire for yourself should be desired also for other people." One poet says, "Decent people show love toward all creatures because these resemble themselves."[6] The virtues of compassion and mercy are prominent. After all, life is a disaster, so all living creatures are to be pitied, and compassion and the inclination to provide relief from

2. Ed. note: Bavinck uses the term *Daçaçíla* (dasa sila) here, which he takes from Kern, *Geschiedenis van het Buddhisme in Indië*, 1:424.

3. Kern, *Geschiedenis van het Buddhisme in Indië*, 1:428–30.

4. Kern, *Geschiedenis van het Buddhisme in Indië*, 1:428–30.

5. Regarding the virtues between parents and children, teachers and pupils, husbands and wives, masters and servants, spiritual people and laity, and among friends, see Kern, *Geschiedenis van het Buddhisme in Indië*, 1:434–37.

6. Ed. note: Bavinck's source for all three quotations is Kern, *Geschiedenis van het Buddhisme in Indië*, 1:442.

suffering are the fundamental values.[7] But women are despised. The Buddha himself said that "women are bad."[8]

Confucianism

Confucianism teaches deep reverence for ancestors and parents.[9] To worship them is the primary duty. In this way, ancestors become tutelary spirits.[10] Human duty is "confined to the five constituent relationships of society":[11] "Between father and son there should be affection; between ruler and subject righteousness; between husband and wife attention to their separate functions; between old and young a proper distinction; and between friend and friend fidelity."[12]

Taoism[13]

Lao-Tse taught especially compassion, thrift, humility, and repaying evil with good.[14] Both Confucius and Lao-Tse knew the golden rule (in its negative form): What you would not want people to do to you, do not do to them.[15]

Greeks and Romans

The Greeks and Romans were unfamiliar with the universal love of humanity. Slaves and foreigners were generally viewed as belonging to a lower, inferior kind of people. Nor did philosophical ethics discover this virtue. Aristotle awarded to masters a despotic power over their slaves, and he said that love toward the slave was as impossible as love from the gods toward human beings,[16] even though the notion of a common human nature was not foreign to Aristotle. It was the cosmopolitan Stoics who first realized that all rational

---

7. Kern, *Geschiedenis van het Buddhisme in Indië*, 1:442n2.

8. DO: *het vrouwvolk is slecht*; Kern, *Geschiedenis van het Buddhisme in Indië*, l:446. Ed. note: The Pali Buddhist Scripture, The Majjhima Nikaya, III.III.2.5 (115), "The Discourse on Many Elements," teaches that while it is possible for a man to become "the perfect rightfully Enlightened One," "the Universal Monarch," "the King of Gods," "King of Death," or "Brahmaa," all of these are impossible for women (The Majjhima Nikaya, BuddhaSasana, https://www.budsas.org/ebud/majjhima/115-bahudhatuka-e.htm).

9. Legge, *Religions of China*, 69–72.

10. Legge, *Religions of China*, 76–77, 84–85.

11. Legge, *Religions of China*, 104–12.

12. Legge, *Religions of China*, 106.

13. Legge, *Religions of China*, 157–237.

14. Legge, *Religions of China*, 184–88, 220–30.

15. Legge, *Religions of China*, 262–65.

16. Zeller, *Die Philosophie der Griechen³*, 2/2:692–96, 865; 3/1:607.

creatures were related, constituting a political entity;[17] each person is merely a member[18] of the whole. Two virtues ought to be practiced in relation to human beings: justice and love. The earlier Stoics emphasized the former: a wise man must be strictly just, without leniency or pity. But the later Stoics, like Seneca, Epictetus, and Marcus Aurelius, expanded especially on the latter virtue.[19] Still later, peripatetics [Aristotelians], too, insisted on a general love for the human race.[20] Ever since then, this has been a commonplace[21] of ethics.

The Teaching of Holy Scripture

In the Old Testament, the human race descended from a single pair. Humanity is one. And neighbor love is clearly taught there. Yet it is noteworthy that Holy Scripture never talks about universal human love, but always about *neighbor* love:[22] Christ's love is always called love toward people, toward the world, never toward the neighbor; but our love toward people is always called neighbor love (Lev. 19:18). What that love toward the neighbor entails is worked out in the Ten Commandments and in other places as well: Leviticus 19:17: "You shall not hate your brother in your heart, but you shall reason frankly with your neighbor, lest you incur sin because of him." Exodus 23:4–5: Your neighbor's stray ox or donkey should be returned (cf. Deut. 22:1–4).[23] But in the Old Testament who is one's neighbor? Leviticus 19:18 alternates the term "neighbor"[24] with the phrase "children of your people" (NKJV). The word itself is indefinite, but the neighbors of an Israelite were, of course, Israelites. Thus "neighbor" occurs mostly with that meaning. But Exodus 11:2 understands an Egyptian man and woman to be neighbors of the Israelites. Sojourners (foreigners)[25] had to be shown respect and love: Exodus 22:21, 23:9 commands, "You shall not wrong a sojourner or oppress him," for "you know the heart of a sojourner, for you were sojourners in the land of Egypt."[26] Leviticus 19:33–34 explicitly includes this command: "You shall love him as yourself." Deuteronomy 10:17–19: God himself loves the sojourner, it says, so the Israelites are to love him, too (cf. Deut. 23:7; Isa. 58:7; Mic. 6:8; Zech.

---

17. GrO: πολιτικὸν σύστημα.
18. GrO: μέλος.
19. Zeller, *Die Philosophie der Griechen*[3], 3/1:287–98.
20. LO: *caritas generis humani*; Zeller, *Die Philosophie der Griechen*[3], 3/1:607n3.
21. LO: *locus communis*.
22. Cf. Wuttke, *Christian Ethics*, 2:254–57 (§124).
23. See below in connection with the six commandments of the second table; cf. Carl Friedrich Keil, *Manual of Biblical Archaeology*, 2:363–74 (§§154–55).
24. HO: רֵעַ.
25. Proselytes (Exod. 12:48).
26. Pagans were to be eradicated from Canaan.

7:9). The stray ox and donkey, even if they belonged to an enemy, had to be returned (Exod. 23:4–5).

Nevertheless, it is true that Israel was sharply isolated from other nations and soon began to boast of its privileges and to despise the uncircumcised. Jesus calls neighbor love a commandment "like" the first and great commandment (Matt. 22:39–40) and puts in our hand the positive rule "So whatever you wish that others would do to you, do also to them" (Matt. 7:12). He says that our enemies also are to be understood as belonging to our neighbors (Matt. 5:43–48). And in response to the question "Who is my neighbor?" (Luke 10:29–30), Jesus shows in the parable of the good Samaritan how one *becomes someone's neighbor*—namely, through serving love; for Jesus asks (v. 36), "Which of these three [priest, Levite, Samaritan], do you think, proved to be a neighbor to the man who fell among the robbers?" Thus the questioner receives a practical answer—namely, Don't ask theoretically who your neighbor is, but show that you are the neighbor of anyone who needs your serving help.[27] Paul too subsumes all the commandments of the second table under neighbor love (Rom. 13:8–10), and even the entire law (Gal. 5:14; cf. Col. 3:14; 1 Tim. 1:5; James 2:8, 10; 1 Pet. 3:8–9; 2 Pet. 1:7).

The proof of love is the *kiss*. A kiss is given with bowed head on the forehead and cheeks, given out of respect on the hand, given in submission on the feet, and given on the mouth in familiar intimacy. It appears repeatedly in the Old Testament, between parents and children, brothers and sisters and relatives, and so on. In the early Christian church, the brotherly kiss was a common practice (Rom. 16:16; 1 Cor. 16:20; 2 Cor. 13:12; 1 Thess. 5:26; 1 Pet. 5:14).[28]

Biblical revelation has taught us that the human race is one and was the first to teach us the idea of "humanity." Every human being is incomplete, onesided, and requires and possesses the supplementation of others. Angels and animals do not form a single race, as humanity does. All of humanity together is the true human (Goethe).[29] And that humanity was successively realized within time by people themselves.[30] All people are blood relatives. The moral, spiritual community of love is constructed upon that natural community.[31] Love presupposes especially both identity and difference. Two exactly identical persons would not love each other, nor would two people who were

---

27. Cf. H. Meyer, *Critical and Exegetical Handbook to the Gospels of Mark and Luke*, 2:126; Martensen, *Christian Ethics, Special Part*, 1:202 (§89).

28. Wuttke, *Christian Ethics*, 2:256 (§124).

29. In Rothe, *Theologische Ethik*, 1:502 (§134).

30. Rothe, *Theologische Ethik*, 1:500–505 (§§134–36); J. T. Beck, *Vorlesungen über christliche Ethik*, 2:229–30.

31. Rothe, *Theologische Ethik*, 1:505–8 (§§137–38).

totally unlike one another. "Love does not take place among even-tempered souls, but among harmonious ones."[32] This community of love must be absolute: it must include all people, also those who have died, and thus is not complete until humanity itself has come to completion. It must include all people in total, in all their aspects; in other words, it has to be complete both extensively and intensively.[33] The true relation of one human being to another is that of love. Only to the extent that someone stands in that relationship of love is a person truly human. Only then can one define oneself.[34] That love is respect for and self-surrender to one's neighbor; it regards this neighbor as inherently an end,[35] and oneself as the instrument for the neighbor's end.[36] This love is the pursuit and acceptance of the neighbor's fellowship, goodness, and gratitude.[37] It gives and it receives, but it does not give in order to receive, from selfish motives, but gives in order to share. For love, to give is more blessed than to receive (Acts 20:35). It does not seek its own interests, but always the interests of others (Phil. 2:4). However, it also accepts and receives; it does not, in a pretense of self-sufficiency, haughtily refuse what others give to it. It finds its own satisfaction in satisfying others. It excludes all work for wages.[38] Love, according to Plato, is the child of wealth and want.[39] Wealth has need of want in order to be able to share itself, and want is in need of wealth in order to be able to receive.[40] Love is the opposite of covetousness, forbidden in the Tenth Commandment.

Both excessive love of and contempt for human beings is therefore wrong. The idolizing of human beings—of children by their parents, of lovers by each other, the cult of genius, servile homage to princes, the religion of humanity (Auguste Comte), ancestor worship (China), and the like—is wrong because no one is good except God (Mark 10:18). Philanthropic naïveté, gullibility, optimism, sentimental infatuation with people as if they would have been good if only they hadn't been corrupted by their environment (Rousseau)—all are to be repudiated.

---

32. GO: *Liebe findet nicht statt unter gleichtönenden Seelen, aber unter harmonischen.* Ed. note: Bavinck attributes this statement to Franz von Baader and provides Rothe, *Theologische Ethik*, 507n (§138) as his source. Rothe provides the following source: "Baader, *Tagebücher* (S. W. XI.,), s. 181." See von Baader, "Tagebücher," 181.

33. Rothe, *Theologische Ethik*, 1:508–9 (§139).

34. Rothe, *Theologische Ethik*, 1:513–15 (§142).

35. GO: *Selbstzweck.*

36. Rothe, *Theologische Ethik*, 1:520–21 (§147).

37. Rothe, *Theologische Ethik*, 1:525–26 (§150).

38. Rothe, *Theologische Ethik*, 1:530–34 (§154).

39. GrO: πλοῦτος, πενία.

40. Rothe, *Theologische Ethik*, 1:532–33, Observation 1 (§154).

But it is equally wrong to have contempt for people, as is common especially among pagans, such as looking down on slaves, on women (Buddhists,
China), and on others in general: "I despise the masses."[41] A similar point of
view is found in Seneca, Tacitus, and Lucian, and in the nineteenth century
particularly in Schopenhauer: egoism is the inevitable basic drive of all people,
the essence of all people;[42] the surest way to safeguard oneself against the evil
of bipeds[43] is to hold them in contempt. This aristocratic, haughty pessimism
is on the rise again in many circles, after the French Revolution and in resistance to universal suffrage. It is characteristic of our liberal schoolteachers
and expressed against a particular segment of the population—for example,
farmers.[44]

The foundation of neighbor love is love toward God. The second table of
the law follows the first, and only one heading appears above all the commandments: "I am the LORD your God." Our neighbors must be loved not
only because they are sweet, sociable, friendly, rich, handsome, and so on,
but also quite apart from all that. In the parable in Luke 10, nothing is told us
about the man who fell among thieves, nor about his social standing, family
background, race, ethnic identity, religion, morality, and so forth, but only
this one thing: that he was a human being.

Human beings, even if there is nothing attractive about them, must still be
loved simply because God obliges us to do so. He alone can do this, binding
us not only to act but to will, obligating us to this in our conscience. All duty
is obligatory, by his word and for his sake.

Now it is certainly true that we cannot actually and factually love all people,
nor show that love in one act or another. It is impossible to embrace all humanity with our love. Holy Scripture never speaks of that universal love of
humanity. As the saying goes, "Unknown is unloved."[45] What can we feel for
those whose names we don't even know? Scripture speaks of neighbor love.
And our neighbor is everyone, no matter who and what they are, who needs
our help; and we are *their* neighbor. Thus, according to Luke 10 there are two
kinds of neighbors: passive ones and active ones. That person is a neighbor

---

41. LO: *odi profanum vulgus*. Ed. note: Bavinck provides no reference, but the full statement
"I despise the masses and avoid them" (*odi profanum vulgus et arceo*) comes from Horace, *Odes*
III.1 (trans. Rudd, LCL 33:140). Bavinck adds the expression "the masses are bad" (*de massa
is slecht*), attributing it to "Bias." Undoubtedly, he is referring to Bias of Priene (sixth century
BC), one of the Seven Sages of Greece to whom is attributed the saying "Most people are evil"
(Wikipedia, s.v. "Bias of Priene," https://en.wikipedia.org/wiki/Bias_of_Priene).

42. Schopenhauer, *Two Fundamental Problems of Ethics*, 202–6.

43. The term "bipeds" comes from the Latin *bipes* = two-footed; "bipeds" means humans.

44. Martensen, *Christian Ethics, Special Part*, 1:200 (§88).

45. DO: *onbekend in onbemind*.

who has a need, of whatever kind (Mark 7:27), and then we must not first ask if they belong to our race, nation, or religion, or if they are needy through their own fault, and so on.

We are to love such a person *in God*. All people are creatures of God, his offspring (Acts 17:28). God himself models to us that universal love[46] (Matt. 5:45). He is good to all his creatures. This neighbor love in its true essence is not "natural," since we are inclined by nature to hate our neighbor.[47] To be sure, we do by nature possess a natural love, as between parents and children, between friends, or as a moral love in the form of virtue. But these are not yet instances of *the* Love; they can occur entirely apart from God.[48] Real and genuine neighbor love is a gift of the Holy Spirit, a supranatural habitude (1 John 4:7; Gal. 5:22), a fruit of faith (Gal. 5:6; Eph. 6:23; 1 Tim. 1:14).[49]

§44. Degrees of Neighbor Love (Fifth Commandment)

The command to show love toward everyone (1 Thess. 3:12; 2 Pet. 1:7) does not preclude different degrees of that love. Some people are much closer to us than others. Some are bound to us by a physical relationship, by social or political relations, by spiritual unity, by friendship, and the like. Some of those neighbors ought to be discussed a bit more thoroughly here.

1. Love toward Those Who Have Died

The religions of China consist especially in the veneration of ancestors.[50] In Egypt, corpses were embalmed due to belief in the transmigration of the soul.[51] Only among the coarsest peoples were corpses simply placed in the open field, as food for animals. Everywhere else, corpses were always cared for. To not be cared for is a dishonor (Prov. 30:17). The oldest practice seems to have been to bury the corpse in the ground, as we read in Cicero[52] and as we have discovered today from recent excavations of burial grounds. People

46. GrO: φιλανθρωπία, φιλοκτισία. Ed. note: The rare Greek term φιλοκτισία can be found in Turretin, *Institutes of Elenctic Theology*, III, qu. 20, §4).
47. Heidelberg Catechism, Q&A 5.
48. Kuyper, "De Liefde I."
49. Wittewrongel, *Oeconomia Christiana*, 2:371.
50. Legge, *Religions of China*, 69–95.
51. See also K. Sartorius, *Die Leichenverbrennung*; Kuyper, *Ons Program*, 802–43. Ed. note: Bavinck provides only the reference "802v.," without a terminus. Pages 802–43 are devoted to the topic of cremation in general and not to the specific point about Egyptian embalming. The ET, *Our Program*, has a much shorter treatment of cremation on pp. 243–46 (§200).
52. Cicero, *On the Laws* II.22.56 (LCL 213:166–68).

preferred to leave the corpse undisturbed, untouched, to commit them to the earth, for sleep and rest in peace. "May the earth rest lightly upon you! Let it lie softly on your bones!"[53] At first fire did not exist. That was discovered later. And when it was discovered, cremation did not yet follow immediately. It came into use only gradually. Fire was sacred, carried sacrifices to the gods in the heavens, and was also suited to lead corpses upward. Burial and cremation existed alongside each other for a long time. Cremation did not supplant burial in prehistoric times. Even throughout history, the two practices continued together—for example, among the Indo-Germanic tribes. Burial was more common in the one tribe, cremation in the other.

As for the Greeks, Lucian said simply, "The Greeks burn their dead, the Persians bury them."[54] But according to Hermann, burial was the custom, with cremation occurring only during wartime or epidemics.[55] It has been demonstrated that in fact both occurred simultaneously: Patroclus,[56] Hector,[57] and Achilles[58] were cremated. In Plato's *Phaedo*, Socrates was indifferent about whether he would be buried or cremated. Among the Romans, according to Cicero,[59] the oldest custom was burial. Sulla is supposed to have been the first to have opted for cremation, as did Pompey, Julius Caesar, Mark Antony, Brutus, and others. But even with cremation, the remaining bones and ashes were buried in the columbarium of the burial chambers. There was no separate cemetery, except for one designated for slaves and convicts behind Esquiline Hill.[60] People killed by lightning[61] were not allowed to be cremated, not even among the Greeks.

Cremation is also found from the Gauls in the West to India in the East, and from Italy to Scandinavia. It is still in use in India and among the Japanese. But the Egyptians buried their dead, as did the Assyrians, Babylonians (cf. Isa. 14:18–20), Persians, Chinese, the native peoples of North America, and the black peoples of Africa. Why some of these buried and others cremated cannot be determined with any certainty. When both customs existed

53. LO: *Sit tibi terra levis! Molliter ossa cubent!* Ed. note: Bavinck's source is K. Sartorius, *Die Leichenverbrennung*, 3. The first phrase is from Martial, *Epigrams* XI.29.11 (trans. Bailey, LCL 480:252); the second is from Ovid, *Amores* I.8.108 (LCL 41:354–55).

54. Lucian, *Works of Lucian of Samosata*, 3:217 ("Of Mourning," para. 21).

55. Ed. note: Bavinck's source may be Hermann, *Lehrbuch der Griechischen Antiquitäten*, 4:373–87 (§40, "Leichenbestattung und Grabmäler").

56. Homer, *Iliad* XXIII.

57. Homer, *Iliad* XXIV.

58. Homer, *Odyssey* XXIV. Ed. note: Bavinck may have borrowed these references to the *Iliad* and the *Odyssey* from Hermann, *Lehrbuch der Griechischen Antiquitäten*, 4:374.

59. Cicero, *On the Laws* II.22.56 (LCL 213:166–68).

60. Ed. note: The Esquiline Hill is one of the seven hills of Rome.

61. LO: *fulguriti*.

side by side, cremation seems to have been the more noble and respectable custom. Cremation occurs more commonly, though not exclusively, among nomadic tribes and warring people, burial among agricultural people. But what appears to have been influential were the religious ideas about the soul and the hereafter. That is evident among the Chinese and Pythagoreans, who rejected cremation.

Among *Israel* we find the following:[62] Before the time of Saul, only Achan and his family were stoned and then burned with fire (Josh. 7:15, 25). Saul and his sons were burned (1 Sam. 31:12–13), but that was done to prevent more indignity at the hands of the Philistines. In 2 Chronicles 16:14 and 21:19, we read of a great fire at a burial, but this consisted only in the burning of spices; the corpse itself was buried, as is expressly noted in 2 Chronicles 16:14. In Amos 6:10 [NIV] mention is made of the burning of the dead, but that was during a period of pestilence and as an especially regrettable deviation from custom. Cremation is nowhere forbidden, however. The fixed custom was burial, and it was conducted with the greatest of reverence. To remain unburied was a dishonor (1 Kings 13:22; 14:11; Jer. 16:4). The graves were usually located outside the city (though Samuel's grave was inside his own house, 1 Sam. 25:1). Graves were decorated (Matt. 23:29). Jacob and Joseph were embalmed (Gen. 50:2, 26). A period of mourning lasted seven days, sometimes seventy days (Gen. 50:3).[63] Grief was expressed in clothing, fasting, the tearing of clothes, sprinkling the head with dust and ashes, and shaving the beard. In Leviticus 20:14 and 21:9, being burned in the fire is ordered for serious offenders, thus as a form of capital punishment.

Among Christians the only custom is burial.[64] Jesus was buried. The grain of wheat must fall into the ground in order to bear fruit (John 12:24). All who are in the grave will one day hear his voice (John 5:28–29). Rising from the grave became inseparable from burial (1 Cor. 15:42–44). In AD 785, Charlemagne prohibited the Saxons from cremating their dead, and in 1249 the Teutonic Knights did the same with the recently converted Prussians. The dead continued to belong to the church. The early Christians preferred to assemble near the graves of the martyrs. There they built their churches and were themselves buried. The churchyard was the graveyard, and burials occurred even inside the churches. In AD 386, Gratian, Valentinian, and Theodosius prohibited burials in consecrated places of worship dedicated to the apostles and martyrs.

---

62. Cf. also Rüetschi, "Begräbnis, bei den Hebräem"; Kuyper, *Ons Program*, 819.
63. Ed. note: We have corrected Bavinck's manuscript, which had "thirty days."
64. K. Sartorius, *Die Leichenverbrennung*, 18–19; Jacobson, "Begräbnis, bei den Christen"; cf. Kuyper, *Ons Program*, 820–22; Kuyper, *Our Program*, 244–46 (§200).

The church ordered interment to take place outside the wall of the basilica.[65] Only bishops, abbots, elders, and faithful laity[66] were permitted to be buried in the church, though not close to the altar. However, this rule was not rigorously enforced. The number of family graves inside the church increased. In the present century this practice is prohibited by law in most jurisdictions.

Our day is seeing a revived interest in cremation.[67] The renewal of this practice has come over from India to Italy, where voices in favor had been heard occasionally. But it so happened that in 1869, an Indian prince, the Maharaja of Kolhapur, died in Florence, and according to his last will and testament he was cremated. This unusual incident was widely discussed. Many physicians declared themselves in favor of cremation and wanted to have it legalized. In early 1872, Albert Keller, a count (who was actually a merchant from Zurich staying in Milan), expressed his desire to be cremated. Keller died in 1874, but his wish could not be fulfilled immediately, since cremation was not yet permitted. On September 6, 1874, it was permitted by law in exceptional cases and for special reasons. At this point, Dr. Polli, the professor in Milan to whom Keller had expressed his wish, proceeded to have a crematorium constructed in Milan. And on January 22, 1876, Keller's corpse was burned there. The building was donated to the city. This incident was widely discussed. A society for cremation was organized in Milan. By 1885, five hundred corpses had been cremated there. Later, crematoria were constructed in Lodi, Varese, Cremona, Bologna, Brescia, Rome, and Padua.[68]

From Italy this interest spread to France: on July 28, 1885, the city council of Paris approved the building of three crematoria at Père Lachaise cemetery for burning the remains of cadavers that had been used for medical research, and the Chamber of Deputies voted, 323 to 180, in favor of making cremation legal. In Germany, there are societies for cremation in Vienna, Münich, Hamburg, and Berlin. Cremation is legal in Gotha, where a crematorium was built as early as 1878 and where, until 1884, about 110 corpses were cremated (by Oct. 31, 1887, 473 corpses were cremated), and it is legal in Hamburg as well.[69]

---

65. LO: *de foris circa murum basilicae.* Ed. note: Bavinck derived the quotation from Jacobson, "Begräbnis, bei den Christen," 214.

66. LO: *Episcopi aut abbates aut digni presbyterivelfideles laici*; from Jacobson, "Begräbnis, bei den Christen," 214.

67. Cf. K. Sartorius, *Die Leichenverbrennung*; Wittmeyer, *Über die Leichenverbrennung.*

68. According to *Algemeen Handelsblad*, Sunday supplement, June 19, 1887, p. 2, in the years 1876–85 there were 606 cremations in Italian cities and 291 in Gotha. The highest numbers of cremations were in Milan (402) and Rome (90). Last year a crematorium was built in Como, and preparations are being made for one in Codogno, Mantua, Bologna, Sena, Venice, and Turin.

69. In England (cf. Thompson, "De vooruitgang der lijkverbranding"), The Cremation Society of Great Britain was established in 1874, with Henry Thompson as its president. In 1879

In Switzerland efforts are underway in Zurich, Geneva, and Basel for legalizing cremation.[70] In the Netherlands, cremation was defended in 1874 by the newspaper *Nieuwe Rotterdamsche Courant*. It wanted to have cremation available as an option and have the councils of large cities adopt measures to gradually clean up substandard cemeteries and to give serious consideration to install a Siemens oven and construct a municipal crematorium.[71]

Grounds for cremation are especially these:

1. The poetry of it.[72] It is an inspiring notion to surrender our dead to the clear pure flame instead of letting them slowly rot in the ground. Jacob Grimm made this point already in 1849. However, although it may seem that way to us when reading Homer, our cremating ovens, first conceived by Küchenmeister and Reclam and then developed and manufactured by Siemens, eliminate all poetry from the business.[73] In these ovens, the corpses are actually not burned by flames but by the air, whose temperature is raised to a white heat.

2. The economy of it,[74] as well as the crowding in many existing cemeteries, thus saving cost and space. However, these are insignificant arguments. People then need to make new cemeteries.

3. The main reason is hygiene. Cemeteries are said to be the source of polluting the air, soil, and water and the cause of illnesses and the like. There is no hygienic argument against cremation.[75] However, the hazards of cemeteries are highly exaggerated. Very miserable burial plots were used as examples, such as burial plots for the poor in Naples and cemeteries in the center of London. No proof has been forthcoming that cemeteries are the cause of epidemics or higher death rates. Even water from wells located close to cemeteries turned out, upon inspection, to

---

a crematorium was built in Woking, and first used on March 20, 1885; by November 30, 1887, there were twenty-three cremations. Ed. note: This crematorium was built by Italian scientist Paolo Gorini (1813–81), whom Bavinck mentions in n. 71 below.

70. Ed. note: Bavinck's source is K. Sartorius, *Die Leichenverbrennung*, 28–29.

71. Kuyper, *Ons Program*, 812. In Denmark the first cremation was performed in an oven of Paolo Gorini, September 1886. Ed. note: Friedrich Siemens developed ovens that used only hot air (not flames) to cremate bodies (Mattogno, "Crematoria Ovens"). A detailed description (with diagrams) of the Siemens oven can be found in Wilhelm Heepke, *Die Leichenverbrennungsanstalten*, 41–58.

72. DO: *poëzie*.

73. Ed. note: This is a reference to the German physicians Gottlieb Heinrich Friedrich Küchenmeister (1821–90) and Karl Heinrich Reclam (1821–87) and the German industrialist Friedrich Siemens (1826–1904).

74. Kuyper, *Ons Program*, 836, 839.

75. K. Sartorius, *Die Leichenverbrennung*, 34–35; Kuyper, *Ons Program*, 833–34.

be very pure—for example, in Augsburg around 1860 and in Berlin in 1865. Also, at burials, potent disinfectants can be used—for example, during a plague.[76]

Arguments against cremation:

1. The system leads to compulsion. Its proponents ask first for permission to have themselves cremated, but only in order later to ask to close all cemeteries because they are harmful to health.[77] If cemeteries are indeed unhygienic, then proponents of cremation should not quit until all cemeteries are eliminated.

2. The justice system will not be able to investigate certain crimes or establish the identity of victims. Cremation can never be made obligatory and universal.

3. Proponents clearly betray their materialist worldview, their antipathy to Christianity, their return to pagan practices. Modernist theologians like the German Heinrich Lang (1826–76) and others were at the head of the movement. Theologian Karl Heinrich Wilhelm Schwarz (1812–85) was cremated at his wish in Gotha on March 28, 1885. So was Multatuli.[78]

4. Cremation breaks with Christian custom, historically and liturgically. In all their statements about death, resurrection, and so on, the Bible and liturgy assume burial. The sensitivity and consciousness of Christian peoples and of all denominations oppose it; such sensitivity and consciousness are shattered by cremation. The poetry wrapped around the grave is turned into prose.

5. Cremation militates against the reverence we owe our dead. A corpse inspires respect and awe. It is a coarse gesture to our natural sensitivity to mar or abuse a body. On the contrary, we treat a dead body as tenderly as possible, as though it still had feeling: we close its eyes, press a kiss on it, yet almost recoil from touching it. We leave it alone as we place it in the earth and entrust it to God. But to destroy it ourselves, to burn it, to cause its decomposition, to assist in destroying it—our feelings

76. DO: *pest.*
77. Kuyper, *Ons Program*, 813.
78. Ed. note: Multatuli was the pen name of the Dutch novelist Eduard Douwes Dekker (1820–87), best known for his satirical novel *Max Havelaar*, which denounced the abuses of colonialism in the Dutch East Indies. His pen name comes from the Latin *multa tuli* ("I have borne much"—referring both to himself and to the victims of the injustices he saw as a colonial administrator).

revolt against such behavior. In their body, too, people are the image of God. That body may not be desecrated by us. Mutilating and tattooing are forbidden in Holy Scripture (Lev. 19:28; 21:5; Deut. 14:1). It is up to God, not us, to destroy the body.

6. Cremation is in conflict with the entire biblical presentation of death as a punishment and an act of God. It conflicts also with the idea of resurrection that is bound to the grave, not absolutely but nonetheless for us as Christians. Christians do not preserve corpses artificially (as the Egyptians did), but neither do they destroy them mechanically.[79] They entrust them to God.

7. Cremation as such also faces objections. A good method has not yet been found. Will it be performed so that people can see it? Charring and the production of smoke and residue cannot be prevented. There is little truth in the poet's claim about "glimmering ash in an elegant urn."[80]

Holy Scripture gives us no specific prescriptions with regard to burial. We have an example in the tender way Jesus was buried by his disciples; the same is true of Stephen (Acts 8:2). We are allowed to mourn and to be sad,[81] as appears from both the Old Testament (Gen. 23:2; 37:34–35; 50:1–3; 1 Sam. 25:1) and the New Testament (Luke 7:12–13). Jesus himself (John 11:33–35),[82] Mary (John 20:11), and the disciples (Mark 16:10; Luke 24:17; John 16:20) mourned, and the church at Ephesus mourned for Paul (Acts 20:37). Death is an evil. Yet Christian mourning is different from pagan mourning. No sorrowing without hope (1 Thess. 4:13), no worldly sorrow (2 Cor. 7:10). The Christians changed a funeral into a feast of celebration and triumph. They buried their dead not at night but during daytime, in the full light of day, dressed in white robes, accompanied by retinues and spectators,[83] without wailing women, without wreaths on the body or the coffin. In the eighth or ninth century, burials began to feature bell ringing. Beginning in the fourth century, burials featured carrying palm and olive branches at the head of the procession as signs of victory and peace. All of this occurred while those in attendance sang psalms and hymns,

---

79. Martensen, *Christian Ethics, Special Part*, 272 (§118).

80. DO: *blanke asch in een sierlijke urn*; Kuyper, *Ons Program*, 831; cf. also Wuttke, *Handbuch der christlichen Sittenlehre*³, 2:566n79 (§263).

81. Funeral meals are objectionable; cf. von Jhering, *Der Zweck im Recht*.

82. Cf. Augustine, *Confessions* IX.12–13. Ed. note: Bavinck's source is K. Sartorius, *Die Leichenverbrennung*, 25.

83. LO: *comites* and *spectatores*.

alternating with prayers and funeral orations. Mourning clothes were not worn at first.[84] Today's Hutterites also frown upon mourning clothes (what about the Quakers?).[85] Nevertheless, such apparel is not impermissible and is often useful and beneficial, protecting against temptations that are an affront to people's sensitivities.[86] Intercessory prayer for the deceased, a common custom in the early church, was rejected by the Reformation, although the Lutheran church does not forbid it absolutely.[87]

A respectful burial alone, however, does not complete the respect we owe the dead. The Roman Catholic Church celebrates an "All Saints' Day" and an "All Souls' Day." Auguste Comte venerated humanity, particularly in its most outstanding representatives. In our day, commemoration days for famous people occur frequently, such as those for Luther, Zwingli, and others. On national holidays people celebrate great men and great deeds from the past. These holidays involve a lot of exaggeration, a cult of genius, deification of people, and humanism, but also many good things. We have a bond with our ancestors, we stand on their shoulders, we are what we are thanks to them. Two virtues are fitting with respect to our ancestors:

a. Gratitude for the spiritual and material goods that they acquired, bequeathed, and gave to us. We have received all of that from their hands for nothing, as a foundation for our own diligence, effort, and so on.

b. Piety, so that we do not criticize them beyond measure nor whitewash[88] their wrongdoings, but explain them in the context of their time. There is truth in this saying: Say "nothing but good about the dead";[89] through their death, their guilt toward us is atoned. And so, in communion with our forebears, we are to work so that we can pass on to the next generation what we have been given, together with what we have added.

Our love should also embrace our offspring.[90] We ought to leave behind a good, rich heritage: God's Word the greatest treasure, a pure confession

---

84. K. Sartorius, *Die Leichenverbrennung*, 23–24.

85. Ed. note: A quick internet search will show that "Quakers do not wear black as a symbol of mourning" (see "Quaker Funeral Traditions"). Gratitude for the life of the deceased is emphasized rather than mourning.

86. Wuttke, *Handbuch der christlichen Sittenlehre*[3], 2:337 (§263).

87. Wuttke, *Handbuch der christlichen Sittenlehre*[3], 2:338 (§263); Martensen, *Christian Ethics, Special Part*, 269–70 (§117).

88. DO: *vergoelijken*.

89. LO: *De mortuis nil nisi bene*.

90. Martensen, *Christian Ethics, Special Part*, 1:274–76 (§119).

even more pure, a fine remembrance, our treasures in art and scholarship, an honorable, untarnished reputation. We must guard against creating debt, both material and spiritual. Entirely wrong is the epigram from the days of Louis XV: "After us comes the flood."[91]

Anatomical dissection of corpses was first performed by Galen in the second century AD but became more common in the fourteenth century.[92] In previous centuries it was performed only on the corpses of criminals, whereas today it is done especially on the corpses of the poor in hospitals. Anatomical dissection always conflicts somewhat with Christian sensitivities, and though it should not be condemned or prohibited, it certainly ought to be restricted and be done with true reverence toward the deceased, the relatives, and so on. The doctrine of "human rights" has not brought significant progress with respect to this issue.

2. Love toward Sinners[93]

This is a very difficult duty. On the one hand, God commands us with utmost seriousness always and everywhere to hate sin and flee from it, both in ourselves and in others. Whoever excuses, denies, or condones sin in themselves or in others angers God and violates love toward him. We may not place our trust in any fellow believer; each of us must beware of our friends (Jer. 9:4; Mic. 7:5); and we must not believe even our blood relatives when they speak friendly words to us (Jer. 12:6). Place trust in no person (Jer. 17:5; Ps. 118:8). Jesus himself admonishes us to beware of people (Matt. 10:17). Blind love that winks at everything is to be disapproved, as in the case of Aaron, who yielded to the people (Exod. 32), and Pilate. Indeed, sin in the neighbor must be punished (Matt. 18:15–20; 2 Cor. 13:2, 10); we must admonish and punish with all seriousness (Titus 2:15). We must be diligent in reproving neighbors and not tolerate the sin in them (Lev. 19:17). We are to rebuke the unfruitful works of darkness (Eph. 5:11).

Thus, judging our neighbor is permissible and obligatory. We must not call what is sinful good; we must discern the spirits (1 Cor. 12:10; 1 Thess. 5:21; 1 John 4:1). The one who is spiritual judges all things (1 Cor. 2:15; 2 John 10).

But on the other hand, we are now being commanded to love our neighbor; hence, to love a sinner. These can go together. Leviticus 19:17 connects

---

91. FO: *Après nous le deluge.*
92. Wuttke, *Handbuch der christlichen Sittenlehre*[3], 2:336 (§263); Martensen, *Christian Ethics, Special Part,* 1:269–70 (§116).
93. Wuttke, *Handbuch der christlichen Sittenlehre*[3], 342–48 (§§265–66).

them in such a beautiful way: "You shall not hate your brother in your heart, but you shall reason frankly with your neighbor, lest you incur sin because of him." God himself does the same. Hating sin, he loves sinners and gave his Son for them. In the neighbor, we are to distinguish between the human being created after the image of God—whom we may therefore not kill (Gen. 9:6)—and what is sinful in the neighbor. In fact, the one must be done for the sake of the other. Loving the neighbor can be done genuinely only if we hate the sin in the neighbor. Only then can we intend their true well-being. Another love, the kind that yields to evil, is pseudo-love, is weakness, and is sin. But genuine love can at the same time fulminate against the sin and grieve over it, as "Samuel grieved over Saul" (1 Sam. 15:35). "Let a righteous man strike me—it is a kindness" (Ps. 141:5). To reprove sin is to be serious but also gentle and loving. Restore the sinner in the spirit of meekness (Gal. 6:1). The Christian does not judge and condemn the neighbor haughtily (Matt. 7:1; Rom. 2:1; 14:4, 13; James 4:11–12). We know that we ourselves will be judged (Matt. 7:1); that we too were once unwise, disobedient, deceived, and so forth (Titus 3:2–3); that we will be measured with the measure with which we measure (Matt. 7:2); that we ourselves will have to give an account (Rom. 14:10, 12; Gal. 6:5) and carry our own burden. Nor does love judge quickly: love hopes, believes, and bears all things (1 Cor. 13:7); it does not infer from a neighbor's disaster that a special sin has been committed (Luke 13:1–5; John 9:2–3; Acts 28:4); it does not insult; it does not mock someone's weaknesses or sins.

Not all mockery, however, is wrong. God himself mocks the idols (Deut. 32:37–38; Judg. 10:14); Elijah mocked the priests of Baal (1 Kings 18:27); Isaiah mocked the idols (Isa. 44:12–17; cf. Jer. 19:3–5); Paul did as well (1 Cor. 4:8, 10; cf. 2 Cor. 11:5, 19; 12:13?).[94] Jesus did not use irony (Matt. 15:24–26; 26:45; Mark 7:9; Luke 13:33–34; John 7:28 do not prove that he did).[95] In relation to the imperfections of our neighbor, our love should be manifested in long-suffering (1 Thess. 5:14; James 5:7–8), even as God does toward us (Exod. 34:6; Num. 14:18). That, after all, is the nature of love (1 Cor. 13:4), and it is worlds apart from Stoic indifference.

3. Love toward Enemies

Love of one's enemy is generally unknown among pagans, although we do encounter it occasionally. According to Xenophon, Socrates, in keeping

---

94. Ed. note: Bavinck takes all of these Scripture references—and also the question mark following 2 Cor. 12:13!—from Wuttke, *Handbuch der christlichen Sittenlehre*[3], 2:348 (§266).
95. Wuttke, *Handbuch der christlichen Sittenlehre*[3], 2:348 (§266).

with all Greek morality, judged that "a man's excellence consists in outdoing his friends in kindness and his enemies in mischief."[96] However, in Plato's work, Socrates says that it is unjust to harm another, for committing harm and injustice are one and the same thing, and one may not commit injustice even against a person from whom one has suffered injustice.[97] This is contradictory, and it is not clear what Socrates actually taught on the subject.[98] Plato, however, emphatically teaches that true virtue harms no one, for the good can do only good, even apart from any benefit and reward.[99] The Stoics likewise taught that one may not fulminate against one's enemies[100] and that all people are members of one body, are brothers and sisters,[101] and that all have God as their father.[102] Each person, simply as a human being, is the object of my sympathy: "Wherever there is a human being, there is a place for kindness."[103] Seneca says, "Our Stoics tell us that we should not cease working for the common good, helping individuals, giving strength even to our enemies."[104] Musonius, Epictetus, and Marcus Aurelius say that all people are our kinfolk, that the same divine spirit dwells in all, that we are also to love those who stumble, ingrates, and foes, and that we must forgive

---

96. GrO: νικᾶν τοὺς μὲν φίλους εὖ ποιοῦντα, τοὺς δε ἐχθροὺς κακῶς; Xenophon, *Memorabilia* II.6.35 (LCL 168:154–55). Ed. note: Bavinck also added here: "and to grieve about the good fortune of one's enemies," citing Xenophon, *Memorabilia* III.9.8 (LCL 168:240–41). At best, this is an inference from Socrates's understanding of envy, which, according to Xenophon, "he found to be a kind of pain, not, however, of a friend's misfortune nor at an enemy's good fortune" (τὴν ἐπ' ἐχθρῶν εὐτυχίαις γιγνομένην). Bavinck's source for the two references to Xenophon and the Greek citation is Zeller, *Die Philosophie der Griechen*[3], 2/1:142nn2–3.

97. For example, in Plato, *Crito* 49A–E (LCL 36:170–75). Ed. note: Bavinck borrows these references from Zeller, *Die Philosophie der Griechen*[3], 2/1:142n4.

98. Zeller, *Die Philosophie der Griechen*[3], 2/1:143.

99. Plato, *Meno* 71E (LCL 165:268–69); *Crito* 49B–E (LCL 36:72–75); *Republic* I.334B (LCL 237:68–71); see Zeller, *Die Philosophie der Griechen*[3], 2/1:503.

100. Cicero, *On Duties* I.xxvi.88 (LCL 30:86–91); see Zeller, *Die Philosophie der Griechen*[3], 3/1:278.

101. Seneca, *Ad Lucilium epistulae morales III*, 90–91 (XCV.52 [LCL 77:90–91]: "We are the parts of one great body" [LO: *membra sumus corporis magni*]); Seneca, *Moral Essays III*, 192 (*De beneficiis* III.28.2 [LCL 310:192]). Ed. note: Bavinck's source for the Seneca references is Zeller, *Die Philosophie der Griechen*[3], 3:299n1.

102. Epictetus, *Discourses, Books 1–2*, 98 (*Discourses* I.13.3 [LCL 131:98]). Ed. note: Bavinck's source for the reference to Epictetus is Zeller, *Die Philosophie der Griechen*[3], 3/1:299n2.

103. LO: *Ubicumque homo est, ibi beneficii locus est.* Ed. note: Bavinck borrows the Seneca quotation found in *Epistulae morales ad Lucilium* XCV.52 from Zeller, *Die Philosophie der Griechen*[3], 3/1:299n3.

104. LO: *Stoici nostri dicunt, non desinemus commzmi bono operam dare, adjuvare singulos, opemferre etiam inimicis*; Seneca, *Moral Essays II*, 182 (*De Otio* I.4 [LCL 254:182]); Zeller, *Die Philosophie der Griechen*[3], 3/1:299n4.

their shortcomings.[105] And Marcus Aurelius practiced these virtues in his personal life.[106]

Love toward one's enemy certainly appears in the Old Testament as well: "If you meet your enemy's ox or his donkey going astray, you shall bring it back to him. If you see the donkey of one who hates you lying down under its burden, you shall refrain from leaving him with it; you shall rescue it with him" (Exod. 23:4–5). "If I have rejoiced at the ruin of him who hated me, or exulted when evil overtook him (I have not let my mouth sin by asking for his life with a curse)" (Job 31:29–30). While love is restricted to one's own people[107] in Leviticus 19:18 ("You shall not take vengeance or bear a grudge against the sons of your own people, but you shall love your neighbor as yourself"), Wisdom[108] releases this restriction entirely:

> Do not rejoice when your enemy falls,
>   and let not your heart be glad when he stumbles,
> lest the LORD see it and be displeased,
>   and turn away his anger from him.
> Fret not yourself because of evildoers,
>   and be not envious of the wicked,
> for the evil man has no future;
>   the lamp of the wicked will be put out. (Prov. 24:17–20)

Similarly, the following passages: "Do not say, 'I will do to him as he has done to me; I will pay the man back for what he has done'" (Prov. 24:29). In Proverbs 25:21–22 we read: "If your enemy is hungry, give him bread to eat, and if he is thirsty, give him water to drink, for you will heap burning coals on his head, and the LORD will reward you." (In this metaphor, the burning pain is a symbol of the burning sense of shame about those undeserved benefits; but it is the cheeks, not the head, that burn with shame; in this manner, you will cause your enemy the greatest pain and best satisfy your revenge; but nevertheless, doing good for the purpose of avenging oneself and causing pain is wrong; this metaphor of burning coals refers to self-incriminating remorse.)[109] And this love toward an enemy was indeed practiced in the Old

---

105. Zeller, *Die Philosophie der Griechen*[3], 3/1:762.

106. Zeller, *Vorträge und Abhandlungen*, 96–97; cf. also Grotius, *Truth of the Christian Religion*, 201–7 (book IV, xii): "The principal things of the Christian religion were approved by the wisest heathens; and if there be any thing in it hard to be believed, the like is found amongst the heathens." Cf. Reinhard, *System der christlichen Moral*, 3:257, note *b*.

107. DO: *volksgenoot*.

108. DO: *Chokma*. Ed. note: This is a transliteration of the Hebrew word חָכְמָה.

109. Delitzsch, *Biblical Commentary on the Proverbs of Solomon*, 2:167–68 (on Prov. 25:21–22). Ed. note: Delitzsch speaks of burning coals as "a figure of self-accusing repentance" and

Testament by David; see Psalm 35:12–13: "They repay me evil for good; my soul is bereft. But I, when they were sick—I wore sackcloth . . ."; and again by David toward Saul (1 Sam. 24; 26; 2 Sam. 1:11–16; 2:5–7; 4:9–12).

But this commandment is especially clear in the New Testament (Matt. 5:38–47). Jesus does not want "an eye for an eye" or "hate your enemy," as was said of old (not in the Old Testament) and was practiced by the tax collectors. Rather, we are not to resist the evil person, but instead to turn the left cheek to whomever smites us on the right cheek (cf. also Luke 6:32–36). Jesus himself prayed, "Father, forgive them" (Luke 23:34). Similarly, Stephen (Acts 7:60) and Paul (2 Tim. 4:16). In Romans 12:14–21 we read things like "Bless those who persecute you; bless and do not curse them," "Repay no one evil for evil," "If your enemy is hungry, feed him; if he is thirsty, give him something to drink," and "Do not be overcome by evil, but overcome evil with good." "When reviled, we bless; when persecuted, we endure; when slandered, we entreat" (1 Cor. 4:12–13). "Do not repay evil for evil or reviling for reviling, but on the contrary, bless, for to this you were called, that you may obtain a blessing" (1 Pet. 3:9). Nor did Jesus threaten when he suffered (1 Pet. 2:23); he ordered Peter to sheath his sword and he healed Malchus's ear (Luke 22:51; John 18:11).

Jesus's saying about turning one's cheek (Matt. 5:38–42) has often been misunderstood and wrongly applied. It was taken too literally by the imitators of Jesus in the Middle Ages, and it is taken too literally by the Quakers, who on the basis of this passage do not want to go to court or serve in the armed forces, who forgo self-defense and remain passive in the face of all kinds of affronts. That cannot have been the intention. When a servant strikes him on the cheek, Jesus himself does not offer him the ether cheek, but says, "If what I said is wrong, bear witness about the wrong; but if what I said is right, why do you strike me?" (John 18:23; cf. also Paul in Acts 22:25). To suffer needlessly, to remain purely passive, is not right either.[110] On the other hand, this saying is also not an exaggeration, not a boast, nor a "counsel of perfection"[111] as Rome declares; it is definitely a precept for every disciple of Jesus.[112] The metaphors of turning the other cheek, walking the extra mile, surrendering your coat, and adding the cloak are explained in Matthew 5:44: "But I say unto

---

parenthetically refers to Augustine and Zöckler, general references that Bavinck also includes in his note. Bavinck also refers to Friedrich Adolph Philippi, *Commentary on St. Paul's Epistle to the Romans*, 2:287–88 (on Rom. 12:20), where Philippi specifies the Augustine references as *De doctrina christiana* III.16 (Augustine, *On Christian Doctrine* [NPNF² 6:563]). The Zöckler reference could not be determined.

110. Martensen, *Christian Ethics, Special Part*, 257–58 (§113).

111. LO: *consilium*.

112. Ed. note: Bavinck explores this matter thoroughly in *RE*, 1:315–40.

you, Love your enemies, bless them that curse you, do good to them that hate you, and pray for them which despitefully use you, and persecute you" (KJV). The idea is that evil must be repaid with good, curses with blessing, hatred with love, sin with forgiveness, misery with compassion. God acts this way, too (Matt. 5:45, 48).[113] Once more, that is not apathy, no Stoic passivity, no condoning the enemy's behavior. On the contrary, Jesus rebukes his enemies and pronounces woe upon the Pharisees. But while he is reprimanding the sin, he is loving and blessing the enemy.

Indeed, he commands us to forgive those who wrong us as often as seventy times seven—that is to say, countless times, again and again (Matt. 18:21–34). The Pharisees said that one must forgive three times. Peter boldly[114] says: Isn't seven times enough? But Jesus will have nothing to do with numbers or calculations here. The Christian should be an inexhaustible source of for-giveness.[115] After all, Christians need forgiveness themselves (Matt. 18:33). Certain evidence that we love our enemies is when we pray for them in all sincerity.[116] Righteous anger is certainly permissible and obligatory, but it must be an anger without sin, not long-lasting, and not rising rashly (Eph. 4:26–27; cf. Pss. 4:4; 37:8). "The anger of man does not produce the righteousness of God" (James 1:20; cf. Col. 3:8; Titus 1:7). And vengeance is never fitting; it belongs to God (Deut. 32:35). Love thinks no evil (1 Cor. 13) and covers a multitude of sins (1 Pet. 4:8).

In a sense, those enemies include worldlings.[117] The children of this world hate the light, do not know Jesus, and thus also do not know his followers (John 17:25; 1 John 3:1); they hate (John 15:18; 17:14) and persecute Christians, Jesus's followers. The world simply cannot love them. The Christian cannot and must not keep ecclesiastical company with them (Rom. 16:17; 1 Cor. 5:9, 11; 2 Cor. 6:14–17; Eph. 5:7, 11; 2 Thess. 3:6, 14; 1 Tim. 6:5; 2 Tim. 3:5; Titus 3:10; 2 John 10; cf. Matt. 10:14; Acts 13:51; 18:6), but may have civic concourse with them (1 Cor. 5:10). Jesus ate with tax collectors and sinners (Mark 2:15–17), with Pharisees (Luke 7:36; 14:1), and sought out sinners. But although the Christian loves worldlings as human beings, intimate interac-tion and bosom friendship[118] with them is impossible. The gap is too wide.

---

113. Wuttke, *Handbuch der christlichen Sittenlehre³*, 2:352 (§267).

114. DO: *kras*.

115. Martensen, *Christian Ethics, Special Part*, 258 (§113).

116. Martensen, *Christian Ethics, Special Part*, 261 (§114).

117. Wuttke, *Handbuch der christlichen Sittenlehre³*, 2:356–57 (§267). Ed. note: The term "worldlings" (DO: *wereldlingen*) is Bavinck's interpretation of Wuttke, *Handbuch der christ-lichen Sittenlehre³*, 2:356, where the word *Weltmenschen* is used. Cf. van Mastricht, *Theoretico-Practica Theologia*, III.vii.8 [IV, 761–65].

118. DO: *zielenvriendschap*.

But how must we act toward the *enemies of God*?[119] Holy Scripture has us adopt a completely different stance toward them than toward our personal enemies. Already to Abraham God said, "I will bless those who bless you, and him who dishonors you I will curse" (Gen. 12:3; cf. 27:29 [to Jacob]; Exod. 23:22 [to Israel]; Num. 24:9 [through Balaam]). God identifies his cause with that of Abraham and of Israel. On this basis believers then pray for the destruction of God's enemies. In Numbers 10:35 Moses prays, "Arise, O Lord, and let your enemies be scattered, and let those who hate you flee before you." God himself says that he will whet his glittering sword, make his arrows drunk with blood (Deut. 32:41–42). Moses prays, "Crush the loins of his [Levi's] adversaries, of those who hate him" (Deut. 33:11). Deborah sang, "So may all your enemies perish, O Lord!" (Judg. 5:31). Hannah sang, "He will guard the feet of his faithful ones, but the wicked shall be cut off in darkness. The adversaries of the Lord shall be broken to pieces; against them he will thunder in heaven" (1 Sam. 2:9–10).

In this context, especially the so-called *imprecatory psalms* come into view.[120]

> Arise, O Lord, in your anger;
>> lift yourself up against the fury of my enemies;
>> awake for me; you have appointed a judgment. (Ps. 7:6)

> Arise, O Lord! Confront him, subdue him!
>> Deliver my soul from the wicked by your sword. (Ps. 17:13)

> Indeed, none who wait for you shall be put to shame;
>> They shall be ashamed who are wantonly treacherous. (Ps. 25:3)

> But God will break you down forever;
>> he will snatch and tear you from your tent;
>> he will uproot you from the land of the living. (Ps. 52:5)

> He will return the evil to my enemies;
>> in your faithfulness put an end to them. (Ps. 54:5)

> But you, O God, will cast them down
>> into the pit of destruction;

119. Cf. the beginning of §34. Ed. note: Bavinck is referring to his discussion of cursing, pp. 180–82.

120. Barwasser, "Die sogenannten Rachepsalmen"; Beardslee, "Imprecatory Element." Ed. note: Bavinck's source for this paragraph is Wuttke, *Handbuch der christlichen Sittenlehre*[3], 2:350 (§267). Unlike Wuttke (who provides only a series of references), Bavinck gives citations from the *Statenvertaling*.

men of blood and treachery
    shall not live out half their days. (Ps. 55:23)

In wrath cast down the peoples, O God! (Ps. 56:7b)

O God, break the teeth in their mouths;
    Tear out the fangs of the young lions, O LORD! (Ps. 58:6)

Rouse yourself to punish all the nations;
    spare none of those who treacherously plot evil. (Ps. 59:5)

God shall arise, his enemies shall be scattered;
    and those who hate him shall flee before him! (Ps. 68:1)

Pour out your anger on the nations
    that do not know you,
and on the kingdoms
    that do not call upon your name! (Ps. 79:6)

Why should the nations say,
    "Where is their God?"
Let the avenging of the outpoured blood of your servants
    be known among the nations before our eyes! (Ps. 79:10)

Return sevenfold into the lap of our neighbors
    the taunts with which they have taunted you, O Lord! (Ps. 79:12)

Do to them as you did to Midian,
    as to Sisera and Jabin at the river Kishon,
who were destroyed at En-dor,
    who became dung for the ground.
Make their nobles like Oreb and Zeeb,
    all their princes like Zebah and Zalmunna,
who said, "Let us take possession for ourselves
    of the pastures of God."
O my God, make them like whirling dust,
    like chaff before the wind. (Ps. 83:9–13)

O LORD, God of vengeance,
    O God of vengeance, shine forth! (Ps. 94:1)

He will bring back on them their iniquity
    and wipe them out for their wickedness;
    the LORD our God will wipe them out. (Ps. 94:23)

Be not silent, O God of my praise!
For wicked and deceitful mouths are opened against me,
    speaking against me with lying tongues. (Ps. 109:1–2)

Appoint a wicked man against him;
    let an accuser stand at his right hand.
When he is tried, let him come forth guilty;
    let his prayer be counted as sin!
May his days be few;
    may another take his office!
May his children be fatherless
    and his wife a widow!
May his children wander about and beg,
    seeking food far from the ruins they inhabit!
May the creditor seize all that he has;
    may strangers plunder the fruits of his toil!
Let there be none to extend kindness to him,
    nor any to pity his fatherless children!
May his posterity be cut off;
    may his name be blotted out in the second generation!
May the iniquity of his fathers be remembered before the LORD,
    and let not the sin of his mother be blotted out!
Let them be before the LORD continually,
    that he may cut off the memory of them from the earth! (Ps. 109:6–15)

Grant not, O LORD, the desires of the wicked;
    do not further their evil plot, or they will be exalted! (Ps. 140:8)

Let the wicked fall into their own nets,
    while I pass by safely. (Ps. 141:10)

The leitmotif of all these passages is found in Psalm 139:21–22:

Do I not hate those who hate you, O LORD?
    And do I not loathe those who rise up against you?
I hate them with complete hatred;
    I count them my enemies.

This is not personal vengeance, which is explicitly forbidden in the Old Testament in several passages: "You shall not take vengeance or bear a grudge against the sons of your own people" (Lev. 19:18); "Vengeance is mine, and recompense" (Deut. 32:35; cf. 1 Sam. 24:12, 15; 25:33; Ps. 7:3–8; Prov. 20:22; 24:29). Rather, what Psalm 139 is speaking of is specifically hatred against the enemies of God.

We find the same in the New Testament. Peter says to Simon the sorcerer, "May your silver perish with you, because you thought you could obtain the gift of God with money! . . . Repent, therefore, of this wickedness of yours" (Acts 8:20–22). Paul pronounces an anathema upon those who do not love Jesus (1 Cor. 16:22) or who bring any other gospel (Gal. 1:8). He says of Alexander the coppersmith, who caused him much evil, "The Lord will repay him according to his deeds" (2 Tim. 4:14). He delivers Hymenaeus and Alexander unto Satan "that they may learn not to blaspheme" (1 Tim. 1:20), the purpose of which was probably to save their spirit (1 Cor. 5:5).

Indeed, God himself, Christ, hates the sinners and will wipe them out (Pss. 2:9; 104:35; 119:21). His wrath and curse rest upon them (John 3:36; Matt. 25:41). Jesus even commands his disciples to hate father, mother, wife, and so on—even their very own lives (Luke 14:26). And it is permissible to rejoice about God's triumph over his enemies (see Exod. 15, about Pharaoh's destruction). "The righteous see it and are glad; / the innocent one mocks at them" (Job 22:19). "The righteous shall see and fear, / and shall laugh at him, saying, / 'See the man who would not make / God his refuge, / but trusted in the abundance of his riches / and sought refuge in his own destruction!'" (Ps. 52:6–7; cf. 54:7; 59:11; 68:22; 107:42). "Rejoice over her, O heaven, and you saints and apostles and prophets, for God has given judgment for you against her!" (Rev. 18:20; cf. Ps. 2; Prov. 1:26; Deut. 32:37–42).

With this, Heidelberg Catechism, Q&A 52, agrees completely: "Christ will cast all his and my enemies into everlasting condemnation."[121] That is why Scripture never says that we must love Satan or the demons, even though they are creatures of God.[122]

4. Love toward Those in Distress[123]

Those in distress are the poor, the sick, widows, orphans, strangers, prisoners, and so on.[124] The world outside of Christ was and is "a world without love." The virtue of compassion toward those in distress was unknown to pagans. In Scripture, that is different. There, in all kinds of ways, the poor are given care, preventively by means of the Year of Jubilee (Lev. 25), but

---

121. See Wuttke, *Handbuch der christlichen Sittenlehre*[3], 2:349–50; Kuyper, *E Voto Dordraceno*, 1:57–64; originally published in *De Heraut*, no. 466 (November 28, 1886).

122. Cf. also Kuyper, "Zetten tot een wit."

123. DO: *ellendigen*.

124. Wuttke, *Handbuch der christlichen Sittenlehre*[3], 2:330–31. Marginal note by Bavinck: "These people in distress are of eminent importance in the field of ethics. They are there in order that we lead others better to appreciate the benefits that we have received from God, so that they thus fulfill a calling toward us; they are there in order to teach us beneficence, compassion, etc."

also through benevolence and granting rights to the poor. A cloak given in pledge must be returned to a poor person before nightfall (Deut. 24:12–13); the poor and needy day-laborer may not be oppressed and must have their wages paid out before sunset (vv. 14–15). One may not harden one's heart nor close one's hand against the poor, but must freely give and lend to them (Deut. 15:7–8).

The poor must not be given favored treatment in court out of sentimental sympathy (Exod. 23:3), but neither may one defer to the great (Lev. 19:15). Poor foreigners, widows, and orphans must be allowed to glean in the harvest field (Lev. 19:9–10; Deut. 24:19–22). The harvest of the Sabbath year was to be shared with the servants, hired hands, maids, and foreigners (Lev. 25:5–7). Participation in the sacrificial meals was to be open to Levites, foreigners, orphans, and widows (Deut. 14:28–29; 16:10–12; 26:12–13). Slaves were to be released in the seventh year (Exod. 21:2; Deut. 15:12). Debts were to be forgiven in the Sabbath year (Deut. 15:1). Interest on loans was not to be charged to an Israelite (Exod. 22:25; Lev. 25:37; Deut. 23:20), but only to a foreigner (Deut. 23:20). One may not mistreat the widow and the orphan, nor wrong the foreigner (Exod. 22:21–24). The elderly were to be honored (Lev. 19:32). The disabled, the deaf, and the blind may not be cursed or led astray (Lev. 19:14; Deut. 27:18). There will always be poor in Israel (Deut. 15:11). The poor are made by the Lord (Prov. 22:2), but they are also spared by him[125] (Ps. 72:13). Punishment awaits those who oppress or mock the poor (Prov. 14:31; 17:5; 22:16), but whoever takes pity on the poor lends to the Lord (Prov. 19:17; 28:8, 27). In this way, God is Father and Judge of the orphan and the widow (Ps. 68:5). He upholds them (Ps. 146:9), loves their cause (Deut. 10:18; Job 29:12–16), and admonishes us to do the same (Ps. 82:3; Isa. 1:17). He severely punishes those who oppress the widow and the orphan (Exod. 22:22–24; Deut. 24:17; Job 24:3; Isa. 1:23; Jer. 5:28; 7:6; 22:3; Ezek. 22:7; Zech. 7:10; Mal. 3:5).

This is still more clear in the New Testament, now that the compassionate High Priest has come, who heals the sick and commends mercy (Luke 6:36) and requires it from his disciples (Matt. 10:42; 25:35–40; Luke 10:30–37; Col. 3:12; 1 Pet. 3:8). The poor must be remembered and given alms (Matt. 6:2; 19:21; 25:34–40; Luke 19:8; 1 John 3:17). Care for the poor is exemplified by Dorcas (Acts 9:36) and Cornelius (Acts 10:2) and taught in exhortations such as the following: "You always have the poor with you" (Mark 14:7); "Contribute to the needs of the saints" (Rom. 12:13); "Do not neglect to do good" (Heb. 13:16); "Mercy triumphs over judgment" (James 2:13). Widows

125. DO: *maar worden ook door Hem verschoond.*

and orphans must be visited and supported (James 1:27; 1 Tim. 5:16), and Jesus reprimands the Pharisees for devouring widows' houses (Matt. 23:14; Luke 20:47). Foreigners are to be given lodging (Matt. 25:35; Rom. 12:13; Heb. 13:2; cf., in the Old Testament, Gen. 18:2–8; Lev. 25:35; Deut. 10:19; Judg. 19:15–21; Job 31:32; Isa. 58:7). Prisoners should be visited (Matt. 25:36; Heb. 13:3; 2 Tim. 1:16). In the church, a vehicle for this work of mercy was instituted in the form of the diaconate (Acts 6).

The aim of these forms of mercy (benevolence, hospitality, etc.) is to heal and relieve human distress—a continuation of Christ as the compassionate High Priest. Mercy has its roots in a heart full of love, but it is easily externalized altogether and focused on the alms themselves (Matt. 6:1–4; Luke 18:12), as the Pharisees did and Roman Catholics still do, making a meritorious work out of it. But giving alms to gain honor or salvation or to be rid of the problem (Luke 11:8; 18:4–5) is definitely wrong and is without blessing (2 Cor. 9:5, 7). Giving alms ought to be done from love (2 Cor. 8:9–10), quietly (Matt. 6), without display[126] (Rom. 12:8), and cheerfully (2 Cor. 9:7). This also condemns the worldly habit of promoting benevolence through charity fundraising dances, plays, fireworks, concerts, lotteries, and bazaars. All of these mock true Christian benevolence; these are not at all about the sufferers, but about the enjoyment.[127]

5. Love toward Brothers and Sisters [in Christ][128]

Jesus himself was the first to call his disciples brothers. He tells them, "If your brother sins against you . . ." (Matt. 18:15), and "for you have one teacher, and you are all brothers" (Matt. 23:8). He tells Peter, "Strengthen your brothers" (Luke 22:32). They are each other's brothers because they are brothers of Christ: "For whoever does the will of my Father in heaven is my brother and sister and mother" (Matt. 12:50; cf. Matt. 25:40; 28:10; Luke 8:21); "You are my friends if you do what I command you. No longer do I call you servants" (John 15:14–15). Jesus is their eldest brother, "the firstborn among many brothers" (Rom. 8:29), and has made them children of one God and Father (John 20:17); "he is not ashamed to call them brothers" (Heb. 2:11), and he became like them in every respect (Heb. 2:17). They all have one God as Father (John 1:13; 1 John 3:9; Gal. 3:26), one Lord (Eph. 4:4–6), one mother—namely, the Jerusalem that is above (Gal. 4:26)—and one inheritance (Rom. 8:17). That is

126. DO: *eenvoudigheid.*
127. Wuttke, *Handbuch der christlichen Sittenlehre*[3], 2:333 (§261).
128. Wuttke, *Handbuch der christlichen Sittenlehre*[3], 2:338–42 (§264); J. T. Beck, *Vorlesungen über christliche Ethik*, 2:261–75.

why they are bound to each other through intimate love, like children of one family. And that love is specifically distinct from neighbor love. Jesus calls it a new commandment: "A new commandment I give to you, that you love one another: just as I have loved you, . . ." (John 13:34–35; similarly, 15:12–13). It is a love that Jesus shows brothers and sisters through us. Christ in us loves the brothers and sisters (". . . that the love with which you have loved me may be in them, and I in them" [John 17:26]). But why does Jesus call this a new commandment? Is he really, as the Socinians claim, a new legislator?[129] Did he supplement and improve the incomplete Old Testament law? Vilmar argues that neighbor love is an ancient commandment and is the fulfillment of the law. But here, Vilmar continues, Jesus is giving not merely a different standard but also a different principle of love. With the law the principle is self-love; but the love of the gospel transcends that of the law as highly as Christ transcends Moses. Here in the gospel, Christ is the principle, and his love is the standard for our love.[130]

But Vilmar is not correct. Jesus's love commandment is *new* for the following reasons:

a. The church became disconnected from Israel and came to stand on its own feet. In Israel, brother love and neighbor love (or ethnic love) coincided and were not yet distinguished. But the ethnic, tribal love now ceased. Brotherly love alone was to keep the church together and thus became independent, and therefore was sensed more distinctly, more profoundly, more intimately, and more valuably.

b. The Holy Spirit now became the life-principle of the church. Working in the Old Testament more by means of objective things like the temple, the cult, and so on, upon the individual person, he now became immanent within believers, binding them together through a holy love.

c. Thereby three relationships were changed: to Christ, who had become incarnate and ascended again; to each other; and to the world. The relationship to each other, which now had a distinctive role, is fraternal[131] love.[132]

129. LO: *novus legislator.*

130. Vilmar, *Theologische Moral,* 2/3:146.

131. DO: *broederlijke.* Ed. note: Since Latin does not have gender-neutral roots, the word "fraternal" can include both sexes (e.g., "fraternal twins"); a literal translation of Bavinck's original is of course "brotherly," which in his day was not restricted to the male sex.

132. Kuyper, "De Liefde XIII"; also Kuyper, *E Voto Dordraceno,* 2:232–40; originally published in *De Heraut,* no. 693 (April 5, 1891).

That fraternal love is therefore also the hallmark and proof that believers are Jesus's disciples (John 13:35). Especially John speaks repeatedly about it (1 John 2:7–11); it is a new (cf. 1 John 2:8) yet also an old commandment that believers have heard from the beginning. "Anyone who does not love remains in death" (1 John 3:14 NIV; cf. 3:16, 23). It is the proof that we have passed from death into life, obligating us to give our life for the brothers and sisters, a love that is rooted in God's love for us (1 John 4:7, 11, 21). Believers have learned that love from God (1 Thess. 4:9) and therefore do good, especially to those of the household of faith (Gal. 6:10). This love is manifested in the sign of the holy kiss[133] (Rom. 16:16; 1 Cor. 16:20; 2 Cor. 13:12; 1 Thess. 5:26; 1 Pet. 5:14), in the love feasts (Jude 12),[134] in their greetings (Rom. 16:5, 16; 1 Cor. 16:20), in their collections (Acts 11:29; Rom. 15:25–26), and in their intercessory prayers. The Holy Spirit prays in us for the saints (Rom. 8:27), just as Christ intercedes for us (Rom. 8:34). James 5:16 admonishes us to pray for one another. Paul prays for his churches (Col. 1:3, 9) and asks for their intercessory prayers (Col. 4:3; 1 Thess. 5:25; 2 Thess. 3:1; Heb. 13:18).[135] This fraternal love is manifested also in both personal and written communication (Eph. 6:21; Phil. 2:19; Col. 4:7, 16; 1 Thess. 3:2, 5–13; 5:27), as well as in visiting each other and longing for one another (Acts 15:36; 19:21; Rom. 1:10–15).[136]

Complete agreement, with respect to both natural and spiritual things, is impossible here on earth. No one should therefore be wise in their own sight (Rom. 12:16); each should esteem the other better than oneself (Phil. 2:3). Everyone should be fully persuaded in their own mind about many things (Rom. 14:5) and leave each other free (Rom. 14:1–13; 1 Cor. 10:19–33). But arguing must be avoided (1 Tim. 6:5; Titus 3:9–11), and harmony must be promoted (Rom. 12:16). Let there be no disputing, but instead a communal seeking after the truth (Acts 15:7).[137] Let offense be avoided, both in taking it and giving it. Not everything that is lawful is edifying (1 Cor. 6:12; 10:23, 32). Instead, brothers and sisters should edify, console, admonish, teach, and correct one another (Luke 22:32; Col. 3:16; Heb. 10:24; 2 Thess. 3:14–15; James 5:19–20).[138]

To the various forms of neighbor love already discussed, I add the remainder of this section as an appendix.

133. DO: *broederlijke kus*.
134. GrO: ἀγάπαις.
135. Cf. Löber, *Die Lehre vom Gebet*.
136. Wuttke, *Handbuch der christlichen Sittenlehre³*, 2:340 (§264).
137. LO: *disputatio*; GrO: συζήτησις; Wuttke, *Handbuch der christlichen Sittenlehre³*, 2:567n81 (§264).
138. Wuttke, *Handbuch der christlichen Sittenlehre³*, 2:342 (§264).

6. Love toward Angels[139]

Angels minister to us (Heb. 1:14; cf. Pss. 34:7; 91:11; Isa. 37:36; Dan. 10:13; Matt. 4:6; Luke 15:10; 16:22; 18:10; Acts 12:15). And we have duties toward them as well. Roman Catholics contend that we must show them religious honor, consisting not of worship,[140] but nevertheless of veneration[141] (in conflict with Judg. 13:15–16; Col. 2:18; Rev. 19:20; 22:8–9). Religious honor is due to God alone (Deut. 6:13; 10:20; Matt. 4:10). Still, we do have duties toward the angels: we must show them civil honor[142] (Gen. 18:3), as we do our fellow human beings. We must speak about them in a respectful manner and through our holy walk make known to them the manifold wisdom of God (Eph. 3:10; 1 Cor. 11:10); we are to speak the truth before them (1 Tim. 5:21). By contrast, toward evil angels we have in particular the duty to hate them, to flee from them, and to resist them (Matt. 8:29; 10:1; 15:22; 17:21; 2 Tim. 2:25–26; 1 Pet. 5:8).

7. Love toward Animals and Nature in General

God has spread his power and beauty throughout nature. We may be lovers of plants, flowers, and animals. Scripture points to that repeatedly; it sees God's hand and power everywhere (Pss. 19; 65; 104). The law, too, provides for the animals: an ox that treads out the grain must not be muzzled (Deut. 25:4); on the Sabbath the livestock too must rest (Exod. 20:10); in the seventh year the cattle may graze in the fallow fields (Exod. 23:11; Lev. 25:6–7). If a donkey stumbles under a load, one must help it (Exod. 23:5); if it has wandered off, one must return it to its owner (Deut. 22:1). Two different animal species may not breed (Lev. 19:19); a kid may not be boiled in its mother's milk (Exod. 23:19; 34:26; Deut. 14:21); an ox or sheep may not be slaughtered along with its young on the same day (Lev. 22:28). Mother bird and chick may not both be taken from the same nest at the same time (Deut. 22:6–7).

During the Flood, God saved the animals as well (Gen. 6:19), and after the Flood God also established his covenant with all living things: birds, cattle, every beast of the earth (Gen. 9:10). "Whoever is righteous has regard for the life of his beast, but the mercy of the wicked is cruel" (Prov. 12:10). Therefore, Schopenhauer unjustly accuses the Holy Scripture of not caring about animals.[143]

---

139. Cf. *RE*, 1:59–60.
140. GrO: λατρεία.
141. GrO: δουλεία.
142. DO: *burgerlijke eer*.
143. Schopenhauer, *Two Fundamental Problems of Ethics*, 173 ("On the Basis of Morals," §8), 242 ("On the Basis of Morals," §19.7). Ed. note: Bavinck added an interlinear reference to

The New Testament, however, speaks less about this. Paul asks, "Is it for oxen that God is concerned? Does he not certainly speak for our sake?" (1 Cor. 9:9–10). Paul characteristically understands the passage about the ox treading out the grain allegorically, to refer to ministers of the gospel (1 Tim. 5:17–18). But in other instances, in plants and animals we see symbolized, as it were, moral ideas.[144] It is not mere wordplay to see a maiden's purity in a rose, humility in a pansy, strength of character in an oak tree, shortness of life in withering grass, majesty and pride in a cedar tree (Isa. 2:13; Amos 2:9; Zech. 11:2), royal nobility and splendor in a palm tree (Ps. 92:12–13), victory and peace in its branches (John 12:13; Rev. 7:9), weakness in reeds (Isa. 58:5; 2 Kings 18:21; Matt. 11:7), beauty in lilies (Song 2:1–2; Hosea 14:5; Matt. 6:28), fruitfulness in olive branches (Jer. 11:16; Ps. 128:3; Rom. 11:16–24), love in the pomegranate (Song 4:13; 6:7; 8:2), nobility but also ingratitude in the vine (Isa. 5), evil in thorns and thistles (Judg. 9:14; Isa. 7:23–25), and faith in the mustard seed (Matt. 17:20).[145]

Animals similarly display moral qualities.[146] They are a living textbook, a moral mirror for people. As Novatian once observed, "In the animals it is the characters, and doings, and wills of men that are depicted."[147] Where the evil in animals and the irrational in nature (Schelling) come from is difficult to say.[148] The eagle (Job 39:30) symbolizes royal dignity and strength and is used of Cyrus (Isa. 46:11; cf. Jer. 48:40; 49:22), also of Jehovah spreading his wings over Israel (Deut. 32:11). The wild donkey symbolizes coarseness and disorderliness (Gen. 16:12; Job 6:5). The war horse (Job 39:19–25) symbolizes pride and overconfidence (Deut. 17:16; Isa. 31:3; Jer. 8:6). The lion pictures strength and valor (2 Sam. 17:10), sometimes Jehovah (Isa. 31:4; 38:13; Hosea 5:14), and Christ (Rev. 5:5). The panther portrays violence and swiftness (Jer. 5:6; Hab.

Schopenhauer's *Parerga and Paralipomena*, §178, but this appears to be in error, since there is nothing about either animals or Holy Scripture in §178.

144. Marginal note by Bavinck: "Man transfers to nature his own feelings. Ambition to imitate. See C. B. Spruyt, 'Iets over den oorsprong en het wezen van den godsdienst,' 61ff.; J. L'Ange Huet, *Nieuwe oplossing van een oud vraagstuk*, 24–71." Ed. note: Spruyt's essay is a review of Herbert Spencer, *Ecclesiastical Institutions, Being Part VI of the "Principles of Sociology"* (London, 1885).

145. Zöckler, *Theologia naturalis*, 501–34.

146. See §38 above and *RE*, 1:61–62; Martensen, *Christian Dogmatics*, 212–14 (§112); Zöckler, *Theologia naturalis*, 535–42.

147. LO: *In animalibus mores depinguntur humani et actus et voluntatis*; Novatian, *On the Jewish Meats* III (*ANF* 5:647). Ed. note: Novatian (ca. 200–258) was a Roman priest and theologian who was consecrated as an antipope by three bishops in 251; he adopted a rigorous position against the readmission of Christians who had lapsed during the Decian persecution in 250. Bavinck's source is Zöckler, *Theologia naturalis*, 537.

148. Zöckler, *Theologia naturalis*, 537, 542. Ed. note: Many of the references to animal symbolism in Holy Scripture are taken from Zöckler, *Theologia naturalis*, 549–55.

1:8). The wolf symbolizes fierceness and rapaciousness (Ezek. 22:27; Matt. 7:15; John 10:12). The partridge pictures greed and miserliness (Jer. 17:11). The bee and the ant symbolize industry (Prov. 6:6–8; 30:25). The dove portrays innocence, guilelessness (Ps. 74:19; Matt. 10:16) and symbolizes the Holy Spirit. The rooster pictures vigilance (Matt. 26:34). The dog represents lust, meanness, and robbery (Isa. 56:11), and represents pagans (Matt. 15:26–27; cf. Rev. 22:15). Sheep portray gentleness and innocent weakness, long-suffering (Isa. 5:17; Jer. 11:19; Matt. 10:6), an image of Jesus (Isa. 53:7; John 1:29; Rev. 5:6), and of Jesus's disciples (John 10). The snake points to cunning and nakedness of sin (Gen. 3; Matt. 10:16; Rev. 12:9; 20:2). Nature and the animal world contain rich lessons for us. Animal fables are full of mystical, profound truth. We are attracted to some animals and find others repugnant.

Two things should be avoided: animal worship, as among the Egyptians and many pagans, and animal cruelty. Buddhists see nature as God, eat no meat, and protect animals—the Jains at times to the point of absurdity.[149] Pythagoras?, Empedocles, neo-Pythagoreans, Essenes, Therapeuts, Porphyry, and others ate no meat and killed no animals. In the Christian church as well many favored vegetarianism.[150] Francis of Assisi was so tender and sweet that the animals all loved him.

The nineteenth century saw the rise of the movement for the protection of animals. A law to protect animals was passed first in England, where also a Society for the Prevention of Cruelty to Animals was also first established. From there the movement has spread to many other countries.[151]

Schopenhauer came to the defense especially of animals; he accused Judaism, Christianity, and the entire West of animal cruelty and praised the East.[152] He saw no essential difference between humans and animals. The core—that is, the will—is the same in both. The only difference is the intellect, and from the intellect stem all the other differences. But human beings fancy themselves altogether different creatures, and the same acts done among animals they call by different names: people eat, animals feed; people drink, animals swill; the body of a deceased human is a corpse, the body of a deceased animal is carrion; humans give birth, animals drop their young.[153] The English language considers all animals as neuter in gender.[154]

---

149. Kern, *Geschiedenis van het Buddhisme in Indië*, 2:59–69.
150. See §38, above.
151. Schopenhauer, *Two Fundamental Problems of Ethics*, 242.
152. Cf. Kiehl, *Natuurlijke historie van den Filistijn*, 1:228–29.
153. DO: *eten—vreten, drinken—zuipen, lijk—aas (kreng), baren—jongen*.
154. Schopenhauer, *Two Fundamental Problems of Ethics*, 241. Ed. note: Schopenhauer's point here is beside the point because (a) unlike German, English is an undeclined language; and (b) gender in language is unrelated to biological sex.

Philosophical ethics since Descartes has strayed completely off course. Kant recognized no duties toward animals, only duties of human beings toward themselves with respect to the treatment of animals.[155] Rothe also denies duties toward animals.[156] So did the ancient Stoics.[157]

Now we undoubtedly also have rights with respect to animals: we may eat them, and we may kill them if they thwart us, because otherwise, the created world would have filled up with animals and nothing would have remained for humans. We may use them for our clothing, employ them in our labor (Gen. 1:28; Ps. 8—what would the Lapplander be without reindeer, the Greenlander without seals, the desert dweller without camels?), use them for making life more pleasant (pets, equestrian sport?, zoos), and for scientific research.

Animal cruelty, on the other hand, is sin and callousness. Harsh treatment of work animals—tormenting household pets for amusement, animal fights, harness racing[158] in England, animal sports in the Netherlands in Bussum, and the like—betrays moral callousness, brutish character, lack of love toward God's creation. Other examples include emptying birds' nests; boys' torturing of flies, spiders, and toads; and then especially the current vivisection of frogs, clogs, cats, and so on, which does seem necessary at times in the interest of science but is highly overused and can be mitigated by chloroform.[159]

However, an organization for the protection of animals is unnecessary, is a disgrace for a Christian society, and is a misguided principle. Imagine establishing a separate society for every sin or evil! Exaggerated gentleness, tenderness, and sentimental love toward a lady's lap dog,[160] buying and releasing a cage of birds (as described in a novel by Justus van Maurik),[161] and Pythagoras's releasing of a net full of fish[162] are also exaggerated and wrong. A human being is "of more value than many sparrows" (Matt. 10:31). But God is good also to all his creatures (Ps. 145:9); he feeds the birds (Matt. 6:26). So we ought to treat the animals well, sparing their strength, easing their death, healing their disease (veterinarians), and so on.[163]

---

155. Schopenhauer, *Two Fundamental Problems of Ethics*, 156, 239–45.

156. Rothe, *Theologische Ethik*, 3:449–53 (§858).

157. Cf. Reinhard, *System der christlichen Moral*, 3:124 (§285).

158. DO: *paard-harddraverijen*.

159. Martensen, *Christian Ethics, Special Part*, 1:280–82 (§121).

160. DO: *damesschoothondje*; Wuttke, *Handbuch der christlichen Sittenlehre³*, 2:364 (§269).

161. Ed. note: This is a reference to the Dutch writer Justus van Maurik Jr. (1846–1904)—specifically, to his story "A Stroll on the Amstelveld" ("Een wandeling op 't Amstelveld"), in the collection *Van Allerlei Slag: Novellen en Schetsen*, 45–66. On pp. 52–54 he describes a woman who buys a cageful of finches and then releases them.

162. Schopenhauer, *Two Fundamental Problems of Ethics*, 242.

163. Reinhard, *System der christlichen Moral*, 3:131–34 (§287).

People must treat all of nature with humaneness, according to its intrinsic worth. In Nineveh, God took pity on the people, on the children, but also on the many animals (Jon. 4:10–11). Is hunting purely for sport[164] lawful? Originally hunting served to eradicate wild animals. But today?[165] Sir Walter Scott used to participate in this but could no longer when once a bird cast its dying eye upon him.[166]

§45. Concern for Our Neighbor's Life (Sixth Commandment)

As with all commandments, this one too must be explained literally and spiritually, and the prohibition contains a positive command.[167] Luther is right when he says: It is written, *thou*; *thou* shalt not—that is, not only your hand and fist but all of you shall not, neither in body nor in mind, not with thoughts, passions, or deeds. Jesus himself explains this commandment in Matthew 5:21–22: "Everyone who is angry with his brother will be liable to judgment." And in 1 John 3:11–16 we read, "Everyone who hates his brother is a murderer." The basis for this prohibition is not that we should not kill any living beings (Buddhists, Pythagoreans, Therapeuts, etc.), nor that we, who lived originally in a state of "a war of all against all,"[168] then for the sake of our security contractually promise to spare one another (Hobbes). Rather, the basis for this prohibition is that the image of God in human beings may not be violated, that human beings bear a royal, priestly character, are God's offspring, and thus their lives are sacrosanct (Gen. 9:6; Acts 17:28; James 3:9). That is why Abel's blood cries out to God from the earth (Gen. 4:10).

The Sixth Commandment forbids murder in the literal sense of the word—that is, killing someone's body, including one's own, with external, physical means.[169] One can personally kill another by striking, punching, poisoning, drowning them, and the like. Or one can have someone else do it, as David did in the case of Uriah (2 Sam. 11:15) and Saul's sons (2 Sam. 21:9), or as the Jews did in the case of Christ (Matt. 27:25). One can do it more directly or more indirectly: by striking someone who dies from that wound a week or a month or a year later; by compromising someone's bodily health; by having

164. DO: *jacht voor louter vermaak.*
165. Martensen, *Christian Ethics, Special Part*, 1:279 (§121).
166. Martensen, *Christian Ethics, Special Part*, 1:279–80 (§121).
167. Cf. Calvin, *Institutes*, II.viii.6.
168. LO: *in bellum omnium contra omnes.*
169. Heidelberg Catechism, Q&A 105.

children, women, or men work beyond their strength (think of factories);[170] by withholding their wages; by seducing friends to live an immoral and intemperate life that undermines their health; by damaging someone's reputation, honor, or good name; or by breaking someone's heart—for example, of one's father or mother, through grief.[171]

But one can sin not only against the letter but also against the spirit of this commandment, when one refrains from murder or manslaughter merely from fear of punishment or lack of opportunity or from concern about one's reputation.[172] This commandment is violated through the root of murder, which lives in all of us and sometimes flares up—by envy, which is icy hatred,[173] or by wrath, which is boiling hatred,[174] by animosity, anger, or thirst for revenge.[175] For "everyone who hates his brother is a murderer" (1 John 3:15). Murders arise from the heart (Matt. 15:19). Envy desires the neighbor's death. One who is angry at one's brother is for that reason already punishable (Matt. 5:22). And all of us, hating each other (Titus 3:3), are full of "envy, murder, strife, deceit, maliciousness" (Rom. 1:29), and thus we are all murderers. All egoism harbors a principle of hatred, and we are egoists even toward our friends, who become our enemies as soon as our interests clash with theirs. We are egoists and therefore haters with respect to those indifferent to us, to our competitors, our enemies, and others.

We are murderers also when we kill our neighbor's soul.[176] Satan was such a murderer from the beginning (John 8:44). We kill a soul whenever we seduce someone, causing them to fall into sin through our word or our example. This happens when we flatter our neighbors' pride, incite their evil lusts and desires, feed their anger, encourage their lust for revenge, weaken their tender consciences, shock their faith by our doubt, crush their faith by our ridicule, or offend them in anything whatsoever. We can do this even to our children if we ignore the bad books they read or any irreverent talk about God, his Word, church, or sermons, or if we stroke their pride, appeal to their ambition, and the like. And all of us are murderers—it was our sins that caused Jesus's death.[177]

---

170. Ed. note: Bavinck provides a specific example, "the firm Regout in Maastricht." P. D. Regout (1801–78) was an early industrialist, owner of a factory in glassworks and potteries in the southern Dutch city of Maastricht. See Ubachs, *Een eeuw modern kapitalisme*.

171. Cf. Monod, "Êtes-vous un meurtrier?," 241. Ed. note: The French quotation is the title of the sermon Bavinck references.

172. Monod, "Êtes-vous un meurtrier?," 243–55.

173. DO: *koude haat*.

174. DO: *hete haat*; E. Sartorius, *Die Lehre von der heiligen Liebe*, 3/2:4–5.

175. Heidelberg Catechism, Q&A 106.

176. Monod, "Êtes-vous un meurtrier?," 252–55.

177. Monod, "Êtes-vous un meurtrier?," 255–59.

This prohibition, however, does not preclude capital punishment or war.[178] The death penalty for a murderer was instituted by God himself (Gen. 9:6). To be sure, a commandment like the one in Genesis 9:4 ("But you shall not eat flesh with its life, that is, its blood") has been repealed and abolished. But this particular commandment of Genesis 9:6 was likely not abolished, since it was given to Noah (the new head of the human race), and its warrant (because the person was created in the image of God) is valid always and everywhere. It was reiterated by Jesus (Matt. 26:52: "All who take the sword will perish by the sword"; cf. also Rev. 13:10). The question, however, is whether Genesis 9:6 is a commandment or whether, instead, it is a prophecy whose fulfillment God himself will ensure. God spared Cain even though he deserved the death sentence (Gen. 4:10–16). Simeon and Levi slaughtered the people of Shechem, but they remained alive, though their anger was cursed by Jacob (Gen. 49:5–7). For those who kill a person out of ignorance, God established six cities of refuge in Israel (Num. 35:9–15; Deut. 19:1–10).[179] In addition, Israel had the death penalty (Exod. 21:12, 14; cf. 1 Sam. 15:18; 1 Kings 20:42). Romans 13 says simply that the government does not bear the sword in vain and avenges wrongdoing. The arguments against capital punishment are no longer valid. They arise from an erroneous view of punishment as though its purpose is rehabilitation. Or the arguments against capital punishment rest on the view that when judicial error occurs, it can no longer be rectified.[180] Nevertheless, opponents of capital punishment for murder do not object to sending soldiers off to war, shooting at rioting mobs, executing traitors—for traitors are still executed—and so on.

War is permissible as well (Luke 3:14).[181] God commanded Israel to wage war. Abraham waged war (Gen. 14); so did Moses, the judges, David, and others, who fought the battles of the Lord (1 Sam. 25:28). The centurion (Matt. 8:8–10) and Cornelius (Acts 10:1–2) remained in office after their conversion.[182] Marcion as well as the Mennonites denied the legitimacy of war.[183]

178. Kuyper, "De Liefde X."

179. De Moor, *Commentarius Perpetuus*, 2:878–83.

180. Kuyper, *Ons Program*, 753–54; Kuyper, *Our Program*, 226 (§184).

181. Ed. note: In later years Bavinck, struck by the horrors of the First World War, would write with greater nuance on the subject of war; cf. Bavinck, *Het probleem van de oorlog*; Bavinck, "Ethics and Politics"; Bavinck, "Imitation of Christ and Life in the Modern World"; Bavinck, *Christendom, oorlog, volkenbond*. See also van Keulen, "Herman Bavinck and the War Question."

182. Cf. Calvin, *Institutes*, IV.xx.11–12; Heidegger, *Corpus Theologicae Christianae*, 1:584–85; de Moor, *Commentarius Perpetuus*, 6:508–11. Luther wrote "Whether Soldiers Too, Can Be Saved (1526)" ("Ob kriegsleutte auch ynn seligem stande seyn künden"); Cromwell said, "Pray and keep your powder dry." Ed. note: An abridged version of Luther's tract can be found in J. M. Porter, ed., *Luther—Selected Political Writings*, 101–20.

183. Ames, *Conscience*, V.xxxiii.

Positively, the Sixth Commandment enjoins love toward the neighbor, toward their life in soul and body.[184] This love is made specific in all kinds of other virtues: patience, peace, gentleness, compassion, and kindness.[185] Paul (Eph. 4:26, 31) and James (3:5–12; cf. 1:19–20) condemn wrath (cf. Matt. 5:22–26). As those who are beloved of God, we are to put on compassion, kindness, patience, and the like (Eph. 4:15–16; Col. 3:12–14).

§46. DUTIES TOWARD OUR NEIGHBOR'S CHASTITY (SEVENTH COMMANDMENT)

The origin and institution of proper sexual relations and of marriage is found in Genesis 1:27–31. God created humans as male and female, with the goal of multiplying the human race (cf. Gen. 2:18–24). God desired a humanity that did not consist of coordinated individuals, but rather of one issuing organically from one another.[186] As a result of sin, this noblest of all human qualities, love, has been perverted and corrupted the most. The chief sins forbidden here are the following:

a. *Adultery*—that is, carnal union of a married person with another. It is a sin against God (Gen. 2:23; Matt. 19:8; 1 Cor. 7:2), against ourselves (1 Cor. 6:19), and against our spouse. The Mosaic law prescribed the death penalty for this (Lev. 20:10–11; Deut. 22:22; John 8:9–15; cf. Gen. 26:11). And God himself punishes it for eternity (1 Cor. 6:10; Eph. 5:5; Heb. 13:21). Sometimes people distinguish further between *adulterium*, the sexual union of a married person with another married person, and *stuprum*, the sexual union of a married person with an unmarried person.[187]

b. *Concubinage and polygamy*, which is contrary to Genesis 2:24, Matthew 19:5, 1 Corinthians 7:2, and Ephesians 5:31. Neither was approved or permitted in the Old Testament but tolerated and overlooked.

---

184. Heidelberg Catechism, Q&A 107.

185. Cf. Hoornbeeck, *Theologia Practica*, 2:463–91; Ames, *Conscience*, V.xxvii–xxx; de Moor, *Commentarius Perpetuus*, 2:885–89. Ed. note: Bavinck borrows the references to Hoornbeeck and Ames from de Moor, *Commentarius Perpetuus*, 2:885. This also explains why the reference to Hoornbeeck is to the first edition (1666) of his *Theologiae Practicae*, whereas Bavinck usually refers to the second edition of 1689, which he may have owned himself.

186. E. Sartorius, *Die Lehre von der heiligen Liebe*, 430–53; Riehl, *Die Familie*; Lippert, *Die Geschichte der Familie*.

187. De Moor, *Commentarius Perpetuus*, 2:890.

c. *Fornication*, the sexual union of two unmarried people outside of marriage (Deut. 22:28–29; 23:17–18; Prov. 5:1–7; Sir. 9:3–9; and in the New Testament, 1 Cor. 6:19; Gal. 5:19, 21; Heb. 13:4; Rev. 2:14, 20–22).

d. *Incest*, fornication with relatives, whether within or outside of marriage (Gen. 19:36: Lot with his daughters; Gen. 35:22: Reuben with Bilhah, his father's wife; Gen. 38:18: Judah and Tamar; 2 Sam. 13:14: Amnon and Tamar; 2 Sam. 16:22: Absalom and his father's concubines; Matt. 14:4: Herod and his brother's wife; 1 Cor. 5: a man's incest with his father's wife). Degrees of consanguinity within which a marriage is prohibited are specified (Lev. 18:6–18; 20:11–12, 14; Deut. 22:30; 27:20, 22–23).[188]

e. *Sins against nature*: men lying with men (Gen. 19:5; Lev. 18:22; Rom. 1:26; 1 Cor. 6:9–10; Eph. 4:19), sodomy, onanism (Gen. 38:9), lying with animals (Exod. 22:19; Lev. 18:23; 20:15–16), sins too shameful to even mention (Eph. 5:12), sexual relations with children (think of sex trafficking). The state licenses brothels and protects prostitution. Bellarmine[189] contends that in so doing, the state does not sin but prevents greater evil.[190]

But in addition, forbidden here is all unchastity of the heart (Prov. 6:23–25; Matt. 5:28; 15:19–20).[191] To this is added anything that can seduce people into unchastity: drunkenness, drugs,[192] revelry (Prov. 23:31–33; Hosea 4:11; Rom. 13:13), for "without Ceres and Bacchus, Venus grows cold."[193] Seductions to unchasity include idleness (2 Sam. 11:2–4), for "if you remove *all* idleness, the bow of Cupid is broken, and his torch lies despised and without its light."[194]

---

188. Ed. note: Bavinck discusses this topic more extensive in *RE*, vol. 3, chap. 23, §§52 and 53.

189. Ed. note: Bavinck borrows the following citation from de Moor, *Commentarius Perpetuus*, 2:901: "*Bellarminus, de Amiss. Grat & Statu pecc. lib.* II. *cap.* XVIII." See Bellarmine, *Opera Omnia*, 4/1:114–18 ("*De Amissione Gratiae et Statu Peccati*," book II, chap. xviii, in *De Controversiis Christianae Fidei*).

190. De Moor, *Commentarius Perpetuus*, 2:901.

191. Ames, *Conscience*, V.xxxix.

192. DO: *opium*.

193. LO: *sine Cerere et Libero friget Venus*; alt: *sine Cerere et Baccho friget Venus*. Ed. note: The phrase comes from Roman comedian Terence, *Eunuchus*, act IV, scene 5. Ceres is the Roman "goddess of agriculture, grain crops, fertility and motherly relationships." In Roman mythology Libera (or Proserpine) "was daughter of the agricultural goddess Ceres and wife to Liber, the god of wine and freedom." Liber is the close equivalent to the Greek god Dionysus, "who was Romanised as Bacchus" (Wikipedia, s.v. "Sine Cerere et Baccho friget Venus," https://en.wikipedia.org/wiki/Sine_Cerere_et_Baccho_friget_Venus; Wikipedia, s.v. "Ceres (mythology)," https://en.wikipedia.org/wiki/Ceres_(mythology); Wikipedia, s.v. "Proserpina," https://en.wikipedia.org/wiki/Proserpina; Wikipedia, s.v. "Liber," https://en.wikipedia.org/wiki/Liber).

194. LO: *otia si tollas, periere Cupidinas arcus*; Ovid, *Remedia Amoris*, line 139 (trans. Riley, *Heroïdes*, 468; see also Ovid, *Art of Love* [LCL 232:252]).

They also include lewd paintings (Ezek. 23:14–17); scanty, indecent clothing (contrary to Gen. 3:7); the common baths, formerly outlawed;[195] unchaste movements of the body, the eyes (Job 31:1), and the hands (Isa. 3:16–24); interchanging dress between males and females (Deut. 22:5; 1 Tim. 2:9–10; 1 Pet. 3:3–5). This commandment forbids also unchaste words, books, and poems, as well as erotic verse and pornographic literature (1 Cor. 15:33; Eph. 4:29; 5:3–4), against which even the pagans guarded themselves;[196] all kinds of unchaste questions in the Roman Catholic confessional;[197] and lewd dances[198] and theater pageants.[199]

What is commanded here is, in short, chastity in soul and body, in word, gesture, and deed, both within and outside marriage (1 Cor. 6:15; 1 Thess. 4:3–4).

§47. DUTIES TOWARD OUR NEIGHBOR'S PROPERTY (EIGHTH COMMANDMENT)

To the content of the image of God belongs dominion over the earth (Gen. 1:26–29). To subdue the earth is our human calling. This is the basis of the right of ownership. In this commandment, the apportioning of the earth among humanity is sanctioned by God. Even without sin there could well have been private property, but after the fall, private property became necessary in order to avoid disputes and to stimulate industry. God now wills that there be poor and rich (Prov. 22:2), wants us to pray for *our* daily bread, and so on.[200] Plato, the Essenes, the Apostolic Fathers, the Anabaptists, and the socialists are therefore wrong. Acts 2:44 and 4:32 do not teach common property, but only common use.[201]

The earth itself is not the same everywhere and cannot be divided into a number of equal parts per capita; rather, the one part completes the others. Thus, everyone should be thankful for their modest portion and be content with it (1 Tim. 6:6–8; Heb. 13:5; Sir. 40:18). We have brought nothing into

---

195. De Moor, *Commentarius Perpetuus*, 2:903.

196. Valerius Maximus, *Facta et dicta memorabilia* VI.1; Plato, *Republic* VII. Ed. note: Bavinck's source for both references is de Moor, *Commentarius Perpetuus*, 2:904–5.

197. Cf. Tomás Sánchez, SJ, *Disputationum de Sancto Matrimonii*, cited in de Moor, *Commentarius Perpetuus*, 2:905.

198. De Moor, *Commentarius Perpetuus*, 2:905–6.

199. De Moor, *Commentarius Perpetuus*, 2:907; Rivet, *Opera Theologicorum*, 1:1409–15. Ed. note: Title of this section: "*De spectaculis Theatralibus.*"

200. De Moor, *Commentarius Perpetuus*, 2:918–19.

201. Cf. de Moor, *Commentarius Perpetuus*, 2:921; Ames, *Conscience*, V.xli; Rivet, *Praelectiones Pleniores*, 1:1417–20.

this world and will carry nothing out of it (1 Tim. 6:7). We should therefore possess as though not possessing (1 Cor. 7:30).

A rich person enters the kingdom of God with difficulty, for mammon and one's belly become one's god (Matt. 6:24; Phil. 3:19). The rich seek their salvation in possessions, not in God (Luke 12:20; 16:19–23). The rich fall into many temptations (1 Tim. 6:9), for love of money is the root of all evil and is idolatry (Col. 3:5). The covetous have no share in the kingdom of God (1 Cor. 6:10; Eph. 5:5). On the other hand, however, we are not to despise or disdain what God gives us, but must manage it carefully as being entrusted to us and make it fruitful for our sustenance (2 Thess. 3:10–12), and for the poor (Eph. 4:28).

Forbidden by the Eighth Commandment is theft in every shape and form.[202] We must refrain from this, not so much from an abstract right to property or for the sake of the civil law, but because we may not take from our neighbors what God *gave* them, both their goods and their life. As the saying goes, "Ill-gotten gains never prosper."[203] And, "Easy come, easy go."[204] Also, the neighbor's property includes not only money, land, and the like but also the time, diligence, and effort devoted to his products.

What is being forbidden by this commandment is theft of any kind; this includes theft of church property (*sacrilegium*, church robbing; Josh. 7:20; 2 Chron. 28:21; Prov. 20:25; Matt. 3:8), buying spiritual goods for money (simony), and selling them for money (Gehazi, 2 Kings 5). This also includes things belonging to the state, or the government, stealing from which many people consider permissible. People steal and enrich themselves from the public treasury when they dodge tolls, infringe on patents, bypass excised duties, evade taxes, and the like (Matt. 22:20; Rom. 13:6–7; 2 Pet. 2:3). The commandment also includes stealing private possessions and kidnapping (Gen. 37:28; Exod. 21:16; Deut. 24:7; 1 Tim. 1:10), rustling livestock (Exod. 22:1–4), or stealing any other good. What is forbidden is not only theft by violence or robbery through burglary, rioting, and looting but also theft without violence, through cunning, with a semblance of right, with a perversion of justice (Ps. 15:5; Isa. 1:23; Amos 5:12); theft through wagers, lotteries, playing for money, and casinos;[205] theft through adulteration of merchandise (Lev. 27:9–10; Amos 8:5–6); theft through hoarding (Prov. 11:26); through false weights and measures (Lev. 19:35; Deut. 25:13; Prov. 11:1;

---

202. St. Crispin stole leather to make shoes for the poor (von Jhering, *Der Zweck im Recht*, 2:619).

203. DO: *Onrecht goed gedijt niet.*

204. DO: *Zo gewonnen, zo geronnen.*

205. De Moor, *Commentarius Perpetuus*, 2:931.

20:10; Ezek. 45:9–12; Mic. 6:11); through incurring debts and not paying
them off (Exod. 22:7; Ps. 37:21; Prov. 3:28; Ezek. 18:7); through dishonest
bankruptcies; through reducing the worker's wages or not paying them on
time (Lev. 19:13; Deut. 24:14–15; James 5:4); through idling at work (Prov.
10:4); through borrowing and not returning (Ps. 37:21); through dishonesty
in commerce (Exod. 22:22; Lev. 19:11, 13; 25:14, 17; Prov. 23:10; 1 Cor. 6:8–9;
1 Thess. 4:6), on the stock exchange, the financial market, in bonds, through
speculations, debasing coins, and unfair competition; theft through usury,
allowed by God in dealings with other nations (Deut. 23:19–21), mostly
condemned by the Scholastics.[206]

Positively, we are commanded to promote and protect our neighbors in
terms of their possessions (Exod. 23:4–5; Deut. 22:1–4). Formerly, in the days
of guilds and corporations, this was easier than in our own day of absolute
private property rights.

§48. DUTIES TOWARD OUR NEIGHBOR'S REPUTATION (NINTH COMMANDMENT)

This commandment regulates our verbal interaction with our neighbor. God
gave human beings the gift of language.[207] We sin against this commandment
already in our heart when we think of our neighbor improperly, not according
to truth, or when we suspect them of this or that without any basis (Matt.
7:1; 1 Cor. 13:5; 1 Tim. 6:4). But this also occurs outwardly, when as a judge
in a court (Deut. 1:17; 16:19; 2 Chron. 19:6–7; Pss. 15:5; 82:2; Prov. 17:15;
24:24) we unjustly convict the innocent and acquit the guilty, favor the rich
or pass sentence without hearing the accused (Exod. 23:1; Deut. 1:16; John
7:51). Or it occurs also if in a court of law we give false testimony, when we
twist the truth, when we do not communicate the facts in good faith but shade
the truth, as a rash or unrighteous accuser (1 Sam. 22:9; 1 Kings 21:6; Matt.
26:61; Luke 3:14; 23:2; Acts 6:11), as the accused (Gen. 4:9; Josh. 7:19), as a
witness (Exod. 23:1; Deut. 19:16, 18; Prov. 6:19; 21:28; 1 Sam. 22:9; 2 Sam.
16:3; 1 Kings 21:13; Dan. 6:13; Matt. 6:1; Acts 8:13; 24:9), or as a lawyer
(Exod. 23:6; Isa. 5:23).

206. De Moor, *Commentarius Perpetuus*, 2:932–33; cf. Uhlhorn, *Das Christenthum und
das Geld*.
207. Ed. note: Bavinck added an interlinear comment: "Wonderful ability. What abuse!
Everyone has a reputation" (*Heerlijk vermogen. Wat misbruik! Naam heft ieder.*); and he wrote
a marginal note: "Our name is our self in its impression and appearance to others. A good name
is better than fine oil. God wants us to have a name. Care for our good name. When honor
is lost, much is lost. To Abraham: I shall magnify your name; to David; to Israel (Ezek. 16)."

Forbidden further are all lies and untruth.[208] Lying always consists of speech, in words or gestures. There is a difference between speaking an untruth and speaking untruthfully. It is also lying when you speak objective truth yet say something different from what you really think. When a person says something that is not true while being fully convinced that it is true, are they then lying? When a person says something that is true but labors under the illusion that it is false yet intends to pass it on, false though they think it is, then they are lying. But is it also always part of the definition of a lie that the intention is to deceive the other? That is Richard Locke's view, who therefore holds that lies told in jest or out of politeness or with irony are not really lies.[209] The clear intention must be to deceive rational people,[210] which then excludes children, the insane, public enemies, and criminals,[211] in which cases these are emergency lies.[212] But that is a fallacious concept.[213] Three elements constitute something a lie, says Vermigli: "to speak a falsehood, the will to speak thus, and the desire to deceive" (the first may be absent, however).[214] Formerly a distinction was made between lies that were malicious, jocular lies, and useful lies.[215] Everyone agreed that the first was sin. But the second and the third were not regarded as sins by the Socinians and were classified as venial sins by many Roman Catholics, including Aquinas.[216] Many philosophers considered the second and third kinds of lie to be permissible as well: Socrates, Plato, Xenophon, and the Stoics; so did many church fathers, as did Grotius, Pufendorf, and Saurin.[217] The Reformed accepted the distinctions among the kinds of lies but held all forms of lying to be sinful.[218] Those who defend the second and third types of lie (jocular lies and useful lies) appeal to Genesis 25:23; 27:24;

208. See Locke, *Über die Begriffsbestimmung der Lüge im eigentlichen Sinne.*

209. Locke, *Über die Begriffsbestimmung der Lüge,* 21.

210. Locke, *Über die Begriffsbestimmung der Lüge,* 22, 34–35.

211. Locke, *Über die Begriffsbestimmung der Lüge,* 38–40.

212. Locke, *Über die Begriffsbestimmung der Lüge,* 41.

213. Locke, *Über die Begriffsbestimmung der Lüge,* 42.

214. LO: *dicere falsum, ejus dicendi voluntas, fallendi cupiditas*; Vermigli, *Loci Communes,* Classis Secunda, Locus XIII, §24; de Moor, *Commentarius Perpetuus,* 2:946.

215. LO: *mendacia in perniciosa, jocusa* and *officiosa.* Ed. note: Bavinck's source is de Moor, *Commentarius Perpetuus,* 2:947. This distinction is found for example in Vermigli, *Loci Communes,* Classis Secunda, Locus XIII, §25.

216. Aquinas, *ST* IIa IIae q. 110 art. 4. Ed. note: Bavinck borrows the reference to Thomas from de Moor, *Commentarius Perpetuus,* 2:947.

217. Cf. Grotius, *De Jure Belli ac Pacis,* 478 (Liber III, Caput 1, §9). Cf. Martensen, *Christian Ethics, Special Part. First Division,* 214–24 (§§96–98).

218. De Moor, *Commentarius Perpetuus,* 2:948–49; Vermigli, *Loci Communes,* Classis Secunda, Locus XIII, §§25–46; A. Rivet, *Praelectiones Pleniores,* 1:1434–36; Voetius, *Selectarum Disputationum Theologicarum,* 4:632ff.; Ames, *Conscience,* V.liii (§§1–17); Turretin, *Institutes of Elenctic Theology,* XI, 20.

Exodus 1:17–20; Joshua 11:4–5; Judges 3:20; 1 Samuel 6:2, 5; 2 Kings 6:8–23; 8:10; Jeremiah 38:27.[219] But irony is permissible. To feign ignorance, as Jesus once did (Luke 24:18–19), is also permissible. Scripture forbids even every idle word (Matt. 12:36; Eph. 5:4).

Forbidden as well are all forms of insulting our neighbor, calling them names, vilifying them, and running them down, including making fun of someone's disabilities, using irony and sarcasm,[220] showing favoritism (Exod. 22:28; Matt. 5:21–22; Eph. 4:31; Acts 17:6; John 8:48), all backbiting and slander (Lev. 19:16; Ps. 34:13; Prov. 4:24; Rom. 1:30; 2 Cor. 12:20; James 4:11; 1 Pet. 2:1),[221] all deception, fawning, and flattery (Ps. 12:3–4; Prov. 24:28; 27:6; Acts 12:22), all mental reservations à la the Jesuits (Eph. 4:25; 1 Pet. 2:1), all promise-breaking, all hypocrisy (Gen. 34:13; 2 Sam. 3:27; 20:9–10; Matt. 26:48–49),[222] all silent condoning, accepting, and delighting in slander instead of rebuking it (Eph. 5:11), nosiness, gossiping, and scandal mongering.[223]

Positively, we are commanded here to show concern for our neighbors, for their honor and good reputation as something precious (Eccles. 7:1), examples of which we find in Scripture (1 Sam. 19:4–5).[224] We are commanded to love the truth (Ps. 15:1–2; Zech. 8:16, 19; Eph. 4:25), even though not all truth need always be told (Prov. 29:11; Matt. 22:15–22; John 8:3–7). Further, we are commanded to practice candor, sincerity, trustworthiness, and so on. The Ninth Commandment exhorts us to form true representations of all things—of God, the world, humanity, our neighbor, and books. We are not to create our world of thinking[225] on our own, making it up, but are to derive it from the objective world, like children: "Unless you change and become like little children, you will never enter the kingdom of heaven" (Matt. 18:3 NIV). This holds also for the kingdoms of art and of science. In the academic world, this is important for critics and reviewers, lest they proceed by their own judgment while making no effort first to become acquainted with the

---

219. Ed. note: Bavinck takes these Bible texts from de Moor, *Commentarius Perpetuus*, 2:952–53.

220. Ed. note: Bavinck is not contradicting what he said in the previous paragraph: that "irony is permissible." In the previous paragraph he was speaking about truth-telling and arguing that use of irony does not necessarily involve untruth. In this paragraph he is dealing with verbal attacks on our neighbor; using irony or sarcasm to demean our neighbor is not permissible.

221. Ed. note: Bavinck also included a reference to Ps. 85:3 in this list, a text that does not seem relevant here.

222. Ed. note: Bavinck also included a reference to 1 Sam. 18:16 in this list, a text that does not seem relevant here.

223. DO: *nieuwsgierigheid, babbelzucht, kwaadsprekerij.*

224. Ed. note: Bavinck also included a reference to 1 Sam. 6:17 in this list, a text that does not seem relevant here.

225. DO: *gedachtenwereld.*

other person. And then, finally, this commandment enjoins us to convey the truth we obtained by communicating in our language with objective purity. Be true, when you think and when you speak!

§49. COVETOUSNESS (TENTH COMMANDMENT)

There is some disagreement about this commandment. The question is whether this covetousness extends to the entire Decalogue, and thus also to the first table of the law, or extends only to the second table, particularly to the Sixth, Seventh, and Eighth Commandments. The Heidelberg Catechism and most Reformed exegetes hold the first view.[226]

What is forbidden here is all lust and desire, also with respect to the first four commandments. Strictly speaking, however, mention is made only of coveting our neighbor's goods, and those objects are specifically named. Also, the words "covet" and "lust after" do not fit with the commandments of the first table. Coveting to serve idols and the like hardly makes sense.[227] De Moor writes that one may also apply it to the first four commandments, "due to the similarity of the vice, due to the excellence of the subject."[228] In other words, one could also apply the Tenth Commandment to the first four, but the Tenth Commandment is not really integral to them.

There is another difficulty with this commandment: Was not covetousness forbidden already in the preceding commandments? After all, the law is spiritual, and in the Sixth, Seventh, and Eighth Commandments we saw the internal, spiritual sins judged and condemned. Why then do we receive yet another distinct commandment against covetousness? Does not this Tenth Commandment show that the previous commandments must not be understood spiritually but only literally and outwardly?[229] Commentators, such as Pictet, usually say that this commandment was added to further interpret and explain the previous commandments and because covetousness might easily be excused (Rom. 7:7).[230] This way, no excuse is possible. This way, the Tenth Commandment itself pointed out that the previous commandments,

---

226. Heidelberg Catechism, Q&A 113: "Q. What is the aim of the tenth commandment? A. That not even the slightest desire or thought contrary to any one of God's commandments should ever arise in our hearts. Rather, with all our hearts we should always hate sin and take pleasure in whatever is right." Cf. de Moor, *Commentarius Perpetuus*, 2:962.

227. Cf. Pictet, *De christelyke zedekunst*, 524, footnote.

228. LO: *Ob similitudinem vitii; ob objecti praestantiam*; de Moor, *Commentarius Perpetuus*, 2:962.

229. DO: *letterlijk en lichamelijk*.

230. Cf. Pictet, *De christelyke zedekunst*, 524, footnote; Ursinus, *Commentary on the Heidelberg Catechism*, 605–6.

and therefore the whole law, must be interpreted spiritually, as Jesus also explained them (Matt. 5:21–48).

Now the unique thing about this Tenth Commandment is that it not only forbids covetousness but specifically covetousness with respect to our neighbor— that is,[231] the one next to whom we live.[232] Not just robbing, killing, and so on of the neighbor in general but also specifically not even coveting any of our next-door neighbor's goods—that is what is forbidden here. The house is the neighbor's residence. Owning your own house is a wonderful ideal. And in that house of your own, you have your own spouse, servant, furnishings, and the like. That is the foundation of a nation's health and well-being. Today, however, this ideal is steadily fading; the middle class is disappearing, the proletariat is growing. Our neighbor's house with everything in it must be safe not only against thieves, murderers, and the like (Sixth–Eighth Commandments) but also against the covetousness of the neighbor, the close friend next door.[233] The Tenth Commandment is a fence around one's own house. It demands contentment with one's own lot.

Now not all desiring is being forbidden here. There are good desires:[234] "As a deer pants for flowing streams, / so pants my soul for you, O God" (Ps. 42:1). "Behold, I long for your precepts" (Ps. 119:40). Agur prays:

> Remove far from me falsehood and lying;
>   give me neither poverty nor riches;
>   feed me with the food that is needful for me. (Prov. 30:8)

The apostle James tells us, "If any of you lacks wisdom, let him ask God, who gives generously to all without reproach, and it will be given him" (James 1:5).

Desiring is innate to our human nature.[235] We cannot do otherwise. We are nothing if not needy; we need all kinds of things, so we desire them. Christ himself experienced hunger and thirst. But sin has unhinged these desires

---

231. E. Sartorius, *Die Lehre van der heiligen Liebe*, 502–7.

232. Marginal comment: Looking at others, comparing oneself to others makes one discontent, is revolt against God as the Dispenser, feeds covetousness: if only I was as he, had his wife, house, field, talent, money, health, children, etc.

233. E. Sartorius, *Die Lehre von der heiligen Liebe*, 506.

234. Such as for food and drink and the like: "Give us this day our daily bread" (Matt. 6:11); "If one aspires to the office of overseer, he desires a noble task" (1 Tim. 3:1); "One thing have I asked of the LORD, that will I seek after . . ." (Ps. 27:4). All prayer is desire; Jesus calls the hungry and thirsty blessed.

235. Ed. note: Bavinck develops his understanding of desiring as a faculty of the human soul (DO: *begeervermogen*) in his *Foundations of Psychology*, §8, *TBR* 9 (2018): 177. See especially B. "The Natural Faculty of Desiring," pp. 182–89. https://bavinckinstitute.org/wp-content/uploads/2019/08/BR9_Foundations.pdf.

and misdirected and corrupted them. Sin did not create desire as a human capacity; sin cannot do that; sin creates nothing, is not a substance, can only corrupt, destroy. It has corrupted desire in three respects:

a. We direct our desires to impermissible objects—for example, a neighbor's spouse.

b. We desire these objects in terms of a wrong value and with wrong measures.

c. We strive to satisfy our desires by means other than those intended by God.

These disordered, *sinful* desires are often summarized in Scripture by the term "covetousness" (Rom. 7:7), and as such they are forbidden.[236] Desire in this sense is sin.

On this we disagree with Rome. Rome teaches that this desire is not sin, is implicit in the conflicting nature of flesh and spirit, was reined in before the fall by the *donum superadditum*, and after the fall is eradicated in baptism. This teaching does away entirely with original sin. It holds that such desire or lust remains but that in itself this is not sin; it only tempts to sin. This disordered desire is not sin if one resists it instead of yielding to it. The first stirrings[237] are not sinful, for these occur entirely involuntarily and arise in us automatically; and without consent of the will there is no sin.

By contrast, we believe this:

a. We are accountable not only for our deeds but also for our being, our nature, our condition. Our nature is corrupted, which ought not to be so.

b. We have not personally corrupted our nature; that occurred through Adam. But in Adam we all fell. That is the profound doctrine of original sin.[238] In Adam we are accountable for our nature.

---

236. Ed. note: This passage found its way into Bavinck's *Foundations of Psychology* (*Beginselen der psychologie* [*BdP¹*]) published in 1897 and republished in a revised version, edited by Valentijn Hepp in 1923 (*BdP²*). The passage can be found in the English translation: *TBR* 9:198. This is important for Bavinck studies since it indicates that his theology and ethics were informed by psychology and vice versa from the beginning of his academic career and not just toward the end. In the first edition, Bavinck parenthetically added "ἐπιθυμία, concupiscentia" at the end of the paragraph [*BdP¹*, 148]. His references are also worth noting here: Christopher Love, *The Combat between the Flesh and Spirit*; Dutch translation: "Strijdt tusschen Vleesch en Geest," in *Theologia Practica, dat is alle de theologische wercken*, 40–95; William Perkins, "The Combat of the Flesh and Spirit," in *The Works of William Perkins*, 1:469–74; Dutch translation in *Alle de Werken*, 301–7 [*BdP¹*, 147n87].

237. LO: *motus primoprimi.*

238. See *RD*, 2:362; 3:43, 45, 75–77, 88, 142–43; 4:54, 123, 194, 520, 522.

c. Consent of the will is certainly necessary for there to be sin; the will is the seat of sin. But the will must be taken not only in its fruit, the deed, but also in its capacity, its root. The will is rooted in and arises from desire. Later we can oppose the desire, based on all kinds of considerations; but the desire is evil (Rom. 7:7). Nature, our capacity, is corrupt.[239]

That is why this commandment penetrates so deeply. It condemns covetousness in concrete terms, such as our neighbor's house, wife, and so on. But according to the customary exegesis of all the commandments, here too we may go back and say: All covetousness is forbidden here; forbidden here first of all are the very "first stirrings" of the sins underlying our consciousness, our will, arising from the depth of our nature, our being, from our heart. Our own conscience testifies to and against that and condemns us whenever such impulses, thoughts, and desires arise within us. And we are commanded here always to love righteousness with our whole heart. What is commanded is that our nature be good, perfect. This is possible only through regeneration. This commandment drives us to Christ, to the Holy Spirit; "doing follows being."[240]

---

239. Kuyper, *E Voto Dordraceno*, 4:261–63. Ed. note: This reflection on the Tenth Commandment (Lord's Day 44) first appeared in *De Heraut*, no. 802 (May 7, 1893).
    240. LO: *operari sequitur esse*.

Bibliography

Books

Aalders, Maarten Johann. *De komst van de toga: Een historisch onderzoek naar het verdwijnen van mantel en bef en de komst van de toga op de Nederlandse kansels, 1796–1898.* Delft: Eburon, 2001.

Aalst, Gerardus van. *Geestelijke Mengelstoffen.* 2 vols. in 1. Amsterdam: Hendrik Vieroot, 1754.

Acta et Documenta Synodi Nationalis Dordrechtanae. Vol. 1, *Acta of the Synod of Dordt.* Edited by Donald Sinnema, Christian Moser, and Herman Selderhuis, in collaboration with Janika Bischof, Johanna Roelevink, and Fred van Lieberg. Göttingen: Vandenhoeck & Ruprecht, 2015.

Acta of Handelingen der Nationale Synode . . . te Dordrecht (1618–1619). Edited by J. H. Donner and S. A. van den Hoorn. Leiden: D. Donner, n.d. [1887].

Acts/Proceedings of the Congress for the Observance of Sunday, Held at The Hague, 19 and 20 September 1901. See *Handelingen van het national congres voor zondagsrust.*

Alsted, Johann Heinrich. *Theologia Casuum, Exhibens Anatomen Conscientiae et Scholam Tentationum.* Hanover: Eifred, 1630. Bayerische StaatsBibliothek digital; Münchener DigitalisierungsZentrum Digitale Bibliothek. https://reader.digitale-sammlungen.de//resolve/display/bsb11069648.html.

Alting, Heinrich. *Exegesis logica et theologica Augustanae Confessionis.* Amsterdam: J. Jansson, 1647 and 1652.

———. *Theologiae Problematica Nova.* Amsterdam: J. Jansson, 1662.

Alting, Jacob. *Opera Omnia Theologica.* 5 vols. Amsterdam: Gerardus Borstius, 1685–87.

Ambrose. *Concerning Virgins.* NPNF[2] 10:361–88.

———. *On the Duties of the Clergy.* NPNF[2] 10:1–89.

Ames, William. *Bellarminus Enervatus sive Disputationes Anti-Bellarminiane.* Vol. 2. London: Humpfridum and Robinson, 1632.

———. *Conscience with the Power and Cases Thereof.* Leiden: W. Christiaens, E. Griffin, J. Dawson, 1639. Reprint, Amsterdam and Norwood, NJ: Theatrum Orbis Terraum and Walter J. Johnson, 1975.

———. *The Marrow of Theology*. Edited and translated by John Dykstra Eusden. Boston: Pilgrim, 1968. Reprint, Grand Rapids: Baker, 1997.

———. *Sententia de Origine Sabbati et die Dominico*. Amsterdam, 1658.

Ammon, Christoph Friedrich von. *Handbuch der christlichen Sittenlehre*. 3 vols. in 8. Leipzig: Georg Joachim Göschen, 1823–29.

———. *Handbuch der christlichen Sittenlehre*. 2nd ed. 3 vols. Leipzig: Göschen, 1838.

Amyraut, Moïse, Louis Cappel, and Josué de la Place. *Syntagma thesium theologicarum in Academia Salmuriensi, Pars Tertia*. Saumur: Jean Lesnier, 1664.

Angelus de Clavasio Carletti di Chivasso. *Summa de angelica*. Nuremberg: Anton Koberger, 1492.

Aquinas, Thomas. *S. Thomae Aquinatis Summa Theologica*. Vol. 4, *Secunda secundae, I–XCI*. Paris: Bloud & Barral, 1882.

———. *Summa Contra Gentiles*. Translated by the English Dominican Fathers. London: Burns, Oates & Washbourne, 1924.

———. *Summa Theologica*. Translated by the Fathers of the English Dominican Province. Allen, TX: Christian Classics, 1981.

Aristeas. *The Letter of Aristeas: "Aristeas to Philocrates" or "On the Translation of the Law of the Jews."* Translated and edited by Benjamin G. Wright III. Berlin: de Gruyter, 2015.

Astesanus. *Summa de casibus conscientiae*. Nuremberg: Antoine Koberger, 1482.

Athenaeus of Naucratis. *The Learned Banqueters*. Edited and translated by S. Douglas Olson. 7 vols. LCL 204, 208, 224, 235, 274, 327, 345. Cambridge, MA: Harvard University Press, 2007–11.

Augustine. *City of God*. NPNF[1] 2:1–511.

———. *Enchiridion on Faith, Hope, and Love*. NPNF[1] 3:231–76.

———. *Letters 1–99*. Edited by John Rotelle. Translated by Roland Teske. The Works of Saint Augustine: A Translation for the 21st Century II/1. Hyde Park, NY: New City Press, 2001.

———. *Letters 156–210*. Edited by Boniface Ramsey. Translated by Roland Teske. The Works of Saint Augustine: A Translation for the 21st Century II/3. Hyde Park, NY: New City Press, 2001.

———. *Letters, Volume V (204–270)*. Volume 13 of *Writings of Saint Augustine*. Translated by Sister Wilfrid Parsons, SND. FC 32. Washington, DC: Catholic University of America Press, 1956.

———. *On Christian Doctrine*. NPNF[1] 2:517–97.

———. *Reply to Faustus the Manichaean*. NPNF[1] 4:151–343.

Azpilcueta, Martín de. *Manual de confesores y penitents*. Coimbra, Portugal, 1560. First published in Spanish, 1549.

Baer, A. *Der Alcoholismus: Seine Verbreitung und seine Wirkung auf den individuellen und socialen Organismus sowie die Mittel, ihn zu bekämpfen*. Berlin: A. Hirschwald, 1878.

Bähr, Karl Christian Wilhelm Felix. *Die Bücher der Könige*. Bielefeld and Leipzig: Velhagen & Klasing, 1868. Translated, enlarged, and edited as *The Books of the Kings* by Edwin Harwood (book 1, *1 Kings*) and W. D. Sumner (book 2, *2 Kings*). Critical, Doctrinal, and Homiletical Commentary on the Bible, Old Testament series, 6. Series edited by Johann Peter Lange and Philip Schaff. New York: Scribner's Sons, 1872.

Baird, Robert. *Geschichte der Mässigkeits-Gesellschaft in den vereinigten Staaten Nord-Amerika's*. Berlin: Gustav Eichler, 1837.

Balduin, Friedrich. *Tractatus Luculentus Posthumus, Toti Reipubliae Christianae ac Ultissimus, De Materiâ Rarissime antehac* enucleata, Casibus Nimirum Conscientiae. Wittenberg: Fincelius, 1628.

Baptista de Salis [Baptista Trovamala]. Summa casuum conscientiae. Nuremberg: Anton Koberger, 1488. https://archive.org /details/A336121.

———. Summa Roselle de casibus conscientiae. Argentina: Knobloch, 1516.

Bardenhewer, Otto. Patrology: The Lives and Works of the Fathers of the Church. Translated by Thomas J. Shahan. Freiburg im Breisgau and St. Louis: Herder, 1908.

Bartholomew of Concordia. Summa de casibus conscientiae. Italy, 1390–1410.

Baumann, Johann Julius. Handbuch der Moral nebst Abriss der Rechtsphilosophie. Leipzig: S. Hirzel, 1879.

Baumgarten-Crusius, Ludwig Friedrich Otto. Lehrbuch der christlichen Sittenlehre. Leipzig: Hartmann, 1826.

Baumhauer, M. M. von. Verum philosophorum praecipue Stoicorum doctrina de morte voluntaria. Utrecht: N. van der Monde, 1842.

Bavinck, Herman. Beginselen der psychologie. Revised by V. Hepp. 2nd rev. ed. Kampen: Kok, 1923. ET: Foundations of Psychology. Translated by Jack Vanden Born, John Bolt, and Nelson D. Kloosterman. TBR 9 (2018): 1–244. Bavinck Institute. https://bavinckinstitute.org/wp-content /uploads/2019/08/BR9_Foundations.pdf.

———. Bilderdijk als denker en dichter. Kampen: Kok, 1906.

———. Christendom, oorlog, volkenbond. Utrecht: Ruys, 1920.

———. De ethiek van Ulrich Zwingli. Kampen: G. Ph. Zalsman, 1880.

———. De navolging van Christus en het moderne leven. Kampen: Kok, n.d. [1918]. Also published in Kennis en leven, 115–44. ET: Appendix B in Bolt, Theological Analysis, 402–40.

———. De Vrouw in de hedendaagsche maatschappij. Kampen: Kok, 1918.

———. Essays on Religion, Science, and Society. Edited by John Bolt. Translated by Harry Boonstra and Gerrit Sheeres. Grand Rapids: Baker Academic, 2008.

———. Gereformeerde Ethiek. Edited by Dirk van Keulen. Utrecht: Kok-Boekencentrum, 2019.

———. Het Christendom. Baarn: Hollandia, 1912.

———. Het probleem van de oorlog. Kampen: Kok, 1914.

———. Kennis en leven: Opstellen en artikelen uit vroegere jaren. Kampen: Kok, 1922.

———. Reformed Dogmatics. Edited by John Bolt. Translated by John Vriend. 4 vols. Grand Rapids: Baker Academic, 2003–8.

———. Reformed Ethics. Vol. 1, Created, Fallen, and Converted Humanity. Edited by John Bolt with Jessica Joustra, Nelson D. Kloosterman, Antoine Theron, and Dirk van Keulen. Grand Rapids: Baker Academic, 2019.

———. The Sacrifice of Praise. Translated by John Dolfin. Grand Rapids: Kregel, 1922.

———. Saved by Grace: The Holy Spirit's Work in Calling and Regeneration. Edited by J. Mark Beach. Translated by Nelson D. Kloosterman. Grand Rapids: Reformation Heritage, 2008. Originally published as Roeping en wedergeboorte (Kampen: G. Ph. Zalsman, 1903).

Bayer, Friedrich. Betrachtungen über den Eid. Nürnberg: Reigel & Weissner, 1829.

Beck, Johann Tobias. Vorlesungen über christliche Ethik. 3 vols. in 2. Gütersloh: C. Bertelsmann, 1882–83.

Beets, Nicholaas. Camera obscura. Haarlem: Erven F. Bohn, 1839.

———. Karakter, karakterschaarschte, karaktervorming. Utrecht: Kemink & Zoon, 1875.

Bekker, Balthasar. De betoverde weereld, zynde een grondig ondersoek van 't gemeen *gevoelen aangaande de geesten, deselver aart en vermogen, bewind en bedrijf: Als ook't gene de menschen door derselver kraght en gemeenschap doen.* Amsterdam: D. van den Dalen, 1691–93. ET: *The World Bewitch'd, or, An Examination of the Common Opinions concerning Spirits: Their Nature, Power, Administration and Operations, as Also the Effects Men Are Able to Produce by Their Communication.* London: R. Baldwin, 1695.

Bellarmine, Robert. *De Gratia et Libero Arbitrio, Liber VI.* In *Opera Omnia*, 4:431–59. Naples: J. Guiliano, 1836.

———. *Disputationes de Controversiis Christianae Fidei adversus hujus Temporis Haereticos.* 4 vols. Prague: Wolfgang Wickhart, 1721. ET: *Controversies of the Christian Faith.* Translated by Kenneth Baker. Saddle River, NJ: Keep the Faith, 2016.

———. *Opera Omnia.* 6 vols. Naples: J. Guiliano, 1856–62.

Bilderdijk, Willem. *De dichtwerken van Bilderdijk.* Edited by Isaac da Costa. 15 vols. Haarlem: A. C. Kruseman, 1856–59.

———. *De Dieren, Dichtstuk.* Amsterdam: P. den Hengst & Zoon, 1817.

———. *De ziekte der geleerden.* Amsterdam and The Hague, 1807.

———. *Opstellen van godgeleerden en zedekundigen inhoud.* 2 vols. Amsterdam: J. Immerzeel, 1833.

———. *Verhandelingen, ziel-, zede-, en rechtsleer betreffende.* Leiden: L. Herdingh & Zoon, 1821.

Bohn, F. *Der Sabbat im Alten Testament.* Gütersloh: Bertelsmann, 1903.

Bolt, John. *Bavinck on the Christian Life: Following Jesus in Faithful Service.* Wheaton: Crossway, 2015.

———. *A Theological Analysis of Herman Bavinck's Two Essays on the* Imitatio Christi*: Between Pietism and Modernism.* Lewiston, NY: Mellen, 2013.

Bonaventure. *The Breviloquium.* Vol. 2 of *The Works of Bonaventure: Cardinal,*

Seraphic Doctor, and Saint. Translated by Jose de Vinck. Paterson, NJ: St. Anthony Guild Press, 1963.

Boxhorn, Marcus Zuerius van. *Spiegeltjen Vertoonende 't cort hayr, by de Hollanders ende Zeelanders joncst ghedragen, ende van vreemde ontleent.* Middelburg: Jacques Fierens, 1644.

Brakel, Wilhelmus à. *The Christian's Reasonable Service.* Translated by Bartel Elshout. 4 vols. Vols. 1–3, Pittsburgh: Soli De Gloria, 1992–94. Vol. 4, Grand Rapids: Reformation Heritage, 1995.

Bruijn, J. de, and G. Harinck, eds. *Een Leidse vriendschap: De briefwisseling tussen Herman Bavinck en Christiaan Snouck Hurgronje, 1875–1921.* Amsterdam: Ten Have, 1999.

Buddeus, Johann Franz. *Institutiones Theologiae Dogmaticae.* Frankfurt and Leipzig, 1741.

———. *Institutiones Theologiae Moralis.* Leipzig: Thomas Fritsch, 1727.

Burs, Jacob. *Threnos.* Tholen: no. pub., 1627.

Buurt, Adriaan. *Beschouwende godgeleerdheid.* 6 vols. Amsterdam: Jacobus Loveringh & Petrus Schouten, 1763–75.

———. *Vervolg der Dadelijke godgeleerdheid.* Part III of *Dadelijke godgeleerdheid.* Amsterdam: Jan ten Houten, Petrus Schouten, and Johannes Wessing, 1783.

Buurt, Adriaan, and Josina Carolina van Lynden. *Dadelijke godgeleerdheid.* 4 vols. in 2. Amsterdam: Jan ten Houten, Petrus Schouten, and Johannes Wessing, 1780–86.

Calvin, John. *Come Out from among Them: Anti-Nicodemite Writings of John Calvin.* Translated by Seth Skolinsky. Dallas: Protestant Heritage Press, 2001.

———. *Commentaries on the Epistles to Timothy, Titus, and Philemon.* Translated by William Pringle. Grand Rapids: Eerdmans, 1948.

————. *Commentaries on the Four Last Books of Moses Arranged in the Form of a Harmony*. Translated by Charles William Bingham. 4 vols. Edinburgh: Calvin Translation Society, 1852–55. Reprint, Grand Rapids: Eerdmans, 1950; Grand Rapids: Baker Academic, 2003.

————. *Commentaries on the Twelve Minor Prophets*. Translated by John Owen. 5 vols. Edinburgh: Calvin Translation Society, 1846–49. Reprint, Grand Rapids: Eerdmans, 1950; Grand Rapids: Baker Academic, 2003.

————. *De Offerande van Abraham: Drie Preken van Johannes Calvijn*. Translated by C. van Proosdij. Leiden: Donner, 1887.

————. *Institutes of the Christian Religion*. Edited by John T. McNeill. Translated by F. L. Battles. 2 vols. Philadelphia: Westminster, 1960.

————. *Letters of John Calvin, Compiled from the Original Manuscripts and Edited with Historical Notes*. Edited by Jules Bonnet. 2 vols. Philadelphia: Presbyterian Board of Publication, 1858.

Candidus, Vincentius. *Disquistiones morales*. Lyon: Prost, 1638.

Carmichael, Casey B. *A Continental View: Johannes Cocceius's Federal Theology of the Sabbath*. Göttingen: Vandenhoeck & Ruprecht, 2019.

Cartwright, Thomas. *A Confutation of the Rhemists Translation: Glosses and Annotations on the New Testament*. Leiden: W. Brewster, 1618.

Catechism of the Council of Trent for Parish Priests. Translated by John A. McHugh, OP, and Charles J. Callan, OP. New York: Joseph F. Wagner, n.d. [ca. 1923].

Chateaubriand, François-René. *The Genius of Christianity, or The Spirit and Beauty of the Christian Religion*. Translated by Charles I. White. 15th rev. ed. Baltimore: John Murphy; Philadelphia: J. B. Lippincott, 1884.

Chemnitz, Martin. *Examination of the Council of Trent*. Translated by Fred Kramer. 4 vols. St. Louis: Concordia, 1871.

Christoffel, Raget. *Zwingli, or The Rise of the Reformation in Switzerland: A Life of the Reformer, with Some Notices of His Time and Contemporaries*. Translated by J. Cochran. Edinburgh: T&T Clark, 1858.

The Church Orders of the Sixteenth Century Reformed Churches of the Netherlands together with Their Social, Political, and Ecclesiastical Context. Translated and collated by Richard R. De Ridder, with Peter H. Jonker and Leonard Verduin. Grand Rapids: Calvin Theological Seminary, 1987.

Cicero, Marcus Tullius. *The Letters to His Friends, Volume II*. Translated by W. Glynn Williams. LCL 216. Cambridge, MA: Harvard University Press, 1928.

————. *On Duties*. Translated by Walter Miller. LCL 30. Cambridge, MA: Harvard University Press, 1913.

————. *On Ends*. Translated by H. Rackham. LCL 40. New York: Putnam's Sons, 1914.

————. *On the Nature of the Gods; Academics*. Translated by H. Rackham. LCL 268. Cambridge, MA: Harvard University Press, 1933. Reprint, 1967.

————. *On the Republic; On the Laws*. Translated by Clinton Walker Keyes. LCL 213. Cambridge, MA: Harvard University Press, 1928.

————. *Tusculan Disputations*. Translated by John Edward King. LCL 141. Cambridge, MA: Harvard University Press, 1927.

Cocceius, J. *Indagatio naturae Sabbati et quietis Novi Testamenti*. Leiden: Johannes Elsevir, 1658.

————. *Summa Doctrinae de Foedere et Testamento Dei*. 2nd rev. ed. Leiden: Elsevier, 1654.

———. *Summa Theologiae ex Scripturis Repetita*. 2nd ed. Geneva, 1665.

Cooper, John W. *Panentheism: The Other God of the Philosophers; From Plato to the Present*. Grand Rapids: Baker Academic, 2006.

Courtney, Janet Elizabeth. *Freethinkers of the Nineteenth Century*. New York: Dutton, 1920.

Cramer, Jacob. *Alexandre Vinet als christelijk moralist en apologeet geteekend en gewaardeerd*. Leiden: Brill, 1883.

Cremer, Herman. *Biblico-Theological Lexicon of New Testament Greek*. Translated by D. W. Simon and William Urwick. Edinburgh: T&T Clark; New York: Scribner's Sons, 1895.

Cyprian. "Treatise IV: On the Lord's Prayer." *ANF* 5:447–57.

Daillé, Jean. *De Jejuniis et Quadragesima Liber*. Deventer: Columbius, 1654.

Daneau, Lambert. *Christianae isagoges ad christianorum theologorum locos communes, libri II*. Geneva: Eustachus Vignon, 1583.

———. *Ethices Christianae*. 3 vols. Geneva: Eustache Vignon, 1579.

Darwin, Charles. *The Descent of Man*. 2nd ed. 2 vols. Reprint, New York: American Home Library, 1902.

Daub, Carl. *System der theologischen Moral*. Edited by Philipp Marheinke and W. Dittenberger. 2 vols. in 3. Berlin: Dunkker & Humbolt, 1840–43.

Davies, Tony. *Humanism*. London and New York: Routledge, 1997.

Deleuze, Joseph Philippe François. *Histoire critique du magnétisme animal*. 2 vols. Paris: Mame, 1813.

Delitzsch, Franz. *Biblical Commentary on the Prophecies of Isaiah*. 2 vols. Translated by S. R. Driver. Edinburgh: T&T Clark, 1890.

———. *Biblical Commentary on the Proverbs of Solomon*. 2 vols. Translated by

M. G. Easton. Edinburgh: T&T Clark, 1884, 1882.

———. *A System of Biblical Psychology*. 2nd. ed. Translated by Robert Ernest Wallis. Edinburgh: T&T Clark, 1885.

Dennison, James T., Jr. *Reformed Confessions of the 16th and 17th Centuries in English Translation*. 4 vols. Grand Rapids: Reformation Heritage, 2008–10.

Denzinger, Henry. *The Sources of Catholic Dogma*. Translated by Roy J. Deferrari. Fitzwilliam, NH: Loreto, 2002.

Diana, Antoninus. *Resolutiones morales: XII partes*. Lyon: Boissant & Anisson, 1647–57.

Dieleman, Kyle J. *The Battle for the Sabbath in the Dutch Reformation: Devotion or Desecration?* Göttingen: Vandenhoeck & Ruprecht, 2019.

Diestel, Ludwig. *Geschichte des Alten Testamentes in der christlichen Kirche*. Jena: Mauke, 1869.

Diogenes Laertius. *Lives of Eminent Philosophers, Vol. II*. Translated by R. D. Hicks. LCL 185. New York: Putnam's Sons, 1925. Reprint, Cambridge, MA: Harvard University Press, 1995.

Dock, Friedrich Wilhelm. *Iets over het vegetarianisme: Zijne beteekenis voor de zedelijkheid en voor de gezondheid*. Goes: Wed. A. C. de Jonge, 1879.

Dorner, Isaak August. *History of Protestant Theology: Particularly in Germany*. Translated by George Robson and Sophia Taylor. 2 vols. Edinburgh: T&T Clark, 1871.

———. *System of Christian Ethics*. Edited by August Johannes Dorner. Translated by Charles Marsh Mead and R. T. Cunningham. Edinburgh: T&T Clark, 1887.

Downame, George. *An Abstract of the Duties Commanded, and Sinnes Forbidden in the Law of God*. London: Felix Kyngston, 1620.

Driessen, Antony. *Verhandelingen, redevoeringen, en predicatien over uitgelzene* plaatzen van Gods Heylige Woort. Amsterdam: Jacobus Hayman, 1737.

Drummond, Henry. Natural Law in the Spiritual World. New York: Henry Hurst, 1899.

Dwinglo, Bernardus. Grouwel der Verwoestinghe staende in de heylighe plaetse: Dat is claer . . . Verhael van de voornaemste Mishandelinghen . . . ende Nulliteyten des natiohalen Synodi van Dordrecht, inde Jaren 1618ende 1619. 2 vols. Enghuysen, 1622.

Ebrard, Johann Heinrich August. Das Verhältnis Shakspear's zum Christenthum. Erlangen: A. C. Deichert, 1870.

Eicken, Heinrich von. Geschichte und System der mittelalterlichen Weltanschauung. Stuttgart: J. G. Cotta, 1887.

Engelberts, Willem Jodocus Matthias. Willem Teellinck. Amsterdam: Scheffer, 1898.

Epictetus. Discourses, Books 1–2. Translated by William Abbott Oldfather. LCL 131. Cambridge, MA: Harvard University Press, 1925.

Epiphanius. The Panarion of Epiphanius of Salamis, Books II and III. Translated by Frank Williams. Atlanta: SBL Press, 2017.

Episcopius, Simon. "Disputation 36." In Operum Theologorum, 2/2:429–30. Amsterdam: J. H. Boom, 1665.

———. Opera Theologica. 2nd ed. 2 vols. The Hague: Arnold Leers, 1678.

Episcopius Simon, and Remonstrantse Broederschap. The Confession or Declaration of the Ministers or Pastors Which in the United Provinces Are Called Remonstrants, concerning the Chief Points of Christian Religion. London: Francis Smith, 1676.

Ernesti, H. Fr. Th. L. Die Ethik des Apostels Paulus in ihren Grundzügen dargestellt. 3rd rev. ed. Göttingen: Vandenhoeck & Ruprecht, 1880.

Essenius, Andreas. Dissertatio de Perpetuâ Moralitate Decalogi. Utrecht: Johann à Waesberge, 1658.

Evangelische gezangen om nevens het boek der psalmen bij den openbaren godsdienst in de Nederlandsche Hervormde gemeenten gebruikt te worden. Amsterdam: Johannes Allart, 1806.

Fabius, Dammes Paulus Dirk. De Fransche Revolutie. Amsterdam: J. H. Kruyt, 1881.

Falckenberg, Richard Friedrich Otto. Geschichte der neueren philosophie von Nikolaus von Kues bis zur gegenwart. Leipzig: Veit, 1886.

Fichte, Immanuel Herman von. Psychologie: Die Lehre vom bewussten Geiste des Menschen, oder Entwicklungsgeschichte des Bewusstseins begründet auf Anthropologie und innerer Erfahrung. 2nd rev. ed. 2 vols. Leipzig: Brockhaus, 1864–73.

Fichte, Johann Gottlieb. Johann Gottlieb Fichte's Sämmtliche Werke. 8 vols. Edited by Immanuel Hermann Fichte. Berlin: Veit & Co., 1845–46.

———. The Science of Ethics as Based on the Science of Knowledge. Edited by W. T. Harris. Translated by A. E. Kroeger. London: K. Paul, Trench, Trübner, 1897.

Firnhaber, Friedrich Jacob. De Absolutismo Morali Eoque Theologico. Wittenberg: Gerdesian, 1715.

Fischer, Kuno. J. G. Fichte und seine Vorgänger. Vol. 5 of Geschichte der neuern Philosophie. 2nd rev. ed. Munich: Fr. Basserman, 1884.

Forbes, John. Theologia Moralis. In Opera Omnia, 1/2:1–359. Amsterdam: H. Wetsten, R. & G. Wetsten, 1702–3.

Fouilée, Alfred. Tempérament et caractère selon les individus, les sexes et les races. Paris: Alcan, 1895.

Franck, Adolphe. Morale pour tous. Paris: L. Hachette, 1868.

Frank, Franz Hermann Reinhold. System der christlichen Sittlichkeit. 2 vols in 1. Erlangen: A. Deichert, 1884–87.

Fuchs, Georg Friedrich. *Der Alkoholismus und seine Bekämpfung.* Heilbronn: Henninger, 1883.

Fulke, William. *Confutation of the Rhemish Testament.* New York: Leavitt, Lord, 1834.

Funes, Martín de. *Speculum morale, et practicum.* Konstanz: Kalt, 1598.

Garnsey, Peter. *Food and Society in Classical Antiquity.* Cambridge: Cambridge University Press, 1999.

Gass, Wilhelm. *Geschichte der christlichen Ethik.* 2 vols. in 3. Berlin: G. Reimer, 1881–87.

Gerhard, Johann. *Loci Theologici.* Edited by E. Preuss. 9 vols. Berlin: G. Schlawitz, 1863–75.

Gils, Pascale van. "'Mishandelde vrouw of misdadigster': De media-aandacht rond de cause célèbre van Jeanne Marie Lorette, 1885–1888." Bachelor's thesis in history, University of Utrecht, 2014. https://dspace .library.uu.nl/handle/1874/290107.

Gleïzès, Joh. Ant. *Die Enthüllung des Christenthumes, oder die Glaubenseinheit für alle Christen.* Translated by Ed. Baltze. Leipzig: Eigendorf, 1879.

Goffar, Antonius (with Martino Bonacina). *Operum de morali theologia, omnibusque conscientiae nodis, compendium.* Leiden: Landry, 1639.

Gouw, J. ter. *De Gilden: Eene bijdrage tot de geschiedenis van het volksleven.* 2nd ed. Rotterdam: Bolle, 1886.

Graetz, Heinrich. *History of the Jews.* Vol. 2. Philadelphia: Jewish Publication Society of America, 1893.

Greef, Wulfert de. *The Writings of John Calvin: An Introductory Guide.* Translated by Lyle D. Bierma. Expanded ed. Louisville: Westminster John Knox, 2008.

Gregory the Great. *Moral Reflections on the Book of Job.* Translated by Brian Kerns. 5 vols. Athens, OH: Cistercian Publications, 2014–19.

Grotius, Hugo. *De Jure Belli ac Pacis.* Amsterdam: Johannes Blaeu, 1651.

———. *The Truth of the Christian Religion.* Edited by Maria Rosa Antognazza. Translated by John Clarke. Indianapolis: Liberty Fund, 2012.

Gürlitt, Cornelius. *Geschichte des Barockstiles, des Rococo und des Klassicismus in Belgien, Holland, Frankreich, England.* Stuttgart: Ebner & Seubert, 1888.

Gürtler, Nicolaus. *Institutiones Theologicae, quibus Fundamenta Reformatae Religionis.* Halle an der Saale: Sumptu novi bibliopolii, 1721.

Hagenbach, Karl Rudolf. *Lehrbuch der Dogmengeschichte.* 6th ed. Leipzig: S. Hirzel, 1888. ET: *A History of Christian Doctrines.* Translated by E. H. Plumptre. 3 vols. Edinburgh: T&T Clark, 1883–85.

Hagenmann, Paul. *Was ist Charakter und wie kann er durch Erziehung gebildet werden?* 4th ed. Spandau-Berlin: Oesterwitz, 1888.

Hahn, Georg Ludwig. *Die Theologie des Neuen Testaments.* Leipzig: Dörffling & Franke, 1854.

Handelingen van het national congres voor zondagsrust gehouden op 19 en 20 september 1901 te 's Gravenhage. Groningen: Wolters, 1902.

Harless, Gottlieb Christoph Adolf von. *Christliche Ethik.* 4th ed. Stuttgart: S. G. Liesching, 1849. ET: *System of Christian Ethics.* Translated by A. W. Morrison and William Findlay. Clark's Foreign Theological Library 4/19. Edinburgh: T&T Clark, 1887.

Harnack, Otto. *Goethe in der Epoche seiner Vollendung (1805–1832).* Leipzig: J. C. Hinrich, 1887.

Hartenstein, Gustav. *Die Grundbegriffe der ethischen Wissenschaften.* Leipzig: F. A. Brockhaus, 1844.

Hartlieb, K. *Der Eid und der moderne Staat: Eine theologische Studie, Zeitfragen des christlichen Volkslebens.* Vol. 9, no. 6. Heilbronn: G. Henninger, 1884.

Hartmann, Johann Ludwig. *Tantz Teuffel.* Rotenburg: von Millenau, 1677.

Hase, D. Karl von. *Evangelische-protestantische Dogmatik.* 5th ed. Leipzig: Breitkopf & Härtel, 1860.

Hauerwas, Stanley. *A Community of Character.* Notre Dame, IN: University of Notre Dame Press, 1981.

Haug, Ludwig. *Darstellung und Beurteilung der A. Ritschl'schen Theologie: Zur Orientierung dargeboten.* 3rd ed. Stuttgart: D. Bundert, 1895.

Haupt, Erich. *Der Sonntag und die Bibel.* Hamburg: Oemler, 1878.

Hauranne, Jean Duvergier de. *Question royale et politique, avec sa décision, où il est montré en quelle extrémité, principalement en temps de paix, le sujet est obligé de conserver la vie du Prince aux dépens de la sienne proper.* Paris: P. M. Lamy, 1778.

———. *Question royalle et sa decision.* Paris: T. Du Bray, 1609.

Heepke, Wilhelm. *Die Leichenverbrennungsanstalten (die Krematorien).* Halle: Marhold, 1905.

Hegedus, Timothy Michael. "Jerome's Commentary on Jonah: Translation with Introduction and Critical Notes." MA thesis, Wilfrid Laurier University, 1991. https://scholars.wlu.ca/etd/115/.

Heidegger, Johann Heinrich [Johannes Henricus]. *Corpus Theologiae Christianae.* 2 vols. Zurich: Johann Heinrich Bodmer, 1700.

Heijningen, George Philips Kits van. *De geestenwereld: Bijdrage tot de geschiedenis van het bijgeloof.* Rotterdam: Nijgh, 1869.

Hellwald, Friedrich von. *Kulturgeschichte in ihrer natürlichen Entwicklung bis zur Gegenwart.* 3rd ed. 2 vols. Augsburg: Lampart, 1883–84.

Helvétius, Claude Adrien. *De l'homme, des ses facultés intellectuelles et son education.* 2 vols. Londres [i.e., The Hague]: Chez la Société Typographique, 1773. ET: *A Treatise on Man: His Intellectual Faculties and His Education.* Translated by William Hooper. 2 vols. London: Cundee, 1810.

Hengstenberg, E. W. *Über den Tag des Herrn.* Berlin: L. Oehmigke, 1852.

Henry, Paul. *Das Leben Johann Calvins des grossen Reformators.* 3 vols. Hamburg: F. Perthes, 1835–44.

Hermann, Karl Friedrich. *Lehrbuch der Griechischen Antiquitäten.* Newly edited by H. Blümner and W. Dittenberger. 4 vols. Freiburg im Breisgau: J. C. B. Mohr, 1882–89.

Herodotus. *Histories, I and II.* Translated by A. D. Godley. LCL 117. Cambridge, MA: Harvard University Press, 1920.

Hiortdahl, Thorstein. *Fremstilling af Kemiens Historie.* Christiania: Dybwad, 1906.

Hirscher, Johann Baptist von. *Die christliche Moral als Lehre: Von der Verwirklichung des göttlichen Reiches in der Menschheit.* 3 vols. Tübingen: H. Laupp, 1835–36.

Hobbes, Thomas. *Leviathan, or The Matter, Forme and Power of a Commonwealth, Ecclesiastical and Civil.* Edited by Michael Oakeshott. Oxford: Basil Blackwell, 1946.

Hodge, Charles. *Systematic Theology.* New York: Scribner, Armstrong, and Co., 1873–74.

Hoekstra, Sytse. *Vrijheid in verband met zelfbewustheid, zedelijkheid en zonde: Een psychologische-ethische studie.* Amsterdam: P. N. van Kampen, 1858.

Hoeven, Abraham des Amorie van der, Jr. *De godsdienst, het wezen van de mensch: Brief aan Dr. J. J. van Oosterzee.* Leeuwarden: G. N. T. Suringer, 1848.

———. *Over het wezen der godsdienst en hare betrekking tot het staatsregt: Een tegenschrift tegen Mr. C. W. Opzoomer, tevens eene bijdrage tot de kritiek der antirevolutionaire rigting.* Amsterdam: P. N. Van Kampen, 1854.

Hofmann, J. Chr. K. von. *Der Schriftbeweis: Ein theologischer Versuch.* 3 vols. Nördlingen: Beck, 1852–55.

———. *Weissagung und Erfüllung im alten und im neuen Testamente: Ein theologischer Versuch.* 2 vols. Nördlingen: Beck, 1841–44.

Hofmann, Rudolf. *Symboliek.* Translated by P. J. de Roode. Abridged by M. A. Adrianni. Utrecht: Kemink and Zoon, 1892.

———. *Symbolik oder systematische Darstellung des symbolischen Lehrbegriffs der verschiedenen christlichen Kirchen und namhaften Sekten.* Leipzig: Friedrich Voigt, 1857.

Hooijer, Cornelis. *Oude kerkordeningen der Nederlandsche hervormde gemeenten (1563–1638).* Te Zalt-Bommel: J. Noman & Zoon, 1865.

Hoornbeeck, Johannes. *Heyliging van Godts naam, ende dag.* 2nd ed. Leiden: Johannes Wagens, 1659.

———. *Nader Bewering van des Heeren dags heyliginge.* Leiden: Johannes Wagens, 1659.

———. *Theologia Practica.* 2 vols. Utrecht: Henry Versteeg, 1663–66.

———. *Theologiae Practicae.* 2nd ed. 2 vols. Utrecht: van de Water, 1689.

Horace. *Odes and Epodes.* Translated by Niall Rudd. LCL 33. Cambridge, MA: Harvard University Press, 2004.

———. *The Odes and Epodes of Horace: A Metrical Translation into English.* Translated by Lord Lytton. New York: Harper & Brothers, 1870.

———. *Satires; Epistles; Ars poetica.* Translated by H. Rushton Fairclough. LCL 194. Cambridge, MA: Harvard University Press, 1942.

Hospinian, Rudolf. *Festa Christianorum.* Zurich: Wolphius, 1593.

Huet, Conrad Busken. *Het land van Rembrand: Studien over de noordnederlandsche beschaving in de zeventiende eeuw.* 2 vols. Haarlem: H. D. Tjeenk Willink, 1882–84.

Huxley, Thomas H. *On the Physical Basis of Life.* New Haven: The [Yale] College Courant, 1869.

Huygens, Constantijn. *Batava Tempe, dat is 't Voor-hout van 's Gravenhage.* Middelburgh: Hans vander Hellen, 1622.

———. *Constantijn Huygens' Koselick mal en voor-hout.* 3rd ed. Amsterdam: A. Versluys, 1904.

———. *Tryntje Cornelis: Klucht.* The Hague: A. Vlack, 1657.

Hyperius, Andreas. *Methodi Theologiae.* Basel: Oporinus, 1567.

Israel, Jonathan. *The Dutch Republic: Its Rise, Greatness, and Fall, 1477–1806.* Oxford: Clarendon, 1995.

Jacobi, Friedrich Heinrich. *Werke.* Vol. 3. Leipzig: G. Fleischer, 1816.

Janet, Paul. *La morale.* Paris: C. Delagrave, 1874.

Jerome. *Against Jovinianus.* NPNF[2] 6:346–416.

———. *Commentaries on the Twelve Prophets.* Edited by Thomas P. Scheck. 2 vols. Ancient Christian Texts. Downers Grove, IL: IVP Academic, 2016.

Jhering, Rudolph von. *Der Zweck im Recht.* 3rd ed. 2 vols. Leipzig: Breitkopf & Härtel, 1893–98.

Josephus. *Jewish Antiquities, Books I–IV.* Translated by H. St. J. Thackeray. LCL 242. Cambridge, MA: Harvard University Press, 1930.

———. *The Jewish War, Books III–IV.* Translated by H. St. J. Thackeray. LCL 487. Cambridge, MA: Harvard University Press, 1927.

Juvenal. *Satires*. In *Juvenal and Persius*. Translated by George Gilbert Ramsay. LCL 91. Cambridge, MA: Harvard University Press, 1918.

Kampschulte, F. W. *Johann Calvin: Seine Kirche und sein Staat in Genf*. 2 vols. Leipzig: Duncker & Humblot, 1869–99.

Kant, Immanuel. *Einleitung in die Metaphysik der Sitten*. In *Metaphysische Anfangsgründe der Rechtslehre*, xiii–lii. Königsberg: F. Niclovius, 1797.

———. *Kant's Critique of Judgement*. Trans. J. H. Bernard. 2nd rev. ed. London: Macmillan, 1914.

———. *On the Metaphysics of Morals and Ethics*. Translated by Thomas Kingsmill Abbott. Radford, VA: A & D Publishing, 2008.

———. *Zum ewigen Frieden: Ein philosophischer Entwurf*. Facsimile of 1795 edition. Prepared by Wilhelm Herzog. Berlin: Forum, 1917. ET: "Eternal Peace: A Philosophical Essay." In *Eternal Peace, and Other International Essays*, translated by W. Hastie, 67–127. Boston: World Peace Foundation, 1914.

Keibel, Erich. *Hoe moeten wij rooken? Populair-genneeskundige wenken voor rookers, die hunne gezondheid liefhebben*. The Hague: Morel, 1889.

Keil, C. F., and Franz Delitzsch. *Biblical Commentary on the Books of Samuel*. Translated by James Martin. Edinburgh: T&T Clark, 1891.

———. *Biblical Commentary on the Old Testament*. Translated by James Martin. 25 vols. Edinburgh: T&T Clark, 1878–89.

———. *Manual of Biblical Archaeology*. Vol. 2. Edited and translated by Alexander Cusin. Edinburgh: T&T Clark 1888.

Kemper, Jeronimo de Bosch. *Geschiedenis van Nederland na 1830*. 5 vols. Amsterdam: E. S. Witkamp, 1873–82.

Kepper, George. *De oorlog tusschen Frankrijk en Duitschland*. 2 vols. Rotterdam: Nijgh & Van Ditmar, 1871.

Kern, Hendrik. *Geschiedenis van het Buddhisme in Indië*. 2 vols in 1. Haarlem: H. D. T'jeenk Willink, 1882–84.

Kiehl, Daniël. *Natuurlijke historie van den Filistijn: Prolegomena tot de studie van Arthur Schopenhauer 1*. The Hague: D. N. F. Kiehl, 1895.

Kirchmann, Julius Hermann von. *Die Grundbegriffe des Rechts und der Moral als Einleitung in das Studium rechtsphilosophischer Werke*. 2nd ed. Leipzig: Dürr, 1873.

Kirchner, Friedrich. *Der Spiritismus: Die Narrheit unseres Zeitalters*. Berlin: C. Habel, 1863.

Kist, Nicholas Christiaan. *Neêrland's Bededagen en Biddagsbrieven*. 2 vols. Leiden: S. & J. Luchtmans, 1848–49.

Klopstock, Friedrich Gottlieb. *Der Messias: Ein Heldengedicht*. Halle, 1749. 2nd ed., Carlsruhe: Bureau der deutschen Classiker, 1818.

Knibbe, David. *De Leere der Gereformeerde Kerk volgens de order van de Heidelbergse Katechismus*. Leiden: Samul Luchtmans en Zoonen, 1761.

Koelman, Jacobus. *De historie van den Christelyken Sabbath*. Amsterdam: Pieter Timmers, 1685.

———. *Het ambt en de pligten der ouderlingen en diakenen*. Rotterdam: Reynier van Doesburg, 1694. New edition: Rotterdam: Oskam, 1875.

Köhler, August. *Lehrbuch der Biblischen Geschichte Alten Testamentes*. 2 vols. Erlangen: A. Deichert, 1875.

Kolb, Robert, and Timothy J. Wengert, eds. *The Book of Concord: The Confessions of the Evangelical Lutheran Church*. Minneapolis: Fortress, 2000.

Köstlin, Julius. *The Theology of Luther in Its Historical Development and Inner*

Harmony. Translated by Charles E. Hay. 2 vols. Philadelphia: Lutheran Publication Society, 1897.

Kurtz, John Henry [Johann Heinrich]. *Church History.* Edited by W. Robertson Nicoll. Authorized translation from latest revised edition by John Macpherson. 3 vols. New York: Funk & Wagnalls, 1889–90.

―――. *Lehrbuch der Kirchengeschichte für Studirende.* 7th rev. ed. 2 vols. Mitau: Reumann, 1874.

―――. *Text-Book of Church History.* Edited and translated by J. H. A. Bomberger. 2 vols. in 1. Philadelphia: Lippincott, 1888.

Kuyper, Abraham. *E Voto Dordraceno: Toelichting op den Heidelbergschen Catechismus.* 4 vols. Amsterdam: Höveker & Wormser, 1904–5.

―――. *Ons Program.* Amsterdam: J. H. Kruyt, 1879.

―――. *Our Program: A Christian Political Manifesto.* Translated and edited by Harry Van Dyke. Bellingham, WA: Lexham Press, 2015.

Lactantius. *Divine Institutes.* ANF 7:9–223.

Lampe, Frederik Adolph. *Schets der dadelyke Godt-geleertheid.* Translated by Bernhardus Keppel. Rotterdam: Losel, 1739.

Lange, Johann Peter. *Zur psychologie in der Theologie.* Heidelberg: Carl Winter, 1874.

L'Ange Huet, Josué. *Nieuwe oplossing van een oud vraagstuk: De methode van het positivisme toegepast op het begrip van oorzaak-en-gevolg.* Leiden: S. C. van Doesburgh, 1872.

Lavater, Ludwig. *Nehemias: Liber Nehemiae, qui et secundus Ezrae dicitur, homiliis LVIII.* Zurich: Froschoviano, 1586.

Lechler, Gotthard Victor. *Das Apostolische und das Nachapostolische Zeitalter.* 3rd ed. Karlsrube & Leipzig, 1885. ET: *The Apostolic and Post-Apostolic Times:*

Their Diversity and Unity in Life and Doctrine. Translated by A. J. K. Davidson. 3rd revised ed. 2 vols. Edinburgh: T&T Clark, 1886.

Lecky, William Edward Hartpole. *History of European Morals from Augustus to Charlemagne.* 2 vols. New York: D. Appleton, 1869–70.

Leeuwen, Everardus Henricus van. *De eed en de moderne staat: Eene studie.* Utrecht: C. H. E. Breijer, 1881.

Legge, James. *The Religions of China.* London: Hodder & Stoughton, 1880.

Leibniz, Gottfried Wilhelm. *Discourse on Metaphysics, Correspondence with Arnauld, and Monadology.* Translated by George R. Montgomery. LaSalle, IL: Open Court, 1902. Reprint, Mineola, NY: Dover, 2005.

Lightfoot, John. *Horae Hebraicae et Talmudicae.* 3 vols. Canterbury: J. Field, 1659.

Liguori, Alphonsus. *Moral Theology.* Translated by Ryan Grant. 2 vols. Post Falls, ID: Mediatrix Press, 2017.

―――. *Theologia Moralis.* 6th ed. 3 vols. Venice: Remondini, 1767. English synopsis: *A Synopsis of the Moral Theology of the Church of Rome, Taken from the Works of St. Ligori, and Translated from the Latin into English.* Translated by Samuel B. Smith. New York: Office of the Downfall of Babylon, 1836.

Limborch, Philip van. *Theologia Christiana.* 5th ed. Amsterdam: Balthzar Lakeman, 1730.

Lippert, Julius. *Die Geschichte der Familie.* Stuttgart: F. Enke, 1884. HathiTrust Digital Library. https://babel.hathitrust .org/cgi/pt?id=uc1.b3215648&view=1up &seq=9.

Löber, Richard. *Die Lehre vom Gebet aus der immanenten und ökonomische Trinität.* 2nd ed. Erlangen, 1860.

Lobstein, Paul. *Die Ethik Calvins.* Strassburg: C. F. Schmidt [F. Bull], 1877.

Locke, Richard. *Über die Begriffsbestimmung der Lüge im eigentlichen Sinne.* Leipzig: J. Drescher, 1886.

Lombard, Peter. *The Sentences Book 1: The Mystery of the Trinity.* Translated by Giulio Silano. Toronto: Pontifical Institute of Medieval Studies, 2007.

———. *The Sentences Book 4: On the Doctrine of Signs.* Translated by Giulio Silano. Toronto: Pontifical Institute of Medieval Studies, 2010.

Lotze, Hermann. *Mikrokosmus: Ideen zur Naturgeschichte und Geschichte der Menschheit; Versuch einer Anthropologie.* 5th ed. 3 vols. Leipzig: S. Hirzel, 1885–96.

Lubbock, John. *The Origin of Civilization and the Primitive Condition of Man: Mental and Social Condition of Savages.* London: Longmans, Green & Co., 1870.

Lucian of Samosata. *Lucian in Eight Volumes I.* LCL 14. Cambridge, MA: Harvard University Press, 1913.

———. *The Works of Lucian of Samosata.* Vol. 3. Translated by H. W. Fowler and F. G. Fowler. Oxford: Clarendon, 1905.

Luthardt, Chr. Ernst. *Die Ethik Luthers in ihren Grundzügen dargestellt.* 2nd rev. ed. Leipzig: Dörffling & Franke, 1875.

Luther, Martin. *Disputation concerning Justification.* In *Luther's Works*, vol. 34, *Career of the Reformer IV*, 151–53. Edited by Helmut T. Lehman. Translated by Lewis William Spitz. Minneapolis: Fortress, 1960.

———. *Lectures on Galatians.* Vol. 27 of *Luther's Works.* Edited by Jaroslav Pelikan and Walter A. Hansen. St. Louis: Concordia, 1964.

———. *Luther—Selected Political Writings.* Edited by J. M. Porter. Lanham, MD: University Press of America, 1988.

———. "Whether Soldiers Too, Can Be Saved (1526)." In *Luther's Works*, vol. 46, *The Christian in Society III*, edited by Robert C. Schultz, translated by Helmut T. Lehman, 93–137. Philadelphia: Fortress, 1967.

Mach, Franz J. *Die Willensfreiheit des Menschen.* Paderborn and Münster: Ferdinand Schöningh, 1887.

MacIntyre, Alasdair. *After Virtue: A Study in Moral Theory.* 2nd ed. Notre Dame, IN: University of Notre Dame Press, 1984.

Malins, Joseph. *The Temperance Movement.* New York: Ward, Lock & Co., 1883.

Marheineke, Philipp. *Theologische Vorlesungen.* 4 vols. Prepared by Wilhelm Vatke and Conrad Stephan Matthies. Berlin: Duncker & Humblot, 1847–48.

Martensen, Hans. *Christian Dogmatics: A Compendium of the Doctrines of Christianity.* Translated by William Urwick. Edinburgh: T&T Clark, 1898.

———. *Christian Ethics.* Translated by C. Spence, Sophia Taylor, and William Affleck. 2 vols. Edinburgh: T&T Clark, 1888–89.

———. *Christian Ethics, Special Part, First Division: Individual Ethics.* Translated by William Affleck. Edinburgh: T&T Clark, 1884.

Martial. *Epigrams, Volume I.* Translated by D. R. Shackleton Bailey. Rev. ed. LCL 94. Cambridge, MA: Harvard University Press, 1993.

———. *Epigrams, Volume II.* Translated by D. R. Shackleton Bailey. Rev. ed. LCL 95. Cambridge, MA: Harvard University Press, 1993.

———. *Epigrams, Volume III.* Translated by D. R. Shackleton Bailey. Rev. ed. LCL 480. Cambridge, MA: Harvard University Press, 1993.

———. *Epigrams I: Spectacles, Books 1–7.* Translated by Walter C. A. Ker. LCL 94. New York: Putnam's Sons, 1919.

———. *Epigrams II: Books 8–14.* Translated by Walter C. A. Ker. LCL 95. New York: Putnam's Sons, 1919.

Martius, Wilhelm. *Der Kampf gegen den Alkoholmissbrauch*. Halle: Strien, 1884.

———. *Handbuch der deutschen Trinker- und Trunksuchtsfrage*. Gotha: F. Perthes, 1891.

Mastricht, Petrus van. *Beschouwende en praktikale godgeleerdheit*. 4 vols. Rotterdam: Hendrik van Pelt, et al.; Utrecht: Jan Jacob van Poolsum, 1749–53.

———. *Theoretico-Practica Theologia*. Amsterdam: Boom & Vidua, 1682. 3rd ed. Utrecht: W. van de Water, 1724. ET: *Theoretical Practical Theology*. Edited by Joel R. Beeke. Translated by Todd M. Rester. 2 vols. Grand Rapids: Reformation Heritage, 2018.

Maurik, Justus van, Jr. *Van allerlei slag: Novellen en schetsen*. Amsterdam: Van Holkema & Warendorf, 1882.

Mayer, Gottlob. *Die Lehre von Erlaubten in der Geschichte der Ethik seit Schleiermacher*. Leipzig: A. C. Deichert, 1899. See Otto Kirn review (articles).

Meinhold, Johannes. *Sabbat und Woche im Alten Testament*. Göttingen: Vandenhoeck & Ruprecht, 1905.

Mendoza, Antonio Escobar y. *Liber Theologiae Moralis*. Lyon: Philippi Borde & Laurenti Arnaud, 1644.

———. *Summula Casuum Conscientiae*. Pamplona, 1626.

———. *Universae Theologiae Moralis, Receptiores absque lite Sententiae Problematicae Disquisitions*. 7 vols. Lyon: Philippi Borde, Laurenti Arnaud & Claudii Rigaud, 1652–63.

Merz, Heinrich. *Das System der christlichen Sittenlehre in seiner Gestaltung nach den Grundsätzen des Protestantismus im Gegensatze zum Katholicismus*. Tübingen: L. F. Fues, 1841.

Meyer, Heinrich August Wilhelm. *Critical and Exegetical Commentary on the New Testament*. Vol. 11, *The Pastoral Epistles*. Translated by J. E. Huther. Edinburgh: T&T Clark, 1881.

———. *Critical and Exegetical Handbook to the Gospels of Mark and Luke*. Translated by Robert Ernest Wallis. 2 vols. Edinburgh: T&T Clark, 1880, 1883.

Meyer, Jürgen Bona. *Probleme der Lebensweisheit: Betrachtungen*. 2nd ed. Berlin: Naumburg, 1887.

Milton, John. *A Treatise on Christian Doctrine, Compiled from the Holy Scriptures Alone*. Translated by Charles Richard Sumner. Cambridge: J. Smith, 1825.

Möhler, Johann Adam. *Neue Untersuchungen der Lehrgegensätze zwischen den Katholiken und Protestanten*. Mainz, 1834.

———. *Symbolik, oder Darstellung der dogmatischen Gegensätze der Katholiken und Protestanten nach ihren öffentlichen Bekenntnisschriften*. 9th ed. Mainz: Kupferberg, 1884. ET: *Symbolism, or Exposition of the Doctrinal Differences between Catholics and Protestants as Evidenced in Their Symbolical Writings*. Translated by James Burton Robertson. New York: Scribner, 1894.

Molière. *The Miser and Other Plays*. Translated by John Wood and David Coward. New York: Penguin, 2000.

Moor, Bernardinus de. *Commentarius Perpetuus in Joh. Marckii Compendium Theologiae Christianae Didactico-Elencticum*. 7 vols. Leiden: J. Hasebroek, 1761–71.

Morris, Rosalind C., and Daniel H. Leonard. *The Returns of Fetishism: Charles de Brosses and the Afterlives of an Idea*. Chicago: University of Chicago Press, 2017.

Mosheim, Johann Lorenz. *Kern uit de zedeleer der Heilige Schrift*. 2 vols. Utrecht: Gisbert and Timon van Paddenburg, 1865.

Mouw, Richard J. *The God Who Commands*. Notre Dame, IN: University of Notre Dame Press, 2004.

Mulder, Coenraad. *De geheel-onthouding en de Heilige Schrift*. Amsterdam: Clausen, 1884.

Müller, Johann Tobias, et al. *The Christian Book of Concord, or Symbolical Books of the Evangelical Lutheran Church.* 2nd rev. ed. 2 vols. Newmarket, VA: Solomon D. Henkel and Bros., 1854.

———. *Die symbolischen Bücher der evangelisch-lutherischen Kirche, deutsch und lateinisch.* Stuttgart: S. G. Liesching, 1848.

Müller, Julius. *The Christian Doctrine of Sin.* Translated by William Pulsford. 2 vols. Clark's Foreign Theological Library 27, 29. Edinburgh: T&T Clark, 1852–53.

———. *Die christliche Lehre von der Sünde.* 5th ed. 2 vols. Breslau: J. Max, 1867.

Musculus, Wolfgang. *Loci Communes in usus sacrae Theologiae candidatorum parati.* Basel: Herwagen, 1560.

Neal, Daniel. *The History of the Puritans, or Protestant Non-Conformists.* 4 vols. London: R. Hett, 1732–38.

Neander, August. *Das Leben Jesu Christi in seinem geschichtlichen Zusammenhange und seiner geschichtlichen Entwickelung.* 4th rev. ed. Hamburg: F. Perthes, 1845.

———. *General History of the Christian Religion and Church.* Translated by Joseph Torrey. 5 vols. Boston: Crocker & Brewster, 1854–56.

———. *Geschichte der Pflanzung und Leitung der christlichen Kirche durch die Apostel.* 4th rev. ed. 2 vols. in 1. Hamburg: F. Perthes, 1847.

———. *History of the Planting and Training of the Christian Church by the Apostles.* 2 vols. Translated by J. E. Ryland. London: H. G. Bohn, 1851.

———. *Vorlesungen über Geschichte der christlichen Ethik.* Vol. 5 of *Dr. A. Neander's Theologische Vorlesungen.* Berlin: Wiegandt & Grieben, 1864.

Nepos, Cornelius. *The Lives of Eminent Commanders.* New York: Palantine, 2015.

———. *The Lives of Eminent Commanders.* Translated by John Selby Watson.

1886. The Tertullian Project. http://www.tertullian.org/fathers/nepos.htm.

———. *The Lives of Eminent Commanders.* Translated by John Selby Watson. 1886. Wikisource. https://en.wikisource.org/wiki/Lives_of_the_Eminent_Commanders.

Niemeyer, Herman Agathon. *Collectio Confessionum in Ecclesiis Reformatis Publicatarum.* Leipzig: Klinkhardt, 1840.

Oehler, Gustav Friedrich. *Theology of the Old Testament.* 2nd ed. Translated by George E. Day. New York: Funk & Wagnalls, 1884.

Oettingen, Alexander von. *Die Moralstatistik.* 3rd ed. Erlangen: Deichert 1882.

Oort, Hendrik, with Abraham Kuenen and Isaac Hooykaas. *De laatste eeuwen van Israels volksbestaan.* 2 vols. The Hague: J. Ykema, 1877–78.

Oosterzee, Johannes Jacobus van. *The Two Epistles of Paul to Timothy.* Edited by E. A. Washburn. Translated by E. Harwood. New York: Scribner's Sons, 1868.

Origen. *Homilies on Leviticus 1–16.* Translated by Gary Wayne Barkley. FC 83. Washington, DC: Catholic University of America Press, 1990.

Ovid. *Art of Love, and Other Poems.* Translated by J. H. Mozley. Revised by G. P. Goold. LCL 232. Cambridge, MA: Harvard University Press, 1979.

———. *The Heroïdes, or Epistles of the Heroines, The Amours, Art of Love, Remedy of Love, and Minor Works of Ovid.* Translated by Henry T. Riley. London: Bell and Daldy, 1869.

———. *Metamorphoses.* Translated by Frank Justus Miller. 2 vols. *Books I–VIII,* LCL 42; *Books IX–XV,* LCL 43. Cambridge, MA: Harvard University Press, 1951–58.

Owen, John. *Theologoumena Pantopada, sive de Natura, Ortu, Progressu et Studio Verae Theologiae.* Franeker: Leonard Strick, 1700.

Pacifico da Novara. *Summa confessionis intitulata pacifica conscientia*. Venice: Zoane Tacuino da Trino, 1535.

Palmer, Christian. *Die Moral des Christenthums*. Stuttgart: Liesching, 1864.

———. *Evangelische Pastoraltheologie*. 2nd rev. ed. Stuttgart: J. F. Steinkopf, 1863.

Perelaer, Michael Theophile Hubert. *Baboe Dalima, or The Opium Fiend*. Translated from Dutch by E. J. Venning. London: Vizetelly & Co., 1888.

Perkins, William. *"A Case of Conscience, the Greatest That Ever Was," with "A Brief Discourse, Taken out of the Writings of Hier. Zanchius, wherein the Aforesaid Case of Consience Is Disputed and Resolved."* Edinburgh: Robert Waldegrave, 1592.

———. *Catechesis*. Hanover: G. Antonium, 1608.

———. *The Works of William Perkins*. Vol. 8. Edited by J. Stephen Yuile. Grand Rapids: Reformation Heritage, 2019.

Perrone, Giovanni. *Praelectiones Theologicae*. Edited by J.-P. Migne. 2 vols. Paris: Petit-Montrouge, 1856.

———. *Praelectiones Theologicae*. 9 vols. Leuven: Van Linthout & Vandenzande, 1838.

Peschel, Oscar. *The Races of Man, and Their Geographical Distribution*. New York: D. Appleton, 1906.

———. *Völkerkunde*. 6th ed. Prepared by Alfred Kirchoff. Leipzig: Von Duncker & Humblot, 1885.

Philippi, Friedrich Adolph. *Commentary on St. Paul's Epistle to the Romans*. Translated by John Shaw Banks. 2 vols. Edinburgh: T&T Clark, 1878–79.

———. *Kirchliche Glaubenslehre*. 2nd ed. 6 vols. Stuttgart: S. G. Leisching, 1864–82.

Philo. *On the Special Laws, Book 4; On the Virtues; On Rewards and Punishments*. Translated by F. H. Colson. LCL 341.

Cambridge, MA: Harvard University Press, 1939.

Pictet, Bénédict. *De christelyke zedekunst: Of schriftuurlyke en natuurkundige grondtregels om godvruchtig te leeven, en zalig te sterven*. Translated by François Halma. 2nd ed. The Hague: Pieter van Thol, 1731.

Plato. *Euthyphro; Apology; Crito; Phaedo; Phaedrus*. Translated by Harold North Fowler. LCL 36. Cambridge, MA: Harvard University Press, 1914.

———. *Laches; Protagoras; Meno; Euthydemus*. Translated by W. R. M. Lamb. LCL 165. Cambridge, MA: Harvard University Press, 1952.

———. *The Laws of Plato*. Translated by Thomas L. Pangle. Chicago: University of Chicago Press, 1980.

———. *The Republic I–V*. Translated by Paul Shorey. LCL 237. Cambridge, MA: Harvard University Press, 1937.

Poimenander, Irenaeus [Godfried Udemans]. *Absaloms-Hayr off Discours, Daerinne ondersocht wordt wat daer te houden zy vande wilde vliegende Hayr-trossen off afhangende Hayr-locken die in onsen tijdt van allerley Mans ende Vrouws-persoonen [. . .] gedragen worden*. Dordrecht: François Boels, 1643.

Polanus von Polansdorf, Amandus. *Syntagma Theologiae Christianae*. Hanover: Johann Aubry, 1615.

Porphyry. *Select Works of Porphyry*. Edited and introduced by Esme Wynne-Tyson. London: Centaur, 1965. Reprint, Whitefish, MT: Kessinger, 2004.

Preyer, William T. *Die Erklärung des Gedankenlesens nebst Beschreibung eines neuen Verfahrens zum Nachweise unwillkürlicher Bewegungen*. Leipzig: Grieben, 1886.

———. *Telepathie und Geisterseherei in England*. Berlin: Gebrüder Paetel, 1886.

Primrose, Gilbert. *La trompette de Sion*. Bergerac: Gilbert Vernoy, 1610.

Proudhon, Pierre-Joseph. *De l'utilité de la célébration du dimanche*. Paris: Prévot, 1839. Translated into German by F. H. as *Die Sonntagsfeier aus dem Gesichtspunkte des öffentlichen Gesundheitswesens*. Kassel: J. C. J. Raabé, 1850.

Pruner, Johann. *Lehrbuch der katholischen Moraltheologie*. Freiburg im Breisgau: Herder, 1875.

———. *Lehrbuch der katholischen Moraltheologie*. 2nd rev. ed. Freiburg im Breisgau: Herder, 1883.

Publius Syrus. *The Moral Sayings of Publius Syrus: A Roman Slave*. Translated by D. Lyman. Cleveland: L. E. Barnard & Company, 1856.

Quack, Hendrik Peter Godfried. *Studiën en schetsen*. Amsterdam: P. N. van Kampen, 1886.

Reichenbach, Karl Freiherr von [Carl]. *Der sensitive Mensch und sein Verhalten zum Ode*. 2 vols. Stuttgart: Cotta, 1854–55.

———. *Letters on Od and Magnetism (1852): Published for the First Time in English, with Extracts from His Other Works, So as to Make a Complete Presentation of the Odic Theory*. Translated by F. D. O'Byrne. London: Hutchinson, 1926.

———. *The Mysterious Odic Force*. Translated by Leslie O. Korth. Wellingborough, England: Aquarian Press, 1977.

———. *The Od Force: Letters on a Newly Discovered Power in Nature and Its Relation to Magnetism, Electricity, Heat, and Light*. Translated by J. George Guenther. Boston: Benjamin B. Mussey & Co., 1854.

———. *The Odic Force: Letters on Od and Magnetism*. Translated by F. D. O'Byrne. New Hyde Park, NY: University Books, 1968.

———. *Physico-Physiological Researches in the Dynamics of Magnetism, Electricity, Heat, Light, Crystallization, and Chemism in Their Relations to Vital Force*.

Translated by John Ashburner. New York: J. S. Redfield: B. B. Mussey & Co., 1851.

Reinhard, Franz Volkmar. *System der christlichen Moral*. 5 vols. Wittenberg: S. G. Zimmermann, 1802–15.

Renan, Ernest. *Renan's Life of Jesus*. Translated by William G. Hutchison. London: Walter Scott, 1897.

Richter, Aemilius Ludwig. *Lehrbuch des katholischen und evangelischen Kirchenrechts: Mit besonderer Rücksicht auf deutsche Zustände*. Prepared by Richard Dove and Wilhelm Kahl. 8th ed. Leipzig: Bernhard Tauchnitz, 1886.

Ridderus [de Ridder], Franciscus. *De mensche Godts: Uyt de geschriften en tractaten van Willem Teellingh*. Hoorn: Gerbrandt & Ian Martensz, 1658. Cf. W. Teellinck, *De mensche Godts*, below.

Riedel, Wilhelm. *Alttestamentliche Untersuchungen*. Vol. 1. Leipzig: Deichert, 1902. *See* Riedel, Wilhelm, "Der Sabbath."

Riehl, Wilhelm Heinrich. *Die Familie*. Stuttgart: J. G. Cotta, 1855. HathiTrust Digital Library. https://babel.hathitrust.org/cgi/pt?id=hvd.32044021072798&view=1up&seq=5.

Ritschl, Albrecht. *The Christian Doctrine of Justification and Reconciliation: The Positive Development of the Doctrine*. Edited and translated by H. R. Mackintosh and A. B. Macaulay. Edinburgh: T&T Clark, 1902.

———. *Die christliche Lehre von der Rechtfertigung und Versöhnung*. 2nd rev. ed. 3 vols. Bonn: Adolph Marcus, 1882.

———. *Geschichte des Pietismus*. 3 vols. Bonn: A. Marcus, 1880–89.

Rivet, André. *Praelectiones Pleniores in Cap. XX Exodi*. In *Operum Theologicorum quae Latinè edidit*, vol. 1, *Exegeticus: Continens, Exercitationes in Genesin CXCI. & Commentaria in Exodum*, 1221–339. 3rd ed. Rotterdam: Arnold Lears, 1651.

Robeck, Johannes. *Exercitatio Philosophica De ΕΥΛΟΓΩ ΕΞΑΓΩΓΕ sive Morte Voluntaria Philosophorum et Bonorum Virorum etiam Iudaeorum et Christianorum.* Rinteln, Germany: Enax, 1736.

Rollock, Robert. *In epistolam Sancti Pauli Apostoli ad Colossenses, Commentarius.* Geneva: Crispinus, 1602.

Rothe, Richard. *Theologische Ethik.* 2nd rev. ed. 5 vols. Wittenberg: H. Koelling, 1869–71.

Rousseau, Jean-Jacques. *Julie, or The New Heloise: Letters of Two Lovers Who Live in a Small Town at the Foot of the Alps.* Translated and edited by Philip Stewart and Jean Vaché. Hanover, NH: University Press of New England, 1997.

Saldenus, Guiliemus. *Toetssteen van eens Christens oordeel.* Groningen: Pieter Brandsma, 1728.

Sánchez, Tomás. *Disputationum de Sancto Matrimonii Sacramento.* Venice, 1606.

Sartorius, Ernst. *Die Lehre von der heiligen Liebe, oder Grundzüge der evangelisch-kirchlichen Moraltheologie.* New edition in one volume. Stuttgart: S. G. Liesching, 1861.

———. *Die Lehre von der heiligen Liebe, oder Grundzüge der evangelisch-kirchlichen Moraltheologie.* 3 vols. in 4. Stuttgart: S. G. Liesching, 1840–56.

Sartorius, Karl. *Die Leichenverbrennung innerhalb der christlichen Kirche.* Basel: Detloff, 1886.

Scheffer, Wessel. *Arthur Schopenhauer: De philosophie van het pessimism.* Leiden: S. C. van Doesburgh, 1870.

Schenkel, Daniel. *Die christliche Dogmatik vom Standpunkte des Gewissens aus Dargestellt.* 2 vols. Wiesbaden: Kreidel und Niedner, 1858–59.

Schiller, Friedrich. *Die Braut von Messina, oder, Die feinindlichen Brüder.* Tübingen: J. G. Cotta, 1803.

———. *"The Bride of Messina" and "On the Use of the Chorus in Tragedy."*

Translated by A. Lodge. Project Gutenberg. Last updated July 20, 2014. http://www.gutenberg.org/files/6793/6793-h/6793-h.htm.

———. *The Poems of Schiller.* Translated by E. P. Foster. London: Heinemann, 1910.

———. *Sämtliche Werke.* Edited by Gerhard Fricke and H. G. Göpfert. 3rd ed. 5 vols. Munich: C. Hanser, 1962.

Schleiermacher, Friedrich. *Die christliche Sitte nach den Grundsätzen der evangelischen Kirche im Zusammenhange dargestellt.* In *Sämmtliche Werke,* div. 1, vol. 12. Edited by Ludwig Jonas. Berlin: G. Reimer, 1843.

———. *Die christliche Sitte nach den Grundsätzen der evangelischen Kirche im Zusammenhange dargestellt.* Edited by Ludwig Jonas. 2nd ed. Berlin: G. Reimer, 1884.

———. *Entwurf eines Systems der Sittenlehre.* Prepared by Alexander Schweizer. Berlin: Reimer, 1835.

———. *Erziehungslehre: Aus Schleiermachers handschriftlichem Nachlasse und nachgeschriebenen Vorlesungen.* Edited by Carl Platz. Langensalza: Beyer, 1871.

———. *Friedrich Schleiermachers Monologen, Kritische Ausgabe.* Prepared by Friedrich Michael Schiele. Leipzig: Dürr'schen Buchhandlung, 1902.

———. *Grundlinien einer Kritik der bisherigen Sittenlehre.* 2nd ed. Berlin: G. Reimer, 1834.

———. *Grundriss der philosophischen Ethik.* Foreword by A. Twesten. Berlin: G. Reimer, 1841.

———. *Introduction to Christian Ethics.* Translated and edited by John Shelley. Nashville: Abingdon, 1989.

———. *Lectures on Philosophical Ethics.* Edited by Robert B. Louden. Cambridge: Cambridge University Press, 2002.

———. *Schleiermacher's Soliloquies: An English Translation of the Monologen.*

Translated by Horace Leland Friess. Chicago: Open Court, 1926.

———. *Selections from Friedrich Schleiermacher's "Christian Ethics."* Edited and translated by James M. Brandt. Louisville: Westminster John Knox, 2011.

Schmets, Wilhelm. *Des hochheiligen, ökumenischen und allgemeinen Concils von Trient, Canones und Beschlüsse.* 6th ed. Bielefeld: Belhagen & Klasing, 1868.

Schmid, Christian Friedrich. *Christliche Sittenlehre.* Edited by A. Heller. Stuttgart: S. G. Liesching, 1861.

Schneckenburger, Matthias. *Vergleichende Darstellung des lutherischen und reformirten Lehrbegriffs von M. Schneckenburger: Aus dessen handschriftlichem Nachlasse zusammengestellt und herausgegeben durch Eduard Güder.* 2 vols. in 1. Stuttgart: J. B. Metzler, 1855.

Scholten, J. H. *De vrije wil: Kritisch onderzoek.* Leiden: Engels, 1859.

Schopenhauer, Arthur. *Die beiden Grundprobleme der Ethik.* 2nd rev. ed. Leipzig: F. A. Brockhaus, 1860.

———. *Die Welt als Wille und Vorstellung.* 5th ed. 2 vols. Leipzig: Brockhaus, 1879.

———. *Parerga and Paralipomena: Short Philosophical Essays, Volume I.* Translated and edited by Sabine Roehr and Christopher Janaway. Cambridge: Cambridge University Press, 2014.

———. *The Two Fundamental Problems of Ethics.* Translated by David E. Cartwright and Edward E. Erdman. Oxford: Oxford University Press, 2010.

———. *The World as Will and Idea.* Translated by R. B. Haldane and J. Kemp. 3 vols. London: K. Paul, Trench, Trübner, 1896.

Schotel, G. D. J. *Bijdrage tot de geschiedenis der kerkelijke en wereldlijke kleeding.* 2 vols. in 1. The Hague: P. H. Noordendorp, 1854–56.

Schrader, Eberhard. *Die Keilinschriften und das Alte Testament.* 2nd ed. Giessen: J. Ricker, 1883.

Schulze, Gustave. *Über den Widerstreit der Pflichten.* Halle: H. Niemeyer, 1878.

Schürer, Emil. *A History of the Jewish People in the Time of Jesus Christ.* Translated by John Macpherson, Sophia Taylor, and Peter Christie. 2nd ed. 5 vols. New York: Scribner's Sons, 1896.

———. *Lehrbuch der neutestamentlichen Zeitgeschichte.* Leipzig: J. C. Hinrichs, 1874.

Schwane, Joseph Anton. *De Operibus Supererogatoris et Consiliis Evangelicis in genere.* Monasterii: Typis Theissingianis, 1868.

Scot, Reginald. *The Discoverie of Witchcraft.* Annotated by Brinsley Nicholson. London: Elliot Stock, 1886. First published 1584. Internet Archive. Uploaded February 5, 2009. https://archive.org/details/discoverieofwitc00scot/page/n6.

Seidel, Christoph Matthäus. *Christliches und erbauliches Gespräch von Zechen Schwelgen Spielen und Tanzen etc.* Halle: Salfeld, Renger, 1698.

Selling, Joseph A. *Reframing Catholic Theological Ethics.* Oxford: Oxford University Press, 2016.

Seneca. *Ad Lucilium Epistulae Morales I.* Translated by Richard M. Gummere. LCL 75. Cambridge, MA: Harvard University Press, 1917.

———. *Ad Lucilium Epistulae Morales II.* Translated by Richard M. Gummere. LCL 76. Cambridge, MA: Harvard University Press, 1926.

———. *Ad Lucilium Epistulae Morales III.* Translated by Richard M. Gummere. LCL 77. Cambridge, MA: Harvard University Press, 1925.

———. *Moral Essays I.* Translated by John W. Basore. LCL 214. Cambridge, MA: Harvard University Press, 1928.

———. *Moral Essays II.* Translated by John W. Basore. LCL 254. Cambridge, MA: Harvard University Press, 1932.

———. *Moral Essays III.* Translated by John W. Basore. LCL 310. Cambridge, MA: Harvard University Press, 1935.

Sharpe, John. *Symphonia propetarum et apostolarum.* Geneva, 1625.

Shelley, Percy Bysshe. *On the Vegetable System of Diet.* Folcroft, PA: Folcroft Library Editions, 1975.

———. *A Vindication of Natural Diet: Being One of a Series of Notes to Queen Mab; A Philosophical Poem.* London: Smith and Davy, 1813.

Spencer, Herbert. *First Principles of a New System of Philosophy.* New York: D. Appleton, 1864.

———. *System of Synthetic Philosophy.* 10 vols. 1862–92. Various editions. Available from the Molinari Institute, http://praxeology.net/HS-SP.htm.

Spinoza, Benedictus de. *Spinoza's Ethics and "De intellectus emendatione."* Translated by Andrew Boyle. London: J. M. Dent & Sons, 1910.

Splittgerber, Franz. *Schlaf und Tod.* 2nd ed. 2 vols. Halle: Julius Fricke, 1881.

Spohnholz, Jesse. *The Convent of Wesel: The Event That Never Was and the Invention of Tradition.* Cambridge: Cambridge University Press, 2017.

Stahl, Friedrich Julius. *Philosophie des Rechts.* 2nd ed. 2 vols in 3. Heidelberg: J. C. B. Mohr, 1845–47.

———. *Philosophie des Rechts.* 3rd ed. 2 vols. in 3. Heidelberg: J. C. B. Mohr, 1854–78.

Stapfer, Johann Friedrich. *De zeden-leer.* Translated by Johannes Willem Haar. 6 vols. The Hague: Pieter van Cleef, 1760–70.

———. *Institutiones Theologiae Polemicae Universiae, Ordine Scientifico Dispositae.* 5 vols. Tiguri: Heidegger, 1750–52.

———. *Onderwys in de gantsche wederleggende Godsgeleertheit, volgens ene wiskundige orde geschikt.* Translated by Antonius de Stoppelaar. 5 vols in 6. Utrecht: G. T. and Abraham van Paddenburg, 1757–63.

———. *Sittenlehre.* 6 vols. Zurich: Heidegger & Co., 1757–66.

Staringh, Jacob Gerard. *Bybels Zakelyk-Woordenboek.* 8 vols. Amsterdam: J. de Groot, 1793–97.

Stassen, Glen Harold, and Gushee, David P. *Kingdom Ethics: Following Jesus in Contemporary Context.* 2nd ed. Grand Rapids: Eerdmans 2017.

Staudinger, Franz. *Die zehn Gebote im Lichte moderner Ethik.* Darmstadt: L. Saeng, 1902.

Stirner, Max. *Der Einzige und sein Eigenthum.* Leipzig: O. Wigand, 1845. ET: *The Ego and Its Own.* Edited by David Leopold. Translated by Stephen T. Byington. Cambridge: Cambridge University Press, 1995. Earlier ET: *The Ego and His Own.* Translated by Stephen T. Byington. New York: Benj. R. Tucker, 1907. Project Gutenberg. Released December 5, 2010. http://www.gutenberg.org/files/34580/34580-h/34580-h.htm.

Stöcker, Adolf, and Heinrich Karl Franz Schwabedissen. *Christliche Wissenschaft und Glaubensheilung: Zwei Aufsätze.* Berlin: Berliner Stadtmission, 1901.

Suicerus [Schweizer], Johann Casper. *Thesaurus Ecclesiasticus, e Patribus Graecis Ordine Alphabetico Exhibens Quaecunque Phrases, Ritus, Dogmata, Haereses, and Hujusmodi Alia Spectan.* 2 vols. Amsterdam: J. H. Wetstein, 1681–82.

Sundby, Thor. *Blaise Pascal: Sein Kampf gegen die Jesuiten und seine Verteidigung des Christenthums.* Translated from Danish by Heinrich Paul Junker. Oppeln: Franck, 1885.

Teellinck, Willem. *De mensche Godts.* Prepared by Franciscus Ridderus. Hoorn, 1658. Cf. Ridderus, *De mensche Godts,* above.

———. *De rust-tydt ofte tractaet van d'onderhoudinge des christelijcken rust-dachs.* Rotterdam: Harmen Huygensz Moinincx, 1622.

———. *De schending van het recht des verbonds gewroken: Eene verhandeling over Lev. 26:23–26.* N.p.: Tractaatgenootschap "Filippus," 1902. Originally published as *Wraeck-sweert, bepleytende het recht van Godts verbondt door bloedige oorloge, diere-tijdt, bleecke pestilentie.* Utrecht: Hermannus Ribbius, Hermannus Specht, en Johannes van Waesberge, 1655.

———. *Noodwendigh vertoogh.* Middelburgh: Hans vander Hellen, 1627.

Tertullian. *De Fuga in persecutione.* ANF 4:116–26.

———. *Of Patience.* ANF 3:707–17.

———. *On Prayer.* ANF 3:681–92.

———. *On the Resurrection of the Body.* ANF 3:545–94.

Teyler's Godgeleerd Genootschap. *Verhandelingen, raakende den natuurlyken en geopenbaarden godsdienst.* 1st series. Vol. 18. Haarlem, 1799.

Thamin, Raymond. *Un problème dans l'antiquité: Étude sur la casuistique stoïcienne.* Paris: Hachette, 1884.

Theocritus. *Idylls.* In *The Greek Bucolic Poets,* translated by J. M. Edmonds, 9–363. LCL 28. Cambridge, MA: Harvard University Press, 1912.

Theodoret of Cyrus. *The Questions on the Octateuch.* Vol. 2, *On Leviticus, Numbers, Deuteronomy, Judges and Ruth.* Greek text revised by John F. Petruccione, translated by Robert C. Hill. Washington, DC: Catholic University of America Press, 2007.

Thiersch, Heinrich W. J. *Voorlezingen over Katholicisme en Protenstantisme.* Translated by Alb. Van Tooerenbergen. 2 vols. Utrecht: Van den Post, 1848–49. Dutch translation of *Vorlesungen über Katholicismus und Protestantismus.* 2nd rev. ed. 2 vols. Erlangen: C. Heyder, 1848.

Tholuck, Friedrich August. *Ausführliche Auslegung der Bergpredigt Christi nach Matthäus.* 3rd rev. ed. Hamburg: F. Perthes, 1845.

———. *Commentary on the Sermon on the Mount.* Translated by R. Lundin Brown. Edinburgh: T&T Clark, 1874.

———. *Vermischte Schriften grösstentheils apologetischen Inhalts.* 2 vols. Hamburg: F. Perthes, 1839.

———. *Vorgeschichte des Rationalismus.* 2 vols. Halle: E. Anton, 1853–62.

Thomas, Louis. *Le jour du Seigneur: Étude de dogmatique chrétienne et d'histoire.* Lausanne: Bridel, 1892.

Tiele, Cornelis Petrus. *Elements of the Science of Religion.* 2 vols. New York: Scribner's Sons, 1897.

———. *Outlines of the History of Relgion: To the Spread of Universal Religions.* Translated by J. Estline Carpenter. 6th ed. London: K. Paul, Trench, Trübner, 1896.

Turretin, Francis. *Institutio Theologiae Elencticae.* Geneva: Samuel de Tornes, 1682. ET: *Institutes of Elenctic Theology.* Edited by James T. Dennison Jr. Translated by George Musgrave Giger. 3 vols. Phillipsburg, NJ: P&R, 1992–97.

Tylor, Edward B. *Primitive Culture.* 2nd ed. 2 vols. London: John Murray, 1903.

Ubachs, Michael. *Een eeuw modern kapitalisme: De Regouts; Leed en strijd van Maastricht's Proletariaat.* Nijmegen: LINK, 1976.

Udemans, Godefridus. *The Practice of Faith, Hope, and Love.* Translated by Annemie Godbehere. Edited by Joel R. Beeke. Grand Rapids: Reformation Heritage, 2012.

Ueberweg, Friedrich. *Grundriss der Geschichte der Philosophie*. 8th ed. (vols. 1–2); 9th ed. (vols. 3–4). Edited by Max Heinze. 4 vols. Berlin: Mittler, 1894–1902.

Ursinus, Zacharias. *The Commentary of Dr. Zacharias Ursinus on the Heidelberg Catechism*. Translated by G. W. Willard. 3rd American ed. Cincinnati: T. P. Bucher, 1851. Reprint, Phillipsburg, NJ: P&R, n.d.

———. *Schat-boek der Verklaringen over den Nederlandschen Catechismus*. Edited by David Pareus. Translated by Festus Hommes. 2 vols. Gorinchem: Nicolaas Coetzee, 1736.

Usener, Herrmann. *Religionsgeschichtliche Untersuchungen*. 3 vols. Bonn: M. Cohen & Sohn (F. Cohn), 1889–99.

Vacek, Edward C. *Love, Human and Divine: The Heart of Christian Ethics*. Washington, DC: Georgetown University Press, 1994.

Vaerst, Friedrich Christian Eugen von. *Gastrosophie, oder Die Lehre von den Freuden der Tafel*. 2 vols. Leipzig: Avenarius & Mendelssohn, 1851.

Valerius Maximus. *Facta et dicta memorabilia*. In *Memorable Doings and Sayings II: Books 6–9, 2–14*. Translated by D. R. Schackleton Bailey. LCL 493. Cambridge, MA: Harvard University Press, 2000.

Vallady, Matyas. *France et Allemagne: Les deux races*. Paris: Ollendorf, 1887.

Vellenga, Gerrit. *Het Geoorloofde: Eene zedekundige studie*. Sneek: J. Campen, 1895.

Vermigli, Peter Martyr. *Loci Communes*. 2nd ed. Zurich: Christophorus Froschouerus, 1580.

———. *Loci Communes*. 10th ed. Geneva: Peter Aubert, 1623.

Vilmar, A. F. C. *Theologische Moral: Akademische Vorlesungen*. 3 vols. in 1. Gütersloh: C. Bertelsmann, 1871.

Vinet, Alexandre Rodolphe. *Essais de philosophie morale et de morale religieuse, suivis de quelques essais de critique littéraire*. Paris: L. Hachette, 1837.

Virgil. *Eclogues, Georgics, Aeneid*. Translated by H. Rushton Fairclough. LCL 63. Cambridge, MA: Harvard University Press, 1916.

Vitringa, Campegius. *Doctrina Christianae Religionis*. 6th ed. 8 vols. Vols. 1–7: Leiden: Johannes le Mair, 1761–79; vol. 8: Leiden: Luzac & van Damme, 1785.

———. *Korte schets van de christelyke zeden-leere, ofte Van het Geestelijke Leven*. Translated by Johannes d'Outrein. Amsterdam: Hendrik Stik, 1717.

Vloten, J. van. *Baruch D'Espinoza: Zijn leven en schriften, in verband met zijnen en onzen tijd*. Amsterdam: Frederik Muller, 1865.

Voetius, Gisbertus. *Lacrymae crocodilli abstersae*. 1627.

———. *Politicae Ecclesiasticae*. 4 vols. Amsterdam: Johannes à Waesberge, 1663.

———. *Politicae Ecclesiasticae, Pars Secunda, Quatuor Libris Adornata*. Amsterdam: Johannes à Waesberge, 1669.

———. *Selectarum Disputationum Theologicarum*. 4 vols. Utrecht: Johannes à Waesberge, 1648–67.

———. *Τα Ασκητικα sive Exercitia Pietatis*. Gorichem: Paulus Vinck, 1679.

Voetius, Gisbert, and Johannes Hoornbeeck. *De praktijk der godzaligheid: Τα Ασκητικα sive Exercitia Pietatis*. Utrecht, 1651. Gorichem: Paul Vink, 1664.

Vos, G. J. *Geschiedenis der Vaderlandsche Kerk*. 2 vols. Dordrecht: J. P. Revers, 1881–87.

Vossius, Gerardus Johannes. *Historiae de Controversiis quas Pelagius*. Amsterdam: Elsevir, 1655.

Waitz, Theodor. *Die Anthropologie der Naturvölker*. 6 vols. Leipzig: F. Fleischer, 1859–72. Volume 1 ET: *Introduction to*

Anthropology. Translated by J. Frederick Collingwood. London: Longman, 1863.

Warneck, Gustav. *Protestantische Beleuchtung der römischen Angriffe auf die evangelische Heidenmission: Ein Beitrag zur charakteristik ultramontaner Geschichtschreibung.* 2 vols. Gütersloh: C. Bertelsmann, 1884–85.

Was lehrt man in der Kirche Christi des Scientisten? Berlin: Schwedtschke & Sohn, 1901.

Weber, Georg. *Geschichte der akatholischen Kirchen und Secten von Grossbritannien.* 2 vols. Leipzig: W. Engelmann, 1845–53.

Weemes, John. *The Christian Synagogue.* London: Thomas Cotes, 1633.

Weiss, Bernhard. *Biblical Theology of the New Testament.* Translated by David Eaton and James E. Duguid. 2 vols. Edinburgh: T&T Clark, 1893.

Weiss, Johannes. *Die christliche Freiheit nach der Verkündigung des Apostels Paulus.* Göttingen: Vandenhoeck & Ruprecht, 1902.

Wendt, Hans Heinrich. *Ueber das sittlich Erlaubte.* Sammlung gemeinverständlicher wissenschaftliche Vorträge 345. Berlin: C. Habel, 1880.

Wernick, Andrew. *Auguste Comte and the Religion of Humanity.* Cambridge: Cambridge University Press, 2014.

Wernsdorf, Gottlieb. *Absolutismus Moralis.* Wittenberg, 1715.

Wette, Wilhelm Martin Leberecht de. *Christliche Sittenlehre.* 4 vols. in 3. Berlin: G. Reimer, 1819–23.

———. *Kurze Erklärung der Briefe an Titus, Timotheus, und die Hebräer.* Leipzig: Hirzel, 1867.

———. *Lehrbuch der christlichen Sittenlehre und der Geschichte derselben.* Berlin: G. Reimer, 1833.

Whitaker, William. *A Disputation on Holy Scripture.* Translated by William Fitzgerald. Cambridge: Cambridge University Press, 1849.

Wichern, Johann Hinrich. *Die innere Mission der deutschen evangelischen Kirche.* Hamburg: Rauhen Hauses zu Horn, 1849.

Willet, Andrew. *Synopsis papismi, or, A General View of the Papacy.* 10 vols. Edited by John Cumming. London: British Society for Promoting the Religious Principles of the Reformation, 1852.

Wiltens, Nikolaas, et al., preparers. *Kerkelyk Plakaatboek.* 5 vols. The Hague: P. & I. Scheltus, 1722–1807.

Windel, C. *Die Grenzen des christlich Erlaubten: Ein Vortag.* Berlin: W. Hertz, 1868.

Winer, Georg Benedikt. *Biblisches Realwoerterbuch zum Handgebrauch für Studirende, Candidaten, Gymnasiallehrer und Prediger.* 3rd rev. ed. 2 vols. Leipzig: C. H. Reclam, 1847–48.

Winkler Prins, Antony, ed. *Geillustreerde Encyclopaedie: Woordenboek voor wetenschap en kunst, beschaving en nijverheid.* 16 vols. Amsterdam: Brinkman, 1870–82.

———. *Geillustreerde Encyclopaedie: Woordenboek voor wetenschap en kunst, beschaving en nijverheid.* 2nd rev. ed. 16 vols. Rotterdam: Elsevier, 1884–88.

Wirth, Johann Ulrich. *System der speculativen Ethik: Eine Encyclopädie der gesammnten Disciplinen der practischen Philosophie.* 2 vols. Heilbronn: Carl Drechsler, 1841–42.

Witsius, Herman. *The Economy of the Covenants between God and Man: A Complete Body of Divinity.* Translated by William Crookshank. 2 vols. London: R. Baynes, J. Maitland, T. Lochhead, and T. Nelson, 1822. Reprint, Phillipsburg, NJ: The den Dulk Christian Foundation, distributed by P&R, 1990.

———. *Miscellaneorum Sacrorum Libri IV.* 2 vols. Leiden: Conrad Meyer, 1736.

Wittewrongel, Petrus. *Oeconomia Christiana*. 2 vols. Amsterdam: Marten Jansz.
Brant and Abraham van den Burgh,
1661.

Wittmeyer, L. *Über die Leichenverbrennung*.
Berlin: Carl Habel, 1876.

Wolff, Christian. *Philosophia Practica Universalis*. Frankfurt and Leipzig: Renger,
1739.

Wuttke, Adolf. *Christian Ethics*. Translated
by John P. Lacroix. 2 vols. New York: Nelson & Phillips, 1873.

———. *Der deutsche Volksaberglaube
der Gegenwart*. 2nd rev. ed. Berlin: Wiegandt & Grieben, 1869.

———. *Handbuch der christlichen Sittenlehre*. 2nd ed. 2 vols. Berlin: Wiegandt &
Grieben, 1864–65.

———. *Handbuch der christlichen Sit-
tenlehre*. Edited and revised by Ludwig
Schulze. 3rd rev. ed. 2 vols. Leipzig: J. C.
Hinrich, 1874–75.

Xenophon. *Memorabilia; Oeconomicus;
Symposium; Apologia*. Translated by
E. C. Marchant and O. J. Todd. LCL 168.
Cambridge, MA: Harvard University
Press, 1923. Revised by Jeffrey Henderson,
2013.

Yoder, John Howard. *The Politics of Jesus*.
Grand Rapids: Eerdmans, 1972.

Ypeij, Anne, and Johannes Izaak Dermout.
*Geschiedenis der Nederlandsche Her-
vormde Kerk*. 4 vols. Breda: W. van Ber-
gen, 1819–27.

Zahn, Theodor. *Skizzen aus dem Leben
der alten Kirche*. Erlangen: A. Deichert,
1894.

Zanchi, Jerome. *Operum Theologicorum*.
Vol. 4. Geneva: Joannis Tornaesij, 1649.

Zegers, J. L. *De geloofsgenezing, hare leer
en hare waarde*. The Hague: Beschoor,
1886.

Zeller, Eduard. *Die Philosophie der
Griechen in ihrer geschichtlican

Entwicklung*. 3rd ed. 3 vols. in 5. Leipzig:
Fues's Verlag (L. W. Reisland), 1869–81.

———. *Die Philosophie der Griechen in
ihrer geschichtlicen Entwicklung*. 3rd
ed. 3 vols. in 6. Leipzig: O. R. Reisland,
1879–92.

———. *Die Philosophie der Griechen in
ihrer geschichtlicen Entwicklung*. 3rd–5th
ed. Leipzig: O. R. Reisland, 1889–1909.

———. *Outlines of the History of Greek
Philosophy*. Translated by Sarah Frances
Alleyne and Evelyn Abbot. London: Long-
mans, Green & Co., 1905.

———. *Socrates and the Socratic Schools*.
Translated by Oswald J. Reichel. London:
Longmans, Green & Co., 1868.

———. *Vorträge und Abhandlungen, Erste
Sammlung*. 2nd ed. Leipzig: Fues, 1875.

Zöckler, Otto. *Das Kreuz Christi: Religions-
historische und kirchlich-archäologische
Untersuchungen; Zugleich ein Beitrag zur
Philosophie der Geschichte*. Gütersloh:
C. Bertelsmann, 1875.

———. *Die Lehre vom Urstand der Menschen, geschichtlich und dogmatisch-
apologetisch untersucht*. Gütersloh:
C. Bertelsmann, 1879.

———. *Handbuch der theologischen Wissenschaften in encyklopädischer Darstellung*. 3 vols. Nördlingen: C. H. Beck,
1883–84. 3rd rev. ed. 4 vols. Nördlingen:
C. H. Beck, 1889–90.

———. *Theologia naturalis: Entwurf einer
systematischen Naturtheologie vom of-
fenbarungsgläubigen Standpunkte aus*.
Frankfurt am Main: Heyder & Zimmer,
1860.

Zwingli, Ulrich. *Huldreich Zwingli's Werke*.
Edited by Melchior Schuler and Johannes
Schulthess. 5 vols. Zurich: F. Schulthess,
1828–35.

———. *Huldrici Zwinglii Opera*. Edited by
Melchior Schuler and Johannes Schulthess. 8 vols. in 9. Zurich: F. Schulthess,
1829–42.

————. *The Latin Works and the Correspondence of Huldreich Zwingli: Volume One (1510–1522)*. Edited by Samuel Macauley Jackson. New York: Putnam's Sons, 1912.

————. *Selected Works of Huldreich Zwingli*. Edited by Samuel Macauley Jackson. Philadelphia: University of Pennsylvania Press, 1901.

ARTICLES, ESSAYS, AND SHORTER WORKS

Alsted, Johann Heinrich. "Tabacologia." In *Encyclopaedia Septem Tomis Distincta*, 7:2383–86. Herbornae Nassoviorum, 1630.

Alt, H. "Advent." *PRE²*, 1:160–63.

Augustine. "Letter 55 to Januarius." *NPNF¹* 1:315.

Baader, Franz von. "Tagebücher, February 24, 1789." In *Sämmtliche Werke*, edited by Emil August von Schaden, 11:181–82. Leipzig: Herrmann Bethmann, 1850.

Barwasser, Pfarrer A. "Die sogenannten Rachepsalmen in neuer Beleuchtung." *Neue Kirchliche Zeitschrift* 4 (1893): 219–51.

Bavinck, Herman. "Christian Principles and Social Relationships." In *Essays in Religion, Science, and Society*, edited by John Bolt, translated by Harry Boonstra and Gerrit Sheeres, 119–44. Grand Rapids: Baker Academic, 2008.

————. "Ethics and Politics." In *Essays on Religion, Science, and Society*, edited by John Bolt, translated by Harry Boonstra and Gerrit Sheeres, 261–78. Grand Rapids: Baker Academic, 2008.

————. "General Biblical Principles and the Relevance of Concrete Mosaic Law for the Social Question Today (1891)." Translated by John Bolt. *Journal of Markets & Morality* 13, no. 2 (Fall 2010): 437–46.

————. "The Imitation of Christ and Life in the Modern World." Translated by John Bolt. In *A Theological Analysis of Herman Bavinck's Two Essays on the* Imitatio Christi, by John Bolt, 402–42. Lewiston, NY: Mellen, 2013.

Beardslee, J. W. "The Imprecatory Element in the Psalms." *Presbyterian and Reformed Review* 8 (1897): 490–505.

Beck, Carl. "Gotteslästerung." *PRE²*, 5:320–23.

Belinda, Jack. "Goethe's *Werther* and Its Effects." *Lancet*, April 30, 2014. https://doi.org/10.1016/S2215-0366(14)70229-9.

Bergh, A. J. Th. van den. "Akte van Beschuldiging in zake Jeanne Marie Lorette." *Haagsche Courant*, September 2, 1885, 1–2.

Bertheau, Carl. "Feste, kirchliche." *PRE²*, 4:547–55.

Beza, Theodore. "Homilia decima (Luke 24:29–35)." In *Homiliae Theodori Bezae Vezelii: In historiam Domini resurrectionis*, 231–60. Geneva: Jean Le Preux, 1593.

————. "Homily 18." In *In historiam passionis et Sepulturae domini nostri J. Christi Homiliae*, 424–56. Paris, 1592.

Bilderdijk, Willem. "Over het Dierlijk Magnetismus." In *Opstellen van godgeleerde en zedekundige inhoud*, 1:103–18. Amsterdam: J. Immerzeel, Jr., 1833.

Böhmer, E. "Geistesgaben." *PRE²*, 4:738–39.

Breithaupt, A. "Die Mitteldinge." *Kirchliche Monatsschrift* 19 (November 1900): 661–83.

Brunetière, F. "Une apologie de la casuistique." Review of *Un problème dans l'antiquité: Étude sur la casuistique stoïcienne*, by Raymond Thamin. *Revue des deux mondes* 67, no. 1 (January 1885): 200–213.

Buchrucker, Karl von. "Das dritte Gebod im Unterricht." *Neue Kirchliche Zeitschrift* 4/8 (1893): 613–32.

Buddensieg, Rudolf. "Quäker." *PRE²*, 12:425–55.

Bunz, G. "Kleider und Insignien, geistliche, in der christlichen Kirche." *PRE³*, 8:44–54.

Burger, Karl. "Keuschheit." *PRE²*, 7:661–63.

———. "Liebe." *PRE²*, 8:664–67.

———. "Pflicht." *PRE²*, 11:570–73.

———. "Selbstsucht." *PRE²*, 14:66–69.

Calvin, John. "Adultero-German Interim, with Calvin's Refutation, M.D.XLVII." In *Tracts Relating to the Reformation*, translated by Henry Beveridge, 3:189–239. 3 vols. Edinburgh: Calvin Translation Society, 1844–51.

———. "Answer of John Calvin to the Nicodemite Gentlemen concerning Their Complaint That He Is Too Severe." In Calvin, *Come Out from among Them*, 97–125.

———. "Calvin's *Response to a Certain Tricky Middler*." Translated by R. Victor Bottomly. *Confessional Presbyterian* 8 (2012): 254–75, 290–91.

———. "Four Sermons from John Calvin Treating Matters Which Are Very Useful for Our Times, as One May See from the Preface: With a Brief Exposition of Psalm 87 (1552)." In Calvin, *Come Out from among Them*, 129–237.

———. "On Shunning the Unlawful Rites of the Ungodly, and Preserving the Purity of the Christian Religion." In *Tracts Relating to the Reformation*, translated by Henry Beveridge, 3:359–411. 3 vols. Edinburgh: Calvin Translation Society, 1844–51.

———. "Response to a Certain Dutchman Who under the Guise of Making Christians Very Spiritual Permits Them to Defile Their Bodies in All Idolatries: Written by Mr. John Calvin to the Faithful in the Low Countries." Translated by Rob Roy McGregor. *CTJ* 34 (1991): 291–326.

———. "A Short Treatise Setting Forth What the Faithful Man Must Do When He Is among Papists and He Knows the Truth of the Gospel." In Calvin, *Come Out from among Them*, 45–95.

———. "The True Method of Reforming the Church and Healing Her Divisions, MD, XLVII." In *Tracts Relating to the Reformation*, translated by Henry Beveridge, 3:240–358. 3 vols. Edinburgh: Calvin Translation Society, 1844–51.

"Carl Reichenbach." In *The New American Cyclopedia*, edited by George Ripley and Charles A. Dana, 14:20. New York: D. Appleton; Boston: Elliot & White, 1862.

Chambers, T. W. "Substitutes for the Fourth Commandment." *Prebyterian and Reformed Review* 1 (1890): 480–88.

Costa, Isaäc da. "Het Genie." In *Da Costa's kompleete dichtwerken*, edited by J. P. Hasebroek, 1:85–86. 3 vols. Leiden: A. W. Sijthoff, 1881.

———. "Vijf en twintig jaren: Een lied in 1840." In *Da Costa's kompleete dichtwerken*, edited by J. P. Hasebroek, 2:379–404. 3 vols. Leiden: A. W. Sijthoff, 1881.

Delitzsch, Franz. "Dekalog." *PRE²*, 3:535–37.

———. "Psalmen." *PRE¹*, 12:268–99.

Deutsche Rundschau. Unsigned review of *France et Allemagne: Les deux races*, by Matyas Vallady. 55 (May/June 1888): 471–72.

"Die Duellfrage im Reichstag." *Schorers Familienblatt* 6, no. 4 (1887): 162–64.

Emants, G. "Normale werkday, zondsrust en vrouwen- en kinderarbeid." *Vragen des Tijds* 12, no. 1 (1886): 99–118.

Feuerbach, Ludwig. "Das Geheimniss des Opfers, oder Der Mensch ist, was er isst." In *Sämtliche Werke*, vol. 10, *Gottheit, Freiheit und Unsterblichkeit vom Standpunkte der Anthropologie*, 1–31. Leipzig: Otto Wigand, 1890.

Freybe, A. "Die deutsche Volksoberglaube und seine pastorale Behandlung." *Beweis des Glaubens* 31 (1895): 66–77, 103–17, 144–56, 181–202.

Fuchs, Georg Friedrich. "Der Alkoholismus und seine Bekämpfung." *Zeitfragen des christlichen Volkslebens* 8, no. 8 (1883): 409–75.

Gillespie, George W. "Superstition." *Schaff-Herzog*, 11:167–71.

"Gisting." In Winkler Prins, *Geillustreerde Encyclopaedie* (1st ed.), 7:575ff.

Gomarus, Franciscus. "Investigatio sententiae et originis Sabbathi." In *Opera Theologica Omnia*, 2:256–76. Amsterdam: J. Jansson, 1644.

Greene, William Benton, Jr. "Christian Science or Mind-Cure." *Presbyterian and Reformed Review* 1, no. 1 (1890): 88–95.

Grosheide, F. W. "Hebreën (Secte der)." *Christ. Encycl.¹*, 2:490–91.

Grüneisen, Carl von. "Heilige, deren Anrufung und Verehrung." *PRE²*, 5:708–23.

Harding, Brian. "The Virtue of Suicide and the Suicide of Virtue: A Reading of Cicero's *On Ends* and *Tusculan Disputations*." *Epoché* 14, no. 1 (Fall 2009): 95–111. Scribd. https://www.scribd.com/document/88366621/Cicero-on-Suicide-2009.

Hauck, Albert. "Reliquien." *PRE²*, 12:689–92.

Henke, Oskar. "Zur Geschichte der Lehre von der Sonntagsfeier." *Theologische Studien und Kritiken* 59 (1886): 597–664.

Herman, Th. "Eid, Schwur, schwören." In *Calwer Bibellexikon: Biblisches Handwörterbuch illustriert*, edited by P. Zeller, 161–63. Calw and Stuttgart: Calwer Verlagsvereins, 1885.

Herzog, J. J. "Bibellesen der Laien und Bibelverbote in der katholischen Kirche." *PRE²*, 2:375–81.

———. "Epiphanienfest." *PRE²*, 14:261–63.

———. "Geißler." *PRE²*, 4:796–802.

Hofmann, Rudolf. "Aberglaube." *PRE²*, 1:62–69.

Holtzmann, H. "Zur synoptischen Frage, II, III: Die Stellung Jesu zum Gesetz." *Jahrbücher für protestantische Theologie* 4 (1878): 328–82, 533–68.

Houten, S. van. "Charles Bradlaugh." *Mannen van beteekenis in onze dagen: Levensschetsen en portretten* 16 (1885): 208–30.

Huet, Conrad Busken. "Molière en de Moliéristen." *De Gids* 50 (1886): 1–40.

Hume, David. "Of Suicide." Hume Texts Online. https://davidhume.org/texts/su/.

———. "Of Suicide." In *Essays on Suicide and the Immortality of the Soul*. Whitefish, MT: Kessinger, 2010.

Issleib, I. "The Augsburg Interim." *Schaff-Herzog*, 6:21–22.

Jacobson, H. F. "Begräbnis, bei den Christen." *PRE²*, 2:214–17.

Jacobson, H. F. (Otto Meyer). "Fasten." *PRE²*, 4:505–9.

Kahnis, Karl Friedrich. "Häresie." *PRE²*, 5:521–27.

Keulen, Dirk van. "Herman Bavinck and the War Question." In *Christian Faith and Violence*, edited by Dirk van Keulen and Martien E. Brinkman, 1:122–40. Zoetermeer: Boekencentrum, 2005.

Kirn, Otto. "Das Gesetz in der christlichen Ethik." *Theologische Studien und Kritiken* 69 (1896): 506–60.

———. Review of *Die Lehre von Erlaubten in der Geschichte der Ethik seit Schleiermacher*, by G. Mayer. *Theologisches Literaturblatt* 22, no. 18 (May 3, 1901): 213–14.

Klöpper, A. "Zur Stellung Jesu gegenüber dem mosaischen Gesetze (Matth. 5, 17–48)." *Zeitschrift für Wissenschaftliche Theologie* 39 (1896): 1–23.

Kolb, C. "Kornthal." *Schaff-Herzog*, 6:376–77.

König, Eduard. "Der Christ und das alttestamentische Gesetz, mit besonderer Beziehung auf die adventistischen Bewegungen der Neuzeit dargestellt." *Neue Kirchliche Zeitung* 18, no. 12 (1907): 895–906.

———. "The Emphatic State in Aramaic." *The American Journal of Semitic*

Languages and Literatures 17, no. 4 (July 1901): 209–21.

Köstlin, Julius. "Eid." *PRE²*, 4:120–24.

———. "Studien über das Sittengesetz: Das Erlaubte." *Jahrbücher für deutsche Theologie* 14, no. 3 (1869): 464–527.

Kübel, Robert. "Adiaphora." *PRE²*, 1:143–51.

———. "Ehre." *PRE²*, 4:103–6.

Kuyper, Abraham. "De Liefde I." *De Heraut*, no. 420 (January 10, 1886).

———. "De Liefde X." *De Heraut*, no. 430 (March 21, 1886).

———. "De Liefde XIII." *De Heraut*, no. 433 (April 11, 1886).

———. "In eerbaar gewaad." *De Heraut*, no. 515 (November 6, 1887).

———. "Lijdzaamheid I–II." *De Heraut*, nos. 1–2 (December 7 and 14, 1877).

———. "The Twelve Sons of Jacob." *Amsterdamsche Kerkbode: Officieel Orgaan van de Nederduitsche Gereformeerde Kerk (doleerende)*. Volume 1:1–9, 11, 13–14 (February 6–May 8, 1887).

———. "Uit de pers." *De Heraut*, no. 537 (April 8, 1888).

———. "Uniformity: The Curse of Modern Life." In *Abraham Kuyper: A Centennial Reader*, edited by James D. Bratt, 19–44. Grand Rapids: Eerdmans, 1998.

———. "Zetten tot een wit." *De Heraut*, no. 537 (April 8, 1888).

Kuyper, H. H. "Genezing door geloofsgebed, I–IV." *Friesch Kerkbode* 12, nos. 582–84, 586 (December 23 and 30, 1898; January 6 and 20, 1899).

"Laatste berichten." *Haagsche Courant*, September 25, 1885, 2–3.

Laguna, Gabriel. "The Expression 'Après Moi le déluge' and Its Classical Antecedents." *Tradición Clásica* (blog), January 13, 2006. http://tradicionclasica .blogspot.com/2006/01/expression-aprs -moi-le-dluge-and-its.html.

Lange, Johann Peter. "Zauberei." *PRE¹*, 18:390–400.

Laveleije, Emile de. "Hamlet." In *Bibliotheek van Moderne Theologie en Letterkunde*, edited by M. A. N. Rovers, 7:341–42. 's Hertogenbosch: Van der Schuyt, 1887.

"Law." In *Encyclopaedia of Religion and Ethics*, edited by James Hastings, 7:805–89. New York: Scribner's Sons; Edinburgh: T&T Clark, 1915.

Leyrer, E. "Kleider und Geschmeide der Hebräern." *PRE²*, 8:33–44.

———. "Los bei den Hebräern." *PRE²*, 8:762–63.

———. "Speisegesetze bei den Hebräern." *PRE¹*, 14:594–613.

———. "Wein und Weinbau bei den Hebräern." *PRE². 16:708–15.

Linde, Simon van der. "Hattem, Pontiaan van." *Christ. Encyl.²*, 3:378–79.

Lowrie, Samuel T. Review of *Skizzen aus dem Leben der alten Kirche*, by Theodor Zahn. *Presbyterian and Reformed Review* 9, no. 33 (January 1898): 101–28.

Luthardt, Chr. Ernst. "Die christliche Ethik." In Otto Zöckler, *Handbuch der theologischen Wissenschaften in encyklopädischer Darstellung³*, 3:461–566.

———. Review of *Zur Duellfrage*, by A. von Oettingen. *Theologisches Literaturblatt* 10, no. 5 (February 1, 1889): 45.

Maitland Club. "Acts and Proceedings: 1618, August." In *Acts and Proceedings of the General Assemblies of the Kirk of Scotland, 1560–1618*, 1143–67. British History Online. http://www.british-history.ac.uk /church-scotland-records/acts-proceedings /1560-1618/pp1143-1167.

Martin, Rudolf. "Vleeschverbruik in de Middeleeuwen en in den tegenwoordigen tijd." *Wetenschappelijke bladen: Een bloemlezing uit buitenlandsche tijdschriften voor Nederland* 40, no. 2 (1896): 175–91.

Mattogno, Carlo. "The Crematoria Ovens of Auschwitz and Birkenau." In *Dissecting the Holocaust: The Growing Critique of "Truth" and "Memory,"* edited by Ernst Gauss, 373–412. Capshaw, AL: Theses & Dissertations Press, 2000. Available online at http://www.vho.org/GB/Books/dth/14.pdf.

Mejer, Otto. "Bußbücher, Bußordnungen, Beichtbücher." *PRE²*, 3:20–23.

Merz, H. "Kreuzerhebung." *PRE²*, 8:273–74.

———. "Kreuzeszeichnen." *PRE²*, 8:274–79.

———. "Kruzifix." *PRE²*, 8:300–303.

Moll, W. "Bijdrage tot de kennis van het middeneeuwsch bijgeloof." *Studiën en bijdragen op 't gebied der historische theologie* 2 (1895): 387–97.

Monod, Adolphe. "Êtes-vous un meurtrier?" In *Sermons, Première Série*, 237–63. 2nd ed. Paris: Ch. Meyrueis, 1855.

Nitzsch, Karl Immanuel. "Die Gesammterscheinung des Antinomianismus, oder Die Geschichte der philosophirenden Sünde im Grundriss." *Theologische Studien und Kritiken* 19 (1846): 7–72.

Oehler, Gustav F., and Franz Delitzsch. "Feste der alten Hebräer." *PRE²*, 4:538–42.

———. "Feste der späteren Juden." *PRE²*, 4:542–47.

Oehler, Gustav F., and Hans Konrad von Orelli. "Sabbath." *PRE²*, 13:156–66.

O'Neill, James David. "Antonio Escobar y Mendoza." *Catholic Encyclopedia*, edited by Charles G. Herbermann et al., 5:534. New York: Robert Appleton Company, 1909.

Orelli, C. von. "Speisegesetze bei den Hebräern." *PRE²*, 14:495–99.

Palmer, Christian. "Ueber das Gesetz und das Erlaubte: Bemerkungen zu Köstlins Studien über das Sittengesetz." *Jahrbücher für deutsche Theologie* 14, no. 4 (1869): 698–705.

Paret, Heinrich. "Adiaphora." *PRE¹*, 1:124–26.

———. "Adiaphoristischer Streit." *PRE¹*, 1:126–29.

Pressel, W. "Gebet bei den alten und bei den heutigen Hebräern." *PRE²*, 4:763–67.

Preyer, William T. "Telepathie und Geisterseherei in England." *Deutsche Rundschau* 46 (1886): 30–51.

"Quaker Funeral Traditions." Everplans. https://www.everplans.com/articles /quaker-funeral-traditions.

Reudecker, Christian Gottlieb. "Sabbatharier." *PRE²*, 13:166–67.

Riedel, Wilhelm. "Der Sabbath." In *Alttestamentliche Untersuchungen, Erstes Heft*, 74–89. Leipzig: Deichert, 1902.

Rietschel, Ernst. "Das Verbot des Eides in der Bergpredigt." *Theologische Studien und Kritiken* 79 (1906): 393–418.

Rivet, André. "De aequivocationibus Jesuiticis." In *Operum theologicorum Praelectiones Pleniores in Cap. XX Exodi*, 1:1280–81. See Rivet, André, *Praelectiones Pleniores*.

Rüetschi, Rudolf. "Begräbnis, bei den Hebräern." *PRE²*, 2:217–20.

———. "Bilder bei den Hebräern." *PRE²*, 2:460–63.

———. "Eid bei den Hebräern." *PRE²*, 4:117–20.

Scheurl, C. T. Gottlob von. "Oath, III. In Canon Law." In *A Religious Encyclopedia, or Dictionary of Biblical, Historical, Doctrinal and Practical Theology*, edited by Philip Schaff, 2:1675–76. New York: Funk & Wagnalls, 1883.

Schleiermacher, Friedrich. "Ueber den Begriff des Erlaubten." In *Friedrich Schleiermacher's Sämmtliche Werke*, 3/2 (philosophy), edited by L. Jonas, 418–45. Berlin: Reimer, 1838.

———. "Ueber Platons Ansicht von der Ausübung der Heilkunst." In *Friedrich Schleiermacher's Sämmtliche Werke*, 3/3 (philosophy), edited by L. Jonas, 271–90. Berlin: Reimer, 1835.

Schrader, E. "Die babylonische Ursprung der siebentägigen Woche." *Studien und Kritiken* 47 (1874): 343–53.

Schwarz, E. "Collision der Pflichten." *PRE¹*, 2:787–88.

———. "Consilia evangelica." *PRE²*, 3:345–48.

———. "Kasuistik." *PRE²*, 7:554–58.

———. "Kollision der Pflichten." *PRE²*, 8:125–27.

———. "Selbstliebe." *PRE¹*, 21:22–24.

Schweizer, Alexander. "Alsted, Joh. Heinrich." *PRE²*, 1:307–8.

Siegenbeek van Heukelom, D. E. "De zelfmoord als peilschaal van het maatschappelijk geluk." *De Gids* 63 (1899): 58–89.

Slater, Thomas. "Antonino Diana." In *The Catholic Encyclopedia*, vol. 4. New York: Robert Appleton Company, 1908. See http://www.newadvent.org/cathen/04773a.htm.

Smeth, J. "J. Uytenbogaert." *Nieuw Archief voor kerkelijke geschiedenis* 2 (1854): 256.

Sommer, J. L. "Busstag." *PRE²*, 2:30–32.

Speight, Allen. "Friedrich Schlegel." In *Stanford Encyclopedia of Philosophy*. Substantive revision November 30, 2015. https://plato.stanford.edu/entries/schlegel/.

Steitz, Georg Eduard. "Passah, christliches." *PRE²*, 11:270–87.

Steitz, Senior D. "Maria, die Mutter des Herrn, ihre Verehrung und ihre Feste." *PRE²*, 9:312–27.

Theologisches Literaturblatt. Unsigned review of *Handbuch der deutschen Trinker- und Trunksuchtsfrage*, by Wilhelm Martius. 12 (1891): 118.

———. Unsigned review of *Het Geoorloofde: Eene zedekundige studie*, by G. Vellenga. 17, no. 4 (January 24, 1896): 46.

Tholuck, August. "Aberglaube." *PRE²*, 1:62–69.

Thompson, Henry. "De vooruitgang der lijkverbranding." In *Wetenschappelijke*

Bladen: Een bloemlezing uit buitenlandsche tijdschriften voor Nederland bewerkt, edited by I. C. van Deventer, 1:31–52. Haarlem: Kruseman, 1888.

"Timeline: History of Addiction Treatment." Recovery.org. https://www.recovery.org/drug-treatment/history/.

Uhlhorn, Gerhard. "Das Christenthum und das Geld." In *Sammlung von Vorträgen für das deutsche Volk*, edited by Wilhelm Frommel and Friedrich Pfaff, 7:7ff. Heidelberg: C. Winter, 1882.

Verwijs, Eelco. "Bijdrage tot de kennis van het oude volksgeloof." *Studiën en bijdragen op 't gebied der historische theologie* 2 (1895): 397–414.

Voetius, Gisbert. "De staurolatria sive cultu et abusu crucis." In *Selectarum Disputationum Theologicarum*, 3:884–931. Utrecht: Johannes à Waesberge, 1648–67.

Wagenmann, J. "Weihnachten." *PRE²*, 16:688–97.

Walther, Fr. "Das Wesen der Liebe zu Gott." *Neue Kirchliche Zeitschrift* 10 (1899): 634–45.

Warneck, Gustav. "Blicke in die römische Missionspraxis." *Allgemeine Missions-Zeitschrift: Monatshefte für geschichtliche und theoretische Missionskunde* 12 (1885): 3–29, 49–66.

Werenfels, Samuel. "Dissertatio de Naamane Syro ab Hypocrisi Vindicato." In *Opuscula Theologica, Philosophica et Philologica*, 1:254–72. 3 vols. Basil: Thurneisen, 1782.

Wijck, B. H. C. K. van der. "Twee pleibezorgers van den godsdienst: Martineau en Rauwenhoff, II." *De Tijdspiegel* 45 (August 1888): 356–81.

Wybrands, Aem. W. "De Dialogus Miraculorum van Caesarius van Hiesterbach, beschouwd als bijdrage tot de kennis van het godsdienstige leven in Nederland, in den aanvang der dertiende eeuw." *Studiën en bijdragen op 't gebied der historische theologie* 2 (1895): 1–116.

Yoder, John Howard. "Walking in the Resurrection." In *Revolutionary Christianity: The 1966 South American Lectures*, edited by Paul Martens, Mark Thiessen Nation, Matthew Porter, and Myles Werntz, 34–46. Eugene, OR: Wipf & Stock, 2011.

"Zaak Lorette." *Haagsche Courant*, September 9, 1885, 1–3; September 18, 1885, 1–3.

Zahn, F. M. "Ist Fetischismus eine ursprüngliche Form der Religion?" *Allgemeine Missions-Zeitschrift: Monatshefte für geschichtliche und theoretische Missionskunde* 6 (1879): 219–28; 241–52.

Zöckler, Otto. "Die Urgestalt der Religion." *Allgemeine Missions-Zeitschrift: Monatshefte für geschichtliche und theoretische Missionskunde* 7 (1880): 337–54 ("Der angebliche Ur-Atheismus"), 437–52 ("Die Fetischismus- und die Animismus-Hypothese"), 485–93 ("Die Animismus Hypothese").

———. "Pfingsten." *PRE*[2], 11:567–68.

———. "Polytheismus." *PRE*[2], 12:107–19.

———. "Probabilismus." *PRE*[2], 12:234–36.

———. "*Reservatio mentalis.*" *PRE*[2], 12:705–7.

———. "Sonntagsfeier." *PRE*[2], 14:428–35.

Selected Scripture Index

Name Index

Subject Index